History and Theory in Anthropology

Anthropology is a discipline very conscious of its history, and Alan Barnard has written a clear, balanced, and judicious textbook that surveys the historical contexts of the great debates in the discipline, tracing the genealogies of theories and schools of thought and considering the problems involved in assessing these theories. The book covers the precursors of anthropology; evolutionism in all its guises; diffusionism and culture area theories, functionalism and structural-functionalism; action-centred theories; processual and Marxist perspectives; the many faces of relativism, structuralism and post-structuralism; and recent interpretive and postmodernist viewpoints.

ALAN BARNARD is Reader in Social Anthropology at the University of Edinburgh. His previous books include *Research Practices in the Study of Kinship* (with Anthony Good, 1984), *Hunters and Herders of Southern Africa* (1992), and, edited with Jonathan Spencer, *Encyclopedia of Social and Cultural Anthropology* (1996).

History and Theory in Anthropology

Alan Barnard
University of Edinburgh

CAMBRIDGE
UNIVERSITY PRESS

PUBLISHED BY THE PRESS SYNDICATE OF THE UNIVERSITY OF CAMBRIDGE
The Pitt Building, Trumpington Street, Cambridge, United Kingdom

CAMBRIDGE UNIVERSITY PRESS
The Edinburgh Building, Cambridge CB2 2RU, UK   http://www.cup.cam.ac.uk
40 West 20th Street, New York, NY 10011–4211, USA   http://www.cup.org
10 Stamford Road, Oakleigh, Melbourne 3166, Australia

First published 2000

Printed in the United Kingdom at the University Press, Cambridge

Typeset in Plantin 10/12pt [VN]

A catalogue record for this book is available from the British Library

Library of Congress cataloguing in publication data

Barnard, Alan (Alan J.)
History and theory in anthropology / Alan Barnard.
      p.   cm
Includes bibliographical references and index.
ISBN 0 521 77333 4 (hardback); 0 521 77432 2 (paperback)
1. Anthropology – Philosophy.   2. Anthropology – History.   I. Title
GN33.B34 2000
301'.01–dc21 00–045362

ISBN 0 521 77333 4 hardback
ISBN 0 521 77432 2 paperback

For Joy

Contents

Figures

Tables

Preface

This book began life as a set of lecture notes for a course in anthropological theory, but it has evolved into something very different. In struggling through several drafts, I have toyed with arguments for regarding anthropological theory in terms of the history of ideas, the development of national traditions and schools of thought, and the impact of individuals and the new perspectives they have introduced to the discipline. I have ended up with what I believe is a unique but eclectic approach, and the one which makes best sense of anthropological theory in all its variety.

My goal is to present the development of anthropological ideas against a background of the converging and diverging interests of its practitioners, each with their own assumptions and questions. For example, Boas' consideration of culture as a shared body of knowledge leads to quite different questions from those which engaged Radcliffe-Brown with his interest in society as an interlocking set of relationships. Today's anthropologists pay homage to both, though our questions and assumptions may be different again. The organization of this book has both thematic and chronological elements, and I have tried to emphasize both the continuity and transformation of anthropological ideas, on the one hand, and the impact of great figures of the past and present, on the other. Where relevant I stress disjunction too, as when anthropologists change their questions or reject their old assumptions or, as has often been the case, when they reject the premises of their immediate predecessors. The personal and social reasons behind these continuities, transformations and disjunctions are topics of great fascination.

For those who do not already have a knowledge of the history of the discipline, I have included suggested reading at the end of each chapter, a glossary, and an appendix of dates of birth and death covering nearly all the writers whose work is touched on in the text. The very few dates of birth which remain shrouded in mist are primarily those of youngish, living anthropologists. I have also taken care to cite the date of original publication in square brackets as well as the date of the edition to be found in the references. Wherever in the text I refer to an essay within a book, the date in square brackets is that of the original publication of the essay. In the references, a single date in square brackets is that of the first publication of a given volume in its original language; a range of dates in square brackets is that of the original dates of publication of all the essays in a collection.

A number of people have contributed to the improvement of my text. Joy Barnard, Iris Jean-Klein, Charles Jędrej, Adam Kuper, Jessica Kuper, Peter Skalník, Dimitri Tsintjilonis, and three anonymous readers have all made helpful suggestions. My students have helped too, in asking some of the best questions and directing my attention to the issues which matter.

1 Visions of anthropology

Anthropology is a subject in which theory is of great importance. It is also a subject in which theory is closely bound up with practice. In this chapter, we shall explore the general nature of anthropological enquiry. Of special concern are the way the discipline is defined in different national traditions, the relation between theory and ethnography, the distinction between synchronic and diachronic approaches, and how anthropologists and historians have seen the history of the discipline.

Although this book is not a history of anthropology as such, it is organized in part chronologically. In order to understand anthropological theory, it is important to know something of the history of the discipline, both its 'history of ideas' and its characters and events. Historical relations between facets of anthropological theory are complex and interesting. Whether anthropological theory is best understood as a sequence of events, a succession of time frames, a system of ideas, a set of parallel national traditions, or a process of 'agenda hopping' is the subject of the last section of this chapter. In a sense, this question guides my approach through the whole of the book. But first let us consider the nature of anthropology in general and the meaning of some of the terms which define it.

Anthropology and ethnology

The words 'anthropology' and 'ethnology' have had different meanings through the years. They have also had different meanings in different countries.

The word 'anthropology' is ultimately from the Greek (*anthropos*, 'human', plus *logos*, 'discourse' or 'science'). Its first usage to define a scientific discipline is probably around the early sixteenth century (in its Latin form *anthropologium*). Central European writers then employed it as a term to cover anatomy and physiology, part of what much later came to be called 'physical' or 'biological anthropology'. In the seventeenth and eighteenth centuries, European theologians also used the term, in this case to refer to the attribution of human-like features to their deity. The German word *Anthropologie*, which described cultural attributes of different ethnic groups, came to be used by a few writers in Russia and Austria in the late eighteenth century (see Vermeulen 1995). However, this usage did not become established among scholars elsewhere until much later.

Eighteenth- and early nineteenth-century scholars tended to use 'ethnology' for the study of both the cultural differences and the features which identify the common humanity of the world's peoples. This English term, or its equivalents like *ethnologie* (French) or *Ethnologie* (German), are still in use in continental Europe and the United States. In the United Kingdom and most other parts of the English-speaking world 'social anthropology' is the more usual designation. In continental Europe, the word 'anthropology' often still tends to carry the meaning 'physical anthropology', though there too 'social anthropology' is now rapidly gaining ground as a synonym for 'ethnology'. Indeed, the main professional organization in Europe is called the European Association of Social Anthropologists or l'Association Européenne des Anthropologues Sociaux. It was founded in 1989 amidst a rapid growth of the discipline across Europe, both Western and Eastern. In the United States, the word 'ethnology' co-exists with 'cultural anthropology'.

In Germany and parts of Central and Eastern Europe, there is a further distinction, namely between *Volkskunde* and *Völkerkunde*. These terms have no precise English equivalents, but the distinction is a very important one. *Volkskunde* usually refers to the study of folklore and local customs, including handicrafts, of one's own country. It is a particularly strong field in these parts of Europe and to some extent in Scandinavia. *Völkerkunde* is the wider, comparative social science also known in German as *Ethnologie*.

Thus, anthropology and ethnology are not really one field; nor are they simply two fields. Nor does either term have a single, agreed meaning. Today they are best seen as foci for the discussion of issues diverse in character, but whose subject matter is defined according to an opposition between the general (anthropology) and the culturally specific (ethnology).

The 'four fields' approach

In North America, things are much simpler than in Europe. In the United States and Canada, 'anthropology' is generally understood to include four fields or subdisciplines:

(1) biological anthropology,

(2) archaeology,
(3) anthropological linguistics,
(4) cultural anthropology.

The main concern of this book is with cultural anthropology, but let us take each of these branches of North American anthropology in turn.

(1) Biological anthropology is the study of human biology, especially as it relates to a broadly conceived 'anthropology' – the science of human-kind. Sometimes this subdiscipline is called by its older term, 'physical anthropology'. The latter tends to reflect interests in comparative anat-omy. Such anatomical comparisons involve especially the relations be-tween the human species and the higher primates (such as chimpanzees and gorillas) and the relation between modern humans and our ancestors (such as *Australopithecus africanus* and *Homo erectus*). The anatomical comparison of 'races' is now largely defunct, having been superseded by the rapidly advancing field of human genetics. Genetics, along with aspects of demography, forensic science, and palaeo-medicine, make up modern biological anthropology in its widest sense.

(2) Archaeology (or 'prehistoric archaeology', as it would be called in Europe) is a closely related subdiscipline. While the comparison of ana-tomical features of fossil finds is properly part of biological anthropol-ogy, the relation of such finds to their habitat and the search for clues to the structure of prehistoric societies belong more to archaeology. Ar-chaeology also includes the search for relations between groups and the reconstruction of social life even in quite recent times. This is especially true with finds of Native North American material dating from before written records were available. Many American archaeologists consider their subdiscipline a mere extension, backwards in time, of cultural anthropology.

(3) Anthropological linguistics is the study of language, but especially with regard to its diversity. This field is small in comparison with linguis-tics as a whole, but anthropological linguists keep their ties to anthropol-ogy while most mainstream linguists today (and since the early 1960s) concentrate on the underlying principles of all languages. It might be said (somewhat simplistically) that whereas modern linguists study *language*, the more conservative anthropological linguists study *languages*. Anthro-pological linguistics is integrally bound to the 'relativist' perspective of cultural anthropology which was born with it, in the early twentieth-century anthropology of Franz Boas (see chapter 7).

(4) Cultural anthropology is the largest subdiscipline. In its widest sense, this field includes the study of cultural diversity, the search for cultural universals, the unlocking of social structure, the interpretation of

symbolism, and numerous related problems. It touches on all the other
subdisciplines, and for this reason many North American anthropologists
insist on keeping their vision of a unified science of anthropology in spite
of the fact that the overwhelming majority of North American anthropologists practise this subdiscipline alone (at least if we include within it
applied cultural anthropology). Rightly or wrongly, 'anthropology' in
some circles, on several continents, has come to mean most specifically
'cultural anthropology', while its North American practitioners maintain
approaches which take stock of developments in all of the classic 'four
fields'.

Finally, in the opinion of many American anthropologists, *applied
anthropology* should qualify as a field in its own right. Applied anthropology includes the application of ideas from cultural anthropology within
medicine, in disaster relief, for community development, and in a host of
other areas where a knowledge of culture and society is relevant. In a
wider sense, applied anthropology can include aspects of biological and
linguistic anthropology, or even archaeology. For example, biological
anthropology may help to uncover the identity of murder victims. Anthropological linguistics has applications in teaching the deaf and in
speech therapy. Archaeological findings on ancient irrigation systems
may help in the construction of modern ones.

A survey for the American Anthropological Association (Givens,
Evans, and Jablonski 1997: 308) found that applied anthropology, along
with unspecified topics not covered within the traditional four fields,
accounted for 7 per cent of American anthropology Ph.D.s between 1972
and 1997. Cultural anthropology Ph.D.s accounted for 50 per cent (and
many of these also focused on applied issues); archaeology, 30 per cent;
biological anthropology, 10 per cent; and linguistic anthropology, only 3
per cent. That said, some anthropologists reject the distinction between
'pure' and 'applied', on the grounds that all anthropology has aspects of
both. In other words, applied anthropology may best be seen not as a
separate subdiscipline, but rather as a part of each of the four fields.

Theory and ethnography

In social or cultural anthropology, a distinction is often made between
'ethnography' and 'theory'. Ethnography is literally the practice of writing
about peoples. Often it is taken to mean our way of making sense of other
peoples' modes of thought, since anthropologists usually study cultures
other than their own. Theory is also, in part anyway, our way of making
sense of our own, anthropological mode of thought.

However, theory and ethnography inevitably merge into one. It is

impossible to engage in ethnography without some idea of what is important and what is not. Students often ask what anthropological theory is for;
they could as easily ask what ethnography is for! Ideally, ethnography
serves to enhance our understanding of culture in the abstract and define
the essence of human nature (which is in fact predicated on the existence
of culture). On the other side of the coin, theory without ethnography is
pretty meaningless, since the understanding of cultural difference is at
least one of the most important goals of anthropological enquiry.

It is useful to think of theory as containing four basic elements:
(1) questions, (2) assumptions, (3) methods, and (4) evidence. The most
important *questions*, to my mind, are 'What are we trying to find out?', and
'Why is this knowledge useful?' Anthropological knowledge could be
useful, for example, either in trying to understand one's own society, or in
trying to understand the nature of the human species. Some anthropological questions are historical: 'How do societies change?', or 'What came
first, private property or social hierarchy?' Other anthropological questions are about contemporary issues: 'How do social institutions work?',
or 'How do humans envisage and classify what they see around them?'

Assumptions include notions of common humanity, of cultural difference, of value in all cultures, or of differences in cultural values. More
specifically, anthropologists may assume either human inventiveness or
human uninventiveness; or that society constrains the individual, or
individuals create society. Some assumptions are common to all anthropologists, others are not. Thus, while having some common ground,
anthropologists can have significant differences of opinion about the way
they see their subject.

Methods have developed through the years and are part of every fieldwork study. However, methods include not only fieldwork but, equally
importantly, comparison. *Evidence* is obviously a methodological component, but how it is treated, or even understood, will differ according to
theoretical perspective. Some anthropologists prefer to see comparison as
a method of building a picture of a particular culture area. Others see it as
a method for explaining their own discoveries in light of a more world-
wide pattern. Still others regard comparison itself as an illusory objective,
except insofar as one always understands the exotic through its difference
from the familiar.

This last point begs the existential question as to what evidence might
actually be. In anthropology, as for many other disciplines, the only thing
that is agreed is that evidence must relate to the problem at hand. In other
words, not only do theories depend on evidence, evidence itself depends
on what questions one is trying to answer. To take archaeology as an
analogy, one cannot just dig any old place and expect to find something of

significance. An archaeologist who is interested in the development of urbanism will only dig where there is likely to be the remains of an ancient city. Likewise in social anthropology, we go to places where we expect to find things we are interested in; and once there we ask small questions designed to produce evidence for the larger questions posed by our respective theoretical orientations. For example, an interest in relations between gender and power might take us to a community in which gender differentiation is strong. In this case, we might focus our questions to elucidate how individual women and men pursue strategies for overcoming or maintaining their respective positions.

Beyond these four elements, there are two more specific aspects of enquiry in social anthropology. These are characteristic of anthropological method, no matter what theoretical persuasion an anthropologist may otherwise maintain. Thus they serve to define an anthropological approach, as against an approach which is characteristic of other social sciences, especially sociology. The two aspects are:

(1) observing a society as a whole, to see how each element of that society fits together with, or is meaningful in terms of, other such elements;
(2) examining each society in relation to others, to find similarities and differences and account for them.

Observing a society as a whole entails trying to understand how things are related, for example, how politics fits together with kinship or economics, or how specific economic institutions fit together with others. *Examining each society in relation to others* implies an attempt to find and account for their similarities and their differences. Here we need a broader framework than the one that a fieldworker might employ in his or her study of a single village or ethnic group, but still there are several possibilities. Such a framework can encompass: (1) the comparison of isolated cases (e.g., the Trobrianders of Melanesia compared to the Nuer of East Africa), (2) comparisons within a region (e.g., the Trobrianders within the context of Melanesian ethnography), or (3) a more universal sort of comparison (taking in societies across the globe). Most social anthropologists in fact engage in all three at one time or another, even though, as anthropological theorists, they may differ about which is the most useful form of comparison in general.

Thus it is possible to describe social or cultural anthropology as having a broadly agreed methodological programme, no matter what specific questions anthropologists are trying to answer. Theory and ethnography are the twin pillars of this programme, and virtually all anthropological enquiry includes either straightforward comparison or an explicit attempt to come to grips with the difficulties which comparisons entail. Arguably, the comparative nature of our discipline tends to make us more aware of our theoretical premises than tends to be the case in less comparative fields, such as sociology. For this reason, perhaps, a special concern with theory rather than methodology has come to dominate anthropology. Every anthropologist is a bit of a theorist, just as every anthropologist is a bit of a fieldworker. In the *other* social sciences, 'social theory' is sometimes considered a separate and quite abstract entity, often divorced from day-to-day concerns.

Anthropological paradigms

It is commonplace in many academic fields to distinguish between a 'theory' and a 'theoretical perspective'. By a theoretical perspective, we usually mean a grand theory, what is sometimes called a theoretical framework or a broad way of looking at the world. In anthropology we sometimes call such a thing a *cosmology* if it is attributed to a 'traditional' culture, or a *paradigm* if it is attributed to Western scientists.

The notion of a 'paradigm'

The theoretical perspective, cosmology, or paradigm defines the major issues with which a theorist is concerned. The principle is the same whether one is a member of a traditional culture, an anthropologist, or a natural scientist. In the philosophy of science itself there are differences of opinion as to the precise nature of scientific thinking, the process of gaining scientific knowledge, and the existential status of that knowledge. We shall leave the philosophers to their own debates (at least until chapter 7, where their debates impinge upon anthropology), but one philosopher deserves mention here. This is Thomas Kuhn, whose book *The Structure of Scientific Revolutions* (1970 [1962]) has been influential in helping social scientists to understand their own fields, even though its subject matter is confined to the physical and natural sciences. According to Kuhn, paradigms are large theories which contain within them smaller theories. When smaller theories no longer make sense of the world, then a crisis occurs. At least in the natural sciences (if not quite to the same extent in the social sciences), such a crisis eventually results in either the overthrow of a paradigm or incorporation of it, as a special case, into a newer and larger one.

Consider, as Kuhn does, the difference between Newtonian physics and Einsteinian physics. In Newtonian physics, one takes as the starting point the idea of a fixed point of reference for everything in the universe. In an Einsteinian framework, everything (time, space, etc.) is relative to everything else. In Newtonian physics magnetism and electricity are considered separate phenomena and can be explained separately, but in Einsteinian physics magnetism is explained as a necessary part of electricity. Neither Newton's explanation of magnetism nor Einstein's is necessarily either true or false in absolute terms. Rather, they derive their meanings within the larger theoretical frameworks. Einstein's paradigm is 'better' only because it explains some phenomena that Newtonian physics cannot.

There is some dispute about whether or not anthropology can really be considered a science in the sense that physics is, but most would agree that anthropology at least bears some relation to physics in having a single overarching framework (in this case, the understanding of humankind), and within this, more specific paradigms (such as functionalism and structuralism). Within our paradigms we have the particular facts and explanations which make up any given anthropological study. Anthropology goes through 'revolutions' or 'paradigm shifts' from time to time, although the nature of ours may be different from those in the natural sciences. For anthropology, fashion, as much as explanatory value, has its part to play.

Diachronic, synchronic, and interactive perspectives

Within anthropology, it is useful to think in terms of both a set of competing theoretical perspectives within any given framework, and a hierarchy of theoretical levels. Take evolutionism and diffusionism, for example. Evolutionism is an anthropological perspective which emphasizes the growing complexity of culture through time. Diffusionism is a perspective which emphasizes the transmission of ideas from one place to another. They compete because they offer different explanations of the same thing: how cultures change. Yet both are really part of the same grand theory: the theory of social change.

Sometimes the larger perspective which embraces both evolutionism and diffusionism is called the *diachronic* one (indicating the relation of things through time). Its opposite is the *synchronic* perspective (indicating the relation of things together in the same time). Synchronic approaches include functionalism, structuralism, interpretivism, and other ones which try to explain the workings of particular cultures without reference to time. A third large grouping of anthropological theories is what might be termed the *interactive* perspective. This perspective or, more accurately, set of perspectives, has both diachronic and synchronic aspects. Its adherents reject the static nature of most synchronic analysis, and reject also the simplistic historical assumptions of the classical evolutionist and

Table 1.1. *Diachronic, synchronic, and interactive perspectives*

DIACHRONIC PERSPECTIVES
  evolutionism
  diffusionism
  Marxism (in some respects)
  culture-area approaches (in some respects)

SYNCHRONIC PERSPECTIVES
  relativism (including 'culture and personality')
  structuralism
  structural-functionalism
  cognitive approaches
  culture-area approaches (in most respects)
  functionalism (in some respects)
  interpretivism (in some respects)

INTERACTIVE PERSPECTIVES
  transactionalism
  processualism
  feminism
  poststructuralism
  postmodernism
  functionalism (in some respects)
  interpretivism (in some respects)
  Marxism (in some respects)

diffusionist traditions. Proponents of interactive approaches include those who study cyclical social processes, or cause-and-effect relations between culture and environment.

Table 1.1 illustrates a classification of some of the main anthropological approaches according to their placing in these larger paradigmatic groupings. The details will have to wait until later chapters. The important point for now is that anthropology is constructed of a hierarchy of theoretical levels, though assignment of specific approaches to the larger levels is not always clear-cut. The various 'isms' which make these up form different ways of understanding our subject matter. Anthropologists debate both within their narrower perspectives (e.g., one evolutionist against another about either the cause or the chronology of evolution) and within larger perspectives (e.g., evolutionists versus diffusionists, or those favouring diachronic approaches against those favouring synchronic approaches).

Very broadly, the history of anthropology has involved transitions from diachronic perspectives to synchronic perspectives, and from synchronic perspectives to interactive perspectives. Early diachronic studies, especially in evolutionism, often concentrated on global but quite specific theoretical issues. For example, 'Which came first, patrilineal or matrilineal descent?' Behind this question was a set of notions about the relation between men and women, about the nature of marriage, about private property, and so on. Through such questions, quite grand theories were built up. These had great explanatory power, but they were vulnerable to refutation by careful counter-argument, often using contradicting ethnographic evidence.

For the synchronic approaches, which became prominent in the early twentieth century, it was often more difficult to find answers to that kind of theoretical question. 'Which is more culturally appropriate, patrilineal or matrilineal descent?' is rather less meaningful than 'Which came first?' The focus landed more on specific societies. Anthropologists began to study societies in great depth and to compare how each dealt with problems such as raising children, maintaining links between kinsfolk, and dealing with members of other kin groups. A debate did emerge on which was more important, descent (relations within a kin group) or alliance (relations between kin groups which intermarry). Yet overall, the emphasis in synchronic approaches has been on the understanding of societies one at a time, whether in respect of the function, the structure, or the meaning of specific customs.

Interactive approaches have concentrated on the mechanisms through which individuals seek to gain over other individuals, or simply the ways in which individuals define their social situation. For example, the question might arise: 'Are there any hidden features of matrilineal or patrilineal descent which might lead to the breakdown of groups based on such principles?' Or, 'What processes enable such groups to persist?' Or, 'How does an individual manoeuvre around the structural constraints imposed by descent groups?'

Thus anthropologists of diverse theoretical orientations try to tackle related, if not identical theoretical questions. The complex relation *between* such questions is one of the most interesting aspects of the discipline.

Society and culture

Another way to classify the paradigms of anthropology is according to their broad interest in either *society* (as a social unit) or *culture* (as a shared set of ideas, skills, and objects). The situation is slightly more complicated than the usual designations 'social anthropology' (the discipline as practised in the United Kingdom and some other countries) and 'cultural anthropology' (as practised in North America) imply. (See table 1.2.)

Table 1.2. *Perspectives on society and on culture*

PERSPECTIVES ON SOCIETY
evolutionism
functionalism
structural-functionalism
transactionalism
processualism
Marxism
poststructuralism (in most respects)
structuralism (in some respects)
culture-area approaches (in some respects)
feminism (in some respects)

PERSPECTIVES ON CULTURE
diffusionism
relativism
cognitive approaches
interpretivism
postmodernism
culture-area approaches (in most respects)
structuralism (in most respects)
poststructuralism (in some respects)
feminism (in some respects)

Basically, the earliest anthropological concerns were with the nature of society: how humans came to associate with each other, and how and why societies changed through time. When diachronic interests were overthrown, the concern was with how society is organized or functions. Functionalists, structural-functionalists and structuralists debated with each other over whether to emphasize relations between individuals, relations between social institutions, or relations between social categories which individuals occupy. Nevertheless, they largely agreed on a fundamental interest in the social over the cultural. The same is true of transactionalists, processualists and Marxists.

Diffusionism contained the seeds of cultural determinism. This was elevated to an extreme with the relativism of Franz Boas. Later, interpretivists on both sides of the Atlantic and the postmodernists of recent times all reacted against previous emphases on social structure and monolithic visions of social process. Society-oriented anthropologists and culture-oriented anthropologists (again, not quite the same thing as 'social' and 'cultural' anthropologists) seemed to be speaking different languages, or practising entirely different disciplines.

A few perspectives incorporated studies of both culture and society (as conceived by extremists on either side). Structuralism, in particular, had

society-oriented concerns (such as marital alliance or the transition between statuses in ritual activities) and culture-oriented ones (such as
certain aspects of symbolism). Feminism also had society-oriented interests (relations between men and women within a social and symbolic
order) and cultural ones (the symbolic order itself). Culture-area or
regional approaches have come from both cultural and social traditions,
and likewise are not easy to classify as a whole.

In this book, chapters 2 (on precursors), 3 (evolutionism) and 4 (diffusionism and culture-area approaches) deal mainly with *diachronic perspectives*. Evolutionism has been largely concerned with society, and
diffusionism more with culture. Chapters 5 (functionalism and structural-functionalism) and 6 (action-centred, processual, and Marxist approaches) deal fundamentally with *society*, respectively from a relatively
static point of view and a relatively dynamic point of view. Chapters 7
(relativism, etc.), 8 (structuralism), 9 (poststructuralist and feminist
thought), and 10 (interpretivism and postmodernism) all deal mainly
with *culture* (though, e.g., poststructuralism also has strong societal elements). Thus the book is organized broadly around the historical transition from diachronic to synchronic to interactive approaches, and from
an emphasis on society to an emphasis on culture.

Visions of the history of anthropology

A. SEQUENCE OF EVENTS OR NEW IDEAS (e.g., Stocking 1987; 1996a; Kuklick 1991)
B. SUCCESSION OF TIME FRAMES, either stages of development or Kuhnian
   paradigms, each of which is best analysed internally (e.g., Hammond-
   Tooke 1997; and to some extent Stocking 1996a)
C. SYSTEM OF IDEAS, which changes through time and which should be
   analysed dynamically (e.g., Kuper 1988; and to some extent Harris
   1968; Malefijt 1976)
D. SET OF PARALLEL NATIONAL TRADITIONS (e.g., Lowie 1937; and to some
   extent Hammond-Tooke 1997)
E. PROCESS OF AGENDA HOPPING (perhaps implicit in Kuper 1996 [1973])

The form of anthropological theory really depends on how one sees the
history of the discipline. For example, is anthropology evolving through
stages, that is, developing through a sequence of events or new ideas? Or
does it consist of a succession of larger time frames, either stages of
development or Kuhnian paradigms? Is anthropology undergoing structural transformations? Is it developing through divergent and convergent

threads of influence between distinct national traditions? Or can the history of the discipline be seen essentially as 'agenda hopping'? As Roy D'Andrade explains:

What happens in agenda hopping is that a given agenda of research reaches a point at which nothing new or exciting is emerging from the work of even the best practitioners. It is not that the old agenda is completed, or that too many anomalies have accumulated to proceed with equanimity. Rather, what has happened is that as more and more has been learned the practitioners have come to understand that the phenomena being investigated are quite complex. Greater and greater effort is required to produce anything new, and whatever is found seems to be of less and less interest. When this happens, a number of practitioners may defect to another agenda – a new direction of work in which there is some hope of finding something really interesting. (D'Andrade 1995: 4–8)

Each of the five possibilities shown above is a legitimate view of the history of anthropology. Indeed, each is represented within this book at one point or another. An emphasis on events, as in A, represents the most objective view, but it fails to capture the complexity of relations between ideas. An emphasis on the internal workings of paradigms, as in B, is common among historians of science, but it does not allow the observer the dynamic perspective of C or the comparative perspective of D. In a sense, E is the inverse of B, as it amounts to the suggestion that anthropologists abandon their old questions rather than incorporate them into a new framework. C is tempting, but it is difficult to sustain the notion of anthropology as a single system when viewing its whole history, in all its diversity and complexity.

With some exceptions, A and B tend to be historians' views, and C, D, and E tend to be practising anthropologists' views. My own leanings are towards D and E, the former representing anthropology at its most conservative, and the latter representing it at its most anarchical.

Concluding summary

Theory in social and cultural anthropology is dependent on what questions anthropologists ask. The organizational structure of the discipline, and the relation of theory to ethnographic findings are integral to these questions. Broadly, theories may be classified as diachronic, synchronic, or interactive, in focus. Paradigms in the physical and natural sciences generally have clear-cut, agreed goals. Anthropological paradigms are not as easy to pin down. We may characterize much of the history of anthropology as a history of changing questions (agenda hopping), but it also has elements of paradigm shift and continuing, often nationally based, traditions.

The remainder of this book explores the development of anthropological ideas with these notions as guidelines. It is organized around historical transitions from diachronic to synchronic to interactive approaches, and from an emphasis on society (especially chapters 5 and 6) to an emphasis on culture (broadly chapters 7 to 10).

FURTHER READING

Ingold's *Companion Encyclopedia of Anthropology* (1994) presents a wide vision of anthropology, including biological, social, and cultural aspects of human existence. Other useful reference books include Adam Kuper and Jessica Kuper's *Social Science Encyclopedia* (1996 [1985]), Barnard and Spencer's *Encyclopedia of Social and Cultural Anthropology* (1996), Barfield's *Dictionary of Anthropology* (1997), and Bonte and Izard's *Dictionnaire de l'ethnologie et de l'anthropologie* (1991).

Chalmers' *What is This Thing Called Science?* (1982 [1976]) describes the major theories in the philosophy of science, including those of Kuhn and his critics.

Recent introductions to anthropological theory which take different approaches from mine include Barrett's *Anthropology* (1996), J. D. Moore's *Visions of Culture* (1997) and Layton's *Introduction to Theory in Anthropology* (1997). Barrett divides the history of anthropology into three broad phases: 'building the foundation', 'patching the cracks', and 'demolition and reconstruction'. He alternates discussion from theory to method in each. Moore summarizes the lives and works of twenty-one major contributors to the discipline, from Tylor to Fernandez. Layton concentrates on relatively recent and competing paradigms: functionalism, structuralism, interactionism, Marxism, socioecology, and postmodernism. See also the various histories of anthropology cited in table 1. 2.

2   Precursors of the anthropological tradition

Most anthropologists would agree that anthropology emerged as a distinct branch of scholarship around the middle of the nineteenth century, when public interest in human evolution took hold. Anthropology as an academic discipline began a bit later, with the first appointments of professional anthropologists in universities, museums, and government offices. However, there is no doubt that anthropological ideas came into being much earlier. *How much earlier* is a matter of disagreement, though not particularly much active debate. Rather, each anthropologist and each historian of the discipline has his or her own notion of the most relevant point at which to begin the story.

From a 'history of ideas' point of view, the writings of ancient Greek philosophers and travellers, medieval Arab historians, medieval and Renaissance European travellers, and later European philosophers, jurists, and scientists of various kinds, are all plausible precursors. My choice, though, would be with the concept of the 'social contract', and the perceptions of human nature, society, and cultural diversity which emerged from this concept. This is where I shall begin.

Another, essentially unrelated, beginning is the idea of the Great Chain of Being, which defined the place of the human species as between God and the animals. This idea was in some respects a forerunner of the theory of evolution, and later in this chapter we shall look at it in that context. Eighteenth-century debates on the origin of language and on the relation between humans and what we now call the higher primates are also relevant, as is the early nineteenth-century debate between the polygenists (who believed that each 'race' had a separate origin) and the monogenists (who emphasized humankind's common descent, whether from Adam or ape). Such ideas are important not only as 'facts' of history, but also because they form part of modern anthropology's perception of itself.

Natural law and the social contract

During the late Renaissance of Western culture and the Enlightenment which followed, there came to be a strong interest in the natural condition of humanity. This interest, however, was not always coupled with much knowledge of the variety of the world's cultures. Indeed, it was often tainted by a belief in creatures on the boundary between humanity and animality – monstrosities with eyes in their bellies or feet on their heads (see Mason 1990). In order for anthropology to come into being, it was necessary that travelogue fantasies of this kind be overcome. Ironically to modern eyes, what was needed was to set aside purported ethnographic 'fact' in favour of reason or theory.

The seventeenth century

The first writers whose vision went beyond the 'facts' were mainly jurists and philosophers of the seventeenth and eighteenth centuries. Their concerns were with abstract relations between individual and society, between societies and their rulers, and between peoples or nations. The times in which they wrote were often troubled, and their ideas on human nature reflected this. Politics, religion, and the philosophical discourse which later gave rise to anthropology, were intimately linked.

Let us start with Hugo Grotius. Grotius studied at Leiden and practised law in The Hague, before intense political conflicts in the United Provinces (The Netherlands) led to his imprisonment and subsequent escape to Paris. It was there he developed the ideas which gave rise to his monumental *De jure belli ac pacis* (1949 [1625]). Grotius believed that the nations of the world were part of a larger trans-national society which is subject to the Law of Nature. Although his predecessors had sought a theological basis for human society, Grotius found his basis for society in the sociable nature of the human species. He argued that the same natural laws which govern the behaviour of individuals in their respective societies should also govern relations between societies in peace and in war. His text remains a cornerstone of international law. Arguably, it also marks the dawn of truly anthropological speculation on the nature of human society.

Samuel Pufendorf (Puffendorf), working in Germany and Sweden, extended this concern. His works are surprisingly little known in modern anthropology, but intriguingly they long foreshadow debates of the 1980s and 1990s on human 'sociality'. 'Sociality' is a word of recent anthropological invention. Yet it much more literally translates Pufendorf's Latin *socialitas* than the more usual gloss of his anglophone interpreters, 'sociability'. Indeed, Pufendorf also used the adjective *sociabilis*, 'sociable' (or as one modern editor renders it, 'capable of society'). He believed that society and human nature are in some sense indivisible, because humans are, by nature, sociable beings.

Nevertheless, Pufendorf did at times speculate on what human nature might be like without society and on what people did at the dawn of civilization. His conclusions on the latter are striking. His notion of 'there' is where people lived in scattered households, while 'here' is where they have united under the rule of a state: 'There is the reign of the passions, there there is war, fear, poverty, nastiness, solitude, barbarity, ignorance, savagery; here is the reign of reason, here there is peace, security, wealth, splendour, society, taste, knowledge, benevolence' (1991 [1673]: 118).

Meanwhile in a politically troubled England, Thomas Hobbes (e.g. 1973 [1651]) had been reflecting on similar issues. He stressed not a natural proclivity on the part of humans to form societies, but rather a natural tendency towards self-interest. He believed that this tendency needed to be controlled, and that rational human beings recognized that they must submit to authority in order to achieve peace and security. Thus, societies formed by consent and common agreement (the 'social contract'). In the unstable time in which he wrote, his ideas were anathema to powerful sections of society: the clergy, legal scholars, and rulers alike; each opposed one or more elements of his complex argument. Nevertheless, Hobbes' pessimistic view of human nature inspired other thinkers to examine for themselves the origins of society, either rationally or empirically. His vision is still debated in anthropological circles, especially among specialists in hunter-gatherer studies.

John Locke's (1988 [1690]) view of human nature was more optimistic. Writing at the time of the establishment of constitutional monarchy in England, he saw government as ideally limited in power: consent to the social contract did not imply total submission. He believed that the 'state of nature' had been one of peace and tranquillity, but that a social contract became necessary in order to settle disputes. While human sinfulness might lead to theft and possibly to excessive punishment for theft in a state of nature, the development of society encouraged both the preservation of property and the protection of the natural freedoms which people in the state of nature had enjoyed.

The eighteenth century

Locke's liberal views inspired many in the next century, including Jean-Jacques Rousseau, though ironically Rousseau's essay *Of the Social Contract* fails to mention him at all. Rather, Rousseau begins with an attack on

Grotius' denial that human power is established for the benefit of the governed. Says Rousseau: 'On this showing [i.e. if we were to follow Grotius], the human species is divided into so many herds of cattle, each with its ruler, who keeps guard over them for the purpose of devouring them' (Rousseau 1973 [1762]: 183). For Rousseau, government and the social contract differed. Government originated from a desire by the rich to protect the property they had acquired. The social contract, in contrast, is based on democratic consent. It describes an idealized society in which people agree to form or retain a means of living together which is beneficial to all.

Social-contract theory assumed a logical division between a 'state of nature' and a 'state of society', and those who advocated it nearly always described it as originating with a people, living in a state of nature, and getting together and agreeing to form a society. The notion was ultimately hypothetical. The likes of Hobbes, Locke, and Rousseau, just as much as opponents of their view (such as David Hume and Jeremy Bentham), perceived the 'state of nature' essentially as a rhetorical device or a legal fiction. The degree to which they believed that early humans really did devise an *actual* social contract is difficult to assess.

Most anthropologists today would accept the view that we cannot separate the 'natural' (in its etymological sense, relating to birth) from the 'cultural' (relating to cultivation), because both are inherent in the very idea of humanity. We inherit this view from these early modern writers who sought to humanize our understandings of law and legal systems.

Definitions of humanity in eighteenth-century Europe

A number of important anthropological questions were first posed in modern form during the European Enlightenment: what defines the human species in the abstract, what distinguishes humans from animals, and what is the natural condition of humankind. Three life forms occupied attention on these questions: 'Wild Boys' and 'Wild Girls' (feral children), 'Orang Outangs' (apes), and 'Savages' (indigenous inhabitants of other continents).

Feral children

Feral children seemed to proliferate in the eighteenth century: 'Wild Peter of Hanover', Marie-Angélique Le Blanc the 'Wild Girl of Champagne' (actually an escaped captive, Native North American), Victor the 'Wild Boy of Aveyron', and so on. These were people found alone in the woods and subsequently taught 'civilized' ways. Peter was brought to

England in the reign of George I and lived to an old age on a pension provided by successive Hanoverian kings. He never did learn to say more than a few words in any language. Le Blanc, on the other hand, eventually learned French and wrote her memoirs, which were published in 1768. Victor, a celebrated case, was probably a deaf-mute; and efforts to teach him to communicate were to have lasting effects on the education of the deaf in general (see Lane 1977).

Anthropological interest in feral children has long since dwindled (see Lévi-Strauss 1969a [1949]: 4–5). This is largely because modern anthropologists are less interested in the abstract, primal 'human nature' which such children supposedly exhibited, and much more concerned with the relations between human beings as members of their respective societies.

The Orang Outang

The Orang Outang is a more complicated matter. In Enlightenment Europe this word, from Malay for 'person of the forest', meant very roughly what the word 'ape' means today (while 'ape' referred to baboons). 'Orang Outang' was a generic term for a creature believed to be almost human, and I retain the eighteenth-century-style initial capital letters and spelling to represent this eighteenth-century concept. More precisely, the Orang Outang was the 'species' that Carolus Linnaeus (1956 [1758]) and his contemporaries classified as *Homo nocturnus* ('night man'), *Homo troglodytes* ('cave man'), or *Homo sylvestris* ('forest man'). Travellers reported these nearly human, almost blind, creatures to be living in caves in Ethiopia and the East Indies. Apparently, neither travellers nor scientists could distinguish accurately between the true orang-utans (the species now called *Pongo pygmaeus*) and the chimpanzees (*Pan troglodytes* and *Pan paniscus*). Gorillas (the species *Gorilla gorilla*) were as yet unknown.

The importance of the Orang Outang is highlighted in the debate between two interesting characters, James Burnett (Lord Monboddo) and Henry Home (Lord Kames). Monboddo and Kames were judges of Scotland's Court of Session. Kames (1774) held a narrow definition of humanity. He argued that the differences between cultures were so great that population groups around the world could reasonably be regarded as separate species. He regarded Native Americans as biologically inferior to Europeans and incapable of ever attaining European culture.

Monboddo (1773–92; 1779–99) went to the other extreme. He maintained (incorrectly) that some of the aboriginal languages of North America were mutually intelligible with both Basque and Scots Gaelic. Not only did he regard Amerindians as fully human, he even thought they spoke much the same language as some of his countrymen! Furthermore, Monboddo extended the definition of humanity to include those who could not speak at all, namely the Orang Outangs of Africa and Asia. He believed that these 'Orang Outangs' were of the same *species* as 'Ourselves' (a category in which he included Europeans, Africans, Asians, and Amerindians alike).

Monboddo's views on the relation between apes and humans are rather more cogent than is generally credited. From the evidence he had, it appeared that his 'Orang Outangs', particularly the chimpanzees of Central Africa, might well be human. Travellers' reports claimed that they lived in 'societies', built huts, made weapons, and even mated with those he called 'Ourselves'. The reports said that they were gregarious, and Monboddo accepted this. Today, we know that orangs in Southeast Asia are relatively solitary, but chimps in Africa are indeed gregarious, make tools, and can certainly be said to possess both culture and society (McGrew 1991).

The essence of Monboddo's theory, however, is language. Just as intellectuals of his day accepted the relatively mute Peter the Wild Boy as human, they should, Monboddo argued, accept the speechless Orang Outang as human too (Monboddo 1779–99 [1784], III: 336–7, 367). In his view, natural humanity came first, then the 'social contract' through which society was formed, then speech and language. Kames, in contrast, did not even accept that Native North Americans had spoken the presumed common language of Eurasia before the biblical Tower of Babel. Thus Kames and Monboddo represent the two most extreme views on the definition of humanity.

Notions of the 'Savage'

'Savage' was not necessarily a term of abuse at that time. It simply connoted living wild and free. The prototypical savage was the Native North American who (although possessing 'culture' in the modern sense of the word) was, in the average European mind, closer to the ideal of 'natural man' than was the Frenchman or Englishman.

The idea of the 'noble savage' is commonly associated with Enlightenment images of alien peoples. This phrase originates from a line in John Dryden's play *The Conquest of Granada*, Part I, first produced in 1692:

> . . . as free as nature first made man,
> Ere the base laws of servitude began,
> When wild in woods the noble savage ran.

Dryden's words became a catch-phrase for the school of thought which argued that humanity's natural condition was superior to its cultured condition.

In the seventeenth and early eighteenth centuries the more typical view of human nature was that humans were but 'tamed brutes'. In the words of Hobbes (1973 [1651]: 65), savage life was 'solitary, poore, nasty, brutish, and short'. The relation between nature and society was a matter of much debate. Some conceived this in a Christian idiom. Nature was good, and society was a necessary evil, required in order to control inherited human sinfulness after the Fall of Adam and Eve. Others argued that society represented the true nature of human existence, since humans are pretty much found only in societies. As Pufendorf suggested, humankind's 'natural' existence is social and cultural, and nature and culture are impossible to separate.

Like Monboddo, Rousseau accepted Orang Outangs as essentially human, but unlike Monboddo he thought of them as solitary beings. This in turn was his view of the 'natural' human. He shared with Monboddo an idealization of savage life, but shared with Hobbes an emphasis on a solitary existence for 'natural man' (*l'homme naturel* or *l'homme sauvage*). Rousseau begins the main text of his *Discourse on the Origin of Inequality* (1973 [1755]: 49–51) with a distinction between two kinds of inequality. The first kind concerns 'natural inequality', differences between people in strength, intelligence, and so on. The second concerns 'artificial inequality', the disparities which emerge within society. It is artificial inequality that he tries to explain. Instead of being poor, nasty, or brutish, Rousseau's solitary 'natural man' was healthy, happy, and free. Human vices emerged only after people began to form societies and develop the artificial inequalities which society implies.

Rousseau's theory was that societies emerged when people began to settle and build huts. This led to the formation of families and associations between neighbours, and thus (simultaneously) to the development of language. Rousseau's 'nascent society' (*société naissante*) was a golden age, but for most of humankind it did not last. Jealousies emerged, and the invention of private property caused the accumulation of wealth and consequent disputes between people over that wealth. Civilization, or 'civil society' developed in such a way that inequalities increased. Yet there was no going back. For Rousseau, civil society could not abolish itself. It could only pass just laws and try to re-establish some of the natural equality which had disappeared. The re-establishment of natural equality was the prime purpose of government, a purpose which most European governments of his day were not fulfilling. Yet not all societies had advanced at the same rate. Savage societies, in his view, retained some of the attributes of the golden age, and Rousseau praised certain savage societies in Africa and the Americas for this.

Coupled with earlier doctrines about 'natural law', Rousseau's idealiz-ation of simple, egalitarian forms of society helped to mould both the American and the French republics. This idealization also influenced a generation of philosophers in Britain, especially in Scotland. Adam Smith tried to tackle two of Rousseau's key problems: the origin of language (Smith 1970 [1761]), and the development of the importance of private property (1981 [1776]). Adam Ferguson (1966 [1767]) praised Amerin-dian societies for their lack of corruption and held great sympathy with the 'savages' of all other continents. Indeed, it seems that the 'polished' residents of Lowland Edinburgh thought of him, a Gaelic-speaking High-lander, as a sort of local 'noble savage'.

I believe that we inherit much more than we might at first think from the eighteenth-century imagery of the 'noble savage'. In anthropological theories which emphasize the differences between 'primitive' and 'non-primitive' societies (such as evolutionist ones), the noble savage has survived as the representation of 'nature' in the primitive. In anthropol-ogical theories which do not make this distinction (such as relativist ones), the noble savage is retained as a reflection of the common human-ity at the root of all cultures.

Sociological and anthropological thought

Standing somewhat apart from the romantic concerns with feral children, Orang Outangs, and noble savages was the sociological tradi-tion embodied by Montesquieu, Saint-Simon, and Comte. Paralleling this, successors to the Scottish Enlightenment argued vehemently over the biological relationships between the 'races'. Both of these develop-ments were to leave their mark in nineteenth- and twentieth-century anthropology.

The sociological tradition

The baron de Montesquieu's *Persian Letters* (1964 [1721]) chronicle the adventures of two fictional Persian travellers who make critical remarks on French society. That book foreshadows not only the genre of ethno-graphy, but also reflexivity (see chapter 10). More importantly though, Montesquieu's *Spirit of the Laws* (1989 [1748]) explores the forms of government, the temperament of peoples, and the influence of climate on society, with true ethnographic examples from around the world. Central to his argument is the idea of the 'general spirit' (*esprit général*), which is the fundamental essence of a given culture: 'Nature and climate almost alone dominate savages; manners govern the Chinese; laws tyrannize Japan; in former times mores set the tone in Lacedaemonia; in Rome it was set by the maxims of government and the ancient mores' (1989 [1748]: 310). While Lévi-Strauss once argued that Rousseau was the founder of the social sciences, Radcliffe-Brown gave that honour to Montesquieu; and the styles of the later structuralist and structural-functionalist traditions do owe much to the respective rationalism of Rousseau and empiricism of Montesquieu.

At the dawn of the nineteenth century the comte de Saint-Simon and subsequently his pupil, Auguste Comte, put forward notions which combined Montesquieu's interest in a science of society with a desire to incorporate it within a framework embracing also physics, chemistry, and biology. Saint-Simon wrote little, and he wrote badly. However, in his writings and especially in Comte's famous lecture on social science (1869 [1839]: 166–208), we see the emergence of the discipline that Comte named *sociologie*. The proposed field of sociology comprised the ideas of Montesquieu, Saint-Simon, and other French writers, and also much of what we would later recognize as an evolutionist, anthropological thinking about society.

All the social sciences, sociology included, owe at least part of their origins to what in eighteenth-century English was known as Moral Philosophy. Modern biology grew from eighteenth-century interests in Natural History (as it was then called). Sociology in a sense originated from a deliberate naming of this new discipline by Comte, who clearly saw his sociology as similar in method to biology. Yet, while the linear development of sociology from pre-Comtean ideas, through Comte to his successors is clear, the development of anthropology or ethnology is not. Anthropological ideas preceded both the formation of the discipline and the name for it. As we saw in chapter 1, 'anthropology' and 'ethnology' as labels existed independently and with little association with what later came to be seen as mainstream social anthropology.

Polygenesis and monogenesis

It is often said that the early nineteenth century was an era of little interest to historians of anthropology. Those who might point to the eighteenth-century Enlightenment as the dawn of our science regard the early nineteenth century as a step backwards. Those who would begin in the late nineteenth century regard the earlier part of that century as an age before anthropology's basic principles came to be accepted. Certainly there is truth in both of these views. However, anthropology as we know it depends on the acceptance of the idea of monogenesis, and therefore the controversy between the monogenists and their opponents marks the first stirring of anthropology as a discipline.

Monogenesis means 'one origin', and polygenesis means 'more than one origin'. Monogenists such as James Cowles Prichard, Thomas Hodgkin, and Sir Thomas Fowell Buxton, believed that all humankind had a single origin, whereas their opponents, championed by Robert Knox and later by James Hunt, believed that humankind had many origins and that 'races' were akin to species.

Modern anthropology assumes all humankind to be fundamentally the same, biologically and psychologically. Such a view was inherent in Montesquieu's argument that it was climate, and not biology or mental ability, which made cultures different. In the early nineteenth century such monogenist or evolutionist thinking was regarded as politically liberal, and in some circles downright radical. Theories of cultural evolution, just as much as the later relativist theories of twentieth-century anti-racists (discussed in chapter 7), depend on the acceptance of the essential biological and intellectual similarity of all peoples. While nineteenth-century white European and American evolutionists did feel themselves superior to people of other 'races', they nevertheless believed that all societies had evolved through the same stages. Therefore, they reasoned, the study of 'lower' races could tell them something about the early phases of their own societies. However, polygenists of the early nineteenth century lacked this belief. Therefore, the polygenists did not invent, and could not have invented, anthropology as we understand it today.

Here is where we must part company with the history of ideas and turn instead to the politics of the emerging discipline. The monogenist camp was centred in two organizations: the Aborigines Protection Society or APS, founded 1837, and the Ethnological Society of London or ESL, founded 1843 (see Stocking 1971). The former was a human rights organization, and the latter grew from its scientific wing. Many of the leaders of both were Quakers. At that time, only members of the Church of England could attend English universities, so Quakers wishing to attend university were educated beyond its borders. Prichard (then a Quaker, though later an Anglican) and Hodgkin attended Edinburgh, and Buxton attended Trinity College Dublin. As it happened, Prichard and Hodgkin carried with them views picked up from the last remnant of the Scottish Enlightenment, Dugald Stewart – whose anthropological ideas stem ultimately from Montesquieu. They carried his small monogenist flame through the dark days of polygenist dominance. Prichard, Hodgkin, and Buxton were all medical doctors. They combined their vocation with the passionate furtherance of their beliefs in human dignity through the APS, and the natural, resulting scientific understanding of humankind through the ESL. Hodgkin helped establish ethnology in France, though he achieved greater fame from his important work in pathology. Buxton became an eminent, reforming Member of Parliament, and one of his particular interests was the improvement of living conditions for the indigenous inhabitants of Britain's African colonies.

The early leader of the polygenists was Robert Knox, the anatomist who dissected the bodies of the victims of Edinburgh's infamous grave-robbers turned murderers, William Burke and William Hare. In *Races of Men: A Fragment* (Knox 1850) he argued, as had Kames, that different human 'races' are virtually different species, and that they had originated separately. Prichard, in various editions of his *Researches into the Physical History of Man* (see, e.g 1973 [1813]), put the monogenist case. His book went into five editions and long stood as an early evolutionist tract. Prichard did not necessarily believe that members of the 'races' they defined were equal in intellectual ability, but he did believe that 'lower' races were capable of betterment. While such a view would be rightly regarded as reactionary today, it was a veritable beacon of liberalism then, in anthropology's darkest age.

With hindsight it is ironic that those who held to polygenesis did take an interest in the differences between human groups. They did call themselves 'anthropologists', whereas most in the monogenist camp preferred the less species-centred term 'ethnologists'. Their battles helped to form the discipline, and it would be denial of this fundamental fact if we were to ignore the battle and remember only our victorious intellectual ancestors, the monogenists, in isolation. We should recall too that the discipline encompasses the study of both the human nature common to all 'races' and the cultural differences between peoples.

Concluding summary

It is impossible to define an exact moment when anthropology begins, but anthropological ideas emerged long before the establishment of the discipline. Crucial to the understanding of what was to come were notions of natural law and the social contract, as formulated in the seventeenth and eighteenth centuries. Though these ideas have long since been jettisoned by most social scientists, they mark a baseline for debate about the nature of society.

Eighteenth-century anthropological concerns included feral children, the 'Orang Outang', and notions of 'savage life'. Ethnography as we know it did not then exist. Montesquieu and Rousseau are both today claimed as founders of social science, and the sociological tradition descended from the former has parallels with the anthropological one. One view of the founding of anthropology is that it stems from the debate between the polygenists and the monogenists of the early nineteenth century. All anthropology today inherits the monogenist premise that humankind is one species.

FURTHER READING

Slotkin's *Readings in Early Anthropology* (1965) presents an excellent selection of short pieces from original sources, while Adams' *Philosophical Roots of Anthropology* (1998) covers in more depth some of the issues touched on here. The classic work on natural law is Gierke's *Natural Law and the Theory of Society* (1934).

My essay '*Orang Outang* and the definition of *Man*' (Barnard 1995) gives further details of the debate between Kames and Monboddo. See also Berry's *Social Theory of the Scottish Enlightenment* (1997) and Corbey and Theunissen's *Ape, Man, Apeman* (1995). A useful reference book on the period is Yolton's *Blackwell Companion to the Enlightenment* (1991). See also Daiches, Jones, and Jones' *A Hotbed of Genius* (1986).

Levine's *Visions of the Sociological Tradition* (1995) presents an excellent overview of sociology and general social theory. His approach is similar to the one given in this book for anthropology, though with a greater emphasis on national traditions. Stocking's essay 'What's in a name?' (1991) describes the founding of the Royal Anthropological Institute against a background of dispute between monogenists and polygenists. See also Stocking's introductory essay in the 1973 reprint of Prichard's *Researches into the Physical History of Man*.

3   Changing perspectives on evolution

By the 1860s the stage was set for evolutionist anthropology to come into its own within what was then, in Britain as on the Continent, usually called ethnology. It had already done so in archaeology, especially in Denmark. There the three-age theory (Stone Age, Bronze Age, and Iron Age) had been systematically propagated from around 1836 by Christian Jürgensen Thomsen, Sven Nilsson, and others (see, e.g., Trigger 1989: 73–86). Yet what became British anthropology grew not so much from this source, nor from evolutionary ideas in biology, but from questions of the relation between contemporary 'savage' or 'primitive' societies and Victorian England.

This chapter examines some parallels and disjunctions between the biological and anthropological traditions. It chronicles the rise of evolutionist anthropology, mainly in Britain in the middle of the nineteenth century, and its rapid development as the major paradigm for understanding human society prior to functionalism and relativism. It also covers the return to evolutionist thought in the middle of the twentieth century, mainly in America, and the growth of evolutionist ideas towards the end of the twentieth century.

Essentially, there are just four broad strands of evolutionist thinking in anthropology: unilinear, universal, and multilinear evolutionism, plus neo-Darwinism. The first three have been gradualist approaches, and their labels come from Julian Steward (1955 [1953]: 11–29), a practitioner of multilinear evolutionism. Neo-Darwinism comes in different guises, from 1970s sociobiology and its aftermath to more recent approaches to the origin of symbolic culture.

Biological and anthropological traditions

Encyclopedists of the Middle Ages classified the universe from high to low – God to angels to man; man to apes, and apes to worms; animals to plants. They believed the world was ordered, and they thought they could deduce its order according to principles embodied in the 'Great Chain of

27

Being' which united all living things. The term was in use well into the eighteenth century, and arguably the modern theory of evolution is an elaboration of this notion (see Lovejoy 1936).

However, there are two important differences between the Great Chain of Being and the theory of evolution. First, the concept 'evolution' has a temporal as well as a spatial aspect: things change or evolve through time. Secondly, whereas the classic notion of the Great Chain of Being was based on the idea of the fixity of species, the theory of evolution, in its biological form, depends on the contrary notion of the mutability of species. Lower forms evolve into higher forms.

Social evolution has parallels with biological evolution. This is obvious today, in a world where most book-educated people learn biological evolution before they learn of other cultures. It was also obvious in the late nineteenth century, when social advancement was often seen as analogous to biological evolution. However, to view social evolution *merely* in this way would be to invert historical precedent. The widespread acceptance in intellectual circles of the notion of 'progress' predates the theory of evolution as we know it. Eighteenth-century thinkers accepted the idea of the progress of humankind within the framework of biological immutability; it was only in the late nineteenth century that modern notions of social evolution became associated with ideas like 'mutual struggle' or 'survival of the fittest'.

The boundary between the Great Chain of Being and evolutionism is hardly a precise one, and beliefs concerning the mechanisms of biological change were varied. Linnaeus, essentially an anti-evolutionist, believed in a system of hybridization, whereby hybrids constantly form and produce new genera. The comte de Buffon seems to have changed his mind in the course of completing his forty-four-volume *Histoire naturelle* (1749–1804), at first rejecting any ancestral connection between different species, and later moving towards a degenerativist, or anti-evolutionist view. He argued that a small number of pure, ancestral animal forms developed into a multiplicity of less-pure, modern forms.

In *Philosophie zoologique*, Jean-Baptiste de Lamarck (1914 [1809]) suggested that each line of descent evolves to produce more-and-more-sophisticated life forms, but that the earliest forms continue to be reproduced by spontaneous generation. The earliest amoebas, he claimed, evolved into jellyfish. These evolved eventually into fishes, and later to reptiles, then later to mammals. Meanwhile, more recently generated amoebas evolved into jellyfish and fishes, but they will not yet have become reptiles or mammals. More recently still, other amoebas will have reproduced to form jellyfish, but not yet fishes. Lamarck believed that organs improve or decay according to whether they are used to their potential or not. He also held that individuals acquired characteristics which could be passed on to their descendants. For example, if a girl learned to paint at an early age, later she could pass on such talents to her children in the womb. Plainly, Lamarck had the idea of evolution, but he misunderstood its mechanism.

Charles Darwin (1859) rejected the Lamarckian view. He argued instead that evolution proceeds only through the passing down of what we now call genetic traits. Accidental mutation produced greater variety, and the forms which were most successful in their respective environments would reproduce more efficiently. Darwin, along with Alfred Russel Wallace (who came to similar conclusions), described the mechanism of evolution as 'sexual selection'. Since only those individuals that survive to reproduce will pass on their genes, mutations which enable this survival will be favoured. Isolation encourages greater change, and ultimately the formation of new species. As Darwin's ideas became well known, they came to have wide implications in Western societies, where they were seen as a threat to Christian orthodoxy. Their impact in the social sciences has, of course, been profound too (see Kuper 1994).

However, it would be wrong to see all developments in evolutionist anthropology simply as an extension of Darwinian theory. Evolutionist thinking in anthropology predates Darwin. Darwin published his most 'anthropological' work (he preferred the word 'ethnological'), *The Descent of Man*, in 1871 – the same year as important works by Lewis Henry Morgan and Edward Burnett Tylor. Arguably, Lamarck's theory, though flawed in biology, makes better sense than Darwin's as an analogy to explain gradual, unilinear, or universal, cultural evolution. Although biological traits may not be passed on in the womb as Lamarck thought, nevertheless newly invented cultural traits may be passed rapidly from individual to individual. New culture traits have the capacity to transform existing social relations. Societies become more complex as this process continues.

Unilinear evolutionism

Unilinear evolutionism is the notion that there exists one dominant line of evolution. In other words, all societies pass through the same stages. Since societies will progress at different rates, those societies which have been slower will remain at a 'lower' level than those which progress more rapidly. Of course, all this begs the question of what exactly it means for social institutions to be 'progressing' or 'evolving'. Different unilinear evolutionists have emphasized different things: material culture, means of subsistence, kinship organization, religious beliefs. But unilinear evolutionists, in general, believed that these phenomena are interrelated, and that therefore changes, say in means of subsistence, create evolutionary changes in kinship organization, religious belief and practice, and so on.

Maine, Lubbock, and Morgan

The idea of unilinear evolution grew from the early nineteenth-century monogenist theorists, but its high point was in the late nineteenth century, when it stood as the central idea of anthropological thought. The first major issue was that of the *family* versus the *social contract*: the outcome would lead directly to kinship theory, a central stage of anthropological debate ever since.

The social contract had stood for nearly two hundred years as a cornerstone of legal thought. Then, in 1861, Scots-born jurist Sir Henry Maine turned against the idea. He objected to it because of its artificial nature and its use in what he regarded as faulty legal fictions. Recalling his specialized knowledge of Roman law (and assuming its great antiquity), Maine argued that society originates instead in the family and in kinship groups built upon the family. In the absence of much opposition from inside the anthropological fraternity, family and kinship easily emerged victorious. However, this led ultimately to a host of vehement debates about the prehistory of the family and descent systems, and the relation of those systems to 'primitive promiscuity', the idea of 'private property', totemism, and the incest taboo (see Kuper 1988).

About a decade after Maine's book, two sometime politicians from opposite sides of the Atlantic came to prominence as anthropologists. Sir John Lubbock sat in the House of Commons as the Liberal Member of Parliament for London University, and was later elevated to the Peerage as Lord Avebury. He was a banker by profession, and is remembered today for his bill which established 'bank holidays' (so-called because he knew he could get more support among the Conservative opposition by calling them that than by calling them 'workers' holidays'). He also wrote prolifically on anthropology, archaeology, and the natural sciences.

Lewis Henry Morgan's career had certain similarities: success in business coupled with politics, and indeed amateur authorship of books on natural history. He was a part-time railroad tycoon and an upstate New York Republican state senator. His political renown was far less great than Lubbock's. Nevertheless his influence was profoundly ironic – because his key anthropological ideas were taken up by Karl Marx and especially by Friedrich Engels (1972 [1884]). The Republican state senator's emphasis on private property as the driving force of evolution struck a chord with his Communist admirers. In 1871, Lubbock and

Morgan met and discussed such matters, when the latter visited England.

Morgan is remembered primarily for two things. First, he was one of very few theorists of the nineteenth century to conduct serious field research. After a chance encounter with a Western-educated Iroquois named Ely Parker, Morgan was to spend many years working with Iroquois and other Native American peoples. He studied especially their kinship systems and their traditional political institutions, and he was active on their behalf as a campaigner for land rights. Secondly, after his discovery of 'the classificatory system of relationship' (essentially, the classifying of parallel cousins by the same terms as brothers and sisters), he developed a comparative model for the understanding of kinship systems worldwide. This was, in his view, the key to unlocking the prehistory of human society.

Matrilineality versus patrilineality

Most nineteenth-century scholars believed that matrilineality came before patrilineality, but they had different views about the evidence for this and the reasons why one system of unilineal descent might emerge first and the other evolve from it. Lubbock (1874 [1870]) maintained some scepticism about the significance of primitive matrilineality, but he accepted that existing matrilineal societies had evolved along similar lines. He believed that matrilineality had once been more common, when marriage was not fully developed. With fully developed marriage, he believed, property would go from a man to his own children (patrilineally) rather than to his sisters' children (matrilineally). Yet Lubbock also pointed out that in the most 'savage' of societies, marriage is unknown, 'female virtue' is not highly regarded, and women are treated as inferior to men. Thus he could not support the more radical matriarchal theories which were emerging. On the more clearly patrilineal side, Maine (1913 [1861]) had thought the Romans were quite ancient, and they, along with the Hebrews, Greeks, and Teutonic nations, all had patrilineal descent: he saw no reason to look to distant ethnography or to further speculation beyond the works of his predecessors in jurisprudence.

Those who favoured the primacy of matrilineality debated both with the patrilineal theorists and with other matrilineal theorists. Morgan and his arch-enemy John Ferguson McLennan (also a lawyer, and parliamentary draftsman for Scotland) left the patrilineal theorists behind and reserved their most vehement criticisms for each other. The debate centred on the reasons *why* matrilineality might have preceded patrilineality. McLennan (1970 [1865]) thought that a struggle for food in early times led to female infanticide. The resulting shortage of women led to polyandry (i.e., one woman with several husbands). Members of these ancient societies could not determine the father of any given child, so they came to reckon descent matrilineally. Patrilineality developed later, as men began first to capture, and subsequently to exchange women with men from other bands.

Morgan (1871; 1877) rested his case on kinship terminology – something which McLennan regarded as of little or no significance. Part of Morgan's argument was diffusionist. The Iroquois of New York State and Ontario (with whom Morgan worked in the 1840s and 1850s) had matrilineal descent and inheritance and a relationship terminology similar in some ways to South Asian ones. He noted too that the neighbouring Ojibwa had a terminology of similar structure even though they spoke a very different language. He reasoned that the First Peoples of North America must have migrated from Asia, a fact today firmly established though in his time still one of speculation. He argued, further, that Asian peoples must once have been matrilineal. Their common classification of the father and the father's brother by one relationship term, and their classification of parallel cousins as 'brothers and sisters', implied to Morgan a system of marriage of several brothers to the same woman. From such a system, he reasoned, matrilineal descent emerged.

Morgan believed that relationship terminologies are conservative, and as such reflect ancient social facts. In other words, they preserve hints of past forms of social organization because other aspects of society change faster than the terminology its members use. In his scheme, patrilineality came rather late, with the rise in private property and its associated laws of inheritance, from father to son. The matrilineal Iroquois represented an in-between stage in evolution, before patrilineal descent but long after what he called the stage of 'promiscuous intercourse'. The early phase of promiscuity evolved into a system of cohabitation or intermarriage between brothers and sisters, which gave rise to a 'communal family' and a custom, reported in Hawaii, whereby a group of brothers and their wives, or sisters and their husbands, once held common 'possession' over one another. This was reflected in his own time by the Hawaiian custom of such a kinship grouping still describing their relationship as *pinalua*, or one of intimacy, though no longer maintaining the practice of common sexual possession (if it ever really existed). The relationship terminology system of Hawaiian and other Polynesian languages, in turn, classifies only by generation, with parents and their siblings all called 'father' and 'mother', and both siblings and cousins called 'brother' and 'sister'.

Swiss jurist J. J. Bachofen, in *Das Mutterrecht* (1967 [1861]: 67–210), presented yet another notion of matrilineal pre-eminence. His theory rested on a supposed early feminist movement which overthrew primeval male dominance. This, he said, was followed by a subsequent resurgence of male authority. Bachofen's evidence involved mainly survivals of notions about female deities (from the matriarchal phase) and the ethnographic discovery of South American *couvade* (from the male overthrow of female authority). This French word designates the custom in which husbands of pregnant wives act as if they are pregnant themselves. Native South Americans reportedly did this in order to deflect malevolent spirits and keep them away from the unborn baby. Bachofen, in fact, here confused matrilineality (descent through the mother) with matriarchy (rule by mothers), but his theory had some following in his own time. It also anticipated more recent revolutionist, and indeed feminist, perspectives on 'primitive society'.

It is important to remember that all these arguments were made *within* the framework of unilinear evolution. There was little concern with cultural diversity for its own sake. To the unilinear evolutionists, cultural diversity was only important as an indicator of different stages within a grand evolutionary scheme. Perhaps the fact that most of the key protagonists were lawyers is significant too. As a pastime they debated over descent as in work they might have argued over competing inheritance claims. The logic and nuance of argument was important to them. There is a real sense in which anthropology as we know it began with law – whether with the notion of natural law (and the social contract) or with the squabbles over family and kinship which, from Maine onwards, became a central focus of the anthropological discourse.

Theories of 'totemism'

In the last quarter of the nineteenth century, though interest in kinship remained strong, other aspects of culture became focal points. Among these was religion, especially *totemism*. A short ethnographic excursion into 'totemism' may help to clarify the points of debate.

'Totemism' is today often written in quotation marks because there is a real question as to whether the category itself represents a single, specific phenomenon. Many have argued that when we talk about totemism, we are actually talking about quite different things in different cultures. However, nineteenth-century writers generally perceived totemism as a worldwide phenomenon, found in Native North and South America, Australia, Asia, Africa, and the Pacific. Arguably, elements of 'totemism' – the symbolic representation of the social by the natural – are found in European thought too, but not to the same degree, and certainly not with the same coherence as in, say, Australian Aboriginal thought. Military symbolism is one obvious example – calling units or operations by the names of animal species.

The word *totem* is from the Ojibwa. The word was introduced into the English language in 1791 by a British merchant, but the first good description of Ojibwa totemic ideas was in 1856, by one Peter Jones, who was both a Methodist missionary and an Ojibwa chief. The next ethnographer, in 1885, was also an Ojibwa, and all subsequent cross-cultural notions of totemism emanate, at least in part, from these two indigenous accounts (see, e.g., Lévi-Strauss 1969b [1962]). In Ojibwa thought, the *totem* is contrasted to the *manitoo*. The totem is represented by an animal species, and it symbolizes a patrilineal clan. It appears in mythology, and there is a rule that a person cannot marry one who shares his or her totem. The manitoo is also represented by an animal species, but it is the guardian spirit of an individual rather than a group. It comes in dreams, and a person cannot kill or eat his or her manitoo.

Similar notions are found in other cultures, but there are differences. For example, ethnographers of Australia have recorded some six forms of 'totemism', with each Aboriginal society possessing some two or three. There are (1) 'individual totems' which resemble the manitoos of the Ojibwa, though they often belong specifically to medicine men rather than to ordinary individuals. There are (2) 'clan totems', like the totems of the Ojibwa. These can be emblems of patrilineal clans, or of matrilineal ones. There are also (3) phratry totems, a phratry being simply a group of clans; and (4) moiety totems, where society is divided in 'half' (French *moitié*), on either patrilineal or matrilineal principles. There are (5) section and subsection totems, these divisions being marriageable categories defined by a combination of descent and generational principles. Finally, there are (6) land-based totems, for example, belonging to spirits of sacred sites. Usually in Australia, all these kinds of totem represent beings whose flesh cannot be eaten *and* whose fellow members cannot be taken as lovers or spouses. So they tend to incorporate the abstract principles of both the Ojibwa manitoos and the Ojibwa totems.

As ethnographic literature on 'totemism' grew, especially of the Australian varieties, armchair theorists in Europe used that literature to speculate on the origin and psychological nature of totems. French sociologist Emile Durkheim (1963 [1898]) argued that the most 'primitive' of men were in awe of blood and refused to cohabit with females of their respective clans, since they believed that their totemic gods inhabit this clan blood. Scottish folklorists Andrew Lang and Sir James Frazer emphasized the consubstantial relation between a man and his totem. Sir Edward Burnett Tylor saw totemism simply as a special case of ancestor worship. Yet whatever their considerable disagreements, almost all theorists of the day saw a relation between totemism and exogamy, and most held that totemism had evolved first. Furthermore, by implication at least, almost all of them saw this as an answer to the problem of primal human society, because these evolutionists believed that Australian Aboriginal culture represented a survival of early culture (for further details, see Kuper 1988: 76–122; Barnard 1999). The prime example of 'primal culture' had moved from Sir Henry Maine's Romans to the Aborigines.

Interesting among theories of totemism is that of Sigmund Freud (1960 [1913]: 140–55 *passim*). Though essentially a Lamarckian, he built his theory on the ideas of Darwin and also of theologian William Robertson Smith. What he sought to explain was no less than the origin of totemism, sacrifice, and the incest taboo all at once. Freud imagined a primal horde of males and females in which one male eventually became dominant. This male alone controlled the females, and he alone had sexual access to them. Members of the horde ultimately came to revere him as a god, but the young males resented his authority. They killed him and had sex with their sisters and their mothers. Then they felt guilty for doing such a horrible thing, so, it seems, they invented totemism! More precisely, the alpha-male primate, patriarch of the horde came to be remembered as a totemic being. His descendants invented sacrifices to appease his spirit. They instituted rules forbidding incest to stop the 'natural' proclivity of males to mate with their mothers. Thus, according to the Freudian view, the horrible deeds of murder and incest came to be forgotten, though vestiges of it remained deep in the totemic systems of Australian Aborigines, and very deep in the subconscious of all humanity. Freud saw both the Greek myth of Oedipus and the 'Oedipus complex' as 'memories' of these distant events.

Tylor and Frazer on 'early' religion

Religion attracted the attention of several scholars. Two are worthy of special note because of their position in the discipline, their great influence, and indeed for the high quality of their work: Tylor and Frazer. Both had the advantage of great longevity (Tylor lived from 1832 to 1917, and Frazer 1854 to 1941). Thus, for decades, their successive publications and public pronouncements represented the established, unilinear evolutionist view. Especially in Frazer's case, this view competed with emerging diffusionist, functionalist, and relativist ideas as later generations rebelled against evolutionism.

Sir Edward Tylor's introduction to anthropology came during a trip to North America. In Havana he met Henry Christie, a gentleman adventurer and like himself an English Quaker, who was about to set off for

Mexico. Tylor went with him and later published his first book on what he found (Tylor 1861). There and in subsequent works, especially *Primitive Culture* (Tylor 1871), Tylor explored the evolution of culture through the doctrine of 'survivals'. The idea is that present-day culture retains elements which have now lost their function, but whose present existence is a testimony to their past importance. Morgan's kinship terminologies are an example. Others, which Tylor was fond of, include items of clothing which formerly were functional but which in his time were only decorative: unused buttons behind the waist of a jacket, or cut-away collars always kept turned down. One of the most curious aspects of Tylor's method was his study of school children in London, for he believed that they, being less mature and less educated, might hold clues to primitive thought. In the realm of religion, he argued that survivals of ancient rituals and beliefs continue long after the original meaning has been forgotten, while the more instinctual and primitive thoughts of civilized humanity may still hold hints of the earlier development of religious ideas.

Tylor's theory of religion consisted of a scheme of evolution from 'animism', the all-embracing doctrine that souls (Latin *animi* or *animae*) exist independently of the material world. He noted that in virtually every human society, there is a common belief in a spiritual essence which survives death. People the world over make offerings to the dead, or to revere things such as trees or streams in which souls are believed to dwell. Tylor postulated that the earliest peoples held this notion through dreams in which souls appeared to them; and that societies eventually developed the practices of making offerings, and later, sacrifices, to such souls, fairies, and deities. He believed that fetishism (when humans control their deities through material objects) and totemism (in which animal or plant species are vested with souls) developed from animism.

In a number of respects, Tylor agreed with Lubbock, though it was in fact the latter who more simply stated the unilinear scheme many nineteenth-century anthropologists seem to have accepted: *atheism* (the absence of definite ideas on a deity), to *fetishism*, to *nature-worship* or *totemism*, to *shamanism* (where deities are believed to be remote and powerful, accessible only through shamans), to *idolatry* (when gods become like men), to *theism* (Lubbock 1874 [1870]: 119). Tylor avoided making such an explicit sequence as this, perhaps because he viewed the evolution of religion as a complex matter, with survivals of earlier stages overlapping with newer ideas and different kinds of animism emerging simultaneously. Tylor's contribution therefore was less substantive and more theoretical and methodological, and as such it still stands as an achievement of evolutionist thought – however flawed the paradigm of unilinear evolutionism may be.

Sir James Frazer was, for most of his career, a classics scholar and Fellow of Trinity College, Cambridge. The University of Liverpool granted him the title of Professor of Social Anthropology in 1907, but he held this as an honorary position. A shy man, he is said to have disliked teaching, but earned sizeable royalties from his voluminous, influential, and widely read books. His *Golden Bough* is one of the great books of anthropology, and it was widely read by generations of intellectuals of all kinds (the young Bronislaw Malinowski, then still a mathematician, read it in order to improve his English). On the surface, *The Golden Bough* represents an attempt to explain the origin and meaning of the slaughter of ancient Italian priest-kings, each by his successor. On a deeper level, it merges myth and history, ethnography and reason, to build a fanciful, poetic overview of the human psyche and social order. *The Golden Bough* was first published in 1890, and expanded to twelve volumes in 1900. Let me quote the final words of the 1922 abridged edition:

Without dipping so far deep into the future we may illustrate the course which thought has hitherto run by likening it to a web woven of three different threads – the black thread of magic, the red thread of religion, and the white thread of science . . . Could we then survey the web of thought from the beginning, we should probably perceive it to be at first a chequer of black and white, a patchwork of true and false notions, hardly tinged as yet by the red thread of religion. But carry your eye farther along the fabric and you will remark that, while the black and white chequer still runs through it, there rests on the middle portion of the web . . . a dark crimson stain, which shades off insensibly into a lighter tint as the white thread of science is woven more and more into the tissue. (Frazer 1922: 713)

What is intriguing here is that while Frazer privileges one realm of culture (namely science) over the others, he nevertheless attributes it to the most primitive as well as the most civilized cultures. From a relativist point of view (see chapter 7), magic in so-called primitive societies may be thought of as nothing more than applied science, or technology. Frazer here sees religion as evolving after primitive science, and modern culture as containing both these threads. This is interesting in light of more recent debates between fundamentalist Christians, who call themselves 'creation scientists', and American anthropologists who in their view have blind faith in the 'false doctrine' of Darwinism (see, e.g., Williams 1983; Stipe 1985). Both sides claim for themselves the status of 'scientist' and claim for science the truth which Frazer also believed it represented.

All the unilinear evolutionists, whether they specialized in kinship or in religion, held a vision of anthropology as a science which tied the present and the past. They sought origins, and they found them among their 'primitive' contemporaries. Their methodological flair, however, was dampened as succeeding generations turned away from the question of origins. Anti-evolutionists turned to diffusion, social function, and cultural diversity. We shall take up those stories later. Yet it is important to see the next phase in evolutionist thought, universal evolutionism, as an attempt to return to grand questions, if not of origins then of universal history.

Universal evolutionism

Universal evolutionism emerged in the early twentieth century as a softening of the tenets of unilinear evolutionism. In light of new ethnographic and archaeological evidence, precise unilinear phases, consistent cross-culturally and throughout the world, could no longer be sustained. So instead, broad, 'universal' phases of evolution were postulated, such as the classical division between 'savagery', 'barbarism', and 'civilization' (championed by Morgan, among others). Debates on matters like matrilineality versus patrilineality were jettisoned as too speculative to merit further consideration. Also thrown aside were the *details* of, for example, Frazer's many analyses of totemism (see especially Frazer 1910: vol. IV), in favour of generalities similar to those of Frazer's passage above, which foreshadowed universal evolutionist thinking. Yet it is of the greatest importance that the universal evolutionism which emerged in the 1930s owed more to Morgan's materialism than to Frazer's quest for the aesthetic and esoteric in the human spirit. The new generation of evolutionists reacted against the functionalist, and especially the relativist bent of most anthropologists of their day (see chapters 5 and 7).

The main proponents of universal evolutionism were Australian archaeologist V. Gordon Childe and American cultural anthropologist Leslie White. Their left-wing political concerns led them to review the theories of Marx and Engels, and those anthropologists, notably Morgan, who had influenced Marx and Engels.

V. Gordon Childe

Childe was prominent as a leftist member of the Australian Labour Party, and his views found no favour in the conservative Australian universities in which he sought employment. He emigrated to Britain in 1921 and travelled widely in Europe before accepting a chair in archaeology, in 1927, at Edinburgh. He later moved to the Institute of Archaeology in London, before returning to Australia to end his days. In Britain Childe achieved fame, both as a field archaeologist and as a theoretician. His ideas became widely accepted within archaeology, where universal evolutionism is perhaps a more natural theory than it is in cultural anthropology. The ages of humankind, seen through their technology, are readily apparent in the archaeological record; and Childe's belief that prehistory and history ought to be the same subject, but with different methodologies, was attractive to archaeologists of his time.

Childe wrote many books, but among them two short popular texts stand out as his most influential. *Man Makes Himself* (Childe 1936) examined human history as a whole, and branched out across the continents, whereas his previous work had largely been confined to Europe. It traced evolution from hunting and gathering, to the dawn of agriculture, to the formation of states, the urban revolution and the 'revolution in human knowledge'. *What Happened in History* (Childe 1942), intended as a sequel, turned out to be much more pessimistic. Written during the early part of the Second World War, it suggested that Europe was heading for a new 'dark age' (albeit only a temporary one). At his death in 1957, Childe's desire to see archaeology and universal history established as social sciences was a long way off.

Leslie A. White

White's place as an isleted evolutionist in a sea of relativism (which American anthropology then was) must have been even more problematic than Childe's. For forty years (1930 to 1970) he taught at the University of Michigan, where he gradually built up a following of 'neo-evolutionist' students and colleagues. Although he did publish five ethnographies on Pueblo peoples, White is far better known for his theoretical works. In a series of essays collected as *The Science of Culture* (White 1949), he put forward the notion of culture as an integrated, dynamic, and symbolic system whose most important component is technology. His proposed science, 'culturology', would be the study of that phenomenon. It would steal subject matter from psychology, but it would oppose conventional psychological theory in seeing history as comprised of cultural forces driven by technology. Its relation to sociology would be similar, in that it would explain what sociology, focused as it is on social interaction, could not.

In *The Evolution of Culture* (White 1959), White turned his attention to the course of evolution from the 'Primate Revolution' to the fall of Rome. He argued that 'energy' is the key mechanism of cultural evolution. In the earliest phase, energy existed in the form of the human body alone. Later, men and women harnessed other sources: fire, water, wind, and so on. Advances in the manufacture of tools, in the domestication of animals and plants, and in the intensification of agriculture all increased efficiency and spurred on cultural evolution.

White's style of evolutionism continued after his death through the work of his students. Marshall Sahlins (especially in his early work), Elman Service, and Marvin Harris, among many others, owe an intellectual debt to Leslie White. However, with the dawn of cultural ecology, their vision became more particularistic than White's, and their approaches decidedly more multilinear. It is ironic too that all these later scholars have acknowledged debts to Marx and Engels, whereas White himself remained largely silent on this in his major texts.

Multilinear evolutionism and cultural ecology

Unilinear evolutionism's assertions were problematic, because they were either untestable or (when falsified by ethnographic cases) clearly non-universal. Unilinear evolutionism rested on an assumption that things occur and change everywhere in the world in the same way, if not at the same time. According to a strictly unilinear approach, specific culture changes have but one explanation, though theorists might disagree as to what explanation this might be.

Universal evolutionism was a much less powerful theory precisely because it was harder to debate. Many would agree that technology advances and societies become more complex with time, but what would they do with this information? What was needed was a more sophisticated and more controversial approach.

Julian H. Steward

Multilinear evolutionism was devised by Julian Steward, of the University of Illinois, as an explicit attempt to get away from both the vague generalities of universal evolutionism and the problematic assertions of unilinear evolutionism. It gets around such difficulties by positing diverse trajectories of technological and social evolution in different regions of the world. These trajectories were essentially limited by ecological circumstances, that is, by historical determinations of technology and the very important further limiting factor of the natural environment. Thus multilinear evolutionism became closely bound with the idea of cultural ecology. It also shares a certain similarity with Darwinian thought in biology, by its analogy with the biological theory of speciation.

The main breakthrough came in 1955, when Steward's major essays to that date were published in book form. Although he went on later to look at technologically advanced societies, his ethnographic work on the Shoshone of California and his comparative essays on hunter-gatherers (which formed the major portion of *Theory of Culture Change*) set the scene. Steward, and later Service (e.g., 1962), propounded the notion that hunter-gatherers developed characteristic ways of exploiting resources to their best advantage not only through technology but also through seasonal migrations, territorial arrangements, and group structures suited to the purpose (see Barnard 1983).

George Peter Murdock

Meanwhile, a quite different but equally multilinear and ecological approach was being developed by George Peter Murdock, first at Yale and later at Pittsburgh. Murdock founded the Cross-Cultural Survey, later the Human Relations Area Files, through which he tried to assemble cultural facts from all the cultures of the world. His purpose was to enable scholars to correlate the distribution of culture traits and work out historical trajectories both in general and for particular culture areas or similar culture types. His best known work was the somewhat mis-titled monograph *Social Structure* (1949), which employed a sample of 250 representative societies for such a purpose. A handful of other scholars followed, notably Melvin Ember and Carol Ember at the Human Relations Area Files (New Haven Connecticut), and in some of his work, Jack Goody at Cambridge.

Let me illustrate the method and theory Murdock espoused with an example. It had been known before Murdock's work that certain rules of descent are more commonly found with certain patterns of postmarital residence, for example, patrilineal descent with virilocal residence (with the husband), or matrilineal descent with either uxorilocal (with the wife) or viri-avunculocal residence (with the husband's mother's brother). Murdock established more precisely statistical correlations between such patterns, and then sought to explain the reasons behind them, and relate them statistically to other patterns, such as means of subsistence and kinship terminologies.

Supposing, let us say, hoe agriculture is commonly practised by women. Women in such a society might tend to pass on both their skills and their fields to their daughters, who would bring in their husbands upon marriage. *De facto* matrilineal groups would be established, and an ideology of matrilineal descent might be expected to emerge. Matrilineal descent is further correlated either with what Murdock called 'Iroquois-type terminology', in which cross-cousins are distinguished from parallel cousins, or with 'Crow-type terminology', in which, in addition, father's sister and father's sister's daughter are called by the same term. The apparent reason for this peculiarity is that a person's father's sisters and father's sisters' daughters would reside in the same locale. If matrilineal descent is recognized, they would also belong to the same matrilineal kin group. Actually, 'Crow-type terminology' makes sense in a strongly matrilineal society, and it would make little sense in most other kinds of society. Murdock reasoned that when modes of descent change, so too should kinship terminologies. Therefore, we can posit a causal, and evolutionary, relationship between these elements of culture.

Neo-Darwinism

Neo-Darwinism is a broad set of perspectives comprising two basic and very different schools of thought: sociobiology and what might be called 'revolutionist' (as opposed to narrowly evolutionist) thinking. The former tradition is in continuity with biology. The latter takes up the nineteenth-century quest for origins and even returns to nineteenth-century interests in totemism and primitive promiscuity.

Sociobiology

By the late 1970s a new grand evolutionist tradition was encroaching on the social sciences, especially in the United States. This was 'sociobiology', sparked off by E. O. Wilson's (1975) book by that title – a book which treated human culture and society as simply adjuncts of humankind's animal nature. Wilson pulled together a variety of strands of biological thinking, and like Darwin considered the implications for the understanding of humanity. Yet unlike Darwin, he took on the whole of human culture. Wilson argued that the application of Darwinian principles makes it possible to explain culture in much the same way as one explains the social life of termites, frogs, or wolves. Analysing anthropological data, he considered the effects of group selection on human warfare, sexual selection on the development of political organization, art as a special manifestation of tool use, ritual music as derivatives of communication, and even ethics as an extension of the desire to pass on one's genes. Altruism within family or community, he suggested, fulfils the function of enabling those who share one's genes to do better than those who do not.

One anthropologist who was influenced by the sociobiology movement was Robin Fox. His approach is interesting because it illustrates clearly the view that human society has its basis in animal sociality. Fox (1975) argued that aspects of human kinship systems are found also among non-human primates. Some primate species have the makings of 'descent' (which he defines as pan-generational relations within a group) while others have only 'alliance' (defined as mating relations between groups). This argument contradicts the mainstream theory of structural-ist anthropology, following Claude Lévi-Strauss (1969a [1949]), that the incest taboo marks the boundary between animals and humans. Only humans have the capability of instituting a taboo. For Lévi-Strauss, the incest taboo is part of (human) nature because it is present in all societies, but it is the essence of culture because it is defined differently from culture to culture. Some cultures, Lévi-Strauss points out, prohibit sex between cross-cousins, while other cultures recognize the category of cross-cousins as precisely the one within which sex is allowed.

However, few anthropologists apart from Fox were taken in, and some reacted strongly against the perceived threat. Among the latter were two influential American scholars of broadly evolutionist persuasion: Marvin Harris and Marshall Sahlins. Harris (1979: 119–40) attacked sociobiology as biological reductionism. Taking on the biologists in their own terms, he pointed out that 'genotypes never account for all the variations in behavioural phenotype' (1979: 121): even in simple organisms, learned behaviour is a factor. Culture, as he says, is 'gene free'. Sahlins, in his devastating little book, *The Use and Abuse of Biology*, pointed out that there was a vast gulf between aggression and war, between sexuality and cross-cousin marriage, and between socially functional 'reciprocal altru-ism' and formalized gift exchange. 'Within the void left by biology', as he put it, 'lies the whole of anthropology' (Sahlins 1977 [1976]: 16).

Thus sociobiology turned out not to be the 'new synthesis' its adher-ents hailed it as. Its impact may have been great among biologists, but it never succeeded in overtaking anthropology. There was simply too much it left unexplained.

The symbolic revolution?

Revolutionist thinking was, in retrospect, characteristic of many thinkers in the eighteenth century. We also see it in the work of Morgan, Marx, and Engels, and more especially in Freud's theory of the origin of to-temism and Lévi-Strauss' theory of the incest taboo as the origin of culture. White's notion of a 'Primate Revolution' is also a clear example. Yet it emerged as a paradigm in its own right – at once evolutionist and anti-evolutionist (in the sense that it puts instantaneous change over slow evolution) – only in the 1980s (e.g., Cucchiari 1981). Its central feature today is the search for the origin of symbolic culture, or *culturo-genesis*. It turns Freud on his androcentric head by giving the instigating force of that first human revolution to the females of the species.

One eccentric version of this approach is that of Chris Knight, a British anthropologist who argues that symbolic culture began with a sex strike

Table 3.1. *Evolution (Maine, Morgan, and others) versus revolution (Rousseau, Freud, Knight, and others)*

	Human/animal 'kinship'	Basis of society	Development of ritual
Evolution	continuity	family	gradual, increasing complexity
Revolution	discontinuity	social contract	catastrophic event leading to the invention of ritual, taboo, totemism, and so on.

on the part of anatomically modern women demanding food for sex (see, e.g., Knight 1991; Knight, Power, and Watts 1995). In the 'primal horde' (to use Freud's term) males impregnated females indiscriminately, and the females were left to care for their young themselves. At some point within the last 70,000 years, females – or rather, the women of some specific horde or band – took charge of the situation and collectively demanded that their menfolk hunt for them before sex was allowed. The women symbolized their refusal of sex by menstruating or pretending to menstruate, and they did this together, in synchrony. The period of hunting and sexual taboo was from new moon to full moon, and the period of feasting and sex was between full moon and new moon.

Knight's theory is evolutionist in that it emphasizes the trajectory from pre-symbolic to symbolic-cultural humankind, but the focal point is on instantaneous revolution. Knight's approach to ritual and symbolic activity generally resembles Lévi-Strauss on kinship, and Rousseau on his vision of the social contract as the basis of society. It directly opposes most other theories of evolution on ritual, and implicitly opposes Fox's gradualist view of the relation between human and animal 'kinship', as well as Maine's and Morgan's idea of the family as the basis of society. The problem is that while it is ingenious, it is untestable.

The relation between the most significant of these ideas is illustrated in table 3.1.

Current trends

The debate between gradualists and those who see the origin of symbolic culture as revolutionary is very much the way anthropological evolutionism, in the broad sense, is moving. In Britain, new links are being forged between social anthropology and linguistics, archaeology, and human biology, as all these bear on the issue. This may seem strange in North

America, where these fields have long been seen as anthropological subdisciplines which are moving away from each other.

While some evolutionists today, such as Tim Ingold (e.g., 1986: 16–129) in Britain, and a number of ecological anthropologists in Japan and the United States, are pursuing the boundary between animals and humans, Knight is perusing the boundary between pre-symbolic humanity and humankind as we know it. The former boundary rests on factors such as the social relations of technology use, while the latter rests on affective aspects of culture and society. Clearly, the former is easier to define. While the latter has an intrinsic fascination, its specific theories are essentially untestable and unlikely to survive if presented (as they tend to be) as part of what Leslie White liked to call 'a scientific theory of culture'.

Concluding summary

Evolutionism in anthropology has parallels with evolutionism in other fields, including archaeology and biology. However, it is also unique in having three classic and easily definable forms: unilinear, universal, and multilinear (though the attribution of these Stewardian ideal types to individual theorists is not always as easy as Steward made out). Unilinear evolutionism took monogenesis for granted and treated cultures as so similar that they would all invent things in the same order and pass through the same stages of development. Universal evolutionism, still characteristic of much thinking in archaeology, recognizes greater complexity than this but seeks to simplify by focusing on the broad, general stages rather than the specifics. Multilinear evolutionism has focused on the specifics of historical development, especially those related to ecological factors. Of the three approaches, it bears the closest relation to the Darwinian notion of evolution.

Bachofen once wrote: 'Generally speaking, the development of the human race knows no leaps, no sudden progressions, but only gradual transitions; it passes through many stages, each of which may be said to bear within it the preceding and the following stage' (1967 [1861]: 98). This gradualist statement characterizes much in evolutionist anthropology from the unilinear, to the universal, to the multilinear approaches. Yet it is contradictory to the ideas of both Darwin and Marx (see chapter 6). The debate today between gradualists and revolutionists seems set to continue, whether today's specific theories of culturo-genesis survive or not.

FURTHER READING

Stocking's *Victorian Anthropology* (1987) and *After Tylor* (1996a) present fine overviews of relevant eras in the history of anthropology in Britain. For more of a social history approach, see Bowler's *The Invention of Progress* (1989). His book on Darwin (Bowler 1990) is also of interest, while Kuper's *The Chosen Primate* (1994) is both lighter in tone and wider in scope.

The classic statement on the three evolutionist approaches in social anthropology is in Steward's *Theory of Culture Change* (1955: 11–29). Harris' critical overview, *The Rise of Anthropological Theory* (1968), has a good deal of relevance; though his negative attitude to those he discusses is not to everyone's liking.

In general, the primary sources cited in this chapter are readable, particularly those by Tylor (1871), Childe (1936; 1942), White (1949; 1959), Steward (1955), and E. O. Wilson (1975). There is also an abridged edition of Wilson's *Sociobiology* (1980).

4   Diffusionist and culture-area theories

Diffusionism stresses the transmission of things (material or otherwise) from one culture to another, one people to another, or one place to another. An implicit presupposition of extreme diffusionism is that humankind is uninventive: things are invented only once, and then are transmitted from people to people, sometimes across the globe. This can be effected either by direct transmission between stable populations or through migrations by culture-rich peoples. In contrast, classical evolutionism assumes that humankind is inventive: each population has the propensity to invent the same things as the next, though they will do so at different rates.

By the time diffusionism was dwindling in importance, around the 1930s, it had left behind ideas which were picked up within other traditions: the idea of 'culture areas' is the most prominent example. This had already become an important facet of the ethnographic tradition of Franz Boas and his followers (see chapter 7). It also appeared within the evolutionism of Julian Steward (chapter 3) and within the functionalist and structuralist traditions which emerged in the first half of the twentieth century (chapters 5 and 8). Culture-area and regional approaches are a logical outgrowth of an emphasis on diffusion, and this chapter will cover these approaches with this point in the background.

Antecedents of diffusionism: philology, Müller, and Bastian

Diffusionism originated in the eighteenth-century philological tradition which posited historical connections between all the languages of the Indo-European language family.

The philological tradition: diffusionism before the diffusionists?

The breakthrough came in 1787, when Sir William Jones, an English Orientalist and barrister serving as a judge in India, discovered similarities between Sanskrit, Greek, and Latin. In the early nineteenth century, Wilhelm von Humboldt, Prussian diplomat and brother of the explorer Alexander, Baron von Humboldt, concentrated his interest on Basque – a European but non-Indo-European language. Echoing earlier ideas of Johann Gottfried von Herder, Wilhelm von Humboldt put the case for a close interrelation between language and culture. About the same time, Jacob Grimm, famous along with his brother Wilhelm for collecting European fairy tales (the 'brothers Grimm'), established the sound shifts which distinguish Germanic from other Indo-European languages, and Franz Bopp took up the comparative study of Indo-European grammar. All these writers touched on ideas which later came into anthropology as diffusionism.

The development of theoretical ideas in linguistics has throughout the history of that discipline foreshadowed the development of related ideas in social and cultural anthropology, though in this case their ideas were very slow to catch on. The thread that links early philological or historical linguistic theories to anthropology was of greater influence in evolutionist Britain than in Germany, where diffusionism was to take hold late in the nineteenth century.

The connection to British evolutionism runs through the work of several scholars, but none as obviously as that of the German-British orientalist, Friedrich Max Müller. Dissuaded by his godfather Felix Mendelssohn from studying music, the young Max Müller turned to Sanskrit, first at Leipzig and then, under Bopp, at Berlin. In 1846 further studies took him to Oxford, where he settled and eventually took up chairs in modern languages and comparative philology. Like Lubbock, Müller was active in Liberal politics and knew many in positions of power. Apparently through his friendship with the Royal Family, he was granted the very rare honour of being made a Privy Councillor.

Müller spent much of his life editing a fifty-one-volume series of sacred texts of the East. He also helped to propagate both the essentially evolutionist idea of psychic unity or psychical identity (i.e., that all humankind shares the same mentality) and the diffusionist idea that the religions as well as the languages of ancient Greece and Rome were related to those of India. He explored the latter through both anthropological comparisons of funeral customs and philological comparisons of the names of Greek and Hindu deities (see, e.g., Müller 1977 [1892]: 235–80). It is noteworthy that Müller (1977: 403–10) argued against the notion that there is one kind of 'totemism', and strongly criticized those who believed that all societies pass through the same stages of religious belief. Through both positive contributions in diffusionist thinking and negative comments on the extremes of unilinear evolutionism, Müller helped temper the tendencies of his British evolutionist contemporaries.

Like Müller, Adolph Bastian was an ambiguous figure. His broad approach was evolutionist rather than diffusionist, but he was a staunch opponent of Darwinism. In the late 1860s he helped establish both museum ethnography and theoretical ethnology in Germany. Thus he influenced the rise of diffusionism by providing the institutional base for it to develop from, even though his immediate successors became critical of his own theoretical contributions.

Bastian spent much of his working life as a ship's surgeon, travelling the world and writing on the exotic cultures he encountered. Unfortunately, his writings were absurdly metaphorical and virtually untranslatable, and have hardly ever been rendered into English. Let me quote one sentence, as translated by Robert Lowie, to give the flavour. The topic under discussion is the avoidance of premature generalization:

> Thereby would be tailored for us a beggar's cloak of mottled shreds and patches, whereas if we wait calmly for the facts to be gleaned for a definite survey, a magnificent peplos will be woven, as though spread by Zeus over a sacred oak, as a radiantly reflected image of reality. (Bastian [1881], quoted in Lowie 1937: 33)

But for all that, Bastian did give the world a theoretical contrast which was well ahead of its time: his distinction between *Elementargedanken* ('elementary thoughts') and *Völkergedanken* ('folk thoughts', or more literally 'folks' thoughts'). The former consist of what were later called 'cultural universals' and which, taken together, formed the psychic unity of humankind. Bastian noted the many similarities between cultures in different parts of the world, and he attributed such similarities to evolutionary convergence along lines pre-determined by these 'elementary thoughts'. His notion of 'folk thoughts', in contrast, represents the aspects of culture which differ from place to place. He attributed such differences to the influence of the physical environment and the chance events of history. The eventual focus of German-Austrian anthropology on 'folk thoughts', in turn, paved the way for diffusionism.

Diffusionism proper

Diffusionism came to prominence in the work of German and Austrian geographer-anthropologists in the late nineteenth century. As we shall see, it then fell into obscurity and absurdity (albeit interesting absurdity) in Britain, in the hands of two early twentieth-century Egyptologists.

German-Austrian diffusionism

The first great diffusionist was Friedrich Ratzel. He trained as a zoologist, but soon turned to geography and saw his theory in terms of a discipline which came to be called 'anthropogeography' (*Anthropogeographie*). Ratzel advocated the mapping of regions and the search for routes of migration and diffusion across the globe. He argued against Bastian's assumption of psychic unity and, wherever possible, sought evidence of culture contact as the cause of cultural similarity. This, together with the fact that he regarded humankind as uninventive, made him a true 'diffusionist' though he did not use the label himself.

Ratzel argued that single items of culture tended to diffuse, whereas whole 'culture complexes' (clusters of related cultural features) were spread by migration. His most famous example was the similarity between hunting bows found in Africa and New Guinea (Ratzel 1891). He postulated a historical connection between them and related this to what he regarded as the similar psychological makeup of peoples in the two areas. He argued further that culture *developed* mainly through massive migrations and conquests of weaker peoples by stronger, and more culturally advanced, ones. Thus, just as evolutionists like Morgan and Tylor (without necessarily knowing it) incorporated elements of diffusionism in their theories, Ratzel, the first great diffusionist, retained a strong element of evolution in his theoretical stance. Where they differed was in the mechanism they chose to emphasize: progress itself or the transmission of culture.

From his base at Leipzig, Ratzel taught a great number of scholars. He influenced not only immediate followers in Germany and later proponents of culture-area theory in North America, but also Tylor in England. Specifically, Tylor praised Ratzel's important three-volume masterpiece *Völkerkunde* – which appeared in English translation as *The History of Mankind* (1896–8 [1885–8]). From this time, evolutionism and diffusionism came to be recognized as two logically opposed but nevertheless complementary perspectives, which depended on each other for a full explanation of human culture history.

Ratzel was probably the first to divide the world into what we now call 'culture areas', but Leo Frobenius greatly extended his method and theory. Frobenius, a self-trained African explorer and museum ethnologist, enjoyed looking for parallels in cultural development worldwide. He came up with the idea of 'culture circles' (*Kulturkreise*), conceived as great culture areas which in some cases spread across the globe and overlapped those which had existed before: for example, bow-and-arrow culture over spear culture. The definition of these culture circles was to dominate German and Austrian anthropology from the 1890s to the 1930s.

However, in his later work Frobenius turned his attention to what he called the *Paideuma*. The term is Greek for 'education' (roughly translated), but in Frobenius' usage it took on a meaning akin to the classic romantic idea of the *Volksgeist*. This is the 'soul' of a culture, a basic psychic principle which determined any given configuration of culture traits. Furthermore, through his search for African culture configurations, he helped develop the notion of 'worldview' (German, *Weltanschauung*) which was to dominate American anthropology in its relativist period. For Africa, Frobenius (e.g., 1933) postulated two basic worldviews: 'Ethiopian' (characterized by cattle and cultivation, patrilineality, ancestor cults, cults of the earth, etc.) and 'Hamitic' (characterized by cattle and hunting, matrilineality, avoidance of the dead, sorcery, etc.). The former he located in Egypt and most of East, West, and Central Africa. The latter was supposedly the worldview of the Horn of Africa, much of North Africa and South Africa.

Playing upon these basic worldviews were a set of more specific culture configurations which, Frobenius believed, had spread either within Africa, or in other cases, from Asia or Europe to Africa. These overlay earlier cultural elements, such as hunting and gathering, which either were subsumed under, or remained encapsulated within, the culture areas which formed through successive waves of cultural diffusion. Thus Frobenius' vision of African culture was of a complex of layers whose historical relations could be determined by comparative study. Ethnology in his eyes was akin to archaeology, but with contemporary ethnographic work as its methodological basis.

After Ratzel and Frobenius, Fritz Graebner and Wilhelm Schmidt took the lead in *Kulturkreis* studies. Graebner, a museologist, concentrated on similarities in material culture, first across Oceania and later throughout the world. Ratzel had emphasized the qualities of cultures, and Frobenius had favoured a quantitative dimension. Graebner put these together in stressing both form and quantity as separate criteria for gauging the likelihood of any two cultures being historically related. By this method he defined culture circles such as the 'Tasmanian' (reputedly the earliest and most primitive), 'Australian boomerang', 'Melanesian bow', and 'Polynesian patrilineal', which he believed represented increasingly advanced cultural waves, surging across the Pacific. Graebner's career was hampered by internment in Australia during the First World War (allegedly for smuggling documents), and by mental illness which afflicted him from around 1926 until his death in 1934. Nevertheless, his attempts to place on a scientific basis the search for geographical culture circles and overlapping culture strata marked a high point in diffusionist thinking. His book *Die Methode der Ethnologie* (Graebner 1911) became a classic.

Schmidt, a Catholic priest with a special interest in African religions, argued that 'African Pygmy culture' was more 'primitive' than Graebner's 'Tasmanian culture'. He distinguished four basic culture circles

(Schmidt 1939 [1937]). After the Primitive Culture Circle of hunters and gatherers came the Primary Circle of horticulturists. At this stage, patrilineal and matrilineal descent first appeared. Schmidt argued that the greater confidence people felt in their own technological abilities led to a reduction in the importance of worship and to a dependence on magic. The Secondary Circle consisted in the mixing of Primitive and Primary traits. These led to intensive agriculture, sacred kingship, and ultimately polytheism. His Tertiary Circle consisted of a complex blending of traits from different cultures of the Secondary Circle, creating the ancient civilizations of Asia, Europe, and the Americas.

One of Schmidt's goals was establishing the history of world religion, a subject on which he wrote more than a dozen volumes. He hypothesized that religion began with a primitive monotheism, derived from early humanity's knowledge of his own, one true God. He believed that each succeeding culture circle developed better technology and more complex social organization, while at the same time it moved away from the primal monotheistic religion. Thus Schmidt's stance had elements of both primitivism and evolutionism, a fact which highlights the contradictions of diffusionism as a unitary perspective.

British diffusionism

While diffusionism reigned in Germany and Austria, elsewhere it infiltrated anthropological thinking mainly as a restraint on the simplicity of unilinear evolutionism. In archaeology, Swedish writer Oscar Montelius, in the 1880s and 1890s, refined the typology of the European Neolithic and Bronze Ages. He argued that regional variations and specific small developments across Europe could be accounted for by diffusion, rather than by evolution (see Trigger 1989: 155–61). In ethnology, things were more subtle, but it is important to recall that Morgan's thinking about kinship terminologies depended heavily on both migration and diffusion, and Tylor often spoke of diffusion and described cultures as having 'adhesions', or elements of culture usually found together. German and American anthropologists called these 'culture complexes'.

However, the co-existence of evolutionism and diffusionism was soon to be challenged in Britain, perhaps spurred on by a growing pessimism after Queen Victoria's death in 1901 and the political manoeuvring of European states which foreshadowed the First World War. Nineteenth-century Britons had firmly believed that Victorian values and the scientific inventions and discoveries personified by Prince Albert's sponsorship were pinnacles of human endeavour. In the pessimism of the first decades of the twentieth century, though, these achievements came to be denigrated. The new symbol of human cultural achievement was ancient Egypt, and degeneration rather than evolution marked the British diffusionists' trajectory from Egyptian to Victorian society.

Sir Grafton Elliot Smith (an eminent Australian-born anatomist) and his disciple William James Perry (a geographer) devised the fanciful theory that all great things had come from the Egypt of pharaohs, mummies, pyramids, and sun worship, and that all the cultures of their own times were but pale remnants of that once grand place. Based at Manchester and later at University College London, they propagated their theory both in academic journals and in public discussions. Elliot Smith's inspiration was his studies of Egyptian mummies (he had worked in Egypt between 1900 and 1909), but the stance of both men is perhaps best exemplified by Perry's *The Children of the Sun* (1923). In this widely read book, Perry argues that Egypt, and only Egypt, was the source of agriculture, the domestication of animals, the calendar, pottery, basketry, permanent dwellings, and towns. The extremist position of Elliot Smith and Perry became known as 'heliocentrist' diffusionism, that is, centred on the sun (with reference to sun worship among Egyptian and other ancient cultures). It met with few adherents among professional anthropologists, though it did prove popular among the Edwardian public.

Together with the great pre-Malinowskian fieldworker W. H. R. Rivers (who had been with Elliot Smith in Egypt and announced his own conversion from evolutionism to diffusionism in 1911), Elliot Smith and Perry fought a rearguard action, first against evolutionism. After Rivers' death in 1922 they continued their battle, but now against the growing tide of functionalism, institutionally established in that year through the appointment of both Malinowski and Radcliffe-Brown to chairs of social anthropology.

The heliocentrists had neither the base of a university anthropology department nor the methodological skills to sustain interest among the new breed of functionalist scholars, whose influence rose rapidly in the 1920s and 1930s (see chapter 5). The functionalist concerns were with modern Asia, the Americas, or sub-Saharan Africa, rather than Ancient Egypt; and with fieldwork and comparison, rather than speculation. Ultimately, the scientific advances in archaeology in the 1940s proved beyond doubt that the Egypt of 4000 BC could not have been the source of all human culture, and gave the *coup de grâce* to British diffusionism: Elliot Smith in 1937, and Perry in 1949. Of anthropological writers in the late twentieth century, only Thor Heyerdahl, an eccentric Norwegian adventurer with a penchant for testing diffusionist theories, maintained a belief in historical connections between Egypt and the Americas. British anthropology went in other directions entirely, whereas American anthropology developed from the foundations of German-Austrian rather than British diffusionist methods.

Diffusionism today?

Of all theories, diffusionism is probably the least popular in present-day social anthropology. However, it is not dead. There is today a great debate in archaeology and biological anthropology between those who favour the 'Out of Africa' or 'Replacement Model' and those who favour the 'Regional-Continuity Model' of human expansion (see, e.g., Gamble 1993). This debate bears close relation to an age-old problem within diffusionism: whether similarities stem more from the transmission of genes or culture between stable populations or more from migration of peoples from one place to another. A number of 'diffusionists', including Ratzel, actually favoured the latter, and the nuances of debate within the diffusionist school foreshadow those of modern studies of world prehistory.

In yet another sense, diffusionism lives on through ideas such as that of the 'culture area', now a part of standard anthropological thinking within all schools of thought. World-systems or globalization theory is another indicator that diffusionism lives (see chapters 6 and 10), though practitioners of it would no doubt repudiate a connection between their school of thought and that of Ratzel and his followers, much less Elliot Smith and his. The irony is that if a connection exists between classic diffusionism and such recent trends, it is precisely at a level of high theory or analogy. It is not one of the diffusion of the idea of diffusion itself.

Culture-area and regional approaches

Each and every anthropologist specializes in the study of some culture area – that where he or she does fieldwork. Yet the importance of the culture area varies according to the theoretical interest of the ethnographer. Broadly, it is useful to distinguish two kinds of culture-area approach. The first is that of American anthropology as it developed from German-Austrian diffusionism. The other, a much more diffuse approach, and in no sense a single school of thought or national tradition, is that of 'regional comparison'. This perspective characterizes quests for cause and regularity. Adherents have variously espoused multilinear evolutionism, functionalism, and structuralism, while maintaining an implicit belief in the historical relation between cultures of their respective regions.

The culture-area approach in American anthropology

Anthropology in Germany and Austria was largely destroyed in the 1930s and 1940s. Those who had opposed the Nazis were persecuted during the Third Reich, and those who sympathized with the Nazis found their theories discredited after the Second World War, when new German traditions (Marxism in the East; and an eclectic, foreign-influenced anthropology in the West) emerged. However, already in the 1920s an interest in historical relations between cultures and notions of 'culture area' and 'culture complex' had become commonplace in American anthropology. It is worth remembering that, although North America may have been colonized by the English in the seventeenth century, American anthropology began with the migration of Franz Boas, a German, and became established across the North American continent through the work of people like Robert Lowie, Edward Sapir, A. L. Kroeber, Clyde Kluckhohn, and Abram Kardiner – all of whom either spoke German in the home or studied in Germany or Austria.

Of these, Boas, Lowie, Sapir, and especially Kroeber (e.g., 1939) helped to develop the notion of the culture area. They directed their efforts towards the definition of specific areas and the recording of 'culture traits', the minimal units of culture, within each. From Boas onwards, American anthropologists of the early twentieth century tended to emphasize the particular over the general (see, e.g., Stocking 1974). In the 1930s and 1940s, more-and-more-detailed studies of cultural comparison within culture areas generated longer lists of culture traits to search for. These ran to the many thousands, with any given activity, for example, hunting or fishing, accounting for several dozen. Boas' rejection of evolutionism, his downplaying of diffusion, and above all his insistence on the meticulous gathering of ethnographic data, all contributed towards changing the agenda of anthropology as a whole, from historical questions to other ones (see chapter 7). Yet, as we shall see, some in his school did turn to history and to conjecture, and with some success.

The best-known example of a 'culture complex' or 'trait complex' was one proposed by the famous American anthropologist of Africa and African-America, Melville Herskovits (1926). He called it the 'cattle complex of East Africa'. Where cattle are found, so too are nomadism, patrilineal descent, age sets, bridewealth, the association of livestock with the ancestors, and a host of other interrelated culture traits. Both Herskovits and the German writers spoke of distributions of traits existing in relation to each other, that is, not distributed randomly. The difference is that Herskovits resisted attempts to put their ideas into either diffusionist or evolutionist schemes (see also Herskovits 1930).

In retrospect, the leading theorist of the school and one who did tackle historical questions, was a museum curator called Clark Wissler. However, Wissler was underrated in his own time. His lack of a university job meant that he trained no students to propagate his theories. His originality lay not so much in his specific new ideas (though he did have many), but in his ability to synthesize the mood of his time and present clear and coherent theoretical statements about what others were thinking. While others were content to record the distribution of prehistoric stone ornaments in eastern North America or of decorative pots in the Rio Grande Valley, Wissler (e.g., 1923: 58–61; 1927) explained such distributions in relation to the development, expansion, and contact of culture areas.

Wissler's greatest contribution was the age-area hypothesis, which both developed from and contributed to the interplay between archaeological and ethnological research (see Kroeber 1931). In the days before radiocarbon dating, archaeologists lacked a means to tell the real age of material they dug up. Relative age could be inferred from stratigraphy within a site, but not easily between sites. Moreover, ethnologists were collecting data on living cultures, but cultures known to have changed through the centuries. Wissler's hypothesis was that culture traits tended to spread from the centre to the periphery of any culture area. Therefore those traits found at the periphery were older, and those found at the centre were newer. When put to the test, the hypothesis seemed to work, and it gave a dynamic aspect to culture-area research which had been lacking. Implicitly, it also brought together diffusion and evolution within a framework of culture-area studies: evolution took place at the centre of a given culture area, and diffusion was from centre to periphery.

The interplay between evolution and diffusion became yet more apparent when American anthropology left behind the extreme relativism of Boas to take up evolutionism again. Thus it took on special meaning in Steward's work. We met him in chapter 3 as the architect of multilinear evolutionism, but his theories also had a diffusionist basis. Crucial here is his distinction between the 'cultural core' (which is determined by environment and evolution) and the 'total culture' (which contains elements of culture susceptible to diffusion). Steward developed the culture-area idea within a framework which emphasized natural environment as the limiting factor for culture, and technology as its enabling component (see, e.g., 1955: 78–97).

Wissler had defined fifteen culture areas for all the Americas (including the Caribbean): Plains, Plateau, California, North Pacific Coast, and so on. Kroeber first altered the names and boundaries of the culture areas, but not their number. Later, in his most important culture-area work, Kroeber (1939) mapped eighty-four 'areas' and 'sub-areas' which he grouped into seven 'grand areas' of North America only. He left South America to Steward, who edited a six-volume study of the culture areas of that continent (Steward 1946–50). Frequently culture areas turned out to be correlated with ecological zones: in North America, the Arctic, the Great Plains, the Eastern Woodlands, and others; and in South America, the Andes, Amazonia, and so on. If the environment is a limiting or determining force upon culture, then its influence should be apparent regionally. Steward and his followers both demonstrated this general principle and tested the limits of environmental determinism by comparative studies both within and between culture areas. All this left the problem of what constitutes 'a culture', but it did help both to fill in the ethnographic map and to increase interest in cross-cultural comparison as a goal of anthropological research.

Regional comparison, national traditions, and regional traditions

It is useful to distinguish three types of comparison in anthropology (see Sarana 1975): illustrative, global, and controlled (which includes regional comparison).

Illustrative comparison involves choosing examples to make some point about cultural difference or similarity. This is the basis of much introductory teaching in anthropology. We might choose Nuer as an example of a patrilineal society, and compare Nuer to Trobrianders, as an example of a matrilineal society. We might choose an element of one society which is unfamiliar to our audience, say gift-giving in Bushman society, and compare it to a similar practice in a more familiar case, say gift-giving in American society. Such comparisons may show similarities (e.g., the practice of gift-giving itself), but usually the illustrations are designed to show differences which reveal aspects of the less-familiar society.

Global comparison, or more accurately, *global-sample comparison*, involves comparing a sample of the world's societies to find statistical correlations among cultural features, or (in ecological anthropology) between environmental and cultural features. George Peter Murdock's approach, discussed in chapter 3, is the best-known example.

Controlled comparison lies in-between in scope. It involves limiting the range of variables, usually (though not always) by confining comparisons to those within a region. Regional comparison has been prevalent in the work of a number of anthropologists of a variety of schools. Among the diffusionists, Frobenius (in his studies of African culture areas) followed a mainly regional approach. Among the evolutionists, Steward employed a form of regional comparison. Among the functionalists, A. R. Radcliffe-Brown (writing on Australia) and Fred Eggan (writing on Native North

America) sought an understanding of specific cultures through a wider understanding of their place within regional structures. At a deeper level, structuralist anthropologists have sought to comprehend such regional structures and define generative principles peculiar to a given region, common structures which set the limits of variation, or culture traits which stand in relation to one another in interesting ways – often capable of transformations when they move between cultures.

The Dutch scholars who studied the Dutch East Indies (now Indonesia) in the 1920s and 1930s originated a structuralist form of regional comparison. Their regions are known within Dutch anthropology as 'fields of ethnological study' (*ethnologisch studievelden*), each defined by a set of features known as its 'structural core' (*structurele kern*). In the case of the former Dutch East Indies, the structural core includes, for example, a system of marriage in which a wife's lineage is of higher status than her husband's. Within a given society, each lineage is linked to every other by a circle of intermarrying units. The most articulate statement of the theory of this school is J. P. B. de Josselin de Jong's (1977 [1935]) inaugural lecture at the University of Leiden. Although in recent decades anthropology in The Netherlands has moved on towards Marxist theory, the understanding of indigenous knowledge, and the anthropology of Third World development, nevertheless 'regional structural comparison' (as it is now called) remains strong in the folk perception of the Dutch tradition.

One of the best-known proponents of regional structural comparison is Adam Kuper, a South African-British anthropologist who once taught at the University of Leiden. Indeed, his 1977 inaugural lecture at Leiden echoed that of J. P. B. de Josselin de Jong more than forty years before (Kuper 1979a [1977]), but with Africa as his area of concern. In a number of articles and books, most notably *Wives for Cattle* (1982), Kuper has sought to explain the regional-structural basis of Southern Bantu kinship, traditional politics, household economics, and symbolism. Any given culture trait can best be interpreted, he argues, in relation to corresponding traits in related cultures. What at first may appear to be random traits are intelligible within a framework which takes account of the Southern Bantu region as a whole. Take three examples where close kin marriage is common: Tswana men tend to marry women of lower status, and bridewealth in Tswana society is relatively low; Southern Sotho men tend to marry higher status women, and bridewealth in their society is relatively high; Swazi men may marry either way, but those who marry 'down' (like the Tswana) pay less bridewealth than those who marry 'up' (like the Southern Sotho). By comparing these societies, each set-up can be seen as a transformation of another, and the entire regional system can be analysed in terms of the ability of powerful individuals to perpetuate their power through bridewealth transactions. Interestingly, where close kin marriage is forbidden (e.g., among Tsonga and Chopi), marriage between commoners lends itself much less to such manipulation, and egalitarian marriage structures occur.

Kuper's method shows promise in other ethnographic areas too, both in Africa and elsewhere. As anthropologists become more regionally focused, both because of the plethora of recent ethnographic data and because of the ease of comparison between closely related and well-studied societies, the trend towards regional studies is likely to continue (see Barnard 1996).

Furthermore, as Richard Fardon and his colleagues have pointed out (Fardon 1990), there is an additional twist: 'regional traditions' in ethnographic writing. These work to ensure that regional understanding is a strong determinant of anthropological theory in general. If one does fieldwork in India, for example, one cannot help but develop theoretical insights specifically relevant to the Indianist literature. A Melanesianist cannot help but comment on Melanesianist debates, an Amazonianist on Amazonianist debates. Thus both the cultural characteristics of regions themselves and the interests of those anthropologists who have worked in them, help determine the agenda of new scholars setting off for fieldwork. Theoretical emphases differ accordingly.

Concluding summary

Diffusionism at the end of the nineteenth century, and well into the twentieth, offered anthropologists one of many points of departure from the pervasive dominance of evolutionism. The extreme ideas of the British school, with its emphasis on Ancient Egypt as the source of high culture the world over, proved of little merit. The more moderate notions of the German-Austrian school filtered into American anthropology and emerged transformed as 'the culture-area approach'. Ultimately, a number of culture-area approaches came into being, including evolutionist, functionalist, and structuralist varieties.

Diffusionist and culture-area approaches constitute one of the most interesting sets of ideas anthropology has produced. Yet unlike evolutionist ideas, diffusionist ones today (e.g., globalization theory) have lost continuity with the past. The primary legacy of diffusionism in its classic form is in the study of culture areas – both historical relations between such areas and, more importantly, the intensive study of regions.

FURTHER READING

Zwernemann's *Culture History and African Anthropology* (1983) gives a good overview of German-Austrian diffusionism. Classic studies of that school and of the American culture-area approach include respectively the essays by Kluckhohn (1936) and Wissler (1927). The relations between them are touched on in some of the essays in Stocking's *Volksgeist as Method and Ethic* (1996b). For a contemporary overview of German-Austrian, American, and British traditions, see Lowie's *History of Ethnological Theory* (1937: 128–95, 279–91). For an anti-culture-area approach, see Herzfeld's essay on the Mediterranean (1984).

On British diffusionism, see Langham's *The Building of British Social Anthropology* (1981: 118–99). For an overview of comparative methods, see Sarana's *The Methodology of Anthropological Comparisons* (1975).

Dutch anthropology is well documented as a national tradition. For further discussion of Dutch structuralism, see chapter 8. See also P. E. de Josselin de Jong's *Structural Anthropology in the Netherlands* (1977). Kloos and Claessen have edited three collections on contemporary Dutch anthropology, most recently *Contemporary Anthropology in the Netherlands* (Kloos and Claessen 1991).

5   Functionalism and structural-functionalism

The terms 'functionalist' and 'structural-functionalist' and their corresponding 'isms' are now quite stable in their meanings. However, this was not always the case. Before looking at the theories, a brief tour of the changing nuances of the terms is in order.

'Functionalism' is a broad term. In its widest sense, it includes both functionalism (narrowly defined) and structural-functionalism. I use it mainly in the narrower sense, that is, to refer to ideas associated with Bronislaw Malinowski and his followers, notably Sir Raymond Firth. It is the perspective concerned with actions among individuals, the constraints imposed by social institutions on individuals, and relations between the needs of an individual and the satisfaction of those needs through cultural and social frameworks. 'Structural-functionalism' tends to be concerned less with individual action or needs, and more with the place of individuals in the social order, or indeed with the construction of the social order itself. Typically, the latter term identifies the work of A. R. Radcliffe-Brown and his followers. In Britain these included E. E. Evans-Pritchard (in his early work), Isaac Schapera, Meyer Fortes, and Jack Goody, among many others.

Yet the boundary between structural-functionalism and functionalism was never rigid. Some of Radcliffe-Brown's followers did not mind the term 'functionalist'; others took to the labels 'structural-functionalist' or 'structuralist' (to distinguish their work from that of Malinowski). Furthermore, the term 'British structuralist' was heard in the 1950s to distinguish Radcliffe-Brownianism from Lévi-Straussianism or 'French structuralism' (described in chapter 8). Confusingly, when in the early 1960s a new generation of British anthropologists turned to Lévi-Strauss, they assumed the label 'British structuralist' for themselves. In broader terms, the latter 'British structuralism' was actually a British version of 'French structuralism'!

As if all that is not bad enough, both Radcliffe-Brown and Lévi-Strauss drew inspiration from the sociology of Emile Durkheim. And although he

did not like being called a 'functionalist', Radcliffe-Brown was happy to
call his discipline 'comparative sociology'.

Evolutionist precursors and the organic analogy

Radcliffe-Brown recalled more than once that anthropology has two
points of origin. He dated one to 'around 1870', the heyday of evolutionist
thinking. The other he dated to Montesquieu's *Spirit of the Laws* (published in French in 1748). This sociological tradition respected the idea
that society is systematically structured, and that its structures are the
proper study of the disciplines we now call the social sciences. It also, at
least from Comte onwards, held to the view that its object of study may be
likened to a biological organism, made up of functioning systems. Evolutionists, especially Herbert Spencer (an English member of this otherwise mainly French tradition) saw the transformation of societal types as
the focal point for research. He also made the most explicit statements on
the organic analogy (see, e.g., Andreski 1971 [Spencer 1876]: 108–20).
Spencer argued the case for a science of society based on the science of life
(biology), then decidedly evolutionist and Darwinian in outlook. Spencer
saw societies as passing through stages analogous to infancy, childhood,
adolescence, adulthood, middle life, and old age. He, and Durkheim as
well, saw them as made up of parts, each with its own function. And they
saw the parts as increasing in heterogeneity with evolution. Even the
diffusionist Leo Frobenius joined the organic-analogy bandwagon. The
idea was amenable to synchronic and diachronic, evolutionist and diffusionist approaches alike.

This early functionalist perspective was itself transformed in the early
twentieth century, partly by Durkheim in his more synchronic work, but
decidedly by Radcliffe-Brown. While neither Durkheim nor Radcliffe-
Brown denied the importance of evolution, they became known for their
emphasis on contemporaneous societies. We can imagine a society functioning smoothly like a healthy organism, made of many parts put together in larger systems; and these systems, each with its own special
purpose of function, working together with the others. Societies have
structures similar to those of organisms. Social institutions, like the parts
of the body, function together within larger systems. The social systems,
such as kinship, religion, politics, and economics, together make up
society, just as the various biological systems together form the organism.
A simple representation of this, essentially Radcliffe-Brownian, analogy is
shown in figure 5.1.

To take the analogy further, look at, say French or British society. The
systems which make up each society are composed of parts which Rad-

Reproductive system	Circulatory system
Digestive system	Nervous system

Systems of an organism

Kinship	Religion
Economics	Politics

Systems of a society

Figure 5.1 The organic analogy: society is like an organism

cliffe-Brown called 'social institutions'. How do we understand the relation between these and the systems they form? 'Marriage' in France or Britain might be designated an institution within the kinship system, but it can also have religious, political, and economic aspects. Therefore 'marriage' is not just part of kinship, because it functions within other systems too. This does not make the analogy useless or wrong, but it does make it problematic. It also shows that it is simplistic. Any institution can have a function in fitting together with some other institution. Everything is, therefore, in some sense 'functional'.

To my mind, the reason the organic analogy succeeded is that it was such a simple model, and one capable of being put to use in either diachronic or synchronic analyses. Yet this was also to be its failing, as successive post-functionalist generations have all clamoured for something more sophisticated.

Durkheimian sociology

Perhaps the most important source for structural-functionalist ideas is the sociology of Emile Durkheim. After an undistinguished student career and a spell of philosophy teaching, Durkheim gained a university post (the first in the social sciences in France) at Bordeaux in 1887. He moved to the Sorbonne in 1902 and taught there until his death in 1917. He gathered around him a devoted group of philosophers, economists, historians, and jurists, who shared his vision of an integrated science of society. In 1898, Durkheim and his band of young scholars founded the *Année sociologique*, an interdisciplinary journal which quickly achieved great influence. Several of this band contributed to anthropological ideas, and especially to the anthropology of religion. Marcel Mauss, Lucien Lévy-Bruhl, Robert Hertz, Marcel Granet, and Henri Hubert, in particular, influenced our discipline, though in some cases their influence was slow, only culminating years after death when later generations read their works in posthumous translations.

It has been said that anthropologists and sociologists agree that Durkheim wrote one great book, but that they disagree about which book this might be. The empirical tradition alive today in sociology is derived from Durkheim's early works. In *Suicide* (1966 [1897]), Durkheim reports from archival sources that statistics differ for suicide rates among Catholics and Protestants, rural people and city dwellers, married and unmarried, young adults and older people, and so on. There are also differences for different countries, and these remain constant through time. Thus even that apparently most individual of acts, the taking of one's own life, has at its heart a social basis.

As *their* choice of Durkheim's one great book, most anthropologists would cite *The Elementary Forms of the Religious Life* (Durkheim 1915 [1912]), or perhaps *Primitive Classification* (Durkheim and Mauss 1963 [1903]), which foreshadows it. *The Elementary Forms* deals with religion in 'early' societies. Durkheim first defines 'religion' and asserts its social basis: religions distinguish the 'sacred' from the 'profane' and take the sacred as their special concern. He traces theories of the origin of religion, notably Tylor's animism, Müller's naturism, and McLennan's totemism. Durkheim himself favours totemism, and he puts forward his ideas on the specifics of its evolution. He makes good use of the growing ethnographic literature on Aboriginal Australia, as well as Native North America. Although still couched in evolutionist terms, towards the end of the book, Durkheim's explanations take on a more strongly functionalist flavour as he moves from belief to ritual. In ritual, he argues, people venerate society itself, as the cosmological order is constructed upon the social order. Ritual helps to validate that order in the minds of its participants.

Durkheim co-authored *Primitive Classification* with his nephew and student, Marcel Mauss. In this short work (first published as an article in the *Année sociologique*), they tackle the question of how the human mind classifies. The authors review ethnographic evidence from Aboriginal Australia, from the Zuñi and Sioux of North America, and from Taoist China, and they conclude that there exists a close relation between society and the classification of nature. Furthermore, they see a continuity between primitive and scientific thinking. The advanced culture of

China possesses elements of classification which reflect those of 'primitive' Aboriginal Australian cosmology, and in turn the structural divisions of Australian Aboriginal society. There are cross-cultural similarities in the classification of time, place, animals, and things – all built up from divisions into twos, fours, sixes, eights, and so on. Australia, North America, China, and ancient Greece provide Durkheim and Mauss' examples. The theory they put forward has elements not only of structural-functionalism, but also of evolutionism and structuralism – all theories which rest on an explicit recognition of the psychic unity of humankind.

Mauss' work proved seminal in several areas of anthropology. His writings, mainly in the *Année sociologique*, include essays on aspects of cultural ecology, sacrifice, magic, the concept of the person, and the exchange of gifts (see Lévi-Strauss 1988 [1950]). Probably the most important of these, and certainly the most functionalist, was his 'essay on the gift' (Mauss 1990 [1923]). He argues that though gifts are in theory voluntary, they nevertheless stem from expectation on the part of the recipient. Moreover, though they may be free from expectation of direct return, there is always an element of repayment, either in the form of a later gift or in the form of deference or some other recognition of social status between giver and recipient. The gift, in other words, is not free; and it is embedded in a system of rights and obligations which in any society make up part of the social structure, and in some societies form a system of 'total services'. Mauss' examples include ceremonial exchanges among Polynesians and Melanesians (including Malinowski's Trobrianders) and among North West Coast peoples (including Boas' Kwakiutl). He also records survivals of 'archaic' exchange in Roman, Hindu, Germanic, and Chinese law, thereby enabling his conclusion that the spirit of the gift is a widespread if not universal institution.

Durkheim and especially Mauss remain inspirational for anthropologists of various theoretical perspectives. Sociology has since gone its own way, though with cross-influences and parallel developments (see Swingewood 1984: 227–329). This is not the place to recount that story, though it is perhaps worth keeping in mind the fact that sociology and anthropology once had the potential to become one discipline.

The functionalism of Malinowski

Malinowski's position in British anthropology is analogous to that of Boas in American anthropology (see chapter 7). Like Boas, Malinowski was a Central European natural scientist brought by peculiar circumstances to anthropology and to the English-speaking world. Like Boas, he objected to armchair evolutionism and invented a fieldwork tradition based on the use of the native language in 'participant observation'. Furthermore, both Boas and Malinowski were pompous but liberal intellectuals who built up very strong followings through their postgraduate teaching.

Malinowski was born in Cracow in 1884, the son of a professor of Slavic philology. He graduated from the Jagiellonian University in Cracow in 1908, in mathematics, physics, and philosophy, and with the highest honours in the Austrian Empire. He studied anthropology at the London School of Economics (LSE), under C. G. Seligman and Edward Wester-marck, then set off for Australia in 1914. Although technically an enemy alien, Malinowski (unlike Graebner) was treated well in Australia during the First World War; he was permitted to carry out fieldwork in areas of New Guinea which were administered by Australia. Between September 1914 and October 1918 Malinowski spent some thirty months, in three separate trips from Australia, conducting his work in New Guinea. All except the first six-month stint was spent in the Trobriand Islands. After the War Malinowski turned down a chair at the Jagiellonian University and returned to the LSE, where he taught from 1922 to 1938. It was in this period that his influence was greatest. At the outbreak of the Second World War he was in the United States. He chose to remain there for the duration, but died in 1942, shortly after accepting a permanent post at Yale.

Functionalism and fieldwork

The phrase 'Malinowskian anthropology' evokes two rather different images today. One is an image of the fieldwork method and its implicit theoretical assumptions and ethnographic style reminiscent of Malinowski's monographs on the Trobriand Islanders. The other is a more explicit theory of culture and cultural universals based on assumptions in Malinowski's late writings, especially his posthumous collection, *A Scientific Theory of Culture* (1944).

The functionalism of Malinowski's fieldwork style was not dissimilar to that of Radcliffe-Brown, but Malinowski was the better researcher. Many of Malinowski's students picked up theoretical ideas from Radcliffe-Brown, especially the emphasis on social institutions functioning within larger social systems. Yet the methods of Malinowski's well-known students, such as Raymond Firth, Phyllis Kaberry, Isaac Schapera, Eileen Krige, Monica Wilson, and Hilda Kuper, are best characterized as 'Malinowskian'. Malinowski encouraged long stints of fieldwork, with close contact with informants over a long period of time.

The most famous of Malinowski's works is *Argonauts of the Western Pacific* (1922). *Argonauts* begins with a statement on subject, method, and scope, then describes the geography of the Trobriands and his arrival in the islands. He moves on to the rules of *kula* exchange, facts about canoes, sailing, and canoe magic and ceremony. He then gives more detailed and specific accounts of aspects touched on earlier, including canoe journeys, the *kula* and magic. He ends with a 'reflective' (we would now say 'reflexive') chapter on 'the meaning of the *kula*'. Here he explicitly declines to venture into theoretical speculations, but rather comments on the importance of ethnology for encouraging tolerance of alien customs and enlightening readers on the purpose of customs very different from their own. This is the Malinowski most passionately admired by his students.

For me, the most striking case of Malinowski's insights came a few years after *Argonauts*. This is in his work on parent–child relations, which tested the central tenets of Freudian psychology (Malinowski 1927a; 1927b). For the Trobrianders, the father is a figure of supreme indulgence, not the authority figure postulated as a cultural universal by Freud. Rather, a boy's mother's brother is in the position of authority. This is because the mother's brother's power is derived from his place as a senior member of the boy's matrilineal kin group. According to Malinowski, the Trobrianders were ignorant of physiological paternity; thus the role of the father would be quite different from that in patrilineal societies, where the biological relationship between father and son is considered the basis of their social relationship. Much later, Radcliffe-Brown (1952 [1924]: 15–31) and Lévi-Strauss (1963 [1945]: 31–54) were to debate this classic set of relations between a boy and his father and a boy and his mother's brother. What makes Malinowski's contribution to the 'avunculate' problem of special interest is that his argument is from deep ethnographic insight and not simply from cross-cultural comparison. This is perhaps what gave him the edge, at least against Freud.

In more general terms, Kaberry (1957: 81–2) describes three levels of abstraction in Malinowski's theory of function. At the first, 'function' denotes the effects of an institution on other institutions, that is, the relation between social institutions. This level is similar to that in Radcliffe-Brown's work. The second involves the understanding of an institution in terms defined by members of the community. The third defines the way in which the institution promotes social cohesion in general. Malinowski himself was not very explicit in print about these levels, and it is likely that Kaberry has inferred them from isolated comments in Malinowski's ethnographic writings. However, in a rare venture into theoretical comment cited by Kaberry as an example of the first level, Malinowski argued that custom is 'organically connected' with the rest of culture and that the fieldworker needs to search for the 'invisible facts'

which govern the interconnection of the different facets of social organization. These, he said (Malinowski 1935: I, 317), are discovered by 'inductive computation'.

A scientific theory of culture?

When, late in his life, Malinowski sat down to summarize his perspective
he explained things in a rather different, and indeed quite peculiar way.
This marks the second of the perspectives Malinowski is known for.

Malinowski claimed that the basis of his approach was a set of seven
biological needs and their respective cultural responses (table 5.1). After
defining 'culture', Malinowski (1944: 75–84) proposes a theory of 'vital
sequences', which he says are biological foundations incorporated into all
cultures. There are eleven of these sequences, each composed of an
'impulse', an associated physiological 'act', and a 'satisfaction' which
results from that act. For example, the impulse of somnolence is associated with the act of sleep, resulting in satisfaction by 'awakening with
restored energy' (1944: 77). He follows this eleven-fold paradigm with a
slightly simpler one. This is the one built on the relationship between
seven 'basic needs' and their respective 'cultural responses' (1944: 91–
119). He then goes on to a four-fold one, relating what he sees as four,
rather complex, 'instrumental imperatives' with their respective 'cultural
responses'. The latter comprise economics, social control, education, and
political organization (1944: 120–31). Finally, he tackles 'integrative imperatives' and the 'instrumentally implemented vital sequence' (1944:
132–44).

None of the ideas of Malinowski's *Scientific Theory of Culture* found
favour with his contemporaries, though in a collection of commemorative
essays published fifteen years after his death (Firth 1957) some of his
students tried to find worth in them. As Malinowski's final statement, and
as the most theoretical of all his writings, it does deserve study. However,
the fact is that his students were embarrassed by it. The biological
assertions seem to have little to do with culture, and much of what he said
is either self-evident (e.g., sleep relieves tiredness) or impenetrable (e.g.,
integrative imperatives and the instrumentally implemented vital sequence). Phyllis Kaberry (1957: 83), a favourite among Malinowski's
students, points out that Malinowski's late concerns with biological needs
were of little interest to any, whereas his earlier work on social institutions
was of great interest. The problem was that Malinowski's work on social
institutions remained submerged within his erudite and ethnographic
prose and, unlike his statement on biological needs, was never the subject
of theoretical generalization.

Table 5.1. *Malinowski's seven basic needs and their cultural responses*

Basic needs	Cultural responses
1. metabolism	1. commissariat
2. reproduction	2. kinship
3. bodily comforts	3. shelter
4. safety	4. protection
5. movement	5. activities
6. growth	6. training
7. health	7. hygiene

Sadly, in a way, the relation between the two Malinowskian perspectives is hinted at in Malinowski's introduction to a volume by one of his other students: 'The most important thing for the student, in my opinion, is never to forget the living, palpitating flesh and blood organism of man which remains somewhere in the heart of every institution' (Malinowski 1934: xxxi). S. F. Nadel commented:

Putting it somewhat crudely, Malinowski's thought moved on two levels only – on the level of the particular society, the Trobriands, where he did his fundamental and exemplary field research; and on the level of primitive man and society at large, and indeed Man and Society at large. In his more general writings Malinowski did refer also to other primitive societies; but he did so in the main only for the sake of supporting evidence, of secondary importance. He never thought strictly in comparative terms. His generalizations jump straight from the Trobrianders to Humanity, as undoubtedly he saw the Trobrianders as a particularly instructive species of Humanity. (Nadel 1957: 190)

What comes out in the final assessment of Malinowski by virtually all his students (i.e., in Firth 1957) is Malinowski's failure to grasp the significance of kinship terminology, the intricacies of economic exchange, the precision required for writing on law, or the meaning of anthropological comparison. Yet we still remember him as the founder of the greatest fieldwork tradition of anthropology. If his own analysis did not live up to expectation, his exemplary fieldwork methods and his inspiring teaching at the LSE seminars in the 1920s and 1930s have left a legacy that is the essence of the British tradition.

Malinowski and Boas both died, not far from each other, in 1942. Yet the year of their passing somehow holds less symbolic significance than that of Rivers, twenty years before, which marked the end of a pre-Malinowskian fieldwork tradition as well as that of diffusionism's most respected British proponent. Perhaps in 1942 the anthropological world was too preoccupied with the horrors of war, but the Boasian spirit stayed with American anthropology, while Malinowskian methodology and (for a time) Radcliffe-Brownian theory remained the backbone of the British tradition.

The structural-functionalism of Radcliffe-Brown

Alfred Reginald Brown was born in Birmingham in 1881. Following his older brother's lead, he adopted the style A. Radcliffe Brown (adding their mother's maiden name) around 1920, and became A. R. Radcliffe-Brown by deed poll in 1926. He was known to his friends as Rex, R-B, or in his university days, Anarchy Brown, because of his political inclinations. In fact, he knew the anarchist writer Peter Kropotkin, whose vision of society as a self-regulating system, functioning by mutual aid in the absence of the state, anticipated Radcliffe-Brown's interest in the functions of social institutions (see, e.g., Kropotkin 1987 [1902]: 74–128).

After completing his bachelor's degree at Cambridge in 1904, Radcliffe-Brown did postgraduate work there and subsequently conducted fieldwork in the Andaman Islands (1906–8) and Western Australia (1910–11). During the First World War he served as Director of Education in the Kingdom of Tonga. Then he travelled around the world, establishing chairs of anthropology as he went, at Cape Town (1920–5), Sydney (1926–31), Chicago (1931–7), and Oxford (1937–46). He also taught for shorter periods at other universities in England, South Africa, China, Brazil, and Egypt.

A natural science of society?

In his Australian ethnography, Radcliffe-Brown (e.g., 1931) advocated a comparative perspective and explained the diversity in Aboriginal kinship systems in terms of the full complex of Aboriginal social structure found at the time. An inductivist, he believed that anthropology would one day discover through comparison the 'natural laws of society' (though he himself did not get very far in the effort). As an empiricist, he opposed speculation about the origins of the systems or institutions which make up society and argued that anthropologists should study just what they find. He wanted facts, and the simplest facts to come by were facts about the present, not the past; and the simplest way to connect them was through the study of society as a unit composed of living, interacting parts (see, e.g., Radcliffe-Brown 1952 [1935]: 178–87).

My favourite among Radcliffe-Brown's works is *A Natural Science of Society*, originally presented as a series of lectures at the University of Chicago in 1937 and transcribed for eventual, posthumous publication by his students (as Radcliffe-Brown 1957). These lectures were designed to propose the idea of a single, unified social science. He explicitly rejected the claims of the dominant social sciences at Chicago at that time – psychology, economics, and so on – that *they* might be that unified social science (1957: 45–50, 112–17). He also rejected the idea of a 'science of culture' (1957: 106–9; cf. 1957: 117–23) and implicitly attacked the Boasian emphasis on this. What really mattered to him was that in Boasian anthropology, the dominant version in America at the time, 'society' (as relations between people) was lost to the vagaries of 'culture', which could not be analysed scientifically. In fairness to Boas and his followers though, Radcliffe-Brown's notion of 'culture' was essentially synonymous with *enculturation* or (more accurately) *socialization*: a way of learning to live in a society. Radcliffe-Brown simply could not comprehend Boas' desires to extol differences between peoples and place the highest value on the richness of the human experience.

Radcliffe-Brown summarized his 'natural science of society' lectures as follows:

I HAVE ADVANCED several theses. The first of these was that a theoretical natural science of human society is possible. My second thesis was that there can only be one such science; the third, that such a science does not yet exist except in its most elementary beginnings. The fourth thesis, which seems to me important, was that a solution of any of the fundamental problems of such a science must depend on the systematic comparison of a sufficient number of societies of sufficiently diverse types. The last was that the development of the science therefore depends at this time on the gradual improvement of the comparative method and its refinement as an instrument of analysis . . . (Radcliffe-Brown 1957: 141)

The emphasis on comparison as an objective was crucial. Indeed, he praised his evolutionist predecessors for their comparative objectives, though he rejected their conjectural methods. He rejected the relativist objectives of his American contemporaries, though he found nothing wrong in their methods of observation and description. This contradiction was at the crux of his vision of the discipline (see Leach 1976a; Barnard 1992).

Function, structure, and structural form

In his work on the Andaman Islanders, Radcliffe-Brown (1922) explained rituals in terms of their social functions – their value for the society as a whole, rather than their value for any particular individual member of society. This emphasis on society over the individual was to remain strong in his own work and to influence both the theoretical interests and the ethnographic approaches of the next generation. His clearest statement on *function* is in a paper in which he takes up both diachronic and synchronic implications of the 'organic analogy' he inherited from Spencer and Durkheim (Radcliffe-Brown 1952 [1935]: 178–87). More specifically, he attacks an American critic's assertion that there is a conflict between 'historical' and 'functional' interests. For Radcliffe-Brown, the opposition is rather between the historical and the sociological, and to him they are not in conflict, but rather, represent different kinds of study. He places the emphasis on synchronic (sociological) aspects: the way given institutions 'function' within a social system, rather than how they change through time.

In another famous analogy, Radcliffe-Brown likened the study of society to the study of sea shells (Kuper 1977 [Radcliffe-Brown 1953]: 42). Each sea shell has its own 'structure', but the structure of one may resemble the structure of another. In this case, the two are said, in Radcliffe-Brown's terms, to share a common 'structural form'. The analogy is that *social structure* is about actual observations, that is, what the anthropologist actually sees and hears about individual people, whereas *structural form* is about generalization, that is, what an anthropologist infers about a particular society on the basis of his or her observations of individuals. Suppose Edward is a chief. Suppose George is another chief among the same people. Perhaps George has succeeded Edward after Edward's death. The anthropologist observes the two chiefs in action, and the relation between each chief and his people constitutes an example of social structure. When the anthropologist generalizes about the role of 'the chief' (rather than the role of Edward or George), he or she is now describing the structural form. To Radcliffe-Brown, the concern of an anthropologist should be not with describing individual chiefs and individual subjects (as Boas might have done), but with understanding among a particular people the relationship between the typical chief and his typical subjects, between the typical father and his typical children, a typical lecturer and her typical students, and so on. Then, at a later stage of analysis, an anthropologist can compare the structural form of one society to that of another, and might even (Radcliffe-Brown hoped) come up with general laws about the way in which societies work.

There are two common criticisms of this line in Radcliffe-Brown's thinking. First, confusingly, Radcliffe-Brown used the phrase 'structural form' to mean what others have usually called 'social structure', and the phrase 'social structure' to mean what others call just 'data'. Secondly, and more seriously, he appeared to be going about things backwards. One cannot get at universal, general laws by counting up instances of anything. One can only get there by reasoning from logical premises, a point made repeatedly through structuralist studies such as those of Claude Lévi-Strauss.

Hardly anyone in social anthropology today claims to be a follower of Radcliffe-Brown. Nevertheless, he was right about the basis of the subject. Virtually all anthropological enquiry is in some sense about relationships between things. Evolutionists, structuralists, interpretivists, and even anti-theorists at their best (when relations of interconnectedness lie implicitly in their descriptions) have this in common. Where they differ is in the ways in which they seek such connections, in the kinds of connections they regard as significant, and in the analogies they use in order to explain them.

Let us turn now to a couple of examples from Radcliffe-Brown's work: kinship terminology and totemism. I choose these because they show, in the case of kinship terminology, a facet of structural-functionalism which has won the argument against earlier approaches; and, in the case of totemism, the transformation from structural-functionalist to structuralist thinking.

Semantic structure or social structure?

What are kinship terms for? Are they simply aspects of language, independent of social implications, or are they more closely tied to the society which possesses them? The answer has wide implications, not just for kinship, but for any domain of classification. Essentially there are three viewpoints: the classical formulations of these are attributed respectively to A. L. Kroeber, W. H. R. Rivers, and A. R. Radcliffe-Brown (figure 5.2).

Kroeber's (1909) view was that kinship terminology reflects *not* society, as Morgan and other nineteenth-century theorists had supposed, but what he called 'psychology'. His notion of 'psychology' was not the university subject which is today called by that term. Rather, Kroeber's 'psychology' concerned specifically the formal properties of human thought, and he anticipated Lévi-Strauss in seeing these mainly in terms of binary oppositions. Kroeber suggested that these formal properties, or principles of classification, may have social implications, but he explicitly denied that there is any direct connection between the terminology itself (also ultimately derived from these principles) and the social implications of the underlying 'psychological' principles. 'Psychology' determines kinship terminology through language, of which the terminology is a part; it determines social behaviour independently and only indirectly. The formal properties he defined were: generation, lineal versus collateral, relative age within a generation, sex of the relative, sex of the speaker, sex of the person through whom the relationship is traced, blood relative versus relative by marriage, and 'condition of life' of the person through whom

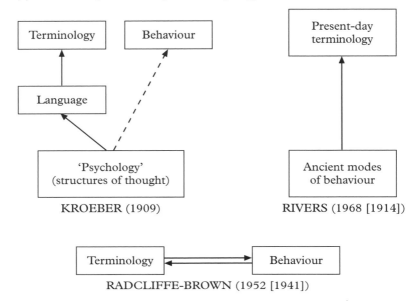

Figure 5.2 Relations between kinship terminology and social facts

the relationship is traced (e.g., living or dead, married or unmarried).

Rivers (1968 [1914]: 37–96) reacted against Kroeber's paper by rearticulating the earlier view which Kroeber was attacking. Rivers' formulation became the best representation of the traditional view that kinship terminology did directly stem from social facts, which was the prevailing theory in the late nineteenth century. Being conservative, he argued, terminology tends to reflect ancient, and often extinct, social facts. Thus it could be used as a kind of linguistic archaeology in order to understand historical changes in social organization. This is precisely what Morgan (1877) had done. Rivers here represented the last of the classic evolutionists, though he had in fact already announced his conversion to diffusionism; and his student, Radcliffe-Brown, was on the verge of a new approach based on a denial of the importance of conjectural history.

Radcliffe-Brown (1952 [1941]: 49–89) rejected Kroeber's claim that terminology was divorced from social behaviour and reflected merely language or 'psychology'. He also rejected Rivers' claim that it reflected only ancient social facts. For Radcliffe-Brown, its importance was its relation to existing social facts: the terminology, no matter what its history, would bear a connection to contemporary society. If one called one's father and father's brother by the same term, then one must treat them in a similar way. The origin of the custom is, in his view, lost in prehistory and can never be recovered. The meaning of the custom, however, is embedded in contemporary society. With few exceptions, Radcliffe-Brown's emphasis on contemporary classification over historical speculation remains with anthropology to this day.

Two theories of totemism

Radcliffe-Brown held not just one, but two theories of totemism. The contrast between them is of significance for understanding the relation between his structural-functionalism and the incipient structuralism which pervades his second theory, devised very late in his life.

Radcliffe-Brown's first paper on the subject is called 'The sociological theory of totemism'. It was delivered at a conference on the island of Java in 1929 and is reprinted in *Structure and Function in Primitive Society* (Radcliffe-Brown 1952: 117–32). There Radcliffe-Brown tries to explain how Australian Aborigines classify the world, and especially how Aborigines classify people as members of social groups. He builds on Durkheim's ideas of totemism, as he agrees with Durkheim that totems have the function of expressing clan solidarity.

However, he disagrees with Durkheim about the relationship between species and ritual. Durkheim argues that because given species represent social groups, these species are made the objects of ritual activity. Radcliffe-Brown argues the opposite. A species is chosen to represent a group because that species is already of ritual importance. But once a species is selected, the interrelationship between ritual, the symbolism of the species, and the solidarity of the group is what is important. For Radcliffe-Brown, totemism is a special development of the symbolism of nature. Totemistic ideas are found in many societies, though only some come to identify local groups specifically with truly totemic species.

Australian totemism, as Radcliffe-Brown points out, is characterized by the relations between four things: (1) the patrilineal local group (or 'horde' as Radcliffe-Brown called it); (2) the totems (certain animals, plants, the rain, the sun, hot and cold weather, and so on); (3) certain sacred spots within the local territories; and (4) certain mythical beings who, in the Dreamtime, made the sacred sites sacred. What Radcliffe-Brown does not quite do is put these relations together into a single framework. He concentrates instead on his disagreement with Durkheim, the relations between one group and another, and the relation between a group and its totemic species.

In his second essay on totemism, 'The comparative method in social anthropology', Radcliffe-Brown goes further. This theory was first presented as a public lecture in 1951 and published in 1952, and is reprinted in the compilations of Radcliffe-Brown's writings by Srinivas (Radcliffe-Brown 1958: 108–29) and Kuper (1988: 53–69). The second theory is not just about how the Aborigines classify people as members of social groups, but also about how they classify animals as members of species. And it concerns the relation between these systems of classification. Radcliffe-Brown anticipates Lévi-Strauss in comparing diverse societies (Australian Aborigines and the Indians of the North West Coast of North America) and expressing a 'general law' based on the notion of structural opposition.

This scheme also goes beyond the social structure into the cosmological structure. Radcliffe-Brown, and following him Lévi-Strauss, have come to ask: Why this particular species? For example, the eaglehawk and the crow represent moieties in parts of Western Australia; and similar birds, the eagle and the raven, represent moieties among the Haida of the North West Coast of North America. The question is not just 'Why have moieties and associate them with species?' It is also 'Why the eagle? Why the crow?' and further, 'What is the symbolic relation between the eagle and the crow?' The last question is answered by appeal to the respective myths of the peoples who revere such species, because myths explain (among other things) the 'kin' relations which connect the species. For example, in Western Australia the mythical Eaglehawk is the mythical Crow's mother's brother.

But for Lévi-Strauss, and I think also Radcliffe-Brown, the question is even deeper. Why do such birds represent exogamous moieties in both Australia and North America? Is it because there is something alike about the indigenous inhabitants of these two continents? Or is there some general principle, or pattern, imprinted on the human mind which is found everywhere, and of which this particular configuration of species and moiety is a trace? Is this, perhaps, a conscious example of an unconscious universal? If this is what Radcliffe-Brown was thinking in 1951, then he had indeed gone beyond his own structural-functionalist paradigm into the realms of Lévi-Straussian structuralism.

The influence of Malinowski and Radcliffe-Brown

Both Malinowski and Radcliffe-Brown demanded loyalty from their students. Between them they persuaded virtually every anthropologist in the British Commonwealth that the old interests of anthropology – in evolution and diffusion – were no longer appropriate areas for major research. Most anthropologists in Britain and many in America followed Radcliffe-Brown's line. They conceived of anthropology as being about filling in the details of ethnography: generalizing about particular societies and comparing them to other societies, working out how the social system functions without conjecturing about the past, de-emphasizing individual action and seeking the broader pattern, and above all, fitting the pieces together to see how elements of the social structure functioned in relation to each other.

Malinowski's greatest influence was in Britain, especially in the establishment of his tradition of 'participant observation'. Radcliffe-Brown's influence was predominant in South Africa and Australia (several famous 'British' anthropologists were in fact South Africans by birth and education). In the United States he left his mark through the work of Sol Tax, Fred Eggan, and others, especially at Chicago. A. P. Elkin and his students at Sydney continued the tradition there, while 'English' South African anthropology through Isaac Schapera (who later emigrated to Britain and worked with Malinowski), Monica Wilson (another student of Malinowski), and others grew to be a major intellectual force, and ultimately a political force against apartheid (see Hammond-Tooke 1997). Radcliffe-Brown's spell also reached India. Indian anthropologist M. N. Srinivas did postgraduate work with Radcliffe-Brown and Evans-Pritchard, then taught for three years at Oxford. In 1951 Srinivas returned to his own country and helped establish there an empirical but essentially structural-functionalist social science tradition.

It has often been said that Radcliffe-Brown's primary influence was as a teacher rather than a writer. He possessed a charismatic personality and was a brilliant lecturer, generally performing without any notes whatsoever. He published relatively little. What he did publish had a conversational style and very little jargon, as more often than not his writings were versions of his public lectures. His writings also exhibit a consistency in theoretical viewpoint through some four decades (see Radcliffe-Brown 1952; 1958; Kuper 1977).

Ironically, the substantive contribution most strongly associated with structural-functionalism is one he wrote little about (but see Radcliffe-Brown 1952 [1935]: 32–48). This is 'descent theory'. Evans-Pritchard (1940: 139–248), Fortes (1945), and others among his followers argued that localized patrilineal or matrilineal descent groups formed the basis of many societies, especially in Africa. Yet the idea was strongly contested, both through confrontation by its opposite, Lévi-Strauss' 'alliance theory' (discussed in chapter 8), and through empirical tests of its validity by close readings of the paradigm cases (see, e.g., Kuper 1988: 190–209).

Radcliffe-Brown intensely disliked being labelled with any 'ism'. The reason he would give (e.g., 1949, included in Kuper 1977: 49–52) is that 'sciences' do not have isms; only political philosophies (Communism,

Liberalism, Conservatism, etc.) have isms. One does not call a botanist interested in the structures and functions of plants a 'structural-functionalist', so why should one call an anthropologist with like interests by this label? He objected most strongly to being put in the 'functionalist' box with Malinowski, whose theory of biological needs and cultural responses he explicitly opposed. Yet outsiders, and some inside, gave the label 'functionalist' to Radcliffe-Brown's work too. And so for a time, this 'functionalist anthropology' did become a 'school' in spite of both its scientific trappings and the ambivalent relationship between its founders. While no one today claims to be a 'functionalist', there remains something 'functionalist' about both anthropological fieldwork and anthropological comparison – in spite of the challenges from processualist, Marxist, and more recent approaches.

Concluding summary

Functionalism had its beginnings in evolutionist thought. It came into its own as an anthropological perspective, partly through the influence of Durkheim (on the cusp of evolutionist-functionalist thinking), but more definitively through the writings of Malinowski and Radcliffe-Brown. Also crucial was the institutional base these latter two and their immediate successors created for the discipline worldwide.

Although Malinowski succeeded in building up a great following, his major venture into grand theory failed. His theory of 'seven basic needs and their cultural responses' never caught on. Radcliffe-Brown's theoretical ventures fared better: especially his emphasis on social structure and his encouragement of comparison. However, his brave vision of 'a natural science of society', analogous to the biological sciences, never bore fruit.

FURTHER READING

Good histories of the sociological tradition are Swingewood's *Short History of Sociological Thought* (1984) and Levine's *Visions of the Sociological Tradition* (1995). The best treatment of functionalism and structural-functionalism (and the aftermath) in anthropology is Kuper's *Anthropologists and Anthropology* (1996 [1973]).

For an evaluation of Malinowski's work by his own students, see Firth's *Man and Culture* (1957). On the fieldwork methods of Malinowski and others, see Stocking's *Observers Observed* (1983). A useful evaluation of the work of Radcliffe-Brown is Firth's (1956) obituary of him.

There are three collections of Radcliffe-Brown's essays: *Structure and Function in Primitive Society* (Radcliffe-Brown 1952), *Method in Social Anthropology* (Radcliffe-Brown 1958), and *The Social Anthropology of Radcliffe-Brown* (Kuper 1977). Some of the best examples of structural-functionalist ethnography are in the edited volumes, *African Political Systems* (Fortes and Evans-Pritchard 1940) and *African Systems of Kinship and Marriage* (Radcliffe-Brown and Forde 1950). A useful reader on kinship, which includes relevant selections from the Kroeber–Rivers debate, is Graburn's *Readings in Kinship and Social Structure* (1971).

Classic functionalist ethnographies include Evans-Pritchard's *Kinship and Marriage among the Nuer* (1951a), Firth's *We the Tikopia* (1936), and Fortes' *Dynamics of Clanship* (1945) and *Web of Kinship* (1949). Two with an ecological twist are Evans-Pritchard's *The Nuer* (1940) and Richards' *Land, Labour and Diet* (1939). One dealing with social change is Schapera's *Migrant Labour and Tribal Life* (1947). A regional-comparative ethnography in the functionalist tradition is Eggan's *Social Organization of the Western Pueblos* (1950).

6 Action-centred, processual, and Marxist perspectives

From the 1950s onwards there were a number of attempts to move anthropology away from the formal, society-centred paradigms, especially structural-functionalism, towards more individual and action-centred ones. Among these are the transactionalism of Fredrik Barth, various interrelated approaches of the 'Manchester School', and 'processual' offshoots of structuralism, including much of the work of Edmund Leach (see chapters 8 and 9).

Earlier ideas on social and cultural processes include the sociological theories of Georg Simmel and Max Weber, some of A. L. Kroeber's perceptive comments on 'culture patterns and processes' (1963 [1948]) and Arnold van Gennep's (1960 [1909]) seminal study of 'rites of passage'. The last was picked up especially by structural processualists such as Edmund Leach and Victor Turner. Relations between structures, processes, and historical events returned with a vengeance in the 1980s in debates such as that between Marshall Sahlins and Gananath Obeyesekere on the death of Captain Cook, and between Richard Lee and Edwin Wilmsen on the political economy of the Kalahari. Meanwhile, a Marxist revolution had succeeded in turning many away from functionalist and structuralist interests towards Marxism, a processual theory based on the social relations of production.

However, Marxism's status in anthropology is ambiguous: it contains aspects of several other theoretical positions. As a trajectory, evolutionist history was firmly in Karl Marx's own mind and in the minds of Marxists of later times. Diffusionism is there too, exemplified by the spread of the revolutions of past and future which so concerned Marx and Engels. Marxism is even more firmly grounded in functionalism, with the idea of societies as self-regulatory systems, but systems which are transformable by revolutionary change. It is also loosely relativist in the sense that different modes of production are said to entail ideologies which need to be understood in their own terms – albeit their own terms of 'false consciousness'. Marxist anthropology has structuralist elements too: a number of its proponents, particularly in France from the 1960s to the

1980s, aligned themselves with structuralist positions in traditional areas such as kinship studies. Marxist-feminists have been prominent in equating class consciousness with gender consciousness (see chapter 9), and Marxism has links with poststructuralism and postmodernism in its concern with power relations.

I group Marxism with processual approaches, as in anthropology (if less so in other disciplines) that is its closest association in both historical time and field of debate. Both processual approaches and Marxism reached prominence in Western anthropology in the 1970s. And while the placement of Marxism with functionalism would have been rejected by mainstream functionalists and Marxists alike, both Marxists and processualists in their heyday saw themselves as at least arguing from common ground. Over the last decade or more Marxism has declined as a predominant paradigm in anthropology. In the West, this has little to do with the revolutionary changes in Eastern Europe and elsewhere. It has more to do with the prior movement of former Marxist scholars away from explicitly Marxist endeavours towards concerns which align them with their former enemies, the (postmodern) relativists, who have in the past couple of decades taken an interest in things like power, oppression, and global politico-economic relations.

Action-centred and processual approaches

Roots in sociology

Two figures stand out among sociological thinkers whose classic understandings of social process and individual action have influenced anthropological ideas: Weber and Simmel.

Georg Simmel was a German philosopher active at the turn of the nineteenth to the twentieth century and author of treatises on social differentiation, the philosophy of history, the philosophy of money, fashion, literature, music, and aesthetics generally (see, e.g., Wolff 1950; 1965). Simmel's approach was formalistic and highly theoretical, but it gave prominence to the individual. He introduced the idea of the *Wechsel-wirkung* (reciprocal effect), which anticipated Mauss' theory (1990 [1923]) of 'the gift', developed not long after. The idea is that the social exists when two or more people engage in interaction with each other, and when the behaviour of one is seen as a response to the behaviour of the other. These dyadic relations provided Simmel with a notion of structural opposition which was dynamic rather than static, and one focused as much on the individual as on society in the abstract.

Max Weber was a German economist and founder of one of the three great traditions of sociology (the others being Marx and Durkheim). Weber wrote on economics, economic history, social science methodology, charisma, bureaucracy, social stratification, differences between Eastern and Western societies, ancient Judaism, and religion in China and India. His fame, though, rests especially on *The Protestant Ethic and the Spirit of Capitalism* (1930 [1922]), which he composed between 1904 and 1905. He died in 1920; most of his works were published after his death, and a collection of his key essays appeared in 1946 (Gerth and Mills 1946).

Weber borrowed from Simmel and, at first glance, he was the more formalist of the two. He developed the anti-empiricist notion of 'ideal types' – our imagined understandings of how things work. He argued that these are necessary in order to comprehend individual events in a social system. In his eyes, social action should be the central concern of sociology, but he also emphasized the notion of 'spirit' (*Geist*) within society. For example, in his study of relations between the feudal economy of rural Germany and the emergent market economy, he argued that not only were these in interaction, but that each was driven by a different 'spirit'. In his work on the Protestant Ethic, he argued that Calvinism and modern capitalism have the same 'spirit', and thus that Calvinist countries are conducive to the development of capitalist economies. Weber made contributions to early debates on the nature of 'interpretation' (*Verstehen*), and his writings consider values, objectivity, and causal explanation. His ideas were picked up by anthropologists, including those of the Manchester School in the 1950s, and they still influence anthropology today. Both transactionalists and interpretivists derive important elements of their thinking from their roots in Weberian sociology.

Roots in anthropology

Within the Boasian tradition, social and cultural change also received some comment, and sometimes even functional analysis. For example, Kroeber (1963 [1948]: 142–4) pointed out that European women's fashion goes through periods of stability and instability. Using statistics on skirt length and width, and waist height and width, for eight selected years between 1789 and 1935, he noted that fashion stability is correlated with times of socio-political stability, and fashion instability with times of strife and restlessness such as those occasioned by revolution and world war.

Transactionalism, the perspective which emphasizes the relations between individuals and the decisions these individuals make in social behaviour, has roots in Malinowski's functionalism, especially as championed by his successor at the London School of Economics, Sir

Raymond Firth (e.g., 1961 [1951]). Firth's approach stresses the importance of 'social organization' (which in sociological terms is made of the
roles people play) rather than 'social structure' (the statuses people
occupy).

   Another precursor was Oscar Lewis, an American anthropologist who
conducted a restudy of Robert Redfield's fieldwork site, the village of
Tepoztlan in Mexico. Redfield (1930), in an apparent mixing of Boasian,
functionalist, evolutionist, and German sociological traditions, had concentrated on the normative rules which are supposed to govern social
behaviour. Lewis (1951) concentrated on behaviour itself, which turned
out not to conform to Redfield's rules at all. Redfield's idealist representation of Tepoztlan portrays a quiet place in which the inhabitants live in
peaceful harmony. Lewis describes it as full of factionalism, with personal
antagonism, drunkenness, and fighting as the prevalent characteristics.
The village described had not so much undergone social change as a
change of paradigm in the hands of these two very different ethnographers.

   It was characteristic of the classic functionalist monographs that they
should end with a section, a chapter, or even a collection of chapters on
'culture contact' or 'social change' – apparently often perceived as the
same thing (e.g., Ottenberg and Ottenberg 1960: 475–564). However, as
social change gradually came to be regarded as the norm and social
dynamics recognized as a subject worthy of study in its own right, new
perspectives appeared which focused directly on change, both linear and
oscillating. At first drawing heavily on both functionalism and structuralism, anthropologists from the 1950s began to examine deficiencies in
their own received paradigms and adapt them to suit their ethnographic
and their archival findings. From the Manchester School to the debates
between Leach and Friedman and between Sahlins and Obeyesekere
(both discussed later in this chapter), the roots of anthropological
discourse in functionalist and structuralist understandings are clearly
present.

Transactionalism

The main proponent of transactionalism has always been Fredrik Barth –
a Cambridge-trained Norwegian, who has taught both in Norway (at
Oslo and later Bergen) and in the United States (at Emory University,
and at Boston). Barth was no doubt influenced by the functionalist
tradition and especially by his teacher Meyer Fortes, but from his earliest
writings he reacted against what he saw as excessive equilibrium in
models of social organization current in 1950s British anthropology.
Working in field areas as diverse as Pakistan, Norway, Sudan, Bali, and

Papua New Guinea, Barth devised an approach which gave prominence to social action, the negotiation of identity, and the production of social values through reciprocity and decision-making.

Barth's (1959) study of politics among Swat Pathan showed that the position of leaders is dependent on maintaining the allegiance of followers through transaction, and a constant 'game' oscillating between conflict and coalition. He developed these ideas further in his short monograph *Models of Social Organization* (1966), as well as in the introduction to his famous edited volume, *Ethnic Groups and Boundaries* (1969). Barth has shown himself to be a consistent thinker, as his recent work, and indeed that of his students and students' students, still echoes his early studies. Barthian models have proved especially valuable in the study of ethnicity and nationalism, where negotiation of identity is readily apparent. Although the specifics of his Swat ethnography were questioned by later writers (e.g., Ahmed 1976), Barth's analytical insights have withstood the challenge.

Transactionalism proceeded through work by, among others, Czech-British Africanist Ladislav Holy, British-American Melanesianist Andrew Strathern, Dutch Mediterraneanist Jeremy Boissevain, American South Asianist F. G. Bailey, and Australian South Asianist Bruce Kapferer. Each has brought his own theoretical twist into the paradigm. For example, Holy was interested in the relation between folk models, normative rules, and the creation of representations (e.g., Holy and Stuchlik 1983). In his last book (Holy 1996), he turned his attention to the understanding of national identity in his native Bohemia as it underwent the transition from Communist Czechoslovakia to the creation of a new Czech Republic. Holy also borrowed from the poststructuralist tradition of Bourdieu, which has parallels with both transactionalist and processualist approaches (see chapter 9). Indeed, there is a sense in which all these perspectives merge into one, though adherents to each school would, for reasons of their own historical, scholastic, national, and literary identities, probably prefer to see them as unique.

Thus transactionalism never fully became a 'school of thought', but remains a powerful analytical tool amenable to use in combination with others. It has both ardent adherents and quiet users among young anthropologists today.

The Manchester School

The Manchester School consisted of a close-knit group of scholars, mainly Oxford educated at first, then transplanted to Manchester and the Rhodes-Livingstone Institute (RLI) in Livingstone, Northern Rhodesia (now Zambia). It was at its height in Manchester between the 1950s and early 1970s, though arguably one could trace its origins to Max Gluckman's arrival at the RLI in 1939. Anthropology at Manchester today is far more eclectic, as testified by the annual debates in anthropological theory held under the auspices of the department there since 1988 (see, e.g., Ingold 1996). However, the term 'Manchester anthropology' once implied an allegiance both to group and to the agreed line, and for a time even to Gluckman's favourite soccer team, Manchester United.

Those associated either with the Institute in colonial times or with Manchester in its heyday include J. A. Barnes, A. L. Epstein, Scarlett Epstein, Elizabeth Colson, Clyde Mitchell, Godfrey Wilson, and Monica Wilson; and those of more recent times include Richard Werbner, John Comaroff, and Jean Comaroff. Each made distinctive and original contributions, and there were variations in approach. For example, Mitchell and (in some of his work) A. L. Epstein favoured 'network analysis', showing the ways in which individuals interacted socially and economically and the lines of connection built up from such interactions. This approach had much in common with Barth's.

However, two names stand out above all the others as providing the distinctive characteristics of the Manchester School: Max Gluckman and Victor Turner. Gluckman was a South African, trained in anthropology and law. He conducted fieldwork with several Central and Southern African groups, including Barotse, Tonga, Lamba, and Zulu, and maintained a strong interest in social change and the relation between 'tribal' and 'town' life. Yet he reacted against the Malinowskian notion that social change was all about culture contact, and sought instead the complex dynamics of African society. He also reacted against functionalist assumptions that African societies were essentially stable, and he set about the study of social action, differences between rules and behaviour, contradictions in social norms, the anatomy of conflict, and the means of dispute settlement. In general works such as *Custom and Conflict in Africa* (1955) and *Politics, Law and Ritual in Tribal Society* (1965), as well as in a number of specific ethnographies, Gluckman examined the relations between stability and change, the ways in which order is maintained in stateless societies, and the role of conflict in creating order. This last issue was one on which he expressed somewhat different views in different publications, but his classic statements in *Custom and Conflict* assert that cross-cutting ties of loyalty strengthen the social order, that social cohesion results from conflict itself, and even that 'the whole system depends on the existence of conflicts in smaller sub-systems' (Gluckman 1955: 21). Gluckman's interest in indigenous African law, including the ways in which disputes are handled, also brought into social anthropology new methodological tools, notably the 'extended case study'.

Perhaps contrary to his own theory of conflict, Gluckman's charismatic leadership fostered a climate of intellectual engagement and general agreement on the central aims of anthropology at Manchester. It also engendered a dread on the part of outsiders when they went to present seminar papers there, that they would be savaged by Gluckman and a room full of his followers. This sense even continued after Gluckman's death in 1975, when his successors were known, on occasion, to kick the wastepaper basket in disapproval of the ideas of visiting speakers.

Turner was a Scotsman transplanted to England, Central Africa, and, from 1964, the United States. In later life he studied pilgrimage in Mexico, Brazil, and Ireland, but he is best known for his research on the symbolism and rituals of the Ndembu people of what is now Zambia. Turner's *Schism and Continuity in an African Society* (1957) has been called 'a centerpiece for understanding the Manchester School's principal currents of ideas, orientations, and empirical concerns' (Werbner 1984: 176). It is built around the idea of 'social drama', with pre-crisis and post-crisis phases. This notion, borrowed in part from the famous study of rites of passage by Arnold van Gennep (1960 [1909]), became a recurrent theme in Turner's rich corpus on Ndembu ritual (cf., e.g., Turner 1967) and his later work on pilgrimage (e.g., Turner and Turner 1978). Others (e.g., Myerhoff 1978) have developed the idea of social dramas further, though Turner's work remains the classic foundation of the 'social drama' approach.

In the ritual process, participants pass through a *liminal phase* (as van Gennep termed it, after the Latin for 'threshold'), which is characterized by what Turner called *communitas*. Communitas is an 'unstructured' realm of 'social structure', where often the normal ranking of individuals is reversed or the symbols of rank inverted. In structural terms (and there is a clear sense in which Turner was *the* structuralist of the Manchester School), one might envisage it as a realm which is simultaneously one thing and not that thing (as in the Venn diagram, figure 6.1)

The diverse interests of Turner and Gluckman provided the Manchester School with a range of pursuits. United by their focus on Central Africa, by their basic theoretical assumptions and, at least at first, by their institutional affiliations, the school they led presented British anthropology with a challenge when perhaps it most needed it. While Gluckman leaned towards the functionalism of the past (even in his concern with rejecting functionalist dogma), Turner turned to structuralist interests in the systematic relations between symbolic aspects of culture. Even Marxism was present in the school – quite apart from the alleged Communist sympathies of Gluckman and others. Specifically, Peter Worsley's (1956) re-analysis of Fortes' (1945) study of lineage organization among

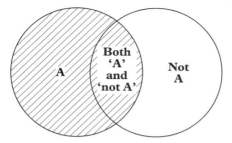

Figure 6.1 The liminal phase as both 'A' and 'not A'

the Tallensi of Ghana emphasized control by elders over the productive power of the land. In contrast, Fortes' functionalist ethnography had stressed merely the continuity of the lineage through association with ancestors buried in the land.

Marxist approaches

In the 1960s a new school was emerging: Marxism. It had a profound influence over the next two decades, especially in France, and also in Britain, South Africa, India, The Netherlands, Scandinavia, Canada, and Latin America. For obvious political reasons, it had less impact in the United States. Even evolutionist Leslie White, though influenced by Marxist thought, remained largely silent on explicitly Marxist issues and debates.

While Marxist ideas had been the established anthropological orthodoxy in the Soviet Union from the 1920s, the more liberal French version offered something different. French Marxists, like Russian ones, were often politically Communist; but they were decidedly more open to theoretical ideas from French structuralism, British functionalism, and non-Marxist materialist approaches such as Steward's cultural ecology. Some writers stuck close to Marx (see especially Marx 1965 [1857–58]), with interests in land, labour, capital, and the like. Others sought to apply the spirit of Marx to questions he had never looked at. For example, one subject of debate in the 1960s and 1970s was whether in West Africa gender and age hierarchy could be analysed in the same manner that classical Marxism analysed class hierarchy (see, e.g., Terray 1972 [1969]; Kahn 1981). Marxists seemed to argue with each other on such matters as much as they argued with non-Marxists, who opposed them at a much deeper level. Nevertheless, a number of widely agreed ideas emerged, and some remain prominent even in our post-Marxist age, both among anthropologists who follow non-Marxist materialist approaches and among those interested in the anthropology of colonialism and imperialism.

Key concepts in Marxist anthropology

The most important of all concepts in Marxist anthropology is *mode of production*, based on Karl Marx's ideas in *Capital*, Vol. 1 (see especially Marx 1974 [1867]: 667–724). The classic commentary on its usage is that by Barry Hindess and Paul Hirst (1975: 9). They define a mode of production as 'an articulated combination of relations and forces of production structured by the dominance of the relations of production'. The notion of 'articulation' here refers to the interaction between these elements, although in Marxist theory more generally it usually refers to an interaction between different modes of production. Hindess and Hirst (1975: 9–10) go on to say that the relations of production 'define a specific mode of appropriation of surplus-labour and the specific form of social distribution of the means of production corresponding to that mode of appropriation of surplus-labour'. Surplus-labour, in their view, is found in all societies, but different societies 'appropriate' it differently. For example, primitive communist and advanced socialist societies appropriate it collectively, whereas in feudal and capitalist societies it is appropriated by classes of non-labourers (i.e., by feudal lords and modern capitalists respectively). Forces of production involve 'the mode of appropriation of nature' (1975: 10). Means of production are simply those economic activities such as food-gathering, horticulture, or pastoralism which individuals practise. Hindess and Hirst (1975: 11) sum up their definitions with the comment that 'there can be no definition of the relations or of the forces of production independently of the mode of production in which they are combined'.

Marxist anthropologists have debated, for example, whether there is a distinctive 'foraging' mode of production, or whether foraging as a means of production is included within a larger mode of production involving other means of production which have similar effects (see, e.g., Lee 1981 [1980]). Those who hold the latter view might argue that what they call the 'domestic' mode, that is, where the household is the unit of producing and distributing goods, characterizes not only foraging societies but also small-scale horticultural ones. Beyond this on a scale of evolving complexity, there are 'lineage', 'feudal', and 'capitalist' modes of production.

On another front, Marx made a distinction between the *base* or *infrastructure* and its *superstructure* (e.g., Godelier 1975). The base consists of elements of a social formation (the Marxist term for 'society') which are closely related to production, such as subsistence technology, settlement patterns, and exchange relations. The superstructure consists of things which are more distant from production, such as ritual and religious belief. Of course, there may be a connection between production and religion, but it is not usually as direct as that between, say, production and politics. In fact by the 1970s, if not earlier, Marxists and cultural ecologists were coming to similar conclusions on a number of issues. Steward (1955) called the Marxist base the 'cultural core' (that related to exploitation of the environment and upon which, he argued, cultural evolution operated). Likewise, the Marxist idea of superstructure resembled Steward's idea of the 'total culture' (upon which cultural diffusion operated).

Yet another distinction common in Marxist anthropology is that between *centre* and *periphery*. The centre, in this sense, is the place where power is exercised, such as the colonial or national capital. The periphery is one of the places affected by decisions made at the centre, such as a rural area where peasants produce for redistribution or trade from the centre. According to Immanuel Wallerstein (1974–89), a centre–periphery relation has characterized economic relations on a global scale since the end of the fifteenth century.

In the 1970s and 1980s, interest grew in the *reproduction* of society through processes involving technology and labour (see, e.g., Meillassoux 1972), and in the articulation of (or interaction between) different modes of production (e.g., Friedman 1975). Interest turned equally towards arguing the rightful place of Marxist theory in anthropology generally (e.g., Kahn and Llobera 1981; Bloch 1983).

The structural Marxism of Godelier

While non-Marxist political anthropologists have sometimes argued an evolutionary trajectory, from band societies to clan-based societies, to chiefdoms, to states, Marxists have always emphasized the significance of economic relations in determining political structures. Still, Marxists differed from each other in how they incorporated non-economic issues, in other words, how important they saw the superstructure.

Structural Marxists regarded superstructure as fundamental. Some even reinterpreted superstructural elements (such as religion or kinship) as being infrastructural, in that they were seen as embedded in a socio-economic framework rather than constructed on top of it. The most prominent member of this school, Maurice Godelier carried out ethnographic research in Melanesia and has long actively undertaken and encouraged research in traditional realms of anthropology. His approach drew on conventional structuralism as well as on Marxism, though his overriding concern in the 1970s was with the description and analysis of modes of production (see, e.g., Godelier 1975; 1977 [1973]). As hinted above, Godelier's structural Marxism also built on cultural ecology and paralleled it in seeking an understanding of relations between environment, technology, and society. The difference was that structural Marxism emphasized relations of production (i.e., social relations) over either technologies or individual activities. Societies as bounded universes remained the units of analysis, though they were called by their Marxian term, 'social formations'. Likewise, culture became 'ideology', and the economy was the 'mode of production'. Structural Marxism had much in common with functionalism too, as both emphasized the synchronic and the functional qualities of ritual, lineage organization, and so on.

Even mainstream economic anthropologists were influenced by the trend. Marshall Sahlins' *Stone Age Economics* (1974 [1972]) is an example. An American anthropologist much taken with Marxism during a year in France, Sahlins eventually repudiated the structural Marxist tradition on the grounds that it gave too little emphasis to culture and therefore had little analytical power to explain the workings of pre-capitalist societies (see Sahlins 1976). Yet it was through *Stone Age Economics* that the notion of the 'domestic mode of production' (where the household is the dominant unit of production and exchange) became popularized.

Another American influenced by but opposed to new directions in Marxist anthropology, Marvin Harris (e.g., 1979: 216–57), built his attack on the notion that the structural Marxists were too structuralist and not materialist enough. Harris' 'cultural materialism' – labelled 'vulgar materialism' in an important Marxist attack by Jonathan Friedman (1974) – sought to reduce culture to virtually pure material forces. Harris argued that even religious taboos, such as that against eating cattle in Hindu India, have a material basis. In this case, it is the preservation of such animals for use in ploughing. Thus, Harris argued, ecological constraints prevail over all others; and culture is essentially a product of material forces (see chapter 3; see also Harris 1977).

The 'land and labour' Marxism of Meillassoux

Claude Meillassoux was critical of Lévi-Straussian structuralism (and perhaps implicitly structural Marxism) for leaving aside the question of exploitation and the material causes of transformation in kinship systems. He distinguishes societies in which land is the subject of labour from those in which it is the instrument of labour. In his view, the domestic economy ensures the reproduction of labour and therefore contributes to the existing power structures. For him, it is control over the means of reproduction (that is, over women) which is most important, not control over the means of production *per se* (see, e.g., Meillassoux 1972; 1981 [1975]). For this reason, Meillassoux's work is often used in feminist anthropology as a starting point for debate.

However, feminists have levelled a number of critiques (see, e.g., H. L. Moore 1988: 49–54). Women are largely invisible in his discussion, though they are central to it. Where they are visible, they form a homogeneous category and are taken out of the essential kinship context in which they belong ('woman' as wife is not the same as 'woman' as mother-in-law). Also, he seems to conflate the notion of biological reproduction with that of social reproduction; and ironically, he seems to see women mainly as reproducers of the labour force rather than as labourers or producers (see, e.g., Edholm, Harris, and Young 1977; Harris and Young 1981).

In fact Meillassoux's Marxism has strong functionalist elements, as well as relying to a great extent on technology as a determinant of mode of production. His arguments reflect his own ethnography, on the Guro of the Ivory Coast (see Meillassoux 1964), perhaps more than is generally the case among Marxists. He argues that capitalism does not destroy pre-capitalist modes of production but rather, maintains them 'in articulation' with a capitalist mode.

Political economy and globalization theory

A third school, still influential, is that of political economy, derived in part from the 'world systems' approach of Immanuel Wallerstein (1974–89) and the 'underdevelopment' ideas of Andre Gunder Frank (e.g., 1967). Whereas structural Marxism and interests in land, labour, and capital within small-scale societies were predominantly European interests, political economy as a school of thought took hold more in North America and the Third World. The influence of this school in Britain is also apparent in the shift in focus, during the late 1970s and 1980s, to large 'regional systems' (e.g., Hart 1982). Unlike other Marxist schools within anthropology, the political economy school stresses history. It also opposes the notion, implied in Meillassoux's work, that capitalist and pre-capitalist modes of production can simply co-exist in a state of 'articulation'.

Wallerstein's idea of a 'world system' which links the economies of the smallest societies to the powerful capitalist economies of the West and the Far East has proved a powerful one. Relations between these economies are unequal, in that developed capitalist ones benefit at the expense of the others. The idea has influenced anthropologists to look in similar directions (see, e.g., Kahn 1980; Wolf 1982), and the relation between the 'global' and the 'local' in cultural as well as economic spheres has become a widespread interest in the discipline. The problem, for mainstream anthropology, is that the political-economy view is outsider-centred. Their 'centre' is remote from the people who should be the objects (if not indeed the subjects) of study. Some writers in the 'subaltern studies' tradition (see, e.g., Guha and Spivak 1988) have put my general point here rather more strongly.

There is no doubt that the capitalist world system has had a global impact over the last few centuries, and little doubt that this impact is on the increase. Commentators have tended to view the phenomenon in Marxist or, more broadly, in evolutionist terms, where the capitalist system represents an evolutionary stage in which this type of society dominates those of the developing world. However, the idea of the 'world system' or 'globalization theory' can also been seen as a diffusionist notion. It is a modern (indeed a 'postmodern') version of grand diffusionism, where the global culture of the West stands in relation to the rest of the world as Elliot Smith and Perry believed Egypt had once stood (chapter 4). Ironically, there is a debate now emerging in archaeology about whether Wallerstein was correct to see the world system as developing only in the last few centuries, or whether it is more useful to consider the impact of prehistoric trade links too. There are also hints of this in the Kalahari debate, as we shall see shortly (cf. Shott 1992).

Three ethnographic debates

Several fierce debates have emerged in processual and Marxist anthropology. Here I want to look briefly at three, which to my mind provide illuminating illustrations of the interplay between the theoretical perspectives touched on in this chapter.

Friedman versus Leach: the political economy of the Kachin

Sir Edmund Leach was an intellectual eccentric who eventually became both an establishment figure and an inspiration to young anthropologists of his day. After training as an engineer, he studied under Sir Raymond Firth and did fieldwork in Sri Lanka (Leach 1961a), Burma (e.g., 1954), and elsewhere. He is usually thought of as one who turned against functionalism at an early date and introduced French structuralism into British anthropology. However, like Turner he advocated broadly a mixture of process and structure as constituting the foundations of social life, and it is his processualism which is our focus here.

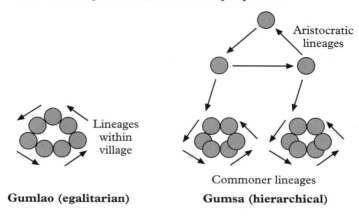

Figure 6.2 Marital alliance between Kachin lineages

Consider Leach's book *Political Systems of Highland Burma* (1954) and related work on the Kachin (notably Leach 1961b [1945/1951/1961]: 28-53, 54–104, 114–23). Before Leach, pre-functionalist ethnographic accounts of the Kachin described them as having an essentially uniform culture and social organization. The functionalist anthropology prevalent when Leach wrote his book assumed a balanced equilibrium, and it took for granted the existence of a single social system within which the ethnographer would work. In contrast to both, Leach focuses on the different structural arrangements in the kinship and political systems of two closely related groupings of clans, one system being egalitarian (*gumlao*) and the other a hierarchical version of the same thing (*gumsa*). A third, also hierarchical system impinges on these, namely that of the Tai-speaking Shan.

Another consideration with regard to kinship is that while *gumsa* is a hypogamous system (women marrying down), the Shan system is hypergamous (women marrying up). In *gumlao*, marriage is in a circle, with each man owing deference to his in-laws but no one clan having absolute priority over the others. This is transformed in the *gumsa* system into a relation of dominance, as men from superior groups give their sisters in marriage to members of lower-status groups. An idealized model is illustrated in figure 6. 2, where arrows indicate the direction of movement of women in marriage. Since bridewealth passes from the groom's family to the bride's, men in higher-status groups end up with fewer potential wives but greater wealth (indeed it seems that wealth was more important than status to those involved). Some marry Shan Chinese, and some become monks. Some Kachin even 'become' Shan.

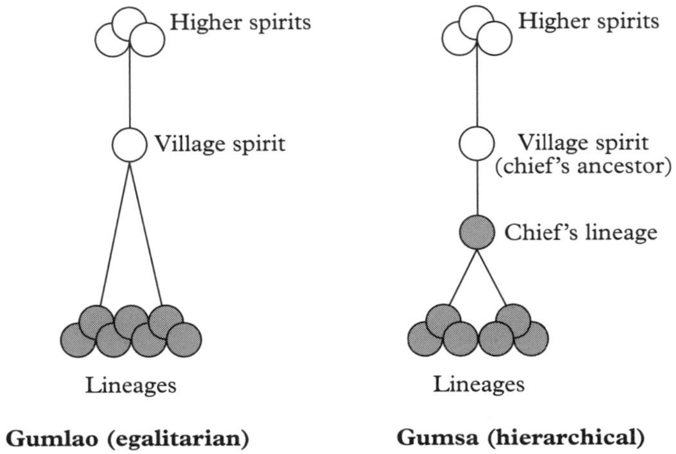

Figure 6.3 Relations between Kachin and their ancestral spirits

For Leach, kinship, class, history, and ideology work together in a complex framework, but not one which would readily be understood by the followers of Radcliffe-Brown or even Malinowski. Leach (1954: 292) summed up his efforts as follows: 'I am not concerned with *average* Kachin behaviour; I am concerned with the relationship between actual Kachin behaviour and ideal Kachin behaviour. And with this in mind I have tried to represent Kachin cultural variations as differing forms of compromise between two conflicting systems of ethics.'

In a now classic library re-study, Jonathan Friedman (1975; cf. 1996 [1979]) analysed Leach's ethnographic data in a structural Marxist perspective, and with particular attention to ecological factors which cause the oscillation and transformation of Kachin social structures. In Friedman's model, instead of the simpler Marxist notion of base and superstructure, we get a more complex four-tier model: the *ecosystem*, which constrains *productive forces*, which constrain *relations of production*, which in turn dominate both the ecosystem and the *superstructure*. Friedman emphasized relations between economics, kinship, and religion in arguing that surplus leads both to feasting and to the accumulation of wives, which entail respectively a gain in prestige and the birth of children, and in turn a higher rank, leading ultimately to the acquisition of prestations and more surplus. A wealthy lineage head would hold feasts for the entire village and thus be seen to have greater influence with the spirit world. This results in the setting apart of such a lineage, as it comes to be recognized as 'closer' to the spirits through its ancestor (as in figure 6.3). Thus the egalitarian *gumlao* system evolves into a *gumsa* one through a sequential combination of environmental, economic, kinship, and religious factors.

In Friedman's model, the social processes described by Leach have been amplified, and Leach's structural-processual framework opened to a framework which emphasizes power and productive relations to a much greater extent. Leach was sceptical of Friedman's Marxist reading of his work, but its existence highlights the potential for multiple interpretations. These may be especially appropriate in the analysis of dynamic social frameworks such as that of Burma in the period Leach described (which is until the Second World War). Marxist anthropology always worked best when it tackled real historical and ethnographic cases, and in this case its interplay with processualism was essential for its insight into Kachin society and social action.

Wilmsen versus Lee: Kalahari history and ethnography

The Kalahari debate concerns the degree to which the Bushmen or San of Southern Africa represent part of a regional or global economic system. It had been simmering for some time, but erupted with a vengeance in response to Marxist-influenced archaeologist-anthropologist Edwin Wilmsen's *Land Filled with Flies* (1989). Ecological-Marxist anthropologist Richard Lee (e.g., 1979: 401–31) and others had long described relations between Bushmen and Bantu-speaking cattle-herders, but they had de-emphasized them and placed them in a context of 'social change'. The real problem is: when does 'traditional' life end and 'social change' begin?

The core of the debate consists of a series of articles and short comments published in the journal *Current Anthropology* (especially Solway and Lee 1990; Wilmsen and Denbow 1990; Lee and Guenther 1991) and one in *History in Africa* (Lee and Guenther 1993). More crucial, though, are the differing assumptions behind Lee's and Wilmsen's ethnographies. Lee often admits that his interest in Bushmen has come from his desire to reconstruct something of the foraging way of life of early humanity:

Foraging was a way of life that prevailed during an important period of human history. The modern foragers do offer clues to the nature of this way of life, and by understanding the adaptations of the past we can better understand the present and the basic human material that produced them both. (Lee 1979: 433)

Lee takes foraging for granted, as a basic and adaptive way of life, an assumption which is anathema to the hard-line revisionists. He also takes for granted the fact that Bushman societies are relevant units of analysis, in spite of the presence of members of other groups within their territories and at their waterholes. Although Bushmen and their cattle-herding neighbours do interact, they are seen as occupying different ecological niches.

Wilmsen (1989) argues that the political economy of the Kalahari is the best unit of analysis, and that this unit has been a meaningful construct since livestock were first introduced to the fringe areas of the Kalahari a thousand years ago. The apparent isolation of Bushmen observed by Lee and others, he says, is a product of the white domination of Southern Africa since the late nineteenth century:

Their appearance as foragers is a function of their relegation to an underclass in the playing out of historical processes that began before the current millennium and culminated in the early decades of this century. The isolation in which they are said to be found is a creation of our view of them, not of their history as they lived it. (Wilmsen 1989: 3)

Traditionalists like Lee emphasize cultural continuity and the cultural integrity of Bushman groups. They see Bushmen as the inheritors of ancient indigenous environmental knowledge, hunting techniques, kinship practices, religious beliefs, and so on. Revisionists like Wilmsen de-emphasize these aspects in favour of greater concern with the integration of Southern African politico-economic structures taken as a whole. The irony is that both sides claim intellectual descent from Marx, and both sides see their approach as one which explains social processes.

Obeyesekere versus Sahlins: the death of Captain Cook

The third debate concerns an intriguing historical problem: why, on 14 February 1779, did Hawaiian warriors kill Captain James Cook upon his return to the islands? To date, each of the two main players, Marshall Sahlins and Gananath Obeyesekere, has contributed some half a dozen publications on the problem (see especially Sahlins 1981; 1985: 104–35; 1995; Obeyesekere 1992), and other protagonists and commentators on the debate are emerging (see, e.g. Borofsky 1997; Kuper 1999: 177–200).

Sahlins, a senior American anthropologist with a specialization in Polynesia, takes an essentially structuralist (or structural-processualist) point of view. He argues that Cook was the victim of mistaken identity and ritual sacrifice. Cook first arrived in the islands in January 1778 at the height of the annual celebrations for their fertility god Lono, and he came back a year later. The Hawaiians, in Sahlins' view, took him for Lono, and duly honoured him as their god. Shortly thereafter Cook set off to continue his expedition, but a storm forced him to turn back. This time his return was decidedly unexpected. More importantly, it was precisely at the wrong time of year for the god. A taboo was in effect, with the change in ritual cycle, and the king had gone inland. Cook's landing and his search for the king led to skirmishing between his marines and the islanders and the death of one of the local chiefs. This action was an apparent reversal of Hawaiian ritual, and 'Lono' had to die.

Obeyesekere, a Sri Lankan anthropologist of religion (based at Princeton), explains away Sahlins' argument as a Western imperialist myth. He argues that the Hawaiians treated Cook as a chief, not as a god. To Obeyesekere, Cook was a 'civilizer' who became a 'savage' when his expedition went wrong. What is more, to Obeyesekere, Sahlins is a myth-maker building his myth of Cook on a wrongful supposition that the Hawaiians had a structuralist mentality, whereas in fact they were pragmatic rationalists. Like Sahlins, Obeyesekere is interested in the relations between culture and historical process, but the focus is entirely different. In a sense, Obeyesekere's focus is on Western culture and the process of exploration and colonization, whereas Sahlins' focus is decidedly on Hawaiian culture and the Hawaiian ritual process.

What is at stake here is not just historical fact. Nor is it merely how to interpret the evidence to come up with a 'correct' retrospective ethnography of eighteenth-century Hawaii. The crux of the matter is two-fold: it relates first to the opposition between 'us' and 'them', which Obeyesekere is trying to break down, and secondly to the issue of who can speak for whom. Is Obeyesekere a legitimate, surrogate 'native voice' because he comes from a culture which was, like the Hawaiian one, the subject of colonial oppression? Or does he go too far in denying Sahlins, with his apparent mastery of the relevant sources, the ability to come up with a competent analysis?

These questions, taken much more broadly, form the theme of the postmodern critique which in the 1980s supplanted Marxism as the leading challenge to traditional lines of enquiry. Embedded in them is one of the central debates of anthropology in our time. Indeed, many would argue that it is *the* anthropological debate of all time. Can anthropology provide objective insights into alien cultures and their social action, or is the discipline forever doomed to implicit subjectivity which ought to be made explicit?

Concluding summary

Action-centred, processual, and Marxist perspectives represent the culmination of the 'social' tradition in anthropology. These perspectives, especially Marxism, have elements of all the preceding ones. Transactionalism, for example, has its roots in Malinowski's ideas on social organization, as well as in the sociology of Simmel and Weber. Different approaches within Marxism emphasize variously social evolution, diffusion (globalization), function, structure, and even reflexivity. On the last point, for example, Hindess and Hirst in their 'auto-critique' (1977: 7) suggest that theories exist only in the context in which they are expressed: their Marxist ideas are, in fact, a product of writing about them.

Plainly, transactionalism, processualism, and the various brands of Marxism are complex perspectives. Even the 'Manchester School' consisted of a blend of ideas and a variety of interests, from ritual to legal processes, from symbolic structures to relations between whites and blacks in the British colonies of south-central Africa.

In the remaining chapters we shall turn our attention away from 'social' to 'cultural' traditions. There is, of course, no absolute divide between them. The difference is one of emphasis: whether it is understanding society which should be our paramount goal, or understanding thought, the symbolic world, communication, or the place of the anthropologist and his or her worldview in relation to that of the alien 'other'.

FURTHER READING

The classic transactionalist monograph is Barth's *Political Leadership among Swat Pathans* (1959). Diverse Manchester ethnographies include Gluckman's *Custom and Conflict in Africa* (1955) and Turner's *Schism and Continuity in an African Society* (1957). An excellent example of structural-Marxist ethnography is Godelier's *The Making of Great Men* (1986 [1982]).

For a review of the Manchester School, see Richard Werbner's 'The Manchester School in South-Central Africa' (1984). Important edited collections respectively on transactionalism and Marxism include Kapferer's *Transaction and Meaning* (1976) and Bloch's *Marxist Analyses and Social Anthropology* (1975). For commentaries on the Kalahari debate, see, e.g., those by Kuper (1992) and Shott (1992). On the Hawaiian debate, see Borofsky (1997).

For a comprehensive review of theoretical developments from the 1960s to the 1980s, including those in Marxist anthropology, see Sherry Ortner's essay 'Theory in anthropology since the sixties' (1984). Bloch's *Marxism and Anthropology* (1983) provides a history of Marxist ideas in social anthropology. The review by O'Laughlin (1975) gives an overview of approaches in the Marxist tradition, while Legros' (1977) critique of evolutionist cultural ecology presents a good picture of the differences between Marxist and non-Marxist understandings of productive forces.

7 From relativism to cognitive science

Melford Spiro (1992), one of several critics of contemporary cultural relativism, defines three types: descriptive, normative, and epistemological. It is useful to follow his classification, and I shall outline each briefly here.

It is a truism that cultures differ one from another. With varying degrees of enthusiasm, anthropologists since the late nineteenth century have been 'cultural determinists', arguing that culture itself (and not merely biology) regulates the ways in which humans perceive the world. A corollary is that cultural variability will produce different social and psychological understandings among different peoples, and this position is called *descriptive relativism*. Virtually all schools of anthropology entail an acceptance of at least a weak form of descriptive relativism.

Normative relativism goes a step further in asserting that, because cultures judge each other according to their own internal standards, there are no universal standards to judge between cultures. Within normative relativism, we can distinguish two logically distinct forms: *cognitive relativism* and *moral relativism*. Cognitive relativism concerns descriptive propositions, like 'The moon is made of green cheese', or 'Pop music causes headaches.' It holds that in terms of truth and falsehood, all statements about the world are culturally contingent, and therefore non-culturally-contingent statements are simply not possible. In other words, all science is ethnoscience. Moral relativism concerns evaluative propositions, like 'Cats are more beautiful than dogs', or 'It is wrong to eat vegetables.' It holds that aesthetic and ethical judgements must be assessed in terms of specific cultural values rather than universal ones. It follows that in social and psychological terms, both appropriate behaviour and processes of thought (i.e., rationality) must also be judged according to cultural values. Boas and his followers, and to a lesser extent Evans-Pritchard and his, all espoused tenets of normative, and especially cognitive, relativism.

Epistemological relativism takes as its starting point the strongest possible form of descriptive relativism. It combines an extreme cultural-determinist position with a view that cultural diversity is virtually limitless. It is important here to distinguish between *generic cultural determinism* (which holds that there is a universal but uniquely human cultural pattern within which cultures vary, i.e., the 'psychic unity' of humankind) and *particular cultural determinism* (which holds that there is no such thing). Epistemological relativists espouse the latter. They argue that human nature and the human mind are culturally variable. Therefore, they claim, both generalizations about culture and general theories of culture are fallacious.

The main concerns of the present chapter will be with 'relativism' as the term was understood prior to the rise of postmodernism; with offshoots, notably cognitive anthropology; and with certain strands of anti-relativism. The first great relativist in anthropology was Franz Boas, whose ideas were essentially of the descriptive relativist type. His follower, amateur linguist Benjamin Lee Whorf, embraced a form of cognitive relativism, as did later cognitive anthropologists and ethnoscientists. Early psychological anthropology of the 'culture and personality' school was characteristically associated with moral relativism. Epistemological relativism is strong in anthropology today, having emerged over the last thirty years or so in the hands of a diversity of thinkers in different countries. Clifford Geertz is perhaps the best-known proponent of it, but other interpretivist and postmodernist thinkers maintain more radical views. We shall return to radical epistemological relativism in chapter 10.

Franz Boas and the rise of cultural relativism

Classic cultural relativism emerged from the work of Franz Boas and his students. For the first half of the twentieth century it was the dominant paradigm of American anthropology. Some adherents (including Boas himself) stressed the richness of cultures then generally thought of as 'primitive', and several (again including Boas) used relativist ideology to argue the case against racism, anti-Semitism, and nationalist zealotry. Others developed their ideas through the study of the relation between language and culture, and still others, through psychological aspects of culture.

Boas was born in Westphalia in 1858. He studied physics and geography at Heidelberg and Bonn and took his Ph.D. at Kiel in 1881. It is said that his Ph.D. research, which was on the colour of water, led him directly to an interest in the subjectivity of perception. In 1883 he began fieldwork with the Inuit of Baffin Island with the intention of comparing their physical environment, measured 'objectively', with their own knowledge of it. He soon came to realize the importance of culture as a determining

force of perception, and consequently he rejected the implicit environ-
mental-determinist position with which he had started. He also began
learning the complex language of the Baffin Island people, recorded
folklore and other aspects of their culture, and eventually published
accounts of his work in both German and English. Boas returned to
Germany in 1884, and in the following year he began to study the cultures
of the North West Coast of North America, first through museum collections in Germany and then, from 1886, through field studies on the North
West Coast.

Boas taught at Columbia University in New York City from 1896 to
1936, and his department quickly became *the* centre of anthropological
research in the United States. He objected to evolutionism, mainly on the
grounds that the task of anthropologists should be to gain first-hand
experience in other cultures and not to speculate about their past. He also
objected to the idea of racial and cultural superiority implicit in evolutionist writings. He countered this with an insistence on ethnographers conducting their fieldwork in the native language, and through use of the
language, gaining an insider's view of the culture under study.

The title of his most famous book, *The Mind of Primitive Man* (Boas
1938 [first edition 1911]), perhaps now seems both evolutionist and sexist,
but the book was written to oppose the incipient racism in America and in
the world. Boas argues that the 'white race' is not intellectually superior,
but just more advantaged than other 'races'. He cites the fact that many
nations made contributions to the origins of world civilization. While
seemingly accepting some aspects of evolutionism in his notion of 'the
progress of culture', Boas rejects any biological basis for culture at all. In
his view, language is independent of 'race', and culture is even more
independent. He points also to the lack of comparability in data used to
support evolutionism. He defines his 'primitive' people in a non-
judgemental way: 'Primitive are those people whose forms of life are
simple and uniform, and the contents and form of whose culture are
meager and intellectually inconsistent' (Boas 1938: 197). He goes on to
point out that different peoples are primitive or advanced in different
respects. Australian Aborigines are poor in material culture but have a
complex social structure. The Indians of California do superb artistic
work, but their culture lacks complexity in other ways. He likens such
differences to those between poor and rich in America and Europe. He
adds that no people are untouched by foreign influences, and concludes
that to assign a whole culture to a uniform category of 'primitive' or
'civilized' is pointless.

Most of Boas' work was of a more specific nature, on topics like art,
mythology, and language, but he often addressed his anthropological

arguments to the general public. His influence was great, partly because of his early monopoly on the training of postgraduate anthropology students in North America, and partly because he wrote prolifically and in plain English. Boas wrote few books, preferring short articles (of which he wrote over 600). The best and most influential of these are included in two collections, one published during his lifetime (Boas 1940) and the other compiled many years after his death by one of his admirers (Stocking 1974). Boas died on 21 December 1942 at a luncheon being held in his honour. He uttered his last words, 'I have a new theory of race . . . ', and before he could finish, collapsed and died in the arms of the person sitting next to him – the great French structuralist, Claude Lévi-Strauss.

Culture and personality

Culture was the abiding abstract interest of American anthropology from Boas to Geertz (with the latter steering clear of static abstraction in favour of a more dynamic approach). This does not mean that there has always been uniformity about what 'culture' is. In a famous overview, A. L. Kroeber and Clyde Kluckhohn (1952) cite over a hundred definitions by anthropologists, philosophers, literary critics, and others. They divide the anthropological definitions into six groups: descriptive (based on content), historical (emphasizing tradition), normative (emphasizing rules), psychological (dealing with learning or problem-solving), structural (having to do with pattern), and genetic (e.g., culture as a product of being human, or simply as that which non-human animals lack). To me, what comes out of their survey is the extraordinary range of perspectives on things which might make up culture. Ironically though, it is not the ideas of Boas or his followers that most anthropology students remember, but Tylor's (descriptive) definition of culture: 'that complex whole which includes knowledge, belief, art, law, morals, custom, and any other capabilities and habits acquired by man as a member of society' (Tylor 1871, I: 1).

While Tylor's definition has remained at the heart of considerations of culture in the abstract, the perspective which emerged as most crucial to its position as the quintessential anthropological concept was that of Ruth Benedict. The key text is her *Patterns of Culture* (1934), written no doubt under the guiding hand of Boas but with a greater emphasis on psychological aspects than in his work. Benedict's undergraduate education was in literature, and her early interest was poetry. Not long after her introduction to anthropology in 1919, she came to the conclusion that her colleagues were making all the wrong sorts of comparison. Just as poetry should be analysed in its cultural context, she argued, so too aspects of culture should be seen in light of the culture in its entirety. She favoured comparison not of kinship terminologies or techniques of pottery-making, but of whole cultures seen through an understanding of their particular 'dominant drives'. In *Patterns of Culture* Benedict compares three peoples: the Zuñi of New Mexico (studied by Ruth Bunzel, Frank Cushing, and others), the Kwakiutl of Vancouver Island (studied by Boas), and the Dobuans of Melanesia (studied by Reo Fortune). She comes to the conclusion that what is normal behaviour in one culture is not normal in another. Even psychological states are culturally determined.

The Zuñi are a ceremonious people. They value sobriety and inoffensiveness above all other virtues. They have cults of healing, of the sun, of sacred fetishes, of war, of the dead, and so on. Each has its own priestly officials, who perform various ceremonies according to the seasonal calendar. The details of these ceremonies are important. If anything goes wrong, it can have adverse consequences: if a priest says a rain prayer in the wrong way, it is likely to be hot and sunny.

All this is very different from what happens among most other Native North American peoples. Benedict contrasts the Zuñi to them, using a distinction invented by the nineteenth-century philosopher and literary critic, Friedrich Nietzsche. He had distinguished two elements of Greek tragedy: the 'Apollonian' and the 'Dionysian'. The Apollonian aspect is that of measure, restraint, and harmony; the Dionysian aspect, that of emotion, passion, and excess. Greek tragedy, according to Nietzsche, had both. American Indian cultures, according to Benedict, have one or the other.

Zuñi are described as Apollonian. They live an ordered life. Everything is done precisely. They do not get worked up, go into trance, or hallucinate. They just perform their rituals as they always have done. They distrust individualism. Supernatural power comes not from individual experience, but from prior membership in a cult. Even in courtship there are absolute and rather tedious rules about what to say and how to say it. Traditionally, there is not meant to be any deep feeling between husbands and wives; they just abide by the rules of proper behaviour. Nor, at least in Benedict's account, do the Zuñi distinguish sharply between 'good' and 'evil'. They say that things just are the way they are.

Kwakiutl are described as the opposite – an example of a Dionysian culture. In their religious ceremonies the chief dancer goes into deep trance. He foams at the mouth, trembles violently, and typically has to be tied up with four ropes (each held by a different person) to keep him from doing any damage. In the past, the most sacred of all the Kwakiutl cult groups was the Cannibal Society. According to accounts by Boas and others, the cannibals would sing sacred songs and dance, while they ate the bodies of slaves specifically killed for the purpose. In the absence of slaves, accounts claimed, the cannibals would just bite chunks out of the arms of the spectators, then vomit them up later.

Kwakiutl used to run their economy along similar Dionysian principles through the institution known as the potlatch. In the nineteenth century, the custom was that chiefs whose waters and lands produced well in a given year would hold great feasts to give away food and other items. Thereby they gained prestige over other chiefs and simultaneously spread their good fortune to members of other clans. In the period when pot-latching was at its most extreme (around the turn of the century), people, through their chiefs, bartered away enormous amounts of subsistence goods in exchange for copper bracelets and blankets. This was not so they could give them away as they previously had done, but so they could destroy them. The more one gives away, the higher one's prestige. And if one can destroy things, they reckoned, one gains even more prestige. Better yet, destruction insults the guests. The chiefs and their retainers even sang 'hymns of self glorification' as they destroyed their wealth.

Dobuans are different again. Their highest virtues, Benedict suggests, are hostility and treachery. For example, marriage begins with the treach-ery of a young man's prospective mother-in-law. A boy will sleep with several girls in sequence. Then one morning, when he wakes up, the mother of whomever he is sleeping with will be standing in the door of her hut. The mother will give him a digging stick and force him to go to work for her, and that means he is married! This does not actually matter very much, because, it seems, almost everyone on Dobu commits adultery. When it is found out, there are violent quarrels, broken cooking pots everywhere, and suicide attempts. There is also sorcery. If anyone has a good crop of yams, it is assumed he must have performed sorcery against those whose yams have not grown well. The Dobuans live in a state of perpetual fear of each other, and (says Benedict) they regard this as normal.

So, what is normal for the Zuñi is not normal for the Kwakiutl. What is normal in Middle America is not normal for the Dobuans, and vice versa. In Western psychiatric terms, we might regard the Zuñi as neurotic, the Kwakiutl as megalomaniac, and the Dobuans as paranoid. In Dobu, paranoia is 'normal'. Of course, in presenting here just the juicy bits from Benedict's account, I have perhaps portrayed her argument as more extreme than she might have preferred. Yet her premise, that culture determines both what is regarded as correct behaviour and what is re-garded as a normal psychological state, remains one of the strongest assertions of relativism in anthropology.

Using the same approach, Benedict herself went on to work with

Japanese immigrants in the United States during the Second World War (Benedict 1946). A number of others followed in her footsteps, notably Margaret Mead, a slightly younger contemporary at Columbia in the 1920s who published her first work in the field even before Benedict (Mead 1928; see also Mead 1930). Clyde Kluckhohn was another well-known figure, who applied Benedict's ideas on psychological aspects of culture in his ethnography of the Navajo (e.g., Kluckhohn 1944; Kluckhohn and Leighton 1974 [1946]). In the last couple of decades their work has come under fire, especially that of Mead on the supposed sexual freedoms enjoyed by Samoan adolescent girls (Freeman 1983). Mead had recorded on Samoa that premarital sex without loving attachment was regarded as normal, that adolescence was not marked by emotional stress, and that teenage rebellion did not exist there, and therefore that it is not a necessary result of the biological facts of puberty. Derek Freeman's alternative view suggests that all these generalizations are false. Yet to me what matters more is that Mead gained insights into American culture *through* her studies in Samoa and elsewhere. Although her writings were less explicit about 'personality' than Benedict's, Mead nevertheless became the most famous representative of the 'culture and personality' school. Her work marked the point of origin of psychological anthropology as we know it today (see, e.g., Bock 1980; 1988).

Primitive thought?

Do peoples who live in different cultures think differently? If so, are some ways of thinking more primitive than others? Can we say that some cultures are more primitive than others? The notion of 'primitive thought' has existed at least since the late nineteenth century, but in the twentieth century it has acquired new meaning. Among twentieth-century questions are: if 'primitive thought' exists, then does it exist only among 'primitive peoples', or is it found universally, perhaps deep within all cultures? Can 'primitive thought' be equated with 'rational thought', or is it different? Indeed is it *more* rational than the scientific thought of the Western world (as the most radical of the Boasians claimed)?

In order to explore these questions, we shall look next at the work of Lévy-Bruhl and Whorf, both active in the 1920s and 1930s. Their ideas are poles apart. Yet they touch on these questions in intriguing and enlightening ways. Then we shall take up briefly another side to relativism – within the 'rationality debate' which lasted roughly from the late 1960s to at least the early 1980s.

The anti-relativism of Lévy-Bruhl

The most important writer on 'primitive thought' was the French philosopher of the social sciences, Lucien Lévy-Bruhl. He rejected the notion of psychic unity and argued that primitive thought is qualitatively different from logical thought. It is not different because it is illogical, but because, in his view, it is *pre*-logical. Its 'pre-logical' nature is defined simply by the presumed absence of a separation of cause and effect. Although part of the *Année sociologique* school and in some respects a functionalist, Lévy-Bruhl's views are better characterized as evolutionist and anti-relativist.

Lévy-Bruhl wrote six books on 'primitive thought', as well as other books and articles on philosophical and political topics. The bibliographical details are not so important, but the French titles of his works on 'primitive thought' are interesting because they hint at his views with regard to the very concept of 'the primitive'. They include: *Les fonctions mentales dans les sociétés inférieures* (translated into English as *How Natives Think*), *La mentalité primitive* (*Primitive Mentality*), *L'âme primitive* (*The 'Soul' of the Primitive*), *Le surnaturel et la nature dans la mentalité primitive* (*Primitives and the Supernatural*), *La mythologie primitive* (not yet translated), and *L'expérience mystique et les symboles chez les primitifs* (not yet translated).

In *How Natives Think*, Lévy-Bruhl (1926 [1910]) divided human thought into just two categories, that of 'primitive mentality' and that of 'higher mentality'. The 'primitive' thinks logically enough in everyday situations, but cannot think logically in the abstract. For example, in 'primitive' cultures one's soul may be equated with one's shadow. The 'primitive', in general, is afraid of phenomena such as shadows because, says Lévy-Bruhl, he or she cannot distinguish between an object and what that object symbolically and mystically represents. A man from Aboriginal Australia does not have a notion of land ownership, since he cannot conceive of himself as being separated from his land. Or, when a South American Indian says she is a parrot, she does not mean (as we would now say) she is a member of the parrot totem. She means that there is an identity between herself and a bird. In the Indian's own view, apparently, she really is a parrot.

For Lévy-Bruhl, 'primitive thought' also differs from logical thought in that it is a product of collective, not individual, thinking. Like other French anthropologists of his time, he frequently referred to the *representations collectives* (collective representations) of peoples. Durkheim, Mauss, and Lévy-Bruhl alike opposed the idea that one can reduce collective action to the actions of a number of individuals, or a culture as a whole to the ideas of each individual bearer of that culture. Yet in

Lévy-Bruhl's case, this applied only, or at least predominantly, with reference to pre-literate cultures, as he regarded the mentality of those cultures with literacy as more individualistic. There is a consistency on this through Lévy-Bruhl's books; yet his private notebooks tell a different story.

Wherever he went, Lévy-Bruhl carried thin, black oilcloth, lined notebooks. Each section had a title, and at the bottom of each page was a note of the date and the place the notes were written. Happily, the notebooks of the last year of his life (1938 to 1939) survived the Second World War, and they indicate an interesting transformation of Lévy-Bruhl's theory. He did not give up the idea of primitive mentality, but he significantly altered its definition. On 29 August 1938, for example, Lévy-Bruhl jotted in his oilcloth pad:

let us rectify what I believed correct in 1910: there is not a primitive mentality distinguishable from the other by *two* characteristics which are peculiar to it (mystical and prelogical). There is a mystical mentality which is more marked and more easily observable among 'primitive peoples' than in our own societies, but it is present in every human mind. (Lévy-Bruhl 1975 [1949]: 100-1)

In other words, it is not the logic which is different, but the knowledge. Cultures are not different in kind, but only in degree.

Chronologically, Lévy-Bruhl's ideas were developed in parallel with those of Boas, Benedict, and Mead – all of whom held romantic attachments towards alien cultures. Lévy-Bruhl's writings challenged their romanticism. They also inflicted a philosophical debate into anthropology which anthropologists of the day were neither equipped to handle nor, in many cases, anxious to argue. Yet Lévy-Bruhl's ideas did make anthropologists think. Looking back on them today, we can see them in light of the work of more recent writers, like Lévi-Strauss. He in some ways follows Lévy-Bruhl (e.g., in distinguishing a profound difference between pre-literate and literate cultures), but in other ways represents an opposite position (e.g., in imputing psychic unity through the notion of *esprit humain*, sometimes translated 'collective unconsciousness').

Lévy-Bruhl still has some admirers, if very few followers. One who does write in the same vein is Christopher Hallpike. He has argued (e.g., 1979: 50-1) that Lévy-Bruhl's work would have been yet more valuable had Lévy-Bruhl been aware of the possibilities of cognitive psychology. Hallpike himself has likened 'primitive thought' to the thought processes of children constructing a correct understanding of the world. He takes his basic ideas from the Swiss psychologist Jean Piaget, but true to his anthropological understanding he develops the notion of 'primitive thought' through the analysis of collective representations.

The linguistic relativism of Whorf

The implication throughout Lévy-Bruhl's work (even in the notebooks) is that 'primitive peoples' are intellectually inferior to people like 'ourselves'. Taking these two categories as given, consider the alternatives.

(1) 'Primitive peoples' are intellectually the same as 'ourselves'.
(2) 'Primitive peoples' are intellectually different, but neither inferior nor superior.
(3) 'Primitive peoples' are intellectually superior to 'ourselves'.

The first two represent views which lie in-between the evolutionist position and the radical relativist one. The third, representing a radical relativism playing as inverse evolutionism, is more interesting than either, because it provides such a sharp contrast to the peculiar brand of evolutionism promoted by Lévy-Bruhl. It is a view best represented by Benjamin Lee Whorf, chemical engineer and amateur anthropological linguist of the Boasian tradition.

Before Boas it had been thought that languages were all pretty much alike. If one knew Greek or Latin grammar, one could describe any language in the world. The Boasians showed that in many respects this is not the case. Inuit and Amerindian languages are much more complex than Greek or Latin. Some have as many as seventeen 'genders', which can be used to make puns, and, no doubt, to confuse the never-ending stream of anthropologists who have gone to study them. Whorf came up with the idea that people who speak such languages have different ways of looking at the world from people who speak simpler languages, like English.

The 'Sapir–Whorf hypothesis', as this idea became known, bears the name of both Whorf and his mentor. (Edward Sapir was himself a student of Boas and a practitioner of both 'culture and personality' studies and anthropological linguistics.) In principle, the hypothesis suggests that there are not just two forms of thought, 'ours' and 'theirs', but a multiplicity of forms of thought, each associated with the language of its thinkers. However, in practice Whorf tended to talk about two main examples which can be taken as exemplary of wider patterns: thought as expressed in the English language, and thought as expressed in the languages of Native North Americans.

The similarities and contrasts between Lévy-Bruhl and Whorf come across well through a comparison of *How Natives Think*, part II (Lévy-Bruhl 1926 [1910]: 137-223), which deals with grammar and counting, and two essays in *Language, Thought, and Reality* (Whorf 1956 [written c. 1936]: 57-86), which deal with relations between expression and

thought in 'primitive communities'. Lévy-Bruhl and Whorf did not disagree about the data. Their ideas converge in that they both understood
the concrete complexity of grammar in the languages of so-called 'primitive' peoples. Where they differed significantly was in their deeper interpretation of that phenomenon.

The same example can be used to support either side of the argument.
Take this one (paraphrased from Lévy-Bruhl (1926 [1910]: 143)). It
illustrates the verbal prefixes and suffixes in the language of the Kiwai
Islanders of Melanesia:

rudo	action of two on many in the past,
rumo	action of many on many in the past,
durudo	action of two on many in the present,
durumo	action of many on many in the present,
amadurodo	action of two on two in the present,
amarudo	similar action in the past,
amarumo	action of many on two in the past,
ibidurudo	action of many on three in the present,
ibidurumo	similar action in the past,
amabidurumo	action of three on two in the present,
	and so on.

To Lévy-Bruhl, the concreteness of these forms reflected a 'primitive'
way of thinking – a lack of abstract thought. To Whorf, such constructions implied great linguistic sophistication. In this example, each word
may be divided into morphemes, that is, smaller units of meaning which
can be put together to form longer words (*ru-*, *-do*, *-mo*, *du-*, etc.). To a
Whorfian, the real concreteness is in these individual morphemes, and
the ability to put them together entails abstract thought. Another contrast
between the two is in their understanding of directionality in the relation
between language and thought. Both believed that language and thought
are related. To Lévy-Bruhl, language reflects thought. Among 'primitives', grammatical categories are built up on the basis of 'primitive
thought'. However, to Whorf, thought reflects pre-existing linguistic
categories. People think only through these categories, and never independently of them.

Whorf realized the possibility that the categories of the English language are not necessarily better than those of other languages. In fact, he
went further than that. He envied the Hopi for their ability to think in
ways 'in advance' of his own. He argued that Hopi grammar is better
suited to the expression of scientific ideas than English is (see especially
Whorf 1956: 59-60, 85). Specifically, the metaphysics underlying English
supposes two cosmic forms: space and time. Space is infinite, three-

dimensional, and static. Time moves in one direction, and it is divided into past, present, and future. The metaphysics underlying Hopi supposes two quite different cosmic forms: objective (manifested) and subjective (manifesting). The former includes the physical universe as experienced through the senses, and also past and present. The latter includes that which exists in the mind, including the Mind of the Cosmos itself, and also what English would characterize as the future tense.

Criticisms of Whorfianism

But is Whorfianism the answer? Did Whorf really explain the relation between language and culture, and the difference between different modes of thought? In fact Whorf has been criticized on several grounds. Let me take a few of the criticisms which have been suggested.

First, some of Whorf's published ideas on the relation between language and culture are just too simplistic. (Indeed Whorf, who disclosed some of his most radical statements in non-linguistic, non-anthropological journals, such as *Technology Review*, the promotional magazine of Massachusetts Institute of Technology, may have realized this.) It is easy to refute Whorf's simplistic notion that language determines thought. Peoples of similar culture sometimes speak very different languages. Speakers of Basque are similar in culture to their French- and Spanish-speaking neighbours. On the other hand, peoples who speak closely related languages can have quite different cultures. Navajo and Apache both speak languages of the Southern Athapaskan group, but the Navajo (culturally but not linguistically influenced by the Hopi) lived in permanent, scattered settlements and were, in early Euro-American contact times, largely peaceful. Their famous artwork is of Hopi origin. The Apache were more nomadic, with an economy based on hunting, gathering, some farming, and raiding. Neither group had a centralized political authority, but the Apache developed a hierarchy of leadership for purposes of raiding and warfare. Their cultures were different, but did they, or indeed do they, think similarly because they speak closely related languages? That question remains open.

Secondly, Whorf's ideas overemphasize linguistic difference. Whorf (along with Sapir, e.g. 1949 [1915-38]: 167-250) was among the first to make systematic studies of Amerindian languages which did not have Euro-centric categories as the foundation of the analysis, and therefore probably among the first outsiders to appreciate the great richness of expression in these languages. However, the pendulum has now swung the other way. Since the 1960s linguists have tended to emphasize universal aspects of language. For example, all peoples speak in sentences, and these are by definition made up of noun phrases and verb phrases. Thus Nootka may not be quite as different from English as Whorf thought it was; and, following his hypothesis, Nootka- and English-speakers may not be as different in their modes of thought.

Thirdly, what evidence do we really have that language determines thought? Whorf's evidence in favour of it is entirely inferential and based on language itself, with little or no attempt to test language against cognition. Proof of the Sapir–Whorf hypothesis would be hard to come by, though linguists are today working on it (see Lucy 1992).

Fourthly, if the thought patterns related through different languages are as different as Whorf suggests, then can a non-Hopi ever understand how a Hopi thinks? If not, then how can we ever compare modes of thought? Though 'weak' versions of the Sapir–Whorf hypothesis remain credible in the eyes of many, the 'strong' version championed by Whorf has never been sustainable. In its essence it denies the possibility of anthropological comparison.

The rationality debate

Since the late 1960s there has been a sporadic resurgence of interest in the question of 'primitive thought', or more accurately, in the question of rationality among 'primitive' peoples. A number of philosophers, sociologists, and anthropologists have participated in the debates, which have been played out at various conferences and in edited collections. The most important of these collections are Bryan Wilson's *Rationality* (1970) and Martin Hollis and Steven Lukes' *Rationality and Relativism* (1982). The former was put together mainly from papers originally published during the 1960s, while the latter consists mainly of specially written papers explicitly designed to supplement and amplify those in the Wilson volume. The former uses ethnographic data, mainly African and 'classic', whereas the latter explores the problem through pre-modern Western science as well.

Let me use just two papers from the latter volume as exemplars of approaches which move beyond a simple 'yea' or 'nay' answer to the question of rationality: those by Dan Sperber and Ernest Gellner.

Sperber (1982) classifies the broadly relativist traditions in social anthropology as either 'intellectualist' or 'symbolist' (see Skorupski 1976). Intellectualists argue that apparently irrational beliefs are not so irrational after all; rather, they are simply mistaken. For example, people believe that the earth is flat because they experience it as such. Symbolists argue that myths, rituals, and so on are only irrational at a literal (and superficial) level. As metaphors for moral values, or whatever, they may be perfectly rational. Sperber's earlier *Rethinking Symbolism* (1975 [1974]) had been an attack on symbolist approaches (Victor Turner, Claude Lévi-Strauss, etc.). Put simply, there he argued that symbolism is a creative mechanism which produces meaning beyond established structures of understanding, and in so doing, helps to develop these very structures. In his 1982 article he does much the same with regard to extreme relativist views. Apparently irrational beliefs are not 'beliefs' at all; they involve a different psychological state. What is more, they are not irrational; they are (in his view) often simply ways of speaking about the world. It is perfectly rational to speak about the world in the same way as do other members of your own culture.

Gellner (1982 [1981]), a staunch anti-relativist, argues here that relativism and the existence of human universals are not incompatible. He defines relativism as 'a doctrine in the theory of knowledge [which] asserts that there is no unique truth' (1982: 183). He targets both cognitive and moral relativist statements, and argues both epistemological and sociological cases against the equation of relativism with diversity. His argument is complex. Essentially, he says that the problem of relativism is whether there is only one world, whereas the problem of universals is philosophically different. Moreover, the search for universals is itself not a universal but is culturally specific (it is found not among all peoples, but, for example, among the sort of people who might read this book). Yet such a search *is* accessible to all human beings, and its diffusion (present-day theorists would say 'globalization') is taking place.

In practice, most relativists in anthropology have been more interested in cultural diversity than in universals. Lévi-Strauss, to the extent to which he is the relativist some of his critics say he is, may be the exception (see chapter 8). In these crucial articles, what both Sperber and Gellner have done is to set aside the philosophical question of relativism by showing its irrelevance to the weak relativist streak in anthropological writing. The fact that other cultures view the world differently from one's own is not, in itself, grounds for seeing all alien understandings as either 'irrational' or expressing valid alternative 'truths'. The existence of human universals does not make relativism untenable; nor does human diversity make it tenable.

Towards cognitive science

After Whorf's untimely death in 1941, within anthropology there was a lull in interest in the topics he studied. When interest in the linguistic aspects of culture re-emerged in the 1950s, the theoretical emphasis in linguistics had changed from the descriptive (pioneered by Boas and

Table 7.1. *Approximate correspondences between words for 'tree', 'woods', and 'forest' in Danish, German, and French*

Danish	German	French
	Baum (tree)	**arbre** (tree)
trae (tree, trees)		
	Holz (woods)	
		bois (woods, woodland)
skov (woods, woodland, forest)	**Wald** (woodland, forest)	
		forêt (forest)

Sapir) to the structural. Ideas drawn from structural linguistics entered anthropology both through structuralism and through the more relativistic concerns of anthropologists interested in aspects of classification. Our concern here will be with the latter.

Structural semantics

Take these famous examples from the work of Danish linguist Louis Hjelmslev (1953 [1943]: 33-4): dark colours and clumps of trees. The terms for dark colours in Welsh differ from those in English, as Welsh has fewer terms. Welsh *gwyrdd* covers fewer shades than the English colour term *green*. Welsh *glas* covers some shades classified by English as *green*, all of *blue* and some of *grey*. *Llwyd* covers some of *grey* and some of *brown* (cf. Ardener 1989 [1971]: 9-12).

Similarly, when we compare words for 'tree', 'woods', and 'forest' in Danish, German, and French, we see a lack of exact correspondence, even between German and French, which have the same number of terms. This is illustrated in table 7.1. (Note here the distinction between English words in inverted commas, when English itself is an example, and in italics, when the English words are used as approximate glosses for foreign terms.) The French category *bois* (roughly 'wood', 'woods' or 'woodland') is wider than the German *Holz* (roughly 'wood' or 'small wooded area'). The French category *forêt* (meaning 'forest'), like its English equivalent, is narrower than the German *Wald* ('woodland' or 'small forest'). To say 'forest' in the French or English sense, a German would normally specify a *großer Wald* ('larger forest').

No language classifies everything. For colours, it would be impossible, since there is an infinite degree of natural variation in both the wavelength of light (red to violet) and the intensity of light (dark to light). Languages make meaning by making structure, and cultures do the same. Sometimes the structure is explicitly linguistic, as in the case of colour classification or words for things to do with trees. At other times, it is not, as for example in rules of etiquette or appropriate styles of dress.

Cognitive anthropology

American linguist Kenneth L. Pike made a great breakthrough in 1954 when he published the first part of an essay of 762 pages called *Language in Relation to a Unified Theory of the Structure of Human Behavior* (completed as Pike 1967). He took the idea of the relation between *sounds* (the phonetic) and *meaningful units of sound* (the phonemic) and postulated a more general relation between *units of any kind* (the etic) and *meaningful units of any kind* (the emic). Phonetics involves the study of all the sounds that humans can make. Phonemics (phonology) concerns sounds distinguished by contrasts with other sounds in a given language. Thus the theory which accounts for differences between sets of sounds in, say, Spanish and Portuguese, could be applied to differences between sets of words in Spanish or Portuguese, or indeed any other level of linguistic or cultural phenomena.

To put it another way, the etic is the level of universals, or the level of things which may be observed by an 'objective' observer. The emic is the level of meaningful contrasts within a particular language or culture. We can explain emic distinctions in terms of various frameworks or grids. Classic examples include Linnaean taxonomy; disease, in medical science; the measurement of the wavelength of light; the chromatic scale in music; and above all, the genealogical grid. While some radical relativists have questioned the universality of such grids, nevertheless their purported existence does highlight the difference between a postulated extra-cultural universal and one's own cultural framework taken (erroneously) as universal (see Headland, Pike, and Harris 1990).

The precise meaning of 'emic' has long been a subject of debate. Harris (1968: 568-604) saw it essentially as equatable with informants' statements, whereas Pike (1967: 37-72) emphasized instead the structured nature of the emic system. Just as informants cannot necessarily describe the grammatical rules behind their own use of language, so too they might be unable to describe the emic system which underlies their cultural understandings and practices. The discovery of that system is the task of the analyst, not the informant.

After Pike's pioneering work, anthropologists tried to formalize the relation between emic and etic categories. Complex methodologies were developed and debated. Following Ward Goodenough's (1956) famous paper on the relationship terminology of the inhabitants of the Truk Islands of Micronesia, several turned their attention to kinship. Emic structures are probably more transparent in relationship terminologies than in any other cultural domain. In them one can easily distinguish 'denotata' (the elements which make up a given class, in this case genealogical points of reference), from 'significata' or 'components' (the principles which distinguish the class), from 'connotata' (principles which, though not defining a class, are loosely associated with it), from 'designata' (the names of classes), from a class or classes of things themselves.

Using English as our example, take the class of kin which English-speakers call *uncle*. The designatum here is the word *uncle* itself. The denotata are genealogical points of reference FB, MB, FZH, MZH, and so on (that is, father's brother, mother's brother, father's sister's husband, and mother's sister's husband; denotata are customarily abbreviated in this way). One could define any class simply by listing all its members, but this is hardly satisfactory. Much more useful is an understanding of the principles of classification, and these are indicated in the significata or components. For the class designated *uncle*, the components are 'male' (to distinguish an uncle from an aunt), 'first ascending generation' (to distinguish an uncle from a nephew), 'consanguineal or consanguine's spouse' (to distinguish an uncle from a father-in-law), and 'collateral' (to distinguish an uncle from a father). By specifying each of these four components, we define what it means to be an *uncle*. Yet in addition to such signification, it is sometimes useful to consider the connotations (connotata) of being an uncle, for example, the characteristic features of 'avuncular' behaviour, whatever that might be in particular. These are not part of the componential analysis proper, but they do hint at its limitations.

Another limitation of componential analysis is the fact that we can have more than one correct analysis for any given set of terms. This is illustrated in table 7. 2, where two different analyses of the English terminology for consanguines (i.e., 'blood' relatives) are shown.

These two componential analyses differ in the technical understanding of the lineal/collateral or direct/collateral distinction and in the hierarchical relation between different distinctions of generation. The first representation (based loosely on that of Wallace and Atkins, 1960) is perhaps the most formally correct. Yet its precise distinction between 'lineals' (defined as ego and his or her ancestors and descendants), 'co-lineals' (siblings of lineals), and 'ablineals' (descendants of siblings of lineals)

Table 7.2. *Two componential analyses of English consanguineal kin term usage*

Componential analysis 1

LINEALS		CO-LINEALS		ABLINEALS
male	female	male	female	
+2 grandfather	grandmother			
+1 father	mother	uncle	aunt	
0 EGO		brother	sister	cousin
−1 son	daughter	nephew	niece	
−2 grandson	granddaughter			

Componential analysis 2

	DIRECT		COLLATERAL	
	male	female	male	female
Generation 2	+ grandfather	grandmother		
	− grandson	granddaughter		
Generation 1	+ father	mother	uncle	aunt
	− son	daughter	nephew	niece
Generation 0	brother	sister	cousin	

seems pedantic and counter-intuitive to me. The second (based on that by Romney and D'Andrade, 1964) was hailed in its time as a psychologically 'real' representation, that is, one which captures in its formal distinctions the thought processes of English-speaking people when they classify their kin. Yet for me as a native speaker of English, the placement of grandparents with grandchildren, of parents with children, and of 'generation 0' by itself, seems to make less sense than the placement of the generations from senior to junior.

The variant examples of table 7.2 show that there is always an element of indeterminacy in componential analysis, and that indeterminacy results from its reliance on lexical structures over actors' perceptions. Though this may be a limitation in some sense, it need not necessarily be very problematic, as long as we are prepared to accept (as postmodern relativists do) that different people, even in the same culture, think in different ways. In linguistics, many scholars hold to the view that the best grammatical analysis is the one which is simplest, whether it is most real to the native speaker or not. There is a place for the alternative view that the best is precisely the one which is most meaningful to the native speaker (while also being formally correct, of course). If native speakers disagree about which one this may be, then so be it. The debate which ensued on this issue is called that of 'God's truth versus hocus-pocus', with the 'God's truth' side favouring the search for cognitive reality and the 'hocus-pocus' side maintaining a scepticism of this very possibility. The debate was played out in the pages of the *American Anthropologist* between 1960 and 1965, and the key papers are included within Stephen Tyler's edited collection, *Cognitive Anthropology* (1969: 343-432).

Ethnoscience

There are two quite different threads of relativist thinking in anthropology today. For convenience these might be labelled the modernist and the postmodernist perspectives. The modernist perspective follows from earlier concerns with formal properties of thought, such as those of the cognitive anthropologists of the 1960s. It therefore follows a formalist methodology (seeking form or pattern in modes of thought) and is most prevalent in the study of scientific thought in traditional cultures, such as in ethnozoology and ethnobotany. The postmodernist perspective rejects formalist methodology altogether in favour of an interpretivist one, which focuses on the interaction of individuals and the negotiation of cultural categories (see chapter 10).

The modernist strand alive today is the culmination of the Whorfian position. In the 1960s proponents of cognitive anthropology took up Whorf's concern of the relation between modern, Western science and the indigenous worldviews they studied. They called their field 'ethnoscience'. That term did not always designate anything at all different from 'cognitive anthropology' (which was how some still saw their enterprise), from 'componential analysis' (which remained their main methodology), or from 'the new ethnography' (a catchword coined in the 1960s to make the comparison between their work and 'the new archaeology' of Lewis Binford). Today however, 'ethnoscience' tends to designate a specialization more than a theoretical perspective – namely the specialized concern with indigenous knowledge systems such as ethnobotany, ethnozoology, ethnomedicine, and so on (see, e.g., Berlin 1992; Ellen 1993). For that matter, the old label 'new ethnography' has in recent times been applied to postmodernist perspectives.

The foremost proponent of ethnoscience in its broadest sense, Charles Frake, has explored both the esoteric and the mundane in his works on ecological systems, interpretations of illness, concepts of law, how to enter a house, and how to ask for a drink in the Subanum, Yakan, and other cultures of the Philippines (see, e.g., Frake 1980). As these examples show, Frake's ethnoscience takes social action as well as the static categories of ethnoscientific discourse into account. Strategies and decision-making come into play. This is true even in the methodology he has espoused, as he makes explicit the eliciting techniques he employs. He shares this view with some of postmodern persuasion. Yet his approach, developed in the 1960s long before postmodernism came into anthropology, differs from postmodernism in its recognition of indigenous, culturally agreed categories, which are to be 'discovered' by an ethnographer through careful question-and-answer sessions.

While some in this tradition do take Western science as a baseline, others (including Frake) prefer to examine the modes of classification employed in traditional societies without necessary regard to such a baseline. Some have even examined Western science itself as a cultural tradition. Scott Atran's (1990) study of the 'folk biology' basis of natural history, from Aristotle to Darwin, is a good example. In its earliest days, ethnoscience was closely tied to linguistics, but in the hands of more recent practitioners it has gradually moved more towards cognitive psychology and now threatens to link up with interests not that far removed from those of the culture and personality school with which it has long been associated (cf. Bloch 1991; D'Andrade 1995: 182-243).

One approach which recognizes the existence of truth in science but nevertheless recognizes also social and cultural determinants within it, is the prevailing perspective of medical anthropology. Cecil Helman's (1994 [1984]) excellent overview of that field cites hundreds of studies in medical science and anthropology to illustrate the cultural, as well as the biological, construction of stress, pain, psychological disorders, and epidemiology. In the last instance, for example, North American psychiatrists are more prone to diagnosing 'schizophrenia' than those in Britain. Likewise, a North American doctor will diagnose 'emphysema' where a British doctor reads the same symptoms as 'chronic bronchitis'. Similar variations have been found in comparative research across Europe (Helman 1994: 270). This does not mean that modern medicine is fallacious (Helman himself is a practising physician), but that culture is everywhere – even in the 'rituals' which surgeons perform in the operating theatre (cf. Katz 1981).

Concluding summary

Boas founded a new anthropology based broadly on relativist principles, or at least on principles emphasizing culture difference and the moral worth of different understandings of the world. Like the functionalists he challenged the old order, but the anthropology which emerged in Boasian America was (for a time) profoundly different from that of Malinowskian, Radcliffe-Brownian Britain. The strongest proponents of relativism were, in their different ways, those of the 'culture and personality school' and the proponents of the 'Sapir–Whorf hypothesis'. Yet the difference was as much one of interest (psychology or language) as of theoretical position.

One of the offshoots of Boasian anthropology has been the interest in cognitive aspects of classification. This interest highlights the sharp divide between the Boasian emphasis on culture as a way of thinking and the Radcliffe-Brownian emphasis on it as a minor adjunct to social structure. The Kroeber/Rivers/Radcliffe-Brown debate on kinship terms discussed in chapter 5 can be seen in these terms. Kroeber's position is in the tradition of Boas and Sapir, and foreshadows the central concerns with the 'emic' in the work of Pike, Goodenough, Frake, and the ethnoscientists of recent times. As we shall see in the next chapter, the structuralism of Lévi-Strauss was to combine elements of both cognitive and social-structural approaches. But, against Boas and his cultural particularism, it would place the emphasis once more on universals.

FURTHER READING

Important works in the Boasian tradition include Boas' *The Mind of Primitive Man* 1938 [1911] and *Race, Language, and Culture* (1940), Lowie's *Primitive Society* (1947 [1920]), Kroeber's *Anthropology: Culture Patterns and Processes* (1963 [1948]), and Kroeber and Kluckhohn's *Culture: A Critical Review of Concepts and Definitions* (1952). The classic text on 'culture and personality' remains Benedict's *Patterns of Culture* (1934). For critical commentaries on the Boasians and the 'culture and personality' school, see Stocking's collections (respectively 1986; 1996b). Boas, Lowie, Kroeber, Benedict, and Mead are all the subject of contemporary or more recent biographical works.

A good overview of relativist thought with reference to the 'rationality debate' is Hollis and Lukes' 'Introduction' to *Rationality and Relativism* (1982: 1-20). Gellner's (1985) *Relativism and the Social Sciences* is also relevant and includes his essay discussed here, 'Relativism and universals'. Two other books, each bearing the title *Modes of Thought* but published a quarter-century apart, together offer an insight into changes in the perception of such modes (Finnegan and Horton 1973; Olson and Torrance 1996).

The classic edited collection on 'cognitive anthropology' is the one by that title, edited by Stephen Tyler (1969). A relatively recent rethink of the Whorfian hypothesis is Lucy's *Language Diversity and Thought* (1992). See also D'Andrade's excellent overview, *The Development of Cognitive Anthropology* (1995).

8 Structuralism, from linguistics to anthropology

'Structuralism' refers to those theoretical perspectives which give primacy to pattern over substance. For a structuralist, meaning comes through knowing how things fit together, not from understanding things in isolation.

There are some similarities between structuralism and structural-functionalism: both are concerned with relations between things. However, there are important differences. Structural-functionalism finds order within social relations. Structuralists are generally as interested in structures of thought as in structures of society. Moreover, the structural-functionalism of Radcliffe-Brown was based mainly on inductive reasoning. One starts with data and sees what generalizations can be made about them. Structuralists often employ a method which is primarily deductive, that is, based on certain premises. Structuralists might follow these premises and see where they lead, rather as in algebra or geometry. They often prefer to work out logical possibilities first, and then see how 'reality' fits. Indeed, for a true structuralist, there is no reality except the relation between things.

Claude Lévi-Strauss has been interested in both the internal logic of a culture and the relation of that logic to structures beyond the culture – the structure of all possible structures of some particular kind. This is especially the case in his work on kinship (e.g., Lévi-Strauss 1969a [1949]; 1966a), arguably the most structured realm of culture. Yet, while Lévi-Strauss is both the best known and the most characteristic of structuralist thinkers, structuralist thought is applicable more widely. It came into anthropology through linguistics, and the work of Ferdinand de Saussure, among others, is significant in its anticipation of the structuralist anthropological enterprise. Structuralist thought has gone through anthropology to literary criticism too, but the last field will not concern us here.

If the French structuralism of Lévi-Strauss is characterized by a concern with the structure of all possible structures, then Dutch structuralism focuses more on regions, as in regional structural analysis (see also

chapter 4). British structuralism, at least in the hands of its early proponents, focuses more on particular societies. These national traditions will
be touched on at the end of this chapter.

Saussure and structural linguistics

Swiss linguist Ferdinand de Saussure is arguably the most important
structuralist of all. However, the theory with which he is associated is not
one he *wrote* on. Rather, we know it through his lectures, collected and
published in his name in 1916 – three years after his death. His influence
in the English-speaking world was slow to catch on. The lectures were
published in English only in 1960. I shall draw here on a subsequently
revised edition (Saussure 1974).

Saussure and his 'Course'

Saussure (de Saussure) was born in Geneva in 1857. He studied there
(initially, physics and chemistry) and in Leipzig (comparative philology),
and he taught philology in Paris before returning to his native city in 1891.
In his lifetime he was best known for comparative and historical studies
on Indo-European vowel systems. Some of this work seems to foreshadow structuralism: later commentators (e.g., Culler 1976: 66–7) have
picked up on the fact that even in historical reconstruction Saussure saw
the relation between elements of language as the key to linguistic analysis.
Like his near contemporary Durkheim, he had a foot in both diachronic
and synchronic camps – indeed he virtually invented the distinction.
While in his published work he maintained the traditional historical view
of language, in his private lectures he anticipated Boas, Malinowski, and
Radcliffe-Brown in stressing synchronic and relational elements of his
subject.

The lectures Saussure gave in Geneva between 1906 and 1911 became
known as the *Course in General Linguistics* or simply the *Course* (Saussure
1974 [1916]). This (along with some of the work of Edward Sapir) marks
the earliest emphasis on synchronic, structural analysis in the study of
language. It also marks the foundation of semiology or semiotics (the
study of meaning through 'signs') and the dawn of structuralism. Saussure hints at the wider, semiological implications of his work, but his
concern in the *Course* was explicitly with language. Indeed, he speaks
disparagingly of the use of linguistics, for example, in reconstructing the
racial history and psychological make-up of ethnic groups (1974 [1916]:
222–8).

Four key distinctions

Saussure made a number of distinctions now commonplace both in linguistics and in the social sciences: diachronic and synchronic, *langue* and *parole*, syntagmatic and associative (paradigmatic), and signifier and signified.

Saussure's distinction (e.g., 1974: 101–2, 140–3) between diachronic and synchronic studies of language was the most significant break with his contemporaries. In the *Course*, he gave at least equal prominence to the latter (language at a particular point in time), whereas linguists of his day tended to be concerned only with the former (language changes through time). In chapter 1, I described evolutionism and diffusionism as diachronic anthropological perspectives and most schools of anthropology as essentially synchronic, while allowing for an in-between set of interactive perspectives. However, for true Saussurians, there is no in-between. The synchronic/diachronic distinction is absolute.

Langue and *parole* (Saussure sometimes uses *langue* and *langage*) are the French words, respectively, for 'language' and 'speech' (e.g., Saussure 1974: 9–15). The French terms are often used in English to represent this distinction, especially in a metaphorical sense. *Langue* is 'language' in the sense of linguistic structure or grammar; and, by analogy, this can be the grammar of culture as well as of language. *Parole* means 'speech' in the sense of actual utterances; and by analogy, it refers also to the social behaviour of real individuals. A fieldworker, in either linguistics or anthropology, moves from the level of *parole* to that of *langue*, that is, from the speech or actions of Tom, Dick, or Harry to a general description of appropriate linguistic or social behaviour.

The third distinction is between syntagmatic and associative relations (Saussure 1974: 122–7). Following Louis Hjelmslev, most structuralists of recent decades have referred to the latter as 'paradigmatic'. Syntagmatic relations are literally those within a sentence. For example, the sentence 'John loves Mary' contains three words: the subject John, the verb 'loves', and the object (of John's love) Mary. If we substitute Sally or Suzie for Mary, we can say that an associative or paradigmatic relation exists between the words 'Mary', 'Sally', and 'Suzie'. Or take traffic lights: a commonly cited cultural example. The colours green, amber, and red stand in syntagmatic relation to each other, as do their respective cultural meanings: go, get ready, and stop. In contrast, a paradigmatic relation exists between the associated elements of these two syntagms or 'sentences'. Red and stop are part of the same paradigm: a red traffic light means to stop. This example illustrates the relational character of elements in a cultural grammar. Red does not mean stop in any absolute sense, but only within this particular framework. In a political context, for example, red means something else: Labour as opposed to (blue) Conservative or (yellow) Liberal Democrat on British politicians' rosettes; or Communist as opposed to (black) Anarchist, in flags carried by revolutionaries. (I should perhaps add that the usage of the term 'paradigm' in this paragraph is different from the Kuhnian usage explained in chapter 1; as Saussurians remind us, words also take their meanings from context.)

This leads to our final Saussurian distinction, that between signifier (the word or symbol which stands for something) and signified (the thing for which the word or symbol stands). These two elements together make up what Saussure (1974: 65–78) called the 'sign', whose salient characteristic is that it is 'arbitrary'. What he meant by this is that there is no natural relation between the phonological properties of a word and its meaning. If I speak Italian, I signify a four-footed, barking, family pet as *il cane*. If I speak French, I say *le chien*. If I speak German I say *der Hund*. If I speak English I say *the dog*. The phonetic makeup of the word, in each case, depends on which language I choose to speak. (Even the noise the animal makes is to some extent arbitrary: Italian dogs say *bau-bau*, French dogs say *oua-oua*, German dogs say *wau-wau*, and British and American dogs say *woof-woof* or *bow-wow*.) Likewise, symbolic elements of culture take their meaning both according to the given culture (say, French or British) and according to context within that culture. As Sir Edmund Leach used to say, a crown may stand for sovereignty (by metonymy – the part stands for the whole), or it may stand for a kind of beer (by metaphor – Brand X, 'the king of beers').

After Saussure

After Saussure, other linguists developed further ideas along the lines he suggested. The centre for such activity was Prague, where the Russian exile Roman Jakobson was based. Others in the 'Prague School' taught elsewhere, notably the Russian prince, Nikolai Trubetzkoy (see, e.g., Anderson 1985: 83–139). These 'functionalist' linguists, as they were sometimes called, developed complex theories of relations within phonological structures. Yet what is important for our purposes is their notion of 'distinctive features', which are analogous to what anthropologists have come to call structural or binary oppositions.

To simplify the basis of such theories, one can define the difference between two sounds in a particular language by the presence or absence of certain features. For instance, take the words *pin* and *bin* in English.

Table 8.1. *English voiced and unvoiced stops*

	Unvoiced	Voiced
Bilabial	p	b
Alveolar	t	d
Velar	k	g

P and *b* are produced in exactly the same part of the mouth (on the lips), and a deaf person reading lips cannot normally distinguish the two words. A foreigner with good hearing, but who speaks a language that does not make the *p/b* distinction, may not be able to 'hear' the difference either. More technically, English makes a distinction between the voiced bilabial stop, which linguists write /b/, and the unvoiced bilabial stop, written /p/. The difference is voicing. In saying 'bit', the English-speaker uses his or her voice on the initial sound, but does not do so in saying 'pit'. (Another subtle difference is the fact that the /p/ at the beginning of a word, in English, is also aspirated or breathed on, whereas the /b/ is not; but that need not concern us here.)

We can represent the structural relation between these two sounds along with other English 'stops' (consonants in which the flow of air in the mouth is stopped) as in table 8.1. The difference between *p* and *b* is replicated in the difference between *t* and *d*, which in turn resembles the difference between *k* and *g*. What distinguishes the first from the second in each pair is the absence of voicing. However, what distinguishes *p* from *t* from *k*, or *b* from *d* from *g*, is position in the mouth (front to back in each series, in terms of the point of articulation).

The recognition of the binary nature of voiceless/voiced distinction (i.e., the absence or presence of the feature 'voiced'), plus the recognition of the place of such a distinction in a wider system (in this case phonological) is what structuralism is all about. As we shall see, Lévi-Strauss' work in kinship, symbolism, mythology, and so on, is all based on similar principles. Fortuitously, Lévi-Strauss, a French Jew, spent the Second World War in exile in New York City, where members of the Prague School had also gone to escape Nazi persecution. Some of the early chapters of Lévi-Strauss' *Structural Anthropology* (Lévi-Strauss 1963 [1945 / 1951 / 1953 / 1958]: 29–97) bear a strong influence of the Prague School, and the first of these chapters (called 'Structural analysis in linguistics and in anthropology', pp. 31–54) was first published in 1945 in the first volume of the exiled Prague School's periodical, *Word: Journal of the Linguistic Circle of New York*.

Lévi-Strauss and structural anthropology

Lévi-Strauss was born in 1908, the son of an artist. He became an accomplished amateur musician, but his early academic training was in law and philosophy and his personal appraisal of his influences include geology, Freudian psychology, and Marxist theory. In 1934 he left France and went to Brazil to teach sociology, read the 1920 edition of Robert Lowie's *Primitive Society*, and ended up doing ethnographic fieldwork with the Bororo Indians.

The contrast between the famous final paragraph of *Primitive Society* (Lowie 1947 [1920]: 441) and Lévi-Strauss' anthropology is interesting. Lowie ends his book with a description of 'civilization' as 'that planless hodge-podge, that thing of shreds and patches' and looks forward to a day when 'the amorphous product' or 'chaotic jumble' will be put into a 'rational scheme'. The paragraph has been much debated, and in his preface to the 1947 edition Lowie (1947: ix) was to declare that it had 'no bearing on anthropological theory'. Yet Lévi-Strauss was to succeed where Lowie dared not, in finding (or creating) the most rational of all anthropological schemes. For Lévi-Strauss, the essence of culture is its structure. This is true both for particular cultures, with their own specific configurations, and for culture worldwide, in the sense that particular cultures exist as part of a system of all possible cultural systems. Nowhere is this more true than in *The Elementary Structures of Kinship* (Lévi-Strauss 1969a [1949]). Lévi-Strauss completed his manuscript in February 1947, exactly five months before Lowie's second preface.

Lévi-Strauss returned to France in 1939. He joined the Resistance, but his superiors thought it wiser for him, as a Jew, to leave for New York. There he met a number of the Central European linguists who were also in exile, borrowed ideas that they had developed within their discipline and applied them to anthropological data. However, it is worth remembering that much of his thought is derived directly from the tradition of Durkheim and Mauss (especially the latter, whose essay *The Gift* influenced his ideas on kinship as marital exchange). It is also important to see Lévi-Strauss as open to anthropological ideas from other countries, especially the American tradition from Boas (who, let us also remember, died in his arms), Lowie, and Kroeber. The complex web of influences on Lévi-Strauss' thinking to about 1960 is illustrated in figure 8.1.

Shortly after the War, Lévi-Strauss went back to France and established his tradition there. His Doctorat d'Etat thesis on 'the elementary structures of kinship' was published in French in 1949. The second edition appeared in French in 1967 and was finally translated for an English edition which came out two years later (Lévi-Strauss 1969a). He

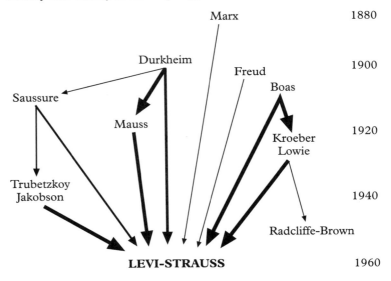

Figure 8.1 Influences on Lévi-Strauss until about 1960

followed *The Elementary Structures* with a widely read travelogue, based partly on his Brazilian fieldwork, *Tristes Tropiques* (1976 [1955]); two brilliant contributions to the study of classification, *Totemism* (1969b [1962]) and *The Savage Mind* (1966b [1962]); three collections of essays; works on language and on art; and four volumes known together as the *Mythologiques*. These latter, peculiarly titled works were published in French between 1964 and 1970 and in English between 1970 and 1981: *Le cru et le cruit* (translated as *The Raw and the Cooked*), *Du miel aux cendres* (*From Honey to Ashes*), *L'origine des manières de table* (*The Origin of Table Manners*), and *L'homme nu* (*The Naked Man*).

In the books on 'mythologics' or 'the science of myth' (as close as an English translation can come), Lévi-Strauss recounts and analyses 813 Amerindian myths, from Lowland South America to the North West Coast of North America. Their essence is contained in a fine, short work, based on radio talks Lévi-Strauss made in Canada in 1977, *Myth and Meaning* (1978a). As Lévi-Strauss spoke this one, rather than wrote it, and as its original is in English rather than French, it is much easier to follow than some of his other works. He wrote many of these in a rather dense academic French, and his translators have almost always attempted to render them as literally as possible. *Myth and Meaning* and *Tristes Tropiques* are easy to read, *The Savage Mind* is perhaps the most inspiring and indicative of his theoretical perspective, while *The Elementary Structures of Kinship* represents structuralist anthropology at its most extreme. In later years, Lévi-Strauss has produced further books on North West Coast mythology, as well as an intriguing text on human aesthetic sensibilities explored through the structural analysis of works of art and music (Lévi-Strauss 1997 [1993]).

Structuralism, pattern, and ideas

Structuralism in its widest sense is all about pattern: how things which at first glance appear to be unrelated actually form part of a system of interrelating parts. In structuralist theory, the whole is seen as greater than the sum of the parts, and most wholes can be broken down by appeal to the idea of distinctive features or binary oppositions. The presence or absence of one particular feature, in culture as in language, can explain a great deal. Structuralism in its 'purest' Lévi-Straussian sense shares this notion with structural (or functional) linguistics, and also with the cognitive anthropology which developed out of the Boasian tradition in North America in the 1950s and 1960s (see chapter 7). The distinctive feature of Lévi-Strauss' own contribution has been his search for the structure of all possible structures. His anthropology represents a culmination of the principle of psychic unity, or as Lévi-Strauss calls it, *l'esprit humain* – a term sometimes loosely translated as 'collective unconscious' (in opposition to Durkheim's 'collective consciousness').

Structuralism in anthropology concerns not merely social structure or structural form in their Radcliffe-Brownian senses, but also the structure of ideas. In Lévi-Strauss' work especially, structures are said to be built on a rational rather than an empirical foundation. That is, a Lévi-Straussian thinks out the logical possibilities for something, and only then looks for examples in ethnography. Take one of Lévi-Strauss' own analogies: the structure of crystals (Lévi-Strauss 1966a: 16). When a physicist studies the mathematical properties of a crystal, he or she is probably not concerned with specific real crystals (which will have flaws in them), but rather with some ideal, perfect crystal. The formation of real crystals is dependent on the effects of variations in heat and pressure, the presence of foreign bodies, and so on. One does not find an absolutely perfect crystal in nature; one finds it in the mind. Lévi-Strauss, therefore, is concerned with ideal structures of society, and in two senses: (1) in the sense of what is in *his* mind, and (2) in the sense of what is in the minds of the people with whom ethnographers work. Not surprisingly, other anthropologists did not take much to the first sense, but they have taken to the second. Yet it is the first sense which is more interesting here. In

Lévi-Strauss' vision, it is important for the anthropologist to hold a view of society which takes in every logical possibility.

It need hardly be said that Lévi-Strauss' output has been varied, complex, and often obscure to the uninitiated, but let me illustrate his contribution through three classic examples: elementary structures of kinship, the culinary triangle, and the Oedipus myth.

Elementary structures of kinship

In his early work (1969a [1949]) Lévi-Strauss was concerned with how rules of marriage affect, and even create, social structure. His 'alliance theory' (*alliance* being a French word for marriage) was set against the then current emphasis in British anthropology on 'descent theory', and true to form he sought to explain descent groups not as the basis of society but as elements in relations of marital exchange which exist between the groups.

As we saw in chapter 3, Lévi-Strauss argued in *The Elementary Structures* that the incest taboo is the essence of culture, and he virtually equated this taboo with the rules governing marriage. He then defined the relations between all human kinship systems, partly by exploring the nature of 'elementary' systems and partly by recourse to the ways in which ethnographic details of 'complex' systems can be seen as reflections of 'elementary' principles of kinship. Essentially, elementary structures are those with positive marriage rules (one must or should marry someone belonging to a particular class of kin, e.g., that of the cross-cousin), while complex structures are those with negative marriage rules (one must not or should not marry someone belonging to a particular class of kin, such as close relatives or members of one's own clan). It does not matter whether we are talking about 'real' or 'classificatory' cross-cousins, because in fact these are imaginary structures. Likewise, it matters little whether people really marry the way they are supposed to marry. Lévi-Strauss was concerned with the 'system of systems' which entails all logical possibilities, and with the formal, almost mathematical relationship of one system to another. He was not directly concerned with the operations of real kinship systems, because no society ever reaches the level of perfection described in his scheme – a point which was lost on his British and British-trained followers-turned-critics (cf. Lévi-Strauss 1966a; Korn 1973; Needham 1973). In more general terms, Lévi-Strauss' structuralism is mainly concerned with culture as an abstraction – not people's actual behaviour, but the idealized pattern it approximates.

Figure 8.2 shows the relations among kinship systems according to Lévi-Strauss' theory of alliance. I should add, though, that this is my

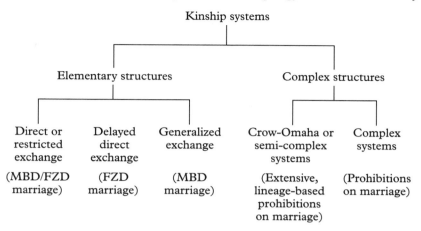

Figure 8.2 Lévi-Strauss' classification of kinship systems

preferred, simplified representation of the essence of his theory. Lévi-Strauss' own diagrams, representing relations between descent and residence (1969a: 216) and cycles of exchange (1969a: 465), are rather different.

Elementary structures include systems of direct exchange, where a group may 'take' wives from the same group it 'gives' wives to. The simplest type is one involving marriage between a man and his mother's brother's daughter (MBD) or father's sister's daughter (FZD), as in some parts of South America and Australia. Elementary structures also include systems of delayed direct exchange. Repeated father's sister's daughter marriage would, if it could be sustained in a real society, create such a structure. However, as Lévi-Strauss' chief critic among alliance theorists, Rodney Needham (1962), showed, such societies remain ethnographically rare if not non-existent. This is for rather technical reasons – among these the demographic unlikelihood of people keeping track of cross-cutting lineage and generational ties when no advantage to them or their society would be gained. In contrast, systems of generalized exchange, such as those involving marriage to the category of the mother's brother's daughter, are very common in parts of Asia. Here it is not necessary to keep track of generation, because one may repeat the marriage of one's parents. For example, if I as a male member of Group A marry a woman of Group B, my son (also Group A by patrilineal descent) may marry a woman from Group B too (such as his actual mother's brother's daughter or anyone classified as such).

Complex structures comprise those systems of Europe, Japan, most of

Africa, and so on, where no such 'elementary' patterns are to be found: one marries anyone, provided he or she is not a close relative. However, some societies, especially in Native North America and West Africa, have such an extensive array of negative marriage rules that their systems, from an individual though not a lineage point of view, come to resemble those of generalized exchange. For example, among the Samo of Burkina Faso, a man must not marry a member of his own patrilineal group, or his mother's, his father's mother's, or his mother's mother's patrilineal group. These 'semi-complex' or 'Crow-Omaha' systems (called after two Native North American peoples) thus lie in-between the more typically complex and the elementary ones (see Héritier 1981: 73–136).

Lévi-Strauss' work on kinship had a profound effect on British anthropology in the 1950s and 1960s, as Leach, Needham, and others sought to apply his methods to the study of particular kinship systems based on alliance. The British structuralists antagonized both Lévi-Strauss, through their rejection of his abstract search for universal patterns, and the structural-functionalists, through their emphasis on alliance over descent (see, e.g., Barnard and Good 1984: 67–78, 95–104). While few in Britain or North America accepted Lévi-Strauss' emphasis on universal structures of kinship in the human mind, the empirical basis of his theory was widely debated (cf., e.g., Hiatt 1968; Lévi-Strauss 1968).

The culinary triangle

One of the most indicative of Lévi-Strauss' excursions into the universality of the human mind is that of our second example: the 'culinary triangle', based on Jakobson's 'consonant triangle' and 'vowel triangle'. Lévi-Strauss first published on the idea in an article in 1965, and this was followed by several discussions, notably in the conclusion to the third volume of the *Mythologiques* (Lévi-Strauss 1978b [1968]: 471–95).

Lévi-Strauss claims that whereas the relations between consonants p, t, and k, and between vowels u, i, and a, can be defined according to relative loudness and pitch, similar relations between states of food substances and between styles of cooking can be defined according to degree of transformation and the intervention of culture. The argument is obscure but interesting. In the 'primary form', the two axes, normal/transformed and nature/culture, distinguish raw from cooked from rotted food (see figure 8.3). In the 'developed form', these same axes distinguish roasted from smoked from boiled food. In terms of means, roasting and smoking are natural processes, while boiling is cultural in that it needs water and a container. In terms of ends, roasting and boiling are natural (boiling is a process similar to rotting), while smoking is cultural (cooked, as opposed

PRIMARY FORM

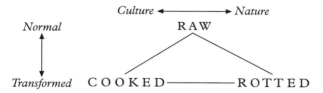

DEVELOPED FORM

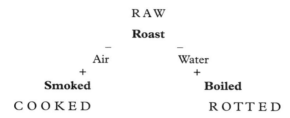

Figure 8.3 The culinary triangle

to raw or rotted). Boiling and roasting of meat are further contrasted in that boiling conserves all the juices (and therefore is naturally plebeian), and roasting destroys some of the meat (and in hierarchical societies, it is associated with high status – the wealthy can afford to be wasteful). While the culinary triangle is one of the most famous examples of structuralist interpretation in anthropology, unfortunately Lévi-Strauss' attempts to generalize about egalitarianism and hierarchy have only lead to puzzlement and ridicule (see Leach 1970: 28–34).

Leach (1976b: 55–9) once analysed aspects of costume and colour symbolism in the same way, but there is a crucial difference between his thinking and that of Lévi-Strauss. Lévi-Strauss' argument is intended to apply universally, whereas Leach's is both comparative and culture-specific. In India, for example, a bride traditionally wears a multi-coloured sari, and a widow wears a white sari. In the West, a bride traditionally wears a white dress, and a widow wears a black dress. The cultural rules are different, though in each case colour symbolizes an activity. Moreover, we cannot say merely that white is for marriage or life, and black is for death in Western culture taken as a whole. In some Christian churches, a priest or minister wears white or coloured garments when engaged in ritual activities, and black in non-ritual contexts. In other Christian churches, the equivalent person may wear black when engaged in ritual activities and ordinary, multi-coloured clothes otherwise. The wearing of white or black in these cases is not only culture-dependent; it is also dependent on very specific culturally significant activities. This is where British structuralism, which emphasizes cultural diversity as well as cross-cultural commonalities of social and symbolic structures, parts company with Lévi-Straussian structuralism with its emphasis on cultural universals embedded in the psychic unity of humankind.

The Oedipus myth

Our third example is Lévi-Strauss' analysis of the myth of Oedipus. There are, of course, a number of different versions of the story, and there are related myths which, in true *Mythologiques* fashion, can be further analysed as permutations of the key myth. Leach (1970: 62–82) does this in his well-known rendition. Here I will recount the version implied by Lévi-Strauss (1963 [1955]: 213–18), with his Latinized Greek names for the protagonists, and simply outline his central explanation.

The main characters are all related (see figure 8.4). Cadmos is the son of the king of Phoenicia. His sister, Europa, is carried off by Zeus, king of the gods, so Cadmos is sent to look for her. However, the Delphic oracle tells him to stop and follow a cow, then to build a city where the cow stops. So he does. Where the cow stops, he founds the city of Thebes. Later, Cadmos kills a dragon. He sows the teeth of the dragon onto the ground, and up come the Spartoi (or *sparti*, which means 'sown'), born from the teeth. Five of the Spartoi help Cadmos to build Thebes. Then they kill each other.

Cadmos subsequently has other exploits, marries a goddess, and has five children, among them Polydorus, who becomes king of Thebes. Polydorus has a son called Labdacos, who succeeds him. Labdacos has a son called Laios, and Laios marries Jocasta. Laios is told by an oracle that he will have a son who will kill him, so, when Oedipus (his son) is born, Laios leaves him exposed, tied to the ground by his foot, on top of a hill. Eventually, a shepherd finds Oedipus and takes him in, and Oedipus is adopted by Polybus, king of Corinth. Later Oedipus is told by the oracle that he will kill his father, so he vows never to return to Corinth again. Instead, he goes to Thebes.

On the way to Thebes he meets Laios (his true father), has a quarrel, and kills him. Later he meets the Sphinx, who has a habit of asking passers-by her riddle, and then killing them if they do not know the answer. None of them do, except Oedipus. The riddle is 'What is it that speaks with one voice, yet becomes four-footed, then two-footed, then three-footed?' The answer, Oedipus knows, is 'man' – who starts as a 'four-footed' baby, then walks on two feet, and finally, in old age, with a

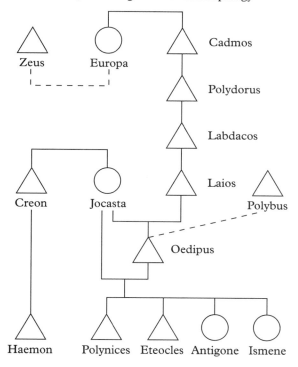

Figure 8.4 Kin relations among characters in the Oedipus myth

stick. So instead of the Sphinx killing Oedipus, Oedipus kills the Sphinx. (In some versions, the Sphinx kills herself.)

Oedipus' reward for killing the Sphinx is the hand in marriage of the widowed queen of Thebes, who is really his mother Jocasta. Oedipus means 'swollen foot'; and Jocasta realises he is 'the child grown into an adult' – the answer to the Sphinx's riddle. Realising too that she has committed incest with him, she kills herself. Then Oedipus blinds himself to become 'the old man' of the riddle. He goes off and is eventually swallowed into the earth, and Thebes comes under the rule of a new king, Creon, Jocasta's brother: Jocasta and Oedipus had had four children – Polynices, Eteocles, Antigone, and Ismene; Antigone and Ismene have gone off to lead Oedipus into the countryside and when they return, they find their brothers quarrelling – Eteocles is defending his crown, and Polynices is outside the city attacking it; eventually, both brothers die, and their mother's brother Creon becomes king. Now, Eteocles has killed his brother Polynices, whom Antigone was very fond of, so Creon, the new king, forbids Antigone to bury her brother Polynices because he,

Table 8.2. *Lévi-Strauss' analysis of the Oedipus myth*

I	II	III	IV
Cadmos seeks Europa who is ravished by Zeus			
		Cadmos kills the dragon	
	The Spartoi kill each other		
			Labdacos='lame'
	Oedipus kills Laios		Laios='leftsided'
		Oedipus kills the Sphinx	
			Oedipus='swollen foot'
Oedipus marries Jocasta despite taboo			
	Eteocles kills Polynices		
Antigone buries Polynices despite taboo			

having tried to take the crown from Eteocles, is now a traitor. There is an elaborate state funeral for Eteocles, but Polynices is condemned to lie unburied. Antigone, however, manages to sneak out and bury Polynices secretly. (In retribution, Creon has Antigone buried alive, walled up in a cave, though she manages to hang herself. Her beloved cousin Haemon, and his mother, commit suicide too, and the story goes on.)

Lévi-Strauss (1963 [1955]: 214) attempts to explain the complexities of the Oedipus myth with a simple diagram, the main features of which are shown in table 8.2. Column I gives details of violations of taboos, specifically taboos of incest and the burial of kin, or in Lévi-Strauss' words 'the overrating of kinship'. Column II gives details of 'the underrating of kinship', the same thing 'inverted': fratricide and parricide. Column III concerns the killing of monsters, by men. The dragon was a male monster who had to be killed in order for humankind to be born from the earth. The Sphinx was a female monster who was unwilling to allow humans to live. In Lévi-Strauss' words, this column represents the 'denial of the autochthonous origin of man' (in other words, the denial of aboriginal association of humankind with the earth). Column IV concerns the meaning of the names of some of the characters. All the meanings are related to difficulties in walking straight or standing upright. They imply that the humans who bear these names are still attached to the earth. The Spartoi were born of the earth without human aid; and in contrast, Oedipus was exposed at birth and staked to the ground. Therefore his foot became swollen, and he was, though born of woman, not fully separated from the earth. So this column, Lévi-Strauss says, indicates 'the persistence of the autochthonous origin of man'. In other words, column IV is the opposite of column III. What is more, column III stands in relation to column IV as column I stands in relation to column II.

The point of all this is that myths are made up of elements known as 'mythemes' (by analogy with phonemes), which myth-makers arrange and rearrange to create meaning, often unconsciously. Myths do not just tell stories; they express symbolic truths, sometimes specific to cultures or culture areas and sometimes universal. The same mythemes may be found in different myths, and may be transposed in myths which occur in different cultures. In any given telling, they may be 'read' either dia-chronically (here, top to bottom, one column at a time or through all the columns) or synchronically (across the columns, showing relations from column to column). Lévi-Strauss himself has always been content to see myth analysis for its own sake, though it has the potential to provide clues to other aspects of culture. It has indeed found use too in the analysis of dreams and dream sequences (e.g., Kuper 1979b).

Structuralism and national traditions of anthropology

While it is easy to think of Lévi-Strauss as the paradigmatic structuralist and his universalistic concerns the epitome of structuralist theory, his thought has both paralleled and influenced structuralist anthropologists working from different premises. Many do not accept his emphasis on psychic unity, favouring either regional or culture-specific foci.

Dutch structuralism emerged from studies of language, culture, and society, by Dutch academics and civil servants in the early twentieth-century Dutch East Indies (now Indonesia). This form of structuralism, described in chapter 4, emphasizes structures which are unique to culture areas or regions (e.g., J. P. B. de Josselin de Jong 1977 [1935]). J. P. B. de Josselin de Jong and other early Dutch structuralists developed their ideas partly independently of Lévi-Strauss, and even anticipated him, especially in studies of kinship. Later Dutch anthropologists utilized Lévi-Straussian methods and replicated Lévi-Straussian studies of mythology and symbolism, generally within a regional framework. Such a regional ap-proach was characteristic of anthropology, especially in Leiden, for sev-eral decades.

Although Lévi-Strauss, rather like Lévy-Bruhl, has often commented on distinctions between 'elementary' structures and 'complex' ones, 'cold' societies and 'hot' ones (with reference to the relative 'heat' of historical change), and societies with mainly 'concrete' and those with 'abstract' thought, his entire approach is predicated on reasoning from the general to the specific. British structuralists have tended to work the other way round, and that is why even those Britons who have been much influenced by Lévi-Strauss' work have found themselves expressing fundamental disagreements with his methodology. This is somewhat true with Leach, but even more so with Rodney Needham (e.g., 1962) in his work on kinship. In the 1970s and 1980s as Professor of Social Anthropology at Oxford, Needham went on to write prolifically on language, religion, symbolic classification, emotion, and what might best be called anthropological philosophy. Sadly, after his disagreements with Lévi-Strauss Needham hardly ever, in this later, non-kinship work, referred to him. Some of Needham's works still carried structuralist theory with them (e.g. Needham 1979), while others obscured it or cast it aside in favour of an emotional variety of interpretivism almost unique to Needham's anthropology (e.g., 1981).

In other countries structuralism caught on in various ways between the 1950s and 1970s, but the Dutch and British traditions have remained the prime exemplars respectively of the regional and culture-specific versions. Belgian anthropology has some parallels with anthropology in Holland. Belgian structuralist Luc de Heusch has applied a regional-structural methodology to the study of political processes, kinship transformations, myth, sacrifice, and symbolism in Central Africa (e.g., de Heusch 1982 [1972]) and in Africa more widely (de Heusch 1985). Roy Willis, a British anthropologist and translator of both de Heusch and Lévi-Strauss, has done similar work in Central Africa (see Willis 1981) and has postulated a common structural basis (but with crucial culture-specific differences) for animal symbolism in African societies outside that region (Willis 1974). As we saw in chapter 6, Sir Edmund Leach and Marshall Sahlins also applied a structuralist approach to the study of social transformations. These writers have all added a historical dimension to Lévi-Strauss' structuralism, giving rise to theories of social transformation which both influenced and drew from processualist and Marxist anthropology from the 1950s to the 1980s.

Meanwhile back in France, Louis Dumont, a student of Mauss and one-time colleague of Evans-Pritchard at Oxford, developed a distinct but seminal, regional-structural understanding of social hierarchy in India (see especially Dumont 1980 [1967]). His work has had its followers, and its critics, in all countries in which the study of the Indian subcontinent is a particular focus. Meanwhile in the United States, studies in ethnoscience and cognitive anthropology developed through interests in human universals, linguistic models, and culture-specific semantic structures which parallel 'structuralism' proper in other countries. Lévi-Strauss himself has frequently praised Americans outside the structuralist tradition as we usually think of it, for their contributions towards his own theories. In Australia and South America too, the intrinsic structuralist thought of the indigenous populations has lent itself well to the development of structuralist ideas among local anthropologists.

Other French anthropologists developed different strands of thought, most broadly structuralist but others less so. Furthermore, the structure of French academia itself, based on research 'teams' (équipes) rather than broad-based teaching departments, fostered the creation of diverse ethnographic and theoretical micro-traditions. Lévi-Strauss and Dumont were key foci, but so too were, for example, Marxist theorists such as Maurice Godelier and Claude Meillassoux (chapter 6).

Concluding summary

Structuralism emphasizes form over content, and in a sense denies that there can be content without form. Structures in language at any level (e.g., phonological, morphological, syntactic) have potential analogies in culture of almost any sphere (e.g., kinship, cooking, mythology). Because of this, structuralism made an easy transition from the linguistics of Saussure and the Prague School to the anthropology of Lévi-Strauss and his followers.

While the influence of Lévi-Strauss has always remained paramount, structural anthropology is a complex tradition. Theoretical stances have always been defined partly by national concentrations of interest, though national boundaries have never been able to contain good ideas (or indeed bad ideas), and structuralism throughout its history has been both an international and a transdisciplinary phenomenon.

FURTHER READING

Culler's *Saussure* (1976) and Leach's *Lévi-Strauss* (1970) are good introductions to the respective ideas of Saussure and Lévi-Strauss. The best source on Saussure's key ideas, however, is the *Course* itself (Saussure 1974 [1916]).

The two volumes of Jakobson's selected writings (1962, 1971) give an idea of Jakobson's influence on Lévi-Strauss. Steiner's *The Prague School* (1982) is another useful source.

There are numerous biographical and analytical studies of Lévi-Strauss, such as those by Boon (1973), Badcock (1975), Sperber (1985 [1982]: 64–93), and Henaff (1998 [1991]). See also *Conversations with Claude Lévi-Strauss* (Lévi-Strauss and

Eribon 1991 [1988]), Lapointe and Lapointe's bibliography (1977), and Pouillon and Maranda's (1970) two-volume collection of papers dedicated to Lévi-Strauss. The A. S. A. conference volume, *The Structural Study of Myth and Totemism* (Leach 1967), also makes interesting reading. It includes Lévi-Strauss' famous analysis of the story of Asdiwal (a North West Coast myth recorded in four versions by Franz Boas), as well as several critiques of Lévi-Strauss' work.

A readable introduction to structuralism in anthropology generally is Leach's *Culture and Communication* (1976b). For a broader understanding of structuralism through key texts, see de George and de George's *The Structuralists: From Mauss to Lévi-Strauss* (1972). For references to poststructuralist and interpretivist critiques of structuralism, see chapters 9 and 10.

9 Poststructuralists, feminists, and (other) mavericks

The poststructuralists, feminists, and mavericks described in this chapter have in common a desire to move away from the more formalist ideas of functionalism and structuralism towards a looser, yet more complex, understanding of relations between culture and social action. The growing interest in power is represented in many of the works touched on here as well.

Poststructuralism occupies an ambiguous position in anthropology. On the one hand, it is in essence a critique of structuralist thought played out mainly in structuralist terms. That is, the poststructuralists, who have practised mainly outside social anthropology (in philosophy, literary criticism, history, and sociology), have offered critiques of Lévi-Strauss and other declared structuralist writers. At the same time, poststructuralists have pointed the way to the explanation of action, the scrutiny of power, and the deconstruction of the writer as a creator of discourses. Thus poststructuralism touches on the interests of transactionalists, Marxists and feminists, and postmodernists alike. In a loose sense, poststructuralism is a form of postmodernism, as structuralism is the primary form of 'late modernism' in anthropology (see chapter 10).

Feminism has its main roots in substantive, as opposed to grand theoretical, issues of sex roles and gender symbolism. However, over the last twenty years it has achieved the status of a theoretical paradigm not only in the substantive area of gender studies, but also more widely in anthropology. It has moved from a concern centrally with women and women's subordination *per se* to a more general commentary on power relations, symbolic associations, and other facets of society at large, as well as a discourse on issues such as reflexivity, the gender of the ethnographer, and therefore the place of the ethnographer in anthropological fieldwork. Thus it too has close links with much in the postmodern agenda, though not all feminists claim to be postmodernists nor all postmodernists, feminists.

It is often all too easy to think of anthropology as definable in terms of grand ideas, competing paradigms, and schools of thought. While these represent a substantial portion of 'anthropological theory' as it is commonly understood, there is nevertheless a place for the maverick. This is true above all on the fringes of structuralist thought, as thinkers have tried to integrate ideas of structure with those of action. Victor Turner and Sir Edmund Leach would certainly be contenders for the status of 'maverick eclectic' (see chapter 6), as would Rodney Needham (chapter 8), David Schneider and Ernest Gellner (chapter 10). For me though, Gregory Bateson and Mary Douglas stand out as especially relevant for treatment here. What they have in common with each other and with much in the poststructuralist and feminist movements is their use of structural (but dynamic) models to explain social action as embedded in culture.

Poststructuralism and anthropology

Poststructuralism, like structuralism, is a mainly French perspective and one which transcends the disciplines. Its adherents sometimes draw heavily on structuralism; indeed, the boundary between the two perspectives is not always a clear one. For me, the most salient feature of poststructuralism is a reluctance to accept the distinction between subject and object that is implicit in structuralist thought, especially that of Saussure.

   The idea of 'poststructuralism' is most closely associated with the literary critic Jacques Derrida, whose writings include some direct criticism (and 'deconstruction') of Saussure and of Lévi-Strauss (see, e.g., Derrida 1976 [1967]). Others, more loosely definable as 'poststructuralists', include Marxist writer Louis Althusser, psychoanalyst Jacques Lacan, and sociologist-anthropologist Pierre Bourdieu. Finally, there is philosopher-historian Michel Foucault, who, along with Bourdieu, has had a profound effect on social anthropology over the last twenty years or more.

Derrida, Althusser, and Lacan

Although less important for anthropology today than the ideas of Bourdieu or Foucault, those of Derrida, Althusser, and Lacan have all had a marked impact in their own spheres of interest. Within anthropology, their impact has been most marked in feminist and late Marxist theory.

   Derrida (e.g., 1976 [1967]; 1978 [1967]) broke with structuralism in an attempt to expose what he saw as the fallacy of any analysis which accepts the totality of a text as a unit of analysis. Any text, he argues, will entail contradictions. The Saussurian notion of 'difference' (referred to by post-Saussurian structuralists in terms of distinctive features or binary oppositions) is transformed into a complex concept where meaning is both 'different' (through *différence*, 'difference') and 'deferred' (through *différance* [*sic*], Derrida's neologism for this phenomenon). The double meaning of the French verb *différer* ('to differ', or 'to defer until later') captures for Derrida the contradictions entailed both in any synchronic analysis of meaning and in the Saussurian priority of speech over writing. Derrida's break with structuralism is also, in a sense, a break with modern Western thought in general and its quest for universal understandings. Texts refer simply to other texts, not to anything beyond that. The notion of 'intertextuality', or relations between texts, has implications for anthropology, especially in the aftermath of Clifford and Marcus' famous edited volume *Writing Culture* (1986), which will be discussed at length in the next chapter. Derrida's method of deconstructing texts has also influenced feminist attempts to understand cultural differences in the perception of male and female.

Of more direct influence on feminism and feminist anthropology, though, is the work of Lacan (1977 [1966]). His work stresses among other things the importance of language in defining identity, and the complexity of sexual identity through complementary images of male and female, and mother and child. Two famous notions of his have given both inspiration and cause for alarm in feminist circles: that 'woman does not exist' (in that there is no ultimate female essence) and 'woman is not whole' (in that a woman lacks a penis, which in turn symbolizes both all that is lacking in male ideology and the social status of women).

Althusser's writings, especially his *Reading 'Capital'* (Althusser and Balibar 1970 [1968]), present a curious mixture of structuralism and Marxism. He argues for a distinction between a 'surface' reading of Marx and a 'symptomatic' reading, the latter being a deeper and truer understanding of Marx's intention. By the latter sort of reading, it is argued, we can gain better insight into the nature of modes of production. This liberating idea was important for Marxist anthropology because it gave anthropologists greater scope to bend Marx's words while maintaining the premise of being true to Marx's intentions. In *For Marx* (1969 [1965]), Althusser considers the ways in which discourse and power enable modes of production to be reproduced through the generations. Here again, his work has proved useful to anthropologists trying to cope with relations between kinship, gender, and production (see, e.g., Meillassoux 1972; 1981 [1975]). Although perhaps more literally a structuralist than a poststructuralist, Althusser pushed at least some Marxist anthropologists towards a confrontation with (Marx's) texts and away from the latent Lévi-Straussian concerns of the structural Marxists (see chapter 6).

Bourdieu's practice theory

Pierre Bourdieu is Professor of Sociology at the Collège de France. Early in his career, as part of his military service, he taught in Algeria (incidentally, the birthplace of both Derrida and Althusser). This led to his ethnographic research on the Kabyles, a Berber people who live in the northern mountainous-coastal area of that country. He has long maintained two diverse research interests: education and social class in French society, and kinship and family organization in Kabyle society. Some of his work, especially in the former, involves a critique of the abuse of power by state authorities. However, he is best known in anthropological circles for his theoretical interest in 'practice', as exemplified in comments on Kabyle patrilateral parallel-cousin marriage, rituals, and the seasonal cycle. The diverse foci perhaps reflect his own 'practice' as both a sociologist of his own society and an anthropologist of an alien one (Reed-Donahay 1995).

The key texts in practice theory are *Outline of a Theory of Practice* (Bourdieu 1977 [1972]) and *The Logic of Practice* (Bourdieu 1990 [1980]). The argument is the same in both. Objective understanding misses the essence of practice, which is an actor's understanding. Structuralists from Saussure to Lévi-Strauss remain at the level of the model, while Bourdieu calls for engagement in the domain of performance. Likewise, distinctions like system/event, rule/improvization, synchronic/diachronic, and *langue/parole* are jettisoned in favour of a new order based on what he calls *habitus* (a Latin word meaning, loosely, 'habitat' or 'habitual state', especially of the body). In Bourdieu's view, the analysis of this should enable the anthropologist to understand the nature of power, symbolic capital, Mauss' 'gift', and more.

Bourdieu is essentially arguing against a static notion of structure. Crucially, habitus lies between the objective and the subjective, the collective and the individual. It is culturally defined, but its locus is the mind of the individual. Habitus is a kind of structure of social action by culturally competent performers. It is analogous to Noam Chomsky's (1965: 3–9) notion of linguistic 'competence', the idea that a native speaker has in his or her mind an intuitive model which generates 'performance' in the speech act. Instead of social institutions, habitus is made up of 'dispositions', which members of a culture know intuitively how to handle. Individuals make choices as to which dispositions to follow and when, according to their understanding of them within the habitus and their own place in the system of events.

Bourdieu variously defines habitus as 'the durably installed generative principle of regulated improvisations' (1977: 78) or 'the system of structured, structuring dispositions . . . always ordered towards practical functions' (1990: 52). Such systems function, he says:

> as principles of the generation and structuring of practices and representation which can be objectively 'regulated' and 'regular' without in any way being the product of obedience to rules, objectively adapted to their goals without presupposing a conscious aiming at ends or an express mastery of the operations necessary to attain them and, being all this, collectively orchestrated without being the product of the orchestrating action of a conductor. (Bourdieu 1977: 72; cf. 1990: 53)

Bourdieu's concern is to move social science away from an emphasis on rules, towards a theory of practice. Yet structure is still there, not so much a constraining structure, but an enabling structure (for those who know how to use it), one of choice.

However, individuals do not all have equal access to decision-making processes. This is where power comes in. Bourdieu's theory of power, implicit in his theory of practice, is that those people who can impose their 'practical taxonomy' of the world on others, by definition, wield power (see, e.g., Bourdieu 1977: 159–97). This may be done through teaching the young, through cultural domination, or through the 'symbolic violence' of, for example, entrusting servants with one's property (and thereby instilling in them one's own values). Bourdieu has been criticized, though, for not going far enough in recognizing individual consciousness. According to Jean Comaroff (1985: 5), Bourdieu's actors 'seem doomed to reproduce their world mindlessly, without its contradictions leaving any mark on their awareness – at least, until a crisis (in the form of culture contact or the emergence of class division) initiates a process of overt struggle'.

Such criticisms notwithstanding, Bourdieu has become one of the most widely cited and most admired figures in our discipline. Indeed Comaroff herself, in toying with the interplay between event, culture, structure, transformation, and consciousness, is building on Bourdieu's strengths as much as she is probing his weaknesses. Virtually all fieldworkers today aim to couple their Malinowskian or Boasian methodological basics (participant-observation, use of the native language, search for connections, and gathering of details over a long period) with a quest for the habitus which might explain the actions of their informants. In a sense, Bourdieu has succeeded where the Marxists failed. He has turned anthropological studies as a whole towards an interest in practice, while maintaining an implicit recognition of cultural diversity as at least one essence of the human condition.

Foucault's theory of knowledge and power

Michel Foucault was Professor of the History of Systems of Thought at the Collège de France. He wrote widely on the history of medicine (especially psychiatric medicine), penology, and sexuality. He argued consistently against a straightforward structuralist approach, though his theoretical focus changed in the course of his career. In the 1960s Foucault emphasized the absence of order in history and articulated the significance of Saussurian *parole* over *langue* (e.g., Foucault 1973 [1966]; 1974 [1969]). In other words, structures are not pre-existing, and discourse should be paramount over cultural grammar. What is more, order is created by the historian or social scientist who writes about an event, not by the actor in a given time and place.

In the following decade, Foucault came to focus on the ways in which power and knowledge are linked (e.g., 1977 [1975]). Power is not something to possess, but rather it is a capability to manipulate a system. In other words, neither social nor symbolic structures are to be taken for granted; nor should they be seen as culturally agreed schemata which each member of society understands in the same way. A related notion has been his idea of 'discourse'. While in linguistics, 'discourse' has generally held the meaning of 'continuous' speech (e.g., what might be analogous to a paragraph or longer segment in writing), in Foucauldian usage it is widened. Here it represents a concept involving the way people talk or write about something, or the body of knowledge implied, or the use of that knowledge, such as in the structures of power which were Foucault's overwhelming concern.

Power is a strong and growing interest in anthropology, and Foucault's influence is very wide. His idea of discourses of power is applicable in feminist theory and has also had great impact in studies of colonial and postcolonial domination of the Third World and Fourth World by the West (see, e.g., Cheater 1999). As Bruce Knauft has put it: 'The trend in anthropology has been to invoke Foucault as a dependable and general-purpose critic of Western epistemological domination' (Knauft 1996: 143). Foucault's ideas have struck a chord particularly with the likes of James Clifford, George Marcus, and others part of or influenced by the *Writing Culture* phenomenon. As with Bourdieu's impact, that of Foucault has altered the direction of anthropology in both fieldwork interests and high theoretical analysis.

Feminism in anthropology

The feminist critique concerns both gender relations in particular societies and the idea of gender as a structuring principle in human society generally (H. L. Moore 1988: vii). While the former may be regarded as essentially a substantive issue, the latter is a theoretical one and therefore merits the same treatment as, for example, Marxism, poststructuralism, or postmodernism – all perspectives with links to feminism in anthropology.

From gender studies to feminist anthropology

In her magnificent overview of feminist anthropology, Henrietta Moore (e.g., 1988: 1) goes to great lengths to point out that although the impetus for feminist anthropology may have been the neglect of women as objects of ethnographic scrutiny, the real issue is one of representation. Women were long represented as 'muted' (as Edwin Ardener put it), as profane, as objects of marital exchange, and so on, and not as prime actors in the centre of social life.

Female anthropologists have been present since the early part of the twentieth century, but through most of that century they did fieldwork as 'honorary males' in small-scale societies. Gradually the significance of females in society became known in the discipline, as more female ethnographers took to describing female roles in activities such as subsistence and (women's) ritual. By the early 1970s, male bias came to be widely recognized: including that of cultures being studied, that of anthropology itself, and that of Western culture generally (H. L. Moore 1988: 1–2). Feminist anthropologists took as their task the deconstruction of these various forms of male bias. So feminist anthropology grew from 'the anthropology of women', the crucial difference being that it is the notion of gender relations and not merely what women do which is central to the feminist enterprise (see H. L. Moore 1988: 186–98). As Moore puts it: 'Feminist anthropology . . . formulates its theoretical questions in terms of how economics, kinship and ritual are experienced and structured through gender, rather than asking how gender is experienced and structured through culture' (1988: 9).

One of the key figures in the early development of feminist anthropology was a man. Edwin Ardener (1989 [1975]: 127–33) argued that dominant groups in society maintain control over expression. Therefore 'muted groups', as he called them, remained in relative silence. Women are the most significant such group in any society, both numerically and otherwise. Even where women are literally vocal, their expression is inhibited by the fact that they do not speak the same 'language' as the dominant group: women and men have different worldviews. Ardener further suggests that anthropology itself is male dominated, but for subtle reasons. Anthropologists are all either male or (in the case of female anthropologists) trained in a male-biased discipline, itself the product of a male culture.

Feminist writers in anthropology have pointed out problems in privileging women as ethnographers of women (see, e.g., Milton 1979; Strathern 1981; 1987a). Moore (1988: 5–10) analyses these problems, which she groups into three kinds: ghettoization, the assumption of a 'universal woman', and ethnocentrism or racism. The first set of problems stems from the idea of the anthropology of women as almost a subdiscipline. For Moore it is a critique of the discipline as a whole, an all-embracing theoretical perspective, and not a specialized branch of the subject.

Moore's second set is related to the erroneous assumption that women are everywhere much the same, as if biological difference itself were enough to create universal cultural differences between men and women. The category 'woman', she argues, needs more careful scrutiny than that, and the mere fact that an ethnographer and her subject may both be women is not enough to assume that they see the notion of 'woman' in the same way. In short, feminist anthropology should rely on ethnography and not on bland but bold assumptions.

The third set of problems is related to the feminist notion of experience. Just as 'economics, kinship and ritual are experienced . . . through gender' (Moore 1988: 9), so too are ethnicity and race. People have multiple identities, but these are not separate but interrelated. A black woman from London, for example, is not just a black, a female, and a Londoner. Her identity is made up of an intricate and simultaneous contextualization of all these statuses and others. Such a view contrasts, if subtly, with the notion of a complex of multiple but separate identities as understood in the traditional functionalist anthropology, for example, of Radcliffe-Brown:

The human being as a person is a complex of social relationships. He is a citizen of England, a husband and a father, a bricklayer, a member of a particular Methodist congregation, a voter in a certain constituency, a member of his trade union, an adherent of the Labour Party, and so on. (Radcliffe-Brown 1952 [1940]: 194)

Gender as a symbolic construction

Anthropologists writing on gender have approached the subject with two perspectives (which are not necessarily mutually exclusive): gender as a symbolic construction, and gender as a complex set of social relations (H. L. Moore 1988: 12–41). The former view is associated, for example, with Edwin Ardener's 'Belief and the problem of women' (1989 [1972]:

72–85), and Sherry Ortner's 'Is female to male as nature is to culture?' (1974).

Consider Ortner's essay. She argues that women everywhere are associated with nature. Her grounds are that the biological fact that women, not men, give birth, bestows on them that universal association. Since every culture (she says) makes a symbolic distinction between nature and culture, men will therefore be associated with culture. She argues further that women's reproductive role tends to confine them to the domestic sphere. Thus women (and to some extent children) represent nature (and the private), while men represent culture (and the public). It is important to note, though, that it is not *her* belief that women are associated with nature in any intrinsic way. Rather it is a cultural-universal belief founded on the structural opposition between nature and culture. Thus Ortner sets herself apart from her analysis.

While Ortner's essay does not represent the basis of all feminist anthropology, it was a major catalyst for debate. Many feminists have indeed been critical of her model, and some have been able to counter it with ethnographic cases which do not fit. Foremost among these are the 'simple societies' described by Jane Collier and Michelle Rosaldo (1981). They point out that hunting-and-gathering societies in Southern Africa, Australia, and the Philippines do not associate childbirth or motherhood with 'nature'. Nor do they associate women simply with reproduction and its aftermath. These societies are essentially egalitarian, and women share child-rearing with men.

Gender as a complex set of social relations

Collier and Rosaldo's perspective is characteristic of the idea of gender as a complex of social relations. This sort of perspective tends to emphasize the social over the cultural, and often seeks the boundary between egalitarian and male-dominant societies. The problem of supposed universal subordination of women is obviously inherent in it, for if there are egalitarian societies then women are not always subordinate. In an overview of women, culture, and society, Rosaldo (1974) argued simply that association with the domestic sphere, rather than with nature, made women subordinate.

Marxist feminists have pushed this case most strongly (see, e.g., Sacks 1979). Eleanor Leacock (1978) went further than others in asserting that previous writers had ignored history, especially the fact that colonialism and world capitalism have distorted relations between men and women. In this well-argued paper, she suggests that the public/private distinction was absent among foragers in pre-contact times, and women's subordination only came about with the growth of private property. Her research on the history as well as the ethnography of the Montagnais-Naskapi of Labrador showed many changes in political authority since the earliest, seventeenth-century, reports. Further research has shown that the same is true in other parts of the world too, notably in Aboriginal Australia.

There have been many attempts to explain universal male dominance, and some have combined the idea of gender as a symbolic construction with that of gender as embedded in social relations. One of the most interesting for its extreme stance is that of Salvatore Cucchiari (1981). Like Knight (see chapter 3), Cucchiari argues that it is possible to reconstruct the prehistory of gender relations. Very simply, his model supposes that in the beginning not only was there equality between the sexes, but also a lack of gender distinction (and bisexuality as a norm). The earliest differentiation was between categories 'Forager' and 'Child Tender', not 'male' and 'female'. However, as people became aware of 'proto-women's' exclusive abilities to bear and nurse children, these proto-women were made a sacred category. Child Tenders became proto-women. From this developed exclusive heterosexuality (as an ideal), sexual jealousy, and sexual control – leading ultimately to universal male dominance.

While most feminists would hold back from such speculations, the search for origins remains permissible in the anthropology of gender. Such big questions as the origin of gender hierarchy link up with feminist interests in exposing power relations of all kinds, with gender differentiation taken as the basis for many. Feminism in anthropology has also helped to reorient much in kinship studies, especially in light of Marxist critiques (see Meillassoux 1981 [1975]). On another front, there is much in broadly feminist anthropology to challenge the image of male dominance as portrayed in traditional ethnographies, and new methods of ethnographic portrayal have resulted in quite different pictures of social life, for example those of Lila Abu-Lughod writing on Bedouin women (e.g., Abu-Lughod 1986). Indeed, that same ethnographer, citing feminist critiques and perspectives of 'halfies' (defined as those 'whose national or cultural identity is mixed by virtue of migration, overseas education, or parentage'; 1991: 137), argues that the critique makes the concept of culture itself problematic. She suggests that anthropologists should write 'against culture' in order to battle against the hierarchies it implies.

Embodiment

Coming out of both feminist theory and Foucault's interests has been a new focus on the body as a source of identity, which logically confounds the separation of sex and gender. The sex/gender distinction actually reproduces some distinctions it serves to question (Yanagisako and Collier 1987).

'Embodiment', even beyond its gender aspects, is an area of increasing interest. In particular, Thomas Csordas (1990; cf. 1994) has built on Merleau-Ponty's (1962) notion that embodiment is indeterminate. His view is much more radical than the notion of the 'anthropology of the body' which emerged in the 1970s. The body is more than the sum of its parts. What is more, one can have 'multiple bodies', for example, physical and social (see Douglas 1969); or individual, social, and body politic (respectively body as self, body as symbol, e.g., of nature, and external control of the body; Scheper-Hughes and Lock 1987).

Andrew Strathern and Pamela Stewart (1998) compare embodiment to communication as modes for the understanding of ritual. In their terms, the embodiment perspective emphasizes the putative effects of ritual on the performers, while the communication perspective emphasizes the social context and the context involving the spiritual powers to which the rituals are directed. Their definition is quite straightforward: 'In the broadest sense, we take the term embodiment to refer to the anchoring of certain social values and dispositions in and through the body . . .' (1998: 237). Others have utilized the concept to explore aspects not only of power and gender, but even species. Thus for Donna Haraway (1988; 1991), both gender and feminism are about embodiment, while embodiment is further both individual and collective, the latter in the sense that it defined the collectivity, for example, of all female human (or primate) bodies.

Two maverick eclectics

My focus in this last section is on just two scholars, whose maverick status is heightened by the fact that neither ended their careers in conventional anthropological writings nor even within anthropology departments. All the same, Gregory Bateson and Mary Douglas are both brilliant exemplars of anthropological theory's contribution to social thought. They remain significant for our discipline, while nevertheless neither leading from the front nor following the trends of their times.

Structure and conflict: Bateson on national character

Bateson was one of the most fascinating figures of twentieth-century scholarship. He neither built up an institutional following nor even gained the conventional recognition of close colleagues and students. Yet he was influential because everyone from Radcliffe-Brown to the postmodernists admired his ability to make sense of what to others was simply the vagary of culture.

Gregory Bateson's father, William Bateson, was a founder of modern genetics, and Gregory's early interests were also in biology. He studied zoology and anthropology at Cambridge, and in 1927 he went off to do anthropological fieldwork with the Iatmul of New Guinea. There he met Margaret Mead, whom he eventually married and with whom he later carried out field research on Bali. Like W. H. R. Rivers, Bateson practised as a psychiatrist, working especially with alcoholics and schizophrenics. He spent much of his later life studying dolphins. He was also heavily involved in the Green movement, and in radical approaches to education at all levels.

Beginning with his ethnographic study of the *naven* ceremony of the Iatmul (Bateson 1958 [1936]), Bateson cultivated a sense of understanding the bizarre through the analysis of form in relation to action. The ceremony lent itself well to such a broadly structural approach, involving as it did transvestism, ritual homosexuality, and the purposeful and (in the ritual context) permissible violation of taboos which (in other contexts) regulate kinship and gender relations. My main example here, though, is drawn from Bateson's essay 'Morale and national character', based on a comparison between aspects of German, Russian, English, and American culture during the Second World War (Bateson 1973 [1942]: 62–79). Let us look at just one of his comparisons: that between the English and the Americans as he (an Englishman working in America) perceived them.

Basically the problem is this: if you put an American in a room with an Englishman, the American will do all the talking. What is more, the American will talk mainly about himself (let us assume, as Bateson did, that these two characters are both male). The Englishman will regard the American as boastful and will resent it. The American will resent the fact that the Englishman appears to have nothing to contribute to the conversation. If the Englishman does talk about himself, he will understate things. He will try to be modest, but in doing that the American will only see in him a false modesty or arrogance. So, both the American and the Englishman are behaving in the way they think is appropriate. However, the Englishman sees the American as boastful, and the American sees the Englishman as arrogant.

Why is this? Bateson's answer rests on two sets of oppositions: dominance v. submission, and exhibitionism v. spectatorship. The dominance/submission opposition, he says, has a clear association with parenthood (dominance) and childhood (submission), while the exhibitionism/spec-

Table 9.1. *Bateson's solution to a problem of national character*

Activity	English interpretation	American interpretation
exhibitionism	dominance (parentlike behaviour)	submission (childlike behaviour)
spectatorship	submission (childlike behaviour)	dominance (parentlike behaviour)

tatorship opposition is variable in the manner in which it is mapped onto dominance and submission. This is illustrated in table 9.1.

By way of further explanation, Bateson suggests this. In England (at least in the upper-middle-class household of the early twentieth century), when the father comes home from work he talks to his children. The children sit and listen. Therefore exhibitionism (doing all the talking) indicates a parentlike role; in other words, dominance. Spectatorship (doing the listening) indicates a childlike role; in other words, submission. In America, says Bateson, the opposite is true. When the father comes home from work, he listens to his children who tell him, and their mother, what they have been up to at school. The parents sit and listen. Thus in America, exhibitionism is associated with childlike behaviour, and spectatorship is associated with parentlike behaviour. These associations are carried through into later life. So, when the adult, male American meets his English counterpart, he tries to show off all his knowledge, abilities, wealth, or whatever. The American, subconsciously perhaps, perceives himself as being submissive and childlike. He treats the Englishman as a parent-figure, which in both cultures is a means of being polite. For the Englishman, exhibitionism is a sign of dominance, and he incorrectly believes the American is trying to be dominant.

Implicit in all this is a distinction between two concepts which Bateson called by the Greek words *eidos* and *ethos*. Culture is made up of both (see, e.g., Bateson 1958 [1936]: 123–51, 198–256). In Bateson's usage, eidos is what we more generally call 'form' or 'structure' (cf. Kroeber 1963 [1948]: 100–3). The sets of oppositions he describes in his study of national character (spectatorship v. exhibitionism; dominance v. submission) are part of the eidos of American and of English culture. Ethos refers to the customs, the traditions, also the feelings, the collective emotions, either of a given culture or of a given event which is defined according to cultural norms. More specifically it refers to their distinctive character or spirit. These concepts are related, and at least in his national-character study ethos seems to depend for its cross-cultural definition on the relation between the eidos of one culture and that of another.

The methods Bateson used seem particularly suited to the analysis of conflict and potential conflict, and he developed a similar approach to understanding conflict between, for example, male and female among the Iatmul, and East and West in the nuclear arms race. Similarly, Canadian anthropologist Elliott Leyton (1974) has analysed conflict in Northern Ireland in terms of direct, eidotic oppositions between aspects of the ethos of Nationalist and Unionist cultures (or Catholic and Protestant) in Northern Ireland. Anthropologists from Northern Ireland have criticized Leyton since then for oversimplifying, as certainly Bateson did on Americans and Englishmen, but the point of this kind of analysis is that conflict is often better understood in terms of structures and processes of interaction than in terms of ethnographic detail alone.

Structure and action: Douglas on grid and group

Mary Douglas' approach is essentially structuralist but played out within a dynamic framework. Like Bateson and Bourdieu, she is interested in the relation between individual actions and the cultural frameworks within which action is interpreted. Douglas read philosophy, politics, and economics at Oxford, and subsequently studied anthropology there under Evans-Pritchard (see chapter 10). She did fieldwork with the Lele of Kasai Province, in the Congo, and taught for many years at University College London. She later became Director of the Russell Sage Foundation in New York and taught at Princeton and Wisconsin, before retiring to London.

Douglas' early work was quite straightforward, with special interests in economics and religion. The latter led her to studies of purity and pollution among the Lele, among the ancient Hebrews, and in Britain. Her first famous book (though not her first book) was *Purity and Danger* (1966). There she examined concepts such as these and hinted at the form of analysis which she was soon to develop in *Natural Symbols* (1969): *Natural Symbols* and most of her many subsequent publications have utilized the framework she calls 'grid/group analysis' (see also, e.g., Douglas 1978; 1982; 1996).

Grid/group analysis is a method of describing and classifying cultures and societies, aspects of culture or society, individual social situations, individual actions, or even individual preferences. The principle is that virtually anything one might want to classify in relation to its alternatives can be measured along two axes, which are called respectively 'grid' and 'group' (figure 9.1). However, Douglas and her followers are not so much concerned with quantitative measurement as with structural opposition,

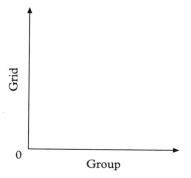

Figure 9.1 The grid and group axes

in other words the presence or absence of high grid or high group constraints.

The *grid* dimension is the measure of 'insulation' or 'constraint' imposed not by group cohesion, but by individual isolation. To be low on the grid scale is to have freedom to act or the scope to interact with others as equals; to be high is to be insulated or constrained in decision-making by the social system. The *group* dimension is the measure of group cohesion, whether people in a group do everything together (high group) or act individually (low group). Douglas' interest lies in determining and accounting for the relative presence or absence of high-grid and high-group features, rather than the establishment of precise co-ordinates along the axes. Thus there are only four logical possibilities, each represented by a different 'box' (figure 9.2). She conventionally labels the boxes with the letters A to D, though unfortunately her usage differs from publication to publication (with no fewer than three different labelling systems). The one shown here is the system used in her booklet *Cultural Bias* (1978), the publication which remains the best introduction to the theory.

Douglas asserts that her method can be used for the study of everything from witchcraft to food preferences (to take examples respectively from her early and recent writings). One which I think brings out the theory particularly clearly is the working environment of research scientists (see Bloor and Bloor 1982). It matters little whether we are talking about astronomers or zoologists, but let us suppose all the scientists are in the same field, say medical research. The differences between them are those of their respective structural positions in their subculture, or their 'sociology' (as Douglas sometimes puts it). They may differ also in the way they

B	C
High grid **Low group** Isolation, by choice or compulsion	**High grid** **High group** Strongly incorporated, with hierarchy
A **Low grid** **Low group** Active individualism, often with competition	**D** **Low grid** **High group** Strongly incorporated, without hierarchy

Figure 9.2 The grid and group boxes

see their work environment, their 'cosmology'. Let us call the protagon-ists Alice, Ben, Carlos, and Deborah (respectively Boxes A, B, C, and D).

Alice is an independent researcher. She goes to work whenever she wants and takes holidays when she chooses. She gets paid according to the amount of work she does, and works on whatever project she wants to. She is not constrained by outside forces; therefore she is *low grid*. She is also *low group* because she is not constrained by group conformity. She belongs to various professional associations, and also to different clubs outside her profession. Sometimes she chooses solitude; sometimes she joins in group activities. Either way, she does not follow the crowd. She is equally free to associate with different groups or with none.

Ben is high grid, low group. He works for a drug company and is on a five-year contract to discover a cure for a rare disease. He has to submit reports to the company every week, detailing what he has been doing. He has to keep accurate records of his activities on a minute-by-minute basis, and is expected to put in exactly forty-eight hours a week. He is therefore constrained by the forces of his high grid predicament. He is also low group. This could mean that he has nobody else working with him. The constraints of time keep him from joining groups, either formal or infor-mal. Unlike Alice, Ben is not low group by choice, but is forced there by the kind of work he does. While all the other boxes have their natural incumbents, Box B is 'unfriendly' (Douglas' term) to almost any person-ality type, and Ben is not happy.

Carlos is high grid, high group. He works in a hierarchical university department. Like Ben, he is constrained by the fact that he has a strict timetable. Yet unlike Ben, he is very much a member of the group. His level within the system does not matter, as he is constrained by the system itself. Even if he is the Dean of Medicine, he is constrained by the money he gets from the university or the research councils, and he never gets enough. Being high group, he has lots of activities related to the main group he belongs to: his department. Supposing he is the head of the department, he might have to chair meetings, organize research and teaching, see visiting scientists, perhaps treat patients, and supervise the activities of his staff. Characteristically in a high-group situation, Carlos would mix business with pleasure. He might be expected to referee the inter-departmental football matches every Saturday, or to invite each of his staff to dinner, one a month, in rotation.

Deborah is low grid, high group. She also works in a university department, but it is one which is run on an egalitarian, democratic basis. She might be the professor, or she might be a junior assistant. It does not really matter, because in this case professors and assistants take turns teaching each other, doing experiments together, and washing the test tubes and coffee cups. She is in a low-grid situation because her group is egalitarian and democratic. Unlike Alice, she is also in a high-group situation, one full of group-oriented constraints. Alice belongs to lots of different societies. Deborah only belongs to her strongly group-oriented department. Like Carlos, she spends lots of time in departmental activities, and whatever the group (her department) all want to do, everyone does.

Mary Douglas and her students have compared a variety of situations in this manner. Her method works best when like is compared to like, as in the case just described. However, her early assumptions about comparing whole societies has not borne fruit. Nor is it particularly meaningful to think in terms of hermits and taxi drivers being Box A, prisoners being Box B, soldiers being Box C, and members of religious cults or hippie communes being Box D – though these are all associations she has described. It may be useful, though, to compare different hippie communes, each as being, in a relative sense, higher grid or group than the next. In other words, if within Western society all hippie communes are relatively low grid and high group, then a small set of boxes for hippie communes (A to D) might be envisaged as lying all within a larger Box D in a grid/group diagram of Western society as a whole.

Grid/group analysis was an interesting idea, and it remains one for many social scientists outside mainstream anthropology. Yet it may also have been an idea (like hippie communes) whose time had come and gone before it took off. It remains to be seen whether some new focus within her paradigm can be made. There may well be hints of poststructuralism and postmodernism hidden in the paradigm, which surely could yield insights into relations between, for example, fieldworkers and their subjects.

Concluding summary

Mavericks, poststructuralists, and feminists possess a diversity of perspectives. Yet these perspectives have in common both roots in structuralist thinking and challenges to mainstream structuralist anthropology, especially in attempts to integrate structure with action and account for relations of power. Functionalism and structuralism had represented both safe perspectives and safe periods for anthropology, indeed in the latter case a period in which anthropology served as a major source for ideas in other disciplines, including literary criticism. Poststructuralist, feminist, and (as we shall see in the next chapter) interpretivist and postmodernist ideas have all challenged the authority of ethnographic reporting and the methods of analysis characteristic of structural anthropology and its predecessors.

If Bateson and Douglas are anthropologists whose thoughts and interests drifted away from the narrow anthropological perspectives of their times, the poststructuralists are just the opposite: practitioners of other disciplines whose insights have offered inspiration for emerging developments within our discipline. Interpretivism in some respects represents the opposite of structuralism – a rejection of meaning as embedded in structure in favour of the intuitive and interactive creation of meaning. In other respects it represents a logical development from poststructuralism, with its breaking down of traditional constructions and opening up of new agendas for anthropology through links with literary criticism and social theory. The last two decades have seen great changes in anthropological perceptions, but they are no greater than the changes which took place in the 1920s or in the 1950s, and the next chapter offers a survey of recent developments in the historical context of a wider interpretive anthropology.

FURTHER READING

Useful commentaries on the leading figures discussed in this chapter include those of Brockman (1977) on Gregory Bateson, Fardon (1998) on Mary Douglas, Jenkins (1992) on Pierre Bourdieu, and Smart (1985) on Michel Foucault.

Among good introductions to poststructuralism is the one by Sarup (1988), which also introduces postmodernism. Ortner's essays 'Theory in anthropology since the sixties' (1984) and 'Resistance and the problem of ethnographic refusal' (1995), along with Knauft's *Genealogies for the Present* (1996), provide excellent overviews of the impact of feminism, poststructuralism, etc. on anthropology.

The best overview of feminist anthropology is H. L. Moore's *Feminism and Anthropology* (1988), and her *A Passion for Difference* (1994) covers a wealth of issues related to current debates. See also Strathern's essay, 'An awkward relationship' (1987a).

10   Interpretive and postmodernist approaches

After Radcliffe-Brown's death in 1955, British anthropology went in four different directions. Some in the next generation simply continued Radcliffe-Brown's line of enquiry (notably Fortes and to some extent Goody). Others, such as Firth, came to emphasize individual action over social structure – an approach drawn partly from Malinowski's early fieldwork-based version of functionalism (chapter 5). This line of thought developed into theories such as processualism and transactionalism (chapter 6). Still others took to at least some of Lévi-Strauss' structuralist ideas (chapter 8), often adapting them to new interests in social process. Finally, a large number came eventually to follow Evans-Pritchard in his rejection of the idea of anthropology as a science, in favour of an interpretive approach which placed anthropology firmly within the humanities.

In the United States, Clifford Geertz began to propound his own style of interpretivism. Anthropology in his hands (and in Evans-Pritchard's) turned the linguistic analogy sideways. Cultures were no longer metaphorical 'grammars' to be figured out and written down; they were 'languages' to be translated into terms intelligible to members of other cultures – or more often than not, the anthropologist's own culture.

In France, outside anthropology, structuralism was under attack as the last bastion of 'modernism'. Philosophers and literary critics there and their followers in North America developed new, 'postmodern' ways of looking at the world. To a great extent, this followed from the idea that the world itself had undergone a quiet revolution. The world had moved beyond modernism, with its hierarchy of knowledge, to a postmodern phase where there was no place for grand theory of any kind (except, a cynic might say, postmodernism itself).

These ideas filtered into anthropology in the late 1970s and early 1980s. There were also developments within our discipline which made it more open to postmodernist ideas. The interpretivism already present served as a foundation – as did latter-day attacks on the alleged colonial mentality and imperialist foundation of anthropology. In the same time period, feminist anthropology grew and further challenged androcentric models, reflexivity became a byword of ethnographic method, and writing and reading took on theoretical significance in the new, literarily aware anthropology. All this culminated in the publication of *Writing Culture* (Clifford and Marcus 1986), and in the eyes of some the discipline was born again.

This chapter focuses on these various strands of thinking. While Evans-Pritchard may be thought of as a thoroughly modernist practitioner of the discipline, his ideas nevertheless foreshadow interpretivism. The eventual move towards postmodernism in the hands of Edwin Ardener and others at Oxford, Evans-Pritchard's old university, lies within the Evans-Pritchardian tradition, or at least possesses a spirit which Evans-Pritchard would have recognized as his own (see chapter 9). At the other extreme, *Writing Culture* signalled a focus on the 'poetics and politics' of writing ethnography. What these strands have in common is a vision of anthropology as a rejection of scientific method, a recognition of the importance of writing, and an attempt to gain insight through human understanding rather than formal methods of research and analysis. In spite of their diversity, it is therefore quite appropriate to see all these threads of interpretive and postmodernist thinking as part of one great movement within the discipline – a movement that all of us have been influenced by, however much some may wish to distance themselves from it.

Evans-Pritchard's interpretive approach

E. E. Evans-Pritchard studied under C. G. Seligman and Bronislaw Malinowski at the London School of Economics. He made six major field expeditions to the Sudan and British East Africa, notably with the Zande (Azande), Nuer, Anuak, Shilluk, and Luo. His accounts of Zande witchcraft (Evans-Pritchard 1937) and Nuer politics and kinship (1940; 1951a) served both to epitomize the British anthropology of their time and to inspire succeeding generations – albeit more on a theoretical than an ethnographic level. In recent years, some of his Nuer work, based on less than a year with the people, has been the subject of criticism for overstating the importance of the lineage in political affairs (e.g., Kuper 1988: 194–201). However, *Witchcraft, Oracles, and Magic among the Azande* (Evans-Pritchard 1937) and *Nuer Religion* (1956) have fared better. Both of these were attempts to understand and relate the inner thoughts of his subjects.

Witchcraft, Oracles, and Magic is an ethnography of Zande thought processes. The author argues that Zande are so obsessed with witchcraft

that to understand their belief in it and how that belief is used to explain
cause and effect is to understand their society. If a grain storage bin falls
and kills someone sitting under it, one cause may well be that termites
have eaten the supports, but the question of why it fell at that time on that
person must be answered by whose witchcraft is involved (Evans-
Pritchard 1937: 69–72).

Nuer Religion concerns, among other things, the definition of *kwoth*.
Like Latin *spiritus*, Greek *pneuma*, and Hebrew *ruah*, it also designates
'breath'. In its metaphorical senses, it can refer to spirits of several kinds,
including the Nuer entity Evans-Pritchard translates as 'God'. Throughout *Nuer Religion*, the author engages his reader in an exercise to picture
and feel the essence of Nuer belief through the words, the symbolism, and
the rituals which characterize the system described by the title of that
book. It is worth remembering, though, that 'Nuer religion' is not itself a
Nuer concept; it is an anthropologist's one (see Evans-Pritchard 1956:
311–22). Evans-Pritchard's monograph, together with a similar one by his
colleague Godfrey Lienhardt (1963) on the religion of the neighbouring
Dinka, formed the foundation of anthropological studies of belief. They
also focused attention on translation, both real and metaphorical. It is
interesting that whereas Evans-Pritchard speaks of 'God' and 'spirits' and
often uses the Nuer term, Lienhardt prefers the English 'Divinity' and
'divinities' – precisely in order to get away from the directness of the more
familiar English terms. It may also be worthy of note that both these
Oxford anthropologists converted to Roman Catholicism; and this, it has
been said, might have played some part in the formulation of their similar
approaches to the interpretation of religious belief and practice.

Evans-Pritchard practised his anthropology within the general theoretical framework of Radcliffe-Brown. However, he rejected Radcliffe-
Brown's notion of the discipline as a science and argued the case for
anthropology as an art (e.g., Evans-Pritchard 1965). This marks the
crucial difference between Evans-Pritchard's vision and the mainstream
British tradition from which it diverged. Especially in his later years,
Evans-Pritchard developed the idea of anthropology as 'translation of
culture', and this became a catch-phrase in the works of many of his
students. What anthropologists are supposed to do is get as close as
possible to the collective mind of the people they study, and then 'translate' the alien ideas they find into equivalent ideas within their own
culture. This is, of course, not the same thing as actual, linguistic translation. Like Radcliffe-Brown's sea shells and Lévi-Strauss' crystals, it is an
analogy (see chapters 5 and 8). Evans-Pritchard rejected the Lévi-Straussian idea of a 'grammar' of culture in favour of a 'meaning' in the more
subtle everyday discourse of culture. The difficulties of translation

(whether to go for a literal one, or an idiomatic one) have precise analogies in ethnography. If we translate Nuer or Zande ideas too literally, then no one outside of Nuerland or Zandeland will understand them. If we translate too idiomatically, then we will fail to capture the essence of Nuer or Zande thought. Anthropology, according to this view, is forever caught in the translator's dilemma.

In his 1951 textbook *Social Anthropology*, derived from a series of six lectures presented on BBC Radio, Evans-Pritchard reviews the scope of social anthropology, its history, methods, and theory, and its potential for applied work. At several points Evans-Pritchard (e.g., 1951b: 62, 116-17) criticizes the 'natural science' analogy and offers instead the vision of anthropology's object as the totality of moral and symbolic systems, which in his view are quite unlike any systems found in nature. They are not governed by natural laws, though they do entail social structures and cultural patterns. Was Evans-Pritchard a structural-functionalist masquerading as an epistemologist? Was he, until his bid for freedom in the 1950s, a philosopher-historian strapped into the straitjacket of functionalist dogma? Or did he simply change his mind, from history to functionalism to epistemology, in the course of his career?

Mary Douglas (1980: 29-38) suggests that Evans-Pritchard's career represented a single, coherent research programme and that he was always an interpretive thinker. Another view is that he broke with functionalism in the 1940s and consolidated his perspective in the 1950s (e.g., Kuper 1996 [1973]: 124-6). In support of Douglas' position, one can cite much in *Witchcraft, Oracles, and Magic* and point to the fact that the text of *Nuer Religion* is made up of papers written and presented up to a decade before its publication. However, Evans-Pritchard's ethnographic work is not all that different from that of any of his contemporaries. The ways in which it differs do not mark him out as having a unique methodological approach or understanding of society, but rather indicate a desire for innovation, especially in his concern with systems of belief. Radcliffe-Brown regarded Evans-Pritchard as one in the same mould as himself and feared that Meyer Fortes would be the rebel. Fortes, though, continued the Radcliffe-Brownian tradition at Cambridge, where it competed with Leach's structuralism and processualism for the favour of the students. Whatever elements of Evans-Pritchard's writing predate *Nuer Religion*, the publication of that book marks a departure from structural-functionalism towards a new kind of reasoning about the nature of religious belief. Evans-Pritchard recalls Durkheim more than he does Radcliffe-Brown, but the emphasis is more on seeing the spirit world as a Nuer sees it and explaining it as if to a Western theological audience, and rather less on demonstrating a relation between belief and social structure.

One of Evans-Pritchard's strongest statements against functionalism lies in his 1950 lecture, 'Social anthropology: past and present', published in his first series of collected essays (1962: 13–28). He argues that the failing of social anthropology since the Enlightenment has been to model the discipline on the natural sciences, and suggests that it is better seen as among the historical sciences or more generally as a branch of the humanities. The fact that historians' issues are generally diachronic, whereas anthropologists' are synchronic, does not bother him. The synthesis of events and the integrative description both aim at is enough for him to assert a methodological similarity. He says that the description of structural form is not antithetical to either history or anthropology. Likewise, 'History is not a succession of events, it is the links between them' (1962 [1961]: 48).

Evans-Pritchard's main influence was at Oxford, where he held the Chair of Social Anthropology from 1946 to 1970. Indeed, he still casts his spell over the Institute of Social and Cultural Anthropology there. It is his bust and not Radcliffe-Brown's or Tylor's which graces that institute's library, and his work which the Oxford tradition has carried forward. In the 1970s, when Oxford anthropology was polarized between Needham's latent structuralism and Ardener's incipient postmodernism, both sides took comfort in Evans-Pritchard's inspiration (see, e.g., Needham 1972: xiv, 14–31; Ardener 1989 [1971]: 35–9). Needham's struggle with the relation between the English word 'belief', the inner state it describes, and the cross-cultural applicability of the concept, is to a large measure attributable to the text of *Nuer Religion*.

Geertz's interpretivism

While Evans-Pritchard showed the way towards interpretivism, it is nevertheless a little harder to justify the appellation 'ism' to his approach than it is to that of Clifford Geertz. Evans-Pritchard's anthropology was, as much as anything, a reaction against the structural-functionalist enterprise, whereas Geertz's marks a positive move towards an understanding of the minutiae of culture as an end in itself.

Geertz, now based at Princeton, was trained at Harvard and has taught at Berkeley and Chicago. He did fieldwork on Java and Bali and in Morocco. His ethnographic work has been diverse in scope and approach. *The Religion of Java* (1960), for example, was fairly conventional, whereas *Kinship in Bali* (Geertz and Geertz 1975) challenges the idea of kinship as an autonomous system which can be understood cross-culturally and argues for its inclusion in a symbolic domain. *Agricultural Involution* (1963), in contrast to both, is in the broad framework of

Stewardian ecological anthropology, while some of his other work on social change in Indonesia lies in the realm of social history. In *Islam Observed* (1968), Geertz turns his attention to comparison, in an attempt to understand Islam in the context of two countries where he has ethnographic experience: Indonesia and Morocco. Unlike Evans-Pritchard (1965 [1963]: 13–36), he does not hold up 'the comparative method' as an impossibility!

The core of his interpretivist anthropology, though, lies in the introductory essay to his book *The Interpretation of Cultures*, which was completed and published in 1973 – the year of Evans-Pritchard's death. There Geertz (1973: 3–30) sums up his approach as one of 'thick description'. Anthropology is about picking through the strata embedded in a particular culture, and revealing them through layers of description. It is not about cognition as anthropologists in America then understood it; nor is it necessarily about large-scale comparison. Critics (e.g., Kuper 1999: 109–14) have pointed out the ambiguity of Geertz's definition of 'thick description' (as detailed and layered) as well as the thinness of some of his own ethnography (in that the sources of his own generalizations are seldom made clear). Yet Geertz's interpretivist challenge is, if in these ways problematic, nevertheless both deeper in ethnographic detail and richer in metaphor than Evans-Pritchard's.

In his two major collections, Geertz (1973; 1983) pushes for an image of society as 'like a text' – for Kuper (1999: 112) 'a metaphor running away with itself'. Geertz also argues for anthropology as the understanding of the 'local' in a tense interaction with the 'global', for an emphasis on the minutiae, even the trivia of culture, and for culture as a symbolic system, but a system within which social action takes place and political power is generated. He deconstructs common anthropological notions such as 'culture', 'worldview', 'art', 'custom', and 'customary law', with a fluency of style that is virtually unmatched. If he were a bad writer, he would undoubtedly have had less influence, but the effect of Geertz's subtle and skilful breaking-down of anthropological conceit and positivist tendencies has been profound. His collected essays are probably as much read outside the discipline as by anthropologists themselves, and (for better or worse) to many are paradigmatic of the discipline as a whole.

In some of his recent work, Geertz has ventured yet further into interpretivism through re-interpreting the ethnography of others. In his award-winning *Works and Lives* (Geertz 1988), he examines the writings of Evans-Pritchard, Malinowski, Lévi-Strauss, and Benedict. Through the analysis of the imagery and metaphors of his chosen authors, Geertz argues that anthropology is simply 'a kind of writing'. This is a major postmodernist challenge to the discipline, and one which is commonplace in the work of both American and French writers over the last two decades (see Clifford and Marcus 1986; Sperber 1985 [1982]). Jonathan Spencer (1989) has argued that Geertz and his followers are mistaken in the view that anthropological texts are merely pieces of writing. Spencer puts the case that anthropology is also 'a kind of working', and demonstrates the logic of putting both the ethnographer, and the diversity of points of view among informants, into the text. Yet whether Geertz's emphasis on writing is exaggerated or not, he has usefully focused attention on anthropology as a creative endeavour.

Today, Geertz remains as one of anthropology's most influential figures, both within and beyond the discipline. His interpretivism undoubtedly paved the way for postmodern anthropology. Some say he is not just a precursor but part of the movement. Before getting into the nuances of postmodernism proper, though, a focus on further foundations, especially with regard to new concepts and interests beyond those of Geertz himself, is worthwhile.

Concepts of changing times

The postmodernist challenge in anthropology has yielded new concepts and areas of new research associated with them. Among the most important are reflexivity and orientalism. Let us consider these with regard to the related concepts of reflexivism (which entails a theoretical emphasis on reflexivity), occidentalism, and globalization.

Reflexivity and reflexivism

All anthropologists do comparison of one kind or another. Those who work far from home might compare more to classic anthropological cases like Nuer or Trobriand society. Others argue that a better kind of comparison is that to societies which are similar, technologically, geographically, or linguistically (see chapter 4). Those who work in societies closely related to their own, either culturally or geographically, tend to make comparisons to their own society more explicit in their writings. At the extreme, there is explicit comparison of one's own culture, described through one's *self* as exemplar, and through the 'self' as vehicle imposed upon the culture purportedly described. In this case, the culture under description can become mere background for the anthropologist's exploration of his or her own cultural and social identity. This is a case of extreme reflexivity.

Reflexivity has formed a major part of the incipient postmodern project within anthropology since the 1970s. Perhaps the first explicit publication in this mould is Judith Okely's essay, originally published in an early issue of the *Journal of the Anthropological Society of Oxford*, 'The self and scientism' (Okely 1996 [1975]: 27–44). However, the roots of reflexivity are yet deeper. Malinowski's fieldwork diary, much commented on by Okely, is the best-known example. Although Malinowski apparently meant it only to record his own private musings, it found its way into print twenty-five years after his death (Malinowski 1967), and it contrasts sharply with his formal ethnographic accounts. In the diary he reveals his sexual fantasies, his heavy use of drugs, his distaste for some aspects of Trobriand culture, and his boredom in the Trobriand Islands. Malinowski's student Jomo Kenyatta, later the first president of Kenya, included reflexive comment in his ethnography of his own people (Kenyatta 1938), but most of the Malinowskians and the Boasians steered clear. Lévi-Strauss included much autobiography in *Tristes Tropiques* (1976 [1955]), though he too separated this from both his ethnographic and his theoretical commentaries. What makes the efforts of most postmodern writers fundamentally different is their assertion that reflexivity itself is ethnography, or at least a central part of it, and that ethnography is at least the major part of anthropological theory itself (see Rabinow 1977).

Reflexivity has strong links with feminist anthropology. Feminist anthropology and gender studies share much of their subject matter, but their approaches are somewhat different. Henrietta Moore (1988: 188) has written that the anthropology of gender is about 'the study of gender identity and its cultural construction', whereas feminist anthropology is about 'the study of gender as a principle of human social life' (see chapter 9). For the last couple of decades, anthropologists interested in the study of gender have moved decidedly away from this 'gender studies' approach to one emphasizing the position of woman as ethnographer as well as that of woman as informant or object. By the middle of the 1980s it was not uncommon for the anthropologist to put herself forward as the main subject of anthropological discourse, as reflexivity gained favour within postmodernist and especially (loosely) feminist circles, and ultimately found favour in anthropology at large (see, e.g., Okely and Callaway 1992). The danger of losing the 'other' for the emphasis on the 'self' became all too easy, as extreme reflexivity became at worst a fetish and at best a theoretical perspective (reflexivism) in its own right.

A further twist is found in the kind of study where the analyst, drawing on her own experiences, speaks for a wider community of oppressed people or attempts to give 'voice' to the oppressed through herself. Writers in this tradition sometimes take their inspiration from the poststructuralist, feminist literary theory of Gayatri Chakravorty Spivak and her 'subaltern studies' associates (see, e.g., Guha and Spivak 1988). Some of Lila Abu-Lughod's writings on Bedouin women (e.g., Abu-Lughod 1990) are in this vein. The idea is that there is something shared among 'subaltern' or subordinate groups, whether subordination is on the basis of gender, class, ethnicity, or history of colonial injustice. Sherry Ortner (1995), on the other hand, points to the Geertzian 'thinness' of work following this approach: a thinness derived from a reluctance to tackle internal politics and problems of representing the 'other' or indeed the (subaltern) self.

Other trends in the last decade have been towards moderation, either allowing personal reflexivity to mingle with reflections on theory, or pursuing the reflective experiences of the traditional objects of ethnography. The former is exemplified by Kirsten Hastrup's (1995) brilliant critique of anthropology's assumptions and directions. The latter includes Pat Caplan's (1997) record of her friendship with 'Mohammed', one of her informants, through the thirty years she has worked with the Swahili of Tanzania. Much of Caplan's text is made up of quotations, and the 'voice' of the informant is heard along with the confessions of the ethnographer. But there is 'fact' as well, especially on spirit cults; and a fine balance is achieved between ethnography and autobiography.

There is still another kind of reflexivity, though perhaps it is less recognized as such. This is the kind of reflexive study which examines not an individual but a collective self: anthropology as a whole, or perhaps a group of anthropologists who share a common interest or ethnographic region. What I have in mind is the kind of study which examines this collective self in interplay, not with individual informants, but with a culture built both of real happenings and of images portrayed through ethnography. A good example is Alcida Ramos' (1992) study of Yanomami ethnography. She remarks that anthropologists who have worked with the Yanomami groups in Brazil have variously presented them as being fierce, erotic, intellectual, or just plain exotic. In some ways, sometimes, they are all these things, but the imagery which has been built up around them is powerful. Ramos notes that media hype has exaggerated ethnographic description to such an extent that some ethnographers, notably Napoleon Chagnon, have been led to tone down new books and new editions of old books which have fuelled that flame.

Orientalism, occidentalism, and globalization

An important component of postmodern anthropology is the interest in power, derived from Foucault among others (see chapter 9). A related concern has been the identification of power as a manifestation of colonial and postcolonial discourses through 'orientalism'. The concept was introduced by Edward Said, a Palestinian literary critic long resident in the United States. In *Orientalism* (1978) and later works, Said attacks the West for creating a notion of the East, the Orient, in order to dominate it, by trade, colonialism, and other forms of exploitation. The West, he says, more polemically, also needs the Orient in order to define itself: what is *not* East is West. Many of his more salient ideas were, in fact, anticipated by anthropologists (e.g., Asad 1973; cf. Goody 1996), who have also pointed out that anthropological studies, at least in colonial times, were embedded in unequal relationships between the West and the Third World. Said is implicitly critical of our discipline and its orientalist discourse, though his main grudges are directed at literary figures, philologists, and archaeologists.

However, recently some anthropologists have turned Said's argument on its head, not so much to negate it as to point out that it is only half the story. James Carrier of the University of Durham has edited a volume called *Occidentalism* (Carrier 1995a), in which nine mainly American anthropologists (some, including Carrier, trained in sociology) comment on the notion of 'the West'. Most of the contributors note that 'oriental' peoples are as likely to have biased and generalized visions of the West as 'occidental' peoples are of the East. Indeed, as Carrier points out in his preface, when he moved from sociology to anthropology, from a training concentrating on the nuances of social complexity in industrial capitalist societies of the West to a specialization in Melanesian society, he was startled by the lack of sophistication in the ways in which anthropologists talk about their own societies.

It struck me at the time as a professional double standard, and it repelled me. These were conscientious scholars who devoted great effort to uncovering the nuances, complexities, and inter-connections of the societies that they studied. Yet they would casually characterize Western society in terms so simplistic that they would not be tolerated of an anthropologist speaking about a village society. (Carrier 1995b: vii–viii)

Carrier goes on to suggest that three trends are prevalent in anthropology today with regard to occidentalism: a tendency towards self-reflection, a growing interest in the 'invention of tradition', and an increasing concern with the ethnography of the West itself (1995b: viii–ix).

The relations between Occident and Orient, whether imagined or real, are now bound up with the process of globalization, also an increasing object of anthropological enquiry. In one of six volumes stemming from the 1993 Decennial Conference of the Association of Social Anthropologists of the Commonwealth, Norman Long (1996) speaks of 'globalization', 'localization', and even 're-localization'. Globalization involves processes of movement in population (e.g., migrant labour), skills, capital, technology and technical knowledge, and also symbolic representations (e.g., notions of 'modernization' and 'globalization' itself, and new concepts of 'citizenship' such as that of the European Union). Localization involves the interplay between local forms of knowledge and external pressures, while re-localization involves the assertion, rediscovery, or invention of locally based knowledge, especially knowledge which can be used in agrarian economic and social development. Long argues for actor-centred research on these issues.

In the same volume, Aihwa Ong (1996) hints at the fallacy in seeing all aspects of globalization, modernization, and industrialization as the same thing, and explicitly opposes the yet bigger fallacy of equating any of these simply with Western culture. Take modernization: China has been in the process of modernizing for a very long time; and the process of modernization and even industrialization in Japan began, not with Commodore Matthew Perry's visit in 1853 (as American school children are taught), but as an ultimate consequence of the expansion of trade from China throughout East and Southeast Asia over a long period.

The true 'postmodern condition', to my mind, is reflected in Marc Augé's (1995 [1992]) intriguing study of the globalized 'non-space' of refugee camps, international hotels, motorways, and airport lounges. As a theme promoted by both evolutionist and postmodernist anthropology as well as a topic visible to anthropologists whenever they do fieldwork or even attend conferences, globalization is a popular and timely concern. The irony is that in theoretical terms it might as easily be seen as most akin to the least trendy of all theoretical perspectives, diffusionism.

Postmodernism and postmodern anthropology

Postmodernism constitutes a critique of all 'modern' understandings. Postmodernists define what is 'modernist' as what is all-encompassing; they reject both grand theory in anthropology and the notion of completeness in ethnographic description. On the latter score, they oppose the presumption of ethnological authority on the part of the anthropologist. Thus reflexivity, and ultimately embodiment, came to the fore. In a wider sense, postmodernist anthropology takes its cue from critical studies of 'orientalist' writing and levels its critique at the creation of the 'other' (and consequent definition of the 'self') as the driving force of all previous positions in the discipline. Postmodernism is also a logical development of both relativism and interpretivism, so much so that it is difficult to isolate these perspectives except superficially – by chronology, vocabulary, or style of writing.

The return to relativism

In a provocative article, Sjaak van der Geest (1990) has suggested that relativism itself is a dogma, not the absence of one. Anthropologists propagate relativism against the cognitive certainties both of those from alien cultures which they study and of non-anthropologists from their own cultures. Yet anthropology has, within the last decade, returned from mildly relativistic notions that each culture has its own value system or semantic structure to stronger views reminiscent of those of Benedict and Whorf. Only now these are couched in the jargon of postmodernism and devoid of any theory of culture as a whole. All this highlights the fact that 'relativism' is not really a monolithic concept (see also chapter 7). The term designates a myriad of theoretical fragments carved from the rock of Boasian anthropology. Yet Boasianism, in one form or another, remains a touchstone to many in American anthropology, both those who oppose relativist dogma and those who espouse insights brought more recently from newer trends in thinking about the relation between anthropology and its objects of study.

Postmodernism came into anthropology long after its early use in studies of art and the practice of architecture. In those fields, from the late 1950s, the term characterized a rejection of formal principles of style and the admission of unlikely blends and especially of local variation. In the social sciences, including anthropology, the term recalls the definition put forward by Jean-François Lyotard, Professor of Philosophy at the Université de Paris VIII (Vincennes), in his report to the government of Quebec on the 'postmodern condition': 'Simplifying to the extreme, I define *postmodern* as incredulity toward metanarratives' (Lyotard 1984 [1979]: xxiv).

In anthropology, following from this, postmodernism involves a rejection both of grand theoretical truth and of the wholeness of ethnographic reality. In other words, to a postmodern anthropologist there is no true, complete statement that can be made about a culture. Nor, for many, can we even come up with an approximation. Therefore, grand theory (what Lyotard calls 'metanarrative') is doomed – except, it seems, the metanarrative of postmodernism itself!

'Writing culture'

Anthropology's premier postmodernist text is *Writing Culture* (Clifford and Marcus 1986), based on a conference on 'The Making of Ethnographic Texts', held in Santa Fe, New Mexico in 1984 (see also Marcus and Clifford 1985). Eight practising anthropologists, a historian of anthropology (James Clifford), and a literary critic (Mary Louise Pratt) presented papers there, and all but one of these appears in the celebrated volume (the missing paper was by Robert Thornton). The unifying theme of *Writing Culture* is a consideration of literary methods within anthropological discourse, though the authors hold a range of views from moderate to radical on the subject. A number of contributors also examine the intrusion of power relations in the ethnographic process. It is worth touching very briefly on each.

James Clifford, in his introduction, attacks the idea of ethnography as a representation of the wholeness of culture and stresses the incompleteness of ethnographic expression, even in the hands of indigenous scholars. He argues for an appreciation of ethnography as writing, but rejects the extremist view that it is only writing or that the recognition of ethnography as a kind of 'poetry' precludes objectivity. His substantive contribution, on 'ethnographic allegory', is decidedly literary in character, and focuses on 'the *narrative* character of cultural representations' (Clifford 1986: 100). George Marcus also offers a literary analysis, but in his case invoking world-systems theory to unmask the 'authority' of the author; and in his afterword he comments briefly on the challenge he believes the Santa Fe conference has given the discipline.

Mary Louise Pratt discusses some diverse ethnographies; she advocates the 'fusion' of object and subjective understandings and the re-examination, on the part of ethnographers, of their enterprise in light of historical precedent and literary genre. Vincent Crapanzano looks at the problems of translation in three quite different texts, including an eighteenth-century one, a nineteenth-century one, and one by Geertz (on the Balinese cockfight). Renato Rosaldo looks at modes of authority in two texts, including Evans-Pritchard's *The Nuer*; and Talal Asad takes as his object of 'translation' an essay by Ernest Gellner on 'translation' in the British anthropological tradition, notably in *Nuer Religion*.

Michael Fischer looks at the dynamism of ethnicity, which, he says, must be re-invented in each generation. Paul Rabinow takes on textual construction in Geertz's interpretivism and Clifford's 'textual meta-anthropology', along with other examples, to illustrate that representations are social facts. Stephen Tyler, a convert from cognitive anthropology, here speaks with the strongest postmodern voice. He comments on the death of scientific thought and celebrates the fragmentary nature of a would-be postmodern ethnography. The latter, he says, aims at a 'discourse', that is, a dialogue, as opposed to the former monologue of the ethnographic 'text'. However, he laments that no postmodern ethnography exists, while asserting at the same time that 'all ethnography is post-modern in effect' (Tyler 1986: 136).

Since *Writing Culture*, a number of anthropologists, both those involved in that project and others, have continued the discourse. Notable examples are Marcus and Fischer's (1986) attempt to justify the experimental and critical nature of recent anthropological writing; Clifford's (1988) treatise on twentieth-century ethnography, literature, and art; Michael Taussig's (1993) highly original study of imitation and the construction of alterity in the self/other opposition; and some of Rabinow's (1997) collected essays. The tempered search for connections figures prominently in the work of Marilyn Strathern (e.g., 1991; 1992), one of the leading anthropologists in Britain today. She argues, among other things, that partial connections are necessary because the amount of data anthropologists have to hand is too great to treat in any other way. American sociologist Norman Denzin (1997) sums up postmodern ethnography as a 'moral discourse'. He says that ethnographers should move beyond the traditional, objective forms of writing about peoples to more experimental and experiential texts, including autobiography and performance-based media; towards greater expression of emotion; to fictionalization, thereby expressing poetic and narrative truth, as opposed to scientific truth; and also towards lived experience, praxis, and multiple points of view.

Postmodernists often stress the arbitrary in culture, descriptions of culture, and theorizing about culture. When commenting on postmodernism itself, postmodernists tend to invoke reflexivity. As Crapanzano (1992: 88) puts it, 'Not only is the arbitrariness of the sign in any act of signification paradigmatically proclaimed but so is the arbitrariness of its syntagmatic, its syntactic, placement.' In other words, whereas some poststructuralists (notably Bourdieu) oppose Saussurian distinctions altogether, here Crapanzano, a decided postmodernist, expands the Saussurian notion of arbitrariness to cover not only signs themselves, but even signs in relation to other signs. For postmodernists, one's vantage point is arbitrary. Therefore the distinction which Saussure, and virtually every linguist and anthropologist since have recognized, that between observer and observed, is called into question.

For reflexivists and other, less self-centred late interpretivists, the nomothetic and the ideographic (see Radcliffe-Brown 1952: 1) blend to form an unbounded mix. Ethnography and theory, and observer and observed (or collective self and collective other), become almost indistinguishable in the course of an anthropological text. It is perhaps no accident that the ethnography of Europeans by Europeans, or of Americans by Americans, form good examples of this genre. Michael Herzfeld (a Harvard-based Englishman who writes on Greeks) epitomizes the soft postmodern tradition in anthropology. His *Anthropology Through the Looking Glass* (Herzfeld 1987) ranges from critiques of more formal and positivistic anthropological theory and exaltations of earlier wisdom, to discussions of contradictions within Greek culture and, more important- ly, contradictions within the anthropological distinctions between self and other and observer and observed. It presents itself as a search for connections which override the contradictions. Herzfeld here draws heavily on the definitive third edition of the *New Science* of Gimbattista Vico (for an English translation, see Pompa 1982 [Vico 1744]: 159–267), an eighteenth-century Italian philosopher, little read in his time, who tried to understand the relations between entities such as history and social evolution, nationhood and religion.

Recent work on the theory of tropes, including metaphor, metonymy, synecdoche, and irony is equally relevant to the postmodernist quest, and James Fernandez (e.g., 1986) of the University of Chicago is the leading proponent of this idea. I read his ethnography of the Fang of Gabon as a search for the deep emic, and therefore within the grand anthropological tradition which includes Malinowski and Boas (as well as Geertz). The spirit of David M. Schneider, great Chicago interpreter of the divergent symbolism of American and Yapese kinship, seems to be there too (see especially Schneider 1980 [1968]; 1984). Often borrowing new ideas from linguistics (e.g., Lakoff and Johnson 1980), Fernandez and the contribu- tors to his edited collection on tropes (Fernandez 1991) see culture as a constant and complex play of tropes. However, whereas George Lakoff and Mark Johnson argued that people map the unfamiliar onto the familiar to create new understanding, Naomi Quinn (1991), for example, argues essentially the reverse. Metaphors are based on culturally agreed understandings, and more often than not they add complexity rather than clarity. For her, as for generations of anthropologists before her, it is culture that is central.

Problems with postmodernism

In one of his many brilliant polemics, the late British philosopher-anthro- pologist, Ernest Gellner (1992: 22–79), attacked relativism and post- modernism as subjectivist and self-indulgent. Postmodernism is the most prevalent form of relativism today, and Gellner saw it as especially prob- lematic in its misplaced attacks on, for example, the stated objectivism of European colonial ethnography. For postmodernists, ethnography in the colonial era represented a tool in the hands of oppressive colonial govern- ments and multi-national corporations. For the anti-postmodernist, post- modernism's attempt to liberate anthropology is misguided, its attacks on earlier anthropological traditions misplaced, and its subjectivity down- right nonsensical. The postmodernist, says Gellner, sees anthropology as a movement from positivism (to postmodernists, a belief in objective facts) to hermeneutics (i.e., interpretation). Yet the postmodernist movement is really a replay of the romanticist one two centuries before, in their overthrow of the classical order of Enlightened Europe. Gellner goes on to attack the contributions to *Writing Culture* for their lack of precision. He concludes: 'In the end, the operational meaning of postmodernism in anthropology seems to be something like this: a refusal (in practice, rather selective) to countenance any objective facts, any independent social structures, and their replacement by a pursuit of meanings, both those of the objects of inquiry and of the inquirer' (1992: 29).

Rabinow and Clifford bear the brunt of Gellner's criticisms, but he blames Geertz for the origins of the obsession with hermeneutics and takes his philosopher's knife to Geertz's (1984) defence of relativism.

Geertz has encouraged a whole generation of anthropologists to parade their real or invented inner qualms and paralysis, using the invocation of the epistemological doubt and cramp as a justification of utmost obscurity and subjectivism (the main stylistic marks of 'postmodernism'). They agonize so much about their inability to know themselves and the Other, at any level of regress, that they no longer need to trouble too much about the Other. If everything in the world is fragmented and multiform, nothing really resembles anything else, and no one can know another (or himself), and no one can communicate, what is there to do other than express the anguish engendered by this situation in impenetrable prose? (Gellner 1992: 45)

Let me sum up the interpretivist and postmodernist enterprises. To soft postmodernists (including Geertzian interpretivists), society is like a text, to be 'read' by the ethnographer as surely as his own text will be read by his readers. Other postmodernists seem to see culture as 'shreds and patches' (to borrow Lowie's phrase) – each shred and each patch, a play on another one. To some, culture is a series of word plays or 'tropes'. Ethnography is much the same thing, and anthropological theory is little more. According to most adherents of these schools, there should be no grand theory and no grand analogy – except that culture is in some unspecified way 'like a text'. The question I would raise about all interpretivist approaches, to a greater or lesser degree, is what they think anthropology would be like if *their* metanarrative were true? Everything is relative; there is no truth in ethnography. Anthropology should dissolve into literary criticism, or at best into that brand of literary criticism that has taken over a big piece of anthropology's subject matter – cultural studies (see, e.g., Bratlinger 1990).

Yet there seems to be a subtle battle among interpretivists and postmodernists generally. One side sees ethnography as an end in itself, or rather an attempt to understand, but one which never quite reaches the level of understanding previously claimed for it. These anthropologists try to understand the human condition through detail, even the detail of ethnographic activity. Radical reflexivists are happy to write more about themselves doing ethnography than about the ethnographees, their subjects. This is the most extreme of all ideographic approaches: ethnography (writing about people) and ethnographic method (doing fieldwork) merge into one. While anthropology as a whole has taken on board and greatly benefited from recent discussions of reflexivity, it is nevertheless important to distinguish this strong version of the phenomenon from the simple awareness of the role of the ethnographer as a social actor as well as a gatherer of data.

The other side sees ethnography as a means to an end, a means to build a wider understanding of human nature. For these anthropologists, interpretivist in temperament and influenced by the more positive aspects of the postmodern critique, there is hope. They may borrow freely from evolutionism and functionalism, from structural Marxism or from biological anthropology. Theirs is a discipline of nomothetic inquiry. In the last section here, I will examine the possibilities for an anthropology in the latter image.

Mixed approaches: towards a compromise?

Robert Layton (1997: 157–215) characterizes present-day anthropology as polarized between socio-ecology and postmodernism. I believe that this characterization, while it has much truth, is too extreme. More and more, anthropologists are showing that they are happy to mix approaches and take from different theoretical traditions. This has been going on at least since the 1950s.

My preference is to look at new developments since the 1950s in terms of three strands of thinking: structural, interactive, and interpretive. These strands are not mutually exclusive. On the contrary, in the hands of diverse theorists and ethnographers, they are intertwined, overlapping, intersecting. While Lévi-Straussian structuralism is concerned unambiguously with structure, transactionalism overwhelmingly with interaction, and Geertzian interpretivism at least primarily with interpretation, there is nevertheless great potential to aim for an understanding which draws on two or even three. Some recent writers, such as Anthony Cohen (e.g., 1985; 1994), have blended interpretive and interactive interests. Edmund Leach (1954), Victor Turner (1957), and Pierre Bourdieu (1977 [1972]) have emphasized both structure and action in their analyses of social process. Roy Willis (1974), Rodney Needham (1979), and a number of others, have mixed structure and interpretation. Some of Ladislav

Holy and Milan Stuchlik's work makes good use of all three within a single paradigm (e.g., Holy and Stuchlik 1983). The simple answer, then, is that the future of anthropology may lie in the blending of approaches. Sociologists, and some anthropologists, like to think in terms of the three great social theorists – Marx, Durkheim, and Weber. They are like primary colours. You can mix them, or rather mix different strands of their thinking, to come up with almost any theoretical position.

Of course, things may not be quite as simple as this. Italian anthropologist Carla Pasquinelli (1996) has suggested a different interpretation, specifically on the concept of 'culture'. She points out that this concept is quintessentially 'modern' in that it is what modernists employ to define the pre-modern 'other'. It arose within evolutionist theory and remained powerful right through what she sees as the three phases of anthropological thinking: the material phase (concerned with customs and traceable from Tylor to Boas), the abstract phase (concerned with patterns, e.g., Kroeber and Kluckhohn), and the symbolic phase (concerned with meaning and typified by Geertz). However, she argues, Geertz's position is liminal, as he sees culture as 'local knowledge', dispersed and fragmentary (i.e., postmodern), while nevertheless seeking, through 'thick description', the totality of culture which Tylor championed (i.e., modern). The break comes with James Clifford (e.g., 1988), who overthrows the object (culture) in favour of the subjectivity of narrative (i.e., of the ethnographer).

But can there be anthropology without an object? If we are not studying culture or society, what then is cultural or social anthropology? This, in my view, is the dilemma postmodernism has left for the present generation (cf. Strathern 1987b; Fox 1991). At the risk of stating the obvious, throughout this book I hope I have shown that cultural anthropology remains a field of diverse viewpoints. The present generation can take its pick between innovative work within the evolutionist school, it can still lift ideas from structuralist or processualist theories to suit new purposes, or it can accept wholeheartedly the postmodern condition if it is prepared for the consequences. The blending of old ideas, of all sorts, seems the safest bet.

Concluding summary

Interpretivism and postmodernism fit into anthropology in a very straightforward way, as aspects of a time-honoured set of analogies between language and culture. An understanding of that relationship, and its historical transformation, lies at the root of new developments in anthropology and in other social sciences.

Anthropological theory has paralleled linguistic theory in uncanny ways through its history. This is not simply fortuitous. Rather it has been recognized and utilized by generations of anthropologists through linguistic and related analogies. Analogy expresses form, but anthropology also shares some content with linguistics, both in that language is an aspect of culture and in that debates on language and writing have become prominent in anthropology itself. It is commonplace to talk of the 'linguistic analogy', though it might be more accurate to think of a set of linguistic analogies which have competed both against each other and against other analogies (the biological analogy, for example) through much of the history of anthropology.

Lévi-Strauss (1963 [1952]: 67–8) once drew attention to three levels of relations between linguistics and cultural anthropology: the relation between a language and a culture, that between language and culture in the abstract, and that between the two disciplines. I would choose a different set of relations to cover the whole realm of linguistic ideas within cultural anthropology: society or culture as grammar, ethnography as translation, and society and ethnography as 'discourse'.

The analogy of grammar was implicit in the work of Radcliffe-Brown and his followers, though they tended to speak more of anthropology as like biology and societies as 'organisms' than of anthropology as like linguistics and culture as 'language'. Later it was made explicit by Lévi-Strauss and structuralist anthropologists generally. For them culture and society have at their root a form which is analogous to the grammar of language. This may be a specific cultural grammar, or (in much of Lévi-Strauss' work), it may be a universal grammar held in common between all cultures.

The analogy of translation was implicit, and occasionally explicit, in the work of Evans-Pritchard. It is still more explicit in the work of Geertz with his notion of religion as a cultural system (Geertz 1966) and in his collections on 'interpretive anthropology' (1973; 1983). For Evans-Pritchard alien cultures are like foreign languages, to be 'translated' into terms familiar in the 'language' of one's own culture. For Geertz, culture is embodied in the symbols through which people communicate. Geertz has moved away from cognitive anthropology and its concerns with thought in the abstract, towards an understanding of action from the actor's point of view. In this he shares much with his early mentor, sociologist Talcott Parsons (e.g., 1949 [1937]), also with processual and action-oriented anthropologists, notably Victor Turner (e.g., 1967), and to some extent with the proponents of the 'embodiment' perspective to the study of ritual.

The discourse analogy, borrowed from Foucault (e.g., 1974 [1969]), features prominently in social anthropology, especially but not exclusively in the work of those who see themselves as part of the postmodern project. Anthropology itself is a discourse. The older, modern anthropologies are discourses partly representing the interests of the segments of society from which they stem. Yet it would be too simplistic to define functionalism, for example, simply as a discourse produced by the British colonial enterprise (cf. Asad 1973). Rather, it is more meaningful to view anthropology throughout its history as a discourse on the human condition, played out in a dialogue between those under the scrutiny of anthropologists on the one hand, and the anthropologists themselves on the other. This view would unite postmodern and modern anthropology in a common enterprise – indeed one consistent with the definition of anthropology given in the first edition of the *Encyclopaedia Britannica* (1771: 1, 327): 'ANTHROPOLOGY, a discourse upon human nature'.

FURTHER READING

Douglas' *Evans-Pritchard* (1980) is the best guide to the basics of that thinker's anthropology. See also Pals' *Seven Theories of Religion* (1996), which contains interesting essays on both Evans-Pritchard and Geertz. Geertz's own *Works and Lives* (1988) makes stimulating reading on the ideas of a number of the other major anthropologists. The most important of Geertz's works though are his two collections of essays (1973; 1983). See also Shankman's essay 'The thick and the thin' (1984).

Knauft's excellent *Genealogies for the Present* (1996) reviews the debates in postmodernist anthropology and other recent trends. Lechte's *Fifty Key Contemporary Thinkers* (1994) is a useful guide to the ideas of structuralist, poststructuralist, and postmodernist thinkers, mainly outside anthropology but who have influenced our discipline. There are many guides to postmodernism in general, among the most interesting is Smart's *Postmodernism* (1993). On cultural studies and theoretical ideas within related fields, see Milner's *Contemporary Cultural Theory* (1994).

H. L. Moore's essay 'Master narratives: anthropology and writing' (1994 [1993]: 107–28) offers a stimulating and highly readable review of the problem of writing. See also James, Hockey, and Dawson's edited volume *After Writing Culture* (1997) for further British approaches to the problems highlighted in *Writing Culture* (Clifford and Marcus 1986). A similar edited collection touching on reflexivity is Okely and Callaway's *Anthropology and Autobiography* (1992).

11 Conclusions

This book has dealt with the 'content' of anthropological theory. Yet anthropological theory is not a vessel to be emptied of old ideas and filled with new ones, or stuffed with more virulent paradigms to strangle the weak ones. Anthropological theory undoubtedly has 'form' as well as content, and in this final chapter we shall focus initially on the question of what form this might be, then return to the issue of the relation between form and content, first with some reflections on the future of anthropological ideas and then with a concluding summary.

National traditions and the future of anthropological theory

It is commonplace to think of anthropology in terms of national traditions, and often useful to do so. I think it is especially useful when trying to envisage the roots of and relations between the Boasian and Malinowskian/Radcliffe-Brownian traditions, and also the relation between anthropology and sociology (which at least had the potential to become part of our discipline, or ours part of theirs). Each new development is partly the product of individual thinking, of course, but also very much the product of the circumstances in which these thinkers found themselves. Some of these circumstances were, in fact, single events or clusters of events occurring at around the same time. Among dates to remember, I would pick out 1748 (which marks the publication of Montesquieu's highly influential book, *The Spirit of the Laws*), 1871 (the date of publication of numerous important works, and that of the founding of the Anthropological Institute), 1896 (when Boas established anthropology at Columbia University), and 1922 (Rivers' death, the publication of important works by Malinowski and Radcliffe-Brown, and the approximate date each of them began teaching in earnest their functional theories). Figure 11.1 illustrates this vision of the history of anthropology, together with the development of sociology and the false start of the mainly German philological tradition.

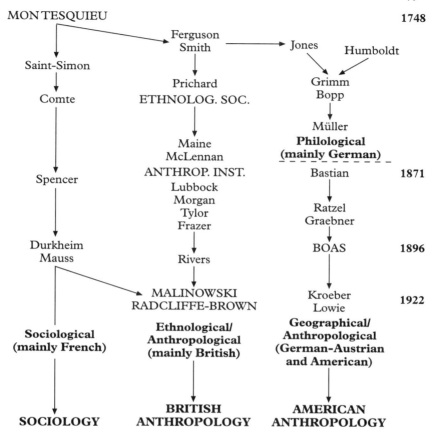

MONTESQUIEU   **1748**

Figure 11.1 Three traditions

That said, it is not always easy to define traditions in anthropology along national lines. Fortes more than once remarked that modern social anthropology contains 'two distinct lines of descent':

> I see one as going back through Radcliffe-Brown, Lowie, and Rivers, to Morgan and Maine in particular, and the other as going back through Kroeber, Malinowski, and Frazer, to Tylor and to some extent Boas. I see the first line as the source of our structural concepts and theories, the second as the source of our speciality in the study of facts of custom, or culture. (Fortes 1969: 14)

This confounds the notion that American anthropology is the tradition concerned with culture, while British anthropology is the tradition concerned with society (Radcliffe-Brown, Rivers, Maine, Malinowski,

Frazer, and Tylor were British; and Lowie, Morgan, Kroeber, and Boas were American). Fortes went on to say that in the metaphorically 'double descent system' which makes up anthropology, each anthropologist belongs to both descent groups and takes from each according to the task at hand.

Integration of all theoretical approaches is one logical possibility. However, it is not likely that a single agreed paradigm will emerge, at least in the short term. What is likely is that there will be an integration of ideas on the part of individuals. This has been in practice for many years, beginning with people such as Edmund Leach (with his blend of structuralist and action-oriented ideas). Nowadays many anthropologists fall, at times, within the scope of more than one paradigm, and some blend two or more. Very broadly three contemporary approaches or emphases may be noted: interpretation, action, and structure. The relation between paradigms associated with such approaches has already been noted (in chapter 10), but others may be possibilities. For example, another set sometimes discussed is that of structure, event, and history (see Augé 1982 [1979]). In their different ways, regional comparison and Marxism may be said to have elements of both structure and history, whereas other approaches could potentially mix event with either of these two (see Holy and Stuchlik 1983).

Today there are a great number of theoretical perspectives for anthropologists to choose from, and these are each made up of many lines of influence. The possibilities for combining them are enormous. This is a positive and truly postmodern tendency. The danger is that the narrower postmodernist project might hold sway, with non-postmodernly correct positions being rejected simply because they make explicit their pre-postmodern origins. However, the acceptance of a diversity of approaches – with the utilization of theoretical ideas according to topic of concern – is at least as old as the early relativism of Franz Boas. Indeed, even before that, anthropologists were free to accept other influences and combine perspectives. For example, Morgan and Tylor happily incorporated diffusionist elements into their specific unilinear-evolutionist schemes.

Anthropologists also operate at different levels of theory: in grand theory, in middle range theory, and increasingly in specific theoretical debates. Anthropology as a whole (including biological as well as cultural anthropology) retains a long-standing concern with two quite different problems: the understanding of human nature and the study of cultural diversity. In the eighteenth-century Enlightenment the former was the main interest. With the development of anthropology proper, in the nineteenth century, cultural diversity became prominent in the hands of the polygenists. Later it came to be what unilinear evolutionism was trying to explain. With Boas and the early relativists, diversity was extolled as a wonder of humanity, and it has seen some resurgence in recent years. Since the 1970s, relativism has come back and swamped both the old functionalist interests in social laws and the structuralist (including structural-Marxist) interests in cultural universals.

Further thoughts on histories of anthropology

Can there ever be a true history of a discipline? Or, the converse, is all history 'Whig history'? I think there are good grounds for favouring the latter, inherently relativistic, view, or at least for admitting that whenever anthropologists put pen to paper they will come out with a somewhat Whiggish version of events. 'Whig history' is a phrase coined by Sir Herbert Butterfield around 1931, when he said that historians have all too often seen history as a conflict between progressives and reactionaries, where the progressives (Whigs) eventually win and bring about changes effecting the present situation. Whig history is thus subjective and 'presentist', and that is why true historians do not like it (see, e.g., Stocking 1968 [1965]: 1-12). Good history, they say, is 'historicist', in a very precise sense of that word.

Yet much of the history of anthropology, especially that written by practising anthropologists, is presentist because that history is relevant to today's concerns. It is also, in the hands of several practitioners, *mythical* in the sense that Malinowski (1948 [1925]: 79, 120) used the word. By this I mean that history gives anthropologists a 'mythical charter' by which to view their own place in the discipline. I would not deny that my own history of the discipline is somewhat 'mythical', 'presentist', and 'Whiggish'. Such a heretical view is acceptable to me because in this book I do not claim to be presenting *the history* of anthropology, but only one possible history among many. More accurately, I am presenting snippets of history chosen and juxtaposed to show the complex connections among the different ideas which make up, not the history of anthropology, but anthropological theory.

There are other possible histories, and there can be more complex uses of history to illustrate ideas. The simple 'great man' view is found in many books, for example, in Adam Kuper's *Anthropology and Anthropologists* (1996 [1973]) or Jerry Moore's *Visions of Culture* (1997). In contrast, L. R. Hiatt chooses a unique method of historical portrayal in *Arguments about Aborigines* (Hiatt 1996). He focuses on aspects of Aboriginal society (gender relations, conception beliefs, political organization, land issues, etc.) and the ways in which each has been interpreted by successive generations of anthropologists.

In *A Century of Controversy* Elman Service (1985) focuses on the specifics of anthropological debate, with issues like the status of kinship terminologies or the nature of culture coming to the forefront. Murray Leaf, in *Man, Mind, and Science* (1979), virtually sets aside anthropological debate in favour of a history of anthropology seen in terms of philosophical questions. Robert Layton's recent book, *An Introduction to Theory in Anthropology* (1997), lies in-between. Layton touches on both debates and philosophical questions (as well as questions of ethnographic interpretation), but largely ignores pre-functionalist anthropology and downplays national traditions. Jack Goody's *The Expansive Moment* (1995) and Henrika Kuklick's *The Savage Within* (1991) present social histories of British anthropology, but they differ profoundly in method and the interpretation of that history. James Urry, in *Before Social Anthropology* (1993), blends several approaches, as his is a collection of his own diverse essays on the history of British anthropology.

This list is certainly not exhaustive, but it gives some idea of the range of possibilities that have, to date, been realized. I hope also that it confirms my feeling that there is no such thing as *the* history of anthropology, any more than an ethnographer today could claim to be writing *the* ethnography of his or her 'people'.

Concluding summary

I do not accept that old anthropological theories die with their proponents. Rather, I hold that in general they are either incorporated into new theoretical trends, or they return in some later generation in a different guise. The foundations of our discipline were there in the Enlightenment, especially in the notion of the social contract (the seventeenth- and eighteenth-century basis of all social science), but the discipline itself emerged in the nineteenth century. The arguments of early theorists remain worthy of close scrutiny, partly because they illustrate so well the character of incipient and past anthropology. They are important equally because anthropologists of later times, and even today, define their own positions in relation to those of earlier writers – either in opposition to them or, not uncommonly, in the augmentation and transformation of their theoretical notions.

Evolutionism is often thought of as a nineteenth-century theory. But then, what about the preconceptions of the late twentieth century? Evolution is not entirely unrelated to the commonplace idea of progress or to the notion of social development. 'Progress', in fact, was a very nineteenth-century concept, and it is retained in our thinking today. The word 'development', with its present-day meaning of helping out people in poorer countries to be economically, at least, more like people in richer countries, is only about forty or fifty years old. Yet in some respects, this concept represents a re-invention of Victorian evolutionary theory. It suggests similar ways of thinking about relations between technology, economics, and society to those pursued by nineteenth-century reformers and social theorists. What many nineteenth- and late twentieth-century anthropologists have in common is a desire to understand causal relationships within a framework of 'progress' or 'advancement'. Some late twentieth-century anthropologists have even taken up the search for human cultural origins, and this represents a promising development – given especially the much greater sophistication of relevant cognate disciplines, such as archaeology, linguistics, and human genetics.

Diffusionism in its pure and extreme forms is long dead, but ideas which grew from diffusionist schools, such as an interest in historical particularities and the notion of the culture area, have, if anything, increased in importance in the last few decades. Regional studies within various theoretical traditions are also increasing in prominence, as anthropological studies focus more on similarities and differences between closely related cultures. The increase in regional focus stems directly from the sheer number of ethnographic studies done by modern anthropologists.

Relativism has been a prominent feature of anthropological traditions, especially in North America, since Boas. In a sense, all anthropology is relativistic, as by its very nature the study of variety in human culture does, or at least should, lead to an appreciation of cultures in their own terms. This does not mean that all anthropologists are relativists in any pure sense. On the contrary, both 'pro' and 'anti' positions on relativism are prominent today, and the new relativism of reflexivity and discourse analysis stems not only from a renewal of interest in Boasian ideas, but equally from the influence of interdisciplinary postmodernist foci.

Functionalism, like diffusionism, is a word few anthropologists would be associated with today. However, functionalist methodology remains the basis of anthropological fieldwork. As Edmund Leach used to say, all anthropologists are functionalists when in the field, because they need to see how social institutions are related and how individuals interact with one another. When anthropologists return from the field to their respective universities, he claimed, they reformulate their ideas in frameworks which go beyond functionalism. In Leach's own case, this resulted in a mixture of structuralism and processualism. For others, it results in different mixes, but the functionalist basis of anthropology itself, like its relativist basis, is still there.

Structuralism achieved great notoriety, thanks especially to the work of Lévi-Strauss, which was influential well beyond the boundaries of anthropology. Within anthropology, Marxist thought frequently had a strong structuralist element. Regional comparison as a theoretical paradigm took much from Lévi-Straussian structuralism and from the Dutch school which preceded it. To some extent too, interpretivist and postmodern perspectives build on structuralism and functionalism precisely by making explicit their rejection of the tenets of these earlier paradigms. They depend, at least in anthropology (perhaps less so in literary criticism, for example), on their own structural opposition to structuralism itself.

Processual and interactive approaches had their heyday in the immediate post-functionalist era, but they too have strengthened with each challenge to the conservatism of static approaches of all kinds. Probably they will never die, as all anthropologists now realize that they must take account of the nuances of social interaction and social change. Processual approaches offered a good antidote to overly formal ideas within functionalism and structuralism. They also enabled function-minded and structurally inclined anthropologists to look more closely at the nuances of social life through their studies of relations between different social or symbolic structures.

Early British interpretive approaches, such as the diverse ones of Evans-Pritchard, Needham, and Ardener at Oxford, built upon functionalism and structuralism while rejecting the analogies on which they are based. They sought structures which are intuitive, and encouraged scepticism of formal approaches and universalistic comparisons. Postmodernist, poststructuralist, feminist, and Marxist approaches all amplify this through their emphasis on the relation between the culture of the anthropologist and the culture of the informant, and more particularly on the relationship between anthropologist and informant as people, each with their own understanding of the other. An added dimension is that the anthropologist, knowing this, must reinterpret his or her own actions and consciousness of purpose in the very process of engagement with the 'other'.

Finally, it is worth reiterating the fact that anthropology is a discipline very conscious of its past. Anthropological theory has a complex history, but its structure can be seen through the influences of individuals, the interplay within and between national traditions, and the development of new foci of interest, new ideas from within and from beyond anthropology itself, and (every few decades) new grand perspectives. Yet there are many ways in which to envisage that history and these relationships. I have put them together in the way that I read them. Others may read, interpret, construct, or deconstruct them differently.

Appendix 1
Dates of birth and death of individuals mentioned in the text

Albert, Prince (Franz Albrecht, Prinz von Sachsen-Coburg-Gotha), 1819–61
Althusser, Louis, 1918–90
Ardener, Edwin, 1927–87
Aristotle, 384–322 BC
Asad, Talal, 1927–
Atran, Scott, 1952–
Avebury, Lord, see Lubbock, Sir John, Bt.

Bachofen, J. J., 1815–77
Bailey, F. G., 1924–
Barnes, J. A., 1918–
Barth, Fredrik, 1928–
Bastian, Adolph, 1826–1905
Bateson, Gregory, 1904–80
Bateson, William, 1861–1926
Benedict, Ruth Fulton, 1887–1948
Bentham, Jeremy, 1748–1832
Binford, Lewis R., 1930–
Boas, Franz, 1858–1942
Boissevain, Jeremy, 1928–
Bopp, Franz, 1791–1867
Bourdieu, Pierre, 1930–
Buffon, Georges-Louis Leclerc, comte de, 1707–88
Bunzel, Ruth, 1898–1990
Burke, William, 1792–1829
Burnett (Burnet), James, see Monboddo, Lord
Butterfield, Sir Herbert, 1900–79
Buxton, Sir Thomas Fowell, Bt., 1786–1845

Caplan, Pat, 1942–
Carrier, James G., 1947–

Chagnon, Napoleon A., 1938–
Childe, V. Gordon, 1892–1957
Chomsky, Noam, 1928–
Clifford, James, 1945–
Cohen, Anthony P., 1946–
Colson, Elizabeth, 1917–
Comaroff, Jean, 1946–
Comaroff, John, 1945–
Comte, Auguste, 1798–1857
Cook, Captain James, 1728–79
Crapanzano, Vincent, 1939–
Cushing, Frank, 1857–1900

Darwin, Charles, 1809–82
De Groot, Huig, see Grotius, Hugo
De Heusch, Luc, 1927–
De Saussure, Ferdinand, see Saussure, Ferdinand de
Denzin, Norman K., 1941–
Derrida, Jacques, 1930–
Douglas, Mary, 1921–
Dryden, John, 1631–1700
Dumont, Louis, 1911–98
Durkheim, Emile, 1858–1917

Eggan, Fred, 1906–91
Einstein, Albert, 1879–1955
Elkin, A. P., 1891–1979
Elliot Smith, Sir Grafton, 1871–1937
Engels, Friedrich, 1820–95
Epstein, A. L. (Bill), 1924–
Epstein, T. S. (Scarlett), 1922–
Evans-Pritchard, Sir Edward E., 1902–73

Fardon, Richard, 1952–
Ferguson, Adam, 1723–1816
Fernandez, James W., 1930–
Firth, Sir Raymond, 1902–
Fischer, Michael M. J., 1946–
Fortes, Meyer, 1906–83
Fortune, Reo F., 1903–79
Foucault, Michel, 1926–84
Fox, Robin, 1934–

Frake, Charles O., 1930–
Frank, Andre Gunder, 1929–
Frazer, Sir James, 1854–1941
Freeman, J. Derek, 1916–
Freud, Sigmund, 1856–1939
Friedman, Jonathan, 1946–
Frobenius, Leo, 1873–1938

Geertz, Clifford, 1926–
Gellner, Ernest, 1925–95
George I, King of Great Britain and Elector of Hanover,
    1660–1727
Gluckman, Max, 1911–75
Godelier, Maurice, 1934–
Goodenough, Ward H., 1919–
Goody, Jack, 1919–
Graebner, Fritz, 1877–1934
Granet, Marcel, 1884–1940
Grimm, Jacob, 1785–1863
Grimm, Wilhelm, 1786–1859
Grotius, Hugo (Huig de Groot), 1583–1645

Hare, William, d. 1860
Harris, Marvin, 1929–
Hastrup, Kirsten, 1948–
Helman, Cecil, 1944–
Herder, Johann Gottfried von, 1744–1803
Herskovits, Melville J., 1895–1963
Hertz, Robert, 1881–1915
Herzfeld, Michael, 1947–
Heyerdahl, Thor, 1914–
Hiatt, L. R., 1931–
Hjelmslev, Louis, 1899–1965
Hobbes, Thomas, 1588–1679
Hodgkin, Thomas, 1798–1866
Holy, Ladislav, 1933–97
Home, Henry, see Kames, Lord
Humboldt, Alexander von, 1769–1859
Humboldt, Wilhelm von, 1767–1835
Hume, David, 1711–76
Hunt, James, 1833–69
Hunter, Monica, see Wilson, Monica

Ingold, Tim, 1948–

Jakobson, Roman Osipovich, 1896–1982
Jones, Sir William, 1746–94
Josselin de Jong, J. P. B. de, 1886–1964

Kaberry, Phyllis M., 1910–77
Kames, Lord (Henry Home), 1696–1782
Kapferer, Bruce, 1940–
Kardiner, Abram, 1891–1981
Kenyatta, Jomo (Johnstone Kemau), 1889–1978
Kluckhohn, Clyde, 1905–60
Knauft, Bruce M., 1954–
Knight, Chris, 1942–
Knox, Robert, 1791–1862
Krige, Eileen Jensen, 1904–95
Kroeber, Alfred Louis, 1876–1960
Kropotkin, Peter, 1842–1921
Kuhn, Thomas, 1922–96
Kuper, Adam, 1941–
Kuper, Hilda Beemer, 1911–92

Lacan, Jacques, 1901–83
Lamarck, Jean-Baptiste de Monet, chevalier de, 1744–1829
Lang, Andrew, 1844–1912
Layton, Robert, 1944–
Le Blanc, Marie-Angélique ('Wild Girl of Champagne'),
    b. c. 1721
Leach, Sir Edmund R., 1910–89
Leacock, Eleanor, 1922–88
Lee, Richard B., 1937–
Lévi-Strauss, Claude, 1908–
Lévy-Bruhl, Lucien, 1857–1939
Lewis, Oscar, 1914–70
Leyton, Elliott, 1939–
Lienhardt, Godfrey, 1921–93
Linnaeus, Carolus (Carl von Linné), 1707–78
Locke, John, 1632–1704
Long, Norman, 1936–
Lowie, Robert H., 1883–1957
Lubbock, Sir John, Bt. (Lord Avebury), 1834–1913
Lyotard, Jean-François, 1924–

Maine, Sir Henry Sumner, 1822–88
Malinowski, Bronislaw, 1884–1942
Marx, Karl, 1818–83
Mauss, Marcel, 1872–1950
Max Müller, F., see Müller, Friedrich Max
McLennan, John Ferguson, 1827–1881
Mead, Margaret, 1901–78
Mendelssohn, Felix, 1809–47
Mitchell, J. Clyde, 1918–
Monboddo, Lord (James Burnett), 1714–99
Montelius, Oscar, 1843–1921
Montesquieu, Charles-Louis de Secondat, baron de la Brède et de, 1689–1755
Moore, Henrietta L., 1957–
Morgan, Lewis Henry, 1818–81
Müller, Friedrich Max, 1823–1900
Murdock, George Peter, 1897–1985

Nadel, S. F., 1903–54
Needham, Rodney, 1923–
Newton, Sir Isaac, 1642–1727
Nietzsche, Friedrich, 1844–1900
Nilsson, Sven, 1787–1883

Obeyesekere, Gananath, 1930–
Okely, Judith, 1941–
Ortner, Sherry B., 1941–

Pasquinelli, Carla, 1939–
Perry, Commodore Matthew, 1794–1858
Perry, William James, 1887–1949
Peter ('Wild Peter of Hanover'), c. 1710–85
Piaget, Jean, 1896–1980
Pike, Kenneth L., 1912–
Prichard, James Cowles, 1786–1848
Pufendorf (Puffendorf), Samuel, Freiherr von, 1632–94

Radcliffe–Brown, A. R., 1881–1955
Ratzel, Friedrich, 1844–1904
Redfield, Robert, 1897–1958
Rivers, W. H. R., 1864–1922
Rosaldo, Michelle Z., 1944–81

Rosaldo, Renato, 1941–
Rousseau, Jean-Jacques, 1712–78

Sahlins, Marshall, 1930–
Said, Edward W., 1935–
Saint-Simon, Claude-Henri de Rouvroy, comte de, 1760–1825
Sapir, Edward, 1884–1939
Saussure, Ferdinand de, 1857–1913
Schapera, I., 1905–
Schmidt, Pater Wilhelm, 1868–1954
Schneider, David M., 1918–95
Seligman, C. G., 1873–1940
Service, Elman R., 1915–96
Simmel, Georg, 1858–1918
Smith, Adam, 1723–90
Smith, William Robertson, 1846–94
Spencer, Herbert, 1820–1903
Spencer, Jonathan, 1954–
Spiro, Melford, 1926–
Spivak, Gayatri Chakravorty, 1942–
Srinivas, M. N., 1916–
Steward, Julian H., 1902–72
Stewart, Dugald, 1753–1828
Stocking, George W., Jr, 1928–
Strathern, Andrew, 1939–
Strathern, Marilyn, 1941–
Stuchlik, Milan, 1932–80

Tax, Sol, 1907–95
Thomsen, Christian Jürgensen, 1788–1865
Trubetzkoy, Nikolai Sergeyevich, 1890–1938
Turner, Victor W., 1920–83
Tyler, Stephen A., 1932–
Tylor, Sir Edward Burnett, 1832–1917

Urry, James, 1949–

Van Gennep, Arnold, 1873–1957
Vico, Giambattista, 1668–1744
Victor ('Wild Boy of Aveyron'), b. *c.* 1788
Victoria, Queen of the United Kingdom and Empress of India, 1819–
    1901

Wallace, Alfred Russel, 1823–1913
Wallerstein, Immanuel, 1930–
Weber, Max, 1864–1920
Werbner, Richard P., 1937–
Westermarck, Edward, 1862–1939
White, Leslie A., 1900–75
Whorf, Benjamin Lee, 1897–1941
Willis, Roy G., 1927–
Wilmsen, Edwin N., 1932–
Wilson, Edward O., 1929–
Wilson, Godfrey, 1908–1944
Wilson, Monica (Monica Hunter), 1908–82
Wissler, Clark, 1870–1947
Worsley, Peter, 1924–

Appendix 2
Glossary

ablineal relative A blood relative (e.g., a cousin) who is neither in ego's line of descent nor the brother or sister of one who is (cf. **co-lineal relative, collateral relative**).

action-centred approaches Approaches which emphasize social action over social structure, such as transactionalism.

affine, affinal relative A relative by marriage.

age-area hypothesis Wissler's notion that older culture traits tend to be those on the periphery of a culture area, rather than in the centre. His hypothesis is based on the idea that things are invented in the centre and diffuse outwards.

age set A category of people united by common age, often those initiated into adulthood at the same time.

agenda hopping D'Andrade's notion of researchers changing their interests when old paradigms yield fewer and fewer insights (cf. **Kuhnian**)

androcentric Male-centred.

animism A belief in a spiritual presence within things such as rocks and trees.

anthropogeography The nineteenth-century German university subject, roughly equivalent to human geography. It gave birth to diffusionism.

anthropology In its widest sense, the subject which includes social or cultural anthropology, anthropological linguistics, prehistoric archaeology, and biological or physical anthropology (cf. **four fields**). In a narrower sense, a short name for social anthropology.

Apollonian An aspect of drama or culture characterized by measure, restraint, and harmony (cf. **Dionysian**).

articulation of modes of production Interaction between different modes of production, for example as when colonial capitalist and lineage-based societies come into contact.

associative Saussure's term for what are now usually called paradigmatic relations in a language or symbolic system.

avunculate   The relationship between a child and his or her mother's brother. More specifically, the term usually refers to accepted informal behaviour between a boy and his mother's brother, contrasted to formality between the boy and his father.

avunculocal   Another word for viri-avunculocal (residing with the husband's mother's brother).

barbarism   In evolutionist theory, the stage of society which lies between savagery and civilization. It is characterized by the possession of things such as pottery, livestock, etc. (cf. **savagery, civilization**).

base   The material aspect of society, believed by Marxists to be determinant of the superstructure or ideological aspect of society (cf. **infrastructure, superstructure**).

basic needs   In Malinowskian theory, the seven biological needs (e.g., safety) which are served by seven corresponding cultural responses (e.g., protection).

Boasian   Referring to the ideas of Franz Boas, especially with reference to his cultural relativism.

bridewealth   Marriage gifts or payments made from the family of the groom to the family of the bride.

British structuralism   Originally a synonym for structural-functionalism (in the 1950s), but later used to refer to the work of British anthropologists who had taken up French structuralist ideas (from the 1960s). British structuralists (in the latter sense) tended to be interested in structural elements of one culture at a time (cf. **Dutch structuralism, French structuralism**).

centre   In opposition to periphery, the economically dominant place. Its centrality does not have to be geographical. For example, in world-systems theory a colonial power may be defined as the 'centre' and its colonies the 'periphery'.

civil society   In the eighteenth century, generally a synonym for government or the state. (More recently the term has been used to refer to anti-state groupings or occasionally to 'society' in contrast to 'the state'.)

civilization   In evolutionist theory, the highest level of society, characterized by urbanization, social hierarchy, and complex social structure (cf. **savagery, barbarism**).

cognitive anthropology   The branch of anthropology or perspective within anthropology which emphasizes the relation between cultural categories and structures or processes of thought.

cognitive relativism   The form of relativism which holds that all statements about the world are culturally contingent (cf. **moral relativism**).

cognitive science   A somewhat broader term for cognitive anthropology, or any field which emphasizes the relation between cultural categories and structures or processes of thought.

'cold' societies   Lévi-Strauss' term for societies he believed to be essentially static. 'Cold' societies have a concern with myth rather than history (cf. **'hot' societies**).

co-lineal relative   Ego's brother or sister or the brother or sister of someone who is in ego's line of descent (e.g., an uncle or nephew) (cf. **ablineal relative, collateral relative**).

collateral relative   A blood relative who is not in ego's line of descent (e.g., a cousin). Sometimes brothers and sisters are included and sometimes not (cf. **lineal relative, direct relative**).

collective conscience, collective consciousness   Durkheim's term for the collective understandings which people within a given society share (French, *conscience collective*).

collective representation   Any of the collective understandings which people in a given society share (cf. **collective conscience**).

communitas   Turner's term for an unstructured realm of 'social structure', where often the normal ranking of individuals is reversed or the symbols of rank inverted. This sense of 'community', he said, characterizes rites of passage.

community   A group of people who share common values. The term has come to be regarded as safer than 'society', whose existence has been challenged by some postmodernist thinkers (as well as some politicians).

comparative philology   An older term for the study of historical or structural relations between languages.

comparative sociology   A term occasionally used by Radcliffe-Brown to mean 'social anthropology'.

competence   In linguistics, the ability or knowledge required by a native speaker to tell intuitively whether a construction is grammatical or not (cf. **performance**).

complex structures   According to Lévi-Strauss, those kinship systems based on rules about whom one may not marry (e.g., that marriage between close relatives is forbidden) (cf. **elementary structures**).

component   In componential analysis, a synonym for 'significatum'.

componential analysis   A method or theoretical perspective which examines the relation between cultural categories as parts of a system of such categories, for example the system of colour terms in a given language.

conjectural history Originally an eighteenth-century term for the methods of historical reconstruction favoured by thinkers such as Adam Smith and much later by evolutionists and diffusionists.

connotatum An element in componential analysis which implies connotation rather than signification (e.g., 'uncle-like behaviour' as opposed to a more formal defining feature of the category 'uncle') (cf. **significatum**).

consanguine, consanguineal relative A relative by blood.

conscience collective Durkheim's term for the collective understandings which people within a given society share (in English, 'collective conscience' or more commonly 'collective consciousness').

consonant triangle Jakobson's term for the structural relations between p, t, and k as representing a system defined according to relative loudness and pitch (cf. **vowel triangle**).

controlled comparison Any form of comparison which involves limiting the range of variables, such as by confining comparisons to those within a region.

couvade A custom whereby a man feels or pretends to be pregnant when his wife is about to give birth, often to draw malevolent forces away from his wife and child.

cross-cousins The children of a brother and those of a sister. In many societies, cross-cousins are marriageable whereas parallel cousins are not (cf. **parallel cousins**).

'Crow' terminology A type of kinship terminology in which the father's sister's daughter is called by the same term as the father's sister, or more generally one in which ego calls several members of his or her father's matrilineal kin group by the same term (cf. **'Omaha' terminology**).

Crow-Omaha systems Lévi-Strauss' term for systems lying in-between elementary and complex ones: systems with 'Crow' or 'Omaha' terminologies in which all those called by kin terms are forbidden as possible spouses.

culinary triangle A structural model proposed by Lévi-Strauss in which roast, smoked, and boiled foods are seen as analogous to raw, cooked, and rotted foods.

cultural anthropology The branch of anthropology or the academic discipline which is concerned with the study of cultural diversity. The term is typically used in the North American traditions, whereas in other traditions 'ethnology' or 'social anthropology' are the more common terms, often with slightly different subject matter (cf. **ethnology**, **social anthropology**, **four fields**).

cultural core, culture core In Steward's cultural ecology, the aspects of culture most susceptible to ecological influence (e.g., subsistence, patterns of migration) (cf. **total culture**).

cultural determinism   The notion that culture, rather than biology, regulates the ways in which humans perceive the world.

cultural ecology   The study of relations between culture and the natural world, especially in the theoretical perspective of Julian Steward.

cultural materialism   The theoretical perspective of Marvin Harris, who argues that there is a direct causal relation between material forces and aspects of culture (cf. **vulgar materialism**).

cultural relativism   Any of several theoretical perspectives in anthropology, including descriptive relativism, epistemological relativism, and normative relativism.

cultural responses   In Malinowskian theory, the seven basic aspects of culture (e.g., protection) each of which serves a biological need (in this case, safety).

cultural studies   The discipline concerned with the study of mass culture, popular culture, etc. Although it touches on anthropological interests, it has its origins in and its most direct links with literary criticism and sociology.

culture   In anthropology, usually taken as the totality of ideas, skills, and objects shared by a community or society. In other contexts, it is sometimes useful to distinguish the 'high culture' of the elite or the (often transient) 'popular culture' of the majority.

'culture and personality'   The perspective of Ruth Benedict and her followers which emphasizes the 'personality' of whole cultures rather than individuals.

culture area   A cluster of related cultures, normally those occupying a geographical region.

culture circle   A cluster of related culture traits, or the geographical area where these are found. The idea is fundamental to German-Austrian diffusionists, who saw these circles as spreading progressively over earlier culture circles (German, *Kulturkreis*).

culture trait   Any individual item of culture, either material or non-material.

culturo-genesis   The origin of culture, or more usually, of symbolic culture.

Darwinian   Referring to the ideas of Charles Darwin, for example in his opposition to Lamarckian ideas (cf. **Darwinism**).

Darwinism   Any of several related perspectives derived from the evolutionist theory of Charles Darwin, and especially the idea of evolution through natural selection.

deconstruction Derrida's term for a method of literary analysis which seeks to expose the underlying assumptions of a text.

deductivism, deductivist Any approach which proceeds from general assumptions to specific conclusions (cf. **inductivism**).

degeneration theory, degenerativist theory The anti-evolutionist notion that organisms or societies decline in physical or moral quality.

delayed direct exchange Lévi-Strauss' term for a type of marital exchange between kin groups where women move in one direction in one generation, and in the opposite direction in the next. It is a logical consequence of men marrying fathers' sisters' daughters (cf. **direct exchange, generalized exchange**).

denotatum In componential analysis, a member of a given category.

descriptive relativism The form of relativism which holds that culture regulates the ways in which humans perceive the world, and therefore that cultural variability will produce different social and psychological understandings among different peoples (cf. **epistemological relativism, normative relativism**).

designatum In componential analysis, the term for a given category.

diachronic perspective A perspective through time (e.g., evolutionism), rather than one in the same time frame (cf. **synchronic perspective**).

différance Derrida's term implying roughly 'a delay in difference', in that the differences which define something in opposition to what it is not, cannot, in his view, be fully conceptualized. There is always, he argues, something beyond such differences.

diffusion The movement of culture traits from one people to another.

diffusionism, diffusionist A perspective which emphasizes diffusion (or sometimes migration) over evolution as the greater cause of cultural change in the world.

Dionysian An aspect of drama or culture characterized by emotion, passion, and excess (cf. **Apollonian**).

direct exchange Lévi-Strauss' term for a type of marital exchange between kin groups where exchanges of women may go in either direction. It is a logical consequence of men exchanging sisters with each other or marrying women of a category which includes both mothers' brothers' daughters and fathers' sisters' daughters (cf. **delayed direct exchange, generalized exchange**).

direct relative A lineal relative or the brother or sister of a lineal relative (cf. **collateral relative**).

discourse A complex concept involving the way people talk or write about something, the body of knowledge implied, or the use of that knowledge, such as in structures of power (e.g., in the work of

Foucault). The term can also have the meaning (as in linguistics) of units of speech longer than a sentence.

dispositions   In Bourdieu's terminology, tendencies or choices individuals have within the habitus (see also **habitus**).

distinctive features   Those features whose presence or absence defines a given phenomenon. For example, in phonology the feature of voicing defines the difference between a p (voiceless) and a b (voiced).

Durkheimian   Referring to the ideas of Emile Durkheim, especially his emphasis on social structure as a determinant of belief and ideology.

Dutch structuralism   Structuralism in The Netherlands, arguably as early as the 1920s, which emphasized regional structures such as that of the cultures of the Malay Archipelago taken as a whole (cf. **British structuralism, French structuralism**).

ecosystem   In ecology and ecological anthropology, the system which includes both social and natural environments.

ego   In discussions of kinship, the person from whose point of view a relationship is traced (meaning 'I' or 'self').

eidos   According to Bateson, the form or structure of culture or cultural phenomena (cf. **ethos**).

Elementargedanken   'Elementary thoughts', those beliefs and aspects of culture held by Bastian to be common to all humankind (cf. **psychic identity, Völkergedanken**).

elementary structures   According to Lévi-Strauss, those kinship systems based on categories between which marriage is prescribed (e.g., the category of the cross-cousin) (cf. **complex structures**).

embodiment   The notion that social or cultural categories are inseparable from the bodies of the individuals who possess them.

emic   Relating to a culture-specific system of thought based on indigenous definitions (cf. **etic**).

empiricism, empiricist   The doctrine which holds that knowledge is derived from experience rather than from prior reasoning (cf. **rationalism**).

enculturation   The process by which people, especially children, acquire culture (cf. **socialization**).

Enlightenment   The mainly eighteenth-century movement which stressed the importance of reason for the critical understanding of nature and society.

epistemological relativism   The form of relativism which holds that human nature and the human mind are culturally variable, and therefore that all general theories of culture are fallacious (cf. **descriptive relativism, normative relativism**).

epistemology In philosophy, the theory of knowledge.

esprit general Montesquieu's term (meaning 'general spirit') for the fundamental essence of a given culture.

esprit humain Lévi-Strauss' term (meaning 'human spirit') for the psychic unity or collective unconsciousness of humanity as a whole. In his usage it implies a structure of thought universal among humanity.

ethnography Literally, 'writing about peoples', the term also implies the practice of anthropological fieldwork.

ethnology The study of ethnic groups, broadly a synonym for social or cultural anthropology. The term was in general use in Britain prior to the 1870s, but since then has been more common on the Continent and to some extent in North America (cf. **cultural anthropology, social anthropology**).

ethnoscience Most literally, the scientific notions of indigenous peoples. More commonly the term implies methods such as componential analysis, designed to elucidate such knowledge.

ethos According to Bateson, the distinctive character or spirit of an event or a culture (cf. **eidos**).

etic Relating to categories held to be universal or based on an outside observer's objective understanding (cf. **emic**).

evolution A change or development, such as from simple to complex. Usually this change is regarded as gradual (cf. **revolutionist**).

evolutionism, evolutionist Any perspective which stresses change for the better or advancement from simple to complex. In contrast to diffusionism, a perspective which emphasizes evolution over diffusion or migration as the greater cause of cultural change in the world. In contrast to a revolutionist perspective, one which argues for gradual over revolutionary change.

extended case study A case study presented in detail within an ethnographic article or book, in order to illustrate a more general point. The idea came into anthropology from legal studies and is characteristic of the Manchester School.

feminism, feminist The movement which developed to counteract male-dominant representations and male dominance generally.

feral child A child existing in a 'natural' state, unsocialized by humans but sometimes believed to have been reared by wild animals.

fetishism The belief in fetishes, or objects believed to have supernatural power.

fetishization The act of treating something as a fetish or as being like a fetish. It is used especially in the latter, metaphorical sense (e.g., Marxist references to the 'fetishization of commodities').

forces of production   In Marxist theory, things such as raw materials and technology which form the material as opposed to the social aspect of the economic base; or the interaction of these elements of the means of production with labour (cf. **base, mode of production, relations of production**).

Foucauldian, Foucaultian   Referring to the ideas of Michel Foucault (cf. **discourse**).

four fields   The classic division of American and Canadian anthropology: cultural anthropology, anthropological linguistics, prehistoric archaeology, and biological or physical anthropology. In other countries these 'four fields' tend to be treated as separate disciplines rather than as branches of the same subject.

French structuralism   In its widest sense, the ideas of Claude Lévi-Strauss and his admirers. In a narrower sense, the perspective within anthropology which emphasizes structures of the human mind rather than structures in the minds of members of particular cultures or people from particular culture areas (cf. **British structuralism, Dutch structuralism**).

function   A term variously used to denote the purpose of a custom or social institution in the abstract, or its relation to other customs or social institutions within a social system.

functionalism, functionalist   Any perspective which emphasizes the functions of customs or social institutions. In anthropology it refers especially to the perspectives of either B. Malinowski (regarded as a 'purer' functionalist) or A. R. Radcliffe-Brown (a structural-functionalist).

Geertzian   Referring to the ideas of Clifford Geertz (cf. **interpretivism**).

Geist   Literally, the 'ghost' or 'spirit' of a society.

genealogical grid   The set of statuses believed to lie at the foundation of all kinship systems, no matter how relatives are classified in any given culture or society.

general spirit   Montesquieu's term (*esprit general*) for the fundamental essence of a given culture.

generalized exchange   Lévi-Strauss' term for a type of marital exchange between kin groups where 'exchanges' of women are in one direction only, for example where a son may marry into the same kin group as his father but a daughter may not. It is a logical consequence of men marrying mothers' brothers' daughters (cf. **delayed direct exchange, direct exchange**).

genotype   The genetic makeup of an organism (cf. **phenotype**).

global comparison, global-sample comparison   Comparison on a world-wide basis in the search for universal cross-cultural generalizations or predictions.

globalization   The process of increasing contact between societies, especially in the economic sphere, across the globe (cf. **localization, re-localization**)

'God's truth'   In linguistics and cognitive anthropology, the view that a good analysis of a set of emic categories will represent the true psychological reality of informants (cf. **'hocus-pocus'**).

Great Chain of Being   The view of the world as consisting of a hierarchy of entities from God to humanity to animals to plants, etc. It was prevalent in the sixteenth, seventeenth, and eighteenth centuries and, in contrast to the theory of evolution, based on a notion of the fixity of species.

grid   Mary Douglas' term for the 'dimension' of constraint through individual isolation (cf. **group, grid/group analysis**).

grid/group analysis   The analysis of 'grid' and 'group' constraints in the style of Mary Douglas.

group   Mary Douglas' term for the 'dimension' of constraint on individuals as members of groups (cf. **grid, grid/group analysis**).

gumlao, gumsa   Among the Kachin of Burma, the two social formations, *gumlao* being egalitarian and *gumsa* being hierarchical.

habitus   In Bourdieu's terminology, the culturally defined system of knowledge and social action made up of 'dispositions' or choices available to individuals (see also **dispositions**).

heliocentrism, heliocentric   Literally 'with the sun at the centre', the extreme diffusionist perspective of the early twentieth century which held that the sun-worshipping ancient Egyptians were the source of greatest invention in human culture.

historicist   Any approach which emphasizes historical or diachronic aspects of culture or society.

'hocus pocus'   In linguistics and cognitive anthropology, the view that a good analysis of a set of emic categories will be one which correctly accounts for the data but which will not necessarily represent the (elusive) 'true' psychological reality of informants (cf. **'God's truth'**).

'hot' societies   Lévi-Strauss' term for societies he believed to be essentially dynamic. 'Hot' societies have a concern with history rather than myth (cf. **'cold' societies**).

hypergamous   Involving marriage where the man is of higher status than his wife (cf. **hypogamous**).

hypogamous   Involving marriage where a woman is of higher status than her husband (cf. **hypergamous**).

ideal types   Weber's notion of the basic forms of social phenomena, simplified from observed cases. For example, his studies of Protestantism assume an ideal type which is not necessarily an accurate representation of *all* Protestant societies.

ideographic   Referring to the specific rather than the general (e.g., the description of exact instances rather than generalizations on social processes) (cf. **nomothetic**).

ideology   Literally, the study of ideas. It generally carries the meaning of a system of values, such as those Marxists and some postmodernists argue give power to one group over another.

illustrative comparison   Comparison of specific ethnographic cases, for example to highlight some feature of culture or social structure which may be unusual.

inductive computation   Malinowski's term for the process of discovery of the 'invisible facts' which govern the interconnection of facets of social organization.

inductivism, inductivist   Any approach which proceeds from specific examples to general conclusions (cf. **deductivism**).

infrastructure   Another word for the 'base' or material aspect of society (cf. **base, superstructure**).

interactive perspective   Any perspective in anthropology which emphasizes action over structure.

interpretation   Intuitive understanding, or more precisely the understanding of culture as being like a language, to be 'translated'.

interpretive   An approach or method based on interpretation.

interpretivism, interpretivist   A perspective which emphasizes the interpretation of culture over the quest for formal structures. Geertz's anthropology is the most commonly cited example.

intersubjective   Referring to methods which privilege equally the ethnographer and his or her informants.

intertextual, intertextuality   Referring to relations between texts, where each represents a commentary on another.

irony   A verbal construction, often humorous, in which words are used to mean the opposite of what they normally mean.

'Iroquois' terminology   A type of kinship terminology in which cross-cousins are distinguished from parallel cousins. Often parallel cousins are classed together with siblings.

Kuhnian   Referring to the ideas of Thomas Kuhn, especially his notion of science as a sequential series of paradigms.

kula   In the Trobriand Islands and surrounding areas, the formalized system of exchange of bracelets for armshells.

Kulturkreis   A cluster of related culture traits, or the geographical area where these are found. The idea is fundamental to German-Austrian diffusionists, who saw these circles as spreading progressively over earlier culture circles (English, 'culture circle').

Lamarckian   Referring to the ideas of Jean-Baptiste de Lamarck, especially that learned traits can be passed from parent to child.

langue   Saussure's term for language in the sense of linguistic structure or grammar; by analogy, this can be the grammar of culture as well as of language as such (cf. **parole**).

Lévi-Straussian   Referring to the ideas of Claude Lévi-Strauss (cf. **structuralism**).

lineal relative   A relative who is in ego's line of descent (e.g., a grandmother or granddaughter).

localization   The interplay between local forms of knowledge and external pressures (cf. **re-localization, globalization**).

Malinowskian   Referring to the ideas of Bronislaw Malinowski, either as a fieldwork methodologist or a functionalist theorist.

Manchester School   The school of thought centred around Max Gluckman at Manchester in the 1950s, 1960s, and 1970s.

manitoo   In Ojibwa belief, the guardian spirit of an individual (cf. **totem**).

Marxism, Marxist   Referring to the ideas of Karl Marx. In anthropology, the term implies a theoretical interest in the connections between material forces and relations of power but not necessarily adherence to Marx's political ideology.

matrilineal descent, matrilineality   Descent through women, from mother to child, etc. (cf. **patrilineal descent**).

means of production   In Marxist theory, the organized arrangement of raw materials, tools, and know-how; the technological system of a society, especially in relation to subsistence (cf. **mode of production**).

metanarrative   Lyotard's term for grand theory.

metaphor   An analogy, or relation of similarity across different levels of analysis (e.g., a red traffic light means 'stop').

metonymy   A relation between objects in the same level of analysis (e.g., a red traffic light in relation to a green traffic light).

mode of production   In Marxist theory, the combination of either the means of production or the forces of production (mode of subsistence plus the social capability to exploit the environment), coupled with the relations of production (the ways in which production is organized) (cf. **means of production, relations of production**).

modern   In contrast to postmodern, emphasizing a holistic, coherent view of the world.

moiety   Literally 'half' a society, defined by membership in one or the other of two unilineal descent groups.

monogenesis   One origin for all human 'races' (cf. **polygenesis**).

monogenist   A person who believes in monogenesis (also the adjectival form of 'monogenesis').

monotheism   Belief in only one deity (cf. **polytheism**).

moral relativism   The form of relativism which holds that aesthetic and ethical judgements must be assessed in terms of specific cultural values (cf. **cognitive relativism**).

morpheme   The smallest meaningful unit of language (e.g., the English word *cars* consists of two morphemes: 'car' and 'plural').

morphological   In linguistics, referring to the level of the morpheme.

multilinear evolutionism   The theory of social evolution which emphasizes cross-cultural diversity and the influence of the environment in the process.

mytheme   In Lévi-Strauss' terminology, a unit within a mythological corpus which may be combined with similar units to make up a given myth.

Mythologiques   Literally, 'mytho-logics', Lévi-Strauss' four volumes on mythology.

naiscent society   Rousseau's notion of an idyllic, egalitarian society before the emergence of 'artificial' inequalities.

natural law   The theory of law or the essence of law in that theory, as embedded in human nature. It was characteristic of Enlightenment legal theory, but opposed by later conceptions of law as a set of rules.

natural selection   The Darwinian notion (also called sexual selection) that individuals with superior characteristics will tend to breed more often than other individuals, thus giving rise to better-adapted individuals in later generations.

naturism   Not to be confused with nudism, F. Max Müller's notion of early religion as nature-worship.

naven   Ceremonies of the Iatmul of Papua New Guinea involving transvestism and other ritual reversals of ordinary behaviour.

neo-Darwinism   In its most usual meaning today, the perspective in human biology which combines Darwinian theory with modern genetics in seeking biological explanations of human social behaviour.

neo-evolutionism   A broad concept embracing late twentieth-century evolutionist ideas in anthropology, including especially those of Julian Steward.

network analysis   A methodological tool which emerged as part of the Manchester School. It seeks an understanding of social relations through chains or networks of individual associations.

new archaeology   In the 1960s, a perspective in archaeology which emphasizes ethnographic analogy.

new ethnography   In the 1960s, a perspective essentially synonymous with the cognitive anthropology of the time. In the 1980s, a rather different perspective essentially synonymous with the approach or approaches typified by Clifford and Marcus' edited volume, *Writing Culture*.

noble savage   A seventeenth- and eighteenth-century notion of the goodness of natural humanity or primitive social humanity embodied in 'savages'. Typically, these were identified with the populations of Native North America.

nomothetic   Referring to the general rather than the specific, e.g., the search for regularities or general laws rather than the description of specific instances (cf. **ideographic**).

normative relativism   The form of relativism which holds that because cultures judge each other according to their own internal standards, there are no universal standards to judge between cultures. There are two positions within normative relativism: cognitive relativism and moral relativism (cf. **descriptive relativism, epistemological relativism**).

normative rules   Idealized descriptions of correct social behaviour, as distinct from actual social behaviour.

occidentalism   A relatively recent term for the stereotyping of the West by oriental or other non-Western peoples (cf. **orientalism**).

Oedipus complex   In psychiatry, the complex of emotions of desire for the parent of the opposite sex (especially a boy for his mother).

Oedipus myth   The Greek myth in which, by a strange sequence of events, Oedipus kills his father and marries his mother.

'Omaha' terminology   A type of kinship terminology in which the mother's brother's son is called by the same term as the mother's brother, or more generally one in which ego calls several members of his or her mother's patrilineal kin group by the same term (cf. **'Crow' terminology**).

Orang Outang   In the eighteenth century, a term roughly equivalent to the modern generic concept of the 'ape', but often believed to be human or nearly human. Not to be confused with the orang-utan of Southeast Asia as known to science today.

organic analogy   The notion that society is 'like an organism' in being composed of evolving or interrelated parts or systems.

orientalism   In anthropology, the stereotyping of the East by Western peoples, especially as described by Edward Said (cf. **occidentalism**).

Paideuma   Greek for 'education', though in Frobenius' German usage it identifies the 'soul' of a culture (cf. **Volksgeist**).

paradigm   Thomas Kuhn's term for a set of suppositions common to practitioners of a given science at a given time. It constitutes a large theory or perspective (e.g., Newtonian physics, Einsteinian physics). In the social sciences, the term bears much the same meaning (e.g., evolutionism and functionalism are anthropological paradigms).

paradigmatic   In structuralist usage, the relation between elements which might occupy the same position in a syntagmatic chain (e.g., Mary and Sally, in the sentences 'John loves Mary' and 'John loves Sally'). In the anthropology of symbolism, paradigmatic relations are those of metaphor as opposed to metonymy.

parallel cousins   The children of two brothers or two sisters. In many societies parallel cousins are treated as brothers and sisters and sharply distinguished from cross-cousins (cf. **cross-cousins**).

parole   Saussure's term for speech in the sense of actual utterances; by analogy, it refers also to the social action as opposed to social structure (cf. **langue**).

participant observation   The fieldwork methodology in which the ethnographer learns through both observation and participation in the social life of the people under study.

patrilateral parallel-cousin marriage   Marriage of a man to his father's brother's daughter (or a woman to her father's brother's son).

patrilineal descent, patrilineality   Descent through men, from father to child, etc. (cf. **matrilineal descent**).

performance   In linguistics, the actual utterances which make up language (cf. **competence**).

periphery   An economically weak or dependent place or region, in contrast to the 'centre'. The concept is important in Marxist anthropological theory (cf. **centre, world system**).

phenotype   The physical makeup of an organism, as produced by both genetic and environmental factors (cf. **genotype**).

phone   A sound. In phonetics, the smallest unit of speech.

phoneme   The smallest meaningful unit of sound, more specifically one which exists within a language-specific system of sounds.

phonemics The study of systematic relations between sounds (as phonemes).

phonetics The study of speech sounds (phones) in their fundamental essence.

phonological Relating to sounds as part of a system of phonemes.

phonology The systematic relations between sounds (as phonemes), or the study of these (in the latter sense, synonymous with phonemics).

phratry A large unilineal descent group, usually a cluster of smaller groups such as clans.

pinalua In Hawaii, a relationship of intimacy or of common sexual possession.

polygenesis Multiple and separate origins for the different human 'races' (cf. **monogenesis**).

polygenist A person who believes in polygenesis (also the adjectival form of 'polygenesis').

polytheism Belief in more than one deity (cf. **monotheism**).

postmodern A term originally employed in architecture and the arts to denote a reaction against 'modernism' (e.g., modern architecture) and a revival of classical traditions, often mixed indiscriminately (cf. **postmodern condition**, **postmodernism**).

postmodern condition Jean-François Lyotard's term for the state of society characterized by, among other things, globalization and a complexity of social groupings.

postmodernism, postmodernist Any perspective which emphasizes a breakdown of Enlightenment ideals. In anthropology and other social sciences, the term implies the rejection of the validity of purported objective categories or scientific methods (cf. **postmodern**, **postmodern condition**).

poststructuralism, poststructuralist Any perspective based on a rejection of structuralist methodology or classic structuralist distinctions such as *langue/parole* or synchronic/diachronic.

potlatch A ceremony performed by peoples of the North West Coast of North America involving feasting and the giving away (or sometimes the destruction of) their own movable property, thereby redistributing goods and gaining prestige for themselves.

practice theory Any perspective which emphasizes practice (or individual action) over social structure.

Prague School In linguistics, the school of thought whose analysis was based on the identification of distinctive features, especially in phonology. It originated in Central Europe and was transplanted to New York during the Second World War.

praxis Especially in Marxist theory, practice or action related to the furtherance of social good.

pre-logical mentality Lucien Lévy-Bruhl's term for the supposed thought processes of peoples who are culturally not equipped to distinguish cause from effect.

presentist In the study of the history of anthropology, the position which sees the past through the concerns of the present. The term is usually used disparagingly.

processualism, processualist Any perspective which emphasizes social process over social structure, or which sees social or symbolic structures in terms of their propensity for transformation.

psychic identity, psychic unity The idea that all humankind shares the same mentality (cf. **logical mentality, pre-logical mentality**).

Radcliffe-Brownian Referring to the ideas of A. R. Radcliffe-Brown (cf. **structural-functionalism**).

rationalism, rationalist The doctrine which holds that knowledge can be derived from reason without the necessity of prior experience (cf. **empiricism**).

rationality debate A debate among philosophers and anthropologists, roughly from the 1960s to the 1980s, over the degree to which 'primitive peoples' were culturally capable of rational thought.

reciprocal altruism In sociobiological theory, the notion of performing acts for others with the expectation of a return gain.

reflexivism, reflexivist A perspective which holds reflexivity as central to anthropological method and theory.

reflexivity The reflection on the place of one's self (the ethnographer) in ethnographic practice.

regional comparison A form of controlled comparison which confines comparisons to those within a region (e.g., Aboriginal Australia, Great Plains North America, etc.).

relations of production The social relations around which production is organized; more technically, the appropriation of surplus labour on the basis of control over the forces of production and especially the means of production (cf. **mode of production**).

relativism, relativist A view of the world which opposes the assumption of cultural universals or universal values. In anthropology, broadly a synonym for 'cultural relativism'. In other words, any of several theoretical perspectives which include descriptive relativism, epistemological relativism, and normative relativism.

re-localization The assertion, rediscovery or invention of locally based knowledge, especially knowledge which can be used in agrarian economic and social development (cf. **localization, globalization**).

representations collectives   French for 'collective representations'.

reproduction   In Marxist theory, not merely reproducing children but reproducing existing aspects of culture or society through the generations.

restricted exchange   A synonym for 'direct exchange' (as opposed to 'delayed direct' or 'generalized'). Lévi-Strauss and his followers use the terms interchangeably.

revolutionist   The view that social evolutionary change is the result of revolutionary events such as a literal 'social contract' or the invention of symbolism.

rites of passage   Rituals to mark the transition from one stage of life to another (such as adolescence to adulthood).

role   What an individual does, or more technically the dynamic aspect of a social status (cf. **status**).

Sapir–Whorf hypothesis   The hypothesis that the structure of the language people speak has an unconscious determining effect on their worldview. It was formulated by Benjamin Lee Whorf on the basis of his own research and that of his mentor, Edward Sapir, on Native North American languages. Also known as the Whorfian hypothesis.

Saussurian   Referring to the ideas of Ferdinand de Saussure (e.g., his distinction between *langue* and *parole*).

savage   In earlier times and to some extent in Lévi-Strauss' usage, 'wild' or 'natural'. In the eighteenth century the term often had positive overtones (in opposition to 'polished' or 'civil' society, believed to exhibit less of human nature). In the nineteenth century, it was a term identifying the earliest and lowest level of society (cf. **savagery**).

savagery   In evolutionary theory the earliest and lowest level of society, characterized by egalitarianism and a low level of material culture (cf. **barbarism, civilization**).

semantics   In linguistics, the study of meaning; the highest level of linguistic analysis (above phonetics, phonology, and syntax).

semi-complex systems   A synonym for 'Crow-Omaha systems', so-called because in Lévi-Strauss' theory of kinship they contain attributes of both 'elementary structures' and 'complex structures' (cf. **Crow-Omaha systems**).

semiology, semiotics   The study of 'signs', which include signifiers and the objects signified (cf. **signifier, signified**).

shamanism   The practice of mediation between the ordinary world and the spirit world by a ritual specialist (a shaman). The term is from Tungus, a Siberian language, and refers especially to such practices as trance, out-of-body travel, etc., as practised by Siberian, Arctic, and Amerindian shamans.

sign   In Saussurian linguistics, the combination of the signifier (a word) and what is signified by it. By extension, any similar pairing in the study of symbolism.

significatum   An element of componential analysis which, along with other significata, defines a given category (cf. **connotatum**).

signified   An object or concept which is represented by a signifier (cf. **sign**).

signifier   The word or symbol which stands for something (the object 'signified'; cf. **sign**).

sociability   An eighteenth-century concept implying both sociality and conviviality (cf. **sociality**).

social action   In opposition to social structure, what people actually do, i.e., the roles they play as opposed to the social statuses they occupy.

social anthropology   The branch of anthropology or the academic discipline which is concerned with the study of society in cross-cultural perspective. The term is typically used in British and certain other traditions, whereas in North America 'cultural anthropology' is the more common term (cf. **cultural anthropology, ethnology**).

social drama   Turner's characterization of a ritual process, such as a pilgrimage or a rite of passage, with pre-crisis and post-crisis phases.

social fact   Durkheim's term for the smallest unit of social structure: a custom, institution, or any aspect of society.

social institution   An element of a social system (e.g., marriage is an aspect of the kinship system).

social organization   The dynamic aspect of social structure, i.e., the activities people engage in as part of the social structure.

social processes   A general term employed for cyclical changes in society or changes in society over time.

social structure   The relations between elements of society, either with reference to specific individuals (Radcliffe-Brown's usage) or to the statuses they occupy (cf. **structural form**).

social system   A term variously referring to specific systems within society (economics, politics, kinship, religion) or to the society as a whole in its systematic aspects.

social theory   The branch of sociology which deals with grand theoretical problems, or any area of the social sciences concerned with similar phenomena.

social values   The values people acquire by virtue of membership in a community or society.

sociality The capacity for living in a society, a concept of importance in theoretical perspectives as diverse as seventeenth-century political philosophy and late twentieth-century sociobiology.

socialization The process by which people, especially children, acquire a knowledge of how to live in society (cf. **enculturation**).

society A social unit equivalent variously to a language group, a cultural isolate, or a nation state. Also the social relations which exist between members of such a unit.

sociobiology The study of social relations in a biological framework. More specifically, a discipline or theoretical position which treats human culture and society as adjuncts of humankind's animal nature.

sound shift A systematic change in a language, such as where one set of sounds is transformed into another set (e.g., voiced stops b, d, g become the equivalent voiceless stops p, t, k).

state of nature The notion of humanity without society, an idea prevalent in the eighteenth-century European social theory.

status The position an individual occupies within a social structure (cf. **role**).

Stewardian Referring to the ideas of Julian H. Steward (cf. **cultural ecology**).

stratigraphy In archaeology, the relation of layers of earth in a site. From these the relative age of artefacts, the remains of dwellings, etc. can be inferred.

structural form Radcliffe-Brown's term for generalities based on observations of the social structure. As his notion of 'social structure' was more concrete than that of others (referring to individuals), his term 'structural form' thus carried the more generic meaning which others ascribed to the term 'social structure'.

structural-functionalism, structural-functionalist Referring to the ideas of A. R. Radcliffe-Brown, who emphasized functional relations between social institutions (cf. **functionalism**).

structural opposition In structuralist theory, the relation between two elements of a structure according to the presence or absence of some distinctive feature.

structuralism, structuralist Any perspective which emphasizes structural relations as a key to understanding. For structuralists, things acquire meaning through their place in a structure or system. In anthropology, it is the perspective identified most closely with Claude Lévi-Strauss.

subaltern studies A perspective in history and literary criticism, and prominent in South Asia, which emphasizes the position of the subordinate rather than the dominant group. It has been of influence in feminist anthropology.

superstructure   The ideological aspect of society, which in Marxist theory is determined by the base or infrastructure (cf. **base**).

surface reading   For Althusser, a reading (of Marx) which focuses on the actual words rather than the deeper meaning of the text (cf. **symptomatic reading**).

symbolic culture   The domain of culture concerned with symbols and symbolism, as opposed to material objects, social relations, etc.

symptomatic reading   For Althusser, a reading (of Marx) which focuses on the deeper meaning of the text rather than the actual words (cf. **surface reading**).

synchronic perspective   A perspective in the same time frame (e.g., functionalism), rather than one through time (cf. **diachronic perspective**).

synecdoche   A figure of speech in which a part represents a whole, or vice versa.

syntactic   In linguistics, either the level concerned with the structure of the sentence or more broadly the domain which lies between the phonological and semantic levels. By extension, any analogous aspect of the structure of culture.

syntagmatic   In structuralist usage, the relation between sequential elements such as words in a sentence. In the anthropology of symbolism, syntagmatic relations are those of metonymy as opposed to metaphor (cf. **associative, paradigmatic**).

theism   Belief in one or more deities (cf. **monotheism, polytheism**).

theory   In science or social science, any discourse, perspective or statement which leads to some conclusion about the world. Anthropological theory is centrally concerned with making sense of ethnography and with generalizations about culture or society.

theory of the gift   Mauss' notion that gifts are given because of social obligations and not simply voluntarily. These social obligations entail relations of reciprocity which are fundamental to society, though perhaps in some parts of the world (e.g., Polynesia, Melanesia, the North West Coast of North America) more than in others.

thick description   Geertz's notion of good ethnography as consisting of a multiplicity of detailed and varied interpretations (both the ethnographer's and those of the people under study).

three-age theory   In archaeology, the idea of human prehistory as consisting of three ages, namely the Stone Age, the Bronze Age, and the Iron Age.

total culture   In Steward's cultural ecology, the general aspects of culture, especially those least susceptible to ecological influence (e.g., language, religious belief) (cf. **cultural core**).

totem   In Ojibwa belief, the spirit of a patrilineal clan, represented by an animal (cf. **manitoo**). By extension, a similar spirit among any people (cf. **totemism**).

totemism   Any belief system which entails the symbolic representation of the social (e.g., clan membership) by the natural (e.g., animal species and their characteristics). As phenomena described as 'totemism' are so varied across the world, some anthropologists have questioned the utility of calling them all by this one term (cf. **totem**).

transactionalism, transactionalist   A perspective which emphasizes transactions between individuals as the basis for social analysis.

trope   A figure of speech, such as metaphor, metonymy, synecdoche, or irony.

unilinear evolutionism   The theory of social evolution which holds that all humankind passes through the same stages of evolution irrespective of environment or specific historical influences.

universal evolutionism   The theory of social evolution which emphasizes broad, general stages rather than specific unilinear sequences of evolution.

uxorilocal   Residing with the wife's group (cf. **virilocal**). Uxorilocal residence repeated through the generations creates localized matrilineal kin groups centred on women.

Verstehen   German for 'understanding' or 'interpretation', the basis of Max Weber's sociology.

viri-avunculocal   Residing with the husband's mother's brother's group (also called **avunculocal**; cf. **uxorilocal, virilocal**). Viri-avunculocal residence repeated through the generations creates localized matrilineal kin groups centred on men.

virilocal   Residing with the husband's group (cf. **uxorilical, viri-avunculocal**). Virilocal residence repeated through the generations creates localized patrilineal kin groups centred on men.

vital sequences   Malinowski's notion of the biological foundations of all cultures.

Völkergedanken   'Peoples' thoughts', those beliefs and aspects of culture held by Bastian to be specific to given cultures and not common to all humankind (cf. **Elementargedanken**).

Völkerkunde   The study of peoples, a German synonym for 'ethnology' but distinguished sharply from *Volkskunde*.

Volksgeist   The spirit or soul of a people or culture.

Volkskunde   In Germany and some other countries, the study of folk-lore and local customs, including handicrafts, of one's own country (cf. **Völkerkunde**).

vowel system   The set of vowels found in a particular language and the structural relations which define them.

vowel triangle   Jakobson's term for the structural relations between *u*, *i*, and *a* as representing a system defined according to relative loudness and pitch (cf. **consonant triangle**).

vulgar materialism   Jonathan Friedman's disparaging term for what Marvin Harris calls 'cultural materialism'. It is 'vulgar' in the sense that it does not distinguish base from superstructure (cf. **cultural materialism**).

Weberian   Referring to the ideas of Max Weber, especially his emphasis on action over social structure (cf. **Durkheimian**).

Wechselwirkung   Simmel's notion of 'reciprocal effect', i.e., that the social exists when two or more people engage in interaction with each other, and when the behaviour of one is seen as a response to the behaviour of the other.

Weltanschauung   German for 'worldview'.

Whorfian hypothesis   Another name for the Sapir–Whorf hypothesis.

world system   Wallerstein's idea of a system which links the economies of the smallest societies to the powerful capitalist economies of the West and the Far East.

worldview   A loan translation of German *Weltanschauung*, the term used especially by Boasian anthropologists for the broad perspective on the world maintained by a people through their culture.

References

Abu-Lughod, Lila. 1986. *Veiled Sentiments: Honour and Poetry in a Bedouin Society*. Berkeley: University of California Press.

1990. The romance of resistance: tracing transformations of power though Bedouin women. *American Ethnologist* 17: 41–55.

1991. Writing against culture. In Richard G. Fox (ed.), *Recapturing Anthropology: Working in the Present*. Santa Fe: School of American Research, pp. 137–62.

Adams, William Y. 1998. *The Philosophical Roots of Anthropology*. Stanford: CSLI Publications (CSLI Lecture Notes no. 86).

Ahmed, Akbar S. 1976. *Millennium and Charisma among Pathans: A Critical Essay in Social Anthropology*. London: Routledge & Kegan Paul.

Althusser, Louis. 1969 [1965]. *For Marx* (translated by Ben Brewster). Harmondsworth: Penguin Books.

Althusser, Louis and Etienne Balibar. 1970 [1968]. *Reading 'Capital'* (translated by Ben Brewster). London: New Left Books.

Anderson, Stephen R. 1985. *Phonology in the Twentieth Century: Theories of Rules and Theories of Representations*. Chicago: University of Chicago Press.

Andreski, Stanislav (ed.). 1971. *Herbert Spencer: Structure, Function and Evolution*. London: Thomas Nelson & Sons.

Ardener, Edwin. 1989 [1970–87]. *The Voice of Prophecy and Other Essays* (edited by Malcolm Chapman). Oxford: Basil Blackwell.

Asad, Talal (ed.). 1973. *Anthropology and the Colonial Encounter*. London: Ithaca Press.

Atran, Scott. 1990. *Cognitive Foundations of Natural History: Towards an Anthropology of Science*. Cambridge: Cambridge University Press.

Augé, Marc. 1982 [1979]. *The Anthropological Circle: Symbol, Function, History*. Cambridge: Cambridge University Press.

1995 [1992]. *Non-Places: Introduction to an Anthropology of Supermodernity* (translated by John Howe). London: Verso.

Bachofen, J. J. 1967 [1859–1916]. *Myth, Religion, and Mother Right: Selected Writings of J. J. Bachofen* (translated by Ralph Manheim). Princeton: Princeton University Press (Bollingen Series LXXXIV).

Badcock, C. R. 1975. *Lévi-Strauss: Structuralism and Sociological Theory*. London: Hutchinson & Co.

Barfield, Thomas (ed.). 1997. *The Dictionary of Anthropology*. Oxford: Blackwell Publishers.

Barnard, Alan. 1983. Contemporary hunter-gatherers: current theoretical issues in ecology and social organization. *Annual Review of Anthropology* 12: 193–214.

1992. Through Radcliffe-Brown's spectacles: reflections on the history of anthropology. *History of the Human Sciences* 5(4): 1–20.

1995. *Orang Outang* and the definition of *Man*: the legacy of Lord Monboddo. In Han F. Vermeulen and Arturo Alvarez Roldan (eds.), *Fieldwork and Footnotes: Studies in the History of European Anthropology* (E.A.S.A. Monographs Series). London: Routledge, pp. 95–112.

1996. Regional comparison in Khoisan ethnography: theory, method and practice. *Zeitschrift für Ethnologie* 121: 203–20.

1999. Modern hunter-gatherers and early symbolic culture. In Robin Dunbar, Chris Knight, and Camilla Power (eds.), *The Evolution of Culture: An Interdisciplinary View*. Edinburgh: Edinburgh University Press, pp. 50–68.

Barnard, Alan and Anthony Good. 1984. *Research Practices in the Study of Kinship*. London: Academic Press.

Barnard, Alan and Jonathan Spencer (eds.). 1996. *Encyclopedia of Social and Cultural Anthropology*. London: Routledge.

Barrett, Stanley R. 1996. *Anthropology: A Student's Guide to Theory and Method*. Toronto: University of Toronto Press.

Barth, Fredrik. 1959. *Political Leadership among Swat Pathans*. London: Athlone Press.

1966. *Models of Social Organization*. London: Royal Anthropological Institute (Occasional Papers no. 23).

1969. Introduction. In Fredrik Barth (ed.), *Ethnic Groups and Boundaries: The Social Organization of Culture Difference*. Bergen: Universitetsforlaget/London: George Allen & Unwin, pp. 9–38.

Bateson, Gregory. 1958 [1936]. *Naven: A Survey of the Problems Suggested by a Composite Picture of the Culture of a New Guinea Tribe Drawn from Three Points of View* (second edition). Stanford: Stanford University Press.

1973 [1972] [1935–71]. *Steps to an Ecology of Mind: Collected Essays in Anthropology, Psychiatry, Evolution and Epistemology*. St. Albans: Paladin.

Benedict, Ruth. 1934. *Patterns of Culture*. Boston: Houghton Mifflin.

1946. *The Chrysanthemum and the Sword*. Boston: Houghton Mifflin.

Berlin, Brent. 1992. *Ethnobiological Classification: Principles of Categorization of Plants and Animals in Traditional Societies*. Princeton: Princeton University Press.

Berry, Christopher J. 1997. *Social Theory of the Scottish Enlightenment*. Edinburgh: Edinburgh University Press.

Bloch, Maurice (ed.). 1975. *Marxist Analyses and Social Anthropology* (A.S.A. Studies 2). London: Malaby Press.

1983. *Marxism and Anthropology: The History of a Relationship*. Oxford: Oxford University Press.

1991. Language, anthropology and cognitive science. *Man* (n. s.) 26: 183–98.

Bloor, Celia and David Bloor. 1982. Twenty industrial scientists: a preliminary exercise. In Mary Douglas (ed.), *Essays in the Sociology of Perception*. London: Routledge & Kegan Paul, pp. 83–102.

Boas, Franz. 1938 [1911]. *The Mind of Primitive Man* (revised edition). New York: Macmillan.

1940. *Race, Language, and Culture.* New York: Macmillan.

Bock, Phillip K. 1980. *Continuities in Psychological Anthropology: A Historical Introduction.* San Francisco: W. H. Freeman & Co.

1988. *Rethinking Psychological Anthropology: Continuity and Change in the Study of Human Action.* San Francisco: W. H. Freeman & Co.

Bonte, Pierre and Michel Izard (eds.). 1991. *Dictionnaire de l'ethnologie et de l'anthropologie.* Paris: Presses Universitaires de France.

Boon, James A. 1973. *From Symbolism to Structuralism: Lévi-Strauss in a Literary Tradition.* Oxford: Basil Blackwell.

Borofsky, Robert. 1997. Cook, Lono, Obeyesekere, and Sahlins. *Current Anthropology* 38: 255–82.

Bourdieu, Pierre. 1977 [1972]. *Outline of a Theory of Practice* (translated by Richard Nice). Cambridge: Cambridge University Press.

1990 [1980]. *The Logic of Practice* (translated by Richard Nice). Cambridge: Polity Press.

Bowler, Peter J. 1989. *The Invention of Progress: The Victorians and the Past.* Oxford: Basil Blackwell.

1990. *Charles Darwin: The Man and His Influence.* Oxford: Basil Blackwell.

Bratlinger, Patrick. 1990. *Crusoe's Footprints: Cultural Studies in Britain and America.* New York: Routledge.

Brockman, John (ed.). 1977. *About Bateson: Essays on Gregory Bateson.* New York: E. P. Dutton.

Buffon, George Louis Leclerc, comte de. 1749–1804. *Histoire naturelle, générale et particulière* (44 vols.). Paris: De l'Imprimerie Royale.

Caplan, Pat. 1997. *African Voices, African Lives: Personal Narratives from a Swahili Village.* London: Routledge.

Carrier, James G. (ed.). 1995a. *Occidentalism: Images of the West.* Oxford: Oxford University Press.

1995b. Preface. In James G. Carrier (ed.), *Occidentalism: Images of the West.* Oxford: Oxford University Press, pp. vii–x.

Chalmers, A. F. 1982 [1976]. *What is This Thing Called Science? An Assessment of the Nature and Status of Science and Its Methods* (second edition). Milton Keynes: Open University Press.

Cheater, Angela (ed.). 1999. *The Anthropology of Power* (A.S.A. Monographs 36). London: Routledge.

Childe, V. Gordon. 1936. *Man Makes Himself.* London: Watts & Co.

1942. *What Happened in History.* Harmondsworth: Penguin.

Chomsky, Noam. 1965. *Aspects of the Theory of Syntax.* Cambridge, MA: M.I.T. Press.

Clifford, James. 1986. On ethnographic allegory. In James Clifford and George E. Marcus (eds.), *Writing Culture: The Poetics and Politics of Ethnography.* Berkeley: University of California Press, pp. 98–121.

1988. *The Predicament of Culture: Twentieth-Century Ethnography, Literature and Art.* Cambridge, MA: Harvard University Press.

Clifford, James and George E. Marcus (eds.). 1986. *Writing Culture: The Poetics and Politics of Ethnography*. Berkeley: University of California Press.

Cohen, Anthony P. 1985. *The Symbolic Construction of Community*. Chichester: Ellis Horwood/London: Tavistock Publications.

1994. *Self Consciousness: An Alternative Anthropology of Identity*. London: Routledge.

Collier, Jane F. and Michelle Z. Rosaldo. 1981. Politics and gender in simple societies. In Sherry B. Ortner and Harriet Whitehead (eds.), *Sexual Meanings: The Cultural Construction of Gender and Sexuality*. Cambridge: Cambridge University Press, pp. 275–329.

Comaroff, Jean. 1985. *Body of Power, Spirit of Resistance: The Culture and History of a South African People*. Chicago: University of Chicago Press.

Comte, August. 1869 [1839]. *Cours de philosophie positive*, vol. IV (third edition). Paris: J. B. de Baillüare et Fils.

Corbey, Raymond and Bert Theunissen (eds.). 1995. *Ape, Man, Apeman: Changing Views since 1600*. Leiden: Department of Prehistory, Leiden University.

Crapanzano, Vincent. 1992. The postmodern crisis: discourse, parody, memory. In George E. Marcus (ed.), *Rereading Cultural Anthropology*. Durham, NC: Duke University Press, pp. 87–102.

Csordas, Thomas J. 1990. Embodiment as a paradigm for anthropology. *Ethos* 18: 5–47.

(ed.). 1994. *Embodiment and Experience: The Existential Ground of Culture and Self*. Cambridge: Cambridge University Press.

Cucchiari, Salvatore. 1981. The gender revolution and the transition from bisexual horde to patrilocal band: the origins of gender hierarchy. In Sherry B. Ortner and Harriet Whitehead (eds.), *Sexual Meanings: The Cultural Construction of Gender and Sexuality*. Cambridge: Cambridge University Press, pp. 31–79.

Culler, Jonathan. 1976. *Saussure*. Glasgow: Fontana/Collins (Fontana Modern Masters).

Daiches, David, Peter Jones, and Jean Jones (eds.). 1986. *A Hotbed of Genius: The Scottish Enlightenment, 1730–1790*. Edinburgh: Edinburgh University Press.

D'Andrade, Roy. 1995. *The Development of Cognitive Anthropology*. Cambridge: Cambridge University Press.

Darwin, Charles. 1859. *On the Origin of Species by Means of Natural Selection*. London: John Murray.

1871. *The Descent of Man, and Selection in Relation to Sex*. London: John Murray.

De George, Richard T. and Ferdinande M. de George (eds.). 1972. *The Structuralists: From Mauss to Lévi-Strauss*. Garden City, NY: Doubleday & Co.

De Heusch, Luc. 1982 [1972]. *The Drunken King, or the Origin of the State* (translated by Roy Willis). Bloomington: Indiana University Press.

1985. *Sacrifice in Africa: A Structuralist Approach*. Manchester: Manchester University Press.

Denzin, Norman K. 1997. *Interpretive Ethnography: Ethnographic Practices for the 21st Century*. Thousand Oaks, CA: Sage Publications.

Derrida, Jacques. 1976 [1967]. *Of Grammatology* (translated by Gayatri Chakravorty Spivak). Baltimore: Johns Hopkins University Press.

1978 [1967]. *Writing and Difference* (translated by Alan Bass). Chicago: University of Chicago Press.

Douglas, Mary. 1966. *Purity and Danger: An Analysis of Concepts of Pollution and Taboo*. London: Routledge & Kegan Paul.

1969. *Natural Symbols: Explorations in Cosmology*. London: Routledge & Kegan Paul.

1978. *Cultural Bias*. London: Royal Anthropological Institute (Occasional Papers no. 35).

1980. *Evans-Pritchard*. Glasgow: Fontana/Collins (Fontana Modern Masters).

1982. Introduction to grid/group analysis. In Mary Douglas (ed.), *Essays in the Sociology of Perception*. London: Routledge & Kegan Paul, pp. 1–8.

1996. *Thought Styles: Critical Essays on Good Taste*. London: Sage Publications.

Dumont, Louis. 1980 [1967]. *Homo Hierarchicus: The Caste System and Its Implications* (revised edition, translated by Mark Sainsbury, Louis Dumont, and Basia Gulati). Chicago: University of Chicago Press.

Durkheim, Emile. 1915 [1912]. *The Elementary Forms of the Religious Life*. London: George Allen & Unwin.

1963 [1898]. *Incest: The Nature and Origin of the Taboo* (translated by Edward Sagarin). New York: Stuart.

1966 [1897]. *Suicide: A Study in Sociology* (translated by John A. Spaulding and George Simpson). New York: The Free Press.

Durkheim, Emile and Marcel Mauss. 1963 [1903]. *Primitive Classification* (translated by Rodney Needham). London: Cohen & West.

Edholm, Felicity, Olivia Harris, and Kate Young. 1977. Conceptualizing women. *Critique of Anthropology* 3 (9/10): 101–30.

Eggan, Fred. 1950. *Social Organization of the Western Pueblos*. Chicago: University of Chicago Press.

Ellen, Roy F. 1993. *The Cultural Relations of Classification: An Analysis of Nuaulu Animal Categories from Central Seram*. Cambridge: Cambridge University Press.

Encyclopaedia Britannica; or a Dictionary of Arts and Sciences, Compiled upon a New Plan (3 vols.). 1771. Edinburgh: A. Bell and C. Macfarquhar.

Engels, Frederick [Friedrich]. 1972 [1884]. *The Origin of the Family, Private Property and the State, in the Light of the Researches of Lewis H. Morgan*. London: Lawrence & Wishart.

Evans-Pritchard, E. E. 1937. *Witchcraft, Oracles, and Magic among the Azande*. Oxford: Clarendon Press.

1940. *The Nuer: A Description of the Modes of Livelihood and Political Institutions of a Nilotic People*. Oxford: Clarendon Press.

1951a. *Kinship and Marriage among the Nuer*. Oxford: Clarendon Press.

1951b. *Social Anthropology: The Broadcast Lectures*. London: Cohen & West.

1956. *Nuer Religion*. Oxford: Clarendon Press.

1962 [1932–61]. *Essays in Social Anthropology*. London: Faber & Faber.

1965 [1928–63]. *The Position of Women in Primitive Societies and Other Essays in Social Anthropology*. London: Faber and Faber.

Fardon, Richard (ed.). 1990. *Localizing Strategies: Regional Traditions of Ethnographic Writing*. Edinburgh: Scottish Academic Press/Washington: Smithsonian Institution Press.

1998. *Mary Douglas: An Intellectual Biography*. London: Routledge.

Fernandez, James W. 1986. *Persuasions and Performances: The Play of Tropes in Culture*. Bloomington: Indiana University Press.

(ed.). 1991. *Beyond Metaphor: The Theory of Tropes in Anthropology*. Stanford: Stanford University Press.

Ferguson, Adam. 1966 [1767]. *An Essay on the History of Civil Society*. Edinburgh: Edinburgh University Press.

Finnegan, Ruth and Robin Horton (eds.). 1973. *Modes of Thought*. London: Faber.

Firth, Raymond. 1936. *We the Tikopia: A Sociological Study of Kinship in Primitive Polynesia*. London: George Allen & Unwin.

1961 [1951]. *Elements of Social Organization* (second edition). Boston: Beacon Press.

1956. Alfred Reginald Radcliffe-Brown, 1881–1955. *Proceedings of the British Academy* 62: 287–302.

(ed.). 1957. *Man and Culture: An Evaluation of the Work of Bronislaw Malinowski*. London: Routledge & Kegan Paul.

Fortes, Meyer. 1945. *The Dynamics of Clanship among the Tallensi*. London: Oxford University Press.

1949. *The Web of Kinship among the Tallensi*. London: Oxford University Press.

1969. *Kinship and the Social Order: The Legacy of Lewis Henry Morgan*. London: Routledge & Kegan Paul.

Fortes, Meyer and E. E. Evans-Pritchard (eds.). 1940. *African Political Systems*. London: Oxford University Press for the International African Institute.

Foucault, Michel. 1973 [1966]. *The Order of Things: An Archaeology of the Human Sciences*. New York: Vintage Books.

1974 [1969]. *The Archaeology of Knowledge and the Discourse on Language* (translated by A. M. Sheridan-Smith). London: Tavistock Publications.

1977 [1975]. *Discipline and Punish: The Birth of the Prison* (translated by Alan Sheridan). London: Allen Lane.

Fox, Richard G. 1991. Introduction: Working in the present. *Recapturing Anthropology: Working in the Present*. Santa Fe: School of American Research Press, pp. 1–16.

Fox, Robin. 1975. Primate kin and human kinship. In Robin Fox (ed.), *Biosocial Anthropology* (A. S. A. Studies 1). London: Malaby Press, pp. 9–35.

Frake, Charles O. 1980. *Language and Cultural Description: Essays by Charles O. Frake (Selected and Introduced by Anwar S. Dil)*. Stanford: Stanford University Press.

Frank, Andre Gunder. 1967. *Capitalism and Underdevelopment in Latin America: Historical Studies of Chile and Brazil*. New York: Monthly Review Press.

Frazer, James George. 1910. *Totemism and Exogamy: A Treatise on Certain Early Forms of Superstition and Society* (4 vols.). London: Macmillan & Co.

1922. *The Golden Bough: A Study in Magic and Religion* (abridged edition). London: Macmillan & Co.

Freeman, Derek. 1983. *Margaret Mead and Samoa: The Making and Unmaking of an Anthropological Myth*. Cambridge, MA: Harvard University Press.

Freud, Sigmund. 1960 [1913]. *Totem and Taboo* (translated by James Strachey). London: Routledge & Kegan Paul.

Friedman, Jonathan. 1974. Marxism, structuralism and vulgar materialism. *Man* (n.s.) 9: 444–69.

1975. Tribes, states, and transformations. In Maurice Bloch (ed.), *Marxist Analyses and Social Anthropology* (A.S.A. Studies 2). London: Malaby Press, pp. 161–202.

1996 [1979]. *System, Structure, and Contradiction: The Evolution of 'Asiatic' Social Formations* (second edition). Walnut Creek, CA: AltaMira Press.

Frobenius, Leo. 1933. *Kulturgeschichte Afrikas: Prologomena zu einer historischen Gestaltlehre*. Frankfurt: Frobenius Institut.

Gamble, Clive. 1993. *Timewalkers: The Prehistory of Global Colonization*. Stroud: Alan Sutton.

Geertz, Clifford. 1960. *The Religion of Java*. New York: The Free Press.

1963. *Agricultural Involution: The Process of Ecological Change in Indonesia*. Berkeley: University of California Press.

1966. Religion as a cultural system. In Michael Banton (ed.), *Anthropological Approaches to the Study of Religion* (A.S.A. Monographs 3). London: Tavistock Publications. pp. 1–46.

1968. *Islam Observed. Religious Developments in Morocco and Indonesia*. New Haven: Yale University Press.

1973. *The Interpretation of Cultures: Selected Essays*. New York: Basic Books.

1983. *Local Knowledge: Further Essays in Interpretive Anthropology*. New York: Basic Books.

1984. Anti anti relativism. *American Anthropologist* 86: 263–78.

1988. *Works and Lives: The Anthropologist as Author*. Stanford: Stanford University Press.

Geertz, Hildred and Clifford Geertz. 1975. *Kinship in Bali*. Chicago: University of Chicago Press.

Gellner, Ernest. 1982 [1981]. Relativism and universals. In Martin Hollis and Steven Lukes (eds.), *Rationality and Relativism*. Oxford: Basil Blackwell, pp. 181–200.

1985. *Relativism and the Social Sciences*. London: Cambridge University Press.

1992. *Postmodernism, Reason and Religion*. London: Routledge.

Gerth, H. H. and C. Wright Mills (editors and translators). 1946. *From Max Weber: Essays in Sociology*. New York: Oxford University Press.

Gierke, Otto von. 1934. *Natural Law and the Theory of Society, 1500 to 1800* (translated by Ernest Barker) (2 vols.). Cambridge: Cambridge University Press.

Givens, David B., Patsy Evans, and Timothy Jablonski. 1997. 1997 survey of anthropology PhDs. *American Anthropological Association 1997–98 Guide*. Arlington, VA: American Anthropological Association, pp. 308–21.

Gluckman, Max. 1955. *Custom and Conflict in Africa*. Oxford: Basil Blackwell.

1965. *Politics, Law and Ritual in Tribal Society*. Oxford: Basil Blackwell.

Godelier, Maurice. 1975. Modes of production, kinship, and demographic structures. In Maurice Bloch (ed.), *Marxist Analyses and Social Anthropology* (A.S.A. Studies 2). London: Malaby Press, pp. 3–27.

1977 [1973]. *Perspectives in Marxist Anthropology*. Cambridge: Cambridge University Press.

1986 [1982]. *The Making of Great Men: Male Domination and Power among the New Guinea Baruya* (translated by Rupert Swyer). Cambridge: Cambridge University Press/Paris: Editions de la Maison des Sciences de l'Homme.

Goodenough, Ward. 1956. Componential analysis and the study of meaning. *Language* 32: 195–216.

Goody, Jack. 1995. *The Expansive Moment: Anthropology in Britain and Africa, 1918–1970*. Cambridge: Cambridge University Press.

1996. *The East in the West*. Cambridge: Cambridge University Press.

Graburn, Nelson (ed.). 1971. *Readings in Kinship and Social Structure*. New York: Harper & Row.

Graebner, Fritz. 1911. *Die Methode der Ethnologie*. Heidelberg: Carl Winter's Universitäts Buchhandlung.

Grotius, Hugo. 1949 [1625]. *The Law of War and Peace* (translated by Louise R. Loomis). Roslyn, NY: Walter J. Black.

Guha, Ranajit and Gayatri Chakravorty Spivak (eds.). 1988. *Selected Subaltern Studies*. New York: Oxford University Press.

Hallpike, C. R. 1979. *The Foundations of Primitive Thought*. Oxford: Clarendon Press.

Hammond-Tooke, W. D. 1997. *Imperfect Interpreters: South Africa's Anthropologists, 1920–1990*. Johannesburg: Witwatersrand University Press.

Haraway, Donna. 1988. Situated knowledges: The science question in feminism and the privilege of partial perspective. *Feminist Studies* 14: 575–99.

1991. *Symians, Cyborgs, and Women: The Reinvention of Nature*. New York: Routledge.

Harris, Marvin. 1968. *The Rise of Anthropological Theory*. New York: Thomas Y. Crowell Company.

1977. *Cannibals and Kings: The Origins of Cultures*. New York: Random House.

1979. *Cultural Materialism: The Struggle for a Science of Culture*. New York: Random House.

Harris, Olivia and Kate Young. 1981. Engendered structures: some problems in the analysis of reproduction. In Joel S. Kahn and Josep R. Llobera (eds.), *The Anthropology of Pre-Capitalist Societies*. London: Macmillan, pp. 109–47.

Hart, Keith. 1982. *The Development of Commercial Agriculture in West Africa*. Cambridge: Cambridge University Press.

Hastrup, Kirsten. 1995. *A Passage to Anthropology: Between Experience and Theory*. London: Routledge.

Headland, Thomas., Kenneth L. Pike, and Marvin Harris (eds.). 1990. *Emics and Etics: The Insider/Outsider Debate*. Newbury Park: Sage Publications.

Helman, Cecil G. 1994 [1984]. *Culture, Health and Illness* (third edition). Oxford: Butterworth-Heinemann.

Hénaff, Marcel. 1998 [1991]. *Claude Lévi-Strauss and the Making of Structural Anthropology* (translated by Mary Baker). Minneapolis: University of Minnesota Press.

Héritier, Françoise. 1981. *L'exercice de la parenté*. Paris: Gallimard.

Herskovits, Melville J. 1926. The cattle complex in East Africa. *American Anthropologist* 28: 230–72, 361–88, 494–528, 633–64.

1930. The culture areas of Africa. *Africa* 3: 59–77.

Herzfeld, Michael. 1984. The horns of the Mediterraneanist dilemma. *American Ethnologist* 11: 439–54.

1987. *Anthropology through the Looking-Glass: Critical Ethnography in the Margins of Europe*. Cambridge: Cambridge University Press.

Hiatt, L. R. 1968. Gidjingali marriage arrangements. In Richard B. Lee and Irven DeVore (eds.), *Man the Hunter*. Chicago: Aldine Publishing Company, pp. 165–75.

1996. *Arguments about Aborigines: Australia and the Evolution of Social Anthropology*. Cambridge: Cambridge University Press.

Hindess, Barry and Paul Hirst. 1975. *Pre-Capitalist Modes of Production*. London: Routledge & Kegan Paul.

1977. *Mode of Production and Social Formation: An Auto-Critique of Pre-Capitalist Modes of Production*. London: The Macmillan Press.

Hjelmslev, Louis. 1953 [1943]. *Prolegomena to a Theory of Language* (Indiana University Publications in Anthropology and Linguistics, Memoir 7). Baltimore, MD: Waverly Press.

Hobbes, Thomas. 1973 [1651]. *Leviathan*. London: J. M. Dent & Sons.

Hollis, Martin and Steven Lukes (eds.). 1982. *Rationality and Relativism*. Oxford: Basil Blackwell.

Holy, Ladislav. 1996. *The Little Czech and the Great Czech Nation: National Identity and the Post-Communist Social Transformation*. Cambridge: Cambridge University Press.

Holy, Ladislav and Milan Stuchlik. 1983. *Actions, Norms and Representations: Foundations of Anthropological Inquiry*. Cambridge: Cambridge University Press.

Ingold, Tim, 1986. *The Appropriation of Nature: Essays on Human Ecology and Social Relations*. Manchester: Manchester University Press.

(ed.). 1994. *Companion Encyclopedia of Anthropology: Humanity, Culture and Social Life*. London: Routledge.

(ed.). 1996. *Key Debates in Anthropology*. London: Routledge.

Jakobson, Roman. 1962. *Selected Writings*, vol. I. The Hague: Mouton.

1971. *Selected Writings*, vol. II. The Hague: Mouton.

James, Allison, Jenny Hockey, and Andrew Dawson (eds.). 1997. *After Writing Culture: Epistemology and Praxis in Contemporary Anthropology* (A.S.A. Monographs 34). London: Routledge.

Jenkins, Richard. 1992. *Pierre Bourdieu*. London: Routledge.

Josselin de Jong, J. P. B. de. 1977 [1935]. The Malay Archipelago as a field of ethnological study. In P. E. de Josselin de Jong (ed.), *Structural Anthropology in the Netherlands*. The Hague: Martinus Nijhoff, pp. 166–82.

Josselin de Jong, P. E. de (ed.). 1977. *Structural Anthropology in the Netherlands*. The Hague: Martinus Nijhoff.

Kaberry, Phyllis. 1957. Malinowski's contribution to field-work methods and the writing of ethnography. In Raymond Firth (ed.), *Man and Culture: An Evaluation of the Work of Bronislaw Malinowski*. London: Routledge & Kegan Paul, pp. 71–91.

Kahn, Joel S. 1980. *Minangkabau Social Formations: Indonesian Peasants and the World Economy*. Cambridge: Cambridge University Press.

1981. Marxist anthropology and segmentary societies: a review of the literature. In Joel S. Kahn and Josep R. Llobera (eds.), *The Anthropology of Pre-Capitalist Societies*. London: Macmillan, pp. 57–88.

Kahn, Joel S. and Josep R. Llobera. 1981. Towards a new Marxism or a new anthropology. In Joel S. Kahn and Josep R. Llobera (eds.), *The Anthropology of Pre-Capitalist Societies*. London: Macmillan, pp. 263–329.

Kames, Lord. 1774. *Sketches of the History of Man* (2 vols.). London: W. Strahan and T. Cadell.

Kapferer, Bruce (ed.). 1976. *Transaction and Meaning: Directions in the Anthropology of Exchange and Symbolic Behavior* (A.S.A. Essays 1). Philadelphia: Institute for the Study of Human Issues.

Katz, Pearl. 1981. Ritual in the operating room. *Ethnology* 20: 335–50.

Kenyatta, Jomo. 1938. *Facing Mount Kenya: The Tribal Life of the Gikuyu*. London: Secker & Warburg.

Kloos, Peter and Henri J. M. Claessen (eds.). 1991. *Contemporary Anthropology in the Netherlands: The Use of Anthropological Ideas*. Amsterdam: VU University Press.

Kluckhohn, Clyde. 1936. Some reflections on the methods and theories of the Kulturkreislehre. *American Anthropologist* 38: 157–96.

1944. *Navaho Witchcraft* (Papers of the Peabody Museum of American Archaeology and Ethnology, vol. 22). Cambridge, MA: Peabody Museum.

Kluckhohn, Clyde and Dorothea Leighton. 1974 [1946]. *The Navaho* (revised edition). Cambridge, MA: Harvard University Press.

Knauft, Bruce M. 1996. *Genealogies for the Present in Cultural Anthropology*. New York: Routledge.

Knight, Chris. 1991. *Blood Relations: Menstruation and the Origins of Culture*. New Haven: Yale University Press.

Knight, Chris, Camilla Power, and Ian Watts. 1995. The human symbolic revolution: a Darwinian account. *Cambridge Archaeological Journal* 5(1): 75–114.

Knox, Robert. 1850. *Races of Men: A Fragment*. Philadelphia: Lea and Blanchard.

Korn, Francis. 1973. *Elementary Structures Reconsidered: Lévi-Strauss on Kinship*. London: Tavistock Publications.

Kroeber, A. L. 1909. Classificatory systems of relationship. *Journal of the Royal Anthropological Institute* 39: 77–84.

1931. The culture-area and age-area concepts of Clark Wissler. In Stuart A. Rice (ed.), *Methods in Social Science: A Case Book*. Chicago: University of Chicago Press, pp. 248–65.

1939. Cultural and natural areas of Native North America. *University of California Publications in American Archaeology and Ethnology* 38: 1–240.

1963 [1948]. *Anthropology: Culture Patterns and Processes* (from the revised edition of Kroeber's complete *Anthropology*). New York: Harcourt, Brace & World.

Kroeber, A. L. and Clyde Kluckhohn. 1952. *Culture: A Critical Review of Concepts and Definitions* (Papers of the Peabody Museum of American Archaeology and Ethnology, vol. 47, no. 1). Cambridge, MA: Peabody Museum.

Kropotkin, Peter. 1987 [1902]. *Mutual Aid: A Factor of Evolution*. London: Freedom Press.

Kuhn, Thomas S. 1970 [1962]. *The Structure of Scientific Revolutions* (second edition). Chicago: University of Chicago Press.

Kuklick, Henrika. 1991. *The Savage Within: The History of British Anthropology, 1885–1945.* Cambridge: Cambridge University Press.

Kuper, Adam (ed.). 1977. *The Social Anthropology of Radcliffe-Brown.* London: Routledge & Kegan Paul.

   1979a [1977]. Regional comparison in African anthropology. *African Affairs* 78: 103–13.

   1979b. A structural approach to dreams. *Man* (n.s.) 14: 645–62.

   1982. *Wives for Cattle: Bridewealth and Marriage in Southern Africa.* London: Routledge & Kegan Paul.

   1988. *The Invention of Primitive Society: Transformations of an Illusion.* London: Routledge.

   1992. Post-Modernism, Cambridge and the Great Kalahari Debate. *Social Anthropology* 1: 57–71.

   1994. *The Chosen Primate: Human Nature and Cultural Diversity.* Cambridge, MA: Harvard University Press.

   1996 [1973]. *Anthropologists and Anthropology: The Modern British School* (third edition). London: Routledge.

   1999. *Culture: The Anthropologists' Account.* Cambridge, MA: Harvard University Press.

Kuper, Adam and Jessica Kuper (eds.). 1996 [1985]. *The Social Science Encyclopedia* (second edition). London: Routledge.

Lacan, Jacques. 1977 [1966]. *Ecrits: A Selection* (translated by Alan Sheridan). London: Tavistock Publications.

Lakoff, George and Mark Johnson. 1980. *Metaphors We Live By.* Chicago: University of Chicago Press.

Lamarck, J. B. 1914 [1809]. *Zoological Philosophy: An Exposition with Regard to the Natural Philosophy of Animals.* London: Macmillan.

Lane, Harlan. 1977. *The Wild Boy of Aveyron.* London: George Allen & Unwin.

Langham, Ian. 1981. *The Building of British Social Anthropology: W. H. R. Rivers and his Cambridge Disciples in the Development of Kinship Studies, 1898–1931.* Dordrecht: D. Reidel Publishing Company (Studies in the History of Modern Science 8).

Lapointe, Francois H. and Claire Lapointe. 1977. *Claude Lévi-Strauss and His Critics: An International Bibliography of Criticism (1950–1976).* New York: Garland (Reference Library of the Humanities, vol. 72).

Layton, Robert. 1997. *An Introduction to Theory in Anthropology.* Cambridge: Cambridge University Press.

Leach, Edmund R. 1954. *Political Systems of Highland Burma: A Study of Kachin Social Structure.* London: The Athlone Press.

   1961a. *Pul Eliya, a Village in Ceylon: A Study of Land Tenure and Kinship.* Cambridge: Cambridge University Press.

   1961b [1945–61]. *Rethinking Anthropology.* London: The Athlone Press (L.S.E. Monographs on Social Anthropology 22).

   (ed.). 1967. *The Structural Study of Myth and Totemism* (A.S.A. Monographs 5). London: Tavistock Publications.

1970. *Lévi-Strauss*. Glasgow: Fontana/Collins (Fontana Modern Masters).

1976a. *Social Anthropology: A Natural Science of Society?* (Radcliffe-Brown Lecture, 1976). Oxford: Oxford University Press.

1976b. *Culture and Communication: The Logic by which Symbols are Connected.* Cambridge: Cambridge University Press.

Leacock, Eleanor. 1978. Women's status in egalitarian society: implications for social evolution. *Current Anthropology* 19: 247–75.

Leaf, Murray J. 1979. *Man, Mind, and Science: A History of Anthropology*. New York: Columbia University Press.

Lechte, John. 1994. *Fifty Key Contemporary Thinkers: From Structuralism to Postmodernity*. London: Routledge.

Lee, Richard B. 1979. *The !Kung San: Men, Women, and Work in a Foraging Society*. Cambridge: Cambridge University Press.

1981 [1980]. Is there a foraging mode of production? *Canadian Journal of Anthropology* 2: 13–19.

Lee, Richard B. and Mathias Guenther. 1991. Oxen or onions? The search for trade (and truth) in the Kalahari. *Current Anthropology* 32: 592–601.

1993. Problems in Kalahari historical ethnography and the tolerance of error. *History in Africa* 20: 185–235.

Legros, Dominique. 1977. Chance, necessity, and mode of production: a Marxist critique of cultural evolutionism. *American Anthropologist* 79: 26–41.

Levine, Donald N. 1995. *Visions of the Sociological Tradition*. Chicago: University of Chicago Press.

Lévi-Strauss, Claude. 1963 [1958] [1945–58]. *Structural Anthropology* (translated by Clare Jacobson and Brook Grundfest Schoepf). New York: Basic Books.

1966a. The future of kinship studies. *Proceedings of the Royal Anthropological Institute for 1965*, pp. 13–22.

1966b [1962]. *The Savage Mind*. Chicago: University of Chicago Press.

1968. The concept of primitiveness. In Richard B. Lee and Irven DeVore (eds.), *Man the Hunter*. Chicago: Aldine Publishing Company, pp. 349–52.

1969a [1949]. *The Elementary Structures of Kinship* (revised edition, translated by James Harle Bell, John Richard von Sturmer, and Rodney Needham). Boston: Beacon Press.

1969b [1962]. *Totemism*. Harmondsworth: Penguin Books.

1976 [1955]. *Tristes Tropiques* (translated by John and Doreen Weightman). Harmondsworth: Penguin Books.

1978a. *Myth and Meaning*. London: Routledge & Kegan Paul.

1978b [1968]. *The Origin of Table Manners: Introduction to a Science of Mythology, 3* (translated by John and Doreen Weightman). London: Jonathan Cape.

1988 [1950]. *Introduction to the Work of Marcel Mauss*. London: Routledge.

1997 [1993]. *Look, Listen, Read* (translated by Brian C. J. Singer). New York: Basic Books.

Lévi-Strauss, Claude and Didier Eribon. 1991 [1988]. *Conversations with Claude Lévi-Strauss* (translated by Paula Wissing). Chicago: University of Chicago Press.

Lévy-Bruhl, Lucien. 1926 [1910]. *How Natives Think* (translated by Lilian A. Clare). London: George Allen & Unwin.

1975 [1949]. *The Notebooks on Primitive Mentality* (translated by Peter Rivière). Oxford: Basil Blackwell & Mott.

Lewis, Oscar. 1951. *Life in a Mexican Village: Tepoztlan Restudied.* Urbana: University of Illinois Press.

Leyton, Elliott. 1974. Opposition and integration in Ulster. *Man* (n.s.) 9: 185–98.

Lienhardt, Godfrey. 1961. *Divinity and Experience: The Religion of the Dinka.* Oxford: Clarendon Press.

Linnaeus, Carolus. 1956 [1758]. *Systema Naturae. Regnum Animale* (tenth edition, vol. 1). London: British Museum (Natural History).

Locke, John. 1988 [1690]. *Two Treatises of Government.* Cambridge: Cambridge University Press.

Long, Norman. 1996. Globalization and localization: new challenges to rural research. In Henrietta L. Moore (ed.), *The Future of Anthropological Knowledge* (The Uses of Knowledge: Global and Local Relations: A.S.A. Decennial Conference Series). London: Routledge, pp. 37–59.

Lovejoy, Arthur O. 1936. *The Great Chain of Being: A Study of the History of an Idea.* Cambridge, MA: Harvard University Press.

Lowie, Robert H. 1937. *The History of Ethnological Theory.* New York: Holt, Rinehart and Winston.

1947 [1920]. *Primitive Society* (second edition). New York: Liveright Publishing Company.

Lubbock, Sir John. 1874 [1870]. *The Origin of Civilisation and the Primitive Condition of Man.* New York: D. Appleton and Company.

Lucy, John A. 1992. *Language Diversity and Thought: A Reformulation of the Linguistic Relativity Hypothesis.* Cambridge: Cambridge University Press.

Lyotard, Jean-François. 1984 [1979]. *The Postmodern Condition: A Report on Knowledge* (translated by Geoff Bennington and Brian Massumi). Manchester: Manchester University Press (Theory and History of Literature, vol. 10).

McGrew, W. C. 1991. Chimpanzee material culture: what are its origins and why? In R. A. Foley (ed.), *The Origins of Human Behaviour.* London: Unwin Hyman, pp. 13–24.

McLennan, John F. 1970 [1865]. *Primitive Marriage: An Inquiry into the Origin of the Form of Capture in Marriage Ceremonies.* Chicago: University of Chicago Press.

Maine, Henry Sumner. 1913 [1861]. *Ancient Law: Its Connection with the Early History of Society and Its Relation to Modern Ideas.* London: George Routledge & Sons.

Malefijt, Annemarie de Waal. 1976. *Images of Man: A History of Anthropological Thought.* New York: Alfred A. Knopf.

Malinowski, Bronislaw. 1922. *Argonauts of the Western Pacific: An Account of Native Enterprise and Adventure in the Archipelagoes of Melanesian New Guinea.* London: George Routledge & Sons.

1927a. *The Father in Primitive Psychology.* New York: W. W. Norton & Company.

1927b. *Sex and Repression in Savage Society.* London: Kegan Paul.

1934. Introduction. In H. Ian Hogbin, *Law and Order in Polynesia: A Study of Primitive Legal Institutions.* London: Christophers, pp. xvii–lxxii.

1935. *Coral Gardens and Their Magic: A Study of the Methods of Tilling the Soil and of Agricultural Rites in the Trobriand Islands* (2 vols.). London: George Allen and Unwin.

1944 [1939–42]. *A Scientific Theory of Culture and Other Essays*. Chapel Hill: University of North Carolina Press.

1948 [1916–41]. *Magic, Science and Religion and Other Essays* (selected by Robert Redfield). Glencoe, IL: The Free Press.

1967. *A Diary in the Strict Sense of the Term*. London: Routledge & Kegan Paul.

Marcus, George E. and James Clifford. 1985. The making of ethnographic texts: a preliminary report. *Current Anthropology* 26: 267–71.

Marcus, George E. and Michael M. J. Fischer. 1986. *Anthropology as Cultural Critique: An Experimental Monument in the Human Sciences*. Chicago: University of Chicago Press.

Marx, Karl. 1965 [1857–8]. *Pre-capitalist Economic Formations*. New York: International Publishers.

1974 [1867]. *Capital: A Critical Analysis of Capitalist Production*, vol. 1 (edited by Frederick Engels [Friedrich Engels] and translated by Samuel Moore and Edward Aveling). London: Lawrence & Wishart.

Mason, Paul. 1990. *Deconstructing America: Representations of the Other*. London and New York: Routledge.

Mauss, Marcel. 1990 [1923]. *The Gift: The Form and Reason for Exchange in Archaic Societies* (translated by W. D. Halls). London: Routledge.

Mead, Margaret. 1928. *Coming of Age in Samoa*. New York: William Morrow and Company.

1930. *Growing Up in New Guinea*. New York: William Morrow and Company.

Meillassoux, Claude. 1964. *Anthropologie économique des Gouro de Côte d'Ivoire*. Paris: Mouton.

1972. From reproduction to production. *Economy and Society* 1: 93–105.

1981 [1975]. *Maidens, Meal and Money: Capitalism and the Domestic Economy*. Cambridge: Cambridge University Press.

Merleau-Ponty, Maurice. 1962. *Phenomenology of Perception* (translated by James Edie). Evanston, IL: Northwestern University Press.

Milner, Andrew. 1994. *Contemporary Cultural Theory: An Introduction*. London: UCL Press.

Milton, Kay. 1979. Male bias in anthropology. *Man* (n.s.) 14: 40–54.

Monboddo, Lord. 1773–92. *Of the Origin and Progress of Language* (6 vols.). London: T. Cadell.

1779–99. *Antient Metaphysics* (6 vols.). London: T. Cadell.

Montesquieu, C. L. de Secondat, baron de La Brède et de. 1964 [1721]. *The Persian Letters* (translated by George R. Healy). Indianapolis: Bobbs-Merrill.

1989 [1748]. *The Spirit of the Laws* (translated by Anne M. Cohler, Basia Carolyn Miller, and Harold Samuel Stone). Cambridge: Cambridge University Press.

Moore, Henrietta L. 1988. *Feminism and Anthropology*. Cambridge: Polity Press.

1994 [1993–4]. *A Passion for Difference: Essays in Anthropology and Gender*. Cambridge: Polity Press.

Moore, Jerry D. 1997. *Visions of Culture: An Introduction to Anthropological Theories and Theorists*. Walnut Creek, CA: AltaMira Press.

Morgan, Lewis Henry. 1871. *Systems of Consanguinity and Affinity of the Human Family* (Smithsonian Contributions to Knowledge, vol. 17). Washington: Smithsonian Institution.

1877. *Ancient Society; or, Researches in the Lines of Human Progress from Savagery through Barbarism to Civilization*. New York: Henry Holt.

Müller, F. Max. 1977 [1892]. *Anthropological Religion*. New Delhi: Asian Educational Services.

Murdock, George Peter. 1949. *Social Structure*. New York: Macmillan.

Myerhoff, Barbara. 1978. *Number Our Days*. New York: Simon & Schuster.

Nadel, S. F. 1957. Malinowski on magic and religion. In Raymond Firth (ed.), *Man and Culture: An Evaluation of the Work of Bronislaw Malinowski*. London: Routledge & Kegan Paul, pp. 189–208.

Needham, Rodney. 1962. *Structure and Sentiment: A Test Case in Social Anthropology*. Chicago: University of Chicago Press.

1972. *Belief, Language, and Experience*. Oxford: Basil Blackwell.

1973. Prescription. *Oceania* 42: 166–81.

1979. *Symbolic Classification*. Santa Monica, CA: Goodyear Publishing Company.

1981. *Circumstantial Deliveries*. Berkeley: University of California Press.

Obeyesekere, Gananath. 1992. *The Apotheosis of Captain Cook: European Mythmaking in the Pacific*. Princeton: Princeton University Press.

Okely, Judith. 1996 [1975–96]. *Own or Other Culture*. London: Routledge.

Okely, Judith and Helen Callaway (eds.). 1992. *Anthropology and Autobiography* (A. S. A. Monographs 29). London: Routledge.

O'Laughlin, Bridget. 1975. Marxist approaches in anthropology. *Annual Review of Anthropology* 4: 341–70.

Olson, David R. and Nancy Torrance (eds.). 1996. *Modes of Thought: Explorations in Culture and Cognition*. Cambridge: Cambridge University Press.

Ong, Aihwa. 1996. Anthropology, China and modernities: The geopolitics of cultural knowledge. In Henrietta L. Moore (ed.), *The Future of Anthropological Knowledge* (The Uses of Knowledge: Global and Local Relations: A.S.A. Decennial Conference Series). London: Routledge, pp. 60–92.

Ortner, Sherry. 1974. Is female to male as nature is to culture? In Michelle Z. Rosaldo and Louise Lamphere (eds.), *Woman, Culture and Society*. Stanford: Stanford University Press, pp. 67–88.

1984. Theory in anthropology since the sixties. *Comparative Studies in Society and History* 26: 126–66.

1995. Resistance and the problem of ethnographic refusal. *Comparative Studies in Society and History* 37: 173–93.

Ottenberg, Simon and Phebe Ottenberg (eds.). 1960. *Cultures and Societies of Africa*. New York: Random House.

Pals, Daniel L. 1996. *Seven Theories of Religion*. Oxford: Oxford University Press.

Parsons, Talcott. 1949 [1937]. *The Structure of Social Action*. New York: The Free Press of Glencoe.

Pasquinelli, Carla. 1996. The concept of culture between modernity and postmodernity. In Václav Hubinger (ed.), *Grasping the Changing World: Anthro-*

pological Concepts in the Postmodern Era. London: Routledge, pp. 53–73.

Perry, William James. 1923. *The Children of the Sun: A Study in the Early History of Civilization*. London: Methuen and Company.

Pike, Kenneth L. 1967. *Language in Relation to a Unified Theory of the Structure of Human Behavior* (second edition). The Hague: Mouton.

Pompa, Leon (editor and translator). 1982. *Vico: Selected Writings*. Cambridge: Cambridge University Press.

Pouillon, Jean and Pierre Maranda (eds.). 1970. *Echanges et communications: mélanges offerts à Claude Lévi-Strauss à l'occasion de son 60ème anniversaire* (2 vols.). The Hague: Mouton (Studies in General Anthropology, 5).

Prichard, James Cowles. 1973 [1813]. *Researches into the Physical History of Man*. Chicago and London: University of Chicago Press.

Pufendorf, Samuel. 1991 [1673]. *On the Duty of Man and Citizen* (edited by James Tully and translated by Michael Silverthorne). Cambridge: Cambridge University Press.

Quinn, Naomi. 1991. The cultural basis of metaphor. In James W. Fernandez (ed.), *Beyond Metaphor: The Theory of Tropes in Anthropology*. Stanford: Stanford University Press, pp. 56–93.

Rabinow, Paul. 1977. *Reflections on Fieldwork in Morocco*. Berkeley: University of California Press.

1997. *Essays on the Anthropology of Reason*. Princeton: Princeton University Press.

Radcliffe-Brown, A. R. 1922. *The Andaman Islanders*. Cambridge: Cambridge University Press.

1931. *The Social Organization of Australian Tribes*. Sydney: Oceania Monographs (no. 1).

1952 [1924–49]. *Structure and Function in Primitive Society: Essays and Addresses*. London: Cohen & West.

1957. *A Natural Science of Society*. Glencoe, IL: The Free Press.

1958. *Method in Social Anthropology: Selected Essays by A. R. Radcliffe-Brown* (edited by M. N. Srinivas). Chicago: University of Chicago Press.

Radcliffe-Brown. A. R. and Daryll Forde (eds.). 1950. *African Systems of Kinship and Marriage*. London: Oxford University Press for the International African Institute.

Ramos, Alcida R. 1992. Reflecting on the Yanomami: ethnographic images and the pursuit of the exotic. In George E. Marcus (ed.), *Rereading Cultural Anthropology*. Durham, NC: Duke University Press, pp. 48–68.

Ratzel, Friedrich. 1891. Die afrikanischen Bögen, ihre Verbeitung und Verwandtschaften. *Abhandlungen der Königlichen Sächsische Gesellschaft der Wissenschaften. Philologischhistorischen Classe* 13: 291–346.

1896–8 [1885–8]. *The History of Mankind* (translated by A. J. Butler) (3 vols.). London: Macmillan.

Redfield, Robert. 1930. *Tepoztlan: A Mexican Village*. Chicago: University of Chicago Press.

Reed-Donahay, Deborah. 1995. The Kabyle and the French: occidentalism in Bourdieu's theory of practice. In James G. Carrier (ed.), *Occidentalism: Images of the West*. Oxford: Oxford University Press, pp. 61–84.

Richards, A. I. 1939. *Land, Labour and Diet in Northern Rhodesia: An Economic Study of the Bemba Tribe.* London: Oxford University Press.

Rivers, W. H. R. 1968 [1914]. *Kinship and Social Organization* (L.S.E. Monographs on Social Anthropology, No. 34.). London: The Athlone Press.

Romney, A. Kimball and Roy Goodwin D'Andrade. 1964. Cognitive aspects of English kin terms. *American Anthropologist* 66(3), Special Publication, part 2: 146–70.

Rosaldo, Michelle Z. 1974. Woman, culture and society: a theoretical overview. In Michelle Z. Rosaldo and Louise Lamphere (eds.), *Woman, Culture and Society.* Stanford: Stanford University Press, pp. 17–42.

Rousseau, Jean-Jacques. 1973 [1750–62]. *The Social Contract and Discourses* (translated by G. D. H. Cole). London: J. M. Dent & Sons.

Sacks, Karen. 1979. *Sisters and Wives: The Past and Future of Sexual Equality.* Westport, CT: Greenwood Press.

Sahlins, Marshall. 1974 [1972]. *Stone Age Economics.* London: Tavistock Publications.

1976. *Culture and Practical Reason.* Chicago: University of Chicago Press.

1977 [1976]. *The Use and Abuse of Biology: An Anthropological Critique of Sociobiology.* London: Tavistock Publications.

1981. *Historical Metaphors and Mythical Realities: Structure in the Early History of the Sandwich Islands Kingdom.* Ann Arbor: University of Michigan Press (Association for the Study of Anthropology in Oceania, Special Publication no. 1).

1985. *Islands of History.* Chicago: University of Chicago Press.

1995. *How 'Natives' Think: About Captain Cook, for Example.* Chicago: University of Chicago Press.

Said, Edward W. 1978. *Orientalism.* New York: Pantheon.

Sapir, Edward. 1949 [1915–38]. *Selected Writings in Language, Culture, and Personality* (edited by David G. Mandelbaum). Berkeley: University of California Press.

Sarana, Gopala. 1975. *The Methodology of Anthropological Comparisons: An Analysis of Comparative Methods in Social and Cultural Anthropology.* Tuscon: University of Arizona Press (Viking Fund Publications in Anthropology 53).

Sarup, Madan. 1988. *An Introductory Guide to Post-structuralism and Postmodernism.* New York: Harvester Wheatsheaf.

Saussure, Ferdinand de. 1974 [1916]. *Course in General Linguistics* (edited by Charles Bally and Albert Sechehaye, translated by Wade Baskin). Glasgow: Fontana/Collins.

Schapera, I. 1947. *Migrant Labour and Tribal Life: A Study of the Condition of the Bechuanaland Protectorate.* London: Oxford University Press.

Scheper-Hughes, Nancy and Margaret Lock. 1987. The mindful body: a prolegomenon to future work in medical anthropology. *Medical Anthropology Quarterly* 1: 6–41.

Schmidt, Wilhelm. 1939 [1937]. *The Culture Historical Method of Ethnology: The Scientific Approach to the Racial Question* (translated by S. A. Sieber). New York: Fortuny's.

Schneider, David M. 1980 [1968]. *American Kinship: A Cultural Account* (second

232   References

edition). Chicago: University of Chicago Press.

1984. *A Critique of the Study of Kinship*. Ann Arbor: University of Michigan Press.

Service, Elman R. 1962. *Primitive Social Organization: An Evolutionary Perspective*. New York: Random House.

1985. *A Century of Controversy: Ethnological Issues from 1860 to 1960*. Orlando: Academic Press.

Shankman, Paul. 1984. The thick and the thin: on the interpretive theoretical program of Clifford Geertz. *Current Anthropology* 25: 261–79.

Shott, Michael J. 1992. On recent trends in the anthropology of foragers: Kalahari revisionism and its archaeological implications. *Man* (n.s.) 27: 843–71.

Skorupski, John. 1976. *Symbol and Theory: A Philosophical Study of Theories of Religion in Social Anthropology*. Cambridge: Cambridge University Press.

Slotkin, J. S. (ed.). 1965. *Readings in Early Anthropology*. Chicago: Aldine Publishing Company.

Smart, Barry. 1985. *Michel Foucault*. London: Routledge.

1993. *Postmodernism*. London: Routledge.

Smith, Adam. 1970 [1761]. *A Dissertation on the Origin of Languages*. Tübingen: Tübinger Beiträge zur Linguistik.

1981 [1776]. *An Inquiry into the Nature and Causes of the Wealth of Nations*. Indianapolis: Liberty Press.

Solway, Jacqueline S. and Richard B. Lee. 1990. Foragers, genuine or spurious? Situating the Kalahari San in history. *Current Anthropology* 31: 109–46.

Spencer, Jonathan. 1989. Anthropology as a kind of writing. *Man* (n.s.) 24: 145–64.

Sperber, Dan. 1975 [1974]. *Rethinking Symbolism* (translated by Alice L. Morton). Cambridge: Cambridge University Press.

1982. Apparently irrational beliefs. In Martin Hollis and Steven Lukes (eds.), *Rationality and Relativism*. Oxford: Basil Blackwell, pp. 149–80.

1985 [1982]. *On Anthropological Knowledge: Three Essays*. Cambridge: Cambridge University Press/Paris: Editions de la Maison des Sciences de l'Homme.

Spiro, Melford E. 1992. Cultural relativism and the future of anthropology. In George E. Marcus (ed.), *Rereading Cultural Anthropology*. Durham, NC: Duke University Press, pp. 124–51.

Steiner, P. (ed.) 1982. *The Prague School: Selected Writings, 1929–1946* (translated by Olga P. Hasty). Austin: University of Texas Press.

Steward, Julian H. (ed.). 1946–50. *Handbook of the South American Indians* (Bureau of American Ethnology, Bulletin 143, vols. 1–6). Washington, DC: Smithsonian Institution.

1955. *Theory of Culture Change: The Methodology of Multilinear Evolution*. Urbana: University of Illinois Press.

Stipe, Claude E. 1985. Scientific creationism and evangelical Christianity. *American Anthropologist* 87: 148–50.

Stocking, George W., Jr. 1968 [1962–6]. *Race, Culture, and Evolution: Essays in the History of Anthropology*. New York: The Free Press.

1971. What's in a name? The origins of the Royal Anthropological Institute. *Man* (n.s.) 6: 369–90.

(ed.). 1974. *A Franz Boas Reader: The Shaping of American Anthropology, 1883–1911.* Chicago: University of Chicago Press.

(ed.). 1983. *Observers Observed: Essays on Ethnographic Fieldwork.* Madison: University of Wisconsin Press (History of Anthropology 1).

(ed.). 1986. *Malinowski, Rivers, Benedict and Others: Essays on Culture and Personality.* Madison: University of Wisconsin Press (History of Anthropology 4).

1987. *Victorian Anthropology.* New York: The Free Press.

1996a. *After Tylor: British Social Anthropology, 1888–1951.* London: The Athlone Press.

(ed.) 1996b. *Volksgeist as Method and Ethic: Essays on Boasian Ethnography and the German Anthropological Tradition.* Madison: University of Wisconsin Press (History of Anthropology 8).

Strathern, Andrew and Pamela J. Stewart. 1998. Embodiment and communications. Two frames for the analysis of ritual. *Social Anthropology* 6: 237–51.

Strathern, Marilyn. 1981. Culture in a netbag: the manufacture of a subdiscipline in anthropology. *Man* (n.s.) 16: 665–88.

1987a. An awkward relationship: the case of feminism and anthropology. *Signs* 12: 276–92.

1987b. Out of context: the persuasive fictions of anthropology. *Current Anthropology* 28: 251–81.

1991. *Partial Connections.* Savage, MD: Rowan & Littlefield Publishers.

1992. Parts and wholes: refiguring relationships in a post-plural world. In Adam Kuper (ed.), *Conceptualizing Society* (E.A.S.A. Monographs Series). London: Routledge, pp. 75–104.

Swingewood, Alan. 1984. *A Short History of Sociological Thought.* Basingstoke, Hants: Macmillan.

Taussig, Michael. 1993. *Mimesis and Alterity: A Particular History of the Senses.* London: Routledge.

Terray, Emmanuel. 1972 [1969]. *Marxism and 'Primitive' Society* (translated by M. Klopper). New York: Monthly Review Press.

Trigger, Bruce G. 1989. *A History of Archaeological Thought.* Cambridge: Cambridge University Press.

Turner, Victor W. 1957. *Schism and Continuity in an African Society: A Study of Ndembu Village Life.* Manchester: Manchester University Press for the Rhodes-Livingstone Institute.

1967. *The Forest of Symbols: Aspects of Ndembu Ritual.* Ithaca: Cornell University Press.

Turner, Victor and Edith Turner. 1978. *Image and Pilgrimage in Christian Culture: Anthropological Perspectives.* New York: Columbia University Press.

Tyler, Stephen A. (ed.). 1969. *Cognitive Anthropology.* New York: Holt, Rinehart and Winston.

1986. Post-modern ethnography: from document of the occult to occult document. In James Clifford and George E. Marcus (eds.), *Writing Culture: The Poetics and Politics of Ethnography.* Berkeley: University of California Press, pp. 122–40.

Tylor, Edward Burnett. 1861. *Anuahac, or Mexico and the Mexicans, Ancient and Modern.* London: Longman, Green, Longman, and Roberts.

1871. *Primitive Culture: Researches into the Development of Mythology, Philosophy, Religion, Language, Art, and Custom* (2 vols.). London: John Murray.

Urry, James. 1993. *Before Social Anthropology: Essays on the History of British Anthropology.* Chur, Switzerland: Harwood Academic Publishers

Van der Geest, Sjaak. 1990. Anthropologists and missionaries: brothers under the skin. *Man* (n.s.) 25: 588–601.

Van Gennep, Arnold. 1960 [1909]. *The Rites of Passage* (translated by Monika B. Vizedom and Gabrielle L. Caffee). London: Routledge & Kegan Paul.

Vermeulen, Han F. 1995. Origins and institutionalization of ethnography and ethnology in Europe and the USA, 1771–1845. In Han F. Vermeulen and Arturo Alvarez Roldan (eds.), *Fieldwork and Footnotes: Studies in the History of European Anthropology.* London and New York: Routledge, pp. 39–59.

Wallace, Anthony F. C. and John Atkins. 1960. The meaning of kinship terms. *American Anthropologist* 62: 58–80.

Wallerstein, Immanuel. 1974–89. *The Modern World-System,* (3 vols.). New York: Academic Press.

Weber, Max. 1930 [1922]. *The Protestant Ethic and the Spirit of Capitalism* (translated by Talcott Parsons). London: George Allen & Unwin.

Werbner, Richard P. 1984. The Manchester School in South-Central Africa. *Annual Review of Anthropology* 13: 157–85.

White, Leslie. 1949. *The Science of Culture: A Study of Man and Civilization.* New York: Grove Press.

1959. *The Evolution of Culture: The Development of Civilization to the Fall of Rome.* New York: McGraw-Hill.

Whorf, Benjamin Lee. 1956. *Language, Thought and Reality: Selected Writings of Benjamin Lee Whorf* (edited by John B. Carroll). Cambridge, MA: The MIT Press.

Williams, Robert Charles. 1983. Scientific creationism: An exegesis for a religious doctrine. *American Anthropologist* 85: 92–102.

Willis, Roy. 1974. *Man and Beast.* London: Hart-Davis, MacGibbon.

1981. *A State in the Making: Myth, History, and Social Transformation in Pre-Colonial Ufipa.* Bloomington: Indiana University Press.

Wilmsen, Edwin N. 1989. *Land Filled With Flies: A Political Economy of the Kalahari.* Chicago: University of Chicago Press.

Wilmsen, Edwin N. and James R. Denbow. 1990. Paradigmatic history of San-speaking peoples and current attempts at revision. *Current Anthropology* 31: 489–524.

Wilson, Bryan R. (ed.). 1970. *Rationality.* Oxford: Basil Blackwell.

Wilson, Edward O., 1975. *Sociobiology: The New Synthesis.* Cambridge, MA: Harvard University Press.

1980. *Sociobiology: The Abridged Edition.* Cambridge, MA: The Belknap Press of Harvard University Press.

Wissler, Clark. 1923. *Man and Culture.* New York: Thomas Y. Crowell Company.

1927. The culture-area concept in social anthropology. *The American Journal of Sociology* 32: 881–91.

Wolf, Eric R. 1982. *Europe and the People without History*. Berkeley: University of California Press.

Wolff, Kurt H. (editor and translator). 1950. *The Sociology of Georg Simmel*. New York: The Free Press.

(editor and translator). 1965. *Simmel: Essays on Sociology, Philosophy and Aesthetics*. New York: Harper & Row.

Worsley, Peter. 1956. The kinship system of the Tallensi: a revaluation. *Journal of the Royal Anthropological Institute* 86: 37–73.

Yanagisako, Sylvia and Jane Collier. 1987. Toward a unified analysis of gender and kinship. In Jane Collier and Sylvia Yanagisako (eds.), *Gender and Kinship: Essays toward a Unified Analysis*. Stanford: Stanford University Press, pp. 14–50.

Yolton, John W. (ed.). 1991. *The Blackwell Companion to the Enlightenment*. Oxford: Blackwell Publishers.

Zwernemann, Jürgen. 1983. *Culture History and African Anthropology: A Century of Research in Germany and Austria*. Uppsala: Acta Universitatis Upsaliensis (Uppsala Studies in Cultural Anthropology 6)/Stockholm: Almqvist & Wiksell International.

Index

Human groups
and social categories

Studies in social psychology

HENRI TAJFEL
Professor of social psychology University of Bristol

CAMBRIDGE UNIVERSITY PRESS

CAMBRIDGE
LONDON   NEW YORK   NEW ROCHELLE
MELBOURNE   SYDNEY

Published by the Press Syndicate of the University of Cambridge
The Pitt Building, Trumpington Street, Cambridge CB2 1RP
32 East 57th Street, New York, NY 10022, USA
296 Beaconsfield Parade, Middle Park, Melbourne 3206, Australia

First published 1981

Text set in 10/12pt Linotron 202 Bembo, printed and bound
in Great Britain at The Pitman Press, Bath

British Library Cataloguing in Publication Data
Tajfel, Henri
Human groups and social categories.
1. Social psychology
I. Title
302   HM251   80-41200
ISBN 0 521 22839 5
ISBN 0 521 28073 7 Pbk

Contents

7032052

Contents

PART III

Insiders and outsiders

Contents

PART IV
Intergroup conflict

For Anne, Michael and Paul

Acknowledgements

I wish to thank my colleagues who were co-authors of some of the work included in this book and who kindly authorized me to use it here. They are as follows:

Dr John D. Campbell, *National Institute of Health, Bethesda, Maryland*
Dr S. D. Cawasjee, *University of Aarhus, Denmark*
Professor John Dawson, *University of Hong Kong*
Professor Robert C. Gardner, *University of Western Ontario, London, Ontario*
Professor Gustav Jahoda, *University of Strathclyde, Glasgow*
Dr Nicholas B. Johnson, *Portsmouth, New Hampshire*
Dr Margaret Middleton, *Australian National University, Canberra*
Professor Charlan Nemeth, *University of California, Berkeley*
Dr Y. Rim, *Israel Institute of Technology, Haifa*
Professor A. A. Sheikh, *Marquette University, Milwaukee, Wisconsin*
Dr A. L. Wilkes, *University of Dundee, Scotland*

This book could not have been put together without the devoted, conscientious and unflagging help of Alma Foster. She knows that I am grateful, but it is a pleasure to be able to express this gratitude publicly.

Foreword

These essays are more than an expression of the creative talents of Henri Tajfel. They are also a sensitive testament to the times in which he has lived and in which the social sciences have grown. Tajfel has contributed to the growth of the social sciences in a notable way, but he has also had the courage and the sensibility to suffer the doubts and the metamorphoses that have been a feature of that growth. The doubts have not all grown in the protected soil of academic research either. He has, like many of his contemporaries, witnessed and survived man's inhumanity to man in our times. He has worked in a practical way to rehabilitate other survivors, looking after the orphaned young of the victims of concentration camps. And he has wondered how or whether the work of the social sciences might have prevented such catastrophes from happening. The essays, substantive contents aside, recount a moving story of change and response – intellectually and politically.

I think that the shape and the energy in Tajfel's rich work derive from two deep conflicts that have beset the social sciences from their start, and he has been honest enough to live with them and give them expression. One grows from the issue of objectivity: whether it is ever possible to describe and understand man's world from a position entirely free of and outside the values that each society cherishes. He doubts profoundly whether, in fact, we can ever be neutral in the sense that the physical sciences can claim neutrality. He offers as a partial answer to this problem the expedient of pluralism, the need for 'a social psychology which grows simultaneously in many places' nurtured by many points of view. Yet, pluralism aside, there is, in his view, no way of escaping the taking of a value position. Eventually, one must relate one's conclusions about particular social behaviour to 'the wider social setting' in which individuals operate. The wider social setting strongly influences and is influenced by individual behaviour, though it has a being of its own as well.

This leads immediately into the second energizing conflict in Tajfel's thinking. It has to do with the locus of explanation. There is a profoundly puzzling relation that exists between individual, human psychological functioning on the one hand and 'the large-scale social processes and events which shape this functioning and are shaped by it' on the other. Tajfel cannot, for example, accept the view that prejudice is an expression only of individual malaise or maladjustment or even of straightforward inter-individual conflict. Its existence also expresses certain structural properties of the broader society as well, these serving to create the categories in terms of which people sort out and evaluate the society immediately around them. Given these 'large-scale processes' and social structures, individual behaviour is channelled along certain lines that are only indirectly determined by the psychology of the individual. There is a constant interaction between the more structural 'superorganic' forces that animate the wider society and the individual reactions that appear superficially to be impelling human behaviour. For Tajfel, there can be no proper microscopic individual social psychology without specification of the social and cultural setting in which it occurs.

Whether viewed as intellectual autobiography or simply as essays in contemporary social psychology, this book is about the resolution of these two sets of conflicts. Substantively, I suppose, one could characterize the main topic of the volume as 'group prejudice', and there are searching essays on this topic, studies that have won the author world-wide renown. But it would, I think, be an error to interpret the main topic in this way. When Tajfel talks about the psychological significance of being a member of a disadvantaged minority, of the social comparisons that such members make between their own group and more privileged ones, he is dealing as well with the much more general question of the sensitivity of people to the social climate of group differentials as they exist in the broader social setting. The study of prejudice may be the manifest content of the research, but the deeper programmatic significance is equally applicable to any social psychological phenomenon – whether political power, aspirations for social mobility, or even migration. Indeed, speaking from my own personal perspective, I find Tajfel's essays speaking directly to issues in human development, particularly to the question of how children enter the society and so quickly take up its standard positions though they have too few exposures ever to have achieved an individual sense of what those positions entail. In this sense, the book provides a propaedeutic to what one might call 'realistic' social learning.

I cannot resist a few personal comments in writing this preface, for I have known the author well for a quarter of a century and value him as a friend. He is a man of huge hospitality in the broadest sense. He listens, reacts, brings you another drink, argues you down and sets you back up. He sets his guests at each other when he fears pseudo-agreement, thunders at them when he thinks their differences finical. Add one further element to that. Tajfel is the canonical European, not only linguistically equipped with several languages deployed with breath-taking speed and fluency, but with a deep sense of European culture. I have already commented on his faith in pluralism as an antidote to parochialism in social psychology. A happy confluence: Henri Tajfel chose to throw his hospitable, European, pluralistic energies into stimulating a 'European' social psychology. I think he was particularly eager to set up a base that would be distinctive to the reigning American social psychology of the time – the post-war decade. It is inconceivable how anybody could have done more to promote the cause – helping found a Society, editing a monograph series, a regular lecturer in Leiden, Paris and Bologna and a peripatetic one in a dozen other centres. I think I speak the complete truth when I say that I have never visited the Tajfels in Bristol without there being an attending Dutch social statistician or a passing-through Italian social developmentalist or a German student of prejudice. It is hard to ascribe causes in history. Tajfel's intellectual enthusiasm, his buoyant hospitality, his European convictions, his faith in pluralism – any of these could have done it alone, could have created a lively and interesting 'European' social psychology. But I must also look to the 'large scale social processes'. I think Tajfel sensed something deeper about the European scene, a point of view waiting to be expressed. And he more than any other helped bring it into being.

This book is a striking example of the genre. If it cannot be said that they are 'European' essays, it can certainly be said with emphasis that their spirit is 'European'. And that is to be welcomed on whatever side of whatever ocean the reader finds himself.

Jerome Bruner
Glandore
Co. Cork
Ireland

1
The development of a perspective

1. Some personal issues

This book is very largely based on previous publications by its author. Its appearance raises therefore the inevitable question as to why it should be published at all. There are two answers to this question, one personal and one 'academic'. The second of these is more important in the long term, but I shall start with the first.

Between the mid-1950s and now, I have become a moderately successful academic, fairly snug and secure inside the variety of ivory towers which it has been my privilege to inhabit or visit. This is a long slice of life. But together with many people of my generation, I share memories of a raging storm which – it seemed at the time – would never stop. Amongst those who died then, there were millions who formed, in the most concrete sense of the term, my 'social background': the generations of European Jews who were born in the half-century straddling the eighteen and nineteen hundreds. The minority who survived came in from very cold and very far. Some of them got back as and if they could to the normal business of living. Others sought a last refuge in a country new to them, continued to fight in other wars, and some of them died again. Some felt guilty forever because there was no sense or reason to their survival while so many disappeared. A very few – those who had the talent – tried to express and reflect what had happened to them and to others.

Sharing their experience and feelings – but not the talent – I became an academic, almost in a fit of absent-mindedness. But this did not happen immediately after the war. In May 1945, after I had been disgorged with hundreds of others from a special train arriving at the Gare d'Orsay in Paris with its crammed load of prisoners-of-war returning from camps in Germany, I soon discovered that hardly anyone I knew in 1939 – including my family – was left alive. In one way or another, this led to six years of working in various ways and in various European countries for organizations which bravely tried with insufficient means to stem the flood of misery; their task was the rehabilitation of victims of war – children and adults. This was the beginning of my interest in social

1

psychology. More years had gone by when, in my final year as an over-ripe undergraduate at Birkbeck College in London, I found myself both very lucky and immensely surprised at having been awarded by the Ministry of Education one of their scarce mature student scholarships. The essay I wrote for the competition, which caused me to be selected for a terrifying interview at Curzon Street, was entitled 'Prejudice'. I still think today that the interviewers must have decided that I was exceptionally well-qualified to know what I was talking about, and this is why they gave me the scholarship.

The ivory towers, more solid then than they are now, had a way of smothering one with their benevolent warmth and comfort. Very soon, first briefly in Durham and then in Oxford, I was talking a new language, I learned a new jargon and discovered 'problems' which I never knew existed. The 'academic' psychology took full hold of me.

I thought at the time that I was deeply and irrevocably steeped in this new life. And yet, when I look back today, I know without any doubt that this has never been true. In a strange way, even my first published paper, unlikely as this would seem from its title, had a lot to do with the past. It was written under the guidance of, and together with, one of my Birkbeck teachers, Richard Peters, who had influenced me a great deal. The title was: 'Hobbes and Hull – metaphysicians of behaviour' (Peters and Tajfel, 1957). The article attempted to present a case against certain forms of reductionism in psychology. I now know what outraged me about Hull was his bland indifference to all that one knew about human society while he was weaving his web of 'hypothetico-deductive' over-simplifications, claiming at the same time that they provided the basis for insights about the complexities of human social behaviour.

And yet, much of my early work seemed far away from these complexities. Some examples of it will be found in chapters 4 and 5 of this book. The awareness of a unifying thread and of a preoccupation of which I really never let go happened as if by chance. There were three incidents. The first was an interview some years ago with a journalist who was preparing a book about psychologists (Cohen, 1977). When I read the interview as a chapter in his book, I disliked it intensely – not because of what Cohen did, but because of what I did to myself. There was obviously something important to me there that I tried to express, but it was done crudely and clumsily. The second incident came as an odd convergence. I was invited one summer to attend a colloquium in Jerusalem concerned with methods of historical research about the Holocaust. Some time later, I was participating in a symposium in Bad Homburg about 'Human ethology: the claims and limits of a new discipline'. When I started preparing my contribution to the symposium

(Tajfel, 1979), I had no idea that the Jerusalem experience would find its way, without any planned intention, into the conclusions of a text concerned, on the face of it, with a completely unrelated theme. The third *prise de conscience* came later, when I was invited to contribute a chapter to a Festschrift for Jerome Bruner (Tajfel, 1980a). The unifying thread became clear long before I wrote the chapter. Thinking about it forced me to consider what possible significance working on such esoteric issues as 'perceptual over-estimation' could have had for me in the early or the mid-1950s.

Within two years of publishing theoretical and research papers on perceptual over-estimation, I was applying some of the ideas contained in them to problems of social stereotyping. It took some more years (which included several excursions in other directions) to get me back to the title of my essay for the Curzon Street interview (see chapter 6). It took even more time to move from chapter 6 to chapter 7 of this book – from a cognitive analysis of sterotypes to their treatment as an indissoluble part of our social reality; and from the first three chapters of Part II to the work described in Part IV which attempts to deal with the social psychological realities of conflict between human groups. The last chapter of the book is a full return to the theme of the third year Birkbeck essay.

This unifying thread – as I see it now – is one excuse for publishing this book. To me, it represents a consistent line of development. There is some arrogance in presenting it to the reader; but I think this is more apparent than real. We all have some kind of an intellectual history; I know now that mine has been deeply enmeshed with the traumatic events of long ago. Being what it is, I think that the book should be of some interest as a reflection of some strands in an important period of development in European social psychology.

My hestitations about producing this book continued for a long time, and I recast it several times as I was working on it. I wish to express my gratitude to Dr Jeremy Mynott of Cambridge University Press whose encouragement to continue always came when it was most wanted. Needless to say, he bears no responsibility for the result.

2. The social dimension

The book is not arranged in chronological order, although chronology is roughly followed whenever it serves the purpose of clarifying the sequence of an argument. Part I on 'Social psychology and social processes' consists of an article which appeared in 1972 followed by a debate directly related to it which was published in 1979. The aim of part

II is to present the widening of a perspective which took as its point of origin the study of certain aspects of perceptual judgement and ended up many years later, through several successive steps, in the conviction that the study of *social* stereotypes by social psychologists is a travesty of our reality unless the term 'social' is taken seriously as the fulcrum of our work on the subject. In following this development of a point of view, part II includes a sequence of general articles and empirical studies published between 1957 and 1980. Part III returns to work done in the sixties and presents, in a sense, a long footnote to the development of ideas reflected in the transition from part II to part IV. It is, however, a necessary footnote since it establishes a continuity of preoccupations between the fifties and the late seventies. But there is also another reason, perhaps a more important one, for including this material. The 'experience of prejudice' described in the first chapter of part III (chapter 8) and the studies on the attitudes of children summarized in the two following chapters deal with the development of ethnic and national attitudes in a variety of social and cultural contexts. Various features of this development led to the asking of many new questions – no more than implicit at the time – about the psychological processes involved in the individuals' affiliation with large-scale social groups and in the conflicts between such groups. Part IV of the book, based on some of the work done throughout the seventies, is an attempt to provide a beginning of a few answers to these questions. But it is no more than a beginning. The first three chapters of part IV (chapters 11, 12 and 13) were published in 1978; but various preliminary versions went as far back as 1972 and 1973. At present, work within this framework is done by many of my colleagues in Britain and elsewhere and plans are made for its future continuation. A list of research reports directly related to the topic and theoretical perspective of part IV of this book, which was prepared in 1978, included nearly 80 items, out of which I was the author or co-author of only a few; a list prepared today would be very considerably longer (see introduction to part IV). This is why I was able to write earlier in this chapter that this book presents 'a reflection of some strands in an important period of development in European social psychology'.

The new-found identity of European social psychology which began developing in the early sixties is inseparable from the themes discussed in part I; it is also closely interdependent with the remainder of the book. The background to the symposium from which chapter 2 was drawn is briefly outlined in the introductory section to that chapter, and therefore I shall not discuss it here. It is the more general issue of the nature of this interdependence which needs to be discussed.

The initial push for this new identity in European work happened

almost by chance, but it would not have led to the subsequent developments had it not happened at the right time in the right place. The
convergence of a visit to Europe of two American colleagues, John
Lanzetta, who was spending two years in London, and John Thibaut,
who was in Paris for a year, led to the creation of a small committee
which, in addition to Lanzetta and Thibaut, consisted of Mauk Mulder,
who was then at the University of Utrecht, Robert Pagès from the
Sorbonne, and myself. After working for over a year, we managed to
organize in 1963 the first ever conference of European social
psychologists.[1] As I wrote later: 'We worked for some time, primarily to
'identify' social psychologists in Europe – a task which appears a strange
one today, ten years later' (Tajfel, 1972b, p. 308). The enterprise
succeeded and continued to expand. Its later developments included the
formalities of the elections of executive committees and of five successive
presidents, each serving for about three years. This formalization started
in the mid-1960s, several years after the first informal group of people
became convinced that the initiative was an important one. But the
underlying validity of all that happened since the beginnings of this
inevitable institutionalization still depended, as it does today, on the
vitality of a need and of the response to it. They were both clearly
identified at the first conference in 1963 and in the initiatives which led up
to it. Accounts of the development of the European Association of
Experimental Social Psychology can be found in the presidential report I
presented in Louvain in 1972 (Tajfel, 1972b) and in the report (to be
published) presented in Weimar in 1978 by Jos Jaspars in his capacity of
Acting President. In this chapter my concern is not with this brief
history, but with the nature of the need that created it and of the response
to this need which took the form of a variety of theoretical and research
developments.

There cannot be, and should not be, any kind of a unified European, or
any other, social psychology. The acquisition of a new identity to which
I referred earlier, must be understood instead in terms of two related
developments. One of them was the progressive creation of an actively
interacting community of people. The diversity of political, social,
linguistic and administrative boundaries in Europe made this convergence of previously isolated small pockets of people in various countries as
difficult as it was necessary. The channels of communication, so easily

---

[1] This conference could not have been organized without the encouragement and support of the Committee
on Transnational Social Psychology of the American Social Science Research Council. Soon afterwards,
the Committee co-opted to its membership several social psychologists from Europe. Until this
connection with the S.S.R.C. was severed some years ago, the Committee, first under the chairmanship of
Leon Festinger and then of Morton Deutsch, continued its support for European activities.

available to our American colleagues, had to be either created or unblocked in Europe. The second development consisted of the creation of a *diversity* of communicating viewpoints, trends of interest and research initiatives. The overwhelming numbers and productivity of our American colleagues were combined with the fact that in the first ten or fifteen years after the war it was, paradoxically, much easier for a social psychologist to travel from a European country to the United States, or vice versa, than to establish contacts much nearer, across a national or a linguistic border. The results were inevitable: the scattered social psychologists in Europe were following at a distance and with due delays, the successive ebbs and flows of the mainstream of American social psychology. It would be a mistake to ascribe the desire to change this state of affairs to some grotesque outburst of a new European chauvinism. As I wrote in 1971, in the Foreword to the first volume of the series of European Monographs in Social Psychology (Carswell and Rommetveit, 1971):

Why a *European* Association and a series of *European* Monographs in Social Psychology? These titles are not meant to reflect some new versions of a 'wider' or 'continental' nationalism – academic, intellectual or any other. The future of social psychology as a discipline and a contribution to knowledge and society is no more 'European', 'American' or 'African' than it is Basque, Welsh, Flemish, German or French . . In the long run . . . an exclusive focus from, and on, one cultural context cannot escape being damaging to the healthy development of a discipline which is in the last analysis one of the social sciences. There was a time, not so long ago, when most of us were quite happy to accept the proposition that the social and human sciences can be 'value free' and independent of their cultural and social framework. It is undoubtedly true that, whatever the case may be, this has become today a highly controversial issue, and not only for social psychology. Even the outwardly neutral description . . . of social psychology as the 'scientific study of human social behaviour' has not managed to remain *au-dessus de la mêlée* . . . For all these reasons, and many others, we must create a social psychology which grows simultaneously in many places . . . [We] do not set out to be 'European' in explicit opposition, competition or contradistinction to anything else . . . But a discipline concerned with the analysis and understanding of human social life must, in order to acquire its full significance, be tested and measured against the intellectual and social requirements of many cultures (pp. vii–viii).

This need for a diversity of social and cultural perspectives found its expression in the last two decades in a variety of new research developments. This book is meant to trace one of these developments, as reflected – and at first only hazily perceived – in the slow crystallization of a conviction and a perspective. A more detailed discussion of both will be found in the two succeeding chapters – this is why they were placed at the beginning of the book. Two additional points need to be made at this stage. The first concerns a very brief and preliminary description of the perspective. The second has to do with the conviction.

The perspective can be simply outlined. It consists of the view that social psychology *can* and *must* include in its theoretical and research preoccupations a direct concern with the relationship between human psychological functioning and the large-scale social processes and events which shape this functioning and are shaped by it. As obvious as this statement may appear to be, it will be seen later (e.g. chapters 2, 3, 7, 11, 14 and 15) that this concern with society at large has been, at best, at the fringes of the mainstream developments, since World War Two. It will also be seen (chapter 11) that connections can be made between this neglect of a *socio*psychological integration and the social and cultural background of most of the post-war social psychology.

As to the conviction, it grew out of the experience to which I referred in the preceding section of this chapter. Today, nearly forty years later, we have seen many new massacres and also some new holocausts. In the face of all this, my belief in a 'value-free' social psychology rapidly grew shaky. At the same time, the sixties and the seventies brought a revival of many semi- or pseudo-scientific attempts, quickly popularized, to provide crude and simplistic 'explanations' of the mayhem that human groups can inflict upon each other, physically, economically and socially (for some of the discussions of these views or of the use made of them, see. e.g. Billig, 1978; Bodmer and Cavalli-Sforza, 1970; Cohn, 1967; Crook, 1978; Kamin, 1977; Ludmerer, 1972; Montagu, 1968; Tajfel, 1976). As will be seen in several chapters of this book, I do not believe that 'explanations' of social conflicts and social injustice can be mainly or primarily psychological. At the same time, a *modest* contribution can be made to what I called elsewhere in this book the unravelling of a tangled web of issues. This is closely related to my conviction that a 'neutral' social psychology is hardly possible (neutrality in the social sciences often amounting to the implicit taking of a position) and that, at the same time it is possible and necessary *to attempt* to understand in one's job as a social psychologist the integration of individual interactions with their wider social settings. This integration can take many forms. The selection of those which are discussed in this book cannot be divorced from the background of personal experience described earlier in this chapter. This is why I must plead guilty to not being a 'neutral' social psychologist despite the respectably aseptic idiom that will be found in some of the chapters to follow.

The discussion about 'social psychology and social processes' to which part I of this book (chapters 2 and 3) is devoted was one only of many debates which engaged social psychologists in the seventies (see e.g. Armistead, 1974; Harré, 1977, a and b; Harré and Secord, 1972; Israel and Tajfel, 1972; Poitou, 1978; Schlenker, 1977; Strickland *et al.*, 1976; Stroebe, 1979). It differed, however, from many other debates in that it was explicitly concerned with the failure of the 'traditional' social psychology to build a bridge between its preoccupation with interacting *individuals*, and the wider social framework of these interactions which was largely neglected. At first sight, the two opening chapters of part II, based on work done between the mid-fifties and the early sixties, hardly seem to do anything much to fill this gap. Chapter 4 starts from a discussion of a half-forgotten issue – perceptual over-estimation – which was very much alive at the time, when controversies concerning the validity of the 'New Look' approach to the study of perceptual pheno- mena filled many pages of psychological journals. The description of this over-estimation and of some of the debate related to it is not relevant at this point; it will be found in the first section of chapter 4. But despite the apparent incongruity between what has been said earlier in the present chapter and this return to the neutrality of a fairly technical issue, the study of perceptual judgement, its inclusion in this book appeared indispensable. The technical problems remained technical for a time, but very soon they acquired a direct relevance to the study of those aspects of social perception which had to do with the divisions of people into social categories and the values associated with these divisions. This progres- sion is reflected in some ways in the formal hypotheses to be found in the last section of chapter 4. It continues with the variety of studies described in chapter 5 which range from an analysis of the effects of classifications on simple judgements of length of lines to a discussion of the effects that intergroup competition and the status of a group as a disadvantaged minority are found to have on the mutual perceptions of two ethnic groups.

But despite this progression, chapters 4 and 5 still remain very much within the tradition of a cognitive analysis of these intergroup pheno- mena. More than that, in presenting a theoretical and empirical progres- sion from the analysis of the judgements of sizes of coins and of length of lines to inter-group stereotypes, they imply that – as social psychologists – we need go no further. This cognitive perspective is widened in chapter 6. It is then *included* in chapter 7, but only as a necessary requirement which is now by no means seen as *sufficient* for the psychological study of social stereotypes. A part of chapter 7 is devoted to a critique of these 'sufficiency' premises, and uses as examples both the earlier work described in the preceding chapters and some very similar recent work which is still continued by a number of people. The latter parts of the chapter widen the scope to consider the *social* functions of stereotypes, the study of which is seen as an indispensable part of the social psychologist's job. In this way, chapter 7 rejoins directly the issues raised in part I of the book and provides an example of the way they relate to one aspect of the social realities of intergroup conflict.

Part III of the book is derived from work done in the sixties. It is included to provide an empirical counterpart to some of the abstractions of part II, but it also leads directly to part IV through the questions it raises about the development of group indentity. Chapter 8 is based on anecdotal evidence about how it felt to be a coloured student in Britain just before the period of the great waves of immigration from the Commonwealth. Chapters 9 and 10 summarize several of the facets of a larger research project, conducted in a number of European countries, about the development of ethnic and national attitudes in children. The 'insiders' and 'outsiders' of the title of part III are shown to play their respective roles early in their lives – with the exception of the outsiders of chapter 8 who describe the strange experience of suddenly *becoming* outsiders.

Part IV of the book represents again, as does chapter 7, a return to the problems of a *social* social psychology raised in part I. The concern of chapter 7 ('Social stereotypes and social groups') was to combine the earlier sequence of a cognitive analysis of stereotypes with the consideration of the functions they serve in the social contexts from which they derive. The first four chapters of part IV take up, in a wider perspective, the relevance to the development of group identity of 'the experience of prejudice' described in chapter 8 and of other forms of intergroup conflict and social divisions. The concluding chapter of the book applies this perspective to the psychological problems thrust upon groups of people who are members of disadvantaged minorities and attempts to describe the finite number of psychological solutions to these problems which appear as being available to them.

This book tries to achieve three aims. The first of these is to reflect a slow convergence of the experiences confronted in the upheavals of the not-so-distant past with the directions taken by some of my academic work, even those directions which appeared, for a time, to have nothing much to do with these experiences. I felt it was important not only to know that this convergence existed, that the work made more sense in relation to the experience, but also to let it be known. This has nothing to do with any inflated view of the importance of what I am, who I am and, most of all, of my academic work. On the contrary, when I look back today at the variety of things I have done between 1945 and 1980, it often appears to me that I have never been as useful again as I was in the few short years immediately after the war, when I had an opportunity of helping to bring back to the surface a few dozen young people, hardly younger than I was myself at the time. But I strongly suspect that many social psychologists and others also reflect in the drift of their work and the selection of their problems the *Weltanschauung* based on the experience which made them what they are. I think this is the case with much of the stubbornly 'non-social' social psychology which dominates the field. As I wrote in concluding chapter 3 of this book:

as social psychologists, we have a duty to attend to these processes [of dehumanization and depersonalization of others]. And even if many of us who wish to ignore them are entirely free to do so, we do *not* have the right to imply through the conclusions we draw from our work that our cosy and equitable inter-individuality can reach beyond the blinkered vision of social reality which we have selected for our special consideration.

I think (but cannot prove it) that this 'inter-individuality' pursued to the exclusion of most other issues has a lot to do with the social background of those who pursue it and the social myths inherent in that background (see chapter 11). I also think the same to be true of some psychologists who, in the name of a presumed scientific objectivity, take strong positions about contentious social and political issues, and in doing so revive some hoary traditions of an earlier period of eugenics and genetics. I have just pleaded guilty not only to having become clearly aware of a connection between my work and my past, but also to aiming at making this connection public. It is my hope (but not a very solid one) that clear-cut statements of *background* positions will become more common in all those fields of our work which relate directly to public issues or public policies. For the time being, the clear *engagement* of some psychologists in some of those issues remains cloaked in a thick fog of claims of objectivity.

The second and third aims of this book have already been mentioned. One of them consists of drawing together the dispersed links of work done over a period of twenty-five years in the hope that the emerging unity and widening of perspective may be of some use to others interested in similar problems. The third aim was to place this slow progression alongside parallel developments in European social psychology which took off in the sixties. The work described in this book can be seen as one of the strands in this wider texture; it has contributed to it while at the same time drawing from it a clearer sense of its own direction.

PART I
Social psychology and social processes

Introduction

The human and social sciences reflected in the seventies the social and economic upheavals of the decade. It was to be expected that the uncertain status of social psychology, poised half-way between being a 'social' and an 'experimental' science, would cause it to be particularly sensitive to the rapid changes in the social and intellectual climate. This sensitivity was reflected in the numerous debates to which reference has already been made in the preceding chapter. Many of these debates concerned what Rom Harré once called, in an article published in 1976 in *The Times Higher Education Supplement*, the drawing of a distinction between 'automatisms' and 'autonomy' in social psychology. 'Automatisms' consist of subjects 'responding' in the artificially rigged situation of laboratory experiments. 'Autonomy' is for Harré, in contrast, 'self-making', and according to him this is what we should study as social psychologists. This autonomy is, as he wrote, 'influenced by what people think they are or think they ought to be'; it is 'the idea that we are free to make ourselves anything we like'.

There can be no quarrel with these statements, although a judgement of their usefulness in the process of gaining new knowledge must await their translation into some empirically *researchable* perspectives. Attempts to achieve this are being made at present (see e.g. Forgas, 1979). But new problems arise when this general conception of 'autonomy' is directly applied to the psychological aspects of the social and political process. The same article of Harré again provides an example. He wrote: 'There is always resistance to the alarming idea of self-intervention and self-reference as the centre of a political process – in other words, to the idea of giving priority to correcting personal practices, the social equivalent of taking care of the pennies and finding the pounds have taken care of themselves.'

This passage is undoubtedly an over-simplification of the arguments for an 'autonomous' social psychology to be found in the writings of Harré and others. It remains, however, a characteristic symptom of the preoccupations which ruled much of the debate. Part I of this book is concerned with the individualistic tendencies of much of social psychology; they are discussed again, in the context of the study of intergroup relations, in Part IV (chapters 11 and 14). The relevance to this

13

discussion of the 'autonomy' views is that the new social psychologies seem to have remained just as individualistic in their approach to social processes as the old one has been.

In an article published in 1977, Billig examined 'the claims of ethnomethodologists, symbolic interactionists and ethogenists to provide an improved basis for social psychology' (p. 393). He chose for this examination the contribution that can be made by these approaches to the study of one large-scale social phenomenon, fascism, which Billig himself later examined in some detail (1978). As he wrote in 1977: 'the new perspectives are inappropriate for a serious examination of a social issue like fascism, because they lack clear political commitment. They are based upon attitudes of either dissociation or sympathetic understanding, both of which are unsatisfactory for an examination of fascism' (p. 393). In the conclusion to the same article, Billig considered Harré's (1974) argument that 'A prominent feature of the approach we are advocating is the respect we pay to the intellectual capacities of ordinary human beings as managers and interpreters of the social world. Everyone is, in a certain sense, a fairly competent social scientist, *and we must not treat his (or her) theory about the social world and his place in it with contempt*' (p. 244, italics in the original). To Billig, 'this seems to be a clear injunction to adopt what has been called the "pallid ideology of cultural relativism" (Bittner, 1973). More than anything else, it betrays a strangely non-empirical stance. It seems curious that the researcher should decide at the outset that there are no beliefs about the world which are contemptible. It can be convincingly argued that the researcher's task is to find which beliefs are worthy of respect and which are not' (1977, p. 427).

The 'non-neutral' stance, to which I confessed in the preceding chapter, is easily found again, here, as applied to a different set of issues. As to the new individualism of the new social psychologies:

Individual autonomy as the core of the 'political process', and of many aspects of social behaviour, is a myth. In many social situations, we are buffeted here and there by powerful social forces beyond our control . . . Individual autonomy (deciding *not* to steal) has strict limits for a child living in a vast slum of an immense city. Or when you have internalized, as a soldier, the powerful social prescription that the enemies are not quite human. Or – as a guard in a concentration camp – that the inmates are a virus in the social 'organism'. These are, of course, extreme cases. My point is that they are no more than one end of a long continuum. Any society which contains power, status, prestige and social group differentials (and they all do), places each of us in a number of *social* categories which become an important part of our *self*-definition. In situations which relate to those aspects of our self-definition that we think we share with others, we shall behave very much as they do . . .

Of course, there will always be exceptions. It will always be interesting to find out why some people are behaving exceptionally. But it is even more important for a social psychologist to find out why so many people behave in unison – which they often do. We cannot train everyone (little by little?) to exercise 'autonomy' which would be independent of the underlying social conditions and norms responsible for crucial uniformities of social behaviour. (Tajfel, 1977, p. 654)

Most of the discussion to be found in part I of this book is concerned with points of view emerging from traditional social psychology which appear very different from those defended by the new. Underlying these differences, there remains, however, a basic similarity between the old and the new: their common neglect of the insertion of individual or inter-individual behaviour and experience into their wider social frameworks.

Harré's 'self-intervention' and 'self-reference' as the 'centre of a political process' are undoubtedly extreme examples of this new individualism. Examples of more moderate positions can also be found in some of the writing which emerged from the 'ethogenic' approach to social psychology advocated by Harré and his co-workers (e.g. Harré, 1977a). But the extremes of the new individualism are easily matched by those of the traditional psychologists. In these cases the individualistic emphasis tends to be associated with claims to scientific objectivity to which reference was made in the first chapter of this book.

A traditional example which mirrors Harré's insistence upon the importance of individual autonomy in the political process can be found in a collection of readings recently edited by Eysenck and Wilson (1978) under the title of *The psychological basis of ideology*. The book consists of a large number of previous publications, from a variety of sources, about the personality determinants of extremist political attitudes. Each of its sections is preceded by an introduction written by the editors who also provide a concluding chapter to the book. 'Ideology' is defined, following the late John Plamenatz (1970), as 'a set of closely related beliefs or ideas, or even attitudes, *characteristic of a group or community*' (p. 303 in Eysenck and Wilson, my italics). From this, the editors draw the strange and cryptic inference that 'this broad definition clearly identifies the notion of ideology with that of a *factor* in the psychometric sense' (p. 303, italics in the original). It follows that, in contrast to 'sociologists and students of political science' who tend to rely on 'uncertain interpretations of historical actions' in order to 'deduce ideologies', psychologists are 'clearly closer to reality by deducing their factors from empirical data gathered along methodologically more sophisticated lines' (p. 303).

The major concern of the book is the question of how *some individuals* tend to adopt extreme political attitudes. This is an important question,

15

but it must be placed in its proper perspective. Ideologies are closely related to social behaviour: there is a continuity between the widespread acceptance of an ideology in a community, a social group or a sub-culture and a social movement related to it. Social movements are not easily explained psychologically in terms of the personality characteristics of masses of people who take part in them. Authoritarian or tough-minded personalities may have contributed to the development of national socialism in Germany; but the question as to why *psychologically* the movement had such an enormous popular success in its time is left just as wide open as before. An analysis in terms of the shared perceptions of social reality by large numbers of people and of the conditions leading to these shared perceptions is not only more realistic; it is also scientifically much more parsimonious. The difficulty of the approach represented by Eysenck and Wilson is that it is based on an implicit vision of a society as consisting of randomly interacting individual particles or 'personalities'. There is no room in this vision for the socially or culturally shared cognitive organizations of a social system based on a commonly perceived social location in that system (see chapter 3 for a discussion of this issue).

This conception of a *collection* of randomly related individual particles is pushed to its extreme in one of the concluding statements of the book: 'Our own interpretation emphasizes first of all the important contribution made by genetic factors in the determination of social attitudes . . . The evidence has been reviewed in a previous section and will not be received again here ' (p. 308). The 'evidence' produced in the book consists in fact of a single study by Eaves and Eysenck (1974) which the editors consider tentative and to which they refer in the Introduction to that same 'previous section' as 'merely the harbinger that betokens the arrival of spring' (p. 219). It seems that these first signs of spring have turned into high summer by the time the final conclusions of the book are reached. So much for scientific objectivity. Thus, the book, far from dealing with *the* 'psychological basis of ideology' reflects much more closely the ideological basis of *some* psychology.

It is in its concern with the shortcomings of this individualistic perspective that the debate presented here differs from many other controversies of the recent years. The immediate background to chapter 2 will be found in its introductory section. Chapter 3 presents a discussion, both sides of which originated in the same stable. The two authors of the article summarized in its first section, Donald Taylor and Rupert Brown, worked in, or around, a research programme on intergroup relations in which we were all engaged at the time their article was written.

2
Experiments in a vacuum[1]

1. Introduction

In the spring of 1969, a plenary conference of the European Association of Experimental Social Psychology was held in Belgium at the University of Louvain. It became increasingly clear during the working sessions and in innumerable extramural discussions that, roughly speaking, two general points of view were represented – and sometimes even schizo-phrenically contained in views expressed at different times by the same people. Some of the papers delivered at the conference followed the long-established tradition of well-disciplined experimental research based on ideas, methods and theories which had become familiar in the last twenty years or so. Others expressed dissatisfaction or searched for new avenues of theorizing and research. The discussions which followed the papers brought into the open something which can perhaps be described as a complex and conflicted collective state of mind. On the one hand, there was genuine respect for much that has been achieved through the well-tried methods of clear-cut empirical hypotheses and their experimental testing. On the other hand, many felt that an unquestioned acceptance of the assumptions – social, scientific and philosophical – underlying much of this research was a heavy price to pay for achieving a modicum of scientific respectability and even for making *some* gains in knowledge. It is possible that the 'student revolution' – very much in evidence in the spring of 1969 – had something to do with these conflicts. If so, this bringing to the surface of latent intellectual conflicts should be chalked up on the positive side of the ledger of the unrest.

But many of the questions discussed from various points of view at the conference were with us long before the recent generations of students replaced the 'silent generations' of the fifties. The most important refer to the following issues: the nature of theory in social psychology; the adequacy of the methods used for the analysis of 'natural' social

[1] This chapter consists of extracts from: Chapter 1: Introduction, and Chapter 3: Experiments in a vacuum, in: J. Israel & H. Tajfel (eds.): *The context of social psychology: A critical assessment*, London: Academic Press, European Monographs in Social Psychology, No. 2, 1972.

phenomena; the nature of the unstated assumptions, values and presuppositions about Man and society determining theories and methods of research; the relevance and significance of the results of science; the relations of theories, problems and methods of research in social psychology to those in the physical and in the natural sciences.

These problems came so clearly to the surface at Louvain that it was obvious that their discussion should be continued. The framework for such a continuation existed in the form of the 'small working group meetings' periodically organized by the Association. The initiative for the one which led to the publication of *The context of social psychology* came from Joachim Israel who took the responsibility for its organization after some preliminary discussions in Copenhagen with Serge Moscovici and myself. The meeting took place in April 1970 in Elsinore,[2] and if the Prince of Denmark had asked 'how to be' instead of asking his other immortal question, he could easily have become one of the participants.

Within this general framework, the aim of the present chapter was to express my preoccupations as a social psychologist whose work has been almost entirely within the experimental tradition of the discipline and who continues to believe that, amongst the approaches to social behaviour open to us, theories which can be tested experimentally contain the least doubtful promise for the future. This belief may be no more than an act of faith or – worse – a demonstration that research can sometimes become a question of clutching at straws. But even if this is so, there are two important reasons for continuing on the straight and narrow path: the first is that a systematic study of social behaviour is an essential task, both intellectual and practical, for our times; and the second, that there is no evidence that other approaches to the psychological aspects of social conduct present even as much solidity as the experimental straw appears to have.

Experimental social psychology as we know it today is 'irrelevant' only to the extent that it is a social science practised in a social vacuum. This vacuum is not due to the fact that we are attempting to do fundamental rather than applied research; it is due to the social psychologists having often taken the wrong decision as to what kind of *homo* their discipline is concerned with: 'biological', 'psychological' or 'sociopsychological'.

Most undergraduate textbooks in social psychology contain in their first few pages some kind of a definition of the discipline. This usually

2 We are grateful to the Danish Social Science Research Council and to the Tricentenary Foundation of the Swedish National Bank for their support. A grant from the Council helped considerably in the organization of the Elsinore conference; a grant from the Foundation enabled the editors to continue working together after the conference on the completion of the book which appeared in 1972.

18

includes at least three assertions: that social psychology is a scientific study of human behaviour; that the kind of behaviour it is concerned with is social behaviour (i.e. interaction between individuals, singly or in groups); and that this social behaviour is 'a function of' or is 'determined by' or is 'related to' the social context in which it takes place. For example, in their *Theories in social psychology*, Deutsch and Krauss (1965) were, not untypically, quite explicit about the issues involved: 'Person-to-person relationships are distinguished not only by the fact that psychological events can take place on both sides of a relationship, but also by their *social* character [italics in the original text], that is to say, human relationships always occur in an organized social environment – in a family, in a group, in a community, in a nation – that has developed techniques, categories, rules and values that are relevant to human interaction. Hence the understanding of the psychological events that occur in human interactions *requires comprehension of the interplay of these events with the social context in which they occur* [my italics]' (pp. 2–3). They add: '. . . the social psychologist must be able to characterize the relevant features of the social environment in order to understand or predict human interaction' (p. 3).

But reading those chapters in the book which are devoted to social psychological theories tested in experimental settings, one must search in vain for further references to the 'interplay with social context' or for a characterization of 'the relevant features of the social environment'. For example, the frustration–aggression hypothesis is presented in the introductory chapter as a typical (and influential) 'middle-range' theory in social psychology; the presentation is concerned – as it must be in order to be faithful to the original product – with the logical relationships between derivations from the main hypothesis and with a brief analysis of some of the key theoretical constructs such as 'aggression', 'interference', 'goal response', etc. This is the beginning and the end of it; how then is this a *'social* psychological theory'?

Quite obviously, its various hypotheses must be tested through predicted *regularities* in the observed social behaviour. One of the most important and pervasive social psychological problems with which we are confronted today is the explanation of the processes involved in intergroup behaviour; I shall return to it later in more detail. This is not a problem which can be characterized as 'applied' or 'theoretical'; it is inextricably both at the same time since it involves some of the basic features of Man's behaviour towards Man as they are adapted to, modified by, and the determinants of, the 'social context' and 'relevant features of the social environment'.

Claims are made that the frustration–aggression theory (or its various modifications) 'explains' some of the aspects of intergroup behaviour, i.e. that it accounts for some of its observed regularities. Support for these claims is sought in data from experiments designed to test the various hypotheses. I am not concerned here with the issue of 'truth' or 'falsity' of the assumed relationships between the variables but with the validity of the claim that a transition can be made from the kind of experimental data that are obtained to intergroup behaviour at large. I shall return later to the issue of extrapolations from experiments. For the present it will be enough to recall that, in the case of frustration and aggression, the experiments range from inducing displaced aggression in frustrated rats to creating ingenious laboratory equivalents of a man berating his wife after having just been reprimanded by his boss. None of this can be relevant to a confirmation or invalidation of the hypotheses as they might apply to *any* social setting of intergroup relations. It is now well known that this cannot be done without taking into account the social reality which gives meaning and definition to 'ingroup' and 'outgroup', to what is and what is not aggression, to the prevailing image of Man that determines the range of application of acts the meaning of which can be described as 'inflicting injury on another organism'. LeVine and Campbell (1972) amongst others (cf. e.g. LeVine, 1965) have shown the close dependence of outgroup aggression upon the *kind* of network of social relations that prevails within the ingroup, and the impossibility of making efficient predictions about the former without a close analysis of the latter. And yet in texts on experimental social psychology the *setting* of discussions about experiments on frustration and aggression, as they relate to intergroup conflict, has remained very much the same as it was thirty years ago.

The objection that hypotheses stated in universal and asocial terms lack predictive power meets the argument that it is the business of science to provide laws of general application; and that no scientific theory can be concerned with particularities of individual cases or of sets of individual cases which contain unknown, unknowable and uncontrolled variables. What matters are the underlying processes which must be discovered and isolated – or, in Kurt Lewin's terms, the appropriate distinctions between genotypes and phenotypes. It was precisely this need to isolate the genotypic aspects of social behaviour which led Lewin to his insistence on the use of experimental methods and was thus responsible for the profound impact of his ideas on the subsequent development of social psychology. But the range of what is genotypic and what phenotypic for the purposes of formulating and testing laws of social behaviour is by no means immediately obvious.

The difficulty concerns the distinction between the 'individual' and the 'general' cases in social behaviour. If I conduct a social psychological experiment, I have groups of subjects who are placed in various experimental and control conditions. These groups can either be representative of mankind as a whole or of particular subsets of it from which they were drawn. If the former is true, then the observed regularities of behaviour are generalizable as a law of wide application. If the latter is true, they are generalizable to the subset. It should be made clear at this point that my concern here is not with the old and hackneyed theme of 'representativeness of samples' in social psychological experiments; there are good reasons why in many cases representativeness may be quite irrelevant to the purposes of the investigation. What is, however, important is a clear realization that the general case is an impossible myth as long as human beings behave as they do because of the social expectations with which they enter an experiment – or any other social situation. If these expectations are shared – as they always are by definition to some degree in any social context – I shall obtain data from my experiment which are neither 'general' nor 'individual'. The observed regularities of behaviour will result from the interaction between general processes and the social context in which they operate.

Without the knowledge of this context the data *may* be irrelevant to the confirmation or the falsification of a hypothesis. What is more, the extent to which the expectations are shared, and thereby the extent to which they determine the pattern of the results, is in itself an empirical question which must be answered before any conclusions can be drawn. If we are dealing merely with random individual differences, then the usual statistical tools will provide all the answers. If, however, the background social context of the experiment and the social task that the experiment itself presents to the subjects provide enough common meaning to determine the observed regularities, then we must provide a kind of interpretation of the data that is specific to many problems in the social sciences, and for which distinctions between the 'general' and the 'individual' do not apply. This will have to be an interpretation concerned with specifying the interaction between what is assumed to be a general process in social behaviour and the conditions under which it may operate, or under which 'phenotypic' differences may conceal 'genotypic' similarities and vice versa. Thus, the observed regularities of behaviour in social psychological experiments fall somewhere in between the general case and the unknowable, individual case. Their range of application is determined by the nature of human social behaviour in which lawful but diverse modifications of pattern occur as a function of interactions between human groups and their social environment. A similar argument underlies many of the quasi-experimental and experimental techniques employed nowadays by ethologists, particularly in their studies of the relationships between ecology and animal social behaviour. It applies even more strongly to the study of human social behaviour in which it can be ignored only at the peril of the continuing 'irrelevance'.

Before proceeding, I should like to make it clear that the above argument is not a plea that experiments must be cross-cultural in order to provide valuable insights. The point is that *all* experiments are 'cultural' and whether the 'cross' adds to their value or not depends entirely upon the theoretical background from which they start. To go around looking for fortuitous similarities and differences may broaden the mind of the researcher as travel is presumed to do, but it will not add much to our fund of relevant knowledge (see Faucheux, 1976, Frijda and Jahoda, 1966 and Jahoda, 1970, 1979 for extended discussions of the cross-cultural issue). An experiment on, for example, conformity may be trivial because of the interpretation of its data in terms of such blunt theoretical instruments as 'universal' needs for affiliation or for approval; and the observed differences between subgroups of subjects may become of little general sociopsychological interest if what we learn from them is that there are individual personality differences in the strength of these needs. On the other hand, one need not rush to other 'cultures' in order to undertake an analysis of the contextual and background conditions which determine the subject's perception of what may be the socially appropriate behaviour in the quandary in which he finds himself when faced with a row of stooges who, to the best of his knowledge, are a random collection of moderately honest citizens.

Thus, the restricted range of applicability of the data from social psychological experiments has three main consequences. First, it places them in a special category which neither relates to the scientifically irrelevant individual case nor to the ideal and unobtainable general case. Second, this middle range of data means that, unless the characteristics of their context are specified, the data can neither confirm nor falsify a general law. Third, these characteristics are inescapably part and parcel of the experimental design. Therefore, a description of the conditions of an experiment must include the analysis or the description of those aspects of the social context that the researcher considers to be relevant to the conclusions he draws; also any conclusion about the confirmation or invalidation of his hypotheses must relate to these conditions.

The need to specify the characteristics of the range is not only due to the impossibility of obtaining amorphous and interchangeable populations of subjects in social psychological experiments. Control of an experiment in the physical or in the biological sciences means that the relevant properties of the substances or organisms on which the experiment is performed are assumed to be explicitly known. It is trivial to say that this is not the case in social psychological experiments. But it is perhaps worth restating that, without ever clearly acknowledging the fact, social psychologists have gone much further than Locke ever did in his dreams of a human *tabula rasa*; many of their experimental designs contain the assumption that the *categories* of subjects used are forever like a clean slate on which our experimental conditions can be written at will. Once again, this is not a plea for respecting individual differences or for what Moscovici once called a 'differential social psychology'; social psychology is not a catalogue of individual, or even group, idiosyncrasies of social behaviour. But, unlike the physicists or the physiologists, we cannot manipulate the properties of the materials which we study before we start the experiment. This need not trouble the 'general' experimental psychologist concerned with, for example, perceptual constancies or short-term memory. There are reasons for believing that, provided certain conditions for obtaining responses are satisfied (and this can be ensured through appropriate preliminary tests), all human beings function very much in the same way. But we cannot assume that this is the case in social or socially determined behaviour.[3] Our experimental conditions are always 'contaminated'; and the nature of this contamination is one of the principal objects of our study.

There are few social psychologists who have not at one time or another felt uneasy about the social vacuum in which most of their experiments are conducted. The feelings of 'irrelevance' to which many people referred are not, in the last analysis, due to the 'tension between basic and applied'. They are directly related to the nature of what is presumed to be basic. And this in turn is a relative matter and depends upon the fit between the kind of questions about human social behaviour

---

[3] But the 'general' psychologist has his own problems, and they centre around a decision as to what is and what is not 'socially determined behaviour'. In this sense, the statement that 'all human beings function very much in the same way' begs the question. Theoretical or empirical problems of this nature arise in the most fundamental areas of 'individual' behaviour. In perception, there is the issue of experiential factors and of the consequent social and cultural differences (see for example, Segall *et al.*, 1966; and Tajfel, 1969a); in motivation, of the effects of free choice and of its constraints (see Zimbardo, 1969); in emotion, of the effects of cognitive and social factors upon the manner in which an individual labels his emotional states and behaves accordingly. As Schachter (1970) wrote in a conclusion to an excellent discussion about the identity between a physiological state and psychological or behavioural event: 'If we are eventually to make sense of this area, I believe we will be forced to adopt a set of concepts with which most physiologically-inclined scientists feel somewhat uncomfortable and ill-at-ease, for they are concepts which are difficult to reify, and about which it is, at present, difficult to physiologize. We will be forced to examine a subject's perception of his bodily state and his interpretation of it in terms of his immediate situation and his past experience. We will be forced to deal with concepts about perception, about cognition, about learning, and about the social situation' (p. 120).

that are being asked and the answers that are being provided. The fit between the questions and the answers is in turn reflected in the experiments being designed.

2. Individual, inter-individual and social psychology

Questions about human social behaviour can be considered as being on a continuum which ranges from biological through psychological and sociopsychological to sociological. Whenever a statement of this kind is made, the current fashion is to add immediately that all these 'levels' obviously interact; that not one of them can be studied without others being taken into consideration; that it has been hard enough to lower the barriers a little between the disciplines and therefore one should not make things difficult by erecting them all over again. The fact remains that 'interaction' is merely a useless slogan unless it can be translated into a way of thinking about research problems and unless it determines the manner in which research is conducted.

It would be a pointless exercise to try to provide here formal definitions of these various levels. They are a matter of emphasis and a focus of interest rather than clearly delimited boundaries. Thus, on the biological level, the questions concerning social behaviour tend to be about the genetic and physiological determinants of human adaptation to, and transformation of, the social environment, and answers are often sought in terms of evolution, ecology, their effects on the structure of the human organism, and the effects of this structure on human behaviour. An example here would be the work of the ethologists on the instinctive aspects of human aggression in their relation to, and continuity with, various forms of intraspecific aggression in other species.

The psychological questions are often addressed to the determination of social behaviour by those characteristics of the human species that are either unique to it or at least drastically different from those displayed by other species: language and other forms of symbolic communication, socially derived secondary motivation, the cognitive and motivational features of socialization. The answers are in terms of general laws of functioning, sometimes closely interacting with the biological level, and sometimes taking this level for granted as providing the range but not necessarily predicting the content of the processes involved. Amongst examples here would be, once again, the relationships between frustration and aggression, the various versions of the theory of cognitive consistency, the role of imitation in social development, laws of competition and cooperation deriving from various forms of the exchange theory, theories of achievement motivation and of affiliation, etc.

24

The sociological questions about behaviour are concerned with its determination by the social, economic and political structures. The answers often tend to formulate predictions from selected properties of these structures to observed behaviour, e.g. as in the relations between economic disparities and outgroup discrimination. Though psychologically-derived concepts such as 'relative deprivation' are sometimes used as a link between the independent and the dependent variables, their psychological context is not the focus of the theoretical analysis.

The sociopsychological human being somehow manages to fall between these several stools. The lack of fit between the kind of questions asked about him and the kind of answers provided depends upon the professional identification of the researcher; so that sociopsychological questions tend to be given biological, psychological or sociological answers.

There could hardly be much disagreement with the suggestion that sociopsychological questions concern the determinants of human social behaviour and that the aim of sociopsychological theories is to understand, explain or predict such behaviour. The determinants can be found, of course, at all of the levels; but this remains one of those empty 'interaction' statements unless it can be shown to work when put to use in the business of explanation and prediction – and sometimes also of postdiction understood as explanation (see Popper, 1961). The lack of fit between questions and answers results from analysing human social behaviour *as if* it could be usefully reduced to the genetic and physiological characteristics of the species as it is in the case of the biological bias; or to non-social human behaviour as in the case of the psychological bias; or to a one-way determination by social structures as in the case of the sociological bias. I do not wish to overstate the issue: there is no doubt that certain aspects of human social behaviour can be usefully analysed in terms of any one of these reductions and I shall happily leave to the reader the task of finding relevant examples. My concern is with the large and crucial areas of social conduct which are uniquely characteristic of the sociopsychological *homo* in the sense that they present empirical discontinuities with his biological background, with his non-social psychological functioning and with the conception of him as being fully accounted for by the social system of which he is a part.

As is the case with other forms of reductionism, our three biases derive from a conception which is fundamentally useful. They provide the *range* of what is possible, i.e. research conclusions in social psychology cannot be incongruent with firmly established evidence deriving from those conceptions in biology, general psychology and sociology which have a direct impact upon the aspects of the functioning of the sociopsycho-

25

logical men and women that are being studied. But from then on they need special treatment adapted to their own problems.

There are some distant parallels between this need for the acknowledgement of the emergence of new variables and systems of behaviour and the study of the emergence of new styles in the history of art. Styles in painting or in music consist, by definition, of certain regularities; these must be isolated, described and analysed. Gombrich's (1960) descriptions of the use of 'stereotypes' in the visual arts provide excellent examples of the use of a general psychological law for providing one important dimension of the range within which the analysis must be conducted. But he, or any other art historian, could hardly stop there. A study of the rules which enable us to refer to a group of painters as 'impressionists' or 'surrealists' or 'fauvists' must be based on familiarity with their conception of what they intended to communicate, how they wished to communicate it, and why they chose their particular idioms. This in turn needs to be related to analysis of what they were reacting to (or against), which may be conducted within the framework provided either by previous stylistic regularities or by the socio-historical background or by both.

The methods of acquisition of knowledge about regularities are, of course, different in the history of art and in social psychology; and so is the relative importance of contributions from a historical type of analysis. But the relationship between the boundaries traced by the range (of human communicative behaviour in the case of art) and the analysis of the nature of selected regularities is similar in both cases. It is undoubtedly useful and important to know that certain processes in perception and in reproduction (such as categorization and stereotyping) make it possible for styles in art to develop, and, at one remove, it is equally useful to know that without our visual apparatus, endowed with a capacity to perceive in perspective, and without our two hands and ten fingers, painting would not have been what it is. It is a far cry from the knowledge of these limiting properties of the range to the kind of knowledge that the art historian needs. If he is interested in style, he has the kind of middle-range populations displaying regularities of behaviour to which I referred earlier when discussing populations of subjects in social psychological experiments. As a matter of fact, even in the case of the limiting feature of perspective, a socio-historical analysis of the development of communicative skills is a prerequisite for understanding how things happen. On the other hand, an excessive fascination with the fact that Man has two hands and ten fingers could provide us with propositions about the development of styles in art which would not be too far removed from certain unilluminating basic propositions in social psychology, such as the more common goals the members of a group have, the more 'cohesive' the group will be; or 'the more often within a given period of time a man's activity rewards the activity of another, the more often the other will emit the activity' (Homans, 1961, p. 54).

Equivalent to 'stylistic regularities' in social behaviour are the conceptions that human groups (selected according to criteria based on the researcher's theoretical interests) have about what they wish to do, their manner of doing it and the reasons for their choice of idioms. But the principal objection to this parallel of 'stylistic regularities' is that it may imply a 'clinical' and descriptive social psychology rather than a systematic science based on general theories of social behaviour. One possible answer to this is that perhaps we do not at present have such a science. In their book on theories in social psychology, Deutsch and Krauss (1965) wrote: 'being in its infancy [social psychology] is still largely dominated by theoretical approaches that are based on implicit conceptions of the nature of Man. None of these approaches is sufficiently explicit in its psychological assumptions, in its mode of logical inference, nor in its empirical reference to permit unambiguous testing of its implications. In short, none of the orientations is a "theory" in the sense of theories in the physical sciences.' (pp. 12–13).

It is true, however, that some of the 'approaches' or 'orientations' that have been influential have led to the formulation of what Merton (1957) called 'theories of the middle range'; these theories, without aspiring to the rigour of the physical sciences, were responsible for an abundance of good experimental research. The frustration–aggression theory is one example; others are provided by theories of cognitive consistency. In particular, Festinger's (1957) theory of cognitive dissonance has stimulated in a period of about fifteen years an enormous amount of research with an increasing range of application. There are many other examples, some of which bear witness to a sudden burgeoning of interest and research in localized and specific problems, such as has recently been the case with the work on 'risky shift', on competition and cooperation in dyads, on the determinants of conformity in small groups or non-verbal communication.

However, many of these theories present one of two characteristics: either they are not primarily theories of social behaviour, or, if they appear to be, it is soon discovered that they are basically about individual, or, at the limit, inter-individual behaviour.

Leon Festinger once said that he had ceased to be a social psychologist long before he developed his more recent interest in research on vision; as his work immediately preceding this interest was concerned with his

27

theory of cognitive dissonance, this seemed at the time a high puzzling utterance. But its original author must not be burdened with my *post hoc* interpretation which is based on a distinction between two types of theoretical questions about human social behaviour. One category consists of questions about what enabled Man, as a species, to become the kind of social animal that he is; the other concerns the behaviour he displays *because* he is the kind of social animal that he is.

Both types of question are relevant to the understanding of social behaviour. The first concerns the range of social behaviour rather than its content because it applies to processes that are preliminary to the social Man, that are no more 'social' in their origin than is colour vision or the generalization of conditioned responses; in other words, the relevance of these processes to social behaviour is theoretically of the same kind as the relevance to it of, for example, the psychophysiology of vision or the role of secondary reinforcement in learning; social behaviour would not have been what it is if these processes were not what they are. But between them and social conduct, as it actually occurs, there is a variety of phenomena of social origin without the consideration of which predictions and explanations are bound to remain as 'irrelevant' as they are often found to be. Itard's savage boy from the Aveyron could have undoubtedly been shown, from the moment he was found, to conform to some lawful relationships between frustration and aggression; and to regulate his behaviour so as to avoid unrewarded effort. Truffaut's sober film about him (*L'Enfant Sauvage*) suggests the dramatic impact on his behaviour of the modification of these processes through social inter-action. Some modifications of behaviour would also probably occur if one changed the social environments of the frustrated and aggressive rats in the experiments on the subject; or of the rats used by Lawrence and Festinger (1962) which 'justified' the effort they expended by doing better work. As in the case of the boy from the Aveyron, an analysis would then be required of the emergent variables without which an understanding of the behavioural transformations would not be possible. It should be clear that terms such as 'transformation' or 'modification' only make sense because in the case of the Itard story we start – uniquely – from something pre-social. In normal circumstances, the 'social' is not a transformation of something that existed before its emergence: it interacts from the beginning with the processes defining the range.

The theories of the second kind are concerned with the behaviour that Man displays *because* he is a social animal. The problems are directly those set by social interaction, such as communicating, competing, cooperating or conforming. The theories from which the experimental hypotheses are derived and the design of the experiments can be

28

considered from two points of view: the image of Man that is implicit in them; and the conception of the relation between Man's 'individual' nature and his social behaviour.

It is the second of these issues which concerns me here. One of the common approaches to it can perhaps be characterized by a quotation from an application by a psychologist for a grant to do cross-cultural research which I recently had the privilege to see. In one of its focal paragraphs it referred to 'this set of environmental circumstances that we call "culture"'.

This is very near to certain research conceptions of the relation between Man's 'individual' nature and the social setting in which his behaviour takes place. The reasoning can be roughly described as follows: there is a bedrock of individual motives such as, for example, striving for reward and avoiding punishment (or striving for gain and avoiding losses); this determines Man's behaviour whether he is reacting to the weather, hunting for food, exploring a new phenomenon or dealing with other people. His capacity to profit from past experience (or learn from past rewards) and his 'cognitive structures' intervene between what he wants and how he gets it. Other people present an additional complication: they too can profit from past experience and use their cognitive abilities. This is the principal reason for the complexities of social interaction. Otherwise, social behaviour is built according to the same matrix of gains and losses as non-social behaviour; in this matrix other people serve as means whereby these gains can be obtained or losses prevented. It is in this sense that they are stimuli which happen to be 'social'.

I know that this is a crude and oversimplified image; but it is not too far off the mark. Let me refer to one of the best and, some years ago, deservedly most widely used textbooks in experimental social psychology: that of Jones and Gerard (1967).

After nearly 600 pages, we reach chapter 15 which gets down to 'The Impact of Group Membership on Individual Behaviour'. The title of the chapter is already of significance since it implies that human groups are in the category of 'sets of environmental circumstances' somehow superimposed on individual behaviour. This is immediately confirmed in the first sentence: 'We have travelled a long and winding road in order to record the major points at which the life of the individual is *touched* [my italics] by the behaviour of other individuals.' (p. 591). The authors continue: 'These other individuals have been characterized variously in preceding chapters as socialization agents, stimulus persons, comparison models, communicators, and actors *linked to the individual through contingencies of outcome* [my italics]. Now we shall attempt to cope more directly with the phenomena of group life and no longer restrict ourselves to the dyad.' (p. 591).

It is indeed the dyad that has been, in previous chapters, the main basis for extrapolations to the wider systems of social conduct. Relations within a dyad, such as, for example, those of competition and cooperation, serve as a model for the study of the psychological aspects of social conflict. Finally, there is only a short step from dyads to groups. Both are governed by the same instrumentalities. Thus: 'Two or more persons become a group when the individual members feel that their purposes are served by continued affiliation. In some groups the members share the same purpose; in others the group holds together because it fulfils a variety of individual purposes.' (Jones and Gerard, 1967, p. 591). We join with others to accomplish our objectives. Hence: 'To say that A is dependent on B or C, or the combination of B and C, implies that A requires the assistance of these others to achieve certain goals important to him.' (p. 591).

Examples of this kind could be multiplied *ad infinitum*. It is true that in other chapters in the book there are discussions of communication in small groups and of the normative aspects of small group structure. But they are still reducible to the same model: Man's social behaviour is an adaptation of his general gain–loss strategy to the special requirements arising out of his being surrounded by other people. Thus, the second of the two kinds of theories referred to above – theories concerned with behaviour that Man displays because he is a social animal – can be reduced to the first: social behaviour is still considered in them in a presocial or an asocial perspective.

3. A perspective for a sociopsychological problem

The main theme so far discussed is that many of the theories which dominate the present research output in social psychology are not sociopsychological. It is therefore unavoidable that most of the experiments designed to test these theories should be equally impervious to the wider realities of social conduct and share their focus on the strategies of individual and inter-individual adjustments. It is in terms of these that we progress without a break from the individual to his relations with another individual in the dyad, then to the relations between a few individuals in a small group, finally to reach the problems posed by the relations between groups. But it seems that at this point the break in the continuity becomes too obvious to ignore. A simpler solution is then adopted: instead the problem itself is ignored. In the late sixties, in a review of experimental work about group processes, Gerard and Miller

(1967) devoted a dozen lines or so to it in a text of about 40 pages. The impact of these few lines was: (a) that indeed very little experimental work on intergroup processes was being done; and (b) that this was due to the methodological difficulties of creating intergroup situations in the laboratory. In the large volume by Jones and Gerard (1967) one must search in vain in the index for terms such as 'intergroup', 'ingroup', 'outgroup', 'identity' (social or any other). 'Conflict' appears in the glossary at the end of the book as 'a state that obtains for an individual when he is motivated to make two or more mutually incompatible responses' (p. 709). It is therefore not surprising that, for example, Sherif's 'field' experiments on conflict between small groups are not even referred to.

Why should this be so? The puzzle becomes even greater if one recalls some obvious propositions, such as that the course of relations between human groups of various kinds is one of *the* fundamental social problems of our times; that in an infinite variety of situations throughout his life, an individual feels, thinks and behaves in terms of his social identity created by the various groups of which he is a member and in terms of his relation to the social identity of others, as individuals or *en masse*. It is equally obvious that this social conduct is determined to a large extent by the relations between the groups to which he belongs as well as other groups, and that the nature of these relations is in turn largely due to the socially shared regularities of intergroup conduct. This is therefore a social phenomenon which can be considered as an example *par excellence* of the interaction between the individual and his social setting. The social setting of intergroup relations contributes to making the individuals what they are and they in turn produce this social setting; they and it develop and change symbiotically. One would expect that the nature of this interaction could hardly fail to become a major focus of interest in social psychology and a point of departure for research and experimentation.

The reasons for the absence of such an analysis and for the poverty of the relevant research are not far to seek. If the basic processes with which social psychology is deemed to be concerned are confined to the motivational and cognitive functioning of an individual (and universal) human being, then intergroup processes can only be conceived in one of two ways: either they are fully explained through these individual processes or they present special problems the study of which would not add very much to our fundamental knowledge. The individual is seen as the genotype of social psychology; the social matrices which act upon him and upon which he acts are no more than a superimposition of phenotypes. As Berkowitz (1962) wrote:

Granting all this, the present writer is still inclined to emphasize the importance of individualistic considerations in the field of group relations. Dealings between groups ultimately become problems of the psychology of the individual. Individuals decide to go to war; battles are fought by individuals; and peace is established by individuals. It is the individual who adopts the beliefs prevailing in his society, even though the extent to which these opinions are shared by many people is a factor governing his readiness to adopt them, and he then transmits these views to other individuals. Ultimately, it is the single person who attacks the feared and disliked ethnic minority group, even though many other people around him share his feelings and are very important in determining his willingness to aggress against this minority. Theoretical principles can be formulated referring to the group as a unit and these can be very helpful in understanding hostility between groups. But such abstractions refer to collections of people and are made possible by inter-individual uniformities in behaviour. (p. 167)

The message is clear: ultimately it is the individual who is the unit of analysis; he reacts to others and others react to him – but otherwise nothing new has happened. Social conduct consists of inter-individual uniformities made up of algebra of individual cognitions and motivations.

Social psychologists still seemed to be steeped in this kind of reductionism at a time when it was being abandoned, or at least seriously questioned, in the very realm of individual behaviour to which they turned for their basic concepts. As Piaget and Inhelder (1969) wrote in a brief discussion of cognitive development:

an action consists in transforming reality rather than simply discovering its existence: for each new action the acts of discovering and transforming are in fact inseparable. This is not only true of the infant whose every new action enriches his universe (from the first feed to instrumental behaviour patterns, like the use of a stick as a means of pulling an object towards one), but it remains true at all levels. The construction of an electronic machine or a sputnik not only enriches our knowledge of reality, it also enriches reality itself, which until then did not include such an object. This creative nature of action is essential. Behaviourists study behaviour, therefore actions, but too often forget the 'active' and transforming characteristic of an action. (p. 128)

There are several reasons for selecting the problems of intergroup relations to exemplify the arguments advanced earlier in this chapter. These problems are at the meeting point of the interests of the biologists, psychologists and sociologists. They involve social conduct in face-to-face interaction which is at the same time guided by highly abstract representations of social reality; they affect profoundly the social experience to which millions of individuals are exposed almost from the moment of their birth.

32

And yet, as we have seen, there are good reasons for maintaining that an experimental social psychology of intergroup relations hardly exists. It is largely replaced by the *as if* approaches to sociopsychological problems to which reference has been made earlier. The focus of some of the biological (and most of the pseudo-biological) writing on the subject is on the evolutionary continuity of human intergroup behaviour with intraspecific aggression and territoriality in other species. This is assumed to explain the less glorious aspects of the human past and present without ever, to my knowledge, an attempt having been made to put forward a set of hypotheses which would meet the criteria of falsifiability or pay serious attention to variables which are unique to human social organization. It would not be useful to return to a discussion of the asocial and presocial nature of these conceptions.

The psychologists have shown, on the whole, more scientific sophistication in considering these problems; or at least it can be said that, as distinct from the previous case, their writings are based on some research on the subject. Roughly four trends can be distinguished in this research: derivations from theories of aggression (mainly but not exclusively centred around the frustration–aggression hypothesis); extrapolations from inter-individual or small group competition and cooperation; a cognitive analysis of judgements, stereotypes, attitudes and beliefs about ingroups and outgroups; and studies of the genesis of prejudice in an individual based on its relevance to, and continuity with, his emotional experiences during early socialization. The first three of these trends of research are, in their own way, concerned as little with the emergence of social interaction and its role in accounting for the regularities of social conduct as is the biological approach. The fourth does take into account the diverse patterns of social relations as they affect early emotional development; but it explicitly focuses its analysis on the subsequent emergence of various types of personality prone to prejudice and thus it cannot, nor is it aiming to, encompass the wider aspects of the social psychology of intergroup conflict.

One way to characterize the approach to the same problems current in much of the sociological writing is to paraphrase the statement by Berkowitz which I quoted earlier (see p. 32). It could then read as follows: Granting all this (i.e. the biological and the psychological considerations), the present writer is still inclined to emphasize the importance of considering the field of group relations in terms of social structure. Dealings between groups cannot be accounted for by the psychology of the individual. Governments decide to go to war; battles are fought by armies; and peace is established by governments. The social conditions in which groups of people live largely determine their beliefs and the extent to which they are shared. Ultimately, a single person's attack on an ethnic minority group that he dislikes or fears would remain a trivial occurrence had it not been for the fact that he acts in unison with others who share his feelings and are very important in determining his willingness to aggress against this minority. Theoretical principles can be formulated based on the individual as a unit and these can be very helpful in understanding hostility between groups. But such abstractions could only refer to unstructured collections of people and are only made possible by inter-individual uniformities in behaviour which are due to the fact that people live in a social context which has its own laws and structure.

This paraphrase is, of course, in many ways unfair to Berkowitz as it skates over some of the serious theoretical problems with which he was concerned.[4] But a critique of his views is not its main point. Rather, it is the fact that the paraphrased statement would readily command the agreement of many of our colleagues who emphasize the social determination of intergroup relations. To take two examples: it could easily be inserted in the influential books by Banton (1967) or by Blalock (1967) without in any way creating inconsistencies with their general argument. But the difficulties this presents for a social psychologist are just as serious as those of Berkowitz's 'psychological individualism'. If this is the beginning and the end of the explanation of social conduct, then we have yet another *tabula rasa* on which nothing has been written about the convergence of the psychological and the social processes and the way in which they shape one another. In a sense, this is like a second sociological version of Skinnerian behaviourism which follows a different direction from the first version proposed by Homans (1961). It is the sociology of the 'empty organism' which relates directly the inputs (e.g. economic situation) to the outputs (e.g. discrimination in employment) without concerning itself with the black box in the middle which contains the mysteries of human social functioning. Even this is not entirely true: unstated assumptions are often made about the black box; some relevant examples can be found in Moscovici's (1972) and Israel's (1972) discussions of the relations between psychological and economic theories (also see Plon, 1972). We are thus confronted simultaneously by the psychological individualism of the psychologists and a sociological or economic version of an implicit 'naive psychologism'.

It is not the purpose of this chapter to produce grand (or even minor)

[4] In particular, it ignores deliberately the inescapable fact that armies, governments etc. are composed of individuals who take decisions for themselves and for others. But this still does not mean that we are dealing here with the 'individual' psychology of presocial men and women who form a society by coming together in a heap.

theories. But it is one of its aims to attempt a discussion of the kind of variables that a theory should include in order to fit the requirements of psycho-social reality. In the case of intergroup relations – and also in other cases, as, for example, in problems of social influence as they relate to the psychological aspects of social change – one could argue that we are confronted at present with a scientific system of separate tiers, with the means of access from one to another hardly ever used; or that we are witnessing something like an exchange of pre-packaged gifts, un-doubtedly selected with the best possible intentions, but without any reference to the needs of the receiver or to the use that he might wish to make of them. The notion of flexibility in the relations between the human organism and his environment, grounded in biology and used in a great many ways in psychological theories and research on cognitive functioning, is the obvious perspective that should be common to ethological theories of intraspecific aggression and to the consideration of the emergent characteristics of human social behaviour. A similar role could be played by the notion of appropriateness of conduct in order to bring the 'psychology of the individual' to a level adequate for many aspects of a sociopsychological analysis.

Very little needs to be said about flexibility. The most important evolutionary weapon of Man has undoubtedly been his capacity to modify his behaviour to accord with environmental requirements, and simultaneously to change the environment to fit his own requirements. And yet, as I have stated elsewhere (see chapter 6), the cognitive models employed to analyse human attempts to understand the environment, biological and physical, in order to act upon it have been ignored in most of the ethological and the psychoanalytic writing concerned with social environment.

Related to these cognitive models of human flexibility is the notion of appropriateness of conduct which leads directly to the conception of Man as a 'rule-following animal' (see, among others, Harré, 1972 and Peters's discussion, published in 1960, of the concept of motivation in psycho-logical theories). In a discussion of the primacy of abstract rules in the determination of behaviour, Hayek (1969) wrote: 'all our actions must be conceived of as being guided by rules of which we are not conscious but which in their joint influence enable us to exercise extremely complicated skills without having any idea of the particular sequence of movements involved.' (pp. 312–13). This rule-integration of motor skills is reflected at a different level in social conduct; or as Peters put it: 'Man is a rule-following animal. His actions are not simply directed towards ends; they also conform to social standards and conventions, and unlike a calculating machine he acts because of his knowledge of rules and

35

objectives.' (p. 5).

In the field of social conduct, rules can be described as notions about appropriateness. This means quite simply that social conduct is to a very large extent determined by what an individual deems to be appropriate to the social situation in which he finds himself. His conceptions of what is appropriate are in turn determined by the prevailing system of norms and values which must be analysed in the light of the properties of the social system in which he lives. It is a crude over-simplification to conceive of social motives as being capable of direct derivation from a hedonic algebra of self-interest – real or fictitious – based on a few universal human drives, whatever the choice of the drives may be. To behave appropriately is a powerful social motive. It is in large part responsible both for the attempts to preserve or to modify one's conduct to fit a situation, and to change, reform or revolutionize a situation or systems of situations which interfere with the possibility (or the free-dom) to act appropriately. This becomes clear if the motive to act according to certain internalized rules and the choice of the mode of action are placed in the context of social stability and social change, of social norms and values as they relate to individual calculations of self-interest, and of a social psychology as contrasted with one which is merely inter-individual. I shall briefly discuss each of these issues.

Notions of appropriateness reflect the system of social norms and values. One could define norms as being an individual's expectations (shared with others) of how others expect him to behave and of how others *will* behave in any given situation. But then – if the system of values were not brought into play – social conduct would consist mainly of unwavering and unchanging conformity. Values are the implicit and explicit ideologies of a society – political, social, moral or religious – and of the subgroups within it. I am not concerned here with the problem of how an individual acquires and internalizes his values, but with the fact that he *has* them. No change is possible in a society without serious tensions occurring between *some* of its norms and *some* of its values. Sometimes changes – e.g. technological ones – are accompanied by tensions, sometimes tensions create change; most often the two interact. If tensions exist, one way to resolve them is to redefine values to fit in with the norms, or to change the norms to conform more closely to values. But if enough individuals or groups – moved by common interests, or a common ideology, or a shared *Weltanschauung* – refuse to do the one or the other, the *status quo* is bound to be shaken sooner or later. In changing it, the individuals change themselves, since by removing one source of tension they create another which stands in a new and different relation to what they are. Thus, to act 'appropriately'

36

is not necessarily to act in conformity with what is or has been. It is also to act as a rebel, an innovator, a saint, a revolutionary and, also, to be capable of genocide.

But to leave out of account motives and strategies of self-interest would be to over-simplify as much as is done in the 'inter-individual' psychology of gain and loss. The notion of 'self-interest' employed in much of the current research, unless closely analysed, is no more than the kind of self-interest about which the researcher knows best because it forms a part of his own background that he assumes he shares with his subjects (as indeed he often does with the legions of undergraduates who gain 'credits' by participating in his research); or if his subjects come from a background which is unfamiliar to him he must assume that he knows what their conceptions of self-interest are. Of course, without independent evidence we shall never know if he was right or wrong in making this assumption. But how then can he pretend to verify general laws of, for example, competition and cooperation?

Even if he happens to be right in his unstated assumptions about his subjects, there are very good reasons why a simple view of 'gain' and 'loss' can only lead to 'trivial' or 'irrelevant' research. The system of values determines to a large extent the conception of gain and loss as soon as we leave the mythical pre-Aveyron 'psychology of the individual' and treat him with the respect due to a member of a species that created its own environment and its own complexities. In turn, the system of norms determines the strategies that are *acceptable* for achieving 'gain'. One of the important contributions to social psychology of Festinger's (1957) theory of cognitive dissonance lies precisely in the fact that it is capable of throwing additional light on the effects of the betrayal of a value on the genesis of subsequent norms. Otherwise, there is not very much excitement in knowing that subjects who expressed opinions contrary to their own for a reward of one dollar subsequently changed their original opinions more than those who did it for ten dollars (Brehm and Cohen, 1962). This finding, and others like it, are 'non-obvious' only if we have finally and sadly reached a conception of the 'obvious' which consists of ingredients taken from the simplistic versions of reinforcement theory and from the philosophy of life of a small-time businessman or politician.

The *shared* psychological processes of social change can be the subject of a proper sociopsychological theory only if betrayals of values, or discrepancies between values and emerging norms, or between norms and emerging values, repeated over a period of time, are seen as leading to the creation of new forms of acceptable conduct which themselves lead to a refitting of values or of their order of priority. This is how we can begin perhaps to understand why – at some points of time – many people may be ready to die because 'it is my country, right or wrong', and – at the other extreme – to take decisions to create concentration camps, to drop the first A-bomb, to burn Dresden or the ghetto of Warsaw, or to kill 'suspect' women and children in Vietnamese villages. It is always possible to 'explain' all these actions in terms of motives of 'self-interest' or as an expression of the ubiquitous 'aggressive drive'. This is just about as illuminating as to say that mothers care for their children because they have a maternal instinct and that we know that they have a maternal instinct because they care for their children. The point is that even if this were true, it gets us not a whit further – and the same applies to all explanations of social conduct in terms of 'basic' individual motivation.

A basis of self-interest, or of self-preservation, can be taken for granted both in the actions of head-hunting tribesmen and of the modern mass incendiaries. The aims of their actions cannot be understood without an analysis of their system of values; the means cannot be understood without an analysis of the system of norms. The selection of aims may or may not imply a conflict of values or a conflict between values and norms; if it does, the processes of justification of actual or of *intended* conduct come into play. The interaction between these processes and the system of norms may lead to modifications in the norms if it takes place within a social system which is capable of an effective diffusion of social influence and which also is characterized by the existence of problems that are common to people who define themselves as a 'group' on the basis of social criteria, whatever these criteria may be.

But this is not all that happens: as mentioned above, an action or an intended action using means or aiming to achieve ends which imply a conflict of values or a conflict between norms and values presents the problem of refitting the system; and this is *one* of the determinants of the creation of new ideologies which, if accepted at large, set the process in motion all over again. For example, the diffusion of nationalist ideologies was (and still is) as responsible for the creation of new nations as the 'existence' of nations was responsible for the creation and diffusion of nationalist ideologies (see Tajfel, 1969b and 1970a, for a more extended discussion). In attempting to resolve its tortured conflict of values, racism contributed more to the social significance of 'race' than did all the genetic differences in the shade of skin or the shape of a nose. (The *presumed* genetic differences between races are already part and parcel of the justifying function of the ideology.) Let me make it quite clear that none of this is written with the intention of denying or neglecting the intrinsic importance of economic, social and political factors; but that the

38

intention is to stake out a claim for the kind of contribution to the understanding of a tangled web of problems that can be made by a sociopsychological approach to some of its aspects.

The nature of this contribution becomes even clearer when one considers some of the psychological differences between categories of social conduct that could, for example, all be happily combined within the common denominator of one or another version of universal individual drives or basic motives and secondary derivations from them. Head-hunting or killing all prisoners of war can go on for centuries without causing the slightest tremor of change if it remains an unquestioned part of appropriate conduct in clearly defined categories of social situations. This cannot be so if similar actions take place against a background of potential and socially-shared divergences in the interpretation of the appropriateness of modes of conduct: the *acceptance* of the establishment of concentration camps in the neighbourhood of large European cities or of dropping napalm bombs on jungle villages cannot go on for very long without considerable psychological repercussions on those who accept these actions as well as on those who do not. The seeds of sociopsychological change are both in the conflict between them and in the conflict within them. It is because of the socially derived, shared, accepted and conflicting notions of appropriateness of conduct, because of the social definition of the situations to which they apply, and of the social origin of their manner of changing and of relating to one another, that individual or inter-individual psychology cannot be usefully considered as providing the bricks from which an adequate social psychology can be built. The derivations need to be in the opposite direction.

It is true that if we wish to formulate a theory we must try to find some similarities of principle underlying the apparent diversity of attitudes and modes of conduct. It is also true that one such set of principles can be found, for example, in the relations that are shown to exist in individual behaviour between frustration–aggression, its inhibition and its displacement; and another in the processes of resolution of cognitive dissonance. My conviction that the latter is bound to be more useful than the former in a sociopsychological analysis is based on the fact that the concepts of commitment and of justification are inherent in it. These concepts are as social as they are psychological: they are capable of being analysed in terms of their social derivation, and they have their own derivations in the sharing, diffusing and communicating of conflicting modes of social conduct, i.e. in theories of attitude change.

This is not the case for theories which cannot transcend the limits of an analysis of individual and presocial motivation and of strategies of behaviour arising from it. To return for a moment to some problems in

39

the psychology of intergroup relations and its analysis in terms of frustration–aggression and its displacements: as everybody's life is full of frustration and everybody's ingroup has its outgroups, we have reached the end of the road apart from a few technical embellishments and a few difficulties encountered here and there in defining our terms. Is it surprising therefore that we come up against complaints of irrelevance and triviality? A collection of individual frustrations is a very different matter from the socially shared *conception of the origin* of common difficulties perceived as common because of a notion of collective identity based on criteria of categorization which are again fully derived from their social context. Shared conduct is not shared because we are all frustrated; it is shared by those who have all accepted basically the same theory of social causation (see Billig, 1976). It is the analysis of the principles which determine the nature of these 'theories', their diffusion and acceptance as well as their translation into social conduct that is one of the fundamental tasks of social psychology. If questions of this nature *are* the proper object of sociopsychological theories, it is difficult to resist the notion that explanations of, for example, intergroup conduct such as those provided by the frustration–aggression hypothesis and all other theories of basic individual motivation are a little like the disembodied grin of the Cheshire cat that Alice saw.

3
Individuals and groups in social psychology[1]

1. How 'social' is social psychology?

The main theme of the Introduction to part I and of the preceding chapter was the 'individualistic' nature of the major theories in social psychology and of the bulk of the research deriving from these theories. Before proceeding with the argument, it is important to stress once again its main point so as to avoid possible misunderstandings about the main reasons for discontent. The complaint is *not* that a great deal of work has been done on individual and inter-individual processes. The study of these processes is one of the main functions of social psychology, and there is no doubt that much progress has been achieved in the last thirty or forty years. The fact remains that this is not the *only* task of social psychology, and that the overwhelming domination of the subject by its almost exclusive concern with individuals in interaction led us to lose sight of two other large-scale issues which are (or should be) equally important: the study of collective behaviour (about which more will be found in chapter 7 and part IV of this book; see also several chapters in Tajfel, 1981, in press); and the study of the *direct* effects that the location of individuals in various parts of the social system inside which they live has on an enormous variety of person-to-person encounters.

The debate about these issues, of which chapter 2 provided an example, continued throughout the seventies. The issues raised in that chapter were taken up directly some years later in an article published by Taylor and Brown (1979). They agreed that social psychology did not manage, in most of its theories and research, to contextualize individual or inter-individual social behaviour within the framework of its wider social determination; and in this, they wrote, they agreed with the views expressed in the previous chapter and by other people (e.g. Billig, 1976; Moscovici, 1972; Steiner, 1974). They also complained however, that two crucial issues were not fully resolved in the manner in which these criticisms were made:

[1] This chapter reproduces parts of a debate which was published in 1979 in the *British Journal of Social and Clinical Psychology* (**18**, pp. 173–9; 183–90). The first section of the chapter is a summary of the article by Taylor and Brown which initiated the exchange of views; the second section is the reply by the author, published in the same issue of the *British Journal of Social and Clinical Psychology*.

the distinction between an individualistic and a group approach to social psychology is not entirely clear, and hence it is difficult to develop guidelines for concrete ways of redressing the balance of individualistic and more social orientations. Second, at what point on this continuum does one cease to focus on psychological issues and posing questions, albeit important ones, which lie outside the domain of social psychology? (p. 173)

In order to resolve these questions, Taylor and Brown (to be referred to as T and B from now on) introduce a distinction between individualism in social psychological *research* and individualism in social psychological *theory*. They agree that research has been individualistic in its preoccupations and has ignored the wider social context of much individual social behaviour. They feel, however, that – on condition that this social context should be explicitly included in the designs and aims of the research – theories in social psychology *should* be, in the last analysis, concerned with individuals, since this is the primary task and function of psychology.

They follow some of the critics in providing examples of such non-contextualized research. This has been the case with 'the gaming approach to conflict' (e.g. Deutsch, 1973); the research by Asch (1956) as re-analysed by Moscovici and Faucheux (1972); and with the progressive loss of the tradition represented earlier by Newcomb (1943) when 'social psychology emphasized the *social* origins of our perception of people' (Taylor and Brown, p. 174). The alternative tradition took over in concentrating almost entirely on dyadic relationships, such as was the case with 'the voluminous literature on interpersonal attraction' (Byrne, 1971). Even those fields of research which, by the very nature of the problems they dealt with, should have been clearly and obviously concerned with issues transcending the dominant 'inter-individuality' ended up in that tradition. Thus, the work on relative deprivation, 'with one noticeable exception', represented by Runciman (1966) ended up with Crosby (1976) proposing an explicitly individualistic 'model of egoistical relative deprivation'; equity theory is only concerned with individuals' relations with other individuals (Berkowitz and Walster, 1976); Rokeach's (1960) theory of prejudice is based on inter-individual perceptions of belief similarity or dissimilarity; the study of attitude formation and change ranging from earlier balance theories (see e.g. Abelson *et al.*, 1968) to more recent formulations (e.g. Triandis, 1971; Fishbein and Ajzen, 1975) is primarily concerned with *intra*-individual processes. The final step has been to treat even intergroup behaviour in these individual and inter-individual terms despite the early research by the Sherifs (e.g. Sherif and Sherif, 1953) and the anthropological evidence (e.g. Brewer and Campbell, 1976) that groups' reciprocal perceptions need to be related to a wider cultural and social framework.

Thus, T and B agree with the critics that *research* on all these issues has been largely conducted in a social vacuum. They do not agree, however, with the view that *theories* in psychology can or should transcend the level of individual analysis.

It is our contention that an individualistic level of theorizing is entirely appropriate; that it can incorporate social or group dimensions in a dynamic fashion; and that an examination of the works which purport to represent a new non-individualistic orientation are in fact not fundamentally different from traditional individualistic approaches, at least at the *level* of theorizing. (p. 176)

In order to pursue this argument, T and B analyse in the remainder of their article two theories which purport to transcend individualism (Moscovici, 1976; Tajfel, 1974, 1978a; Tajfel and Turner, 1979) and argue (i) that these theories remain essentially 'individual'; (ii) that their value lies precisely in the fact that they have remained 'individual' while managing to contextualize social behaviour in its interaction with group phenomena; and (iii) that the sooner this is openly acknowledged, the easier it will be for these theoretical developments, which they consider important, to influence beneficially the mainstream of social psychology.

In other words, T and B state that social behaviour originates from and pertains to, individuals. Whatever 'non-individual' variables may affect it (such as 'groups', 'social context', etc.) useful social psychological theories must remain at this individual level. The two recent theories discussed by T and B have done precisely this, despite their protestations to the contrary. Like M. Jourdain we were speaking prose, but we did not know it.

My agreement with T and B stops at the end of the first sentence of the above summary paragraph. The statement about social behaviour originating from, and being performed by, individuals is entirely unexceptionable and trivially true. But immediately afterwards the difficulties begin. The *bourgeois-gentilhomme* may have been speaking prose without knowing it, but Molière never informed us whether the result was good prose or bad prose. To say that in the last analysis we are concerned with individual social behaviour is as true as it is meaningless until and unless some useful and interesting statements are made about the characteristics of this behaviour and the kind of theoretical approach which will be needed to understand these characteristics.

2. Individualistic and group theories
(a) Research and theory in 'individualistic' social psychology.
Let us start with the T and B distinction between 'research' and

'theories'. The examples of research provided by T and B originate from the frustration–aggression theory as applied to 'the collective discontent of a group'; gaming approaches to conflict; the theories of attribution, of dissonance, of interpersonal attraction, of attitude formation and change, of social comparison, of social influence. For some reasons (unexplained in the T and B paper) *all* these social psychological theories have led to research which can be, as T and B agree, justifiably criticized for its neglect of the social context of social behaviour. An obvious question arises: if this has really happened because of some (haphazardly determined?) directions of research rather than *the nature of the theories*, how come that the above list includes practically all of the 'mainstream' of the last 40 years or so, with no more than a few half-forgotten puddles left behind here and there? As I wrote a few years ago: 'many of the theories which dominate the present research output in social psychology are not socio-psychological. It is therefore unavoidable that most of the experiments designed to test these theories should be equally impervious to the wider realities of social conduct and share their focus on the strategies of individual and inter-individual adjustments'.

In other words, the problem seems to lie not with directions of research, as T and B write, but with the nature and explanatory targets of the theories from which the research derived. But I suspect that T and B would agree with this despite the confusing distinction between 'research' and 'theories' introduced in their paper. Within their self-imposed limitations these theories have been extremely useful in helping us to explain some fundamental aspects of human social behaviour. But it looks as if *other* theories are needed to do the job not previously done: namely, to take into account the 'dynamic interaction' between individual behaviour and its wider social scenario. As already stated, T and B see no difference of principle between these other theories and the earlier ones, since – in the last analysis – they must all be concerned with 'individuals'.

It is because of this essential agreement that we must all share about individuals that T and B have led themselves into something which looks like a semantic confusion whirling around a strawman. As they wrote: 'Only when social reality is accounted for, not just as it influences behaviour in a static function but as a truly dynamic and interactive relationship of the individual and social structure, will social psychological theory be sufficiently comprehensive.' But also, the 'basic theoretical building blocks' of the intergroup theory which they describe (e.g. Tajfel and Turner, 1979) 'are individualistic in nature' and, according to them, should remain so.

(b) Individual processes and collective behaviour in the theory of intergroup behaviour

The 'individualistic' description of the intergroup theory in the T and B paper is simply achieved: of its three important aspects one only is described because, presumably, T and B consider it to be more funda-mental than the other two. In a recent text (see chapters 11 to 13 in this book) the theory is described as a 'conceptual tripod' which enables us, because of the convergence of all of its three lines of thought, to make predictions and achieve more understanding about the social psycho-logical aspects of intergroup relations. The 'support' of the tripod described by T and B is the sequence of social categorization–social identity–social comparison. This sequence, as they rightly say, consists ultimately of individual processes. They admit that 'group processes are, of course, fundamental to the theory; however, it is their dynamic and bi-directional interaction with the individual and his motivations and aspirations which makes it truly a social psychological theory of inter-group behaviour'.

If there was no more to it than that, T and B's argument would have been entirely justified. The processes of social categorization, social identity and social comparison, as used in the theory, cannot be conceived to originate outside of their social contexts. But they can also be shown to function in some ways which are basically the same in group, inter-individual and even non-social settings. For social categor-ization this has been shown to be the case, in some conditions, in the study of the general judgement processes (see chapter 4 in this book; Eiser and Stroebe, 1972). The notion of social identity is based on the simple motivational assumption that *individuals* (at least in our culture) prefer a positive to a negative self-image. The idea of social comparison originated with Festinger's fully inter-individual theory (1954). In view of these important similarities between the 'individualistic' conceptions of social categorization, social identity and social comparison and those used in the presently-discussed theory of intergroup behaviour, what is the nature of the *differences* between this kind of theory and others?

A full description of these differences is obviously not possible here (see chapters 11 to 13). It will be useful, however, to outline the general structure which will help to locate the concepts of social categorization, social identity and social comparison in the total pattern and show that they cannot be considered, as they are by T and B, to be the core of the whole enterprise. Let me state that the emphasis chosen here reflects my own views and need not be shared by some of my colleagues who have contributed in crucial ways to the development of our work – including amongst others Rupert Brown and Donald Taylor. It is perhaps super-fluous to add that our past and present disagreements are and have been as useful as our agreements in enabling us to extend our work in new directions.

An important aspect of 'social reality' is that most social systems contain collections of individuals who differ from each other in a variety of ways. Some of these differences can easily be ascertained to exist by an outside objective and uncommitted observer; e.g. differences in sex, age, wealth, power, forms of work, forms of leisure, dress, language, etc. The observer has certain tools which will enable him to structure these differences in one way of another, i.e. to establish his own 'construction' of any particular social 'reality'. This is often attempted in an 'outside' stance by sociologists, social anthropologists or social historians. The individuals inside the system have also tools to do this kind of job; the tools used by both the outsiders and the insiders are not dissimilar. But the *criteria* for accepting the validity of one construction or another may differ vastly between those who engage in the 'outside' construction for their professional (scientific) purposes and those inside the system who need guidelines for their behaviour and thus attempt to construct a coherent system of orientation in their social environment.

Social categorization is one of these tools (see chapters 4, 6 and 7). But the fact that this tool exists (i.e. that it is a part of human cognitive equipment) provides us with no more information as to whether, when or how it will be used than knowing that a man has bought a do-it-yourself kit would by itself inform us whether, when, how and for what purposes he will use it. We only know that there are some things he can do with his kit (there may be some we do not know about if we underestimate his ingenuity); and we also know that some constructions are definitely impossible because of the limitations of this particular box of tricks. For example: an outside observer may notice (and check with other outside observers) that in a society he is looking at some individuals are black and some are white. This information, however objective it is, would not by itself enable him to conclude that his black–white distinction is one on which the tool kit of social categorizing has been put to use, i.e. that this distinction is in any way relevant to the social behaviour inside the system.

As I wrote above, the aim of a theory of intergroup behaviour is to help us to understand certain selected uniformities of social behaviour. In order to do this, we must know (i) something about the ways in which groups are constructed in a particular social system; (ii) what are the psychological effects of these constructions; and (iii) how the constructions and their effects depend upon, and relate to, forms of social reality.

These are the primary aims of the theory of intergroup behaviour which was discussed by T and B in their paper, although it would be idle to pretend that they were not much hazier in the early stages than they are now in hindsight.

The first of the above three questions requires an answer in two stages. We need, first of all, a definition of a group which refers to the way the notion is *constructed* by those inside the system. This definition must enable us to make the transition from what we assume is 'constructed' by the individuals involved to data showing whether our assumptions were correct or incorrect. The notion of social categorization discussed by T and B is undoubtedly and crucially implied in this process of definition. If we did not know about the human capacity to categorize the environment in certain ways, we could not even begin to make the assumption that collections or heaps of individuals in a social system can be cognitively organized into a complex matrix of overlapping categories. But this by itself tells us nothing about the nature of the categorizations and their uses or effects in social behaviour.

The second stage of the answer to the question about the ways in which groups are constructed concerns the fact that a theory of intergroup behaviour has for its aim the explanation (or a better understanding) of certain uniformities of intergroup behaviour. It is therefore necessary to state the basic conditions for groups to be constructed in such a way that the consequent behaviour of members of one group towards another shows uniformities rather than a random variation from individual to individual. The theory makes two testable and interdependent propositions about these conditions. They consist of stating that certain uniformities of intergroup behaviour will appear if (i) members of a group believe that there is no possibility for them (or at least that there are considerable difficulties) of moving from one group to another; and that (ii), consequently or in interaction with the former condition, the boundaries between the groups are fairly sharply drawn. One of the results of the conjunction of these two conditions is that it may powerfully determine the course of interpersonal interaction independently of the individual characteristics of the interactants or of the detail of their past or present personal relations (see chapters 11 to 13).

The second question above concerned the psychological effects of the above conditions. This is the aspect of the theory briefly summarized by T and B and presumably considered by them to be more fundamental than the others. It is the sequence from social categorization to social identity and social comparison (see Tajfel, 1974; Turner, 1975; Tajfel and Turner, 1979; chapter 12 in this book). There is no doubt that T and B are quite correct in stating that the *focus* of these psychological effects is in *individuals*. It could hardly be anywhere else. What is more, as I wrote earlier, there are some important similarities in these processes as they appear in individual, inter-individual or intergroup behaviour. There are also some important differences which are discussed elsewhere in this book (see chapters 2, 7 and 11).

The third question formulated earlier concerned the relationships between, on the one hand, social intergroup constructions and their effects, as just discussed, and, on the other hand, various forms of social reality. Providing a set of testable answers to it is quite fundamental if the theory is to have any predictive value at all. There are several reasons for this. All the theoretical considerations summarized so far would not be capable of making clear-cut and testable distinctions between a multi-group social system which retains its stability and one which is in the process of change, attempted change or resisted change in the relations between the groups of which it is composed. The fact that individuals in a social system perceive the system as having sharply drawn and fairly impassable group boundaries does not, by itself, lead to the conclusion that they will engage in common action either to change it or to preserve it. The fact that they are capable of making social comparisons which are relevant to their self-image does not, by itself, mean that these compari- sons will result from the perceived position of their group as relating to other groups rather than remaining at an inter-individual level (see Turner, 1975, 1978a, for a more detailed discussion). The construction of a social system in terms of sharply drawn social categories and the *capacity* to categorize and compare oneself with others in certain ways and for certain purposes are the *necessary* conditions for the appearance of certain forms of intergroup behaviour; they are not *sufficient* conditions.

The translation from potentiality to actual social behaviour must be sought elsewhere. 'Social reality' can be described or analysed in terms of socio-economic, historical or political structures. Such descriptions or analyses are not within the competence of the social psychologist. But he *can* ascertain that, for whatever reasons, the system of the relations between social groups is perceived by the individuals located in the various parts of the system as being capable or incapable of change; as being based on legitimate or illegitimate principles of social organization. He can also ascertain whether, as a result, group actions are being considered or undertaken in common by those who feel that their location (and 'social identity' as defined by Taylor and Brown and elsewhere) in the system is capable or incapable of change; is secure or insecure. A combination of these shared interpretations of social reality with the location of social groups within the system as perceived by their members provides the possibility of formulating a number of hypotheses. These hypotheses and some of the research deriving from them are described elsewhere (see chapters 13 to 15 and Tajfel, 1978a).

It will now be clear, I hope, why I find it difficult to agree with T and B who, after having summarized in their paper the sequence of social categorization–social identity–social comparison, and described it as containing the 'basic postulates' of the theory, relegate all the rest to the following single sentence: 'It is from these basic postulates that a variety of important concepts emerge including social mobility, social change, cognitive alternatives, legitimacy and stability.' It is the use of this truncated version of a more complex structure which enables them to write immediately below that their aim was 'to point out that the focus of the theory is ultimately the individual', although 'group processes are of course fundamental to it'. The focus of the theory is not the individual but the explanation of uniformities of intergroup behaviour. No one would deny that ultimately we are concerned with individuals who behave in one way or another. But a clear distinction must be made between theories which are 'individualistic' and one which is concerned with socially-shared patterns of individual behaviour. An 'individualistic' theory contains the (most often) unstated assumption that individuals live and behave in a homogeneous social medium. This medium consists of a collection of undifferentiated individual particles which are assumed to relate to each other inter-individually following the laws of basic psychological processes. There is no room in this vision of randomly floating particles for the cognitive and socially-shared *organization* of the system within which the particles float. Or if it is admitted that the lines along which the system is structured, both objectively and subjectively, have a great deal to do with the social behaviour of its individual elements, this is considered to be no more than a set of 'variables' superimposed on something more 'fundamental'. It has been the contention of this chapter so far that this kind of approach cannot get us very far in understanding those crucial uniformities of social behaviour which pertain to the *psychological* aspects of the social systems in which we live, i.e. it will get us no nearer to an adequate social psychology of social conflict, social stability, social change, social movements or social unrest. Taylor and Brown wrote that 'the individual should and will remain the ultimate target of understanding'. My view is that if this were really to be the case, then social psychology 'should and will remain' as incapable as it has been until now of providing any new psychological insights into some of the most important aspects of our functioning in society. In the next section of this chapter, I hope to support this statement using as examples two theories which were also briefly mentioned by T and B in their paper.

(c) Individualistic assumptions in social psychology: Belief similarity and equity

As T and B wrote, Rokeach's belief-similarity theory of prejudice (e.g. Rokeach, 1960) marked the introduction of a social variable like 'race' into '*research* on interpersonal attraction' (my italics). As they also wrote, 'nevertheless, even in these studies the emphasis was still predominantly interpersonal, i.e. subjects rated a black or white *individual* and the salience of the social category was minimized'. The patent absurdity of the theory as applied to some social contexts is acknowledged by T and B when they write that 'it would be bordering on the absurd to suggest . . . that the hostility between blacks and whites in southern Africa today is caused principally by a perception of belief similarity. To ignore the gross inequities of power and wealth institutionalized by a long history of colonialism would be truly to do "experiments in a vacuum".' T and B also add that their 'point is not that the similarity–attraction relationship is invalid but rather that its validity is specific to certain contexts'.

One can think of a few such contexts: for example, a debating society, an arts college with strongly liberal norms and prescriptions, or any other context which would make it socially undesirable to show racial prejudice in a polite psychological experiment. It is interesting that when T and B discuss this issue, they refer once more to research and not to the nature of the theory underlying it. The only thing which, according to them, is missing in this kind of approach is the introduction of just one more independent variable: an increase in the salience of a social categorization.

The result is therefore an unchanged theory of interpersonal attraction, one of whose elements is the perception of belief similarity or dissimilarity. Then, an independent variable of social categorization is stuck on somewhere or other as a scaffolding which will hopefully prop up the venerable structure. The homogeneous social medium of freely-floating individual particles has remained unchanged. As in the example of the study by Taylor and Guimond (1978) quoted by T and B, the induction by the experimenter of a more salient social categorization 'affected' the 'paradigm', as was shown in the responses of the individuals concerned (see also e.g. Billig and Tajfel, 1973; Doise and Sinclair, 1973, showing similar effects of the increased salience of social categorization).

So far so good: we all agree that social categorizations of various kinds may have profound effects on some interpersonal responses. But unless this is seen in a much wider theoretical context (see the previous section), the underlying assumptions have not changed at all. Our particles have continued their random floating. It so happens that *some* of them (for reasons unexplained, apart from the experimenter's induction or, perhaps in 'real life', owing to some individual motivational patterns) are using salient social categorizations which apply to one or another aspect of their social environment.

The 'individualistic' counter-argument to this objection is quite simple and it has a short-term research plausibility: there are undoubtedly some social contexts in which these salient social categorizations are generally induced in many individuals, for one reason or another; there are other social contexts in which they are not. But all the rest remains a deep mystery to the social psychologist. Thus, social categorization is still conceived as a haphazardly-floating 'independent variable' which strikes at random as the spirit moves it. No links are made, or attempted, between the conditions determining its presence and mode of operation, and its outcomes in widely diffused commonalities of social behaviour. Why, when and how is a social categorization salient or not salient? What kind of shared constructions of social reality, mediated through social categorizations, lead to a social climate in which large masses of people feel that they are in long-term conflict with other large masses? What, for example, are the *psychological* transitions from a stable to an unstable social system? It is not my contention that the theoretical approach briefly outlined in the previous section of this chapter and described in detail elsewhere necessarily provides the best answers to these very difficult questions. For all I know, most of the hypotheses deriving from it will be disproved in future research. The point is that we shall never be able to formulate adequate guidelines for research on collective social behaviour if we do not go beyond constructing sets of independent variables seen as functioning in a social environment which is assumed to be psychologically unstructured in its homogeneous and all-embracing 'inter-individuality'.

A very similar argument applies to equity theory which has recently come back into fashion. Its claims are not modest. The subtitle of a recent book on the subject (Berkowitz and Walster, 1976) promises to lead us through equity theory 'towards a general theory of social interaction'. This claim is restated in the first chapter of the book in which we are told that its 'first section elucidates a general theory of social behaviour – equity theory' (Walster *et al.*, 1976, p. 1). In a recent paper Caddick (1977) succinctly summarized the major proposals of the theory, two of which are particularly relevant here: '(i) When individuals find themselves participating in inequitable relationships they become distressed. (ii) Individuals who discover they are in an inequitable relationship attempt to eliminate distress by restoring equity.' As

Caddick wrote, 'There is a considerable amount of experimental evidence' to support these proposals. But, as he added:

The experimental evaluation of equity theory has generally involved face-to-face interactions between the experimental Ss. It seems fairly obvious that, at this level of interpersonal closeness, esteem-damaging accusations of inequitable behaviour would be hard to avoid or ignore, the possibility of retaliation and the difficulty of sustaining equity-producing psychological distortions would increase and, as a result, the restoration of equity by actual compensation might well become the most attractive resolution. Furthermore, inequitable relations between experimental Ss are almost invariably created by the investigator and not by the intentional behaviour of the S who stands to gain from the inequity. This, of course, places the disadvantaged S in a situation which he can either exploit or reject but, if we keep in mind the fact that behaving equitably is a means by which the S can attain personal regard in his own and the other person's eyes, and if we compare this payoff with the usually trivial one which would result from accepting the E's manipulations, then the commonly observed tendency to compensate comes as no real surprise.

These points are not just methodological. Implied in Caddick's criticism of the experimental procedures is the admission that equity theory *does* work. In many situations there is indeed discomfort due to an inequitable relationship, and attempts are made to eliminate it. The major problem that arises concerns the conditions when this does *not* happen. It is, of course, not difficult to think of innumerable social situations in which the proposals summarized above seem blatantly wrong. The relationships which are created and observed in the studies on equity share one characteristic: no social differentiations, apart from being equitably or inequitably advantaged or disadvantaged as individuals, are supposed to exist between the subjects. Once again, as in the case of the belief-similarity theory, we are inside an unstructured and homogeneous social environment. As Caddick wrote, 'equity theory is basically an intragroup theory in its orientation'. It assumed that 'equitable treatment of others, as a social value, extends to cover members of outgroups as well as members of ingroups'. The intragroup orientation determines the kind of research that is undertaken; and by the same token the data that are obtained. Its universal stance leads to the kind of extrapolations from interpersonal to intergroup behaviour about which T and B complained in their paper.

Here again, it would not be enough simply to introduce the independent variable of a salient social categorization in order to see whether its effect would be to decrease the discomfort caused by inequity and/or the tendencies to restore equity. Our social history is full of familiar and horrifying examples of dehumanization of outgroups and even more so of milder forms of their depersonalization. The psychological processes which produce this dehumanization or depersonalization would require a discussion which is well beyond the scope of this chapter. But the point must be made that, as social psychologists, we have a duty to attend to these processes. And even if many of us who wish to ignore them are entirely free to do so, we do *not* have the right to imply through the conclusions we draw from our work that our cosy and equitable inter-individuality can reach beyond the blinkered vision of social reality which we have selected for our special consideration. As T and B wrote, the individual is the target of understanding for social psychology; but he cannot remain the only target.

PART II

From perceptual judgement to social stereotypes

Introduction

Part II of this book includes general discussions and reports of research related to them which were published between 1957 and 1980. Their principal theme was already mentioned in the introductory chapter. The logical and chronological sequence, together with some related research developments, needs to be presented here in a little more detail.

The issues of the sociopsychological integration discussed in the introductory chapter and part I of this book, and returned to again in part IV, do not make their appearance until the concluding chapter of part II. But the progression in the four chapters, 'from perceptual judgements to social stereotypes', reflects the development of the perspective described in chapter 1. This development can be retraced in the succession of the following stages:

(1) A re-analysis of perceptual over-estimation. The original findings and some of their implications are described in the first four sections of chapter 4. The re-analysis consists of reinterpreting the finding that the magnitudes of stimuli which have value to the subjects are perceived as larger than identical neutral stimuli. This over-estimation is seen here as a by-product of an exaggeration of perceived or judged differences between the stimuli in a series in which the value of the stimuli varies concurrently with their size, as is often the case in, for example, series of coins of various denominations. The functional grounds on which this is expected to happen are discussed in the second section of chapter 4 which, together with its fourth section, also provides examples of experimental studies confirming the 'accentuation theory'.

(2) The same principles are then transposed from judged differences between *individual* stimuli in a series endowed with value differentials to *groups* of stimuli. This applies to stimuli which are subjectively classified in such a manner that there is a predictable relationship between their assignment to different classes and their magnitudes. An important aspect of this transposition is that the criteria on the basis of which the stimuli are assigned to one class or another can be unrelated to, or independent of, the physical dimension along which the judgements of magnitude are made. The 'value differentials' enter the picture again when the distinctions between the classes of stimuli acquire an additional

significance because they are related to subjective differences in value between the classes. These transpositions are discussed in the final section of chapter 4 and some of them are exemplified in an experimental study summarized in section 2 of chapter 5.

(3) Further transpositions are made in sections 3 and 5 of chapter 4 from the 'physical' judgements just discussed to judgements of individual people and of *groups* of people. Experimental illustrations of these principles, as they apply to social perception, can be found in the last two sections of chapter 5. Together with the theoretical principles outlined in chapter 4, these studies provide the cognitive basis for a theory of social stereotypes.

(4) This theory is further developed in chapter 6 which is thus concerned with the 'cognitive etiology' of prejudice. The chapter presents an argument for the need for such an etiology and for an appropriate theory of social categorization which would counteract the over-simplified notions of intergroup prejudice as being fully 'explained' in terms of irrational human urges or equally over-simplified notions of evolutionary continuity.

(5) The last chapter of part II includes the cognitive emphasis of the previous chapters but moves beyond it to present a *socio*-cognitive view of the functioning of social stereotypes. In doing this, it uses some of the principles and arguments which form the basis of discussions about intergroup conflict to be found in part IV of the book and which were first very briefly outlined as one aspect of the general issues discussed in part I.

Chapter 5 is inserted in this sequence in order to reflect the empirical progression from the earlier instances of 'accentuation' in the judgements of physical dimensions of stimuli to judgements of people on various dimensions of 'person perception'. It provides at the same time selected examples of the various principles involved. An experimental example dealing with perceptual over-estimation is briefly summarized in one of the sections of chapter 4. This is followed in chapter 5 by descriptions of studies which concern: accentuation of differences between, and similarities within, classes of stimuli in simple judgements of length; accentuation of differences between certain characteristics of *individual* people when judgements of those people are made on dimensions which are of particular salience or importance to those who are making the judgements; accentuation of stereotyped *similarities* between people who are assigned to the same social category; and finally, accentuation of *differences* between people belonging to two different social groups when these differences are highly significant to the relationship between the groups as it is perceived by the members of one of the groups.

Part II: Introduction

As pointed out in chapter 7, some of the earlier hypotheses discussed in chapter 4 have been very recently rediscovered in a truncated form (e.g. Taylor *et al.*, 1978) and reconfirmed again using a different, and at times uncertain, methodology. It is also argued in the chapter that, in some important ways, these reformulations represent a 'theoretical retreat' as compared with the earlier work. In contrast to this narrowing of a borrowed and displaced perspective, there have been in recent years some research developments which, in building upon it, and finding new integrations, have extended the range of issues to which useful applications can be made. Three of these developments will be briefly mentioned here.

The first of these emerged from the work done over a number of years at the laboratory of social psychology in the University of Mannheim. The work in Mannheim went in two directions. One direction consisted of extending, refining and testing some of the earlier hypotheses, such as those concerned with the effects on judgements of socially-derived value differentials; with the relationships between these effects and the cognitive complexity of the stimuli; with the role of accumulated past experience; etc.[1] The second direction of the work used social contexts of judgement in order to establish a convergence between the social accentuation theory and some of the principles of the signal detection theory (e.g. Upmeyer, 1971; Upmeyer and Layer, 1974).

The second development consisted of an application of the accentuation principles to the polarization of judgements on attitude scales, which is found in people who have extreme attitudes, favourable or unfavourable, towards the issues with which the attitude scales are concerned. This work has been conducted during several years by Eiser and his co-workers. He addressed himself to a problem which has remained unresolved since the early work of Hovland and Sherif (1952) and can be stated as follows: the polarization of judgements is found in people who feel intensely about an issue. When they are presented with a series of statements relating to that issue, they tend to exaggerate the degree of extremity of the statements which are relatively favourable or unfavourable as compared with people who are less involved in the issue. There was, however, a hitch. In a number of studies, this principle was proved to work well when applied to statements at the *unfavourable* end of the series; it did not work with any degree of consistency at the favourable end.

Eiser resolved the inconsistency by combining the 'classification'

---

[1] Some of this work is summarized in Irle (1978); other reports and summaries can be found in e.g. Eiser and Stroebe (1972), Irle (1975), Lilli (1975), Lilli and Winkler (1972, 1973).

principles of the accentuation theory, outlined in chapter 4, with a study of the social significance of the 'evaluative language' used in the formulation of a series of statements which usually constitutes an attitude scale. The details of this analysis and of the studies originating from it can be found in a number of his publications, which he summarized in some of the chapters of a book on *Cognitive social psychology* published in 1980. The convergence of his views with the emphasis adopted here on the social dimension of social psychology, and their significance which extends beyond the merely technical issues of attitude measurement is well expressed in the conclusion to the chapter on 'Social judgement' in his book:

[The study of] social judgement . . . is not a reductionist attempt to dismiss as troublesome or irrelevant anything intrinsically social about our appraisals of social objectives and events, nor is it just a technological appendage to the field of attitude measurement which may serve to enhance the reliability of conventional instruments. Instead, it asks fundamental questions not only about how individuals categorize social stimuli along given dimensions, but also how they choose and symbolically define the dimensions in terms of which to categorize. It is this element of choice and symbolic definition which is of greatest theoretical significance to the social psychologist, and which is the basis of the constructive role of individual judgements in social interaction.

It is this symbolic definition of 'dimensions in terms of which to categorize' which has been at the focus of the third development concerning us here, mainly centred around studies conducted at the University of Geneva. The major hypotheses of this work are the same as those outlined in chapters 4, 5 and 6 of this book. As Doise (1978a) wrote:

Let us distinguish between three levels in intergroup relations: actions, evaluations and representations. These levels are interconnected. All intergroup behaviour is associated with judgements which are either evaluative or objective. At the same time, judgement is itself a form of action, it always represents the taking of a position in relation to another group and it often justifies or anticipates actions relating to that group. Our thesis is that differentiation at the level of cognitive representations is always associated with evaluative and behavioural discriminations, and that it is sufficient to elicit a change at one of those levels in order to create corresponding changes at the two other levels. (p. 23, translated from the French)

The cognitive and 'value' hypotheses described in chapter 4 were applied to a number of new social contexts in the studies emerging from Geneva.[2] The conception that interconnected changes between the levels

[2] Examples of these applications or their reviews can be found in, e.g. Dann and Doise, 1974; Deschamps, 1977; Doise, 1978b; Doise, *et al.*, 1978; Doise and Weinberger, 1972–3.

are a *sufficient* condition for intergroup discrimination to occur has not, however, remained unchallenged (e.g. Turner, 1975, 1978a and review of the controversy in Tajfel, 1980b).

At the same time, an application to intergroup representations of some principles of the accentuation theory described in this book led the Geneva workers to a direct and important inference from it: namely, that the more complex 'criss-cross' intergroup categorizations (i.e. when, for example, two groups in the presence of each other are each further subdivided, and some of their memberships overlap) might cause a *decrease* in intergroup discrimination. There is some evidence from field studies in social anthropology that this might be the case (see e.g. Jaulin, 1973; LeVine and Campbell, 1972). This was further confirmed in experimental studies conducted by Deschamps and Doise (1978); but a subsequent study by Brown and Turner (1979) threw some doubt on the earlier results. Thus, the issue still remains unresolved. Its direct relevance to a better understanding of some of the processes which *may* be underlying a decrease in the acuity of intergroup conflicts should make it one of the research priorities in the social psychology of intergroup relations. A simpler instance of category differentiations appearing in one of its symbolic and linguistic forms discussed by Eiser and by Deschamps (see also Billig, 1976, ch. 9) has recently been shown by Schönbach (1981, in press) to exert its predicted effects on intergroup attitudes. It concerned in this case the effect on public attitudes of the designation in West Germany of migrant workers either as *Gastarbeiter* or as *Fremdarbeiter* (guest workers or foreign workers).

Thus, to return to the general progression of part II of this book as it relates to the introductory chapter and to part I, the full circle is completed. Starting from judgements of size of coins and similar issues, we have come back to one of the social dimensions of social psychology. The intention was to outline the connections between the various seemingly disparate links and, at the same time, to establish once again their association with the personal issues and the social dimension discussed in the opening chapter of this book.

4

The importance of exaggerating

1. Introduction

The New Look in the study of perception is by now a half-forgotten memory. Its rapid accumulation of research started with the publication in 1947 of the then famous paper by Bruner and Goodman on 'Value and need as organizing factors in perception'. By the time I became interested, in the mid-1950s, in one of the aspects of this research, the phenomenon of perceptual over-estimation, the general interest in the New Look and the amount of work devoted to it were already beginning to wane.

But the point of this half-nostalgic paragraph was not to plead with the reader to share in the nostalgia. Research on the 'organizing factors in perception' internal to the human organism went on in many directions from the late forties and early fifties. The ideas initiated with the New Look (and going back for centuries to several intellectual forefathers) were integrated, sometimes explicitly but often without much acknowledgement, with the new interests and findings concerning such issues as information processing, the operation of expectancies, decision processes or perceptual development in childhood.

The phenomenon of perceptual over-estimation shared this fate. To begin with, starting with the work of Jerome Bruner and his various collaborators, it was used as an intriguing example of the internal 'organizing factors'. It was found in some studies (and disconfirmed in others) that when the stimuli presented to the subjects had some value (e.g. coins), their magnitudes tended to be over-estimated as compared with control valueless or neutral stimuli. A different perspective I adopted for an explanation of this apparent oddity developed into a theory of social categorization mentioned in the Introduction to this part of the book and discussed in more detail in the chapters to follow. The beginnings of this integration of an approach to perceptual over-estimation with a much wider set of issues in social perception and social categorization were reflected in a paper on 'Value and the perceptual judgement of magnitude' which was published in 1957 in the *Psychological Review*. Some relevant extracts from this paper follow directly.

At that time, about twenty experiments on various aspects of over-estimation had been conducted in the preceding fifteen years or so. Of those, only two yielded unambiguously negative results (Bevan and Bevan, 1956; Lysak and Gilchrist, 1955). Partly negative results were reported by Carter and Schooler (1949), and by Klein *et al.* (1951). All other workers were able to conclude that, in the situations which they were using, 'motivational' or 'value' variables had an effect on their subjects' perceptual judgements of magnitude. Shifts in judgement of size, weight, number and brightness had been reported.

All this evidence cannot be dismissed as an accumulation of experimental artifacts. Furthermore, perceptual accentuation need not be considered as a 'maladaptive' phenomenon. The fact that it may represent a departure from 'objective reality' led to a general criticism which consisted of pointing out that in order to survive we must perceive the world as it is, that we usually do, and that therefore the fleeting phenomena of over-estimation are more typical of the specific laboratory situations in which they were demonstrated than of perception under normal conditions. There is, however, a possibility that these shifts in the judgements of magnitude do not interfere with adequate handling of the environment. They may even be of help.

The experiments on over-estimation fall naturally into two classes. In one group, changes in the magnitude of the stimuli under investigation are relevant to the changes in value. The experiments on coins provide an example here: in general, the larger the coin, the greater its value. On the other hand, several experiments have been reported in which changes in value have in no apparent way been related to changes in the physical dimension which the subjects were requested to judge. Thus, in the experiment by Lambert *et al.* (1949), the colour of the disc was the determinant of its value, as red discs only were associated with reward; but judgements of size were requested of the subjects. In the experiments by Bruner and Postman (1948) and by Klein *et al.* (1951), discs containing a swastika were among the stimuli used. Judgements of their size were compared with judgements of size of discs containing neutral symbols. Here again, the size of the swastika has no easily conceivable relationship to its degree of relevance.

2. 'Relevant' dimensions in the accentuation of differences

In the 'relevant' group of experiments, the stimuli whose magnitudes were judged, form, by definition, a series varying concurrently in at least two dimensions: the physical dimension (size or weight), and the 'dimension' of value. The concern of most experimenters has been to show (or to deny) that the stimuli of the series in which a variation in magnitude was paired in the environment with a variation in value were judged larger than stimuli of objectively equivalent magnitudes belonging to a different, neutral, series. Thus, judgements of size of coins were compared with judgements of size of cardboard or metal discs, or judgements of weight of jars filled with 'candy' with similar judgements of jars filled with sand. Little attention has been paid to the perceived differences *between* the magnitudes of the stimuli in the valued series, as compared with the corresponding relationships in the neutral series.

It seems that some, at least, of the apparent contradictions between the various experimental results can be resolved if this intraserial aspect of the situation is considered. On the basis of an argument to be developed later, a prediction can be made that in a 'relevant' series, where value changes concurrently with the dimension subjected to investigation, the differences between the stimuli of the series will be perceived as larger than the objectively equivalent differences between the stimuli of a neutral series, where no such association exists between value and magnitude.

The results in the 'relevant' group of experiments support this contention. The quantitative difference, as expressed by subjects' judgements, between the two extremes of a series has been adopted here as a rough measure of the accentuation of differences.

The early study by Bruner and Goodman (1947) shows that the perceived difference between the smallest and the largest coins (extension of the scale of judgements) is much larger than the corresponding extensions for discs. A conversion of the data in the experiment by Carter and Schooler to similar extensions, for all subjects combined, shows that: (a) In all series of stimuli (coins, aluminium and cardboard discs) the perceived extensions are larger than the actual ones; (b) The relative differences between the actual and perceived extensions are about twice as large for the series of coins as for both series of discs.

Carter and Schooler imply this when they 'suggest that there is a constant error involved in making these size judgements such that small coins are under-estimated and large coins are over-estimated in size' (1949, p. 205); but they do not seem to draw any further conclusions.

Bruner and Rodrigues (1953) have introduced in their well-controlled experiment the notion of 'relative increase in over-estimation' in which some of the suggestions made here were already implicit. Half of their subjects were assigned to a 'value set' in which the instructions to the subjects emphasized the purchasing power of money. The other half were assigned to an 'accuracy set' in which the experimenters' concern with accurate judgements of size was stressed. A conversion of their data similar to the conversion of Carter and Schooler's data gives similar results. The relative extensions for the value series are considerably larger than for both neutral series. (See section 7 of this chapter for tables showing these conversions, and a discussion of some other aspects of the intraserial accentuation of differences.)

One further example: Dukes and Bevan (1952) found that for their positive series (jars filled with 'candy') the variability of responses was less marked than for the neutral series (jars filled with sand). This is related to smaller j.n.d.'s (just noticeable differences) in the positive than in the neutral series. In other words, the differences between the stimuli of the positive series were more clearly and consistently perceived than the objectively equivalent differences in the neutral series, and the scale of judgements was more extended for the positive than for the neutral series.

This summary of evidence suggests that the results of the 'relevant' experiments on over-estimation cannot be solely the product of some simple and rather mysterious process of over-estimation. As has already been pointed out, the interest of the experimenters was confined mainly to the comparisons of the perceptual judgements of stimuli in a value series with the judgements of physically equivalent stimuli in a neutral series. The subjects were invited to make comparisons between the valued stimuli and either a neutral standard or elements of a parallel neutral series. However, the implications of the fact that the stimuli associated with value do form a series cannot be ignored; during the experiments the subjects were repeatedly exposed to the various elements of this series, and the 'belongingness', in the case of coins, would be further enhanced by familiarity.

In view of the evidence concerning the effects that all elements of a series, past and present, have on the quantitative judgements of its individual members (e.g. Helson, 1948), it may reasonably be assumed that the judgements of magnitude given by the subjects in the 'relevant' overestimation experiments were not only determined by the perceived relationship, at the time of judgement, between a stimulus of the value series and a standard. They must have been affected as well by the background of perceived relationships between this particular stimulus and all other stimuli of the same series. This assumption is further supported by the evidence that the effects exercised by a particular stimulus on judgements pertaining to a series of stimuli increase as a function of the extent to which this stimulus is perceived as forming part of the series which is being judged (Brown, 1953).

In other words, in the 'relevant' experiments on over-estimation two aspects of the situation must be taken into account: the *inter*serial and the *intra*serial. The first consists of the perceived relationships of magnitude between any stimulus of the value series and the neutral stimuli; the second is concerned with the perception of relationships between the stimuli of a value series as compared with the corresponding relationships in an objectively identical neutral series.

The phenomenon of accentuation of differences between the stimuli in a value series can be isolated in its 'pure' form when the following two requirements are satisfied: the subjects' judgements must be based on comparisons between the various stimuli of this series, and not between these stimuli and some extraneous ones; and the value and neutral series must be objectively identical, value being the only experimental variable in which they differ. These requirements were satisfied in some experiments conducted by the writer.

An ordered series of ten weights was used, and the subjects were requested to judge their heaviness in terms of seven category numbers. Each subject underwent an equal number of sessions under the 'value' and under the 'neutral' conditions. An experimental session consisted of two parts: in the first part, the entire series was presented several times in random order, but no judgements were reported by the subject. In the second part, following the first after an interval of about three minutes, all the stimuli were presented again several times, and judgements of weight were requested at each presentation. In the 'value' condition, a small paper bonus (gift certificate, exchangeable for a book) accompanied each presentation of one of the two heaviest (or two lightest) stimuli of the series during the first part of the session. No rewards were given in the first part of the neutral sessions. In this way, the effects of the two experimental conditions, introduced in the first part of the sessions, on judgements of weight in the second part could be assessed. A total of sixty adult subjects were used in the four experiments. They were told, as part of the instructions, that the purpose of the experiment was to investigate the effects of monotony on the speed of performing a simple task which consisted of discriminating between weights. The 'small paper tokens', which they were to receive from time to time were being introduced in order 'to vary the degree of monotony'.

Data consisted of differences in the extensions of the scales of judgement between the two conditions. Results can be briefly summarized as follows: in the first two experiments, in which rewards were associated with the two heaviest or the two lightest stimuli of the series, extensions of the scales of judgements were significantly larger for the 'value' than for the 'neutral' condition. In a third experiment, in which rewards were associated indiscriminately with all the stimuli of the series, no such effect occurred. In a fourth experiment, the procedure was the same as in the first and second experiments, apart from the fact that the paper 'bonuses', passed by the experimenter to the subjects at each presentation of either one of the two heaviest or one of the two lightest stimuli, were devoid of all value. Once again, no significant effect on the extension of the scale of judgements was observed (see Tajfel, 1959, for more detail).

All this evidence is, to say the least, strongly suggestive. The advantages of using accentuation of differences as an explanatory device for over-estimation are that: (a) It accounts for seemingly contradictory results, such as the under-estimation of the small end of the value series reported in some studies (Bruner and Rodrigues, 1953; Carter and Schooler, 1949); it also accounts for Bruner and Rodrigues's (1953) 'relative over-estimation'; (b) It does not require an introduction of *deus ex machina* principles to account for the phenomenon of over-estimation in the 'relevant' class.

The first point above does not require further elaboration. The second can be supported by some lines of argument, independent of each other.

What is the nature of the experience with coins, or with any series of stimuli, where it is important to discriminate sharply between the elements of the series? Discriminative responses to stimuli in such series are not usually made in terms of precise quantitative labels attached to individual stimuli. They are made in terms of 'larger than', or 'smaller than', the neighbouring elements of the series. Minimizing the differences entails a risk of confusion; accentuating them is an additional guarantee of a successful response. However, the normal routine of responding in terms of 'larger' or 'smaller' is upset in most experiments on over-estimation. The usual technique for correct handling of coins, for example, which is based primarily on an awareness of the relevant differences between a particular coin and other coins of the series, present or absent, is not quite adequate, as unusually precise individual quantitative labels are requested in the experiments. These absolute labels, whether obtained through matching or through some kind of verbal categorizing, may be expected to reveal an accentuation of differences between the stimuli, since they would reflect, and possibly exaggerate, what is otherwise implicit in the relative judgements of comparison pertaining to the series.

It is in this sense only that the results yielded by the studies on over-estimation can be treated as experimental artifacts. In this context, it is not particularly important to find out whether the stimuli are really 'seen' as larger or smaller. They are *reproduced* as such; to ask the subject to match a variable standard to a stimulus, or to assign to the stimulus a quantitative verbal label, is essentially asking him to reproduce its size.

This reproduction, which involves an activity very different from stating vaguely that an object is larger or smaller than something else, lends itself easily to a sharpening of the relevant distinctive feature of it, which is, in this instance, its difference in size from the next object in the series. The phenomenon is not unfamiliar: Gibson reported some time ago (1953) that a sharpening of differences occurred in the early stage of aircraft recognition training, when his subjects were asked to draw the silhouettes of the various aircraft.

A prediction is possible here to the effect that shifts in the estimates of magnitudes would either not occur or promptly disappear if the training to discriminate between the elements of a series, along which discrimination is important for the subject, was directed towards the accuracy of individual quantitative labels rather than towards a clear distinction in relative terms between the stimuli. This is exactly what happened in an experiment by Smith, Parker and Robinson (1951) in which accuracy of report was a condition of obtaining the reward. Prizes were offered to the subjects who would report correctly the greatest number of *dots* forming clusters which were flashed successively on a screen. In a control group, prizes went to those subjects who reported correctly on the number of dots in the greatest number of *clusters*. No information about the accuracy of their estimates was available to the subjects during the experiment. The first group showed over-estimation in the early stages of the experiment, but after a certain number of trials the performance of both groups converged.

These assumptions of a 'functional' mechanism underlying the accentuation of differences may be supplemented by some evidence coming from a different quarter. It consists of the findings about the effects of multidimensionality on the acuity of discrimination along a series. Eriksen and Hake (1955) have reported that when the method of absolute judgements is used, the number of discriminable steps for a series of stimuli is greater when the stimuli vary concurrently in two or more dimensions than when they vary in one dimension only. More specifically, they found that discriminability was considerably greater when the 'stimuli varied in size and hue, size and brightness, hue and brightness, and size, hue and brightness' (p. 159) than when they varied in only one of these dimensions. Eriksen and Hake suggest that their results were due to a kind of summation, to 'the ability of Ss to make fairly independent judgements of stimulus values along each of the component dimensions' (p. 158). They add, however:

We cannot assume that this is always the case for compound stimuli. For some stimuli, judgements made of values in the separate dimensions may be inter-related. That is, the evocation of a particular response tendency by a component of a compound stimulus may change the likelihood of evocation of other response tendencies by other components of the stimulus. We could expect this to occur when Ss have learned by long experience to associate the occurrence of certain values in one dimension with the occurrence of particular values in another.

Two conclusions can be drawn from the above: the first, supported by Eriksen and Hake's results, is that under some conditions of judgement, and in a situation new to the subject, compounding of concurrently varying dimensions will result in a clearer perception of differences between the stimuli along a series. The second is related to the first, and already outlined in the above quotation from Eriksen and Hake: when the association between dimensions has been a long-standing one, new training may not be capable of inducing changes in discriminability. In such cases, judgements along one of the dimensions have already been influenced, previous to the experiment, by concomitant changes in other dimensions. In other words, it is likely that the Eriksen and Hake situation represents the incipient stages of a process which develops when there is a consistent pairing, in the environment, of changes in more than one dimension.

Such pairing exists by definition in series where magnitude and value vary concurrently. The difficulty is that value is not a 'dimension' in the physical sense. It is, however, an important attribute of the stimuli in such series, if only because efficient discrimination between the stimuli in terms of differences in value is, in most cases, more important than discrimination in terms of the physical dimension.

In the experiment on weights described earlier, value is the only 'dimension of difference' between the two series. It would also be a supplementary and important difference between two series which differ not only with regard to value, but also with regard to some other dimensions. In the first case, the difference in value is the only contributing factor to a more pronounced accentuation of differences in the value than in the neutral series; in the second, it is one of the contributing factors. Once again, this does not necessarily mean that the subjects 'see' the stimuli in the value series as being more different from each other, or larger, or smaller. They respond *as if* they perceived them as such, and this is as far as the phenomenology of it can go for the time being.

3. Social perception

Some implications of the present discussion go well beyond the problems raised by the phenomenon of over-estimation. It may be said that, in a sense, 'over-estimation' as discussed in this chapter is a special case and a convincing experimental paradigm of a more general aspect of social perception. Many social objects and events are sharply classified in terms of their value or relevance. When judgements concerning some quantifiable or rateable aspects of stimuli which fall into distinct categories are called for, differences in value or relevance cannot fail to influence the quantitative judgements in the direction of sharpening the objectively existing differences between the stimuli.

These judgemental effects of categorization are probably fairly general: it is likely, however, that they are particularly pronounced when judgements are made in dimensions in which scaling in magnitude is simultaneously a scaling in value. Thus, it may well be that an accentuation of differences in size will hardly occur between two paintings, one liked and one indifferent or disliked. But when skin colour, or height, or some facial traits of social 'value' are concerned, there will be a marked sharpening of differences in the degree of these characteristics perceived as belonging to individuals who are assigned to different categories. Some evidence of this is provided by a study on 'perceptual accentuation and the Negro stereotype' conducted by Secord, Bevan and Katz (1956). Their results suggest that a group of prejudiced Ss sharpened the differences in the degree of negroid physiognomic traits possessed respectively by negroes and whites, more than did a group of non-prejudiced Ss. It is likely that the same is happening in the case of more abstract social judgements which are implicitly quantitative, such as, for example, those concerning the relative frequency of crimes in various social groups, as perceived by people who have an axe to grind against one group or another.

4. An experimental illustration: value and the accentuation of judged differences[1]

As was pointed out earlier in this chapter, the numerous experiments concerned with the phenomenon of perceptual over-estimation due to motivational or value variables fall into two classes. In one group, there is no relationship of any kind between the physical magnitudes of the stimuli judged by the Ss and the value of these stimuli to them; in the second group there is a consistent relationship between the physical magnitudes and value. For example, larger coins tend to be more valuable than smaller ones; but there is no relationship between the size

[1] Most of this section of the chapter consists of extracts from: H. Tajfel and S. D. Cawasjee: Value and the accentuation of judged differences: A confirmation. *Journal of Abnormal and Social Psychology*, 1959, **59**, 436–9.

of a swastika and the degree of its emotional relevance to the subject (Klein *et al.*, 1951).

Coins took a rather undue prominence in experiments in this field; since they served again as stimuli in the present experiment, it may be worth adding that the writers did not consider the judgement of size of coins as a problem of intrinsic importance and interest. The results obtained have, however, some interesting implications for phenomena of much greater generality: namely the effects of abstract attributes of stimuli on the judgement of their physical characteristics. As will be argued in section 5, value is no more than one instance of an abstract attribute, and coins are only one instance of its operation.

In 'natural' conditions the denomination of a coin is judged through a swift and implicit comparison with other members of the series. The identifying decision may be based on differences between the coins in colour, design, or simply on the fact that the value is specified. When none of these cues exist, and size is the main differential, a weighting in terms of size cues must become the prominent feature of the process of judgement. Again, in many natural situations one is not allowed to base one's decision on a comparison between two members of the series present simultaneously; a coin must be quickly and correctly identified when it is seen in the absence of others. The concern is not with the size of the coin expressed in terms of absolute units of measurement; it is with the difference between this coin and those near to it in the order of size.

Theoretical reasons were given earlier why this situation should lead to an accentuation of judged differences. This 'implicit' accentuation should manifest itself explicitly when all the elements of the natural situation are maintained, with the addition of a request to the Ss to verbalize in quantitative terms their estimates of the size of coins. The Ss, when confronted with this request should, on the present assumptions, judge the differences between the coins to be significantly larger than the corresponding differences between the control stimuli.

Method

The British coins of two shillings and two shillings and sixpence (2s and 2s 6d) offered the advantage of differing, for all practical purposes, in size only. At the time of this study the tails design consisted of coats of arms. These, though not identical in both coins, were very similar; in addition, coins of the same denomination minted at various dates differed in the design of their coats of arms. The value of the coins was not stated in numbers; the 2s coin displayed the words 'one florin', and the 2s 6d coin the words 'half crown' in the middle of an identical Latin inscription in small letters running round the circumference in both coins. Heads on both coins were identical: they displayed the profile of the monarch reigning at the time of minting.

Selection of control stimuli presented some difficulty, as they had to achieve a maximum similarity with the coins, without being confused with them at the same time. The control stimulus for the 2s coin was an 1896 South African coin with the profile of Krueger on one side and a coat of arms with an inscription on the other. The coin, originally very slightly larger than the 2s piece, was filed down to size. The control stimulus for the 2s 6d coin was an 1834 2s 6d coin (which still had official currency, but was extremely rare and practically unknown) with the profile of William III on one side and a coat of arms on the other. The texture and brightness of the current and control coins were identical. The profiles on the two current coins were not the same in order to approach, as far as possible, a distinct lack of resemblance between Krueger and William III. The diameter of the smaller stimuli was 2.858 cm; of the larger – 3.175 cm.

Two hundred subjects each made one judgement of either the experimental or the control pair of stimuli, presented successively. The experimenter held the coin flat in the palm of his hand at a distance of about 40 cm from the subject's eyes and asked him to estimate the diameter in terms of tenths of an inch. Those Ss who worried about the difficulty of the task were told to stop worrying and try as best they could. The subjects were recruited for several weeks *au hazard des rencontres:* in restaurants, hotels, canteens, libraries, colleges, coffee (non-alcoholic) parties, trains, etc. No one who had the opportunity of hearing someone else's estimates was used as a subject. The two hundred subjects were divided into eight groups of twenty-five each: half judged the current coins, half the control coins; half judged heads, half tails; half judged the larger stimulus first, and half the larger stimulus second. Assignment of Ss to groups was randomized.

Results

Results in terms of mean estimates are shown in Table 1. Table 2 shows the judged size relationships between the two coins. For each subject the basis of scoring here was his judgement of the diameter of the smaller coin; the difference between his estimates of the larger and of the smaller coin was then expressed as the percentage of the judged diameter of the smaller coin. The actual difference between the two coins was 11.1% of the diameter of the smaller coin.

As can be seen from Table 3, an analysis of variance conducted on these scores shows a highly significant difference in the expected direction between the judged size relationships of the two current coins

An experimental illustration

Table 1
Mean estimates (in inches) of length of diameter of stimuli

	Current coins					Control coins				
	Heads		Tails			Heads		Tails		
					Mean					Mean
	A	B	A	B		A	B	A	B	
Large stimuli	1.42	1.45	1.53	1.57	1.49	1.36	1.47	1.26	1.30	1.35
Small stimuli	1.15	1.18	1.21	1.26	1.20	1.16	1.23	1.08	1.12	1.15
Difference	0.27	0.27	0.32	0.31	0.29	0.20	0.24	0.18	0.18	0.20

Note: A – large stimuli presented first
      B – large stimuli presented second

Table 2
Mean percentage differences between estimates of large and small stimuli

| | Current coins | | Control coins | |
	Heads	Tails	Heads	Tails
Large stimulus first	23.5	26.4	17.6	17.5
Large stimulus second	22.9	23.5	18.7	15.8
Over-all mean	24.2		17.4	

Table 3
Analysis of variance of percentage differences between the estimates of large and small stimuli

Source	SS	df	MS	F
Value (Current v. control coins)	2231.12	1	2231.12	19.55★
Sides (Heads v. Tails)	1.25	1	1.25	–
Order of presentation	53.46	1	53.46	–
V × S	127.68	1	127.68	–
V × O	25.78	1	25.78	–
S × O	79.38	1	79.38	–
V × S × O	0.67	1	0.67	
Error	21913.22	192	114.13	

★$p < 0.001$

and the two control stimuli respectively. None of the other variables approach significance.

Analysis of variance was then conducted for the actual estimates of the larger and smaller stimuli separately. None of the variables reaches significance for the smaller stimulus. There is a significant over-estimation of the larger coin in relation to the larger control stimulus (see Table 4).

Table 4

Analysis of variance of size estimates of the larger stimulus

Source	SS	df	MS	F
Value (Current v. control coins)	102.39	1	102.39	4.57*
Sides (Heads v. Tails)	0.86	1	0.86	–
Order of presentation	14.31	1	14.31	–
V × S	79.51	1	79.51	3.55
V × O	2.02	1	2.02	–
S × O	0.86	1	0.86	–
V × S × O	2.18	1	2.18	–
Error	4301.16	192	22.40	

*$p < 0.05$

The hypothesis of an accentuation of judged differences between the stimuli in a series varying concomitantly in size and value finds very clear support in the data. The possibility that the small differences in design between the current coins and the control stimuli may have somehow contributed to the results seems extremely remote in view of the fact that they are equally clear-cut for both sides of the coins.

The evidence for over-estimation *per se* as function of value is much more ambiguous; it is moderately consistent for the larger coin, and non-existent for the smaller one. The expectation was that some amount of over-estimation would be found for the larger coin, and some amount of under-estimation for the smaller one. The latter prediction was not borne out. It is possible, however, that the smaller coin was not under-estimated because it was not the smallest member of the series to which it belonged. This series consisted of four coins (sixpence, one shilling, two shillings, and two shillings and sixpence) which differed mainly in size and value.

However, as Eiser and Stroebe (1972) wrote later, on the basis of subsequent evidence:

It is not a necessary requirement of accentuation theory . . . that accentuation or polarization effects should operate systematically at either extreme of the response continuum. One subject's set of ratings may differ from another both in terms of their dispersion or extremity, and also in terms of the centre or average rating of the series as a whole. Accentuation theory is properly concerned only with differences in the first of these two parameters. Neither the theoretical principles nor the empirical findings . . . suggest that the direction of the value-size correlation should affect the extent of polarization of the subject's judgements. Nevertheless, it is quite conceivable that the direction of the correlation may have an effect on the subject's reference scale, that is, on whether the stimuli as a whole tend to be over- or under-estimated. When the two effects are superimposed, the result should show an assymetrical extension of the subject's range of judgements relative to judgements made in the absence of value correlation, such as was observed in the coin studies. (p. 82)

An experimental postscript

Some time after the data for the above study were collected in the streets of Oxford and other such places, and at about the time when they were being published in the *Journal of Abnormal and Social Psychology*, I was spending a year (1958/9) at Harvard University. The four stimuli of the experiment (the two British coins and the two control coins) were carefully transported across the Atlantic. A few students who took part in a seminar I was conducting at Harvard volunteered to run a control study in the streets of Cambridge, Massachusetts, and other such places. The design and the number of subjects were the same as described earlier in this chapter, with one exception. Each subject was asked, before giving his estimates of size, whether he had ever visited Britain. Those who had were eliminated from the study. The hypotheses (and a control for the Tajfel and Cawasjee study) was that, since the pair of British coins had not acquired in the past any 'value' for the subjects, nor did they experience habitually any differences in value between the two coins, the judgements of the two pairs of stimuli should be virtually the same. In particular, we were interested in comparing the judged *differences* between the stimuli of each of the two pairs. The data showed no trace of any accentuation effects or any other effects of 'value'. Thus, the results of this moderately natural control condition provided fairly convincing support for the data of the original study and for the hypothesis on which the study was based.

5. Values, classifications and stereotypes

The previous sections of this chapter were concerned with the accentuation of differences between individual stimuli of a valued series. In the present section the argument is extended to shifts in judgement which can be expected when the array of physical or social stimuli which an individual assesses in terms of their relative magnitudes is *subjectively* classified in one way or another. The use of the term subjective classification does not mean that we are concerned here with some kind of an 'autistic' view by individuals of their physical or social environment. It simply recognizes the fact that, whatever categorizations are made of the surrounding world, they are the result of an interaction between the information obtained from the outside and its active internal organization by human beings.

The attribution of differences in value to different classes of stimuli (or objects, or people) in the environment is considered here to be one of the fundamental principles of this internal organization. No doubt, the straightforward model presented here is a bare over-simplification of what really happens when the environment, particularly the social environment, is organized in certain ways by the human individual. On the other hand, the usefulness of such over-simplifications can only be assessed by seeing how far they can get us in a *partial* understanding of more complex phenomena. As will be seen in the remainder of this chapter and the chapters to follow, the simple principles offered for consideration here have shown a certain continuity of usefulness all the way from constricted judgements of length of lines, classified in one way or another, to certain aspects of judgements we make about other people as individuals, but mainly so in terms of their memberships of social groups.

As we have previously seen, the accentuation of judged differences between the stimuli of a series probably accounts for a number of phenomena in the field of perceptual over-estimation.[2] It is important to note that in most experiments on over-estimation, and in those concerned with the effects of prejudice on judgements of physical characteristics, data were collected by presenting the stimuli individually. This has been done either by asking the subjects to assign quantitative verbal labels to the stimuli presented one by one, or by asking them to match a variable standard to each stimulus in turn. As Bruner (1957) has argued, it is very possible that most perceptual activities 'depend upon the construction of an adequate system of categories against which stimulus inputs can be matched' (p. 127). He continued as follows:

There is probably one condition where perceptual acts are relatively free from such influences, and that is in the task of discriminating simultaneously presented

---

[2] The remainder of the chapter mainly consists of extracts from: H. Tajfel: Quantitative judgement in social perception. *British Journal of Psychology*, 1959, **50**, 16–29.

stimuli as alike or different . . . Ask the person to deal with one stimulus at a time, to array it in terms of some magnitude scale, and immediately one is back in the familiar territory of inferential categorizing. Prentice, in his able defense of formalism in the study of perception, seems to assume that there is a special status attached to perceptual research that limits the set of the observer to simple binary decisions of 'like' and 'different' or 'present' and 'absent', and to research that also provides the subject with optimal stimulus conditions, and Graham has recently expressed the credo that no perceptual laws will be proper or pure laws unless we reduce perceptual experimentation to the kinds of operations used in the method of constant stimuli . . . [But] the point must be made that many of the most interesting phenomena in sensory perception are precisely those that have been uncovered by departing from the rigid purism of the method of constants. (pp. 127–8)

The main assumption discussed in the previous sections was that in a series of stimuli 'where value changes concurrently with the dimension subjected to investigation, the differences between the stimuli of the series will be perceived as larger than the objectively equivalent differences between the stimuli of a neutral series, where no such association exists between value and magnitude' (section 2).

The experiment by Secord *et al.* (1956), already mentioned earlier, can serve as a starting-point for further discussion. They reported that a group of prejudiced subjects accentuated the differences in skin colour (and in some other physical features) between negroes and whites more than did a group of non-prejudiced subjects. The situation can be described in the following manner: the physical characteristic, the skin colour, is a dimension which varies continuously from light to dark. On this continuous variation a classification is superimposed: the distinction between whites and negroes. Skin colour is one of the determinants of this classification; in other words, there is a fairly consistent relationship between the discontinuous classification and the continuous physical dimension. So far, the situation is identical for the prejudiced and the non-prejudiced subjects. The difference between the two groups of subjects can be defined only in terms of the emotional or, if one prefers the term, value relevance of the classification to the subjects. The continuous dimension of skin colour is broken by the discontinuous classification which, in the case of prejudiced subjects, is more sharply accentuated. As in the case of studies on coins, the object of judgement is perceived for what it is, in this instance 'black' or 'white', before judgements of skin colour are made. Prediction can be made to the effect that judgements on any dimensions which are in some way relevant to a value classification by providing cues to it (and thus acquire value in themselves) will show a shift in opposite directions for stimuli falling into the distinct classes. The situation is not, in principle, different from that encountered in a series of coins. Instead of dealing with individual stimuli which differ concurrently in a physical attribute and in the attribute of value, we have here groups of stimuli which differ in precisely the same manner.

6. Statement of predictions

A value differential, a classification, and a physical dimension enter into a specific relationship in the example just discussed. This particular combination of attributes is, of course, only one of many possible combinations. Before proceeding to a more detailed discussion of these, the predictions concerning the judged relationships between the elements of the various series which result from the combination of attributes should be stated more formally.

(1) When a variation in value (v) is correlated in a series of stimuli with a variation in a physical dimension (p), the judged differences in this physical dimension between the elements of the series will be larger than in a series which is identical with regard to the physical magnitudes of the stimuli, and in which the stimuli do not possess the attribute of value.

(2) When differences in value exist in a series of stimuli, but are in no way correlated with the variation in a physical dimension, these differences in value will have no effect on the judged relationships between the physical magnitudes of the stimuli of the series.

(3) When a classification in terms of an attribute other than the physical dimension which is being judged is superimposed on a series of stimuli in such a way that one part of the physical series tends to fall consistently into one class, and the other into the other class (c_1), judgements of physical magnitudes of the stimuli falling into the distinct classes will show a shift in the directions determined by the class membership of the stimuli, when compared with judgements of a series identical with respect to this physical dimension, on which such a classification is not superimposed.

(4) When a classification in terms of an attribute other than the physical dimension which is being judged is superimposed on a series of stimuli, and the changes in the physical magnitudes of the stimuli bear no consistent relationship to the assignment of the stimuli to the distinct classes, this classification (c_2) will have no effect on the judged relationships in the physical dimension between the stimuli of the series.

(5) When a classification in terms of an attribute other than the physical dimension which is being judged is superimposed on a series of stimuli in such a way that one part of the physical series tends to fall consistently

78

into one class, and the other into the other class, and this classification is of inherent value or of emotional relevance to the subject (c_1v), judgements of physical magnitudes of the stimuli falling into the distinct classes will show a shift in directions determined by the class membership of the stimuli when compared with judgements of a series identical with respect to this physical dimension, on which such a classification is not superimposed; this shift will be more pronounced than the shift referred to in (3) above.

(6) When a classification in terms of an attribute other than the physical dimension which is being judged is superimposed on a series of stimuli, this classification being of inherent value or of emotional relevance to the subject, and the changes in the physical dimension bear no consistent relationship to the assignment of the stimuli to the distinct classes, the classification (c_2v) will have no effect on the judged relationships in the physical dimension between the stimuli falling into the distinct classes.

7. Application of predictions to the various series

Table 5 contains a list of the various possible series with a brief description of their characteristics. They can now be considered in more detail.

(a) The pv series

This series has already been discussed in the previous sections. Not only are the judged differences between the stimuli larger in pv than in the p series, but there are also some indications that, when the differences in value between the stimuli can be quantitatively assessed, a larger difference in value between the stimuli leads to a greater accentuation of size differences between them. A conversion of the data from the experiments by Bruner and Goodman (1947), Carter and Schooler (1949), and Bruner and Rodrigues (1953) shows that the percentage increase from the actual to perceived differences between the sizes of coins is very much smaller for the difference between a 'penny' and a 'nickel' than between a 'nickel' and a 'quarter' (see Table 6; a 'penny' is one cent, a 'nickel' is five cents and a 'quarter' is twenty-five cents). As can be seen from Table 6, the percentage increases from the actual to the perceived distances tend to become *smaller* for all control stimuli in all three experiments as the larger end of the series is approached. They tend to become considerably *larger* in the case of coins. It is possible that the over-all differences in percentages between the three experiments are due to differences in the experimental procedure; but the general trend of

Table 5
A list of the various possible series

Series	Characteristics of the series
1. p	Ordered change in a physical dimension
2. pv	Ordered change in a physical dimension correlated with a change in value
3. pc_1	Ordered change in a physical dimension consistently related to a classification in terms of another attribute
4. pc_2	Ordered change in a physical dimension; a classification in terms of another attribute superimposed on the series bears no consistent relationship to the change in the physical dimension
5. $(pv)c_1$	Ordered change in a physical dimension correlated with value; a classification in terms of another attribute consistently related to the change in the physical dimension is superimposed on the series
6. $(pv)c_2$	Ordered change in a physical dimension correlated with value; a classification in terms of another attribute superimposed on the series bears no consistent relationship to the changes in physical dimension
7. $p(c_1v)$	Ordered change in a physical dimension is consistently related to a classification in terms of another attribute; this classification is of inherent value or of emotional relevance to the subject
8. $p(c_2v)$	Ordered change in a physical dimension; a classification in terms of another attribute superimposed on the series bears no consistent relationship to the change in the physical dimension; this classification is of inherent value or of emotional relevance to the subject
9. $(pv)(c_1v)$	Ordered change in a physical dimension correlated with value; a classification in terms of another attribute superimposed on the series is related to change in the physical dimension: this classification is of inherent value or of emotional relevance to the subject
10. $(pv)(c_2v)$	Ordered change in a physical dimension correlated with value; a classification in terms of another attribute superimposed on the series bears no consistent relationship to change in the physical dimension; this classification is of inherent value or of emotional relevance to the subject

relative increase in the perceived differences between the coins with the increase in the differences in value between them appears in all the three studies. The possibility that this is due to factors other than value, such as differences in design between the coins, must not be overlooked. This seems, however, unlikely in view of the finding, reported by Vroom (1957), that judgements of size of defaced coins (i.e. with their design practically removed through use) did not differ from judgements of coins with their design intact. Also, as was seen in section 4, accentuation of differences between two coins was independent of the differences in their design; it was present both for 'heads' and for 'tails', and *not* present for both in a control condition. Still other factors may play a role; but the evidence is strongly suggestive.

Table 6

Percentage increase from actual to perceived differences between stimuli

Converted from data in experiments by:	Stimuli	Penny–nickel	Nickel–quarter
Bruner and Goodman	Coins	86.3	131.0
	Discs	36.3	20.7
Carter and Schooler	Coins	36.4	53.4
	Aluminium discs	22.5	19.3
	Cardboard discs	24.0	12.1
Bruner and Rodrigues	Coins (on table)	55.5	83.4
	Metal discs	52.7	40.0
	Paper discs	50.0	16.9

(b) The pc_1 series

In the preceding series, value and a physical dimension – two of the three variables considered here – were seen in a specific relationship. In the present series, the relationship is between a physical dimension and a classification. The differences between the stimuli in the physical dimension along which judgements are made are relevant to the classification since they provide cues for assigning the stimuli to one class or another; but they are not the primary basis of the classification. The classification itself may be based on another physical attribute, on an abstract attribute, or on a combination of several attributes. When the stimulus is identified as belonging to one of the classes before the judgement of its magnitude in the physical dimension is made, this class identification serves in turn as a cue to the judgement of the physical magnitude, and causes the shift of judgement in the direction consistent with the general relationship between the physical magnitudes and the classification. The judgement of the skin colour of a man labelled as 'white' should, according to the present argument, differ consistently from the judgement of the skin colour of the *same* man labelled as 'Negro'. This is one example of a situation arising frequently in the judgement of physical characteristics of stimuli in the social environment. Classifications of people into ethnic, or sometimes other, groups often imply consistent differences between the groups in terms of some physical features. Industrial or agricultural products originating from different sources may be known to differ consistently in their size, colour, texture, weight, etc. The shifts of judgements could be demonstrated by comparing judgements pertaining to such series with those of other series, identical with the pc_1 series with regard to the physical dimension, and not broken by a discontinuous classification (p series).

81

One further hypothesis can be formulated concerning what might be called the 'zone of uncertainty' between two classes of stimuli in a pc_1 series. Class identification of a stimulus in this series, when it precedes an absolute judgement of the physical magnitude, has so far been considered as capable of exercising a shift in this judgement, since it acts as a cue helping to characterize the object of judgement as possessing the physical attribute to a greater or lesser degree. However, this effect cannot be expected to be of the same extent along the entire range of stimuli. The darker the skin of a negro, or the lighter the skin of a white man, the more the information provided by the pre-existing classification is redundant, and the more the judgement will be based on the actual physical characteristics of the stimulus. This information will, however, increase in importance in the more ambiguous cases towards the middle of the range, such as those of relatively light-skinned negroes and dark-skinned whites. It is here that the largest shifts, consistent with the classification, may be expected (see chapter 5).

(c) The pc_2 series

In such a series there is no orderly relationship between the physical dimension judged and the classification: the physical magnitude of a stimulus does not help in its assignment to one of the various classes, and the identification of a stimulus as belonging to one of the classes does not provide any cue as to its physical magnitude. In this situation, the classification is not expected to have any effects on judgements of physical magnitude. Size of books and their classification into the subjects with which they deal may be taken as one example. There is no consistent relationship between the two, and one would not expect a book to be judged larger or smaller because it is known to be concerned with physics, biology or psychology. Judgements of physical magnitudes of stimuli belonging to a pc_2 series should thus not differ from judgements relating to a simple p series, and consequently they should differ from pv and pc_1 series in the same way as a p series differs from them; i.e. differences between the stimuli in a pv series should be more accentuated than the corresponding differences in a pc_2 series; and the shifts in opposite directions in the judgements of stimuli belonging to different classes, predicted for a pc_1 series, should not occur in pc_2 series.

It will be obvious that pc_1 and pc_2 series, as characterized above, are no more than two extremes of a continuum, running from a perfect correlation between an orderly progression in the physical dimension and a classification, as in the case of a pc_1 series, to a complete lack of correlation in the case of a pc_2 series. If it can be assumed that the shifts in the judgements of physical magnitudes are determined by a long-

standing relationship between the physical dimension and the classification, then a further hypothesis can be formulated to the effect that the
extent of these shifts will be a function of the degree of consistency of this
relationship, experienced in the past. Thus, the correlation between skin
colour and the classification into whites and negroes is presumably very
high, and consequently noticeable shifts in judgements of skin colour
may be expected; on the other hand, it may well be true that the
Scandinavians tend to be taller, on the average, than the Italians, but as
the overlap between the two classes is bound to be very large, shifts in
judgements of height may either be non-existent or hardly noticeable.

This hypothesis has direct relevance to the general problem of
stereotyping, as it formulates a testable relationship between the strength
of a stereotype and the nature of past experience which supports it. The
fact that stereotypes are essentially consequences of sharpened or accentuated classifications has not been sufficiently exploited in research.
Judgements of almost any aspects of objects which are stereotyped are
not made in a vacuum, they are always implicitly comparative.[3] The
statement that Italians are 'lively' means that they are more lively than
some other people. The problem is to find out to what extent an Italian is
judged as being 'lively' (i.e. more lively than somebody else) not because
he is lively, but because he is known to the 'judge' to be an Italian. An
investigation of this problem must proceed along two lines: first, it is
possible to create experimental conditions in which the amount of
correlation between a discontinuous classification and a continuous
dimension, along which judgements are made, can be varied; secondly,
shifts in judgement due to the effects of the various degrees of consistency of this relationship can be investigated by presenting the subjects
with identical stimuli variously characterized at different times as belonging or not belonging to a particular class (see chapter 5).

(d) The $(pv)c_1$, $p(c_1v)$, and $(pv)(c_1v)$ series

In these series there is an interaction between a change in a physical
dimension, a classification and value. The three series will be treated
together, as it is doubtful whether they can be empirically distinguished,
though they may differ in their origin. In the $(pv)c_1$ series there is a
correlation between value and a physical dimension, as in the previously
discussed pv series. The physical dimension is in turn consistently related
to a classification, as was the case in the pc_1 series. The example of

---

[3] As will be seen in part IV of this book, the inherently *comparative* nature of intergroup relations, as
reflected in the processes of social comparison, has acquired a central importance in later theoretical
developments concerning intergroup behaviour. Also see Tajfel, 1974, 1978a; Tajfel and Turner, 1979;
Turner, 1975.

industrial or agricultural products originating from two sources, which was used above for pc_1 series, applies here when a change in the quality of the products is related to a change in the physical dimension, such as size, colour or texture. When products from one of the sources are consistently found at the favoured end of the physical range, a $(pv)c_1$ series will ensue. The effects on judgements of the physical dimension could be assessed by comparing judgements given when the origin of the items present is unknown with judgements given when each of the items is labelled according to its origin.

The $p(c_1v)$ series presents a different case. The classification is here one of value, and the changes in the physical dimension, not themselves related to value, are related to the classification in a manner described previously for the pc_1 series. In the case of the $(pv)c_1$ series the classification which is related to a change in the physical dimension has come to be associated with value, as the change in the physical dimension had such an association in the past. In the $p(c_1v)$ series, the change in the physical dimension would come to be associated with value by a similar process in which the initial association of the classification with value would play the intermediary role.

These two series would thus converge empirically towards a $(pv)(c_1v)$ series, in which value is associated both with the classification and with the change in the physical dimension. Skin colour and other physiognomic traits, as judged by the prejudiced group of subjects in the experiment by Secord *et al.* (1956), are examples of such series; it is probable that the degree of darkness of skin or of flatness of nose would not have had a value connotation for these subjects if possession of these attributes in various degrees had not been consistently associated with the classification into negroes and whites which is for them of inherent value. It has been argued above that such an association tends to shift judgements of the 'relevant' physical characteristics of the stimuli falling into the distinct classes in opposite direction. In a corresponding pc_1 classification these shifts were attributed to the fact that the classification, which has built up specific expectations, provides information concerning the physical magnitudes, especially in the middle part of the range. Here, the classification, which is the same, should exercise similar effects; but these effects should be further accentuated as the classification, or the identification of an individual as negro or white, is decidedly more important for the prejudiced than for the non-prejudiced subjects. This special attention paid by prejudiced individuals to physical cues, which has for its purpose the efficient identification of members of the group against which they are prejudiced, has been demonstrated in other contexts by Allport and Kramer (1946), and by Lindzey and Rogolsky

(1950).[4] In the context of judgement, Stevens and Galanter (1956) have argued that 'what happens when O rates an apparent magnitude on an N-point scale is the result of the interplay of three important "forces" plus an unknown number of lesser ones. The three important forces that interact are: intent, discrimination, and expectation' (p. 7). By 'intent' Stevens and Galanter mean that 'a properly instructed O tries to make the intervals on his category scale equal in width and thereby produce a linear scale' (p. 7). Discrimination is the subject's ability 'to tell one magnitude from another' (p. 7). Expectation plays a role since the subject 'inevitably has expectations regarding how the experimenter will distribute the stimuli, and consequently regarding the relative frequency with which he should use the various categories' (p. 7). The differences between judgements of skin colour given by prejudiced subjects and judgements of magnitude given in a 'neutral' psychophysical experiment are in the different ways in which the factors of intent and of expectation influence judgement in these two situations. In the former case, expectation is not determined by the subjects' guesses about the experimenter's distribution of the stimuli falling into the various categories; it is based on the long-standing past experience of a consistent relationship between the classification and the various categories in terms of which judgements are made. And it is not the subject's intent to produce a linear scale: intent can be replaced by the 'intention' of producing a scale whose close correspondence to the classification represents a perceptual 'vested interest'.

Shifts in opposite directions of judgements of the stimuli falling into the distinct classes should thus be larger in a (pv) (c_1v) series than in a corresponding pc_1 series. Some evidence of this is provided by the fact, mentioned above, that the prejudiced subjects perceived negroes as more negroid in physiognomic traits than did the non-prejudiced subjects. In this case, the photographs were first identified by the subjects as belonging to the 'negro' or 'white' category, and the judgements of 'negroidness' were subsequent to this identification. A study by Pettigrew, Allport and Barnett (1958) provides some interesting indications about the converse phenomenon: the assignment of stimuli to various classes based on ambiguous cues from the physical dimensions which are correlated with a value classification. The experiments were conducted in South Africa; subjects from the five South African ethnic groups (Afrikaans-speaking Europeans, English-speaking Europeans, Coloureds, Indians and Africans) were asked to identify the 'race' of faces after 'a brief stereoscopic presentation of pairs of racial photographs'.

[4] Also see Tajfel (1969a) for a more extensive discussion of the relations between prejudice against certain groups and the recognition of members of these groups by the prejudiced individuals.

These pairs were of two kinds: either the same face presented to both eyes, or ethnically mixed pairs in all possible combinations. The differences between the Afrikaners and all the other groups are of interest here. (1) For the 'one-race pairs' this group gave the largest percentages of 'European' and 'African' judgements, and the smallest of 'Coloured' and 'Indian' ones; the Europeans and the Africans representing, of course, the extremes of the range. (2) An analysis of the distribution of incorrect identifications for the 'one-race pairs' revealed that the Afrikaners gave fewer incorrect identifications as 'Coloured' and 'Indian' than all other groups, and twice as many 'African' judgements as all other groups combined. (3) For the 'two-race pairs', when responding to the combination with an identification of ethnic group which did not correspond to either of the two presented photographs, the Afrikaners gave the smallest percentage of 'Coloured' responses, and the largest percentage of 'African' responses. Pettigrew *et al.* conclude that 'throughout the results, the Afrikaners deviate most consistently in their judgements from the other four groups. They tend to respond in an either–or, bifurcated manner'. If it is assumed that a racial classification in terms of 'white' and 'non-white' has a more pronounced connotation for the Afrikaner group than for the other groups (including the English-speaking European group), these results are entirely consistent with the above discussion of the $(pv)(c_1v)$ series. Similar results in a different context were obtained some years later in Texas by Lent (1970).

Predictions concerning the differences between the $(pv)(c_1v)$ series and the p and pc_2 series need not be detailed here, as they would be similar to those outlined above in the comparison between these two series and the pc_1 series.

No prediction can be made concerning the direct comparison of a $(pv)(c_1v)$ series with a pv series, as this raises the problem of the interaction, within one series, between the variable v and a c_1 classification. There is the possibility that a classification of this nature leads to a decrease in the efficiency of discrimination between the stimuli *within* each of the classes; on the other hand, v should lead to an increase in the judged differences between the stimuli along the entire range. The effects of the resulting complex interaction may either cancel each other, or produce differences between pv and (pv) (c_1v) similar to those expected when p is compared with (pv) (c_1v).

(e) The $(pv)c_2$ series

One of the main implications of the preceding discussion was that a c_2 classification, which bears no relationship to the changes in the physical dimension, has generally no effects on the judged relationships between the physical magnitudes of objects which fall into the distinct classes. Thus, a $(pv)c_2$ series should not differ in this respect from a pv series; for example, judged differences in size between coins are not likely to be affected by a classification of the coins according to the date of their minting, whether or not the subjects are informed of the date for each coin before they give their judgements of size.

(f) The $p(c_2v)$ series

The above implication concerning the c_2 classification applies also to this series. Some supporting evidence can be found in experiments on perceptual over-estimation which yielded negative results. One example is provided by the experiment of Klein *et al.* (1951) in which judgements of size of discs bearing the sign of a swastika were compared with similar judgements of discs bearing neutral signs. No over-estimation of the swastika discs was found, and the authors' conclusion was that this went some way towards invalidating other results in this field. On the assumptions outlined here, the results of this experiment *had* to be negative. It is difficult to conceive of a consistent relationship between the size of a swastika and the degree of its emotional relevance. Therefore, a series of discs of various sizes bearing the emblem is, in the terminology adopted here, a p series and not a pv series in which results similar to those found in the experiments on coins could be expected. In the experiment by Klein *et al.* (1951) the subjects were presented with the swastika and other discs in random order; this resulted in a combination of two p series which together amount to a $p(c_2v)$ series. In this series, there was no association between size and value, there was a value classification into emotionally relevant and emotionally neutral stimuli and the stimuli belonging to the two classes were, as far as their size was concerned, randomly distributed along the series.

(g) The $(pv)(c_2v)$ series

This is a combination of the two preceding series. It is introduced here only for the sake of completeness, as concrete examples of it are difficult to find; it could, however, be produced without much difficulty in the laboratory. Predictions concerning this kind of series are difficult to make in the context of the present argument, and possibly of little interest, as they are neither crucial to the discussion nor readily applicable in 'real-life' situations. Difficulty of prediction is due to the fact that if the value classification does not bear any relationship to the progression in the physical magnitude, the random distribution of stimuli with and without the attribute of value along the physical dimension would necessarily destroy the pv aspect of the series, i.e. the correlation between value and the physical dimension.

8. Abstract continua

The schema outlined so far may be applicable not only to the effects of various kinds of classifications on judgements of physical magnitudes, but also to their effects on 'abstract' judgements which imply the existence of a continuous attribute. This kind of judgement can hardly be considered 'perceptual'; but there are no *a priori* grounds to assume that principles which are found helpful in the prediction of judgements made under certain conditions, and concerned with the physical aspects of stimuli, should not be capable of application to judgements of abstract attributes made under similar conditions. Many objects in our environment, especially in the social environment, are often rated along some quantifiable, or rather, comparative abstract continuum, such as beauty, pleasantness, intelligence, etc. Such 'dimensions' are often, by their very nature, inherently possessed of, or correlated with, value, and they may be, in this sense, compared to the previously-discussed pv series. On this abstract equivalent of a pv series discontinuous classifications in terms of other attributes may be superimposed in a manner similar to those intervening in a pv series. Such classifications may or may not be of inherent value to the subject. If a series of paintings, half of which are Dutch and half Italian, are presented for rating in terms of beauty to someone who has no previous bias in favour of either, the fact that the subject knows which paintings are Dutch and which Italian should not affect the results. This is a near enough equivalent of the previously-discussed c_2 classification, when it is considered that beauty is now the continuum along which judgement is made, just as was the physical dimension before. If, on the other hand, the classification in terms of another attribute is itself of value, the judgemental results should be similar to those discussed above under the headings of c_1 and c_1v classifications. In an experiment on stereotypes, Razran (1950) asked his subjects to rate photographs of faces in terms of their pleasantness and other similar attributes. The same photographs were presented later, together with a number of new ones, and ethnic labels were attached to each one of them. The new judgements, as compared with the original ones, tended to show displacements which might be expected on the basis of a value classification originating in prejudice. This is, of course, an example of a familiar phenomenon which occurs in an infinite variety of social situations. It is introduced here because it relates theoretically to the preceding argument, and because predictions of effects on the basis of this argument could be made in each case in which the attribute determining the value classification could be identified.

5

Differences and similarities: some contexts of judgement

1. Introduction

The aim of this chapter is to bring together a few examples of the functioning of the general principles outlined in the previous chapter. It is not the purpose of this collection of examples to provide definite 'proofs' of what has been said earlier. The research examples have been chosen from a variety of contexts; but in their empirical diversity they exemplify the principles discussed in the preceding chapter. Other studies related to the same (or modified) principles were conducted in the sixties and later by my colleagues and myself, and by other people. Reviews of theory together with various forms of theoretical analysis, can be found in, for example, the books by Eiser and Stroebe (1972), Irle (1975), Deschamps (1977), Doise (1978b), Eiser (1980) and a number of journal articles. The studies summarized in this chapter[1] provide examples of the following:

(i) The effects of a classification on judgements of stimuli varying in physical dimension (length); this corresponds to the pc_1 and pc_2 series described in the previous chapter.

(ii) The polarizing (or 'stretching') effects of value differentials in the judgements of characteristics of individual people. This is a 'transfer' from a pv series as previously discussed to equivalent phenomena in the 'person perception', i.e. in the judgements we make of various characteristics of other people.

(iii) The role of categorization in accentuating similarities between people who are placed in the same social category. This again represents a transposition of one aspect of the pc_1 series to an equivalent aspect of the functioning of social stereotypes.

(iv) The discussion of an apparent exception which reduces itself to the

---

[1] The full versions are as follows: H. Tajfel and A. L. Wilkes: Classification and quantitative judgement, *British Journal of Psychology*, 1963, **54**, 101–14; H. Tajfel and A. L. Wilkes (1964): Salience of attributes and commitment to extreme judgements in the perception of people, *British Journal of Social and Clinical Psychology*, **2**, 40–9; H. Tajfel, A. A. Sheikh and R. C. Gardner: Content of stereotypes and the inference of similarity between members of sterotyped groups, *Acta Psychologica*, 1964, **22**, 191–201; H. Tajfel: A note on Lambert's 'Evaluation reactions to spoken languages', *Canadian Journal of Psychology*, 1959, **13**, 86–92.

same underlying process: an accentuation of differences between certain traits attributed to various social groups which works *against* a positive self-evaluation of the groups making the judgements. This represents one of the social equivalents of the $p(c_1v)$ series described in the preceding chapter.

The four studies also vary in the degree of their remoteness from 'natural' situations. The first is a straightforward controlled laboratory experiment; the second lets go of the 'controls' a little in the sense that it is based on judgements of other people in terms of categories of descriptions of others freely selected by the respondents; the third is based in part on judgements of other people made in a fairly 'natural' situation; and the fourth, which is a re-analysis of an earlier study, is directly relevant to the mutual perceptions of two social groups which were at the time (twenty years ago), and still are today, in a traditionally competitive relationship.

2. Classification and judgements of length

(a) Introduction

The experiments reported here are concerned with classification as an independent variable. A series of stimuli may be classified in a number of ways, and there can be a number of possible relations between a classification and the physical magnitudes which are subjected to judgement. A series of stimuli may be classified in terms of a discontinuous attribute (e.g. a group of people classified into, say, Swedes and Italians); the dimension along which the judgements are made (e.g. height) may be a continuous one. If in our group of people *all* the Swedes were taller than *all* the Italians, there would be a perfect correlation between the classification and the physical attribute under judgement, though the series was not classified in terms of that attribute. If our group of people consisted of, for example, French and Italians, and there was no difference between the means and the spreads of the heights of individuals in both groups, we would have a classification standing in no relation to the physical attribute under judgement.

The problem with which the present experiments are concerned can be stated as follows: how does the subject's knowledge that stimuli fall into various classes affect the judgements of a physical dimension of the stimuli when this dimension stands in certain relation to the classification?

Two of the predictions stated in the previous chapter were as follows:

(i) 'When a classification in terms of an attribute other than the physical dimension which is being judged is superimposed on a series of stimuli in

91

such a way that one part of the physical series tends to fall consistently into one class, and the other into the other class, judgements of physical magnitudes of the stimuli falling into the distinct classes will show a shift in the directions determined by the class membership of the stimuli, when compared with judgements of a series identical with respect to this physical dimension, on which such a classification is not superimposed.'

(ii) 'When a classification in terms of an attribute other than the physical dimension which is being judged is superimposed on a series of stimuli, and the changes in the physical magnitudes of the stimuli bear no consistent relationship to the assignment of the stimuli to the distinct classes, this classification will have no effect on the judged relationships in the physical dimension between the stimuli of the series.'

The effect of this situation on judgement can be stated in terms borrowed from the experimental literature on anchoring (e.g. Sherif and Hovland, 1961). An anchoring stimulus placed outside a series of stimuli may determine either a contrast or an assimilation effect in the judgements of the stimuli of the series. In the case of contrast, judgements of the stimuli shift away from the value of the anchor stimulus; in the case of assimilation they shift towards that value. There exists a good deal of evidence that when the anchor stimuli are placed relatively far outside the original series, they determine a contrast effect; when they are placed very near or at the extremes of the series, they often lead to an assimilation effect.

It is a fair assumption that the judgemental process underlying the contrast and assimilation effects reduces itself to the perceived extent of similarity and of difference between the anchoring stimuli and the stimuli of the series. When the anchoring stimulus is perceived as definitely different from those nearest to it in the original series, the judgements of these stimuli reflect this differentiation by shifting away from the judged value of the anchor; when the anchoring stimulus is perceived as very similar to the stimuli of the series, the opposite happens: the judgements of the stimuli nearest to the anchor reflect the subjective equivalence by shifting towards the judged value of the anchor stimulus.[2] This would fit in with the general results of experiments on anchoring which show that when the values of anchoring stimuli progressively approach the values of the end stimuli of the original series, the extent of contrast is reduced (e.g. Heintz, 1950) until finally assimilation takes over (Sherif, *et al.*, 1958).

---

[2] This prediction about the relationship between the distance of an anchor from the series of stimuli and its categorization as the 'same' or 'different from' the series was confirmed in a study by Wilkes and Tajfel (1966).

A classification superimposed on a series of stimuli may be regarded as determining the same type of shifts in the extent of judged similarities and differences between the various stimuli. The nature of these shifts will depend on the relationship between the division of the stimuli into classes and the pattern of variation in the magnitudes of the stimuli which the subjects are requested to judge.

In a series in which a classification is directly and consistently related to the physical dimension under judgement, the class identification of a stimulus provides a supplementary source of information about the relationship of its magnitude to the magnitudes of other stimuli, whether identified as belonging to the same class or to a different class. In absolute judgements of a series of stimuli which are presented in successive random orders, an identity in the labelling should therefore produce assimilation or convergence in the assessments, whereas a difference should produce contrast or divergence. Therefore, the differences between the judgements of magnitude of stimuli belonging to the distinct classes should be greater in such a series than in an identical series on which a classification has not been superimposed. At the same time, differences between the judged magnitudes of stimuli belonging to the same class show a tendency to be smaller than the corresponding differences in an unclassified series.

There is no reason to assume that any consistent shift in the differences between the judged magnitudes of stimuli belonging to distinct classes should be observed when a classification superimposed on a series stands in no coherent relation to the magnitudes of the stimuli. In this situation, 'the physical magnitude of a stimulus does not help in its assignment to one of the various classes, and the identification of a stimulus as belonging to one of the classes does not provide any cue as to its physical magnitude'.

These effects should become accentuated in direct relation to the amount of past experience in judging the classified series.

(b) Method

The purpose of the experiments was to assess the effects of classifications on simple quantitative judgements. Judgements of length of series of lines were used. This choice was dictated by the relative simplicity of judgements of length; if it is found that classification exercises its predicted effects in this context, that 'stereotypes' can be formed about the length of lines, then such effects are likely to be even more marked when the complexity of the task of judging increases, with the corresponding tendency of the subject to rely increasingly on all the available sources of information about the stimuli.

A series of eight lines differing from each other by a constant ratio of approximately 5% of length were used as stimuli in all the experiments. The shortest line was 16.2 cm long; the longest 22.9 cm. Each line was drawn diagonally on a sheet of white cardboard whose dimensions were 63.5 cm × 50.8 cm. The relatively large size of the sheets of cardboard was chosen in order to minimize the cues about the differences in the length of lines that could be provided by comparisons with the frame. Each length of line was presented several times (see below), but a separate sheet was prepared for each presentation of each stimulus, in order to avoid the possibility of an identification of a stimulus on the basis of irrelevant cues.

Sixty-one subjects took part in the first two experiments (Expts. ia and iia). They were volunteers, men and women, drawn from students at Oxford University, Westminster Training College and Manchester University. Of those sixty-one subjects, fifty-four were available for the second sessions (Expts. ib and iib).

Procedure common to all experimental situations
The eight lines were presented one by one six times in successive random orders. The subjects were requested to judge the length of each line in centimetres. Judgements in centimetres rather than inches or fractions of inches were used because in this way the differences in length between the stimuli could be made fairly small while avoiding at the same time the tendency for rough judgements in terms of the nearest inch. Before the beginning of judgements, a ruler was shown and several examples of relationship between centimetres and inches were given. The subjects were tested individually. They were seated facing the stimuli which were presented by the experimenter at a distance of about 2.5 metres. They called out their judgements which were recorded by the experimenter. There was no time limit for the presentation of stimulus which was held in front of the subject until the judgement was made. The interval between the presentation of successive stimuli was 4 sec. The subject was not told how many different lengths of lines were presented to him. Each subject was requested to come for a second session a week after the first.

Table 1 presents the summary of the procedures used in the four experiments.

Classification
Three groups of subjects served in Expts. ia and ib, and two groups in Expts. iia and iib.
Experiment ia. Group C (classified). This group was presented with a

94

Table 1

Summary of the experimental procedure[3]

Experiment	Groups*	Mode of prior presentation	Number of presentations of the series of stimuli
ıa (first session)	C, R, U	Successive	6
ıb (second session)	C, R, U	Simultaneous	11
ııa (first session)	C_1, U_1	Simultaneous	6
ııb (second session)	C_1, U_1	Simultaneous	6

* C and C_1, classified series; U and U_1, unclassified series; R, randomly classified series

classification superimposed on a series in such a way that there was a stable and predictable relationship between the lengths of lines and their labels. Each of the four shorter lines had a large letter A drawn above its middle at each presentation; each of the four longer lines a letter B drawn in the same way. The group consisted of twelve subjects.

Group R (randomly classified). This group was presented with a classification which bore no relationship to the lengths of lines. The stimuli was labelled with letters A and B as for group C, but each of the eight stimuli was labelled A at half of its presentations and B at the other half. The order of appearance of labels A and B was randomized for each stimulus. The group consisted of thirteen subjects.

Group U (unclassified). Conditions of presentation of stimuli for this group were identical to those for groups C and R, the only difference being that the lines were presented without any labels. The group consisted of twelve subjects.

Experiment ıb. A week later, the subjects in groups C, R and U were tested again. The conditions of presentation of stimuli were the same for each group as in Expt. ıa. In group C, ten out of the original twelve subjects were still available; all the thirteen subjects from group R reappeared; and eleven out of twelve from group U.

Experiment ııa. Group C_1 (classified). Conditions of presentation of stimuli were the same as for group C in Expt. ıa. The group consisted of twelve subjects.

[3] The 'successive' v. 'simultaneous' prior presentations of the stimuli were designed to vary the salience of the classifications to the subjects. As this variation in salience did not prove successful and the issue was of secondary importance in the study, the data and discussion concerning the effects of this variable are omitted here.

Group U_1 (unclassified). Conditions of presentation of stimuli were the same as for group U in Expt. ɪa. The group consisted of twelve subjects. *Experiment ɪɪb*. The same subjects were tested again a week later. The conditions of presentation of stimuli were the same for each group as in Expt. ɪɪa. Eleven out of twelve subjects were still available for group C_1, and nine out of twelve for group U_1.

Past experience

Effects of past experience at successive sessions: as each group of subjects underwent two experimental sessions at an interval of a week, the data allowed an assessment of the cumulative effects of classification on judgements of length.

Effects of past experience within a session: this was investigated in Expt. ɪb, which was, it will be remembered, the second experimental session for groups C, R and U. After these three groups had completed their judgements of the series of stimuli presented six times, the series was presented without interruption in five additional successive random orders, identical for all groups, and identical in their respective conditions to the previous six presentations for each of the groups. Thus, the effect of past experience within a session was assessed by comparing the judgements of the first six with the last five presentations of the series in this experiment.

(c) Results

Description of the general pattern of results

Table 2 sets out the general results: means of all the control groups (randomly classified and unclassified) were combined, as their patterns are highly similar. The table shows the means of the judgements of each

Table 2

Mean judgements of stimuli in the various experimental conditions

Stimuli	Class A				Class B			
	1	2	3	4	5	6	7	8
Actual values	16.2	17.0	17.9	18.8	19.7	20.7	21.7	22.8
	Expts. ɪa and ɪɪa (first sessions)							
Groups C and C_1	16.0	17.3	18.1	19.3	21.1	22.3	23.6	25.3
Groups R, U and U_1	16.4	17.3	18.2	19.3	20.3	21.5	22.6	24.2
	Expts. ɪb and ɪɪb (second sessions)							
Groups C and C_1	15.6	16.5	17.2	18.3	20.3	21.6	22.4	24.4
Groups R, U and U_1	16.6	17.4	17.9	19.0	20.3	21.3	22.8	24.6

stimulus. Stimuli have been numbered from 1 to 8 in order of increasing length. Stimuli 1 to 4 belong to class A, stimuli 5 to 8 to class B in the classified series (groups C and C_1). Therefore, the *inter*-class difference is between stimuli 4 and 5. All the other differences between adjacent stimuli are *intra*-class differences. The data from Expt. ıb include only the first six presentations of the series.

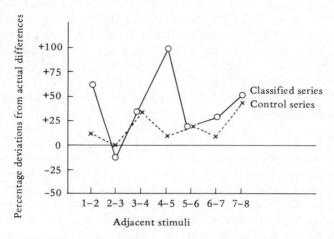

Fig. 1. Comparison of actual and apparent differences between adjacent stimuli in Expts. Ia and IIa

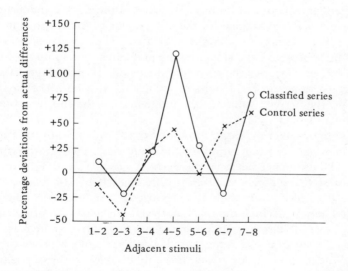

Fig. 2. Comparison of actual and apparent differences between adjacent stimuli in Expts. Ib and IIb

In Figs. 1 and 2 the actual difference between each two adjacent stimuli was taken as a basis, and the deviations of the judged differences from the actual ones are expressed as percentages of the actual differences. These deviations are plotted as positive when the judged differences are greater than the actual ones; as negative when they are smaller.

An inspection of Figs. 1 and 2 will show that, as predicted, the inter-class differences (between stimuli 4 and 5) are larger by far for the classified series (groups C and C_1) than for the randomly classified and unclassified ones, both in the first and in the second sessions. In the first sessions the relevant percentage figures are as follows: apparent difference 100% greater than the actual difference for the classified series; 11% greater for the randomly classified and unclassified ones. In the second sessions: 122% greater than the actual for the classified series, 44% for the unclassified ones.

Analysis of results

It was assumed in the introduction to this section that a stable and predictable relationship between a classification and a variation in physical magnitudes would lead to an increase in the apparent differences between the classes, and a decrease in the apparent differences within the classes. Therefore, an analysis of results was required which would take into account the combined effects on judgements of both these predicted phenomena. In order to do this, the judgements of stimuli belonging to each of the classes were treated separately, and a linear function was fitted to the judgements of the stimuli from each of the classes, independently of the other. This was done for the judgements of each subject in all the groups. The method of averages was used. The calculations yield the following scores: m_s, the slope for the judgements of stimuli belonging to the shorter class; m_1, the corresponding slope for the longer class; Y_4, the derived value for the judgement of the longest stimulus of the shorter class; Y_5, the derived value for the judgement of the shortest stimuli of the longer class.

Thus, the m_s and m_1 slopes provided direct measures of the apparent differences between the stimuli of the same class, the intra-class differences. The difference between the derived values Y_4 and Y_5 provided a measure of the apparent inter-class difference. This last measure is, of course, affected both by the difference between the judged values of the stimuli 4 and 5 at which the break between the classes occurred, and by the intra-class slopes. It would increase as a function of an increase in the judged differences between the stimuli 4 and 5 and of a decrease in one or both of the intra-class slopes, and it would decrease in the opposite case. It fulfils, therefore, the conditions for testing the combined predicted effects of the classification. At the same time, the separate contribution to the results of the intra-class differences could be assessed by a statistical analysis of the slope indices.

Table 3

Mean inter-class differences and intra-class slopes

Groups	Inter-class differences $(Y_5 - Y_4)$	Intra-class slopes
	Expts. 1a and 11a (first sessions)	
C and C_1	1.9	1.22
U and U_1	1.1	1.18
R	1.1	1.06
	Expts. 1b and 11b (second sessions)	
C and C_1	2.1	1.08
U and U_1	1.4	1.17
R	1.1	1.01

Table 3 provides the group means of the scores relevant to the analysis, namely: mean intra-class slopes $\frac{1}{2}(m_s + m_1)$ and the inter-class differences $(Y_5 - Y_4)$.

The results of the statistical analysis were as follows:

(a) The analysis of variance for the inter-class differences $(Y_5 - Y_4)$ in Expts. 1a and 11a shows that the classification, as predicted, determines an increase in the apparent inter-class difference (F ratio for the classification is 6.12; $p < 0.025$).

(b) The analysis of variance for mean slopes $\frac{1}{2}(m_s + m_1)$ shows that the classification did not determine any consistent differences in the apparent intra-class differences. This does not confirm the prediction that an introduction of the classification would lead to an increase in the judged similarity of stimuli belonging to the same class.

(c) Analysis of variance for Expts. 1b and 11b shows results parallel to the previous analysis. The predicted effects of classification for inter-class differences are significant (F ratio = 4.40; $p < 0.05$). No other differences between the groups are significant.

(d) A comparison of apparent inter-class differences between groups C (classified) and R (randomly classified) in the first session (Expt. 1a) yields a strong tendency for the differences in group C to be larger, as predicted; but this tendency does not reach statistical significance. In the second session (Expt. 1b), this difference between the groups is significant in the predicted direction at p<0.01. A comparison of the two groups taking as a score for each subject the means of his performance in the first and second sessions is significant at p<0.025 in the direction of larger inter-class differences for group C. There are no differences between the intra-class slopes of the groups, either in the first or in the second session.

(d) Effects of past experience

The possible cumulative effects of classification as a function of past experience from the first session to the second were assessed by comparing the relevant scores in Expts. ia and iia with those in Expts. ib and iib. The effects of cumulative experience with the classification within a session were assessed by comparing the scores in the first six presentations of the series in Expt. ib with those obtained in the last five presentations in that experiment.

Comparisons of first and second sessions: A 2×2 analysis of variance was conducted on the shifts of the inter-class differences from Expts. ia to ib and iia to iib for groups, C, C_1, U and U_1. The effects of past experience (Expts. ia to ib and iia to iib) are not significant. The same is true of the analysis of intra-class slopes, and of a separate comparison made of the shifts from first to second sessions in inter- and intra-class differences for groups C and R (Expts. ia to ib).

Effects of past experience within a session: It will be remembered that in Expt. ib there were three groups of subjects, (C, R and U) who after having completed their judgements of the series presented six times, judged the length of lines in five additional presentations of the series. Table 4 sets out the group means obtained from these additional presentations. Figure 3 presents the percentage differences between the actual and apparent differences for judgements of each two adjacent stimuli; these percentages have been plotted as positive when the apparent differences exceeded the actual ones; as negative in the opposite case.

As can be seen from Table 4 and from Fig. 3, it is only at the predicted point of inter-class break (stimuli 4–5) that the apparent difference between the stimuli for group C exceeds considerably both the actual differences and the corresponding differences for the two control groups.

Linear functions were fitted to these data in the manner previously described. Group C was then compared separately with group R and with group U, both for its derived inter-class differences $(Y_5 - Y_4)$ and mean intra-class slopes $\frac{1}{2}(m_s + m_1)$. The two control groups R and U do not differ from one another (see Table 5); the inter-class differences in

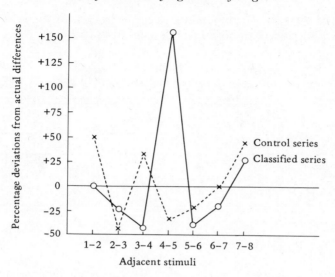

Fig. 3. Comparison of actual and apparent differences between adjacent stimuli in the second part of Expt. Ib

group C are significantly larger than those in group U at $p < 0.01$; than those in group R at $p < 0.001$.

At the same time, the intra-class slopes show a tendency to be less steep in group C than in the two other groups; but this tendency does not reach statistical significance when group C is compared with each of the two control groups separately.

An inspection of these results shows indirectly the accentuated effects of the classification as function of repeated trials within the same session. A direct assessment of these cumulative effects of classification was made by calculating for each subject the shift of his scores for inter-class differences and for intra-class slopes from the first six to the last five presentations of the series. The statistical significance of the difference in these shifts between group C and each of the control groups was assessed separately. An inspection of the data in the second part of Table 2 and in Table 4 will show that, as function of practice within a session, apparent differences between the stimuli tended to decrease with the only clear exception of the inter-class difference in group C. The stability of the inter-class differences in group C within the session as compared with the decrease of the corresponding differences in the control groups does not quite reach statistical significance at $p = 0.05$. The decrease in the intra-class differences (i.e. the flattening out of the intra-class slope)

101

compared with the corresponding decrease in each of the two control groups is significant in both cases at $p < 0.01$.

Table 4

Mean judgements of stimuli in the last five presentations of the series in Expt. 1b

Stimuli	Class A				Class B			
	1	2	3	4	5	6	7	8
Actual values	16.2	17.0	17.9	18.8	19.7	20.7	21.7	22.8
Group C	17.1	17.9	18.6	19.1	21.4	22.0	22.8	24.2
Groups R and U	16.9	18.1	18.6	19.8	20.4	21.2	22.2	23.8

Table 5

Mean inter-class differences and intra-class slopes in the last five presentations of the series in Expt. 1b

Groups	Inter-class differences $(Y_5 - Y_4)$	Intra-class slopes
C	2.0	0.83
R	0.7	0.99
U	0.09	1.02

(e) Discussion and summary of results

Before the results can be summarized and conclusions drawn, certain problems of control arising from the data and from the experimental procedures must be briefly discussed.

The results concerning the effects of classification on judgement cannot be attributed to extraneous factors irrelevant to the experimental variables:

(i) The mean scale values of the classified (C and C_1) and control (U, U_1 and R) groups were compared; there are no significant differences between the experimental groups and any of the control groups.

(ii) Variability scores for the judgements of each stimulus by each subject in all the groups were calculated, and comparisons of mean scores made. There are no significant differences between the experimental and the control groups.

102

(iii) An inspection of Fig. 1 shows that there is a marked difference between groups C and C_1 and the three other groups not only at the predicted point of inter-class break (stimuli 4–5) but also, to a lesser extent, between stimuli 1 and 2. An analysis of variance, parallel to the one conducted on the inter-class differences, was done on these data. There is not even a hint that the difference between the experimental and the control groups is statistically significant (the F ratio for the classification variable is 0.47). It seems therefore safe to conclude that the only consistent difference between the experimental and the control groups is at the predicted point of the inter-class break.

(iv) There was a possibility that the larger inter-class differences found in all the experiments for groups C and C_1 were due not to the effects of classification but to some measure of differential over- or under-estimation in one direction or another inherent in the use of letters A and B as labels. This could be checked by inspecting the data from group R where these two labels were used in random alternation for each of the stimuli. The mean judgements of each stimulus were calculated separately when it was labelled A or B. They are practically identical; the mean scale value for label A is 19.5 and for label B is 19.6. The same applies to the mean differences between the judgements of adjacent stimuli when they were labelled in the same way (both A or both B), and when one was labelled A and the other B; the respective means are 1.07 and 1.12. This eliminates the possibility that the experimental results could have been due not to the predicted effects of the classification but to some inherent differences in the judgements of the same stimulus when labelled A or B.

The following conclusions can therefore be drawn from the experimental results:

(i) A classification superimposed on a series of stimuli in such a way that there is a consistent and direct relationship between the magnitudes of the stimuli and the division of the stimuli into two classes determines a significant increase of the apparent differences between the stimuli at the point of transition from one class to another. This does not happen when the classification superimposed on the series does not stand in a coherent relationship to the physical dimension.

(ii) There is no direct evidence that this relationship between a classification and the judged physical dimension determines an increase in the judged similarity of the stimuli belonging to the same class.

(iii) There is no evidence that a repeated experience of the same classification after an interval of a week increases its effect on judgement.

(iv) The evidence is, however, very clear that the classification increases its predicted effects on judgement as a function of repeated experience during the same experimental session. This seems due to two judgement trends happening concurrently: the apparent inter-class differences in the classified series do not follow the trend of the control groups towards a progressive decrease in the apparent differences between the stimuli in the middle of the series; and there is a definite increase in the judged similarity of stimuli belonging to the same class. It is therefore possible that repeated and frequent experience of the same type of classification would lead, despite the negative results reported in (iii) above, to an accentuation of its effects on judgement which would include both a relative increase in the subjective differences between the classes and in the subjective similarity within the classes.

These findings have some fairly wide implications for a variety of judgement situations. They represent, in a sense, a simplified exercise in stereotyping. An essential feature of stereotyping is that of exaggerating *some* differences between groups classified in a certain way, and of minimizing the same differences within such groups. It may be important to note that these effects were shown to exist in the present experiments despite the relative ease and simplicity of judgements, the minimal amount of experience with the classification, and its minimal significance to the subject. The drastic effects of a small but consistent and direct increase in the amount of experience with the classification can be seen when one considers the results of the additional trials in one of the experiments.

3. Polarization of judgements in the perception of people

(a) Introduction

A recurrent theme in the previous and present chapters was that judgemental shifts acquired a special importance when their orderly operation was transferred from judgements of simple physical characteristics of objects to apply to judgements of characteristics of people. The present section of this chapter and those to follow provide three examples of this transposition from the 'physical' to the 'social'. In the present section we are dealing with the perception of attributes of other *individuals*; in the next two, with individuals seen as members of *social groups*. The three studies described here are experimental, in the sense of having been fairly tightly controlled and conducted more or less in laboratory conditions. But they also have in common the attempt to arrange for situations which would be as natural as possible and would allow us to draw conclusions which are easily applied to 'real-life' conditions of judgements of other people. The present section is primarily concerned with the effects of the attribute of value, as discussed in chapter 4 of this book; the next two sections derive directly from one of the theoretical formulations and empirical findings described earlier in this chapter and in the preceding one.

Experimental work on perception of people has always been beset with difficulties inherent in the nature of the problems studied. These investigations attempt to extend the scope of generalizations that can be made about the ways in which people perceive, assess or judge other people. Reliable generalizations are, of course, most easily established in properly controlled experiments, but adequate controls imposed on the fleeting, variable and rich contexts of impressions about people have a way of yielding predictions which seem to apply above all to other equally well-controlled situations. The main reason for the existence of this vicious circle of prediction from experiment to experiment instead of prediction from experiment to natural phenomenon is probably in the difficulty (or sometimes impossibility) of identifying the relevant deter-mining variables in 'real' situations.

The experiments described in this section were designed as one attempt in this direction. The hypotheses were based on a fairly well documented set of findings in the field of quantitative judgement; the results seem applicable without undue qualifications to a variety of settings in which people assess other people.

The aim of the studies was to explore the possibility of extending to judgement of human attributes a group of converging results reported in other areas of quantitative judgement. The common denominator of these findings is that a 'polarization' of judgements occurs when the dimensions along which these judgements are made are of high relevance to the subject. Another way to describe the phenomenon is to state that when the differences between the stimuli judged by the subject have in the past acquired some form of emotional or 'value' significance for him, he will tend to use in his estimates of magnitude a relatively high proportion of extreme judgements, placed at one or at both ends of his response scale. Hovland and Sherif (1952) and Sherif and Hovland (1961) reported similar results about the placement of series of statements concerning a controversial social issue. They found that groups of subjects who were highly involved in the desegregation issue in the United States tended to place more of the statements at the extremes of a prescribed category scale than did less involved subjects. The phe-nomenon was particularly marked for statements which expressed opinions strongly at variance with those held by the subject. Manis (1960) described the same phenomenon for groups of students in relation to the issue of fraternities in American colleges. The mean standard deviations of judgements made by students who held strong views for or against fraternities were greater than of judgements made by students who did not feel strongly about the issue.

The determining condition of all these findings seem to be the subject's involvement with his judgements on a particular dimension. Different degrees of such involvement have an obvious parallel in the perception of people. We assess other people in terms of a very large number of attributes; each of these attributes can be conceived as a 'dimension' varying from 'more' to 'less', e.g. from 'intelligent' or 'kind' or 'honest' to their opposites. The relative importance of the various attributes is bound to vary from individual to individual; e.g. to one person 'intelligence' may be more important than 'kindness', to another 'honesty' more important than 'strength of character'. A simple inference from the variety of findings discussed previously would be that judgements of subjectively important attributes should tend to cluster more in the regions of extreme responses than judgements of attributes which are less important to the individual.

However, this inference loses much of its simplicity when one considers two stumbling blocks in the way of subjecting it to some sort of valid empirical test. In the first place, it is by no means easy to ascertain the relative importance of various attributes to an individual. Secondly, terms such as 'intelligent' or 'kind' or 'honest' used by one person are not necessarily equivalent in their connotations to the same terms used by another. 'Intelligence' or other such attributes cannot *by definition* be specified in *a priori* objective terms when one is concerned with the subjective aspects of their use, with the private connotations which determine the extent of their salience for an individual.

The investigation described here was an attempt to circumvent these difficulties in the testing of the prediction just stated. The main preoccupation in the designing and conducting of the experiments was to isolate the relevant variables without at the same time distorting them beyond recognition through rigidity of the experimental controls. This was attempted in the following successive stages:

(i) Identifying and isolating for each subject an equal number of salient and non-salient attributes *defined in his own terms*.

(ii) Designing a rating situation in which each subject was able to use his own previously identified salient and non-salient attributes.

(iii) Adopting an assumption concerning differences in the free use of attributes which differ in the degree of their importance to the subjects.

(iv) Validation of the assumption just referred to.

The first assumption above is closely related to a discussion by Hastorf, Richardson and Dornbusch (1958). One of the main points put forward by Hastorf *et al.* is that it is crucially important 'to study the qualities of a person's experience of others in terms of the verbal categories he uses in reporting that experience' (p. 56). They assumed that in such a study the frequency and the sequence of the categories used by a subject may become fairly important as indices of his manner of perceiving others. A more specific assumption related to the problem at hand was made for the purposes of the present study: that when categories of description of others are used freely by the subjects, those that are related to attributes which are subjectively important will tend to be used earlier in a sequence and more frequently than categories related to the less important attributes.

The hypothesis of the study can therefore be rephrased in the following terms: the most frequent and earliest categories used in free descriptions of others will tend to be related in a subsequent rating task to more extreme judgements than the less frequent categories of description appearing later. The dual task of the experiments was to test this hypothesis and the validity of the assumption linking it to the problem of subjective importance.

(b) Method

Free use of categories

The aim of the first phase of the experiments was to elicit fairly free descriptions of other people. Ten photographs (heads only) of youngish men (approximately between the ages of twenty and thirty) were selected from various sources and reproduced on slides. The group of subjects consisted of seventeen young men (students at Oxford University and at Ruskin College). Each subject was provided with ten sheets of paper. The sheets were numbered from one to ten, one for each photograph, and each sheet was divided into ten spaces, also numbered from one to ten. The subjects were told that their task would be to describe the personal characteristics of each of the men whose photographs would appear on the screen; they should try to find, as far as they could, ten items of description for each photograph, to be written on the sheet in the order of their occurrence; they should describe each characteristic in their own words, using adjectives, short sentences or any other form of short description.

Following these instructions, the photographs were presented on the screen one after another. Each photograph remained on the screen until all the subjects completed the work on the sheet corresponding to it.

Determination of salience of attributes

Not all the subjects were able to specify as many as ten characteristics for each of the photographs. However, the work of each subject yielded a total of between fifty and one hundred separate items of description. These items ranged from single adjectives or nouns to short sentences.

The descriptions provided by each subject were then coded by two judges working together. The aim of this coding was to determine for each subject the clusters of expressions which (a) were identical, synonymous or closely related; (b) overlapped as little as possible with other clusters of expressions used by that subject. In this way, the original number of items supplied by each subject was reduced to about ten to fifteen clusters.

Each of the clusters was then evaluated from the original response sheets in terms of its priority for each of the photographs and of its overall frequency of occurrence. An item appearing first in a description of a photograph was assigned a score of ten; the second item a score of nine, and so on, until the last item on the sheet was reached. Therefore, the final score for each cluster consisted of the sum of the ranks that the various items belonging to it were given each time one of them appeared on the sheets. The scores were thus determined by a combination of priority and frequency of occurrence of the items belonging to each cluster. A high score represented a salient attribute; a low score a non-salient one. The attributes used by each subject were ranked for salience from the highest to the lowest.

Preparation of individual rating scales for the subjects
For each subject, the top four and the bottom four attributes were selected from his ranking order. Each of these attributes was then arranged in a bipolar way (e.g., intelligent–unintelligent). In this, the subject's own manner of describing each attribute was used (e.g. one subject may have used descriptions such as 'strong' and 'weak', another 'forceful personality' and 'weak personality').

Ten small booklets were then prepared for each subject. Each booklet consisted of eight pages. On each page, one bipolar attribute was presented in the form of a non-verbal seven-point scale, consisting of the two opposites separated by seven clearly spaced positions. In this way, each subject was provided with ten booklets each consisting of eight rating scales, four for his salient attributes and four for the non-salient ones. The sequence of the attributes and the position of the positive and negative opposites were randomized for each booklet.

Rating of the attributes
The same subjects participated in a second experimental session which took place about four weeks after the first. Sixteen out of the original seventeen subjects were still available. The stimulus material consisted of

ten new photographs of young men obtained in the same way as the photographs for the first session. The subjects were requested to rate each photograph on the eight rating scales, using one booklet per photograph. The rating was done by placing a tick above the appropriate position. The ten photographs were presented one by one on a screen, each remaining on the screen until all the subjects completed all the ratings in the appropriate booklet.

To summarize the procedure: the first experimental session provided descriptions of personality characteristics from photographs. The salience for each subject of the attributes he had used was determined from these descriptions. Rating scales for the four most salient and the four least salient attributes were prepared separately for each subject. In the second experimental session, the subjects rated ten new photographs, each on eight rating scales representing each subject's own salient and non-salient attributes.

(c) Results

The seven points on the rating scale were assigned numbers from -3 for the most unfavourable rating through 0 for the neutral one to $+3$ for the most favourable one. The prediction that the subjects would tend to use more extreme ratings for the salient attributes than for the non-salient ones could thus be tested by comparing the frequency of ratings assigned by each subject to the categories -3, -2, $+2$ and $+3$ for each of the two groups of four attributes.

The general pattern of results is presented in Table 6. An inspection of this table will reveal two trends in the data:

(i) The frequency of the more extreme ratings ($+3$, $+2$, -2, -3) is consistently higher (with one small exception at $+3$) for the salient attributes than for the non-salient attributes. These ratings represent 52.3% of the ratings for the salient attributes; and 45.8% for the non-salient attributes.

Table 6

Over-all mean frequencies of ratings for each point of the rating scale

	-3	-2	-1	0	$+1$	$+2$	$+3$	Totals
Salient attributes	2.6	5.7	5.5	4.7	8.9	9.3	3.3	40.0
Non-salient attributes	1.9	4.9	6.3	5.8	9.6	8.0	3.5	40.0
Totals	4.5	10.6	11.8	10.5	18.5	17.3	6.8	80.0

(ii) The frequency of favourable (positive) ratings is consistently higher, both for the salient and for the non-salient attributes, than the frequency of unfavourable (negative) ratings. The percentage of favourable ratings is 53.3; of the unfavourable ones, 33.6; of the neutral ones (0), 13.1.

The statistical significance of these two trends in the data was assessed in the analysis of results.

Extreme ratings for salient and non-salient attributes
The Wilcoxon matched-pairs signed-ranks test (Siegel, 1956) was applied in order to test the prediction that the frequency of the more extreme ratings will be higher for the salient than for the non-salient attributes. The frequencies of each subject's ratings of -3, -2, $+2$ and $+3$ for salient and non-salient attributes were taken as scores, and the significance of the differences between the pairs of scores was assessed. The prediction of higher frequency of more extreme ratings for salient attributes was confirmed at p nearly 0.01 ($T = 21$ for $N = 15$, one-tailed test; there was no difference between the two scores of one of the subjects).

The same analysis was applied separately to the favourable and to the unfavourable ratings. The higher frequency of more extreme ratings for salient attributes is statistically significant for the unfavourable ratings ($T = 14.5$ for $N = 13$; $p < 0.025$); the same tendency in the case of favourable ratings does not reach the level of statistical significance.

The preponderance of favourable ratings
The frequencies of each subject's positive and negative ratings were taken as his scores, and a Wilcoxon test applied to the differences between each pair of scores. The higher frequency of favourable ratings is statistically significant at $p < 0.01$ ($T = 5$ for $N = 16$; two-tailed). The same analysis was then conducted separately for the scores obtained for the salient attributes and for the non-salient attributes. In both cases the higher frequency of favourable ratings is significant at $p < 0.01$ ($T = 9.5$ for the salient attributes; $T = 12.0$ for the non-salient ones).

(d) Validation of the assumption concerning priority and frequency

The results reported in the previous section show that the salient attributes (those which tend to appear early and to be repeated frequently in the descriptions of other people) are related to frequent use of the more extreme categories of a response scale. The assumption was made in the introductory section that priority and frequency of appearance of an attribute are indices of the degree of its importance to the subject. The confirmation of the initial prediction relating the importance of an attribute to higher frequency of extreme judgements depends therefore on the possibility of validating this assumption.

Method

A separate experiment was conducted for this purpose. The first stage of the procedure was identical to the first stage of the experiment previously described: a group of twenty-one male subjects (students at Ruskin College) who did not take part in the first experiment described personal characteristics of young men in the set of ten photographs used in the previous experiment, and projected in the same way on a screen. An independent judge went through each subject's descriptions and reduced them to a smaller number of near-synonymous and non-overlapping clusters. Out of these, eight were again selected for each subject, four ranking highest in their combined frequency and priority, and four ranking lowest.

A list of eleven trait names was then prepared for each subject: four of these were the highest ranking attributes he had used, four the lowest ranking attributes, and three 'buffer' attributes were added, usually taken from another subject's list. These eleven attributes were then arranged in all their possible paired combinations (fifty-five in all), and each pair written on one page of a booklet separately prepared for each subject. Using a method devised by Ross (1939), the fifty-five pairs were so arranged that (i) each item was paired with every other item; (ii) each item appeared equally often at the top and at the bottom of a page; (iii) the same item was never involved in adjacent pairs; and (iv) as far as possible an item alternated from the top to the bottom of a page in its successive presentations.

Of the fifty-five pairs, only sixteen involved a choice between one of the four highest and one of the four lowest ranking attributes; i.e. only sixteen choices were directly relevant to the validation of the assumption about frequency and priority.

The second part of the experiment took place three weeks after the first session. Fifteen subjects were still available – some did not reappear, and some of the original descriptions could not be used as they mainly consisted of details about physical characteristics of the faces shown. The booklets were distributed to the subjects. The following instructions were given:

'The booklet in front of you contains a series of paired characteristics of people. I want you to attend carefully to each pair and to underline that item in the pair which you feel is more important in a person.

Sometimes the choice will be difficult, but please make a choice for every one of the pairs given.'

The hypothesis was that if the assumption relating the subjective importance of an attribute to the priority and the frequency of its appearance was justified, then there should be a statistically significant preponderance of choices of the four highest ranking attributes as 'the more important in a person'.

Results

Table 7 sets out the relevant frequency distribution of the choices. It will be noted that none of the subjects chose less than seven high-ranking attributes and that most of them chose considerably more. The mean number of such choices is ten out of the sixteen possible ones.

The Chi square test for one sample was used to assess the statistical significance of the results on the assumption that under a null hypothesis an equal number of subjects would choose a majority of high-ranking attributes and a majority of low-ranking attributes. The observed distribution, which can be seen from Table 7, is as follows: twelve subjects chose a majority of high-ranking attributes; one subject chose an equal number from each of the two categories; two subjects chose a majority of low-ranking attributes. For this distribution $\chi^2 = 7.14$. It can therefore be concluded that the greater frequency of choice of high-ranking attributes as 'more important' is statistically significant at $p < 0.01$.

Table 7

Frequency distribution of choices of highest ranking attributes as 'more important'

Number of Ss	Number of highest ranking attributes chosen out of 16 possible choices
3	13
2	11
4	10
3	9
1	8
2	7
15	

(e) Conclusions and discussion

The results can be summarized as follows:

(i) Attributes which appear early and which are repeated frequently in

112

free descriptions of other people tend to be assigned more extreme ratings than attributes which have low frequency and priority.

(ii) This is an overall finding. It conceals the fact that a significantly higher frequency of such extreme ratings was found only for the distribution of the unfavourable judgements. The favourable judgements show a tendency in the same direction, but this tendency does not reach statistical significance.

(iii) Attributes which have high rank in terms of frequency and priority tend to be judged as 'more important in a person' than the low-ranking attributes.

(iv) The ratings made by our subjects show a consistent preponderance of favourable judgements about other people.

This last finding is quantitatively more convincing than all the others. There are, however, several reservations in the way of interpreting it as a general phenomenon. First, our subjects and the young men shown in the photographs had a good deal in common: age, nationality, probably much of their background. Secondly, the subjects knew that their ratings would be subsequently seen by the experimenters: presumably many of them would hesitate to produce gratuitously a string of spiteful judgements about people who were unknown to them.

None of these reservations seems to hold in relation to the first finding. There are no apparent reasons which could determine a greater use of the extreme rating categories for one class of attributes rather than for another. It must not be forgotten that the *content* of these classes changed from subject to subject; an attribute which appeared as salient for one subject often appeared as non-salient for another, or did not appear at all in other lists. The only common feature of the division of attributes was the one determined in advance: in terms of the criteria of priority and frequency. Despite these variations in content, the results, though not quantitatively impressive, show a marked degree of consistency.

This consistency is more marked for the unfavourable than for the favourable judgements; but this finding is perhaps less mysterious than it appears to be. It is well in line with the initial prediction considered in the light of the data. The prediction referred to a greater use of extreme-judgement categories for the salient attributes. The extreme categories were defined in advance as the two outer pairs of rating points at the favourable end and the unfavourable ends of the rating scale; but, in view of the skewed distribution of judgements, the unfavourable extremes are more extreme for our groups of subjects than the favourable ones. The overall median of ratings is not at the neutral point of 0, but somewhere between 0 and +1.

This skewness of extreme choices is also in line with results reported by Hovland and Sherif (1952) whose subjects tended to cluster their ratings of statements at the end of the scale far removed from their own position on the issue. This clustering tendency was less marked at the end of the scale near to the subject's own position. If one defines 'position' in our experiments in terms of the subjects' general tendency to view rather favourably the people whose characteristics they were requested to evaluate, then our finding bears a close similarity to the one reported by Hovland and Sherif.[4]

The fourth finding concerning the assumption about priority and frequency establishes – in conjunction with the other findings – the validity of the hypothesis as initially formulated: that in the evaluation of other people's characteristics there is a tendency to use more extreme judgements for those attributes which are more important to the rater.

Two final points, related to those raised earlier in the introduction to this section, remain to be made. First, that the findings reported here are coherent with, and extend the scope of, a general judgement phenomenon already established in related fields and discussed previously. Secondly, the generalizations emerging from the present study can be applied as predictions and checked without too much difficulty in a variety of 'real', out-of-laboratory situations. Knowing what is important to the rater may enable us to predict how and when he will tend to use his more extreme judgements. This information about salience is quite often available: for example, when we know someone fairly well, or when we are confronted with situations in which the aims and the functions of judgements are clearly defined, as is the case in various selection interviews.

4. Accentuation of social similarities and differences: two examples in ethnic stereotypes

(a) Introduction

If we return to the theoretical scheme outlined in chapter 4, the polarization of judgements of *certain* kinds of personal attributes described in the preceding section of the present chapter would represent an 'abstract' equivalent of a pv series (see Table 5, chapter 4); i.e. of a series in which differences between the stimuli have a value connotation to those making the judgements. The two studies described in the present section make a simultaneous shift in two different directions: from judgements of individuals to judgements of groups; and correspondingly

---

[4] This assymetry of polarization, which has been found in various contexts of judgement, was later extensively studied and discussed by Eiser and his collaborators. For a recent review and analysis see Eiser, 1980.

– from judgements of single stimuli to judgements which are made as a function of the *class* to which the stimuli belong. In terms of the notation employed in chapter 4, we are concerned here with series on which a c_1 classification has been superimposed.

The two studies do not, however, explore the same aspects of a c_1 classification. It will be remembered that in the experiments on judging lengths of lines, two predictions were made about the effects on judgements of a c_1 classification, that is a classification biserially correlated with a progression in the dimension being judged. The first of these predictions was that differences between stimuli belonging to the two classes will be accentuated as compared with differences between identical stimuli which were not classified in this manner. This prediction received clear support in the data (see e.g. Fig. 1 in this chapter). The second prediction was that a corresponding effect of a c_1 classification would be a subjective *decrease* in the differences between the stimuli belonging to the same class. In two of the three relevant conditions in the experiments on judgements of length, this decrease in intra-class differences was neither clear nor consistent. In the third condition, however, the effect of a c_1 classification on the decrease in the subjective intra-class differences was very marked. This was when the whole series of stimuli was judged several more times during the *same* experimental session, i.e. when the subjects acquired more continuous experience with the classification. The consequent 'decrease in the intra-class differences compared with the corresponding decrease in each of the two control groups was significant in both cases at $p < 0.01$'. Some of the possible reasons for this lack of confirmation in the first two conditions and a clear confirmation of the hypothesis in the third condition were discussed earlier in this chapter.

The phenomenon of relative decrease in intra-class differences is explored in this section in a setting very different from the Spartan conditions in which the simple judgements of length previously described were given. We move directly to a fundamental aspect of stereotyped judgements of other people. A social stereotype consists of assigning certain traits in common to individuals who are members of a group and also of attributing to them certain differences in common from members of other groups. A direct inference from our previous discussion of a c_1 classification is that, as a result of stereotyping, individuals who are members of a social group to which a stereotype is applied should be judged as more similar to each other *only* in certain attributes; namely, in those of their assumed characteristics which form part of the culturally accepted stereotype of their group.

The discussion of the Canadian study by Lambert *et al.* (1960), which

115

follows the 'similarity' study, explored another major effect of a c_1 classification: the increased accentuation of *differences* between social groups when a classification is combined with a value differential, in the manner previously described for the (c_1v) series.

Two further points need to be made in this introduction. The first is that the Canadian origin of both studies described here is a pure coincidence. One resulted from a month's visit to the University of Western Ontario in the early part of 1964; the other, from a brief visit to Wallace Lambert at McGill University in the autumn of 1958. The second point is that neither the study on stereotyped similarities nor the reinterpretation of the data of Lambert *et al.* have been selected for inclusion here because, by themselves, they are assumed to provide a satisfactory validation of the general principles of social categorization discussed in some of the previous chapters. The reasons for their selection is that both, despite their experimental origins, happen to sail fairly close to the wind of 'social reality'. In the case of the Western Ontario study this is so, as will be seen, because of the relatively 'natural' conditions in which the judgements of the individuals belonging to the stereotyped groups were obtained; in the case of the Montreal study, because the issues involved in it have proved, in the twenty years since it was conducted, to be of increasing social and political importance in Canada. As has just been said, these studies do not *prove* anything; but they provide useful indications that the introduction of certain experimental 'controls' need not create an unbridgeable gap between such controlled studies and 'real' social situations.

(b) Content of stereotypes and the inference of similarity between members of stereotyped groups

The purpose of this study was to test the hypothesis of minimization of differences within a class in the context of stereotyped judgements. The hypothesis can be formulated as follows: individuals of an ethnic group are perceived as being more similar with regard to traits which form a part of the stereotype concerning that group than with regard to traits which are not considered to be characteristic of that group. In addition, the study set out to test this hypothesis in a situation in which judgements made by the subjects approached as nearly as possible judgements that would have been made by them in a natural setting.

A stereotype about an ethnic group is generally defined in terms of a consensus of opinion concerning the traits attributed to that group. If subjects are presented with a list of attributes and asked to indicate those which they believe apply to a specific group, those chosen most frequently can be assumed to belong to the culturally held stereotype,

116

and those selected least frequently not to be part of it. This method of eliciting stereotypes has been used in a number of studies (e.g. Gilbert, 1951; Katz and Braly, 1933), and it has been demonstrated that such stereotypes remain relatively constant over long periods of time (e.g. Child and Doob, 1943; Gilbert, 1951; Katz and Braly, 1933; Meenes, 1943).

Most studies on the effects of stereotypes have generally been conducted under conditions where subjects obtain a minimum of information about the individual members of the groups which they are requested to characterize. Photographs, recorded voices and written characterizations have generally been used as stimuli. In such situations the effects of stereotypes are likely to be more pronounced than they might be in 'real life': the paucity of specific information about the individual causes the subjects to fall back on what they know, or think they know, about the ethnic group to which that individual belongs. In addition, few of the studies have attempted to demonstrate that specific individuals of an ethnic group were actually attributed traits which are presumed characteristic of that ethnic group. Sheikh (1963) made such an attempt in his study. His subjects first rated on twenty-five traits two Indians (from India) and two Canadians who were interviewed in front of them in a fairly free and unstructured situation. Some time later, the same subjects rated on the same twenty-five rating scales 'people from India' and 'Canadians' in general. As will be seen below, closer relationships were found for the Indians than for the Canadians between the general stereotype and the ratings of the individual members of the national groups. These results raise some problems with regard to the possible interaction between the two sets of judgements; they are, however, tangential to our present purpose.

The data for the present study were drawn in part from Sheikh's investigation, but since that study was not designed to test the present hypothesis, additional data had to be gathered to permit its testing.

Method

Two groups of students enrolled in undergraduate psychology courses acted as subjects. One group (Sheikh's study) was tested in April 1962, the other in January 1964.

Twenty-five subjects were tested in 1962 in two testing sessions. During the first session, subjects were asked to listen carefully to each of four interviews which would be conducted in front of the class and after each interview to rate the interviewee on a series of seven-point descriptive scales. Each interview lasted approximately eight minutes. For the first two interviews, a male Canadian and then a male Indian (from India) individually discussed their views concerning films. Then two other males, one Canadian and one Indian, were individually interviewed about their favourite books.

Each of the interviews were partly rehearsed in that the interviewees had been previously contacted and told of the kind of questions they would be asked. While a pattern of questions was prepared in advance, it was freely varied so that interviews were relatively spontaneous and reflected somewhat unrehearsed reactions to the questions. Subjects rated each interviewee immediately after the interview was terminated. The ratings were made on twenty-five semantic differential scales (Osgood, *et al.*, 1957).

One week later the same twenty-five subjects rated the concepts 'people from India' and 'Canadians' on semantic differential scales identical to those used to rate the interviewees.

A second group of thirty-seven subjects were tested in January 1964. They were presented with twenty-five adjectives, one from each of the scales referred to above, and asked to select those which they thought characterized most people from India and those which described most Canadians. They were invited to add adjectives not included in the list if they thought that these were useful in the descriptions of members of the two groups. The adjective used to represent each scale was previously determined by the ratings which the previous group of 1962 had given to the concepts 'people from India' or 'Canadians'. For each scale, the mean rating was determined and the adjectival end closest to that mean rating was selected to be included in the list.

The hypothesis of a more marked minimization of differences for traits which are part of a stereotype than for those which are not can now be stated as follows: the traits which were assigned the most frequently to people from India and to Canadians by the subjects who characterized these groups in 1964 can be considered as more closely approaching the respective stereotypes than the traits which were assigned to these groups least frequently. Therefore the inference from the hypothesis would be that the judged differences between the two 'real' members of each of the national groups should be smaller for the first class of traits than for the second in the ratings of another and comparable groups of subjects tested independently in 1962.

Results

Since it is necessary to determine first which adjectives were included in the stereotypes of people from India and Canadians, the results of the group of subjects tested in 1964 are presented first. Table 8 presents the frequency with which each of the twenty-five adjectives was chosen as descriptive of people from India and Canadians. The first adjective in each pair (see Table 8) was the one presented in the list of adjectives; the second adjective (in brackets) is its opposite on the semantic differential scale, and was not presented in the list of adjectives. These adjectival descriptions of people from India and Canadians cannot therefore be unambiguously assumed to represent *the* stereotypes about these two groups. If other adjectives had been included, it is quite possible that some would have been chosen more frequently. The ordinal positions indicated in Table 8 describe the extent to which the adjectives with higher frequency of assignment approach the stereotype of people from India and Canadians.

The nine adjectives chosen most frequently to characterize people

Table 8
Frequency with which adjectives were selected to characterize two ethnic groups

People from India	F	Canadians	F
Spiritualistic (materialistic)	26	Conservative (progressive)	28
Religious (irreligious)	24	Sociable (unsociable)	27
Family-oriented (self-oriented)	20	Friendly (unfriendly)	25
Submissive (dominant)	20	Peace-loving (quarrelsome)	21
Relaxed (tense)	19	Flexible (rigid)	20
Peace-loving (quarrelsome)	13	Optimistic (pessimistic)	16
Artistic (inartistic)	12	Follower (leader)	15
Follower (leader)	12	Talkative (taciturn)	14
Unassuming (boastful)	10	Neat (messy)	12
Friendly (unfriendly)	8	Praising (critical)	12
Considerate (inconsiderate)	7	Confident (diffident)	9
Complex (simple)	7	Family-oriented (self-oriented)	8
Emotional (unemotional)	7	Considerate (inconsiderate)	8
Subtle (obvious)	6	Complex (simple)	8
Romantic (unromantic)	5	Idealistic (practical)	6
Conservative (progressive)	5	Emotional (unemotional)	6
Imaginative (unimaginative)	4	Relaxed (tense)	6
Idealistic (practical)	4	Submissive (dominant)	6
Neat (messy)	4	Unassuming (boastful)	5
Flexible (rigid)	4	Imaginative (unimaginative)	4
Optimistic (pessimistic)	3	Romantic (unromantic)	3
Confident (diffident)	3	Artistic (inartistic)	2
Talkative (taciturn)	3	Religious (irreligious)	2
Praising (critical)	2	Spiritualistic (materialistic)	2
Sociable (unsociable)	1	Subtle (obvious)	1

The first of each pair of adjectives were included in the list; the adjectives in brackets are their polar opposites on the rating scales.

from India were selected as representing the stereotype about Indians (within the restriction of the adjectives presented). The nine adjectives selected least frequently were used to indicate those traits which were definitely not part of that stereotype.

Because of ties in the frequency with which certain adjectives were selected, the stereotype of Canadians was defined as consisting of the seven most frequently chosen adjectives; the seven least frequently chosen adjectives were selected as those not representing the Canadian stereotype.

The major hypothesis previously formulated was that individuals belonging to the same ethnic group will be judged as more similar to one another on traits which are part of the stereotype applying to their group than on traits which are not part of the stereotype. Consequently the mean difference score of each subject's rating of the two Indian interviewees on the nine traits which were selected as part of the Indian stereotype was compared with that obtained from the nine traits not included in the stereotype. A non-parametric sign test indicated that the two Indians were rated more similarly on the traits included in the stereotype than those not in the stereotype ($p < 0.011$, one-tailed test).

A similar analysis was performed on the mean difference scores for the ratings of the two Canadian individuals on the seven traits included in the stereotype compared with those seven not included. The non-parametric sign test was significant ($p < 0.039$, one-tailed test).

As described in the Method section, each subject in the group tested in 1962 rated each interviewee as well as the two ethnic groups which were represented. Consequently, it was possible to determine a score for each subject on the similarity of his ratings of each interviewee and that interviewee's ethnic group. An index of stereotyped perception was determined by squaring the difference between each subject's rating of an interviewee on a particular trait and his corresponding rating of the appropriate ethnic group. These squared difference scores were totalled for the two interviewees of an ethnic group over the traits included in the stereotype and those not included in the stereotype, as defined on the basis of data from the second group of subjects. Non-parametric sign tests indicated that there was a significant difference ($p < 0.014$, one-tailed test) between the index of stereotyped perception of the Indian interviewees on those traits included in the stereotype as compared with those not in the stereotype. That is, on the stereotype traits the Indian interviewees were rated as being more similar to people from India than they were on those traits not included in the stereotype. A similar analysis for the Canadian interviewees indicated that the results were in the predicted direction (i.e. ratings of the two Canadians were more similar to ratings of Canadians on those traits included as part of the stereotype than on those not in the stereotype but this difference was not significant ($p < 0.115$, one-tailed test).

Discussion

Since numerous studies have demonstrated that ethnic stereotypes are relatively constant over long periods of time assuming no incident develops to change them, it appears reasonable to use the results of data obtained in 1964 as indicators of a stereotype existing in 1962. Even if such an assumption is not tenable it is none the less reasonable to assume that using such data would tend, if anything, to weaken the association between the data concerning stereotypes and those obtained from judgements of individual members of the ethnic groups. Notwithstanding this, it is clear from the results obtained that stereotypy of judgement did occur. Both the Indian and the Canadian interviewees were judged as more similar to the other interviewee of the same ethnic group on those traits included in the stereotype than on those not included. That is, evidence was presented indicating a minimization of the differences between members of an ethnic group on traits which subjectively characterize that group. This effect was stronger with reference to the Indians than for the Canadians. Such results are to be expected, since subjects are much more likely to respond to individual differences when judging members of their own group than when judging outgroup members. Despite this, however, it is clear that stereotypes were operating in both instances to reduce judged differences between individuals within an ethnic group.

Although minimization of differences in judging members of an ethnic group suggests that a stereotype is operating, it does not demonstrate what stereotype it is. It is possible, for example, that university students have a stereotype about Indian university students which is different from that concerning 'most people from India'. Such a possibility would result in a minimization of differences between individuals perceived to be Indian university students, but no conclusion could be reached as to whether these individuals were identified with the total ethnic group.

Since the objects of judgement in this study were live individuals reacting more or less spontaneously in a reasonably natural setting, it seems clear that stereotypes do in fact operate in the 'real world' where information additional to that concerning ethnic group membership is transmitted to the observer. The interviewees in this study were cautioned not to give explicit information to the subjects which would aid in the ratings, but were told to react as spontaneously as they could to the questions. The material discussed was relatively neutral and provided little information of direct use to the subjects, but it is just such situations to which individuals normally respond. Even under such free situations, it is clear that ethnic group stereotypes operated to effect the subjects' judgements of the individuals in a manner consonant with the hypothesis.

(c) Twenty years ago: some problems of French identity in Montreal

Lambert *et al.* (1960) have reported a study which is of uncommon interest for our understanding of the functioning of stereotypes. Some aspects of the study seem to be of special theoretical importance, and the results, though they appear to be unexpected in some ways, are consistent with general considerations about the nature of shifts in judgements.

Lambert's subjects were groups of French-speaking and English-speaking Montreal students. They were asked to evaluate the personality characteristics of four bilingual speakers who recorded on tape French and English versions of a two and a half minute passage of prose. The subjects were not aware of the fact that each speaker read the passage in both languages, 'so that the evaluational reactions to the two language guises could be matched for each speaker'. The cumulative results for all the speakers showed that the English subjects evaluated the English speakers more favourably on seven out of fourteen traits; the French subjects evaluated the *English* speakers more favourably on ten out of fourteen traits. Already at this general level, and without further analysis, this finding is of interest: it contradicts the over-simplified view that national stereotypes are determined by an autistic, uncritical, and wish-fulfilling image of one's own group, especially when this group is contrasted with another in a context of latent or explicit tension or conflict.

Lambert *et al.* examine and reject a number of explanations which might account for the French preference of the English speakers:

(1) The possibility that the lower rating of the French speakers by the French subjects was due to the selection by the experimenters of traits which did not have 'value' for French-speaking Canadians. This does not meet the facts, as some of the traits used were rated as highly desirable by the French group of subjects.

(2) The possibility that the results were due to 'the greater probability in the Montreal community of finding English people in more powerful social and economic positions', and therefore to the existence of powerful stereotypes common to both sections of the community. This would not explain the emergence in the data of the fact that the French group makes a *greater use* of these stereotypes than the English group.

(3) The possibility that data from various questionnaires designed to elicit the subjects' attitudes towards their own and the contrast groups might yield some convincing correlations with the ratings of voices. Lambert *et al.* conclude 'that the comparatively unfavourable perception of French speakers is essentially independent of the perceivers' attitudes towards French and English groups'.

Our main interest is in the judged *differences* in various traits between the French and English guises of the speakers in the Lambert *et al.* study. These differences provide a clue to the finding that on some traits the French subjects, as compared with the English subjects, underrate the French, or overrate the English, speakers. There exists in the Montreal community a discrepancy in socio-economic status in favour of the English group. Both groups of subjects were aware of this: when estimating the likely occupations of the speakers, they ascribed significantly higher status to the English than to the French guises.

This in itself does not account for the findings for reasons already discussed. However, the fact is established that the classification into French and English was correlated with socio-economic status, both objectively and subjectively. The subjects judged the speakers on a number of traits: some of these traits were related to socio-economic status or success, some not. So far, the situation was identical for the French and English groups of subjects. The only difference between the groups was in *the relevance* to them of the Franco–English discrepancy. It is a fair assumption that this discrepancy caused more concern, was in a sense more salient, worrying, and relevant to the French than to the English subjects, especially as the French subjects were all college students, future direct competitors of the English group. If this is so, *some* differences between the French and the English were of greater impact to them than to their English counterparts. Therefore, the prediction could be made that the classification into French and English would determine larger shifts in both directions for the French group on those dimensions which are correlated with the 'value' or relevant aspect of this classification – the socio-economic status.

The comparison between the judgements of the French and the English subjects should show that (a) the French subjects tend to accentuate the English superiority on traits related to socio-economic success more than the English subjects; (b) the French subjects, as compared with the English subjects, should not show this trend on traits not related to socio-economic success.

The comparison *within* the French group of judgements on traits related to socio-economic success with those on traits not related to it, should show greater accentuation of differences in favour of the English on the former than on the latter.

Lambert *et al.* reported that the English of their four speakers was 'faultless'. As to their French, two of them (Cou and Bla) spoke with a French-Canadian accent, one (Leo) 'spoke with a marked French-Canadian accent characteristic of those who work in the "bush"' (they described it later as a 'caricatured French-Canadian'), and the fourth (Tri) 'spoke French with an accent that was judged indistinguishable from that used in France'. If the French of the French guises was identified in this way by the French group of subjects, the inference from the predictions just stated would be that the French subjects would accentuate the differences in the relevant traits between the French and English guises in their judgements of the first two speakers; they should still be concerned, but perhaps less so, with the 'bush' accent; and not at all concerned with the 'Parisian' accent.

Table 1 in the Lambert *et al.* study provides all the data needed to assess these inferences. It contains quantitative statements of significance of differences in evaluations of each trait for each speaker between his French and English guises for both groups of subjects.

These data have been reclassified (see Table 9) into eight classes. The first six columns contain traits for which there are significant differences between the judgements of the English and the French guises of the same speaker, the last two the non-significant ones.

The columns in the table contain the traits on which:

A. Both groups of subjects judged the English guise of a speaker more favourably than his French guise.
B. Both groups of subjects judged the French guise more favourably.
C. English group judged the English guise more favourably.
D. French group judged the English guise more favourably.
E. English group judged the French guise more favourably.
F. French group judged the French guise more favourably.
G. In the English group no significant differences were noted between the English and French guises of a speaker.
H. In the French group no significant differences were noted between the English and the French guises of a speaker.

As can be seen from Table 9, the patterns for Bla and Cou, the two French-Canadian accents, are almost identical. Both groups agreed that the English guises were better looking and taller. However, the French group had for both a cluster of traits (leadership, intelligence, self-confidence, dependability, sociability) clearly related to socio-economic success in which it judged the differences between the French and the English guises to be significantly in favour of the English; for the English subjects all these traits can be found in the non-significant column (G).

124

A reclassification of data from the Lambert et al. study

Speaker	A	B	C	D	E	F	G	H
COU	Height Good looks Character		Kindness Likeability	Leadership Sense of humour Intelligence Self-confidence Dependability Ambition Sociability			Leadership Sense of humour Intelligence Religiousness Self-confidence Dependability Entertainingness Ambition Sociability	Religiousness Entertainingness Kindness Likeability
BLA	Height Good looks Ambition		Kindness	Leadership Intelligence Self-confidence Dependability Sociability Character		Religiousness Kindness	Leadership Sense of humour Intelligence Religiousness Self-confidence Dependability Entertainingness Sociability Character Likeability	Sense of humour Entertainingness Likeability
LEO	Height Good looks Intelligence Dependability Ambition Character		Sense of humour	Leadership Self-confidence Sociability Likeability		Kindness	Religiousness Self-confidence Entertainingness Kindness Sociability Likeability Leadership	Sense of humour Religiousness Entertainingness
TRI			Height Intelligence Dependability		Sense of humour Entertainingness Sociability	Self-confidence	Good looks Leadership Religiousness Self-confidence Kindness Ambition Character Likeability	Height Good looks Leadership Sense of humour Intelligence Religiousness Dependability Entertainingness Kindness Ambition Character Likeability Sociability

125

To this can be added 'character' for Bla where the difference is significant for the French subjects and not significant for the English; and, in the same way, 'ambition' for Cou. For Bla, the French guise is at the favourable end for the French subjects on the traits of religiousness and kindness, not related in any clear manner to socio-economic success. For Cou, these traits are in the non-significant column (H).

The pattern for Leo, the 'bush' accent, is similar, apart from two differences: the French subjects significantly disliked him – or liked him less than his English counterpart; and the English subjects joined the French in estimating his intelligence and dependability to be significantly lower than that of his English counterpart.

The case of the 'Parisian' Tri is strikingly different. The French subjects did not think that the English were better at anything than he was. The entire 'success' cluster travels from column D to column H. A comparison between the judgements of the French and the English subjects shows that the differences in these traits are not relatively accentuated in favour of the English guise by the French subjects.

In summary, it seems that the hypothesis of accentuated differences in the judgement dimensions relevant to a value classification does account for the results of the Lambert *et al.* study. For the French group of subjects the differences between the English and the French in those traits which are relevant to socio-economic status were more pronounced than the same differences for the English group of subjects; these differences were in the direction, consistent with the classification, of *relatively* overrating the English or underrating the French. No such tendency was shown by the French subjects (a) for traits not relevant to socio-economic status (kindness, likeability, religiousness, entertainingness); (b) for traits relevant to socio-economic status, but inherent in an individual who is not 'one of them' in the Franco-English competition: a Frenchman from France.

6
Cognitive aspects of prejudice[1]

1. Introduction

The diffusion of public knowledge concerning laws which govern the physical, the biological and the social aspects of our world is neither peculiar to our times of mass communications nor to our own culture. These public images are as old as mankind, and they seem to have some fairly universal characteristics. The time of belief in a 'primitive mind' in other cultures has long been over in social anthropology. For example, at the turn of the century, Rivers (1905) could still write about differences in colour naming between the Todas and the Europeans in terms of the 'defective colour nomenclature of the lower races' (p. 392). Today, Lévi-Strauss (1966) bases much of his work on evidence showing the conceptual complexity of the understanding of the world in primitive cultures rooted in the 'science of the concrete' with its background of magic. As he wrote:

To transform a weed into a cultivated plant, a wild beast into a domestic animal, to produce, in either of these, nutritious or technologically useful processes which were originally completely absent or could only be guessed at; to make stout water-tight pottery out of clay which is friable and unstable, liable to pulverise or crack; to work out techniques, often long and complex, which permit cultivation without soil or alternatively without water; to change toxic roots or seeds into foodstuffs or again to use their poison for hunting, war or ritual – there is no doubt that all these achievements required a genuinely scientific attitude, sustained and watchful interest, and a desire for knowledge for its own sake. For only a small proportion of observation and experiments (which must be assumed to have been primarily inspired by a desire for knowledge) could have yielded practical and immediately useful results (pp. 14–15).

At the same time, the new anthropological disciplines of ethnobotany

[1] Reprinted (with minor changes) from the *Journal of Biosocial Science*, 1969, Supplement No. 1, 173–91. The article was awarded the first annual Gordon Allport Intergroup Relations Prize by the Society for the Psychological Study of Social Issues (SPSSI). Its inclusion in this book has a purpose additional to that of providing a link between the previous chapters, mainly concerned with the study of judgement processes, and the one to follow which takes a much more definite 'social' stance. It is also meant to express my debt to, and admiration for, the late Gordon Allport who was a great mentor and a good friend.

and ethnozoology are concerned with the study of biological classifications developed in primitive societies, and with the principles underlying these classifications. We are very far indeed from Rivers's 'defective nomenclatures'.

An image of Man emerges from these considerations, and from very many others. When we think of human attempts to understand the physical or the biological environment, Man appears essentially as an exploring and rational animal, stumbling heavily on his way, pulled back by his insufficiencies and stupidities, but still imperfectly rational, still engaged in what Sir Frederick Bartlett (1932) called many years ago the 'effort after meaning'. This effort does not translate itself into some mystical concept of a 'group mind'. It works within the limits imposed by the capacities of individual human minds, and within the socially-determined processes of the diffusion of knowledge. It is essentially a rational model, however imperfect the exploring rationality often appears to be. But there seems to be one exception to this model, one set of problems for the consideration of which we seem to have adopted a very different set of ideas. It is as if we were suddenly dealing with a different and strange animal that uses some of his abilities to adapt to some aspects of his environment, and is quite incapable of using them in order to adapt to others. The prevailing model of Man as a creature trying to find his way in his social environment seems to have nothing in common with the ideas of exploration, of meaning, of understanding, of rational consistency. We have the rational model for natural phenomena; we seem to have nothing but a blood-and-guts model for social phenomena. In this new blood-and-guts romanticism so fashionable at present in some science and semi-science, Man's attitudes and beliefs concerning the social environment are seen mainly as a by-product of tendencies that are buried deeply in his evolutionary past or just as deeply in his unconscious.

This seems to be particularly true in a field in which the acquisition of knowledge about the springs of human behaviour is perhaps the most urgent and ominous task confronting us at present. This is the field of relations between large human groups which includes, of course, race relations and international relations. The psychological aspects of inter-group relations include the study of behaviour in intergroup situations, of behaviour related to these situations, and of beliefs and attitudes concerning an individual's own group and various other groups which are relevant to him. The competitive or cooperative, hostile or friendly, relations between groups are determined, to a very large extent, by the logic of the situations within which they arise. Once this is taken for granted it is equally true that these situations have their effects on the motives and attitudes of millions of individuals, that these motives and attitudes in turn determine behaviour, and that this behaviour partly determines in turn the subsequent relations between the groups.

A psychological theory of intergroup relations must provide a two-way link between situations and behaviour, and it can do this through an analysis of the motivational and the cognitive structures which intervene between the two. But it is in this analysis that Man's search to understand his environment often seems to be forgotten, and a peculiar one-way causation is established. In this, ideas and beliefs seem to be considered as no more than projections and rationalizations of powerful motivational forces, and somehow or other it has implicitly been taken for granted that inferences can be made directly from motivation and the evolutionary past of the species to complex intergroup behaviour without paying much attention to the flimsy cognitive by-products thrown out as if at random by the subterranean springs of emotion and 'instinct'. Our image of a social man is that of a man who has lost his reason. Otherwise, the argument usually runs, how can we explain the perennial hostility of man to man? Not much attention has been paid to the fact that cooperation between groups also needs to be explained; or that hostility need not be based on unconscious motivational factors, that it can also follow as a result of attempts to explain to oneself in the simplest and most convenient way the causal sequence of relations between groups.

Two intellectual traditions form the background from which arises this denial of the autonomy of cognitive functioning. One consists of extrapolating from the background of animal behaviour to human behaviour in complex social situations; the other, of assuming that theories of unconscious motivation provide the necessary and sufficient basis for the understanding of social attitudes. There is no shortage in either of these trends of thought of carefully considered attempts to look in all directions before leaping. But it is just as true that the general climate of opinion favours the blood-and-guts model which at present is having quite a run. It has been blessed and speeded on its way by a number of books, some of which have quickly become bestsellers. The act of blessing has been performed not only in the protected gentility of academic discussions; it has burst through again and again to the public forum owing to serialization in newspapers, television appearances and other public pronouncements. And thus, suddenly, tentative views concerning a complex problem about which we know very little have become public property and are already being used here and there to buttress and justify certain political opinions and actions.

The relevance to this discussion of both the biological and the

psycho-analytic points of view has been succinctly summarized by
Lorenz (1964) when he wrote:

> There cannot be any doubt, in the opinion of any biologically-minded scientist,
> that intraspecific aggression is, in Man, just as much of a spontaneous instinctive
> drive as in most other higher vertebrates. The beginning synthesis between the
> findings of ethology and psycho-analysis does not leave any doubt either, that
> what Sigmund Freud has called the 'death drive' is nothing else but the
> miscarrying of this instinct which, in itself, is as indispensable as any other (p.
> 49).

I do not wish to quarrel on this occasion with all of this statement and
to discuss its several ambiguities. From the point of view of the present
discussion, its major difficulty lies in the gaps which persist when the
usual extrapolations are made to complex social behaviour in Man.
There is no doubt that under *some* conditions all men can and do display
hostility towards groups other than their own, be they social, national,
racial, religious or any other. There is also no doubt, however, that
under other conditions this hostility either does not appear or can be
modified. The scientifically-minded biologist (as distinct from Lorenz's
biologically-minded scientist) would have to specify for us in the case of
human behaviour, as he does so often and so successfully for animal
behaviour, the invariances of the waxing and waning of the aggressive
drive. Until he does so, statements such as that of Lorenz are just about
as useful as would be statements relating the development of the rich
variety of gastronomic traditions to our undeniably innate need for food
and drink, or as have been the attempts to explain the complex forms of
the use of language with the help of a few basic laws of conditioning.

It is hardly startling to say that the best way to predict whether a
person will harbour hostile attitudes towards a particular group and what
will be the content of these attitudes is to find out how he understands
the intergroup situation. And it is hardly any more startling to say that
this understanding will in turn affect his behaviour. This does not mean,
of course, that emotional and motivational factors are unimportant. But
it is just as true that the greatest adaptive advantage of the human species
is its capacity to modify its behaviour as a function of the way in which
individuals perceive and understand a situation. It is difficult to see why
it should be assumed that they lose this capacity as soon as they confront
human groups other than their own, and that it is in these situations
alone that most of their concepts, attitudes, beliefs and modes of thinking
are no more than powerless and pale projections of instinctive or
unconscious drives.

It is not, however, the purpose of this chapter to present a detailed methodological analysis of inferences about complex social behaviour that are made from some of the more extreme positions in ethology and in psycho-analysis. At any rate, their present importance lies more perhaps in their impact on public opinion than in the durable scientific contributions that they are likely to make to the study of intergroup relations.

We know only too well that prejudice is part and parcel of intergroup relations, and in particular of race relations. Klineberg (1968), for example, proposed the following general definition:

The English term 'prejudice' and its equivalents in many other European languages refer primarily to a prejudgement or a preconcept reached before the relevant information has been collected or examined and therefore based on inadequate or even imaginary evidence. In contemporary social science this notion has been retained but is usually regarded as constituting only one aspect of the complex phenomenon of prejudice, namely, the conceptual, or cognitive, aspect – the ideas or opinions we have about those individuals or groups who are the objects of such prejudgement. (The term 'stereotype' is usually applied to this aspect.) Prejudice also involves an attitude for or against, the ascription of a positive or negative value, an affective, or feeling, component. Usually there is in addition a readiness to express in action the judgements and feelings which we experience, to behave in a manner which reflects our acceptance or rejection of others: this is the conative, or behavioural, aspect of prejudice. (The resulting actions are also described as representing varying degrees of discrimination.) Prejudice may therefore be defined as an unsubstantiated prejudgement of an individual or group favourable or unfavourable in character, tending to action in a consonant direction (p. 439).

In the context of Klineberg's definition, the purpose of this chapter is to present an outline of the cognitive etiology of prejudice, mainly with regard to its *unfavourable* aspects. The principal argument will be clear from the preceding general considerations: it is that the etiology of intergroup relations cannot be properly understood without the help of an analysis of their cognitive aspects, and also that this analysis cannot be derived from statements about motivation and about instinctive behaviour. We live in a social environment which is in constant flux. Much of what happens to us is related to the activities of groups to which we do or do not belong; and the changing relations between these groups requires constant readjustments of our understanding of what happens and constant causal attributions about the why and the how of the changing conditions of our life. These attributions are based on three processes which will be discussed in turn. They are the processes of categorization, of assimilation and of search for coherence.

2. Categorization

Much work has been done in social psychology on the so-called stereotypes which can be defined as the attribution of general psychological characteristics to large human groups. There is no doubt that the content of various stereotypes has its origins in cultural traditions, which may or may not be related to over-generalized common experience, past or present. But what is perhaps more important is their general structure and function. As the late Gordon Allport (1954) and many others pointed out, stereotypes arise from a process of categorization. They introduce simplicity and order where there is complexity and nearly random variation. They can help us to cope only if fuzzy differences between groups are transmuted into clear ones, or new differences created where none exist. They represent, of course, tendencies towards simplification rather than sharp dichotomies: in other words, in each relevant situation we shall achieve as much stereotyped simplification as we can without doing unnecessary violence to the facts. But there is good evidence that even when facts do turn against us and destroy the useful and comfortable distinctions, we still find ways to preserve the general content of our categories.

In a rather formal way, the problem of stereotypes is that of the relation between a set of attributes which vary on continuous dimensions and classifications which are discontinuous (see chapter 4). For example, classifications into nationalities or racial groups are, on the whole, discontinuous; most people are clearly X or Y and rarely something rather indefinable in between. Height of people or colour of skin are continuous dimensions. If it were true that all the Scandinavians were taller than all the Italians, we would have a perfect bi-serial correlation; and one could predict the class membership of an item from its value on a certain dimension, and vice versa, despite the fact that these values were not the original criterion on which the classification was based. It will be obvious that theoretically the possible bi-serial correlations of that nature may vary all the way from fully predictable relations to cases where there is no relationship at all; and that in the world of human groups there will be very many cases where there is no relationship, hardly any 'perfect' ones, and quite a number which show a strong positive correlation, such as, for example, some physical characteristics associated with race.

Three empirical statements need to be inserted at this point, all of which are based both on common experience and on a good deal of evidence from experimental work in social psychology. The first is that personal traits or characteristics can be empirically treated as dimensions much in the same way as height and weight would be if we could conceive them only in comparative terms of 'more' and 'less', 'shorter' and 'longer', 'heavier' and 'lighter'. This is the kind of statement that I make if I say that someone is 'intelligent' or 'honest' or 'lazy'; these are essentially comparative judgements which could hardly be made in a vacuum of absolute assertions (see chapter 5).

The second statement is that, through personal and cultural experience, dimensions such as 'intelligent', 'lazy' or 'honest' are subjectively associated with classifications of people into groups. As long as we have little specific knowledge about an individual, we shall tend to ascribe to him the characteristics which we derive from our knowledge of his class membership, be it a class of trade unionists, undergraduates, animal lovers, or Patagonians. Two inferences follow directly: one is that, in many social situations which present notorious ambiguities of interpretation, it will always be easier to find supporting evidence for the assumed class characteristics of an individual than to find contradictory evidence. The second inference is perhaps socially more important: whenever we are confronted with the need to interpret the behaviour *en masse* of the members of a particular group, there is bound to be very little clear negative feedback following the ascription of this behaviour to the assumed class characteristics.

The third statement refers to two consequences of the tendency to simplify in order to cope. They are but two aspects of the same phenomenon and can be described as follows: when a classification is correlated with a continuous dimension, there will be a tendency to exaggerate the differences on *that* dimension between items which fall into distinct classes, and to minimize these differences within each of the classes (see chapters 4 and 5).

There is one obvious and essential difference between the judgements of lines in the experiments described in chapter 5 and stereotyped judgements of human beings when these are associated with prejudice. In the case of our lines it would have been enough to present some form of reward to the subjects for accurate judgements and to penalize them for the inaccurate ones in order to eliminate quite rapidly the biases that were obtained. This is certainly not the case when hostile stereotypes are used. Their rigidity and resistance to information which contradicts them is undoubtedly one of their most salient features. This does not present, however, much of a mystery. In the first place, judgements of human characteristics in complex social situations are much more uncertain and ambiguous than the judgements of lines in a laboratory setting. The negative feedback of contradictory information is therefore much less clear and much easier to ignore. In the second place, and this is probably more important, the consequences of a mistake in judgement are radically different in the two situations. If a man is prejudiced, he has an emotional investment in preserving the differentiations between his own group and the 'others'. Inaccurate judgements are not followed by the obvious dire consequences of inaccurate judgements about the physical properties of the environment. On the contrary, the preservation of these judgements is self-rewarding, and this is particularly so when prejudiced judgements are made in a social context strongly supportive of hostile attitudes towards a particular group. We are then confronted with a spiral effect in which the existence of prejudice at large not only provides additional support and rewards for hostile judgements; it also removes the possibility of a 'reality check' for these judgements which then feed upon each other and become more and more strongly entrenched in the form of powerful social myths.

3. Assimilation

The content of the categories to which people are assigned by virtue of their social identity is generated over a long period of time within a culture; the origin and development of these ideas are a problem for the social historian rather than for the psychologist. The task of the social psychologist is to discover how these images are transmitted to individual members of a society, and it is here that the second of the three processes previously mentioned, that of assimilation, comes into play.

The wider problem of assimilation of social information as a form of social learning is well beyond the scope of this chapter. I should like to concentrate on two points which appear the most relevant to the autonomy of cognitive functioning in attitudes towards other groups. One is concerned with the learning of evaluations (or preferences), the other with the balance that occurs early in life between a child's identification with his own group and the pressure of notions about various groups, including his own, which are generally accepted in his society.

In his work on the development of moral judgement in the child, Piaget (1932) described the transition from the stage in which the value of pronouncements are judged by their source rather than by their content, to a stage in which the child begins to interact and to cooperate with equals. At this point it is beginning to learn to take conceptually the role of the other. This ability 'to see the same data from more than one point of view' (Holmes, 1965, p. 134) is not only the basis for the development of intellectual operations, but also for 'the emergence of a new morality', the progress from constraint to cooperation. According to Piaget, this progress cannot take place when the child is exposed to only one source of information and 'when it remains in awe of this source of truth' (Holmes, 1965, p. 135). These tend to be precisely the conditions under which the child learns his socially-sanctioned truths about a variety of human groups other than his own. It is not surprising, then, that later in life the ordinary categories of moral judgement, governed by conceptual reciprocity, apply with difficulty to individual members of these groups or to the groups as a whole. Thus, 'bad' and 'good', even 'liked' or 'disliked' become incontrovertible statements of fact not different in their mode of assimilation from, for example, 'large' or 'small', (see chapters 9 and 10).

There are many minority groups in the world today which stand low in the evaluative pecking order of human groups that each society constructs for itself. If it were true that the identification with one's own group is based on some kind of a universal and self-generating process, then the fact that a group is considered as inferior in the social order should not considerably affect the affiliation with it shown by its own young children. If, on the other hand, a system of preferences in the society at large does affect all of its members, then children of the groups assumed to be inferior should be exposed to a conflict in which the progressive acquisition of their own group identity, and the formation of their own social self that goes with it, should clash with the ordering that is generally accepted and socially transmitted.

There are many relevant studies in existence. For example, Mary Goodman (1964), working in New England in the late forties, elicited by various means preferences for Negroes and whites in a group of nursery school children between the ages of three and a half and five and a half: 92% of the white children expressed a preference for their own group; the corresponding figure for Negro children was 26%. There is an earlier and famous study by Clark and Clark (1947) in which Negro nursery school children were shown a brown and a white doll and were asked which of the two they preferred and which of the two they looked like: 66% of the children identified themselves with the brown doll; exactly the same proportion expressed a preference for the *white* one; in an answer to another question, 59% declared that the brown doll 'looked bad'.

The sensitiveness of the children to the social context was particularly well brought out in a study conducted by Morland (1966). He worked with groups of nursery school children in Lynchburg, Virginia, and in Boston: 46% of Negro children expressed preference for their own group in Boston; only 22% did so in Lynchburg. The trend was reversed for the white children's preferences for their own group: the figure was 68% in Boston and 80% in Lynchburg. Similar results were obtained in an inter-racial situation less tense than in the United States. Vaughan (1964) found that, at the ages from four to eight, the proportion of Maori children in New Zealand expressing preference for their own group was about half of the corresponding proportion of the white children.[2]

All this evidence points to the high sensitivity of children to the context of social influences in which they live – even when these influences are at cross-purposes with the powerful forces working towards an identification with the child's own racial or ethnic group. The enduring basis for future prejudices and conflicts is laid most crucially in childhood. And – as might be expected – the sensitivity to the social context continues throughout life. This was well brought out in a study by Pettigrew (1958) who worked in South Africa and in the United States.

In South Africa, he applied three attitudes scales to his subjects: an F-scale roughly comparable to the one used by Adorno, Frenkel-Brunswik, Levinson and Sanford (1950); a C (conformity) scale and an A (anti-African) scale. The C-scale was nearly as predictive of the attitudes towards the Africans as was the F-scale; students born in Africa were found to be more prejudiced, but not more authoritarian, than those not born in Africa; the same was true of students belonging to the Nationalist party as compared with others; the Afrikaners 'are both more anti-African and more authoritarian, and, when the F-scale differences are corrected for, they remain significantly more hostile to the Africans' (p. 35). Results which point in the same direction were obtained by Pettigrew (1958) in a comparison of four small towns in Georgia and North Carolina with four similar locations in New England. He concluded that 'in areas with historically embedded traditions of racial intolerance, externalizing personality factors underlying prejudice remain important, but socio-cultural factors are unusually crucial and account for the heightened racial hostility' (p. 40). To this it may be added that the scores on the F-scale which are designed to elicit the personality correlates of prejudice are themselves by no means free of conforming influences in societies which display a high incidence of one form or another of an authoritarian ideology. Thus, Pettigrew's conclusion can be viewed as a rather conservative estimate of the psychological importance in prejudice of 'socio-cultural factors'.

4. Search for coherence

The process of categorization provides the mould which gives shape to

---

[2] For further evidence, see chapters 9 and 15. A summary of much of the work in this field together with a description of more recent studies can be found in Milner (1975).

intergroup attitudes, and the assimilation of social values and norms provides their content. But this does not tell us very much about the manner in which individuals react to specific intergroup situations which confront them and about the way in which they try to come to terms with constant changes that occur in these situations. It is here that the consideration of the third process previously mentioned, that of the search for coherence, may be of some help. Instead of introducing this search for coherence in general terms, I should like to illustrate it with an example. We were once piloting one of our studies on national attitudes in children (see chapters 9 and 10) in a primary school in a suburb of Vienna. A boy of about eleven was being interviewed and stated, like many others, his dislike for the Russians. He was then asked why he disliked the Russians. The answer was: 'because they occupied our country, and Hitler was their chief'.

If the individual is to adjust to the flux of social change, he must attempt to understand it: in other words, in order to deal with change an individual must make constant causal attributions about the processes responsible for it, and these attributions must fulfil at least two criteria: they must equip him to deal with new situations in a manner which appears consistent to him, and they must do this in a way which will preserve, as far as possible, his self-image or integrity. This need to preserve the integrity or the self-image is the only motivational assumption that we need to make in order to understand the direction that the search for coherence will take.

One of the most important classes of events within the stream of constant social change arises directly from the fact that an individual is a member of numerous social groups which interact with other groups. Theoretically, two types of change (and consequently, of the need for cognitive adjustment to change) can be distinguished: intragroup and intergroup. The former consists of the individual's changing circumstances within the group or groups to which he belongs; the latter, of those aspects of the changing relations of his group with other groups which affect directly some important aspects of his life. In both cases, he needs to build a cognitive structure which provides him with a satisfactory explanation of the causes of change. A 'satisfactory' explanation will manage to preserve personal integrity while at the same time – for reasons of cognitive economy – it will tend towards as much simplification as the situation allows for.

The effects of change – whether intra- or intergroup – on the manner in which an individual relates himself to his own group can only be of two kinds: an increase in the intensity of affiliation with the ingroup, or a decrease, i.e. alienation from it. In both cases, the change of attitude towards the group requires a causal attribution. In all cases in which this attribution is confined to social agents (as distinct from physical causes, such as natural catastrophes, etc.) it can go in two directions only: the determinants of change may be attributed to some characteristics and actions of the individual himself and/or other individuals; or they may be attributed to the characteristics and actions of his own and/or other groups.

It is this second category of causal attributions which is of interest here. All that we know about causal attributions regarding social events points to the conclusion that, unless situational explanations are easily available (and often even when they are), actions of others tend to be explained in terms of their individual and fairly permanent characteristics. In the case of individual attributions, this type of explanation provides obvious advantages in terms of simplification and of predictability of further events. There is no reason to assume that this need for simplification and for predictability is any less relevant in causal attributions to groups.

There are, however, some important differences: the first is that explanations in terms of group characteristics obviously must represent a considerably greater degree of simplification than in the case of individual characteristics; the second (already referred to) that, with regard to the predictability of future events, the feedback of causal attributions to group characteristics is much more complex, ambiguous, and difficult to interpret than in individual cases. It is therefore likely that internal requirements will play a much greater part in the causal attributions to groups, and that for the same reason these attributions will be much more resistant to change than the individual ones. However, the fact that group attributions are bound to be resistant to change does not mean that they can never change. If one considers a sequence of events which would generate individual causal attributions in one case and group attributions in another, the prediction is that the modification of the latter would lag much more behind the events than would that of the former. It is not the purpose of this chapter to suggest experimental designs; but it is certainly possible to think of experimental situations in which the relevant variables could be manipulated.

The requirement of simplification implies *ipso facto* that of personalization. If there is to be an explanation in terms of the characteristics of a group, these must be characteristics which are relevant to the situation and *common* to the group as a whole, with a corresponding neglect of individual differences between the members of a group. There is abundant evidence, both in the psychological literature and in common experience, of this personalization of even very large human groups.

138

Starting from this, some fairly general statements can be made:

(i) Any change in the *status quo* between social groups imposes a need to construct a causal explanation to account for the change on the individuals involved. This explanation can be of two kinds: (a) situational or (b) referring to the characteristics of the groups.

(ii) Situational explanations are in terms of preceding events that do not originate in the groups involved (such as a natural catastrophe). When events of this nature are not concrete, clear-cut, and easily discernible, causal attributions will tend to be made in terms of the characteristics of groups.

(iii) Causal attributions to group characteristics can be of two kinds: either referring to the non-psychological characteristics of a group (e.g. its wealth or power, ecological conditions in which it lives, its skin colour), or in terms of its psychological characteristics. This is, however, an uneasy distinction, since the non-psychological characteristics are often assumed to be related to, or be the cause of, various psychological characteristics, and vice-versa.

(iv) In view of this, a more appropriate dichotomy appears to be between explanations in terms of group attributes which are assumed to be situational, transitional and flexible, and those which are assumed to be inherent and immutable.

(v) Causal group attributions of complex social events must tend towards cognitive simplicity. Attributions in terms of 'inherent' group characteristics satisfy this requirement.

(vi) In their attribution of causality to inherent characteristics of groups, these 'ideologies' are also best fitted to shift the locus of responsibility for change either from the individual himself to a group, or from the ingroup to an outgroup. They will therefore be more likely to appear when other types of causal attributions either conflict with the prevailing values and beliefs, or represent a threat to the individual's self-image.

It follows therefore that not just *any* kind of intergroup conflict or competition should lead to the creation and spread of these attributions. It would be interesting to seek examples of those which do not end up in this way, and to recreate them experimentally. It would be equally interesting to create sequences in which the initial 'inherent' attribution weakens, despite the intergroup competition or conflict remaining, as a function of the disappearance of the conflict of values or of threat to the self-image. This is not easy, as that kind of social engineering has rarely been attempted, though some instances of it can be found in the management of industrial disputes.

Most changes in the structure of intergroup relations do tend to involve the creation of inherent ideologies with very little planned or unplanned social therapy in sight to deal with them. It is interesting that this occurs whether the position of a group deteriorates or improves; whether the group becomes better suited to fulfil the needs of its individual members, or is in the process of becoming less and less effective in doing so. The common feature of those determining conditions which result in inherent group ideologies is in their association with a conflict of values or with the threat to the individual's self-image.

As distinct from the previous case, examples here are only too easy to find. It may be of some interest, however, to mention one or two in order to illustrate the variety of pertinent conditions and the underlying uniformity of the postulated processes.

An improved group position and the resulting stronger affiliation of its members is often achieved at the cost of using the group's capacity to put another group at a disadvantage. This is, of course, a one-sentence history of colonialism and of related forms of successful expansion. One of the better examples can be found in the heyday of Victorian England; the principal beneficiary of the successful expansion was a social class which was also imbued with a fairly definite code of values and morals. The advantages accrued from the colonial gains had to be explained away in terms which would not conflict with the code – thus, 'white man's burden' with its conceptions of inherent superiority and inferiority quickly came into being. The ideologies themselves may vary in content depending upon the cultural background from which they arise – e.g. the religious elements in the hierarchy of human groups built by the Bible-carrying early Boers of South Africa, the 'degeneration' of other peoples in the blood myths of Nazi Germany going back to a background of the eighteenth and nineteenth centuries, the 'moral' justifications of slavery – but their formal features remain constant.

We witness today an interesting special case of this general category of processes. An intensified affiliation with a group is only possible when the group is capable of supplying some satisfactory aspects of an individual's social identity.[3] This can be defined as the attribution by the individual to the ingroup of certain characteristics from the sharing of which he derives some satisfaction; i.e. the group is an adequate reference group. The case of Negroes in the United States is one where the only clear definition of the group which is generally shared is in terms of skin colour, hardly a satisfactory point of reference. Many (or most) of the

[3] Part IV (chapters 11 to 15) of this book is devoted to a description of a theoretical framework concerned with this issue of 'social identity' and to its various implications for intergroup behaviour and social conflict.

other presumed attributes of the Negro group originate from the conceptions of it held by the outgroups. In a situation of increasing tension, a search for a satisfactory and distinctive definition of the ingroup becomes desperate, and it can find expression, once again, in the creation of inherent attributions, both about the ingroup and the outgroup. These ideologies again fulfil here the function of preserving personal integrity, and they fulfil it rather better – for reasons already stated – than ideologies in which group differences would be conceived to be more ambiguous and flexible. This is not to say that other solutions are not being found and used, but rather to reiterate the point that the kind of sequence suggested here provides an explanation for one of the solutions being adopted.

5. Summary and conclusion

The aim of this chapter was to stress the importance of the adaptive cognitive functioning of Man in the causation of prejudice. It was felt that this approach has the merits of economy, credibility and testability of explanation which are not always shared by views seeking the psychological causes of intergroup tensions in the evolutionary past of the species or in unconscious motivation. Three cognitive processes were considered from the point of view of their relevance to the genesis of prejudice in an individual: categorization, assimilation and search for conceptual coherence.

Though the chapter was not concerned either with discussing ways to reduce prejudice or with outlining in any detail designs for future research, it is my belief that the general approach adopted here has implications, both for social action and for research, which have not been as yet consistently and fully taken into account.

There is no easy way to deal with intergroup prejudice in its manifold varieties, and all one can hope for is that its more vicious and inhuman forms can be made less acute sooner or later. It is patently obvious that beliefs and views about causes of social events which are held by great masses of people are more easily accessible to change than their motives; and that there is at least a chance that a change of beliefs and views may affect in turn the management of conflicts, real or imaginary. This would be particularly true if such changes were to be planned against a background of strong legislation preventing public forms of discrimination against minorities. It is therefore important and *useful*, for the purposes of science as well as for those of the society at large, that a consideration of prejudice as a phenomenon in the minds rather than in the guts of people should take precedence over views which are, on the whole, not only untestable but also useless in the planning of any form of relevant social change.

7
Social stereotypes and social groups[1]

1. Introduction: stereotypes and social stereotypes

The Oxford English Dictionary, in its definition of stereotypes, draws a tight circle in admitting only that they 'make [things] unchangeable, impart monotonous regularity . . ., fix in all details, formalize'. This static formability of the semi-officially recognized use of the term contrasts nicely with the awareness of its social significance shown by the late Oliver Stallybrass, co-editor of *The Fontana Dictionary of Modern Thought* (1977). He wrote in it that a stereotype is 'an over-simplified mental image of (usually) some category of person, institution or event which is *shared*, in essential features, by large numbers of people. The categories may be broad (Jews, gentiles, white men, black men) or narrow (women's libbers, Daughters of the American Revolution) . . . Stereotypes are commonly, but not necessarily, accompanied by prejudice, i.e. by a favourable or unfavourable predisposition towards any member of the category in question' (p. 601, my italics).

This definition will do for our purposes. By using the term 'shared' as a central part of his statement, Stallybrass went further than have done many social psychologists in encompassing the *social* psychological significance of stereotypes and of the processes on which their functioning is based. He was not unique in doing so. The important social functions of unfavourable stereotypes have recently been at the forefront of the discussions held at the Edinburgh International Television Festival in August 1978. Some extracts of the statements made at the Festival by various playwrights, producers and executives, as reported in *The Times* (30 Aug. 1978), are worth quoting:

Stereotyping should be seen as a part of the comic method by which we tried to diminish what we feared: in the case of contemporary Britain, not only the Irish but also Afro-Asians and Arabs (John Bowen).

It was appalling . . . to find programmes like the *Black and White Minstrel Show* or *Mind Your Language* being broadcast in a multiracial society under strain, when what they did was reinforce stereotypes of black and brown people as being lovable but ridiculous (Brian Winston).

[1] From: J. C. Turner and H. Giles (eds.): *Intergroup behaviour*. Oxford: Blackwell, 1981 (in press).

143

A socially damaging caricature becomes a stereotype (Fay Weldon).

A distinction [needs to be made] between the creation of a dramatic 'type', which meant achieving the subjectivity of another person or group, and the creation of stereotypes, which were essentially weapons in the struggle for power constantly being waged in society (John McGrath).[2]

It is clear from all this that some of the people whose jobs put them in daily contact with the creation and diffusion of social stereotypes are keenly aware of the variety of social functions served by these stereotypes. After some years of relative neglect, we have also recently seen a revival of interest amongst social psychologists in the study of stereotypes. Their approach stands, however, in stark contrast to the awareness of the social dimension of the problems shown by the practitioners of the media. This will become clear from our second series of quotations:

Illusory correlation refers to an erroneous inference about the relationship between two categories of events. [The hypothesis] suggested that the differential perception of majority and minority groups would result *solely* from the cognitive mechanisms involved in processing information about stimulus events that differ in their frequencies of co-occurrence (Hamilton and Gifford, 1976, p. 392, italics mine).

There is no theoretical or empirical reason to assume that forming generalizations about ethnic groups is radically different from forming generalizations about other categories of objects (Taylor *et al.*, 1978, p. 778).

The present writers believe that stereotypes are not a unique structure or process but exist and operate in the same manner that cognitive processes in general influence an individual when he deals with any aspect of his environment (Taylor and Aboud, 1973, p. 330).

The group's impression may depend on the way in which data on individuals are organized in memory . . . Specifically, the proportion of extreme individuals in a group was retrospectively over-estimated; this was true for both physical stimuli (height) and social stimuli (criminal acts) (Rothbart *et al.*, 1978, p. 237).

All this is a consistent echo of earlier views:

These judgemental effects of categorization [of physical objects] are probably fairly general . . . It is likely that the same is happening in the use of more abstract social judgements which are implicitly quantitative, such as, for example, those concerning the relative frequency of crimes in various social groups (Tajfel, 1957, pp. 202–3, see chapter 4).

---

[2] These statements are not *verbatim* reproductions of what was said at the Festival. They are quotations from the account of the proceedings as published by *The Times*.

Or:

One of the aims of the investigations reported here was to show that evidence for the *essential unity* of judgement phenomena, social or physical, can be slowly accumulated and that . . . it is possible to attempt an understanding of seemingly varied phenomena in terms of the same general judgement principles (Tajfel and Wilkes, 1963, p. 114, italics added, see chapter 5).

An important point must be stressed at this juncture. It is emphatically *not* the argument of this chapter that general cognitive processes can be neglected in the study of the formation, diffusion and functioning of social stereotypes. On the contrary, as will be seen later, I fully agree with the views expressed in the above quotations that the understanding of the cognitive 'mechanics' of stereotypes is essential for their full and adequate analysis. The question that arises is whether such a study is all that is needed – a view which, as we have seen, seems to be adopted in some of the recent (and also earlier) work on the subject.

Two definitions of stereotypes were provided at the beginning of this chapter, the 'formal' one from the *O.E.D.*, and the more 'social' one formulated by Stallybrass (1977). The difference between the two illustrates (although rather crudely) the difficulties which are bound to arise in an approach to the study of stereotypes which remains exclusively or primarily cognitive. Stereotypes are certain generalizations reached by individuals. They derive in large measure from, or are an instance of, the general cognitive process of categorizing. The main function of this process is to simplify or systematize, for purposes of cognitive and behavioural adaptation, the abundance and complexity of the information received from its environment by the human organism (see e.g. Bruner, 1957; Bruner and Klein, 1960; Bruner and Potter, 1964; Tajfel, 1972a, 1978b; see also chapter 6). But such stereotypes can become *social* only when they are 'shared' by large numbers of people within social groups or entities – the sharing implying a process of effective diffusion. There are at least two important questions which cannot be answered if we confine our interest to the cognitive functions alone. The first concerns an analysis of the functions that stereotypes serve for a social group within which they are widely diffused. The second question concerns the nature of the links between these social or group functions of stereotypes and their *common* adoption by large numbers of people who share a social affiliation. It is the asking of these two questions which defines the difference between the study of stereotypes *tout court* and the study of *social* stereotypes.

145

2. The four functions of social stereotypes

The cognitive emphasis, just discussed, in the recent revival of interest in the study of stereotypes is but one instance of a much more general trend of work and thought in social psychology. This is based on two assumptions, implicitly adopted or explicitly made in some of the highly influential traditional texts in the subject (e.g. Berkowitz, 1962; Jones and Gerard, 1967; Kelley and Thibaut, 1969; see chapter 2). The first is that the analysis of individual processes, be they cognitive or motivational, is necessary *and* also (very often) sufficient for the understanding of most of the social behaviour and interactions. The second assumption follows from the first: such an analysis need not take into account *theoretically* the interaction between social behaviour and its social context. The latter is seen as providing classes of situations in which the general individual laws are displayed. Alternatively, the social context is conceived as providing classes of *stimuli* which 'impinge' upon social interactions, i.e. they selectively activate certain individual 'mechanisms' or modes of functioning which are already fully in existence. These 'individualistic' views have recently been contested in a number of publications (e.g. Doise, 1978b; Moscovici, 1972; Perret-Clermont, 1980; Stroebe, 1979; Tajfel, 1978a; see chapters 2 and 3) and therefore the detail of the arguments will not be rehearsed here once again. It will be enough to say that, in the case of social stereotypes, 'social context' refers to the fact that stereotypes held in common by large numbers of people are derived from, and structured by, the relations between large-scale social groups or entities. The functioning and use of stereotypes result from an intimate interaction between this contextual structuring and their role in the adaptation of individuals to their social environment.

The remainder of this chapter will be concerned with outlining these individual and social functions of stereotyping and with the nature of the interaction between them. In the case of individual functions, stereotypes will be discussed first (as they have been in the earlier and recent work mentioned in the previous section) in relation to their cognitive aspects; this will be followed by a consideration of stereotypes as a tool which helps individuals to defend or preserve their systems of values. Two social functions of stereotypes will then be considered: first, their role in contributing to the creation and maintenance of group ideologies explaining or justifying a variety of social actions; and, second, their role in helping to preserve or create positively-valued differentiations of a group from other social groups. Finally, we shall attempt to specify the links that possibly relate these two social functions of stereotypes to their individual counterparts.

3. The cognitive functions of stereotypes

When Allport discussed 'the process of categorization' in his classic book on prejudice (1954; pp. 20–2), he assigned to it the following 'five important characteristics':

(1) 'It forms large classes and clusters for guiding our daily adjustments.'
(2) 'Categorization assimilates as much as it can to the cluster.'
(3) 'The category enables us quickly to identify a related object.'
(4) 'The category saturates all that it contains with the same ideational and emotional flavour.'
(5) 'Categories may be more or less rational.'

In his later discussion in the same book of 'the cognitive process' in prejudice, Allport assigned to it the characteristics of selecting, accentuating and interpreting the information obtained from the environment. He distinguished, however, between a category and a stereotype. The latter was 'an exaggerated belief associated with a category. Its function is to justify (rationalize) our conduct in relation to that category' (p. 191). In this way, Allport combined the cognitive and the 'value' functions of stereotyping. But his definition of stereotyping located the phenomenon as no more than an adjunct to his fourth 'important characteristic' of the process of categorization (see above), as something which itself 'is not a category' but an 'image' which 'often exists as a fixed mark upon the category' (p. 192). Since then, we have gone beyond Allport's static conception of a 'fixed mark' or an image.

This section is concerned with the details of the functioning of categories which, as Allport put it, guide 'our daily adjustments'. As it is not possible within the brief of this chapter to go back to the extensive literature on the subject (see chapters 4 to 6), we shall summarize the issue of 'adjustments' by a few statements. Categorizing any aspect of the environment, physical or social, is based on the adoption of certain criteria for the division of a number of items into more or less inclusive separate groupings which differ in terms of these (and associated) criteria and resemble each other on the same (or associated) criteria within each of the groupings. The 'differing' and the 'resembling' need not necessarily be based on any easily ascertainable concrete similarity or dissimilarity. A common linguistic labelling may be sufficient, as in Wittgenstein's (1953) example of games. As he wrote, 'for if you look at them you will not see something that is common to *all*, but . . . we see a complicated network of similarities overlapping and criss-crossing' (see Billig, 1976, chapter 9, for an extensive discussion of this issue as it applies to social categorization). It might be argued that, for example, the social category of 'nations' represents some of the characteristics attributed by Wittgenstein to the category of 'games'.

Whatever these classifying criteria may be, *some* of the attributes of the items separated into, for example, two categories may present varying degrees of bi-serial correlations (or subjectively-experienced bi-serial correlations) with the division into categories. In turn, these correlated attributes, which are associated in an orderly fashion with the categorial division *need not* be the original criteria for the categorization.

The major hypotheses and a number of others following from them were discussed in chapter 4 and extended to the following social phenomena: accentuation of differences between people belonging to different social categories on those personal attributes of the individuals concerned which were subjectively correlated with the division into categories; and accentuation of the corresponding similarities within each of the categories. Secondary hypotheses were concerned with the effects of the amount of past experience with the correlation; the strength of the correlation; and its salience in any particular social situation. Most of these hypotheses were subsequently confirmed in experiments using both physical stimuli and categorizations of people into social groups (see Billig, 1976; Doise, 1978b; Irle, 1975; Eiser, 1980; Eiser and Stroebe, 1972; Lilli, 1975; Tajfel, 1969a, 1972a for general reviews of the earlier work). Some of the same hypotheses were rediscovered and tested again in very recent experiments (see e.g. Taylor *et al.*, 1978, pp. 779–80).

In one sense, some of these recent reformulations represent a theoretical retreat from the earlier work. This is so for two reasons. The first concerns the crucial role played in stereotypes by value differentials associated with social categorizations. This 'value' aspect of categorizations was one of the cornerstones of the earlier theories (see chapters 4 and 5 and most of the references mentioned above). It has lost its explicitness through the emphasis in the more recent work upon the near-monopoly of 'pure' cognitive processes in the functioning of stereotypes. The second reason for the theoretical retreat is a lack of specification in some of the more recent work of the *nature* of dimensions on which differences between social groups and categories or similarities within such groups would or would not be accentuated. As was seen above, clear specifications of this kind were amongst the principal aims of the earlier hypotheses. The understanding of the use of categorizations in simplifying and ordering the social environment clearly depends upon these specifications. They help us to predict when and how various aspects of these categorizations fit or do not fit the requirements posed by the need to systematize the information which individuals receive or select from their environment. What is equally important, they provide predictions as to when and how the various social differentiations or accentuations will or will not occur.

In view of all this cognitive research on stereotypes done, and multiply-described, from the late fifties onwards, it is a little odd to find a report of a recent study on stereotype formation (Rothbart *et al.*, 1978) starting with the statement that: 'Research on the nature of group stereotypes has focused far more on the description of social stereotypes than on the mechanisms or processes implicated in their formation' (p. 237). And again, in the conclusion to the same report, that: 'Traditionally, research and theory on stereotypes have emphasized the motivational functions of group stereotypes, with particular attention paid to the inaccuracy, irrationality and rigidity of such judgements' (p. 254). The frequent complaints about the non-cumulative character of much social psychological research find here, once again, their unwelcome vindication. We seem sometimes to be working by a series of successive starts or jerks, separated from each other by a few years during which a topic drops more or less out of sight; each of the new starts then claims in turn to be the harbinger of a fresh and previously neglected 'approach'.

Be that as it may, the recent work of Rothbart and his colleagues, as well as that of Hamilton (1976; Hamilton and Gifford, 1976), draws our attention once again to another cognitive aspect of the functions of social stereotyping. This has to do with the subjective inflation or exaggeration of the significance of social events which either occur or *co*-occur with low frequency in the social environment. Rothbart's research is concerned with the fact that impressions of *groups* of people are affected by 'the way in which data on [some individual members of these groups] are organized in memory' (Rothbart *et al.*, 1978, p. 237). Extreme events or extreme individuals are more accessible to memory retrieval than are more average instances. In turn, following Tversky and Kahnemann (1973), Rothbart *et al.* argue that this affects judgement in the sense that those instances from a class of events which are the most available for retrieval serve as a cue for judging the frequency of their general occurrence in the class as a whole. In this way, *negative* behaviour of members of *minority* groups is likely to be over-represented in memory and judgement.[3] The attitudinal aspects of these interactions between social categorizations and memory have recently been studied by Eiser *et al.* (1979).

There is a family resemblance between some of this research and the work on 'illusory correlations' reported in Hamilton (1976) and Hamilton and Gifford (1976). As the latter wrote, the concept of 'illusory

[3] This is a brief summary of a more complex argument made by Rothbart *et al.*

149

correlation' was introduced by Chapman (1967) who defined it as 'the report by observers of a correlation between two classes of events which, in reality, (a) are not correlated, or (b) are correlated to a lesser extent than reported' (p. 151). Experiments conducted by Hamilton and Gifford showed that this kind of processing of information (associating, as in Rothbart's views, 'infrequent' events with 'infrequent' people) is directly related to the formation of stereotypes about minority groups. We wrote earlier that the work of Rothbart, Hamilton and their collaborators drew attention 'once again' to this kind of phenomenon. Indeed, a careful reading of Brunswik's (1947) classic work on the uses of 'representative design' in the study of perception and his reports in the same book of the studies in which he applied these ideas to the perception of people, could easily bring us once again to a plea for more cumulative continuity in the theory and research on social stereotyping. Over thirty years ago, Brunswik was able to show how 'illusory correlations' function and how they can be made to disappear in certain conditions.

In sum, there exists a long and reputable tradition of work which shows that the formation and use of social stereotypes cannot be properly understood without a detailed and painstaking analysis of the cognitive functions they serve. We must now turn to the second major function of stereotypes: the role they play in the preservation of an individual's system of values.

4. Social stereotypes and individual values

Much of the argument in the previous section and the studies mentioned in it referred to a general cognitive process which can be briefly restated as follows: once an array of stimuli in the environment has been systematized or ordered through their categorization on the basis of some criteria, this ordering will have certain predictable effects on the judgements of the stimuli. These effects consist of shifts in perceived relationships between the stimuli; these shifts depend upon the class membership and the relative salience of the stimuli in the total array. The resulting polarization of judgements and the special weight given to some of the stimuli serve as guidelines for introducing subjective order and predictability into what would have been otherwise a fairly chaotic environment.

But this is not enough if one is concerned with the issues of social categorization and stereotyping. Many of the categorizations applying to objects in the physical environment are neutral, in the sense that they are not associated with preferences for one category over another, with one category being 'bad' and another 'good', or one being 'better' than

150

another. When, however, this *does* happen in the physical environment, certain clear-cut effects appear which distinguish between 'neutral' and 'value-loaded' classifications (see chapter 4 for a detailed discussion).

As was seen in chapter 4, three consequences followed. The first was that there was no reason why what appeared to be true for judgements of physical magnitudes of individual stimuli should not also apply to judgements of differences between individual people on various 'dimensions' of person perception. The second was that the model of increased polarization of judgements relating to value differentials between *individual* stimuli should also apply to *classes* of stimuli which differed in their respective value to the people making the judgements. The third consequence was a combination of the first two: the increased accentuation of judged differences, due to value differentials, between classes of stimuli and of judged similarities within each of the classes should apply, once again, to value differentials not only in the physical environment but also (and much more importantly) to social categorizations of people into differing groups (see chapter 5 and e.g. Doise, 1978b; Eiser and Stroebe, 1972 for later reviews).

It is at this point that it is important to state the clear-cut *functional* differences between the 'purely' cognitive processes manifested in the shifts of judgement applying to neutral categories, which were discussed in the previous section of this chapter, and the social value differentials with which we are now concerned. Two of these differences are particularly relevant to the present discussion.

The first concerns the nature of the feedback obtained from the environment when the use of categorizations as a guiding device for judgements leads to shifts or biases which are in accordance with the *assumed* characteristics of the stimuli belonging to the different classes. In the case of judgements applying to the physical environment, it can be expected that shifts leading to erroneous responses which are maladaptive will be quickly eliminated. Exaggerating the difference between two coins of different value is a 'good error' as long as it provides an additional guarantee that there will be no confusion between them. But any errors or shifts of judgement which do lead to misidentification or a confusion between objects which should be clearly discriminated will have as a direct consequence the correction of the errors. The speed and accuracy of these corrections will depend upon the degree of clarity of the information received after the response has been made.

In the case of the social environment, it is not only that the information received (about, for example, the personal characteristics of people) is generally much more ambiguous to interpret and lacking in clear-cut criteria for its validity. If we now return to the shared nature of social

151

stereotypes, discussed in the first section of this chapter, the judgements made of people who belong to one or another of social groups or categories which are stereotyped in certain ways are likely to receive, by definition, the positive feedback of general social consensus. Less information than is the case for physical categories will be needed to confirm these judgements, and considerably more to disconfirm them in the face of what appears to fit in with what is generally accepted as a social 'reality'.

The second of these two issues is perhaps even more important. It concerns once again a difference between social categorizations which are neutral and those which are value-loaded. A neutral social categorization means that certain stereotyped traits may be applied to certain social groups ('Swedes are tall') without having a positive or negative value connotation. It is not that the trait 'tall' is necessarily value free; it is the category 'Swedes' which may be neither positive nor negative, and therefore meeting a Swede who happens to be short will not present much of a crisis – if there are enough short Swedes around, this may even modify the general stereotype. But the story is very different if and when a social categorization into groups is endowed with a strong value differential. In such cases, encounters with negative or disconfirming instances would not just require a change in the interpretation of the attributes assumed to be characteristic of a social category. Much more importantly, the acceptance of such disconfirming instances threatens or endangers the value system on which is based the differentiation between the groups. As we have seen, for Allport (1954), the cognitive process in prejudice consisted of 'selecting, accentuating and interpreting' the information obtained from the environment. It is in this way that the process fulfils its function of protecting the value system which underlies the division of the surrounding social world into sheep and goats. There are many and varied daily social situations which enable us to select, accentuate and interpret in accordance with our value differentials the information about different 'kinds' of people; but we shall select here only two instances of the process since both have been subjected to fairly systematic study by social psychologists.

The first of these can be discussed very briefly, as it is no more than a simple extension of the earlier discussion in this and some of the previous chapters about value differentials magnifying *still further* the accentuation of differences between classes, and similarities within classes, which is characteristic of neutral categorizations. Just as the judged differences in size between individual items in a series of coins tend to be larger than the corresponding differences in a neutral series of stimuli (see chapter 4), so the judged differences on certain dimensions *correlated* with the classifica-

152

tion tend to be larger in the case of social categorizations related to value differentials than they are in neutral categorizations. One way to test this hypothesis has been to compare the ratings of personal attributes of people belonging (or assigned) to two different social categories and made by two groups of subjects; one of these groups of subjects was previously ascertained to be prejudiced against one of the two categories while the other group of subjects was not. The underlying assumption was that the categorization presents a stronger value differential for the former than for the latter group. The results usually showed that the prejudiced group judged the differences on certain dimensions between the members of the two categories to be larger than the non-prejudiced group (see e.g. Doise, 1978b, for a recent review of some of the earlier studies). We shall return later, when discussing the group functions of stereotypes, to this issue of intergroup differentiation. For the present, it will be enough to point to the value-preserving function of differentiations of this kind. The ordering by individuals of their social environment in terms of social groups, some of which are viewed favourably and some unfavourably, becomes more efficient and stable if and when various relevant differences between these groups (and similarities within them) can be conceived to be as constant and clear-cut as possible.

The second line of social psychological evidence concerns the identification in ambiguous conditions of members of disliked social categories. Bruner *et al.* (1956, chapter 7) presented an early and detailed analysis of the conditions in which individuals will commit errors of over-inclusion or over-exclusion in their assignment of ambiguous items into one of two categories which are available for such assignments. The first of these errors consists of including into a category an item which, on some specified criteria, does not belong to it; the second, of excluding an item which does belong.

In their analysis, Bruner *et al.* related the frequencies of the type of errors to their perceived consequences, i.e. to the weighing up of the respective risks entailed by making one or the other kind of mistake. This analysis of risk can be extended to the subjective consequences of misidentifying the group membership of individuals when the social categories to which they belong are related to a strong value differentiation for the person making the category assignments. The risks are that a 'bad' person could be assigned to a 'good' category or a 'good' person to a 'bad' one. If this happens too often, it could threaten or even invalidate the value differential. From the empirical evidence we have, it looks as if the former of these two kinds of errors is avoided more persistently than the latter. In other words, there seems to be a preference for not having the wrong person inside an exclusive club over the risk of having the

153

right person out of it. This conclusion can be drawn from a group of studies conducted in the fifties in the United States in which comparisons were made in the accuracy of recognition of Jews by anti-Semites and non-anti-Semites. The prejudiced subjects showed greater accuracy in recognizing Jews. This was due to a response bias: they labelled a relatively larger number of photographs as Jewish (e.g. Scodel and Austrin, 1957). 'The mistakes committed by (this) group . . . tend in the direction of assuming that some non-Jews are Jewish rather than the other way round' (Tajfel, 1969a, p. 331).

Here again, the value differentials guide the use made of ambiguous information. As in the previously discussed case of accentuation of differences and similarities, the maintenance of a system of social categories acquires an importance which goes far beyond the simple function of ordering and systematizing the environment. It represents a powerful protection of the existing system of social values, and any 'mistakes' made are mistakes to the extent that they endanger that system. The scope, frequency and enormous diversity of witch-hunts at various historical periods (including our own) of which the basic principle is not to miss out anyone who *might* be included in the negative category, bear witness both to the social importance of the phenomenon and to the importance of the psychological processes insuring the protection of the existing value systems or differentials. In this section we discussed a few rather undramatic instances of this process. It must not be thought that the 'value' aspects of the functioning of social stereotypes remain equally undramatic in periods of high stress, social tensions and acute intergroup conflicts.

5. The 'ideologizing' of collective actions

The witch-hunts just mentioned bring us to a discussion of the role of *collective* actions in the functioning of social stereotypes. Tens of thousands of 'witches' were tortured and killed in Europe in the sixteenth and seventeenth centuries. As Thomas (1971) wrote:

It was the popular fear of *maleficium* which provided the normal driving-force behind witch prosecution, not any lawyer-led campaign from above . . . Even when the courts ceased to entertain witch-trials, popular feeling against witches continued, as the periodic rural lynchings demonstrated . . . The reason for the new popular demand for witch-prosecution cannot be found in the changing attitude of the legislature and the judiciary. It must be traced to a change in the opinion of the people themselves (pp. 548, 550, 551; 1973 edn).[4]

[4] A fascinating modern example of a *maleficium* first being *invented* and then the people responsible for it being sought and found amongst an 'outsider' minority group is described in Edgar Morin's *La rumeur d'Orléans* (1969).

Thomas's point about witch-hunting having been a massive and *widespread* phenomenon in the population at large is important, since it is likely that it applies to many social situations where causes of distressful social events are sought in the characteristics, intentions or behaviour of outgroups. In his early functionalist analysis of witchcraft, Kluckhohn (1944) characterized witches as being generally 'outsiders'. It is interesting to see that the social psychological parallels to the hotly-contested functionalist views in social anthropology have mainly stressed the individual motivational processes rather than their social equivalents. They consisted, in the main, of adopting perspectives on mass violence or mass hatred which extrapolated from individual displacement or re-direction of aggression to the large-scale instances of social aggression or violence (see chapters 2 and 3, for a discussion of this issue and of the theoretical difficulties presented by extrapolations of this kind).

By contrast, the large-scale diffusion of hostile or derogatory social 'images' of outsiders has not been, to my knowledge, the subject of explicit applications of cognitive theories in social psychology, although such theories might have made a useful contribution to our understanding of the large-scale acceptance and resilience of social stereotypes. These theories would include, for example, the 'justification of behaviour' aspects of cognitive dissonance, the work within attribution theory on the attribution of responsibility and intentionality, the research on internal versus external locus of control, etc. The traditions of social psychological research on stereotypes originate primarily from two sources: the descriptive one, consisting of a detailed analysis of the contents of stereotypes; and the cognitive one which emphasizes, as we have seen, the *individual* cognitive processes.

These two traditions have not, however, come together to work towards the construction of a theory of *contents* of stereotypes as shared by social groups. The outer limit of the social psychologists' interests resided in manipulating the salience of social categorizations in 'natural' or laboratory conditions and finding that, as a result, intergroup stereotypes became more 'active', intense or extreme (see chapter 3).

We have, however, at our disposal all the elements needed to make a modest beginning of such a theory of contents of social stereotypes, we can trace some general *directions* that could be taken. This will be done in two steps. The first consists of a rough classification of the psychological functions that stereotypes can serve for social groups; and the second, of pointing to some potential developments which could provide a theoretical and research articulation for these functions.

The classification of functions is not presented here as an *a priori* or deductive exercise. It is a rough attempt to bring together what is generally known from social psychology, social history, social anthropology and common sense. It appears, from all these sources, that outgroup social stereotypes tend to be created and widely diffused in conditions which require: (i) a search for the understanding of complex, and usually distressful, large-scale social events (see chapter 6); (ii) justification of actions, committed or planned, against outgroups; (iii) a positive differentiation of the ingroup from selected outgroups at a time when such differentiation is perceived as becoming insecure and eroded; or when it is *not* positive, and social conditions exist which are perceived as providing a possibility for a change in the situation. We shall refer to these three functions as, respectively, those of social causality, justification and differentiation.

We can do no more here than give a brief selection of examples in order to illustrate or clarify the nature of each of these categories. To start with causality: something was 'needed' in the seventeenth century to explain the plague, but as Thomas (1971) wrote, its incidence 'was too indiscriminate to be plausibly explained in personal terms'. Thus, the Scots were accused of poisoning the wells of Newcastle in 1639, Catholic sorcery was held responsible for an outbreak of gaol fever in Oxford in 1577, and the local Independent congregation was blamed for an outbreak of plague in Barnstaple in 1644 (Thomas, 1973 edn, pp. 667–8). An even clearer example can be found in anti-Semitism. This is carefully and brilliantly traced in Norman Cohn's (1967) description of the persistence of the myth about the Protocols of the Elders of Zion. As Billig (1978) wrote:

The emotional ferocity of the crudest anti-Semitism makes it easy to forget that anti-Semitism can provide an extensive cognitive interpretation of the world. Above all, crude anti-Semitism is based upon a belief that Jews have immense powers of evil in the world. Modern anti-Semitic dogma asserts that Jews control both communism and capitalism and that they aim to dominate the world in a régime which will destroy Western civilization. All facts are explained in terms of this pervasive and perverse belief (p. 132).

The 'justification' principle is well documented throughout V. G. Kiernan's volume on: *The lords of human kind: European attitudes towards the outside world in the imperial age* (1972). Two examples, taken almost at random, illustrate the principle.

The idea of Europe's 'mission' dawned early, but was taken up seriously in the nineteenth century. Turkey, China, and the rest would some day be prosperous, wrote Winwood Reade, one of the most sympathetic Westerners. 'But those people will never begin to advance . . . until they enjoy the rights of men; and these they will never obtain except by means of European conquest' (p. 24).

An ex-soldier from Tonking whom W. S. Blunt talked to in Paris exclaimed against his government's folly in sending armchair philosophers to run the colonies, who fancied that all men were brothers – it was the English in India who were realistic – *'en agissant avec des brutes il faut être brutal'* (p. 97).

The 'differentiation' principle could be considered as a part of the general syndrome of ethnocentrism understood in Sumner's (1906) sense of the term, but this is an over-simplification. It is a 'dynamic' process which can only be understood against the background of *relations* between social groups and the social comparisons they make in the context of these relations. The creation or maintenance of differentiation, or of a 'positive distinctiveness' of one's own group from others which are relevant to the group's self-image seems to be, judging from the accounts of social anthropologists, a widespread phenomenon in many cultures. As this intergroup differentiation will be discussed extensively in part IV of this book, I shall simply note it here as the third of the major group functions served by stereotyping.

6. Links between the collective and the individual

Two points remain to be made – they concern relating this discussion to the potential development of a properly *social* psychological theory of stereotyping. The first of these two points has to do with the social functions of stereotypes – social causality, justification and differentiation or some combination of them – as they relate to the contents of a stereotype. The analysis of such a relationship cannot be done in psychological terms alone. The competitive and power relations between groups will largely determine the *nature* of the psychological functions which need to be fulfilled by the groups' reciprocal images. But when this is taken for granted as the indispensable background for any social psychological analysis, such an analysis should then be able to make theoretical sense of the *contents* of ingroup and outgroup stereotypes. This can be done through identifying one or more of the major group functions that the stereotype may be serving. A perspective of this kind would undoubtedly be a significant advance upon the 'descriptive' tradition of work which often did not go much further than eliciting a cultural consensus about certain 'traits' attributed to certain groups and, at times, monitoring the stability or changes over time of these collective descriptions.

The second and final point concerns the links between the group functions of stereotyping discussed in the previous section of this chapter and the individual functions discussed in the preceding sections. It seems that, if we wish to understand what happens, the analytic sequence should start from the group functions and then relate the individual functions to them. As we argued in sections 3 and 4 of this chapter, an individual uses stereotypes as an aid in the cognitive structuring of his social environment (and thus as a guide for action in appropriate circumstances) and also for the protection of his system of values. In a sense, these are the structural constants of the sociopsychological situation, it is the framework within which the input of the socially-derived influence and information must be adapted, modified and recreated. No doubt, individual differences in personality, motivation, previous experiences, etc. will play an important part in the immense variety of ways in which these adaptations, modifications and recreations are shaped. It remains equally true, however, that – as we argued at the beginning of this chapter – a stereotype does not become a *social* stereotype until and unless it is widely shared within a social entity. As long as individuals share a common social affiliation which is important to them (and perceive themselves as sharing it), the selection of the criteria for division between ingroups and outgroups and of the *kind* of characteristics attributed to each will be directly determined by those cultural traditions, group interests, social upheavals and social differentiations which are perceived as being common to the group as a whole. As Berger and Luckmann (1967) so cogently argued some years ago, social reality is not 'out there' to be comprehended or assimilated in some manner which approaches asymptotically its faithful reflection in individual attitudes and beliefs. It is constructed by individuals from the raw materials provided to them by the social context in which they live. If this were not the case, the selection and contents of social categorizations and social stereotypes would have to be conceived as arbitrary and random occurrences, capriciously varying from one society to another, from one historical period to another. As it is, the restricted variety of the combination and re-combination of their common elements can be attributed to the restricted number of the major group functions that they generally seem to be serving; and their common structure to the two major psychological functions they serve for the individual.

As was mentioned earlier, social psychological theories of stereotypes have not been much concerned in the past with establishing the links between these collective and individual functions. This is why no grand theory can be offered in this chapter – or perhaps an all-encompassing theory is not possible, or even desirable. Theories in social psychology have often been characterized by a strong positive correlation between the scope of their ambitions and the bluntness of their predictions or explanations. As Hinde (1979) recently argued in relation to another area of social psychology, we are still at a stage in which a strong dose of theoretical eclecticism is not only unavoidable, it is perhaps the most useful way to proceed.

The suggestion made here is that future research in social psychology could relate the group functions of social causality, justification and differentiation (see previous section) to the individual functions of cognitive structuring and value preservation by using two recent theoretical and research initiatives. These concern the study of social groups conceived as social categories, each immersed in a complex and wider structure of many social categories which are *defined as such* by the individuals involved and are related to each other in a variety of definable patterns (such as those of power, status, prestige, majority-minority, perceived stability or perceived possibility of change, flexibility or rigidity of group boundaries, etc.). The first of these two research initiatives relates an individual's self-respect or self-concept (or his 'social identity') – through the process of intergroup social comparison – to the relative position of his group on a number of dimensions in a multi-group social system. This would help to account for the reshaping by individuals of many aspects of the previously-discussed group functions of differentiation and justification (see part IV of this book).

There is a clear theoretical continuity here with some of the processes of accentuation of differences occurring when certain criteria of classification are combined for individuals with value differentials between those categories which have been selected as important in systematizing the social environment (see sections 2 and 3 of this chapter). This is at the same time consonant with the general argument of this chapter and with a good deal of work on the role of social categorization in structuring our views of the social environment (see Tajfel, 1978b). The social context of values and of the requirements for adaptation to the environment helps the individual to seek out, to select for special attention, to exaggerate, and, if necessary, to create, those similarities and differences which fit in with the general consensus about what matters and what does not matter in the potentially infinite number of possible structures of social divisions and social equivalence.

The second of the two initiatives mentioned above mainly concerns the social or group function of social causality, but it also has important implications for the two other functions of justification and differentiation. It consists of some recent attempts to draw attention to the fact that the traditional attribution theory has remained largely individualistic and has neglected both the social determinants and the social functions of the processes of attribution (see Apfelbaum and Herzlich, 1971; Deschamps,

1977, 1978; Duncan, 1976; Hamilton, 1978; Hewstone and Jaspars, 1981; Mann and Taylor, 1974; Stephan, 1977; Taylor and Jaggi, 1974).[5]

The remainder of this brief excursion into 'social' attribution is a paraphrase of some of the arguments put forward by Hewstone and Jaspars (1981) As they wrote:

The main point is that traditional attribution theory has failed to introduce the fact that *individuals* may belong to different social *groups* . . . In this alternative perspective . . . an observer attributes the behaviour of an actor not simply on the basis of individual characteristics, but on the basis of the group or social category to which the actor belongs and to which the observer belongs.

Hewstone and Jaspars provide a number of recent empirical examples of this kind of social attribution, although perhaps the earliest instance can be found in the famous study of rumour by Allport and Postman (1947). As Hewstone and Jaspars argue, this is a dynamic interaction, in the sense that the perceptions of 'causes' and 'reasons' of behaviour of members of the ingroup and the outgroup are determined by the existing relations between the groups, they are interdependent, and they contribute in turn to the future course of the intergroup relations. Following Buss (1978), Hewstone and Jaspars define causes as 'that which brings about a change' and reasons as 'that for which a change is brought about'. They also expect that 'reasons' would tend to be used to explain the behaviour of ingroup members and 'causes' would apply to outgroup members. At the same time, this hypothetical dichotomy would be strongly affected by the positive or negative evaluations of the behaviour to which the explanation is applied. The results such as those from the study of Taylor and Jaggi (1974) in which internal attributions were made of socially desirable acts performed by ingroup members and external attributions to the socially undesirable acts performed by them (with the opposite pattern applying to members of the outgroup) are not too far removed from the 'reasons–causes' dichotomy. It is obvious that this kind of a model can lead to useful predictions of a number of complex interactions in the perception or attribution of social causality.

To return to the main argument of this section, it is also quite obvious that the internal (i.e. dispositional) explanations are an instance of the functioning of social stereotypes. But the static, stable consensus implied by the older descriptive studies of stereotypes is replaced here by shifting perspectives closely related to the individual's evaluation of the equally-shifting social situations which are perceived *in terms of the nature of the*

[5] I am grateful to Miles Hewstone and Jos Jaspars for first drawing my attention to the synthesis that can be made of some of the ideas outlined in this chapter with their attempts to 'socialize' the traditional attribution theory.

160

relations between the groups involved. It is in this way that the potential development of a *social* attribution theory provides the second of our links between the group and the individual functions of stereotyping. Just as the previously-mentioned social identity perspective helps to transpose the differentiation and justification group functions of stereotypes to the level of individual functioning, so the social attribution perspective seems to be a promising tool for a similar link from the group functions of justification and social causality.

7. Concluding remarks

In this chapter we moved from the individual to social functions of stereotypes, and then reversed directions in proposing a sequence of analysis which would *start* from the social functions to reach the individual ones. This is not the usual sequence in social psychological texts. It is, however, justified on two grounds at least. The first is that, in this way, we come closer in our work to a healthy respect for the social realities of intergroup relations, including social conflict, than is often the case in the study of stereotypes focusing exclusively or predominantly upon cognitive or motivational processes 'inherent' in the individual. At the same time, the resulting individual processes of stereotyping are not conceived as some mystical offshoot of a 'group mind' – the theoretical and empirical integrity of moving from one researchable perspective to another and of linking them explicitly seems to be preserved. Much of what has been proposed here is no more than a hazy blueprint for future research. But if we wish our discipline to become more directly and theoretically involved in the study of the tough realities of our social functioning we need to make a start, even if it consists, for the present, of no more than speculations and blueprints. To quote from chapter 3 of this book: 'The point is that we shall never be able to formulate adequate guidelines for research on collective social behaviour if we do not go beyond constructing sets of independent variables seen as functioning in a social environment which is assumed to be psychologically unstructured in its homogeneous and all embracing "inter-individuality".'

PART III
Insiders and outsiders

Introduction

The main theme of the three chapters of part III is the acquisition of group identity. The social stereotypes discussed in various ways in part II are presented there in the form of a 'finished product'. In part IV, it will become clear that the 'relativist' perspective upon social judgement which dominates all the chapters of part II is also, in a different way, fundamental to the understanding of the functioning of group affiliations, intergroup attitudes and intergroup conflict. This is so because no social group in a complex society lives in isolation from others, and therefore the processes underlying the ways in which it compares itself with other groups are crucial to the manner in which it is defined by its members. These 'comparative' notions that the individuals construct of the group or groups to which they belong contribute in turn to some important aspects of their definition of themselves, of their social identity.

These issues will be discussed in detail in part IV of the book. Part III represents a background to it since it provides examples of the development of awareness of group membership (or rather, membership of social categories) in a variety of social and cultural contexts. These examples relate to three separate issues.

The first concerns the attitudes which develop as a function of belonging to a social entity which is, in some ways, a disadvantaged minority. A full discussion of the psychological significance that can be attached to the term 'group' used in this context, and the psychological effects of such a group membership will be found in chapter 15. Examples of the development of some of these effects will be found in part III. Chapter 8 is based on the accounts of coloured students from the Commonwealth who arrived in Britain in the early sixties. This, it will be remembered, was before the time of the rapid growth of immigration and of the correspondingly growing awareness of the 'race relations' problems in this country. Most of the students came not knowing what to expect, or rather expecting something very different from what they had to confront on arrival and later. One of the results was a growing awareness of their 'minority membership' together with the development of new attitudes towards themselves and the host country.

The second section of chapter 9 reflects similar issues, but in very different ways and very different circumstances. It is also concerned with the progressive development of certain minority attitudes. But these 'minorities' are not minorities in any numerical sense of the term. They fit in much better with a social definition of minorities, the discussion of which will be found in chapter 15. The two case studies of 'ingroup devaluation' presented in the concluding section of chapter 9 deal with the development in children of certain simple value-judgements about members of their own ethnic groups in the context of *direct* comparisons with members of another group which is perceived in some ways as being of a higher status. As was said above, these children did not come from numerical minorities: they were Scottish children from Glasgow expressing their 'likes' or 'dislikes' for photographs of people they themselves had categorized as being respectively Scottish or English; and Israeli Jewish children in Haifa of Sephardic origin (mainly from the Arab countries) who were making *implicit* comparisons between their 'likes' and 'dislikes' towards people of their own origin and the Ashkenazi Jews, mainly of European origin. It will be remembered that the former category represent now, as it did at the time of the study, the majority of the Israeli Jewish population.

There is no implication in these two case studies, conducted in the sixties, that some phenomena of a timeless character have been identified. It is fully possible (or rather probable, particularly in the Scottish case) that similar studies conducted today would yield very different results. This issue is discussed in chapter 9. For the present, it will be enough to say that the point of the studies was to present instances of children's sensitivity to the social climate of group differentials in which they live. The studies were like a snapshot of someone taken long ago, and who would look very different in a photograph taken many years later. Such differences do not deny, but confirm, the process of change due to ageing. In the same way, different results which might be obtained in similar studies conducted today would *confirm* that changes in the images of the groups to which the children belong can be ascribed to their sensitivity to the changing social climate and circumstances. That is, such a confirmation would depend upon a careful preliminary study of those social changes on the basis of which the corresponding changes in the ethnic images could be either predicted or clearly understood. An excellent example of the use of such a temporal perspective, extending over a period of fifteen years or more, can be found in the recent accounts by Vaughan (1978a and b) of his studies on the attitudes of Maori children in New Zealand.

The two studies just outlined were part of a very much larger research project, for which I was responsible, on the development of national attitudes in children in several European countries. As will be seen in chapter 9, they were conducted because the initial results from Glasgow differed drastically from those obtained in Leiden, Louvain, Naples, Oxford and Vienna. This more general trend of data defines the second of the three issues mentioned at the beginning of this Introduction. As this is discussed in some detail in chapter 9, it will be enough to state it very briefly here: the suspicion we had that the ethnocentrism of young children, as expressed in their preferences for their own nationals over 'foreigners', crystallizes early in life, long before the concept of 'nation' (which often presents serious difficulties of definition not just for 'ordinary' citizens but also for historians and political scientists) has been grasped even in a most rudimentary form. A description of the findings and their discussion will be found in the first section of chapter 9.

This early development of national preferences and the primacy of their 'affective' over their 'cognitive' components led, within the same research project, to further studies which aimed at a more detailed elucidation of the relationship between 'knowledge' and 'preferences' applying to foreign countries. This is the third theme of part III. The assimilation by children of the socially-prevailing pecking order applied to foreign nations rejoins some of the issues discussed in chapter 6. The studies described in chapter 10 set this socially-derived system of preferences against the background of the acquisition of factual knowledge about foreign countries.

8

The experience of prejudice

1. Introduction

This chapter reproduces parts of the Epilogue to a collection of essays written some fifteen years ago by West Indian, Asian and African students in Britain.[1] The co-author of the Epilogue and co-editor of the book was John Dawson, at present Professor of Psychology at the University of Hong Kong. This is how the book came to be published: In the summer of 1963 the Institute of Race Relations agreed to sponsor an essay competition for African, Asian, and West Indian students. At the beginning of the academic year posters announcing the competition were displayed in colleges and universities throughout the country. They read as follows:

African, Asian and West Indian students who are reading for a first or higher Degree or for a Diploma at Universities, Colleges of Technology, Teacher Training Colleges and similar institutions in Britain are invited to take part in an Essay Competition. The essay should be on the general subject of the writer's attitudes towards the colour problem before he came to this country and the changes in these attitudes, if any, that may have occurred as a result of having spent some time in Britain. Competitors are free to base their essays on personal experience, to deal with the problem in general terms or to combine the two approaches.

We received seventy-three essays, of which sixty-eight were written by men and five by women. Of those, twenty-three were by Nigerian students, twenty by students from other African countries, ten came from West Indian students, nine from Indians, nine from students from other Asian countries, one from Guyana and one from Cuba. Ten of the essays were selected to be published as a book. In the Preface to it we wrote:

The essays are not answers to a questionnaire distributed to a representative population of overseas students in Britain; those published in this book were not chosen on the basis of representativeness of the opinions expressed, experiences described, countries of origin, universities, or subjects studied. We used fairly

---

[1] Henri Tajfel and John L. Dawson (eds.): *Disappointed Guests*. Oxford University Press, 1965.

general criteria of originality, intrinsic interest, liveliness or readability.

Nevertheless we believe that some sort of a coherent image emerges, and that the unpremeditated unity of themes and the core of agreement between people from so many different backgrounds cannot fail to impress. There are two characteristics that all our authors share: they all came from abroad to study in this country; and they are all coloured. These two characteristics seem to determine a common experience of bitterness and disappointment. How much of it is due to colour and how much to a clash of cultural backgrounds? Different views about this are expressed in various essays; but it seems that the weight of opinion is towards the first alternative.

The potential consequences of this are perhaps best expressed in the words of a student from Nigeria who wrote in his essay: 'Down the ages, it has been the traveller who has helped to disseminate knowledge and who served as the unofficial ambassador of his own country. And when this messenger of peace is himself a student or a learner, the problem becomes more threatening, as impressions of scholastic days are erased only with difficulty, and most of the students of today are the leaders of tomorrow in their respective countries.'

The Epilogue to the book was based on an informal content analysis of all the essays received for the competition which were written by men (there were too few essays by women to attempt to draw any conclusions, however tentative). This content analysis followed the lines of the broad categories which were implicit in the terms of the competition:

(a) Experience of the colour problem before arrival in this country: the intention was to include here views, attitudes, and personal experiences concerning Europeans and the image of Britain. However, the content of the essays forced an extension of this to other aspects of intergroup relations at home, such as tribalism, racialism, relations between social classes, etc.

(b) Experience in Britain: this was concerned with the writers' first impressions and their immediate responses; with experience of prejudice and discrimination in personal relations; and with such matters as social class, religion, education, lodgings, work, organizations, other national groups, etc.

(c) Changes in attitude occurring during the visit to Britain.

2. Prior experience

The surveys carried out by Political and Economic Planning (1955) and Carey (1956) have shown that the adaptation of students to the British society and to its educational institutions is considerably influenced by the country of origin, language, culture, social structure, previous experience of Europeans – and the shade of skin. The P.E.P. survey, for example, reported that less than half of the light-skinned West Indian students experienced discrimination in Britain as compared with 80% of dark-skinned West Indians and 72% of Africans. Only about a third of students from Asian and Mediterranean countries reported experiences of discrimination. But it remains true that colour is by no means the only variable affecting students' adaptation. For example, in a book on Indian students in Britain, Singh (1963) described some fairly startling differences in their reactions to this country and in the patterns of adaptation to it related to the social background of the students.

Some of these various background factors were quite clearly reflected in the essays. The determination of views held at home about Britain is complex and often results in ambivalence. But the nature of this ambivalence varies with the nature of the problems encountered at home. Thus, many of the West Indians are thoroughly confused on coming to Britain by the natives' inability to discriminate between finer shades of colour. The crude categorization into 'white' and 'black' or 'coloured' seems to them to miss the finer points of distinction so common in the West Indies. One student writes: 'In the West Indies we find an amazing double vision. For in contemplation of human groups, no society has developed a more delicate instrument of perception. Coming to Britain is like entering a land where the natives suffer from a peculiar kind of colour blindness . . .'

It is interesting, perhaps, to add that the theme of the belief in the inherent superiority of light shades of skin appears also in some essays which are not from the West Indies. This is, for example, a generalized conclusion reached by a student from India, a woman: 'I understand that it is human nature to appreciate fairness of complexion, and hence each race tries to prove its superiority over others from this point of view. When one is bound to admit one's inferiority, one tries to subdue this inferiority complex by a show of hatred towards the privileged opponent.'

But this is hardly typical of Indian attitudes towards colour. And just as the background of the Indian student differs enormously from that of the West Indian, so is the previous experience of the colour problem different for the West Africans on the one hand, and for the East, Central, and South Africans on the other. The presence of large groups of Europeans and Asians has complicated racial issues and created stormy paths to independence in East and Central Africa. Here is, for example, a view from Uganda: 'To the European, the African was an ignorant person deserving education only to become an obedient servant; the Indian was another of those primitive savages. To the Indian, the European was an inevitable but hateable proud master, and the African a

170

primitive native only worthy of exploiting. To the African, the European was an unavoidable, pompous and sometimes brutal master who, though clever and sometimes useful, must be driven out at the earliest possible opportunity.'

It is hardly worth repeating that these views are not necessarily representative. It remains true, however, that in West Africa the same racial issues have not arisen; there have been no European settlers and very few Asians. Thus, the West African students' experience of Europeans has been limited mainly to their role as administrators, teachers, missionaries, medical officers, etc. One should add immediately that this does not necessarily ease the path of of the West African student's adjustment to this country: he has a longer way to go to come to terms with the colour problem in Britain.

Experience of non-settler Europeans reflected in the essays strikes a favourable balance. But of these favourable mentions, nearly half refer to missionaries and teachers – with only one strong expression of disapproval towards a teacher in a mission school. The other categories of Europeans (such as district commissioners, civil servants, medical officers, etc.) are much more evenly distributed in the general range. One of the results of these relatively favourable experiences is an increased sensitivity to what happens on arrival in Britain. As one Nigerian student put it: 'The people encountered in the United Kingdom differ a great deal from the former colonial masters.' In the context of the essay, the implication was that prejudice and discrimination in Britain were much worse than was to be expected on the basis of experiences at home, in Nigeria. And another: 'West Africans find it difficult to appreciate the implications of the colour bar . . . unlike the black South Africans, the East Africans and the American Negroes, they have lived in a homogeneous if not completely free society.'

Colour and race loom large in the instances of various intergroup conflicts or difficulties at home which the essays mentioned. In the total of thirty-three cases which explicitly refer to various conflicts, no less than nineteen are concerned with skin colour or variations on this theme. But reflections on the universal nature of intergroup prejudice transcending colour and manifesting itself in a number of forms (religion, class, caste, tribe) are by no means absent. One of the students writes: 'It is difficult to conceive of a country where one will not encounter racialism in one form or another . . . even as a child in the Sudan I saw the reactions of one tribe to another, of one ethnic group to others, and, of course, the attitudes of foreign races towards our own.' An Indian writes: 'It is essential to grasp that it is not white men *only* who are inclined to this particular type of mistake.'

171

It is, however, the inclination of the white men to commit 'this particular type of mistake' which is the writers' preoccupation within the framework set by the essay competition. According to the retrospective evidence present in the essays, there is a keen awareness before leaving home of the racist tendencies in the world of the white man. 'Events in Alabama, Notting Hill, Sofia and Moscow are an eloquent testimony to the fact that the problem cuts across ideological and regional boundaries', writes one of the students. In this context South Africa is mentioned more frequently than any other country but it is closely followed by the United States.

Though we are not concerned in this section with students' experiences on arrival in Britain, one effect of South African background on the first reactions to this country should perhaps be presented at this point: 'I realized the indescribable human indignity [at home] . . . to breathe the air, to be able to go to any place I pleased, to talk to anyone I chose, to find the London policeman a friend . . . I was worth my qualifications and paid my worth, not a percentage of a white man's pay . . . I re-evaluated the Europeans.'

And here is, like a mirror image, the beginning of another essay from South Africa (which was not submitted for the competition):

For much of my thinking life the question of colour has obsessed me. It has forced moral issues on me which I have been unable to resolve; it has demanded sacrifices of me which I have not always been prepared to make; it has nibbled at my conscience and eaten into my self-respect; it has distorted my social values, it has estranged me from my own community and, finally, it has driven me from my own country. For I am an African born and bred – but a pink one from South Africa.

The concluding paragraph of this essay provides a counterpart to the one just quoted:

I have not met many coloured people in Britain – very few in fact. But I feel cured of a sickness I contracted in early childhood. I don't feel the compulsion to seek out the black face at a party and be nice to it and to demonstrate to it that I am with it all the way. Occasionally though I have relapses when I feel constrained to excuse myself to those whom I suppose to be free of this contamination: this is where these confessions of a colour addict began.

The race problem in the United States is also a salient point of the image of the 'white man's world'. The frequent mention of the United States in terms of racialism is an indication of this general awareness. One Nigerian student commenting on America's role in the world today writes that 'social conscience is much more developed and sustained in Britain than in America. And today nothing has so singularly challenged

172

America's claim to world leadership as the clumsy and dastardly approach to the Negro problem'. This is a fair representation of the views of others who referred to this issue. However, one also meets frequent acknowledgements of the efforts being made in the United States to deal with the problem, and a realization that there is a continuous, if slow, trend towards improvement.

Other 'white' countries are not frequently mentioned; but the rare references to Australia are all in terms of restrictive immigration laws, the white Australia policy, and the lack of full citizenship for the Australian aboriginals; to Portugal in terms of discrimination in the colonies; to Russia in relation to racist outbreaks which occurred shortly before the essays were written. The Scandinavian countries are referred to, and so is France, in both cases for an explicit denial of the existence of the cruder forms of colour discrimination.

How does Britain fare? In order to answer this, a tally was made of 'ideas held about Britain before arrival' in terms of their evaluative content. Of the forty-six relevant statements concerning 'the country and the people', twenty were definitely favourable, twenty-one fairly non-committal and only five definitely unfavourable. This distribution is approximately paralleled by the distribution of views held before arrival concerning the colour problem in Britain. Of forty-four statements made, sixteen confessed to having thought that there was no colour problem here, twenty-one were not very sure one way or the other, and seven were expecting to find on arrival an extensive colour problem.

Some students complained that the image of Britain projected at home does not prepare them for what they find here on arrival. This is due in part to the over-optimistic accounts of those who return: 'When the sophisticated been-to's returned to West Africa they concerned themselves with the delights of the mother country and neglected the colour problem', complains a student from Sierra Leone. Also, lectures and courses tend to display the official brand of optimism: 'In Nigeria cultural organizations usually arrange a series of lectures for students going overseas to acquaint them with the way of life – none of the speakers made even a passing reference to the colour problem.'

It appears that in some cases these idealized accounts do no more than confirm information previously received. A student from Tanzania writes:

All along at school we are shown a number of films depicting life in Britain. The British Council and the American Information Services have been the chief agencies for this. Most of these films have shown life in the West at its best: model schools, welfare services, new towns, technical achievements, scientific and medical progress. All these have tended to support current ideas held by

African school-children about life in Britain. Ignorance about Europeans, the propaganda of the films, and publications of the British information office all combine to bring about this illusive picture of Britain. And this is the root of the problem facing the new student in Britain. One soon discovers that the imagined conception is far from reality. Most of the ideals previously held about Britain are gradually discarded.

In the next two sections we have attempted to summarize, as far as was possible, the ways in which these 'ideals' were 'gradually discarded', the experience which led to the changes of attitudes and to the emergence of attitudes held after some years of study in Britain.

3. Experience in Britain

I have often had occasion to remark that much of the nationalism of the West Indian Negro is born at Paddington, the train station at which I arrived when I came first to England. After a tiring two weeks at sea and a five-hour train ride in from Plymouth one awakes to the scurryings of white porters who not only seem eager to carry one's bags – but are extremely deferential. Little do the porters know what an impact they make on coloured immigrants. The average non-student immigrant will perhaps not have been addressed as 'Sir' very often in his life. And he will most certainly not have seen so many white men doing this type of work before. This last goes for West Indian immigrants of all classes. The educated West Indian, in between spells of bewilderment caused by such an impressive novelty as the London Underground, is likely to be somewhat amused too at the accents of the people round about him. He is naturally surprised to find that he speaks English better than a large percentage of Englishmen. He suddenly feels a great sense of pity for so many countrymen at home who for centuries have been fed the picture of the ideal Englishman, and he desires beyond all else that they should share his experience; if he happens to be a believer in the myth of white supremacy, he is almost suddenly emancipated. As he drives through the streets of Paddington he thinks how much better for the English stereotype it would have been if he had been landed in Trafalgar Square in the midst of bowler hats and brollies that he had so often been shown on newsreels. For the first time he is aware of the effectiveness of selective news reporting. He begins to wonder if he has not been falsely led to believe that his fellow Negroes in Africa have not progressed beyond the shanties and tribal dance displays that so often greet him at the cinema. When he later meets Africans who are cultured and sophisticated, when he learns that there are impressive buildings in Accra and Lagos of which he has possibly not heard at home, he wonders why all this information has never been put over to him before. He concludes – perhaps rashly – that there were forces at work in the world at large which were doing everything to set up the association between blackness and poverty, backwardness and savagery, and realizes that he had been beguiled into regarding himself as inferior to the white man – though perhaps only slightly so – simply because there was this false consolation that way out there in the darkness of Africa there were men vastly inferior to himself. In his new mood of enlightenment he is very likely to become hypersensitive, to look for discrimination and to find it both where it exists and where it does not. The English, he had been told, are, unlike the Americans, 'above colour prejudice, their long dealings with the Commonwealth have broadened them and given them experience of many nations and many colours'. He is soon disillusioned about this last. The milling masses of Englishmen round about him are neither broadminded nor experienced in the affairs of other nations, and though no one has made a move to lynch him he is convinced that the staring eyes around him suggest that he should not be in England where 'he is likely to lower their standard of living and to debase their stock'. These English, he feels, are *vis-à-vis* colour prejudice more subtle than the Americans but their methods of expressing disapproval are, if anything, even more psychologically devastating. Of course he is in no condition to distinguish between those who are prejudiced and those who are having the bewildering experience of seeing their first black man off-screen.

This is one account of first impressions on arrival. There is a quality of shock to some of them, of relief to others. All in all, the balance is not unfavourable, and it is compounded of a selective and complex variety of images. Several of the students are pleased with the manner of treatment accorded to them by the immigration officers, some delight in the lack of discrimination in the coaches at the airport, or respond enthusiastically to the pleasantness of the air hostesses; one remembers clearly the impression made on him by the fact that a taxi-driver 'called me Sir'; another noticed with approval some mixed couples in the street.

At the other end of the range, the English climate is responsible for a good deal of initial misery: 'Cold, miserable and wet'; 'Britain is grey and unfriendly' (this is obviously not just climate). There are complaints of loneliness on arrival, of lack of Christian virtues in a country which teaches them abroad, and a number of more general statements about Britain not being 'up to expectations'. In view of the sort of expectations (described in the previous section) that have often been built up, this is less than surprising.

For quite a number of students, the surprise of seeing Europeans working at manual tasks had immediate and stimulating effects on morale. This is clearly expressed in the extract from the essay quoted above. This is also the immediate – and in some cases unforgettable – introduction to the realities of social class structure in Britain, the discovery to many that thinking of 'whites' as one undifferentiated category cannot fit the realities of their new and complex environment. It is a curious reversal: the British can be so different in so many respects from each other; yet, on the basis of the one and unique clumsy criterion of skin colour, *they* tend to lump together so many people who differ even more from each other. This leads many students to the discovery of a new and wider identity defined through the initially unacceptable criteria imposed by the surrounding society – a discovery which has its powerful consequences.

Sensitivity to class differences in Britain is expressed in quite a number of essays. 'Seeing that the English people are not equal themselves, do I aspire to be equal to an Englishman? If so, what class of Englishman?' asks a Nigerian. In general, it is found that people at the lower end of the socio-economic ladder tend to be friendlier than those higher up with whom, some students complain, they have little contact. One of them refers to the 'class of Britons that make friends with coloured immigrants most genuinely – from the lower strata of society, that is those who themselves know what it is to be subject to any form of indignity; he who is down fears no fall, but this class has intellectual limitations'. At the same time, 'the more secure middle and upper strata of British society', writes another, 'lose no time in condemning race prejudice in the lower class. Why can't they set an example by opening their own doors to those middle and upper middle classes of non-whites?'

These quotations are interesting not only because of the class consciousness that they themselves display; they represent one more expression of the yearning that is perhaps one of the most pervasive characteristics of the essays: to be recognized as an individual and treated as such, to be recognized as having an existence separate from that of 'black' or 'coloured' or whatever. It can be seen in several essays that many of the well-intentioned gestures of acceptance or goodwill flounder because they carry the implication that all coloured students are categorized as a uniform mass. The Nigerian, Indian, West Indian, Ghanaian or any other student does not wish people to be nice to him because he is 'black', and therefore needs support. They wish to enter into individual relations with individuals where each man stands for himself whatever his label.

But instead of this, most of them find evidence of prejudice and discrimination. The incidents vary in nature, and encompass the usual range: difficulty in obtaining lodgings; not being served in hotels; people who avoid sitting next to a coloured man in trains or even in church; milkmen who refuse to deliver; overcharging by taxi drivers; being called a 'nigger bastard', etc. Similar incidents are also reported in the mentions of experiences of prejudice or discrimination found in the content analysis which could be classified as less extreme. Finally, a few statements were found in the essays in which an explicit denial was made of having encountered personally any form of hostile behaviour. Some of these referred to experiences in colleges or universities.

Altogether, concrete instances of hostile behaviour taking various forms are reported by sixty out of the sixty-eight men who sent in essays. The pattern is not particularly consistent, and does not allow any definite statement (if only because of small numbers) about the differences between the African, Asian and West Indian students with regard to their impression of the intensity of the experience. It is difficult to distinguish in reading the essays between those reports of hostile behaviour which are based on genuine hostile intent and those which may well be due to the sensitivity of the writer, between discrimination which is real and that which is imagined. Some of our writers are well aware of this. For example, a Nigerian student comments about one of his compatriots: 'He would complain most bitterly that the attitude of British girls was far from encouraging. But I have personal knowledge that his fortunes at home were no better.' Interpretations of attitudes of others as hostile are determined not only by the objective situation and by the background experiences which have already been discussed, but also by the personality characteristics of those who report them. This too is seen quite clearly by some of our writers, such as the student from Sierra Leone who states flatly, if perhaps a little dogmatically, that 'the reaction to prejudice depends on the personality'. But some of the subtler links between impressions of hostility and personal attitudes are also stated: 'It is precisely those of my Nigerian colleagues apparently most injured by the experience of colour prejudice who utter most wicked and damaging remarks on West Indians.'

Before proceeding to a brief review of the various aspects of their lives which, the students felt, were affected by the hostile attitudes surrounding them, it may be worthwhile to consider their views about the causes of these attitudes. The view that prejudice is a universal phenomenon and that today's attitudes of the white towards the black are caused by a multitude of historical, political, social, and economic factors in addition to the inherence of prejudice in human nature appears in many versions. But sometimes more specific points are made. Several writers feel that some of the difficulty can be attributed to the 'culture shock' felt on both sides when the student arrives in Britain. Specific economic and political issues are also mentioned. One writer, for example, attributes some at least of the difficulty in finding lodgings to political manipulation surrounding the general housing shortage: 'Coloured immigrants are being made scapegoats for the Government's failure to solve its housing problem, and the victims of social distress are made to appear as the causes of it.' Or, in relation to employment: 'Most factory workers on seeing a coloured worker become hostile and nasty, not because they are

177

colour conscious but because they are a threat to their economic position . . . if they later realize the new employee is a student on vacation, they become more friendly.'

A good deal of attention is also paid to the support that prevailing stereotypes find in mass media of communication, advertising, education, etc. Many well-known examples are quoted and there would be no purpose in enumerating them here again. But less obvious instances are also pointed to with some bitterness. Why, asks a student from Nigeria, do so many campaigns concerned with relief from hunger 'choose the coloured man as a symbol of hunger . . . when much of the money is spent on white refugees?' Professor Trevor-Roper's well-known statement about African history comes in for some unflattering comment in at least three essays. One attempt of a student from Uganda to counteract images created by the reading of comics seems worth reporting. He tried to deal with the firm conclusion reached by some children in Edinburgh that, looking as he does, he must be a spaceman. He said he was an African, 'but they refused to believe me. So I told them I was an Englishman but that I had fallen through the chimney – this answer seemed satisfactory.'

Even a brief glance at many essays would reveal the widespread bitterness and disappointment caused by the difficulties in obtaining lodgings and in keeping them. This theme appears in no less than fifty-two essays, with only five students stating explicitly that they had no difficulties. To many this is a stumbling block in achieving a reasonably happy adaptation to life in this country, and it is hardly possible to exaggerate the immense impact that landladies have on the image of Britain that the students will take back with them, and presumably share with others.

The experience of discrimination and restriction is shared by all the three groups of our writers without any hint from the restricted number of cases available that any one of the groups fares better than any other. Twenty-three students report extreme or considerable difficulties which range from the experience of confronting a complete colour bar in seeking accommodation to restrictions imposed on the lodgers once accommodation is found. Twenty-nine students report difficulties of a similar nature though in milder terms.

When considering some of the incidents mentioned, it is possible to come to the conclusion that sometimes the writers may be attributing to colour discrimination restrictions that could have been imposed by some landladies on any lodger (e.g. no girl-friend allowed in, no locking of bedroom when having visitors). It is fully possible that such hypersensitivity exists in many cases; but this is hardly relevant to the problem.

Once someone has gone from house to house, from advertisement to advertisement, finding in place after place the incontrovertible evidence of 'no blacks' 'no coloureds' or of some even more distasteful politer version, it is not surprising that suspicions are aroused and intentions of discrimination sometimes imputed when they do not exist. And then, objectively, there is the 'colour tax': in order to obtain accommodation, the students must frequently pay more than the normal rates or accept lodgings in sub-standard areas. Carey wrote in 1956 that 'colour tax is a process by which the coloured student gets second-rate accommodation, second-rate jobs, and second-rate girl-friends – 'second-rate' in the sense that they are of a standard not normally acceptable to British students.' He goes on: 'Colour tax is symptomatic of the half-way house in which the coloured people find themselves here; a situation that is neither full acceptance, nor outright rejection, but limited social participation: acceptance at a price.'

This does represent a theme which runs continually through the essays in relation to lodgings, to sex, and to employment. No less than eight of the authors have made direct reference to colour tax. As part of a study of the degree of adaptation and integration achieved by African and Asian students at Oxford carried out by Dawson (1961), an analysis was made of the relative costs of accommodation for a group of 160 African and Asian men and women students as well as for a control group of 160 British students. It was found that African and Asian men paid sixteen shillings a week more for lodgings than their British counterparts whilst women students paid twelve shillings a week more than the control group. It was also found that African and Asian students tended to live in lodging-houses of a semi-professional type close to the centre of Oxford, whilst the students from the control group tended to live with the families in the more outlying suburbs. The differences between the groups were statistically of high significance and confirmed the fact that African and Asian students were paying more and tending to live closer together. However, other variables had to be considered before interpretation in terms of 'colour tax' and discrimination could be put forward. For example, evidence was found that many of those students preferred to live together and tended to choose accommodation in which this was possible rather than isolate themselves. On the other hand, there was also considerable evidence that it was easier for African and Asian students to obtain this type of accommodation rather than the 'family' type.

All these difficulties related to lodgings create a sense of loneliness and frustration. Difficulties – real and imagined – in establishing relations with members of the opposite sex accentuate this still further. Eight of our writers seemed quite happy about this aspect of their lives. Of those, three were married to English girls, two were engaged to be married, and one had an English girl-friend. Seventeen students complained of minor difficulties in finding female companionship (refusals to dance and other similar sources of annoyance), while thirty went further and complained of the entire pattern of their relationship with native girls. The type of incidents and the specific nature of the complaints vary: e.g. relationships are only possible with foreign girls, neurotics, or semi-prostitutes; white girls who go out with coloured students are ostracized; parents forbid friendship with a coloured man; a minister of the Church told white girls not to go out with coloured men; a student was attacked by juveniles when out with a white girl. On the whole, this is felt by our writers to be one of the salient aspects of the life of a coloured student in this country. 'Because of the strong emotions rooted in sexual matters', writes a Sudanese student, 'it would not be an exaggeration to say that racialism is deepest rooted here.' As one would expect, it is with respect to sex that sometimes the most painful or embarrassing experiences arise. 'To walk through the streets with a white girl at your side is to run the gauntlet of staring white faces – she could not possibly be decent.' Or, from another student: 'A university woman who forms a love relationship with a coloured man is quietly ostracized.' And another, referring to an English girl who contracted a mixed marriage: 'She is isolated from the rest of society . . . eyes fixed on her as if she had committed a crime.'

But even success in sexual matters may have its bitter ingredients. Some students feel that such success is sometimes not based on a decent human relationship but can be attributed to the legend of Negro sexual superiority. 'No frank discussion could omit a reference to the fact that even in Oxford it is strongly believed that a Negro is sexually superior. Whether or not this is a complaint, few Negroes can decide', writes a West Indian. And so, writes another, 'A West Indian can hardly be blamed for despising a woman who regards him as a foreign phallus.'

Carey interpreted much of this again in terms of a 'colour tax'. 'Because of their colour', he writes, 'these students are usually (only) able to contact women of a social standing and of an educational background below that acceptable to British students.' This statement is perhaps too sweeping. It could be argued that any male group, white or black, visiting another country on a temporary basis may have difficulty in forming normal relationships with women at equal socio-economic levels. There is also some evidence from the essays that the degree of difficulty is related to cultural background and not to colour only. African students in the group apparently have most difficulty, Asian students are next, whilst West Indian students tend to have least difficulty – these differences are statistically highly significant. It is only here that the effect of country of origin on experience and adaptation becomes clearly apparent. The differences in terms of general patterns of prejudice and discrimination, or in terms of lodgings and employment, are not nearly so marked.

As many of the students live on grants that are not quite adequate, the experience of looking for jobs leads to a number of comments concerning discrimination in employment. The main theme running through these comments is the lack of jobs available to students which would be compatible with their qualifications. Of forty-six students who mentioned this issue, three only stated that they found no employment difficulties. There are reports that friendship shown by workers tends to be withdrawn when the students assumes a working role and the threatening characteristics of an economic competitor. A number of students pointed out that the main pressures in terms of economic competition were in the metropolitan areas such as London and Birmingham where there are the largest numbers of African, Asian and West Indian workers. One student wrote that 'it is with the semi-skilled in the large industrial towns where the group pressures are sharpening. Economic insecurity where the supply of semi-skilled labour is abundant creates hostility towards the coloured group.'

Very few examples of academic discrimination are mentioned in the essays – a total of three, none of them of serious proportions. The following quotation from a West Indian is rather more typical of our students' reactions to the ups and downs of their academic career: 'It often works the other way; a Negro student who shows any promise is likely to be even more highly praised than a white one. This might be regarded as a form of patronage.' It is this quality of 'performer' which they think is attributed to them, the implication of delighted surprise in the praise bestowed on them, that seems to annoy some of the successful students among the writers of our essays.

4. The image of Britain

There is no easy way to summarize the extraordinarily varied comments about Britain and the British that we found in the essays. It will be clear from the preceding pages that, on the whole, they are not likely to be enthusiastic. We came to the conclusion that the simplest way of conveying to the reader the general flavour of these comments was in the form of a quantitative summary, although we are keenly aware of the pitfalls of this type of pseudo-statistic: the small number of cases, the

need to interpret comments which are sometimes ambiguous as favourable or unfavourable, the varying degree of intensity of the statements,
etc. A summary of all these statements is set out in Table 1. The

Table 1

Comments by students about the British

Favourable	Number	Unfavourable	Number
Friendly	6	Ignorant (this implies a lack of knowledge of coloured students and their countries)	25
Helpful	4		
Cooperative	3	Reserved	21
Polite	3	Patronizing	13
Courteous	3	Superior	10
Tolerant	2	'Conservative'	9
		Hypocritical	6
		Fear of neighbours' gossip	6
		Suspicious	4
		Condescending	4
		Sexual jealousy	3
		Insular	3
		Pity instead of friendship	3
		Curious	3
		Xenophobic	2
		Aloofness	2
		Self-adoration	1
		Misunderstanding	1
		Self-centred	2
		Coldness	1
Total	21		119

descriptive terms used by the authors were transcribed, as far as it was
possible, to the headings which appear in the table. The assignment to
categories 'favourable' or 'unfavourable' was made, in cases of doubt, on
the basis of the context in which an evaluation appeared.

The general ratio of 5.3 unfavourable comments to 1 favourable is a
disturbing one, and it is unfortunately too striking to be ascribed to the
lame statistics from which it emerges; it does obviously reflect the
balance of opinion. In view of this high frequency of negative evaluations, the statements were analysed further from two points of view:
their distribution in the three groups of students; and their distribution as
function of the length of time spent in Britain.

182

Table 2 presents the pattern yielded by the breakdown according to the area of origin. Here again, the distribution is fairly clear-cut. The African ratio is the most unfavourable, followed by the Asian ratio, with the West Indian distribution far below the others in its relative frequency of unfavourable comment. This confirms the importance of similarity of cultural background in the adaptation to this country.

Table 2
Attitudes according to area of origin and time spent in Britain

Area of origin	Unfavourable	Ratio of number of comments to 1 student	Favourable	Ratio of number of comments to 1 student	Ratio: un-favourable to favourable
Africa					
(42)	75	1.79:1	10	0.24:1	7.5:1
Asia					
(16)	30	1.88:1	5	0.31:1	6.0:1
West Indies					
(10)	14	1.40:1	6	0.60:1	2.3:1
Years spent in Britain					
0–1.9					
(25)	35	1.40:1	6	0.24:1	5.8:1
2–3.9					
(30)	57	1.90:1	10	0.33:1	5.7:1
4+					
(13)	27	2.08:1	5	0.39:1	5.4:1

The same type of analysis was made with regard to the length of stay. As can be seen from Table 2 (lower half) the only slight trend that seems to emerge is an increased readiness to make comments, favourable or not, as function of the length of time spent here. There is a very slight tendency for the 'dislike ratio' to decrease with years, but it would be a bold man who would draw cheering conclusions from figures such as these. Unfortunately, the general conclusion of the preponderance of dislike is based on much clearer evidence.

5. Changes in attitudes

One cannot reach valid general conclusions about changes in attitudes from a collection of essays such as we received: the variety of form and contents precludes any possibility of a systematic analysis. A good deal about these changes can be inferred from the previous descriptions of experiences in Britain as they relate to expectations existing before arrival.

However, one conclusion can be reached based on the content analysis of the explicit statements found in the essays: that the number of those expressing satisfaction is lower than those who held high expectations before arrival; and that the number of those whose final verdict is not favourable is higher than of those whose initial expectations were low.

But statements such as these are not very illuminating. They do not add anything to what has already been seen in the previous sections. A little more information is provided when a tally is made of the statements directly concerned with specific advantages and disadvantages in studying in Britain. The students are often aware of the hypersensitivity which arises from the general situation in which they find themselves. This type of reaction to real or imagined discrimination has been noted previously by P.E.P. (1955) and Carey (1956), and it does present a real problem. Judging from the themes running through the essays, this sharpened sensitivity leads to considerable difficulties of adjustment and sometimes it creates an unbridgeable gap between the student and the surrounding society. Here is one reaction of that nature extracted from an essay written by an Indian student:

At 17, I came over believing in my gifts, my ability to absorb, build, be assimilated by society here . . . At 23, I find most British attempts at friendship disingenuous; think most jokes involving Negroes, darkies and wogs are tasteless; regard most failures to get a room as a deliberate slight, and whenever there's talk of British justice, law and order I pretend I'm not listening.

Many statements are concerned with the sharper realization of racial and colour differences. More often than not this is placed in the context of a new awareness of race prejudice, although for many students the subsequent identification with their own national or racial groups stemming from this experience was considered to be new and enriching. This was particularly evident for West Indian students: 'In this atmosphere it is not strange that many West Indians give birth to Caribbean nationalism.' This same type of reaction concerning 'African-ness' or sometimes *négritude* was also mentioned by some African students.

The colour problem is the principal theme of the essays: it could not be otherwise, and not only because this is the central topic of the essay competition. This topic struck a chord because it related directly and intimately to something which is centrally important in the lives that the writers lead in this country.

A direct proof of this genuine preoccupation is the number of statements containing suggestions about 'what could be done', about ways and means to reduce prejudice and discrimination. We found no less than 147 such suggestions. Some of them do not go beyond a general statement of principle: more tolerance is needed in intergroup relations, more sympathy, efforts should be made to implement the United Nations Charter, etc.

The dominant opinion is that the British public needs to be educated. It must be education for tolerance, and it must also be prevention: something should be done to stop the dissemination of crude and misguided notions about foreign countries, particularly those about Africa and Asia.

There is considerable feeling against the type of film and television programme which emphasizes the primitive nature of the lands and peoples from which the students came. They point out that this type of programme does not present the developments which are taking place today – it only adds to the general ignorance about their countries. One Indian student comments: 'It seems ludicrous that the peoples of the East, the peoples of backward nations, of small nations, should train millions of young people in technologies and sciences originating in Britain and the young British remain so indifferent to them as people.'

Some students wrote of the inflexibility of stereotypes encountered in this country amongst the middle-aged. In contrast to this, many stressed the friendly attitude of the children, and some hoped that the solution to the problem could be found through the children. A Nigerian student wrote:

The average British youngster is most friendly, and has little inhibition when dealing with a foreigner. This is most vividly seen in schools and playgrounds when he plays freely with children from other parts of the world. But before he comes up to the grammar school level he has already been imbued with all sorts of notions about the 'other man'.

Opinions are also expressed that the Church is not making the most of its opportunities and fails to provide strong moral guidance with regard to problems of prejudice and discrimination. This is reflected in a series of comments such as: 'Britain is not a Christian country', 'Britain is a Christian country by name only', or 'It is . . . a pity that the tremendous influence of the various Christian Churches over the faithful has been inadequately used.'

The plea for adequate information before arrival, already discussed in one of the previous sections, is again made in this context by quite a number of students. There is no doubt that this is one of the clear-cut and consistent themes in the essays.

The picture we had to present is not encouraging, and it is part of a larger and even less encouraging pattern. Race prejudice in one form or another appears all over the world. Acts of discrimination must be considered in relation to their background of prejudice, but they must also be seen in the light of economic, social, political, and historical conditions; there can be no easy 'solutions', no simple plans of action. The problems are difficult and they are deeply rooted in the structure of our society and of the societies from which the students come.

But it is possible that something could be done more or less immediately. Some of the problems discussed in the essays could be dealt with to some extent at an institutional level. There are many institutions directly or indirectly concerned with Commonwealth and foreign students in this country, and the responsibility for action should be laid squarely at their doorsteps. Universities and colleges, student bodies, Government departments and agencies, voluntary organizations, etc., have not sufficiently coordinated their efforts and have not devised a coherent programme. It is true that even if such a programme existed and was implemented one could still not hope that drastic improvements would take place. But the problem is sufficiently important to warrant an attempt, even if only moderate success can be expected. The choice is between initiating some form of action on a limited scale or waiting until – miraculously – prejudice and discrimination disappear from our social scene.

9
The beginnings of ethnocentrism[1]

1. The development of children's preference for their own country

There is general consensus of evidence that children come to prefer their own country to others well before they are able to form, understand and use appropriately the relevant concepts of countries or nations (for reviews of evidence, see Jahoda, 1963a and b; Davies, 1968). This discrepancy between the development of concepts and of evaluations exists not only with regard to countries and nations but also in the case of attitudes pertaining to other large-scale human groups – racial, ethnic, religious and social (see Proshansky, 1966). Several studies have shown that evaluations precede understanding whether the relevant groups are or are not in direct contact (e.g. racial, ethnic or religious groups living side by side as contrasted with nations), and whether clear-cut physical or behavioural cues do or do not exist to facilitate discrimination (e.g. racial groups in contact as contrasted with, for example, religious groups in contact). It seems that Horowitz's (1936) early dictum that 'attitudes toward Negroes are now chiefly determined not by contact with Negroes, but by contact with the prevalent attitude toward Negroes' has a much more general application.

Studies such as those by Piaget and Weil (1951) and by Jahoda (1962) have shown that at the ages of six or seven the concept of nation is still rudimentary and highly confused for most children. Our purpose was to show that, at the same age, there is already a highly crystallized and consensual preference in children for their own country, and to trace the course of development of this preference until about the age of twelve. Piaget once wrote that 'what first interests a child in a country is the name' (1928, p. 128). It is this 'nominal realism' underlying preferences that most probably accounts for their early existence and for their relative independence, already mentioned, of direct contact or of supporting

[1] From: H. Tajfel, C. Nemeth, G. Jahoda, J. D. Campbell and N. B. Johnson: The development of children's preference for their own country: A cross-national study. *International Journal of Psychology*, 1970, **5**, 245–53; and H. Tajfel, G. Jahoda, C. Nemeth, Y. Rim and N. B. Johnson: Devaluation by children of their own national or ethnic group: Two case studies. *British Journal of Social and Clinical Psychology*, 1972, **11**, 235–43.

cues. In the present study we wished to use no more than the 'word' or the national label in order to elicit children's preferences, to do this in a manner which would not involve young children in complex verbalizations which are often equally complex to interpret, and to avoid as far as possible the weight on the children's responses of heavy normative pressures – such as exist when, for example, preferences for national flags are requested (Lawson, 1963). We also attempted to establish as much free choice of response as possible by using stimuli which were highly ambiguous and by introducing a considerable time lag between the presentation of the national label and the relevant evaluations. At the same time, we attempted to develop a method which would have the advantage of unambiguous comparability both cross-nationally and across age groups.

(a) Procedure

Subjects for the study were drawn from primary schools in Oxford (England), Leiden (Holland), Vienna (Austria), Glasgow (Scotland), Louvain (Belgium) and Naples (Italy).[2] In each sample, half of the children were male and half female; they ranged from six to twelve years of age. The numbers of subjects in the various samples were as follows: 356 in Oxford, 136 in Glasgow, 120 in Leiden, 418 in Vienna, 110 in Louvain (Flemish subjects) and 118 in Naples.

In each country the same experimental method was used. Twenty-three fairly standardized photographs of young men were prepared in Oxford for the purposes of the study and used in all the countries. Each child was tested individually in two successive sessions, the sessions being separated by two to three weeks. In one session, the child was presented with twenty photographs and asked to put each photograph in one of four boxes respectively labelled 'I like him very much', 'I like him a little', 'I dislike him a little' and 'I dislike him very much'. In the other session, the child was told that some of the photographs were of people of his own nationality (e.g. English in England) and that some were not. He was then asked to decide whether or not each photograph was of his own nationality and then to place it in one of two boxes appropriately labelled (e.g. English and not English). In the Louvain study, half the subjects sorted out the photographs on the basis of

[2] A detailed description of the Leiden study is available in: J. Jaspars, J. P. van de Geer, H. Tajfel and N. B. Johnson: On the development of national attitudes, *European Journal of Social Psychology*, 1973, **3,** 347–69; of the Vienna study in: M. D. Simon, H. Tajfel and N. B. Johnson: Wie erkennt man einen Österreicher?, *Kölner Zeitschrift für Soziologie und Sozialpsychologie,* 1967, **19,** 511–37; of the Naples study in: N. C. Barbiero: *Noi e gli altri: Attegiamenti e pregiudizi nel bambino,* Naples: Guida Editori, 1974, and of the Israeli study in: Y. Rim: The development of national stereotypes in children, *Megamot,* 1968, 45–50.

Belgian–not Belgian, while the other half sorted them on the basis of Flemish–not Flemish. At the start of each session, the child was given three pilot photographs to ascertain his understanding of the instructions. Thus, for example, in the nationality assignment session for an English child, the experimenter first made sure that the child could read the labels on the boxes (i.e. English–not English). After the child was informed that some of the individuals in the photographs were English and some were not English, he was shown the first pilot photograph and was asked whether he thought the individual was English or not English. After the child responded, the experimenter asked him to put it in the appropriate box. The procedure was repeated for the three pilot photographs; if the child had difficulties, the prompting continued. Similar prompting occurred in the like–dislike session for the three pilot photographs. Here, the child was first asked to decide whether he liked or disliked the individual. If the child responded, for example, that he liked him he was instructed to hold the photograph near the two boxes for the 'liked' people, and was than asked if he liked the person 'very much' or 'a little'. After the child responded, he was shown the appropriate box for the photograph. This procedure was repeated for at least three pilot photographs; if the child had further difficulties the prompting continued. Half of the children in each of the national samples had the nationality assignment session first and the like–dislike session later; this order was reversed for the other half of the subjects. The photographs were presented in four different random orders.

(b) Results

In all the samples the proportions of photographs assigned by the children to the categories of 'own' nationals and of foreigners were each close to 50%.

Preference for 'own' nationals
The analysis of data was done in two ways:

(i) An index termed 'd-score' was calculated for each child. The d-score consisted of the mean differences in liking between the photographs the child assigned to his own national category and those he assigned to 'not own', (e.g. English as compared with not English, etc.). A score of 1 to 4 was assigned to the degrees of liking (from 'I dislike him very much' to 'I like him very much') in the like–dislike sessions; the d-score consisted of the mean difference in liking scores between the photographs assigned to own and not own nationality. Thus, a positive d-score reflected a preference in the like–dislike session for photographs assigned to own nationality in the nationality assignment session. Table 1

Table 1
Mean d-scores[1]

Oxford	+0.30*	Louvain		
Glasgow	+0.09		Belgian	+0.24*
Leiden	+0.32*		Flemish	+0.19*
		Naples		+0.17*
		Vienna		+0.32*

[1] Mean rank difference in liking between photographs classified as 'own nation' and those classified as 'not own nation'
*p<0.01

shows the overall mean d-scores for each of the samples. With the exception of Scotland, they are all highly significant, (on the basis of a two-tailed one-sample t-test). Thus, children clearly prefer those photographs they classify as 'own nation' to those classified as 'not own nation.

(ii) In order to facilitate comparisons across countries and age groups, a second index of preference was calculated by means of a correlation coefficient based not on individual data from the subjects but on the photographs. For each photograph the percentage of subjects that assigned it to 'own nation' was correlated with the overall mean 'liking' score for that photograph in each sample. Table 2 sets out these

Table 2
Correlations (r) between liking and nationality (total samples)

Oxford	0.82*	Louvain	Belgian–not Belgian	0.66*
Glasgow	0.07		Flemish-not Flemish	0.54*
Leiden	0.31	Naples		0.51*
Vienna	0.76*			

* p<0.05   N = 20 photographs

correlations. They are positive and statistically significant with the exception of Scotland and the Dutch data which nearly reach significance. Thus, the more a group of children classify a photograph as 'own', the more it is preferred.

Age trends
As can be seen in Table 3, a fairly clear pattern emerges when the nationality-liking correlations for younger children are compared with

Table 3
Correlations between liking and assignment to own nation

		Younger Ss (age 6–8)	Older Ss (age 9–12)
Oxford		0.923★	0.726★
Glasgow		0.342★	0.032
Leiden		0.465★	0.174
Louvain	Belgian	0.407	0.739★
	Flemish	0.230	0.530★
Naples		0.653★	0.099
Vienna		0.779★	0.657★

★ p<0.05

those for the older age groups. With the exception of the Louvain samples, all correlations show a substantial *decrease* with age.

Cross-national comparisons

The studies were first conducted in Oxford and in Glasgow, and later in Leiden, Louvain and Vienna. Of those six samples (i.e. including the Belgian–not Belgian and Flemish–not Flemish versions in Louvain) all excepting Glasgow showed a significant tendency to prefer photographs which were assigned to own national groups. Six kinds of correlation were run subsequently in order to assess and compare the extent of cross-age and cross-national consensus of preferences and of nationality assignments. They were as follows:

(1) Within each national group, a correlation between the younger and the older children of their liking of the twenty photographs.

(2) Within each national group, a correlation between the younger and the older children of the proportions of subjects who assigned each photograph to their own nationality.

(3) Correlations showing the extent of agreement in liking of the twenty photographs between the younger children for all pairings of national groups.

(4) As (3) for the older children.

(5) Correlations showing the extent of agreement in assignment of the twenty photographs to own nationality between the younger children for all pairings of national groups.

(6) As (5) for the older children.

Table 4 shows the correlations obtained for (1) and (2) above. Leaving

191

the Naples data aside for the moment, it can be seen that all intranational correlations are positive and that, with the exception of the Flemish data, they are all statistically significant: i.e. there is fair agreement between the younger and the older children within each national group as to who they like and as to who is their compatriot.

Table 4

Correlations between younger and older children, (a) on liking, (b) on nationality assignment

	Oxford	Glasgow	Leiden	Louvain Belgian	Flemish	Naples	Vienna
(a)	0.949*	0.649*	0.844*	0.530*	0.335	0.846*	0.881*
(b)	0.804*	0.581*	0.680*	0.666*	0.383	0.183*	0.802*

* $p < 0.05$

The sets of correlations (3), (4), (5) and (6) showed unexpected regularities which led to the decision of replicating the study in Naples. These correlations are reproduced in Table 5.

Table 5

Correlations between various countries in younger (Y) and older (O) children (a) on liking, (b) on nationality assignment

(a)	Dutch Y	O	Belgian Y	O	Flemish Y	O	Austrian Y	O	Italian Y	O	Scottish Y	O
English	0.574	0.448	0.507	0.657	0.506	0.670	0.733	0.809	0.667	0.714	0.813	0.865
Dutch			0.595	0.332	0.100	0.104	0.839	0.616	0.579	0.579	0.482	0.505
Belgian					0.282	0.599	0.652	0.357	0.790	0.391	0.369	0.544
Flemish							0.428	0.501	0.376	0.645	0.498	0.577
Austrian									0.803	0.779	0.682	0.786
Italian											0.579	0.754

(b)	Dutch Y	O	Belgian Y	O	Flemish Y	O	Austrian Y	O	Italian Y	O	Scottish Y	O
English	0.711	0.782	0.233	0.493	0.527	0.574	0.690	0.715	0.662	0.551	0.520	0.450
Dutch			0.332	0.601	0.212	0.679	0.431	0.504	0.487	0.405	0.255	0.482
Belgian					0.299	0.653	0.329	0.508	0.013	0.365	0.039	0.044
Flemish							0.526	0.765	0.343	0.230	0.368	0.025
Austrian									0.685	0.491	0.056	−0.013
Italian											0.306	0.463

Ignoring once again for the moment the Naples data, the following can be seen from the table:

(1) The five samples (i.e. except Glasgow) who showed positive relationships between preference and national assignment display no clear-cut pattern or trend from the younger to the older age groups in their agreement as to who they *like*. It can be seen in Table 5a that out of the ten pairs of correlations between samples from Oxford, Leiden, the two Louvain samples and Vienna, there is an increase in the liking correlations from the younger to the older children for six pairs of countries, and a decrease for four.

(2) The over-all pattern is very different for the same ten pairs in the case of correlations of nationality assignments. It can be seen from Table 5b that in *all* ten cases older children in any two countries agree more than younger children do as to who are their compatriots. This was an intriguing finding, particularly in view of the absence of a similar pattern in the case of liking and of the general finding that the correlations between liking and nationality assignment decreased with age (see Table 3).

One possible explanation of this regularity was that, with increasing age, children tend to learn some kind of physical stereotype of their national group and that this stereotype may be similar in the four countries concerned – England, Belgium, Holland and Austria. In order to test this possibility, the study had to be replicated in another location in which two criteria would be satisfied: (1) the same photographs could still be used as presenting a credible choice in the assignment to compatriot and foreigner; and (2), the location should offer the possibility of finding a 'physiognomic ecology' different from the first four countries. Thus, if it were true that children do acquire with age some form of a consensual physical stereotype of their national group which depends to some extent upon the cues which they learn in their environment, the agreement in national assignments between the new location and the other countries should *decrease* with age. The replication was conducted in Naples. Comparison of the data obtained there with the other data provides suggestive evidence that a certain crystallization of physical stereotype may be taking place with increasing age and that this stereotype is not unrelated to what we called the 'physiognomic ecology'.

(1) The younger and the older children in Naples strongly agree, as do the children in the other locations, as to who they like; they do not, however, agree – and in this they are the only exception – as to who are their compatriots (see Table 4). In view of the general tendency for the assignments of younger children to be more closely related to affectivity

193

than those of the older ones (see Table 3), this finding lends support to the possibility that there is a crystallization of a physical stereotype in the older age group.

(2) As stated above, in all ten pairs of correlations from Oxford, Leiden, Louvain and Vienna there is an increase with age of agreement about national assignments. Out of the five correlations with Naples, four show a decrease with age in this agreement (see Table 5b). Once again, there is no sign of a clear-cut pattern for the corresponding set of correlations for liking (see Table 5a).

(c) Conclusions and discussion

The main findings of the study are as follows:

(1) In all the locations except Glasgow there is a significant tendency to assign better liked photographs to own national category.

(2) The strength of this tendency decreases with age with the exception of Louvain, where, both in the case of the Belgian and of the Flemish assignments, there is a marked increase of the correlations with age. For children tested in England, Belgium and Austria the tendency is still strong and significant in the older age-range tested.

(3) There is a marked agreement between all the locations in the selection of photographs that are liked.

(4) There is also a marked agreement between all the locations, with the exception of Naples, in the assignments to own national category.

(5) In all cases of positive relationships between liking and nationality assignment except Naples the cross-national agreement in nationality assignment increases with age. No such general age tendency appears in the case of cross-national agreement on liking. The Naples data provide a marked exception to the assignment pattern: the comparisons of other locations with Naples show a tendency for a decrease with age of agreement in nationality assignments.

(6) In all locations there is a high agreement on liking between the younger and the older children. This also applies to nationality assignments with the exception of the data from Naples.

Discussion of these findings is bound to remain speculative without further data bearing on the various hypotheses that can be generated. This discussion must be mainly concerned with the various exceptions to general trends that were found in the data.

The general findings are as follows: through an association of national verbal labels with preference sorting of photographs one can elicit from young children a clear index of preference for their own national group. This relationship weakens with age. It would be naive to assume that this decrease is due to a decrease in nationalism. It seems more likely that for the younger children both sets of judgements tend to be based more directly on the same affective criterion and that this is the way in which they solve the problem presented to them by the highly ambiguous task of nationality assignments. There is no doubt that this task is also an ambiguous one for the older children – as it would be for adults. But it is possible that in the older age group separate cues begin to function for liking and for nationality assignments, that an effort is made by the children to approach the two kinds of judgements with different criteria. There are indications in the data that a physical national stereotype develops in children with age. It is possible that the subtle cues for this stereotype do not fully overlap with the cues for liking of individual photographs, and that there is an area of random variation in the relationship between the two.

In addition, we know from previous studies, such as those of Piaget and Weil (1951) and of Jahoda (1963), that a 'great intellectual distance (is) traversed within the span of a few years' (Jahoda, 1963) with regard to the concept of nationality. A relatively mature concept of nation could be strongly related to positive attitudes towards one's own country without having to express itself through rudimentary 'preferences' for photographs which appear – rather dubiously – to be one's compatriots. It is likely that in younger children a more primitive kind of national preference which still remains at a pre-conceptual stage makes use of any simple affective symbols that it can find.

The agreement in national assignments between the first four locations in which positive results were obtained led to the Naples study. Cross-national comparisons of the Naples data with the others strengthened the case for the existence of a physical stereotype of own nation which develops with age. If this interpretation were to be supported by further research, it would lead to some interesting questions. Is this an 'ideal' stereotype based on mass communication media such as comics, cinema, television, advertisements, etc. in which certain physical 'types' are used, or is it based more directly on a distillation of cues from the 'real' social environment? The second alternative does not appear very plausible unless one assumes a considerable uniformity in what we referred to above as 'physiognomic ecology'. Physiognomic problems of this nature have always presented extraordinary difficulties for research (e.g. Brunswik, 1947; Tagiuri, 1969). On the other hand, there also exists the possibility that a 'negative' stereotype develops because of frequent presentation of 'undesirable aliens' as having certain physical characteristics in comics, cartoons, films, etc. (see e.g. Johnson, 1966). The difference in the physical stereotypes between Naples and the other locations could be explained on this basis only if it could be shown that the heroes and villains to whom the Neapolitan children are exposed in various forms of visual fiction look different from their equivalents in Oxford, Louvain, Leiden or Vienna. Alternatively, it is of course possible that the general physiognomic ecology of Naples is sufficiently different from that of the other European locations in which we worked to have produced the differences that were found.

The two main findings – of a significant relationship between preference and nationality assignments in the younger children and of its decrease with age – have two exceptions: in Glasgow where this relationship hardly exists; and in Louvain, where it shows a considerable *increase* with age both for the Flemish and for the Belgian assignments. The common feature of Glasgow and Louvain is that, as distinct from the other four locations, nationality assignments present there a task which is altogether more complex. But the effects of this complexity are very different in Glasgow and in Louvain. The early confusion in Louvain (shown also by a weak correlation in the data from younger children between assignments as Flemish and as Belgian, and relatively weak correlations in liking between the younger and the older children in both the Belgian and the Flemish versions of the task) gives way in the older age groups to firm preferences for their own national group – whether expressed as Belgian or as Flemish. One can speculate that the lack of a simple and unique national label for the Flemish children combined with the high salience in the country of the bi-national issue and of the Flemish self-awareness (which, however, is not on the whole *un*Belgian) interferes, in the case of the younger children, with the simple affective reaction to the 'word' or 'label'. Flemish may mean not Walloon but it is also a sub-category of Belgian of which Walloon is another sub-category; not Flemish may mean Walloon and/or Belgian; Belgian and not Belgian may present similar complexities. It is therefore a fair assumption that these difficulties of ethnic and national labels and relationships are sorted out only at later ages when both kinds of national concepts, assignments and preferences have become more firmly established.

The Glasgow children seem to react to a different kind of complexity by not showing a preference for their own national group. One possible reason for this lack of national preference may well be that the well-known phenomenon of the devaluation of ingroup which has been shown in many studies on children of minority or underprivileged groups (for some examples see Vaughan, 1964; Morland, 1966; Jahoda and Thomson, 1970) exists here in a rather unexpected context. As the Scots are by no means a minority in Scotland nor are the intergroup tensions between the English and the Scots comparable to those which form the background of other studies on ingroup devaluation, the data we obtained may well constitute an important example of children's high sensitivity even to those aspects of social influence which remain fairly subtle as distinct from being an all-pervading consequence of a tense intergroup situation (see chapter 6). It is because of this possibility that further studies specifically addressed to this problem were subsequently conducted in Scotland and in England as well as in Israel where data were obtained from children of European and of Oriental origin.

2. The devaluation by children of their own national or ethnic group: two case studies

The previous section presented a report of a cross-national study of the development in children of preference for their own nation. There were two exceptions to the general pattern. In Louvain, two separate groups of children (all Flemish) categorized the photographs into Belgian–not Belgian and Flemish–not Flemish, respectively. Both groups showed an over-all preference for their own national group; but for both, this preference which was rather weak in the younger age group, considerably increased in the older one. These findings were interpreted in terms of the relative difficulty that possibly confronts younger children in Belgium when they have to deal with national categorizations and labels which derive from dual and criss-crossing critera. The second exception was the Glasgow group; it was the only one in which the subjects showed hardly any tendency to prefer their own; photographs classified as 'Scottish' were liked no better than those classified as 'not Scottish'.

One possible interpretation of the discrepant Glasgow results was that the meaning of the dichotomy Scottish–not Scottish was not equivalent to the meaning of the equivalent dichotomies elsewhere. Not English or not Austrian may have simply meant an undifferentiated category of foreigners to whom compatriots were preferred. Not Scottish in Glasgow may have been interpreted as English. If that was the case, the Glasgow results offered a rather unexpected case of relative devaluation by children of their own national group.

There is a good deal of evidence in the literature that, under certain conditions, a consistent devaluation by children of their own national, ethnic or racial group does take place. From the early studies of Goodman (1964) and of Clark and Clark (1947) to the more recent ones, such as those of Vaughan (1964), Morland (1966), Jahoda and Thomson (1970) and Milner (1970), the trend of the data is steady and convincing: children from underprivileged groups tend to show much less preference for their own group than is 'normally' the case, and sometimes they

197

show a direct preference for the dominant group. But all these studies were conducted in social contexts which presented either fairly distinctive and unambiguous sets of cues for differentiation between the groups, or a fairly high degree of intergroup tension or a combination of both these factors. If the interpretation of the negative results in Glasgow in terms of 'devaluation' was to prove correct, the findings seemed of some theoretical importance: the Scots are hardly an underprivileged minority in Glasgow, the Scottish–English intergroup relations hardly display the degree of tension which forms the background of the other findings on the devaluation of own groups. One would therefore have to assume: (i) that the social context does provide some subtle cues for the 'superiority' of the English over the Scottish national identification; and (ii) that children display an unexpectedly high sensitivity to this kind of social influence. The present section describes three further studies, two in Glasgow and one in Oxford, the purpose of which was to test the hypothesis that the absence of Scottish preference in the original study was due specifically to a devaluation by the children of the Scottish identity as compared with the English one.

A similar kind of reasoning led to another study which was conducted in Haifa. The Israeli Jewish population originates in part from Europe and in part from the Middle East and North Africa. According to recent figures, over 60% of the population is in the latter category. Strains have developed and there undoubtedly exists a background of a correlation between socio-economic status and origin (e.g. Shuval, 1963). At the same time, it cannot be said that the Israeli situation presents a set of unambiguous cues differentiating between the two groups or that the degree of intergroup tension is comparable to that existing with regard, for example, to the 'colour problem' in the United States or in Britain. For these reasons, the European–Oriental dichotomy in Israel seemed to provide a possibility for another case study of children's assimilation of fairly subtle influences from their social context in the absence of acute and 'legitimized' intergroup tension.

Study I (Glasgow and Oxford)

Procedure

The general method of the study was the same as that adopted in the earlier study and outlined above. The same set of photographs was used again. Three separate studies were conducted:

(i) Ninety-six Scottish primary school children in Glasgow, aged from six to eleven, underwent two sessions, one in which they classified the photographs by putting each in one of four boxes according to the degree of liking, and the other in which the task was to decide for each

photograph whether it was Scottish or English and to place it accordingly in one of two boxes. As in the earlier study, half of the children had the
like–dislike session first and the nationality assignment session later, and
the order was reversed for the other half; there was an interval of two to
three weeks between the two sessions; each child was tested individually.

(ii) Ninety-six English primary school children in Oxford, of the same
age as the Glasgow children, underwent exactly the same procedure.

(iii) One hundred and forty Scottish primary school children in
Glasgow, of the same age as above, underwent the same procedure with
the exception that the nationality categorization was made in terms of
British–not British.

(iv) All the schools were of generally similar social composition.

Results
To determine the degree of preference for one's own group the same two
measures were used as in the previous studies. A score of 1 to 4 was
assigned to the degrees of liking (from 'I dislike him very much' to 'I like
him very much') in the like–dislike sessions. A score (reflecting the mean
difference in liking between photographs classified as 'own nation' and
those classified as 'not own nation') was computed for each child. The
overall mean difference (d) scores are presented in Table 6; they consist of

Table 6
Difference (d) scores and correlations‡ for liking and nationality assignment

	Mean d-score (total sample)	Correlations	
		Younger children (aged 6–8)	Older children (aged 9–11)
British–not British (Scottish subjects)	+0.177†	0.22	0.663*
Scottish–English (Scottish subjects)	+0.042	0.44	−0.346
English–Scottish (English subjects)	+0.233†	0.70*	0.564*

* Significantly different from 0 with $p < 0.05$.
† Significantly different from 0 with $p < 0.01$.
‡ These correlations are based on photographs ($N = 20$), using for each photograph two
  scores: (1) the percentage of subjects who assigned the photograph to own national
  category; and (2) the mean rank of preference for that photograph in the groups of
  subjects.

the mean difference in liking between the photographs the children assigned to their own national category and those they assigned to 'not own' (i.e. English as compared with Scottish in Oxford and *vice versa* in Glasgow). Thus a positive d-score reflected a preference in the like–dislike session for photographs assigned to own nationality in the nationality assignment session.

Correlations were also computed between percentages of subjects who categorized a given photograph as 'own' and the mean liking score for the whole group of children for the same photograph; these correlations are also shown in Table 6. As can be seen in Table 6, both younger and older English children show a marked preference for photographs classified as English compared to those classified as Scottish. Scottish children, however, do not show a preference for Scottish as compared to English. There are indications of such a tendency at younger ages but at older ages this is reversed and there is a preference for English over Scottish. At the same time, there is little preference for British compared with not British at younger ages; however, this preference does develop with age. (The younger and older groups of children in the three samples referred to in Table 6 were of equal size.)

Discussion

The Glasgow results clearly support the interpretation outlined above of the absence of Scottish preference in the earlier study in which a classification of Scottish–not Scottish was used. An explicit dichotomy into Scottish–English gives very similar results, while the same dichotomy used with the English children elicits a very clear preference for English. In addition, the English preference continues with age, while this is certainly not the case with the Scottish children; on the contrary, there are some indications of the development of relative preference for the outgroup. This fits in with results about the adult stereotypes of Scottish subjects about the Scottish and the English reported by Cheyne (1970). Using Lambert's (Lambert *et al.*, 1960) technique of ratings of various personal characteristics from tape-recordings of accented voices, Cheyne found that the Scottish subjects attributed 'superiority' to English voices on a number of traits (directly or indirectly related to success and status in life) such as wealth, prestige, intelligence, occupational status, ambition, leadership and cleanliness. The Scottish voices were rated higher than the English on fewer traits (one only – sense of humour – for *both* male and female Scottish subjects) which were more related to 'personal interaction' than to success: e.g. friendliness, generosity, goodheartedness, likeability (in the data from male Scottish subjects). These are the articulate stereotypes of the adults which serve a certain function (see chapter 5 for an interpretation of very similar results in the French and English populations in Montreal reported by Lambert *et al.*, 1960). In relation to the present study, Cheyne's data provide some evidence that self-denigrating ideas which might affect the children do exist in the adult Scottish population.

The British–not British classification does not present a problem of conflicting identifications for the Glasgow children. Here the trend of the results is very similar to that found for the Louvain children in the earlier study: preference for own national group increases with age. In Glasgow as in Louvain, there are no simple and unique national labels, such as those which led to clear-cut expressions of national preference by the younger groups of children elsewhere. For the Flemish children in Louvain there is criss-crossing of labels 'Flemish' and 'Belgian' which stand in a relatively complex relationship to one another. A similar relationship obtains in Glasgow between 'Scottish' and 'British', and it seems to have similar effects on the course of development of the children's national identification: a clear-cut preference for the super-ordinate label develops at a relatively later age. But while in Louvain this is accompanied by an increase in preference for the Flemish label in the group of children who categorized in terms of Flemish–not Flemish, this is not the case for the Glasgow children, either when they classified in terms of Scottish–not Scottish in the previous study or in terms of Scottish–English in the present one. This difference between the two locations can, once again, be attributed to the effects of social context on the attitudes of the children: there is little doubt that in recent years the national issue has been more acute and paramount in Flanders than in Scotland.

Study II (Haifa)[3]

Procedure

The subjects of the study were four hundred primary school children in Haifa from Grade two to Grade six (i.e. from about the age of six to about eleven). Eighty children were drawn from each grade, forty boys and forty girls, half of each age group being of European origin and half of Oriental origin. (These two labels are not, of course, an adequate description of origins and they are used as shorthand terms for a complexity and variety of backgrounds.) Twenty photographs of young Israeli men were used; half of these were of European and half of Oriental origin. The photographs were fairly standardized (heads and necks only,

---

[3] The data in Israel were collected before the outbreak of the Six-day War in 1967.

no special distinctive signs, etc.); it is important to stress that the Oriental photographs were generally of the physical type that one would encounter anywhere in Mediterranean Europe; the European photographs were in a more general European range.

The procedure was identical to that of the previous studies, the national categorization being, of course, in terms of 'Israeli–not Israeli'.

Table 7

Preference for 'Israeli' compared to 'not Israeli'

	Mean d-scores† (total sample)	Correlations	
		Younger children (aged 6–8)	Older children (aged 9–11)
European children	+0.447*	0.72*	0.69*
Oriental children	+0.465*	0.91*	0.90*

* p<0.01

† Mean difference in liking between photographs categorized as 'Israeli' and 'not Israeli'.

Results

As can be seen in Table 7, the national preference results which were obtained in other countries are strongly replicated in Israel. The Israeli mean d-scores (mean difference in liking between photographs categorized as Israeli and non-Israeli) are amongst the highest we found; so are the correlations between the overall degree of liking of individual photographs and the frequency of their assignment to the category 'Israeli'. As distinct from other locations, the Haifa results show no age trend: the Israeli preference starts at a high level in the younger group of children and remains at that level for the older age group.

The main purpose of the study was, however, to compare the reactions of the children to the European and the Oriental photographs. This was done in three ways: (i) a comparison of the degree of liking expressed towards the two sets of photographs; (ii) a comparison of the frequency of assignment of the two sets of photographs to the category 'Israeli'; and (iii) age trends if any.

(i) As can be seen in Table 8, the European photographs were preferred by *both* groups of children; the difference in mean preference between the two sets was highly significant. These differences are of the same order

Table 8

Comparison of European and Oriental photographs on liking

(The figures represent the mean ratings of the photographs in which 1 stands for the 'most disliked' and 4 for the 'most liked')

	European photographs	Oriental photographs	p
European subjects	2.73	2.42	<0.01
Oriental subjects	2.92	2.58	<0.02
All subjects combined	2.83	2.50	<0.001

of magnitude as the differences that were found in most other locations between photographs classified as compatriots and as foreigners.

(ii) The differences between the two sets in the frequency of assignment to the category 'Israeli' are also highly significant for both groups of children (see Table 9) – the European photographs were seen more frequently as 'Israeli'.

Table 9

Comparison of European and Oriental photographs on classification as 'Israeli'

(Entries are mean percentages of subjects who classify the photographs as 'Israeli)

	European photographs	Oriental photographs	p
European subjects	62.7	50.6	<0.01
Oriental subjects	64.1	52.5	<0.02

(iii) As can be seen in Table 10, these differences between the two sets in the frequency of assignment to the category 'Israeli' increase steadily as a function of age.

Discussion

The higher preference for the European photographs and their higher assignment to the category 'Israeli' by both groups of children can be interpreted in at least two ways:

(i) The collection of Oriental photographs happened by chance to present sets of cues which elicited dislike, or at least determined weaker preferences than those shown for the European photographs which

203

Table 10

Percentage differences in assignment to category 'not Israeli' between European and Oriental photographs

Grade	Europeans subjects	Oriental subjects
2	9.5	7.2
3	11.9	11.3
4	12.9	14.1
5	13.0	14.7
6	17.0	13.6
Correlations between age and difference scores	0.94★	0.84★

★ $p < 0.01$.

happened to be individually more likeable. In view of the high correlations between preference and national assignment, this also caused a lower frequency of the assignment of Oriental photographs to the category 'Israeli'. With increasing age, there was increasing consensus amongst the children as to which individual faces were more likeable and which dislikeable; given that the same chance distribution was still operating, this increasingly favoured the European photographs and thus determined the growing gap between the frequency of assignment of the two sets of photographs to own national category.

(ii) The Oriental and European photographs were identified by the children with better than chance accuracy as representing people from the two main groups in the population of the country. This accuracy of identification increased with age. The 'devaluation' of the Oriental group by both groups of children reflected itself either in assigning relatively fewer Oriental photographs to the category 'Israeli' or in less liking for these photographs, or in both. In view of the high correlation between the two kinds of assignment, all three tendencies would lead to the results that were obtained.

In view of the likelihood of close correlations between ethnic identification, liking and national assignment amongst Israeli children, any attempts to distinguish between the above two possibilities through further testing in Israel could not have led to unambiguous conclusions. But a choice between the 'random liking' and the 'ethnic identification' possibilities was feasible if it could be shown that an independent group of subjects were capable of identifying the Oriental and the European photographs with better than chance accuracy. The photographs were therefore presented to a group of British adults in Bristol who have never been to Israel or in the Middle East. They were ten women and ten men, all teachers or students of psychology who were tested individually. After a brief introduction in which the two categories of origin of Israeli Jewish citizens were explained to them, they were requested to guess for each photograph in turn whether the person was of Oriental or of European origin. They were not informed that there was an equal number of photographs in each of the two categories. The results are shown in Table 11. As can be seen, accuracy of identification was better

Table 11

Identification of Oriental and European photographs by British adults

	Mean correct identifications		
	European photographs (out of 10)	Oriental photographs (out of 10)	All photographs (out of 20)
Men	7.3	7.5	14.8
Women	8.3	7.7	16.0
All	7.8	7.6	15.4
Mean percentage correct			77.0 $p < 0.001$*
Median percentage accuracy for subjects			77.5
Median percentage accuracy for photographs			80.0

* Significantly different from 10.0 with $p < 0.001$.

than chance at a high level of significance. It is therefore possible to conclude *a fortiori* that the Israeli children, familiar with their 'physiognomic ecology', would have tended to identify correctly the ethnic origin of the faces shown to them. This strengthens the case for the hypothesis of 'devaluation' accounting for the data and fits in with the increasing discrepancies of frequency of assignment as 'Israeli' between the two categories of photographs that was found as a function of age.

Conclusion

All the results referred to (Louvain) or reported (Glasgow, Oxford, Haifa) in this section point to the same conclusion: children are highly sensitive to the socially-prevailing evaluations of national and ethnic groups. The particular interest of the Scottish and Israeli studies is that children are shown to assimilate negative ingroup evaluations even in conditions of nil 'visibility' of ethnic differences in the photographs, as in Glasgow, or of reduced distinctiveness (as compared with 'racial' situations) as in Haifa; and – more importantly – that the social system of evaluations has its clear effects even in situations which are not characterized by manifest and intense intergroup tensions.

The studies reported here did not set out to 'describe' particular social situations as they may exist at present in Scotland or in Israel. It is, for example, fully possible – in view of continuously changing political and social conditions – that studies conducted today in Glasgow or in Haifa would provide data differing from those obtained some time ago. The results are of some importance in a more general sense – in that they provide evidence of the very high sensitivity of young children to the more primitive aspects of the value systems of their societies.

10
Children's international perspectives[1]

1. An exploratory study

The main problem of this chapter is the manner in which mankind becomes classified into groups and the development of differentiations – both cognitive and affective – which underlie these classifications. The 'finished product' at maturity is a division of mankind into distinct large-scale groups. This division, based as it is on class concepts at a fairly high level of abstraction, comes about through a simultaneous development of value judgements and of cognitive differentiations. But the early intervention of value judgements may prevent the development of the capacity to decentralize one's view of events, of other people's actions and intentions, of their attitudes; in other words, of the capacity to understand that the view of the world as structured by members of outgroups may not converge with the 'inside' view, and yet that the principles on which it is based are not different from those guiding one's own view. This failure to grasp the principle that rules remain invariant though their application from different vantage points may give different results can perhaps be referred to as a failure to achieve 'cognitive empathy'.

In brief, the main theoretical preoccupation of our research is the relation between development of affective and cognitive components of attitudes towards large-scale ingroups and outgroups. Before some of the findings are described, a brief discussion is necessary of the role played by inter-cultural variables in an investigation of this nature.

It will be obvious that the study of these attitudinal problems confined to one social or cultural group would not enable one to draw any general conclusions. The results of such a study might be due to some specific characteristics of the social environment of the group involved. For example, lack of conceptual flexibility in the manipulation of ideas concerning outgroups might have resulted from powerful social forces

[1] From: H. Tajfel and G. Jahoda: Development in children of concepts and attitudes about their own and other nations: A cross-national study. *Proceedings of the XVIIIth International Congress of Psychology*, Symposium 36, 17–33, Moscow; 1966; and N. B. Johnson, M. R. Middleton and H. Tajfel: The relationship between children's preferences for and knowledge about other nations. *British Journal of Social and Clinical Psychology*, 1970, **9**, 232–40.

towards early crystallization of value judgements; or it might have been due to severely restricted factual information; or to strongly entrenched cultural myths about the ingroup and the outgroup; or to strong normative pressures towards conformity of attitudes. It is, however, impossible to give an empirical meaning to any of these possibilities unless data from several groups are available. But even when they are available, further methodological problems arise. For example, differences between results from various cultural groups could mean that: (a) the social influences are different; (b) the hypothesis of a general process of which various cultural conditions are assumed to represent special cases is not confirmed; (c) the design of the study did not manage to achieve inter-cultural equivalence of the tasks assigned to the subjects.

It is for these reasons that the findings included in this section cannot be considered to do more than present half of a story. A full inter-cultural investigation of the development of national attitudes would have to be conceived in at least two consecutive stages. The first is that of identifying and eliciting behavioural phenomena which appear theoretically important. These phenomena of inter-cultural convergence and divergence must then provide the basis for the generation of further hypotheses which could well be conceived on the lines of the various alternatives previously mentioned. For example, they could give rise to a second stage of the investigations about the exact nature of social influences in which historical, sociological, economic and anthropological considerations would play a part as important as the more strictly psychological approaches to the problem.

Most of the research we have conducted until now can best be described in terms of attempts to provide answers to a series of empirical questions concerning the development of national attitudes. Some of these questions are as follows:

(a) Can it be said that at the ages of six to eleven there is in children a marked consensus of preferences concerning foreign countries?

(b) If such consensus does exist, how does it relate to the assimilation of factual information about the same countries?

(c) What is the relationship between a country's position on a preference scale and factual knowledge about it?

In our first exploratory study we included a number of tests whose aim was to assess the development of consensus in children about various items of factual information concerning foreign countries and the structure of preferences applying to the same countries. The study was conducted in Britain (Oxford and Glasgow), and Belgium (Louvain and Antwerp). Four foreign countries served as stimuli: America, France, Germany and Russia. The tasks presented to the subjects included

208

amongst others: paired comparisons of preference; and the determination of relative size of all the five countries. This last task consisted of presenting the child with seventeen black plastic squares of different sizes; the square in the middle of the series represented the size of the child's own country. The subject was asked to select the squares which would represent the size of each of the four foreign countries.

Of the number of findings which emerged, the most important are those concerning the relationships between the development of preferences and the assimilation of factual information.

As one would expect, polarization of all judgments increases significantly as function of age. In both age groups polarization for preference in Britain is higher than in Belgium; and, on the whole, factual information is more highly polarized than preferences in Belgium, and the reverse is true of the British subjects.

These data can be presented in a form which brings out the results more clearly. The preference judgements are distributed over four ranks for each foreign country. The same is true of the size judgements. These size judgements can be scored for their correctness in the simplest possible way by considering as correct responses those which assigned America and Russia to categories 1 and 2 (the larger ones), and France and Germany to categories 3 and 4. Thus, only those children who judged either France or Germany to be larger than either America or Russia are considered to have given incorrect judgements. If one also divides the preference judgements for each country into the two higher versus the two lower ranks, the figures provide an estimate of the polarization of preferences as compared with the polarization of correct judgements of size. These figures can be seen in Table 1.

It can be seen from Table 1 that: (a) in Britain, preferences for each of the countries tend to polarize earlier than one of the most elementary items of factual information about these countries, and that this phenomenon does not appear consistently in the Belgian data; and (b) that the general level of polarization of preference judgements is higher at both age levels, with one single exception, in Britain than in Belgium (in the case of the exception for Germany, the trend reverses in accordance with the other data for the higher age level).

The conclusion to be drawn from these data is that, at least in one of the two countries concerned, children learn which foreign countries are 'bad' or 'good' before they learn practically anything else about them; in the other sample, the level of polarization of preferences is also fairly high for two of the countries. At the age of nine to eleven, all preferences are highly polarized with the exception of Germany which obviously presents an ambiguous stimulus for the Belgian children. The second

Table 1

Polarization of preference and size judgements in Britain and Belgium
(in percentages of subjects out of total samples)

	Britain		Belgium	
America	Age 6–7	Age 9–11	Age 6–7	Age 9–11
Preference	63 (cats. 1,2)	85 (cats. 1,2)	54 (cats. 1,2)	69 (cats. 1,2)
Size	58 (cats. 1,2)	90 (cats. 1,2)	59 (cats. 1,2)	88 (cats. 1,2)
Russia				
Preference	70 (cats. 3,4)	85 (cats. 3,4)	60 (cats. 3,4)	83 (cats. 3,4)
Size	52 (cats. 1,2)	70 (cats. 1,2)	58 (cats. 1,2)	78 (cats. 1,2)
France				
Preference	68 (cats. 1,2)	88 (cats. 1,2)	50 (cats. 3,4)	71 (cats. 1,2)
Size	59 (cats. 3,4)	82 (cats. 3,4)	70 (cats. 3,4)	84 (cats. 3,4)
Germany				
Preference	58 (cats. 3,4)	83 (cats. 3,4)	68 (cats. 1,2)	52 (cats. 1,2)
Size	48 (cats. 3,4)	78 (cats. 3,4)	46 (cats. 3,4)	83 (cats. 3,4)

conclusion concerns the difference between the two samples. No inferences can be drawn from the present data about the reasons for the
differences in the pattern of data between Belgium and Britain. It is at
this point that hypotheses of a 'sociological' nature, to which we
previously referred, could be generated from the findings. Their testing
could lead to conclusions about the relative effectiveness of selected social
variables in the creation of firm preference structures applying to foreign
national groups.

2. Knowledge and preferences[2]

Most teachers who attempt to provide children with knowledge about
other countries would hope thus to provide a basis for tolerance and
understanding in international relations. This hope appears to be based
upon a common–sense assumption: that prejudice and emotion are based
upon certain (possibly erroneous) 'facts' which the child may be said to
possess. Thus, if the child believes certain 'good' things about a nation he
will feel positively towards it, while if he believes 'bad' things about it he
will be prejudiced against it. To put this argument in more technical
terms, one would maintain that cognitive components of national

[2] This experiment was carried out while the authors were at Oxford University working within an
international project on the development of national attitudes directed by the author of this book.

attitudes develop prior to – and tend to influence – affective components.

Psychological research on adults (e.g. Carlson, 1956; Rosenberg, 1960)
has also suggested a relationship of reciprocal causality between cognitive and affective components of attitudes. Such a relationship cannot,
however, be assumed to exist for children since they may not fully have
developed the 'meta-value' of attitudinal consistency. Nor do we know
whether the normal process of attitude development involves primarily
the establishment of preferences based upon information or, on the other
hand, the acquisition of information against an evaluative background.
While the study of racial attitudes in children suggests that the affective
component of attitudes towards human groups may be acquired before
the child possesses even rudimentary information about them (see
Milner, 1975), similar studies in the field of national attitudes are rare.

Such studies as there have been of the development of national
concepts in children (e.g. Jahoda, 1962, 1963a and b; James and Tenen,
1951; Johnson, 1966; Lambert and Klineberg, 1959, 1967; Meltzer, 1939,
1941; Piaget and Weil, 1951; see previous section of this chapter) make
reference to the interdependence of cognitive and affective factors, but
leave the causal relations involved less than clear. It has, however, been
suggested in the preceding section of this chapter that British children
may establish an evaluative reaction to other countries before possessing
any information about them, and Jahoda (1962) made a similar suggestion with regard to Scottish children's view of their own country:
namely, 'that favourable self-stereotypes may be acquired *before* any
understanding of the conceptual whole to which they refer' (p. 97).

In asking if there is a relationship between evaluation of a country and
knowledge of it we are attempting to provide information which bears
upon the causal questions asked above. Grace and Neuhaus (Grace and
Neuhaus, 1952; Grace, 1954) have conducted a similar study on American students, in which they related evaluation of countries to the
subject's estimate of the amount he knew about them. Using this
technique they obtained somewhat inconsistent results. One study
suggested that the relationship between knowledge and evaluation was
best approximated by a straight line of negative slope, subjects 'knowing' least about their most disliked nations. Other data suggested a
curvilinear, U-shaped curve with subjects 'knowing' least about countries they felt neutral towards. Their final conclusion was that individual
differences in the form of the relationship accounted for the inconsistency
of their results. The study we report here investigates the relationship, in
British children of primary school age, between liking for and knowledge about other countries using an objective measure of information.

(a) Method

Subjects

Ninety-six children from a North Oxford primary school were selected to comprise a 3 × 2 × 2 factorial design, the factors being age (three groups of mean age 11.0, 9.0 and 7.3 years), sex, and social class (two groups: working class comprising children whose fathers were skilled or unskilled manual workers; and middle class whose fathers were classed as professional, managerial, clerical, business or self-employed). Intelligence measures were not taken. However, since the school was partly 'streamed' and sex–class groups were matched for school class, it is unlikely that large sex or social class differences existed. For further details, see Middleton, Tajfel and Johnson (1970).

Procedure

While the children were tested in three experimental sessions altogether, data from only the first part of the first session and the third session are presented here. Results from the rest of the study are presented in Middleton, Tajfel and Johnson (1970).

Measurement of the direction and strength of *preference* was made in the first session in which children were tested individually.

Each child was given a box containing ten dolls, stylized wooden figures 6 cm high, identical except for their nationality labels which were printed on cards 3 cm × 1 cm and tied around their necks. The ten names represented were Australia, China, England, France, Germany, India, Italy, Japan, Russia and America. (It was explained to the child that the last represented the United States of America. No comments were made about any of the other labels.) The child was asked to stand the dolls on the table, and as he did so to read out the names of the countries for which they stood. Training in reading the labels was given to the 14 seven year olds and 4 nine year olds who showed some reading difficulty; and the 8 seven year olds who failed on the third attempt to read a name correctly were given assistance in reading the names in the subsequent experimental sessions. The child was then asked to place each doll on one of three platforms labelled 'like', 'neither like nor dislike', and 'dislike', according to how he felt about the country the doll represented.

Finally, the ratings on which the main analyses are based were obtained. The child was asked to rate the countries by standing the dolls along a 40 in stick labelled 'like very much indeed' at one end and 'dislike very much indeed' at the other. The stick was marked +20 to −20 on the back, facing the experimenter and not visible to the child. It was

212

explained to him that a pencil mark in the middle of the side of the stick facing him represented the point of neither liking nor disliking and, to make clear to him how placement along the stick indicated direction and intensity of feeling, he was first trained in its use with plastic items of food such as cheese, banana and grapes. The possibility of equal ratings was also explained. Very few children appeared to have any difficulty in understanding the task, and the experimenters were impressed by the apparently deliberate nature of the children's placements. For half the children, selected randomly, liked objects were placed to the left of centre, for half they were placed to the right.

On the basis of these ratings six nations were selected for each child. England (E) was always included, and of the remaining nine, the subject's first and second most liked nations (referred to as L_1 and L_2), his first and second most disliked (D_1 and D_2 respectively), and the doll of the remaining five which was closest to the neutral point (N). These six nations only were used in Session 2. Where equal ratings were involved in the selection of L, N or D nations, orders of liking were sought by paired comparisons. If no distinction was made, one nation among the relevant group of tied ratings was chosen randomly by the experimenter.

Knowledge was assessed in a group test, two and a half to four weeks after Session 1. It was a pencil and paper test with seven items, tapping what were thought to be the first facts a child is likely to acquire about another country. Presentation of items was in such a form as to depend to a minimal extent on the ability to read and write. One experimenter conducted the test and three others watched the children recording their answers. The sizes of the groups varied from seventeen for seven year olds to twenty-five at eleven. Each item, and the response required, was fully explained and, where appropriate, illustrated on the blackboard, and the next item was presented only when all had completed the preceding one. Alphabetical order was used for dealing with the countries in turn for three of the items, and a second order, chosen so as to be uncorrelated with the alphabetical, for the remaining four.

Item content, response required and method of scoring were as follows:

1. *Map* The child was required to indicate the geographical positions of the ten countries by putting the first letters of their names in appropriate places on a foolscap-sized outline map of the world. The names of countries were read out in turn and the required letter put on the blackboard. One point was scored if any part of the letter fell inside the boundaries of the country concerned, half a point if within 1 cm of its borders.

2. *Language* The countries were listed in three rows, well spaced, and

the subject was required to underline those in which he thought that most people speak the same language as he does, English. Scores were 1 if correct, 0 if wrong.

3. *Skin colour* This item was introduced by a brief talk about skin colours and the names used to describe them, and the task was to underline either 'white' or 'not white' in each sentence which took the form of 'Most people in . . . have skins which are (white, not white)'.

4. *Famous people* and 5. *Towns or cities* were more difficult items and required written answers. In item 4 the child was asked to name two people, either dead or alive, from each country, and in item 5 to name two towns or cities. Children were told not to worry about spelling, but to write them as they sound, or to ask an experimenter to write them for them if that proved too difficult. Half marks were given on item 4 to names which could not be deciphered, and on item 5 for suburbs or states. No score was given for clearly incorrect answers such as attributing de Gaulle to Germany, or for naming private citizens (e.g. 'my mother').

6. *War* The child was required to put a tick opposite the name of each country in one of three columns headed 'fought on the same side as England' (in World War Two), 'did not fight', or 'fought against England'.

7. *Population* The last item dealt with the relative sizes of populations compared with England, and required that either 'more' or 'less' be underlined in the nine sentences 'China (France, etc.) has (more, less) people than England'. Again, half marks were given if more than one alternative or none was selected.

(b) Results

Preferences for nations

Mean ratings given by the three age groups to the ten countries are given in Table 2. As can be seen from the table, the agreement of groups results from the three age groups is high. In general, countries are more clearly discriminated in the two older age groups. Analyses of variance carried out on these data show a few over-all sex and class differences in preference: girls like Japan more than do the boys ($F_{1,84} = 10.93$; $p < 0.01$); girls also show higher preference for France ($F_{1,84} = 10.71$; $p < 0.01$) and China ($F_{1,84} = 6.00$; $p < 0.025$). Middle-class children show higher preference for Italy than working-class children ($F_{1,84} = 5.88$; $p < 0.025$). Significant age differences are not reported here.

Concordance in the ranking of the ten countries increases from $W = 0.075$ at age seven ($p < 0.025$) to $W = 0.228$ at age nine

Knowledge and preferences

Table 2
Mean ratings of countries

Country	11	Age 9	7	Total sample
Australia	11.0	9.8	6.7	9.2
China	1.5	−0.3	3.3	1.5
England	16.3	16.3	11.0	14.5
France	10.5	7.8	4.7	7.7
Germany	1.2	−2.3	1.1	0.0
India	0.2	2.2	0.7	1.0
Italy	0.6	5.3	5.2	3.7
Japan	0.1	−0.2	1.2	0.4
Russia	3.0	−1.9	−2.3	−0.4
U.S.A.	8.3	6.8	4.5	6.5

(p < 0.001) to W = 0.340 at age eleven (p < 0.001). Thus, we may say that, while inter-individual agreement on the relative likeability of nations increases over this age range, and there are a few sex and class differences in preference, the over-all picture is one of a fairly stable and consistent set of preferences acquired at an early age.

Knowledge about nations
The relative difficulty of the items in the knowledge questionnaire is indicated by the mean scores obtained on each item and shown in Table 3. Over 90% of subjects gave the correct answer to items 2 and 3 (language and skin colour) for England, indicating a high degree of validity for these forced-choice items.

Mean knowledge scores for each of the nine foreign countries were as follows: Australia, 3.9; China, 2.7; France, 3.8; Germany, 3.8; India, 2.9; Italy, 2.9; Japan, 3.2; Russia, 3.3; and U.S.A., 5.2. For each of the foreign countries, the chance expectation is about 1.8. The mean knowledge score for England, which was based on the five 'non-relative' items, was 5.7.

A total knowledge score was obtained for each child by summing over all countries and items. Not only does knowledge increase significantly with age, but also boys score significantly higher than girls and middle-class children much higher than working-class children. The social class difference is greater than the sex difference, and also larger than the increase of knowledge shown between nine and eleven years, as the mean scores for each experimental group, shown in Table 4, indicate.

215

Table 3

Mean knowledge scores for seven items over nine foreign countries and England

		Map	Lan-guage	Skin colour	Famous people	Cities	War	Pop-ulation	Total
	Item	1	2	3	4	5	6	7	
Nine foreign countries	Age 11	5.1	7.6	7.6	3.9	5.5	5.3	5.8	40.8
	9	3.9	6.5	7.2	2.1	3.3	4.3	5.4	32.7
	7	0.8	6.0	6.1	0.7	1.0	3.0	4.8	22.4
Foreign total		3.3	6.7	6.9	2.2	3.2	4.2	5.3	31.8
England	Age 11	0.8	1.0	1.0	1.9	1.9			6.6
	9	0.7	1.0	1.0	1.8	1.8			6.3
	7	0.3	0.9	0.8	0.8	1.3			4.1
England total		0.6	1.0	0.9	1.5	1.7			5.7
Total		3.9	7.7	7.8	3.7	4.9	4.2	5.3	37.5
Maximum possible		10.0	10.0	10.0	20.0	20.0	9.0	9.0	88.0
Chance expectation	$\simeq$	00.0	5.0	5.0	00.0	00.0	3.0	4.5	$\simeq$18.5

Table 4

Mean total knowledge scores for twelve groups of eight children

Age	WC male	MC male	WC female	MC female
7	18.8	36.8	22.6	27.3
9	37.1	50.0	30.8	37.5
11	45.2	57.0	34.8	52.9

In general, subjects possess less information than one might expect. For example, only about 60% of the total sample report that the French and the Italians are not English-speaking; over 30% of the sample state that the Germans are not-white; and more children see India having fought against, and Italy having fought with, England in the war than the other way round.

Knowledge and preference

As stated earlier, the major aim of the present study was to examine the relationship between the liking shown for a nation and the amount known about it. A comparison was thus made between knowledge

216

Knowledge and preferences

scores for the five nations designated L_1, L_2, N, D_2, D_1 by each subject. Knowledge scores, however, obtained by summing a child's scores over items for each nation, can be usefully related to preference only to the extent to which they index a unitary variable. Two criteria were used to assess the extent to which items met this requirement: (a) total scores, over all nations, for each child on each of the seven items were inter-correlated (N = 96); (b) total scores, over all children for each nation on each of the seven items were inter-correlated (N = 9).

Examination of the two matrices of product–moment correlations led to the rejection of items 7 (population) and 3 (skin colour) from the knowledge score. Item 7 was rejected on criterion (a) since, while the other six items had mean inter-correlations ranging from +0.40 to +0.68, this item gave a mean inter-correlation of only +0.34; it was also, as can be seen from Table 3, a very difficult item on which scores were significantly polarized for only three of the nine countries by the age of eleven. Thus, this item was omitted primarily because children who knew a lot about foreign countries on the basis of the other items did not show a strong tendency to possess knowledge about population. Item 3 was omitted from the total score on criterion (b) since it showed a small negative mean inter-correlation with the other items, which themselves showed mean inter-correlations ranging from +0.11 to +0.40. Thus, countries which appeared well known judging by the other items tended not to be on item 3.

The relationship between knowledge and preference was investigated on the basis of the more unitary score derived from items 1, 2, 4, 5 and 6. Table 5 gives mean knowledge scores for the five nations designated, for each subject L_1, L_2, N, D_2 and D_1.

Table 5

Mean knowledge scores for liked, neutral and disliked nations

		L_1	L_2	N	D_2	D_1
Age	11	4.06	3.78	2.47	2.53	2.80
	9	2.69	2.70	2.02	1.67	2.05
	7	1.50	1.34	1.11	1.22	1.38
Class	WC	2.17	1.78	1.39	1.49	1.68
	MC	3.33	3.44	2.34	2.12	2.47
Sex	M	3.41	2.90	2.26	1.95	2.42
	F	2.09	2.32	1.47	1.67	1.73
	Total	2.75	2.61	1.86	1.81	2.07

As can be seen from the table, the relationship between liking and knowledge is, for most groups, clearly curvilinear, with least knowledge displayed for N or D_2. These children know more about countries they like than those they dislike, but least of all about those they feel neutral towards. Since five scores are used from each subject (repeated measures) in the analysis of variance of the knowledge scores there are two error terms in the analysis. The within-subjects error term is used for assessing the significance of all effects involving liking (L). Since there is no ground for assuming equal correlations between scores for all pairs of values of the L variable, conservative tests (see Lubin, 1965; Edwards, 1968, pp. 301–3) have been applied whenever the within-subjects error term has been used.

The significant age, class and sex differences found in the first analysis of variance, where scores based on all items and nations were used, are found again. The effect of liking on knowledge is also apparent, with linear, quadratic and, to a lesser extent, cubic components of this effect all achieving significance.

While the relationship demonstrated is interesting in its own right, it may tell us more about the 'propaganda environment' in which the child lives than about intra-individual processes involved in the formation of attitudes. It may be that affective tone and quantity of information are related in a similarly curvilinear way in the material with which the child comes into contact through his school, his parents or the mass media. That is to say, there may simply be more information 'in the air' referring to the nations the child is expected to like or dislike strongly and the results presented may simply reflect this societal disproportion. Alternatively (or additionally) there may be an active individual process at work ensuring that the child knows most about the nations *he* likes best, and least about those *he* feels neutral towards. The strength of evidence for an individual effect can be assessed from our data (although negative results would not demonstrate that individual effects were *not* operating). From each child's knowledge score for each of the five selected nations, we subtracted, as a correction term, the mean knowledge score for that country given by the other subjects in the child's age group. The mean corrected scores for the five preference categories for the whole sample are:

L_1	L_2	N	D_2	D_1
+0.13	−0.09	−0.24	−0.14	−0.03

Thus, we can see that, by comparison with his own age group, the child still knows more, on average, about the country he likes best and least about the nation he feels neutral towards. An analysis of variance exactly similar to that previously described was carried out on the corrected scores. While the quadratic component of the liking/knowledge relationship is still significant using a conservative test ($F_{1,89} = 4.43$; $p < 0.05$), its interpretation becomes complicated by two significant interactions: Liking × Sex ($F_{1,89} = 4.11$; $p < 0.05$) and Liking × Class ($F_{1,89} = 4.69$; $p < 0.05$). It appears from further inspection of the data that the curvilinear relationship in the corrected scores is more clearly seen in results from male and from middle-class subjects.

(c) *Discussion*

The results of this study show clearly that there is a relationship between preference for and knowledge about nations in the primary school children tested, and that the form of the relationship is roughly U-shaped. The last part of the analysis of results suggests that the effect is an individual one, and does not solely reflect a property of the propaganda environment. The causal implications of this affective–cognitive link are not entirely clear, but it is hoped that further research will help to answer this question. To the extent ·that the affective component of national attitudes is based upon the knowledge that the child has acquired, one would expect that, while children may know nearly as much about nations they dislike as about nations they like, the knowledge should have different affective implications. Thus, a child who likes Russia, for example, should possess different, and more evaluatively positive, information as compared to the majority of children who dislike Russia. If, on the other hand, the evaluative component of the attitude is learnt first, the result might be simply to make the child sensitive to information referring to those nations he feels strongly about; alternatively, processes of selective attention or recall might operate so as to assure congruence between the early affective learning and the information taken in. Thus, the hypothesis that affect is based upon knowledge requires that children with different evaluations possess different information, while the hypothesis that knowledge is acquired only against a background of early affective learning can tolerate such a finding but does not require it.

A finding by Johnson (1966) suggests the prior emergence of the affective component. In examining the relationship between readership of various types of comics and national preference, he found that children who read comics containing a high proportion of war stories showed a pattern of national preferences more congruent with the alliances of World War Two than children who did not read these comics. In particular, the war-comic readers showed significantly less liking for Germany. If this lower preference had been caused by these children having acquired more *information* about the war, this should have been discernible in the responses given to the question all children were asked, to tell the experimenter 'all you can think of about Germany'.

When responses to this item were analysed, however, it was found that the war-comic readers appeared to possess slightly less information about the war than the other children. Thus, some evidence exists for believing that knowledge is not an essential prerequisite for the development of emotional reactions to other nations. As Horowitz (1940) put it: 'Within the individual the sequence frequently is the development of a prejudice first and the perfection of the techniques of differentiation later.' The results of the present study are certainly congruent with that view.

The other important finding of this study relates to social class differences. On the one hand, the preferences of working-class and middle-class children are very similar. On the other, the middle-class subjects show a knowledge of foreign countries approximately two years ahead of their working-class counterparts. Since the working-class and middle-class children were chosen from the same streamed school forms, it seems clear that no argument based on intellectual differences could account for such a large discrepancy, which is congruent with a similarly marked class difference in the achievement of affective reciprocity reported elsewhere (Middleton, Tajfel and Johnson, 1970).

PART IV
Intergroup conflict

Introduction

We live in a world in which the processes of unification and diversification proceed apace, both of them faster than ever before. In some ways, large-scale human groups communicate with each other more than ever, know about each other more than ever, and have become increasingly interdependent. At the same time, there is a powerful trend, to be seen virtually all over the world, aiming at the preservation or the achievement of diversity, of one's own special characteristics and identity. Part IV will be concerned with this latter trend – the 'differentiation' between social groups. This occurs not only at the level of national, ethnic or linguistic movements towards a clearer group 'distinctiveness', it has also become one of the most important features of industrial relations in many countries. The erosion, preservation or creation of differentials has been, in recent years, one of the fundamental features of some of the most acute social and industrial conflicts. It would be no less than ridiculous to assert that objective rewards (in terms of money, standards of living, consumption of goods and services, etc.) are not the most important determinant of these conflicts. But the main point made in part IV of this book is that, however important they undoubtedly are, they do not represent, by any means, the whole story. Differentiation between social groups (and the conflicts about the differentials, which are a special instance of it) cannot be adequately understood in economic terms alone. Other forms of analysis are needed for this understanding; they cannot *replace* the economic and social analysis, but must be used to supplement it.

One of the principal aims of the theoretical framework presented in part IV is to develop an alternative approach to the social psychology of intergroup relations. In this, the behaviour towards each other of different social groups which are at the same time separate and unavoidably shackled together (in the sense that the fate of each of them depends, to a large extent, upon the nature of its relations with the others) is seen as a joint function of certain social psychological processes and of the structure of the objective relations between the groups. The processes in question are *social* psychological because, as will be seen later, their origins and development are not conceivable outside of the social settings

223

in which they function. Social psychology (or even less, any other kind of psychology) is not, and cannot be, by the nature of the questions it asks, in a position to provide more than a small part of the analysis of the relations between social groups. It would not be very fruitful to engage in a discussion about the relative importance for this analysis of a social psychological approach as compared with, for example, sociological, economic or historical considerations. All of us in our various disciplines are dealing with a common knot of problems seen from different perspectives, and it would be futile to claim a monopoly of some kind of a 'basic truth' or conceptual priority for any one of these perspectives. It seems, however, important to define, even if only in very general terms, the point of insertion, as it were, of one's own brand of work into the bewildering complexity of the spiral of causation in intergroup relations.

This can be done perhaps using as an example a statement once made by the social anthropologist, Robert LeVine, during a conference on ethnic and national loyalties. LeVine asserted: 'Describe to me the economic intergroup situation, and I shall predict the content of the [intergroup] stereotypes.' This assertion was provoked by some remarks about the genesis of group stereotypes which were made during the conference, just prior to LeVine's terse summary:

From Jezernik's work it would appear that economic factors have an overwhelming effect on the content of stereotypes which emerge in new or changing conditions of interaction between groups. Statements from which measures of social distance are inferred are never very far removed from the image that one group holds of another. Stereotypes provide rationalizations for keeping others at bay, whenever the 'distance' stated as preferable is in conflict with a system of moral or social values. I remember presenting some years ago to students in Oxford a set of adjectives mentioned to me at the time by Jezernik as typical of the Slovene characterizations of immigrant Bosnians. When the students were asked where these descriptions came from and to whom they applied, the unanimous guess was that they were the stereotypes used about coloured immigrants in England. (Tajfel, 1970a, p. 130).

It is easy to agree with LeVine that social stereotypes cannot be considered as some kind of a 'primary cause' in the development of relations between the groups (see chapters 6 and 7). Nevertheless, the interweaving of the social (or economic) and psychological causation in the course of these relations is exemplified in the above quotation. An admittedly crude and over-simplified model of this interaction could look as follows: social and economic conditions leading to rivalry between groups for various kinds of objective benefits are associated with a diffusion of certain derogatory notions about the outgroup. These notions, which are related to attitudes and behaviour establishing various forms of social distance between groups (see e.g. Banton, 1967), can hardly be conceived as originating *directly* from a situation of objective struggle for a distribution of resources, since there are no clear 'non-psychological' reasons why such a struggle should be accompanied by the derogation or denigration of the outgroup. One can easily conceive of conflicts, competitions or struggles in which the adversary is seen to be as 'good' as oneself, even if his goals are seen as incompatible with one's own. As we know from common experience, this kind of perception of conflict – i.e. the view that one is dealing with someone not very different from oneself whose aims, however, happen to be at cross-purposes with one's own – is not unusual in conflicts between individuals. It is found much less frequently in conflicts between social groups. The social psychological processes which intervene between the existence of various kinds of intergroup conflicts and the construction of widely diffused systems of beliefs about the ingroups and the outgroups will be discussed in some detail in the next few chapters. But the point that needs to be made at present is that these ideas, attitudes and systems of belief become an inherent part of the intergroup social situation and that, in a variety of conditions, they are able to deflect in one direction or another the course of the relations between the groups involved. To summarize: the existence and functioning of social stereotypes are one example (and by no means the most important one) of the way in which social psychological processes contribute to the texture of an objective intergroup social situation. They do not *create* such situations; on the contrary, as LeVine said, not only the origins of stereotypes but even their contents cannot be dissociated from the prior existence and the special characteristics of a conflict of interests. However, once they *are* in existence, they become in their own right one of the causal factors which needs to be taken into account in the analysis of intergroup relations.

It will be clear by now that, although part IV of this book is concerned with the social psychology of groups in conflict, it will not consist of attempts to 'reduce' the social reality of social conflicts to the consideration of their psychological concomitants. But an attempt will be made to describe psychological processes against their background which is to be found in the various kinds of relations between groups, and to determine what effects these processes may have upon the course of these relations.

Jerome Bruner once wrote that: 'one may speak of the corpus of myth as providing a set of possible identities for the individual personality. It would perhaps be more appropriate to say that the mythologically instructed community provides its members with a library of scripts upon which the individual may judge the play of his multiple identities' (1962, p. 36).

225

Part IV: Introduction

The work described in part II of this book was strongly influenced by Bruner's conceptions of the functioning of cognitive categories (e.g. Bruner, 1957). There are clear links between this early work, as described in chapters 4 and 5, and some aspects of the ideas about intergroup differentiation with which part IV is concerned. As already mentioned in the introductory chapter to this book, writing a chapter for a Festschrift for Bruner was one of the occasions which established for me a convergence between these earlier studies and a theoretical framework developed much later and presented here. The connection was expressed as follows in the Festschrift chapter (Tajfel, 1980a):

The social identity 'library of scripts' [to which Bruner referred in his 1962 essay] does not just 'exist' as an immutable fact of life. It is created out of social realities, it changes with them, it always includes views about 'others' without which the scripts would lose both their meaning and their function. In their continuous interdependence with the social realities of the group's relations with other groups, the scripts contain dimensions of comparisons and values with which these dimensions are endowed. Both the dimensions and the values are selected, enhanced, created or preserved as a function of what is possible and serviceable in the construction of myths and images, and of what is feasible in the undertaking of social action . . . The end result is often in the achievement of certain differentiations from the other groups . . . The continuity of these views about social differentiations with some of the earlier work on accentuation of differences in judgement has found an apt one-sentence summary recently proposed by Commins and Lockwood (1979): 'The social group is seen to function as a provider of positive social identity for its members through comparing itself and distinguishing itself, from other comparison groups, along salient dimensions which have a clear value differential' (pp. 281–2).

These differentiations have much in common with the findings about the combined functions of categorizations and values which followed after 'perceptual over-estimation' had lost its status as an oddity and was reconsidered as an instance of a wider judgemental process [see part I] . . . The systematization of the social world in terms of a *selection* of criteria as to what is important and what is not in a complex and overlapping matrix of social categories is not, as was already said, based on some immutable sets of preordained data. This selection involves at least three phases of social construction. One consists of the cultural creation and development in the society at large of a common background of myths, images, perspectives and interpretations concerning the social system and its organization. The second phase concerns the points of convergence and divergence, within this common background, of the perspectives adopted by various sub-groups which differ from each other in their location within the system. The third consists of the choices made by individuals between the perspectives which are available to them. No assumption is made in this 'constructional' view that we are dealing here with a collection of autistic departures from 'veridicality'. The 'constructions' results from an interaction

226

between, on the one hand, the social and physical realities of the life of a society, a community, a social group or an individual and, on the other, the 'values and needs', collective or individual, combined with the potentialities and the limitations of the cognitive tools we have at our disposal.

One final point remains to be made in this Introduction. The ideas outlined in part IV and the empirical studies mentioned in it have been, in very essential ways, the product of a team of people working together. The development of the theoretical views owes a great deal to the work of my colleagues (e.g. Turner, 1975; also see Billig, 1976 and various chapters in Tajfel, 1978a and Turner and Giles, 1981). This work led to a large number of experimental studies; reference to some of them or to summary reviews will be found in various chapters of part IV.

What may, however, turn out in the long run to be more important than the accumulation of laboratory experiments is the fact that the ideas outlined here have been found to be useful in field studies or interpretations of some social phenomena in a variety of 'real-life' concrete settings. Much of this work continues at present. Examples of recent applications include: linguistic aspects of ethnic identity (e.g. Bourhis *et al.*, 1973; Bourhis and Giles, 1977; Giles, 1978, 1979; Giles *et al.*, 1977a and b; Taylor and Giles, 1979); the effects of mass media on public attitudes concerning minority groups (Husband, 1977, 1979); inter-ethnic attitudes and conflicts in such diverse settings as Northern Ireland, Finland, Italy and Indonesia (Cairns, 1981 (in press) Capozza *et al.*, 1979; Jaspars, 1981 (in press); Liebkind, 1979); differentials and negotiations in industrial and hospital settings (Brown, 1978; Louche, 1976; Skevington, 1980); social status in academic institutions (Bourhis and Hill, 1981 (in press); van Knippenberg, 1978); ethnic attitudes in children (Vaughan, 1978a and b); problems of teenage identity in a period of widespread unemployment (Palmonari *et al.*, 1979); the role of women in society (Smith, 1978; Williams and Giles, 1978). It is the existence of this work which enabled me to write with some confidence in the first chapter of this book about its relevance to a genuinely 'social dimension' of social psychology and to describe it as one of the trends contributing to the recent development of social psychology in Europe.

11[1]

The attributes of intergroup behaviour

1. When does inter-individual behaviour become intergroup behaviour?

The question is of more than 'academic' interest. During the debates in Britain about the Race Relations Act, one of its opponents, a Conservative Member of Parliament, was reported in *The Times* (2 December, 1975) to have said that 'there was deep resentment in Britain at the thought of legislation being used to control what were the ordinary dealings of individuals with individuals'. The statement represents an extreme form of the 'individualistic' approach to intergroup relations (see chapters 2 and 3). Needless to say, its political implications are very far removed from the views and aims of many of the social psychologists who transpose theories and findings from inter-individual to intergroup settings. But the obvious answer that can be made to the M.P. can also be made to other 'reductions' of intergroup to inter-individual behaviour. Although he was right when he said that, in the last analysis, 'individuals' deal with 'individuals', they are not necessarily dealing with each other *as* individuals; quite often they behave primarily as members of well defined and clearly distinct social categories. When in conditions of racial discrimination people find it difficult to obtain accommodation or employment, it is not because they are ugly or handsome, short or tall, smiling or unsmiling, but because they are black. But this kind of an answer offers no more to a social psychologist than an opportunity for asking further questions. What are the conditions in which dealings between individuals will be determined, to a large extent, not by their personal relationships and individual characteristics but by their membership of different social groups? And what are the attributes of this kind of (intergroup) behaviour as compared with inter-individual behaviour?

---

[1] Chapters 11, 12 and 13 are extracts from H. Tajfel: The psychological structure of intergroup behaviour, which appeared as part I of H. Tajfel (ed.): *Differentiation between social groups: Studies in the social psychology of intergroup relations.* (European Monographs in Social Psychology, No. 14), London: Academic Press, 1978.

(a) A social psychological definition of group membership

Sherif's definition of intergroup behaviour is concerned with the distinctions just made, and leads to similar questions. As he wrote: 'Whenever individuals belonging to one group interact, collectively or individually, with another group or its members in terms of their group identification, we have an instance of intergroup behaviour' (1966, p. 12). In the terms of this definition, the questions could be as follows: What is a group and what is not a group? What is meant by group identification? How do instances of intergroup behaviour differ from other instances of social behaviour? To try and answer these questions we shall use the Humpty Dumpty principle of definitions; but although the definitions will be supposed to mean what we choose them to mean, they will remain generally consistent with the argument as it proceeds. Thus, for reasons which will become clear in the next chapter in the discussion of social categorization, social comparison and social identity, we shall adopt a concept of 'group' identical to the definition of 'nation' proposed by the historian Emerson (1960) when he wrote: 'The simplest statement that can be made about a nation is that it is a body of people who feel that they are a nation; and it may be that when all the fine-spun analysis is concluded this will be the ultimate statement as well' (p. 102).

This is a description of what 'is' a group which may include a range of between one to three components: a cognitive component, in the sense of the knowledge that one belongs to a group; an evaluative one, in the sense that the notion of the group and/or of one's membership of it *may* have a positive or a negative value connotation; and an emotional component in the sense that the cognitive and evaluative aspects of the group and one's membership of it *may* be accompanied by emotions (such as love or hatred, like or dislike) directed towards one's own group and towards others which stand in certain relations to it.

Sherif's interactions in terms of 'group identifications' are the more likely the stronger and are the evaluative and the emotional components of one's notion of the ingroup and of one's membership in it. The loose definition just proposed deliberately ignores the distinctions usually made between, for example, membership groups and reference groups or between face-to-face groups and large-scale social categories. Emerson's statement about nations was seen by him as 'ultimate' because, in the last analysis, members of a national group are considered as such when they categorize themselves with a high degree of consensus in the appropriate manner, and are consensually categorized in the same manner by others. His statement is essentially a social psychological one: it is not concerned with the historical, political, social and economic

events which may have led to the social consensus now defining who is
'in' and who is 'out'. But there is no doubt that these events were crucial
in the establishment of the nature of this consensus; and equally true that
the consensus, once established, represents those social psychological
aspects of social reality which interact with the social, political and
economic events determining the present and the future fate of the group
and of its relations with other groups.

From the point of view of a social psychologist whose interest in
conflict between 'groups' also encompasses social conflict, the deliberate
looseness and flexibility of this definition are quite important and useful.
One way to define social conflict, or rather to distinguish it roughly from
other kinds of conflict, is to say that it is a conflict between large-scale
socio-economic or socio-political groupings as distinct from conflicts
inside an individual, between individuals or between small groups. The
three aspects of group membership previously mentioned – the cognitive, the evaluative and the emotional – can be made to apply equally
well to small groups and to large social categories. The definitions have,
of course, nothing useful to say about the social and social psychological
conditions which determine the creation of the social-cognitive consensus about group membership, the development of positive or negative
evaluations of the group and of one's membership in it, and the
corresponding investment of emotion. Nor do they have anything to say
about the *effects* of all this on social behaviour towards the ingroup and
the relevant outgroups. They contribute, however, a useful point of
departure for the asking of appropriate questions both about these
conditions and about their effects.

The mention of the effects on social behaviour of group membership
in terms of our definition of groups raises, of course, the spectre of
tautology. How can this membership be ascertained outside of its
behavioural effects, and what can therefore be meant by its cognitive,
evaluative and emotional aspects *preceding* these behavioural effects? The
methodological problem is not as insoluble as it may appear to be, either
in 'natural' situations or in those contrived in the social psychological
experiments. In the former case, the problem concerns the relationship
between the objective criteria of the membership of a group or a social
category, as they may be used by an outside observer, and their
correspondence with the psychological reality of such a classification to
the people who have been 'externally' assigned to one group or another.
One would not have had to wait for the South Moluccans in Holland to
have held to ransom a train with all its passengers, and a large number of
schoolchildren, in order to know that at least some of them, or perhaps
most of them (i.e. amongst those *objectively* defined on some criteria as

South Moluccans) considered themselves as a separate and distinct group within the Dutch population. Anyone who wished to know would have had to do no more than ask a few questions, or use for the purpose the available methodological tools. It would have also been possible to determine the degree of awareness (i.e. the cognitive component) of this group membership, the extent and direction of the evaluations associated with it, and the degree and nature of the emotional involvement. However, an important point must be made at this stage: even with this knowledge being acquired, predictions of the *effects* on social behaviour of the presumed convergence of the three components of group membership amongst the South Moluccans in Holland cannot be made unless there is in existence some theoretical structure from which these predictions can originate. It is also interesting from our point of view that, what appeared from newspaper reports as a very high degree of intensity of the South Moluccans' ingroup affiliation, need not be related, either in principle or in reality, to any requirement of face-to-face interaction between all, or most, members of the group.

This would therefore appear to be a case for which there exists some correspondence between external or objective criteria of group membership and the definition of group adopted here. Cases in which this correspondence does not exist are just as important, since negative instances are as necessary as the positive ones for the breaking of tautological vicious circles. For example, if one went from a country in which 'colour' distinctions matter profoundly to one in which they are irrelevant to social stratifications or social behaviour, the continuing feedback of one's responses in a variety of social situations would sooner or later modify one's criteria of social categorization. The methodological translation of this kind of example would be on the lines very similar to the South Moluccans' case above, with results in the opposite direction.

It is important, however, at this point to make a clear distinction between two kinds of external criteria of group membership, i.e. those criteria which do not originate from the self-identification of the members of a group. The objective criteria used by naive outside observer or sometimes a social scientist without a sufficient knowledge of the culture which he studies may sometimes go wrong – as would be the case of a Martian social scientist coming to Europe with the deep conviction, embedded in all his past experience, that the clear distinction between blue eyes and brown eyes is endowed with profound social significance. The other kind of external criteria are those consistently used in relation to a selected group by *other* groups in any multi-group social organization. These criteria are highly likely to correspond, in the

231

long run, to the internal ones delimiting the membership of the group in question.

The first of the three components of group membership previously mentioned has been referred to above as social–cognitive. The social aspect of it resides in the consensus about group membership which is necessary if this membership is to become effective as a determinant of social uniformities (as distinct from individual variability) in social behaviour relating to the ingroup and the outgroups. The consensus about 'who is who' will be in many cases shared by the group socially categorized in certain ways and by the surrounding groups by which and from which it is perceived as distinct. But a stronger statement can be made: the consensus may often *originate* from other groups and determine in turn the creation of various kinds of internal membership criteria within the ingroup. It is likely, for example, that the continuation of the Jewish group identity, despite the increasing difficulty in several countries in the last century or so of establishing any set of consistent objective criteria distinguishing Jew from non-Jew, had as much to do with the consensus in the outgroups about the existence of a distinct group known as 'Jews' as with the corresponding ingroup consensus (see e.g. Herman, 1970).

The escape from the possible tautology of our social psychological definition of groups à la Emerson must also be considered in the setting of experimental studies on intergroup behaviour. The point of departure is once again the correspondence, or the lack of it, between the external and the internal criteria of group membership. In this case, the external criteria are those assumed to exist and/or imposed by the experimenter, and the internal criteria are those used by his subjects and presumed to guide their behaviour in the experiment.

In principle, four types of situations can be distinguished from this point of view. In the first type, the experimenter uses 'natural' groups (i.e. those which are assumed to have existed as such before the experiment) and introduces various manipulations whose nature depends upon the questions he asks, his hypotheses, predictions, etc. As natural groups are used, the problems of correspondence are not in this case different, in principle, from those just discussed in relation to the fully 'naturalistic' situations. The second type, represented by the series of Sherif's studies (1951, 1953, 1961, 1966), consists of an explicit imposition by the experimenter of what he considers to be powerful group divisions. These divisions are imposed in the hope that they will be reflected in any or all of the cognitive, evaluative and emotional aspects of the 'subjective' group identifications. The correspondence problems here are also similar to those which exist in the naturalistic situations. For example, Sherif's aim was to ascertain the effects on intergroup behaviour of certain forms of conflict between his experimental groups. He used a variety of measures and informal observations of social behaviour *before* the explicit conflict had developed. There should therefore be no difficulty in establishing that, at the time of the 'manipulation' (i.e. the introduction of the explicit conflict), the subjects considered themselves as members of separate and distinct groups. Consequently, their behaviour during the conflict (and also afterwards) could be considered a reflection in *new* conditions of those previously existing subjective group identifications. In other words, this behaviour was a *joint* function of phenomenally 'real' group memberships and of a certain specific set of new relations between the groups plotted in advance by the experimenter.

The third of our four types is less simple although it represents, in a way, a variant of the second type which has just been discussed. As before, there is an imposition by the experimenter of an explicit intergroup division, but this is considerably less powerful than was the case in Sherif's studies. There can be, of course, various degrees of 'strength' of this external imposition. This depends upon the number and the nature of the variables that the experimenter brings to bear to make it clear to his subjects that they are indeed in two or more separate and distinct groups; and it is a truism that the more powerful is this imposition, the more likely it is that independent evidence will be found for its phenomenal effectiveness. This is why we shall take as our example the *minimal* degree of imposition, on the assumption that if our subjective definition of groups can be shown to be useful in these conditions, it should be useful *a fortiori* in less demanding circumstances.

Examples of these minimal degrees of imposition upon the subjects of an intergroup classification are to be found in several fairly recent experiments (e.g. Rabbie and Wilkens, 1971; Tajfel, 1970b; Tajfel *et al.*, 1971, and several subsequent variations and modifications). They have reached what is probably a limit of being as minimal as possible in an experiment by Billig and Tajfel (1973). The general principles of this minimal imposition are simply stated: the subjects are divided into two 'groups' on the basis of criteria which are assumed to be quite unimportant to them (such as expressing a preference for one or the other of two painters they have never heard of before – although in reality the subjects are randomly assigned to one or the other 'preference' groups, and the paintings of which they see the reproductions on slides are also randomly designated as being by one or the other painter). The subjects do not interact during the experiment, either within or betweeen the 'groups'. Each subject is informed of his own group membership based on his preferences but the membership of all the other subjects, whether in his own group or in the other, remains anonymous to him. Each subject is then isolated for a short time when he is asked to make decisions through which he allots various amounts of money to two *other* subjects only designated by individual code numbers and by their respective group membership. Three types of pairs of recipients are used for the decisions about awards of money: the first consists of someone from the subject's own group versus someone from the other group; in the second, both recipients are from his own group; in the third, both recipients are from the outgroup. Before they make their decisions, the subjects are informed that each of them will receive at the end of the experiment the total amount of money allotted to him anonymously by the others (which is indeed done – very approximately – at the end of the experimental session). In the experiment by Billig and Tajfel (1973), the height of absurdity was reached in the method used to divide the subjects into 'groups'. Even the pretence of differences between the groups in aesthetic preferences was dropped, and each subject was explicitly and visibly assigned to one group or the other on the basis of a random toss of a coin.

We shall have to return to these experiments and their results at various points of the subsequent discussions. For the present, our concern is with the possible circularity of the definition of group proposed earlier when the attempt is made to apply it to 'groups' concocted in these conditions by the imposition of the experimenters' 'minimal' categorizations. Three questions arise: have the subjects accepted the experimenters' arbitrary criteria dividing them into groups; or – in the terms previously used – is there a correspondence between the external (the experimenters') criteria and the internal (phenomenal) criteria of group membership? If so, what are the effects of this phenomenal acceptance? And finally, how – if at all – can these *effects* be conceptually distinguished from what is supposed to precede and determine them, i.e. the reality for the subjects of one or more of the three subjective aspects of group membership (cognitive, evaluative and emotional) which have previously been mentioned?

The question about effects is the simplest one to answer: a variety of measures have shown that, in these initial experiments as well as in all the others which followed them, most of the subjects acted very consistently in the direction of favouring in their decisions anonymous members of their own groups at the expense of the anonymous members of the outgroups. It can therefore also be said that, at some level, there is a correspondence between the experimenters' external criteria and the subjects' internal criteria guiding their behaviour. But is this correspondence due to their 'felt' membership of a group? Or is it due to some other factors, such as the possibility that they were presented by the experimental design with a 'forced choice' of criteria for decisions (as assumed by Gerard and Hoyt, 1974), or at least with strong implicit encouragement to use an externally imposed and otherwise meaningless division?

The 'forced choice' argument is easily dismissed if it is meant to imply that the subjects were not given the opportunity to choose strategies other than those of favouring the anonymous members of their own groups. The 'matrices' on which their decisions were made allowed for a number of other strategies, some of which were used by some subjects on some occasions, and some by many subjects on many occasions. None of them, however, attained anywhere near (with the occasional exception of the use of fairness as a moderator of ingroup bias) the consistency, the level and the frequency of adopting a course of action which led either to giving more to the ingroup member than to the outgroup member, or to giving *less* than might have been possible to either of the recipients when this was the only way open to giving relatively more to the ingroup member than to the outgroup member.

The 'implicit encouragement' argument is, however, more serious and more difficult to deal with, whether it appears in the form relating it to the 'experimenter effect' (Rosenthal, 1966) or to the 'demand characteristics' of an experimental situation (Orne, 1962). As a matter of fact, it was this difficulty that Gerard and Hoyt (1974) had in mind rather than a simple 'forced choice' contention, although the distinction between the two was less than clear in their article. Simply and briefly stated, the argument amounts to the following: the subjects acted in terms of the intergroup categorization provided or imposed by the experiments not necessarily because this has been successful in inducing any genuine awareness of membership in separate and distinct groups, but probably because they felt that this kind of behaviour was expected of them by the experimenters; and therefore they conformed to this expectation.

The first question to ask is: why should the subjects be expecting the experimenters to expect of them this kind of behaviour? The Gerard and Hoyt answer is that the experimental situation was rigged to cause this kind of expectation in the subjects. However, this answer retains its plausibility only if we assume that what was no more than a hint from the experimenters about the notion of 'groups' being relevant to the subjects' behaviour had been sufficient to determine, powerfully and consistently, a *particular form* of intergroup behaviour. In turn, if we assume this (and the assumption is by no means unreasonable), we must also assume that this particular form of intergroup behaviour is one which is capable of being induced by the experimenters more easily than other forms (such as cooperation between the groups in extorting the maximum *total* amount of money from the experimenters, or a fair division of spoils between the groups, or simply random responding) – at least in our culture. And this last assumption must be backed up in its turn by another presupposition: namely, that for some reasons (whatever they may be) competitive behaviour between groups, at least in our culture, is extraordinarily easy to trigger off – at which point we are back where we started from. The problem then must be restated once again in terms of the need to specify why a certain *kind* of intergroup behaviour can be elicited so much more easily than other kinds; and this specification is certainly not made if we rest content with the explanation that the behaviour occurred because it was very easy for the experimenters to make it occur.

The alternative to this explanatory dead end is to assume that the subjects structured the situation for themselves as one involving relations between groups, and that they behaved in ways similar to those habitual to them in situations of this kind. This alternative leaves untouched, of course, the whole matter of explaining what precisely makes this behaviour 'habitual'; but as this issue will be discussed later in this chapter and in the following ones, we shall leave it at present in order to return to the usefulness, in this third type of experimental situation, of our Emersonian definition of group membership.

In the two previous types of experiments, the problem was resolved because of the possibilities inherent in them of cross-validating phenomenal group membership through indices additional to and independent from the observed effects of any particular experimental manipulation. This would be much more difficult in the third 'minimal' type with which we are now concerned. The reason for the difficulty is that the existence and intensity of the subjective group membership in these experiments is probably no less fleeting than the validity to the subjects of the imposed criteria for intergroup categorization. But even here, what is difficult is not necessarily impossible: in the initial Tajfel *et al.* (1971) experiments, the subjects who had already finished their tasks and were waiting together for the others to return one by one from their isolation cubicles, greeted each of the arrivals with half-jocular but eager inquiries about 'which were you' followed by appropriate cheers and catcalls. This is, however, hardly convincing as evidence. It seems much more useful to consider the phenomenal group membership in these circumstances as a respectable and fairly usual kind of intervening variable on condition that it can earn its methodological respectability. In other words, if its effects on social behaviour can be predicted and made to be dependent upon its presumed presence or absence in a social situation, there is no reason why it should not be considered as a heuristic device which adequately serves its purposes.

Many of the studies recently reported (see e.g. Brewer, 1979; Tajfel, 1980b; Tajfel and Turner, 1979; Turner and Giles, 1981, for recent reviews) satisfied either the requirements just mentioned or alternatively those mentioned in relation to the first two types of intergroup experiments. This was also already the case in one of the earlier experiments (Billig and Tajfel, 1973). The study was designed for the explicit purpose of testing the effectiveness of the notion of 'group' in inducing the predicted bias in favour of the ingroup in the subsequent awards of money to members of the ingroup and the outgroup. In one of the experimental conditions, as already mentioned above, the subjects were divided into two groups explicitly on the basis of random tosses of coins. In the other, they were divided on the basis of aesthetic preferences (as in the Tajfel *et al.*, 1971, experiments) but the notion of 'groups' was carefully kept out of all the communications between the experimenters and the subjects. Thus, in one of the conditions, there was a 'pure' categorization into groups devoid of any basis in similarity within the group, as distinct from the earlier experiments in which common group membership was defined by a common preference for the same painter. In the other condition, there was a similarity within each of the two categories of subjects, defined again by a common aesthetic preference, but the stress was on *individuals* and inter-individual similarities and differences, and not on group membership. The results showed clearly on several independent measures that discrimination in awards of money in favour of the 'random' ingroup was significantly more marked and consistent than discrimination in favour of 'similar' other individuals. In a third condition, in which the criteria of 'groupness' and of individual similarity were combined, discrimination was the strongest.

It may be interesting to note, in a parenthesis, the relevance of these findings to one of the points made earlier in this chapter. This was concerned with the powerful impact that the consensus of outsiders may have on the formation of a 'subjective' group membership amongst those who have been lumped together as a group by others, even on the basis of generally inconsistent and varying criteria. This 'empty' group condition in the experiment just described illustrates the *reductio ad absurdum* of this process, but it also shows how easily it can be set in motion (see chapter 15).

The results of the three conditions of the experiment (the fourth was a control condition) lend themselves to a parsimonious explanation if one assumes a successful induction (in the first and third conditions described above) of subjective group membership and its absence in the second condition. A simple 'forced choice' argument would be quite incapable of accounting for the differences in results between the conditions. Various forms of explanations in terms of 'implicit encouragement' lead to the theoretical circularities already described.

The fourth type of intergroup experimental situations can be dealt with very briefly, as it does not present problems which differ from those already discussed. These are the situations in which behaviour favouring the ingroup occurred, although the experimenters either did not predict it, or even strenuously tried to prevent it. Several examples are available, but one will be sufficient for our purposes. Ferguson and Kelley (1964) had two groups of subjects which engaged, each group in common, in various tasks. It was explicitly stated that the idea was *not* to try and do better than the other group but for each group to do as well as it could. The products of each group were subsequently rated by some of its members who did not themselves take part in the work, and therefore had no individual axes to grind. Despite this, they consistently over-estimated the quality of the products of their own group relative to the outgroup although there were no objective grounds for this stubborn partiality.

Instances of this fourth type of experiment can be assigned to one of the preceding three types with regard to their relevance to defining group membership in phenomenal terms. The nature of this assignment will depend, as before, upon the origins and strength of the imposition of external criteria for group membership; this may vary, as before, from the use of previously existing 'natural' criteria to the use of criteria which are either strongly or minimally induced *ad hoc* for the experimenters' purposes. In each case, the social psychological 'reality' of group membership can either be empirically cross-validated or used as a heuristic device, or both.

(b) The interpersonal–intergroup continuum

This discussion of a social psychological notion of group membership and of its applications to the various settings, natural and experimental, of intergroup relations may lead to a serious misunderstanding. Nothing that was said earlier was meant to imply that individuals or groups 'have' stable group identifications of a certain kind; or that the cognitive, evaluative and emotional components of these subjective memberships are indiscriminately expressed in behaviour in any, or even most, social situations or social settings. There is a reciprocal (or 'dialectical') relationship between social settings and situations on the one hand, and the reflection or expression in them of subjective group memberships on the other. The general principles of this relationship need to be briefly stated.

The number and variety of social situations which an individual will perceive as being relevant in some ways to his group membership will increase as a function of: (i) the clarity of his awareness that he is a member of a certain group; (ii) the extent of the positive or negative evaluations associated with this membership; and (iii) the extent of the emotional investment in the awareness and the evaluations. Or, in Sherif's terms, all this will increase the number and variety of situations in which an individual will 'interact, collectively or individually, with another group or its members in terms of their group identification'. Conversely, there will be *some* social situations which will force most individuals involved, however weak and unimportant to them may have been their *initial* group identifications, to act in terms of their group membership. It is likely, of course, that these situations, as they develop and continue, will enhance for many people the significance to them of the initially 'weak' forms of their group membership. A third principle, following from the conjunction of the two previous ones, must therefore also be stated: an important aspect of the interaction between the two principles just mentioned is that there is a positive feedback between them. Social situations which force the individuals involved to act in terms of their group membership also enhance for them some group identifications which had previously not been very significant to them, or perhaps even create or bring to life group memberships which were previously only dormant or potential. As a consequence, and in terms of the first principle, many of those people will be likely to perceive *in common* an increasingly greater number and variety of social situations as relevant in some ways to their group membership.

It is not our purpose here to discuss in any detail the various 'traditional' approaches to the social psychology of intergroup relations. But it may be worth mentioning *en passant* that some of the most influential amongst them are characterized by a curiously truncated view of social psychological reality as it reflects the interaction between the three principles just outlined. For example, an approach to intergroup relations in terms of individual patterns of prejudice – represented in social psychology by a massive literature – often takes into account and develops in various ways the first of the three principles without paying much regard to its interaction with the other two. The same is true of the approaches based on theories of individual motivation most clearly represented by the frustration–aggression hypothesis and its various developments (see chapter 2).

We shall return in the next section of this chapter to a discussion of some of the social situations which are likely to promote an increase in the significance to the individuals of their social group membership. But before this is done, we need to elaborate upon the basic differences between social behaviour which can be considered as inter-individual and behaviour which can be referred to as being of an intergroup character.

These differences can be conceived as lying on a continuum, one extreme of which can be described as being 'purely' interpersonal and the other as 'purely' intergroup. What is meant by 'purely' interpersonal is any social encounter between two or more people in which *all* the interaction that takes place is determined by the personal relationships between the individuals and by their respective individual characteristics. The 'intergroup' extreme is that in which *all* of behaviour of two or more individuals towards each other is determined by their membership of different social groups or categories.

At least one of these extremes – the interpersonal one – is absurd, in the sense that no instances of it can conceivably be found in 'real life'. It is impossible to imagine a social encounter between two people which will not be affected, at least to some minimal degree, by their mutual assignments of one another to a variety of social categories about which some general expectations concerning their characteristics and behaviour exist in the minds of the interactants. This will be true, for example, even of wives and husbands or of old friends who have different jobs or are of different ages, sexes, nationalities, religions, or whatever; and even truer of professional 'role' encounters – as between patient and doctor, student and teacher, car owner and mechanic – however familiar those people may have become and however close their personal relationships may happen to be.

The other extreme – of 'purely' intergroup behaviour – is less empirically absurd in the sense that fairly clear examples of it can be found in real situations. An air force crew bombing an enemy population target is an example, and so is any battle waged by soldiers of opposing armies out of sight of each other. The moment, however, the soldiers come to be able to distinguish individual specimens amongst their opponents, some aspects of their behaviour towards them may be affected by some individual characteristics. This, is, however, *inconsistently* related to the paramount categorization into 'us' and 'them'. For example, an individual attack on a big fellow from the other side may be conducted differently from the attack on a little one; or even on occasions an incipient personal relationship may develop in these highly adverse circumstances and make some difference to what happens between two or more people from the opposite sides of a battle. But it still remains true that even if this happens, the vast majority of inter-individual encounters set within an intensely intergroup context will be much more powerfully determined by that context than by any other social relationships which may develop between the people involved. The selection for the gas ovens in the concentration camps during World War Two was undoubtedly, to some small extent, affected by the individual characteristics of those who were so selected, by the individual whims or 'personalities' of the selectors or by some personal relationships which may have developed here and there. All this hardly amounts to more than a wrinkle if it is our aim to describe and understand the most significant *general* aspects of what happened. Examples – many of them much more frequent and familiar in 'normal' life and less extreme in their tragic significance – could be multiplied.

In returning briefly from this point of view to the experiments on 'minimal' groups described earlier in this chapter (Tajfel *et al.*, 1971), it may be interesting to note that, in a paradoxical sense and seen from a different perspective, they may well be considered as 'maximal' rather than minimal. One of our aims was to simulate in the laboratory – even if crudely – a situation in which members of one group act towards members of another in complete disregard of the individual differences between them. The (imposed) anonymity of the 'outsiders' insured in the experiments that no variations would occur in the way they were treated; this anonymity did not prevent (and undoubtedly contributed to) treating them less favourably than the 'insiders'. The common denominator of all these examples – from the contrived absurdities of the experiments to the tragic realities of the War – is the depersonalization of the members of the outgroup. The next stage is often their dehumanization. In the experiments, the depersonalizing anonymity was created in a *deus ex machina* fashion by the experimenters. In real life it is generated by the actors themselves as a function of the intergroup situation within which they act; but otherwise, certain similarities in the nature of the resulting social behaviour are quite striking.

We have therefore a continuum which goes from the probably fictitious extreme of 'purely' interpersonal behaviour to the rarely-encountered extreme of 'purely' intergroup behaviour. All of the 'natural' (and also experimental) social situations fall between these two extremes, and the behaviour towards people who are categorized as members of the ingroup or the outgroup will be crucially affected by the individuals' perception (or rather interpretation) of the situation as being being nearer to one or to the other extreme. But this statement contains its own limitations, and it is important to make them as explicit as possible. There are the extreme outgroup haters who are likely to perceive all (or most) social situations involving the objects of their hatred as being relevant to the relations between the groups involved. But to most people, the simple appearance of members of an outgroup in a social situation does not necessarily classify the situation as being of an intergroup nature and does not therefore necessarily imply that they will engage in the corresponding forms of social behaviour. This may be true even when the groups in question are involved in a conflict, although the more intense is the conflict the wider will be the range of situations which are likely to be perceived as relevant to it.

The points just made are really no more than a reiteration, in different terms and from a slightly different perspective, of the three interacting principles of salience of 'subjective' group membership which were outlined a little earlier in this section. Their restatement in a slightly different form is an attempt to avoid an ambiguity which could otherwise easily raise its ugly head, and had already done so on occasions. The theoretical framework presented in part IV of this book is *not* an attempt to put forward some kind of a general or universal theory of social behaviour. Although everyone is, on occasion, a committed member of one ingroup or another, and although every ingroup has its outgroups, much (if not most) of our social behaviour in many circumstances may have very little to do with this membership. We are therefore concerned with only one class of social situations, however large, varied and important this class may be, and with forms of social behaviour which are relevant to it. We are *not* concerned with one or another type of individuals or 'personalities' who are forever condemned by their emotional difficulties to act as 'insiders' towards others who are forever and in all circumstances their selected 'outsiders'. A vast majority of people may, in their various social encounters, engage in interactions which have almost everything to do with their respective group memberships, or very little to do with them. No one has illustrated this more cogently than Wilfred Owen in the poem which Benjamin Britten used to conclude the *War Requiem*. In it, one dead soldier says to another: 'I am the enemy you killed, my friend.' The 'enemy' and the 'friend' occurring in the same sentence have both been profoundly true at different times: the former during the horrors of the battle which had just finished, the latter, when it is now all over, the past divisions have disappeared, and the only one that still matters is between the dead and the living, between those who died for nothing and those who managed not to.

Some of the principal attributes of behaviour towards members of outgroups in social situations nearing the intergroup extreme of our continuum have already been mentioned in the previous discussion. They can be briefly summarized as follows: first, social behaviour will be to a large extent independent of individual differences either in the ingroup or in the outgroup. Second, it will be to a large extent independent of the personal relationships which may exist in *other* situations between individual members of the two groups. Third, it will be to a large extent unaffected by temporary motivational states of individuals during an encounter, or just preceding an encounter, or during a series of encounters. The major *common* determining features of social behaviour in these situations are as follows: a *shared* ingroup affiliation of the individuals concerned (in the sense of the social psychological definition of group membership discussed earlier); and a *shared* interpretation of the relations between the ingroup and the outgroup *as applied* to a particular social situation or to a series of such situations. The intergroup instances of social behaviour can therefore be conceived as being a joint function of these affiliations and interpretations.

All the statements just made can be rephrased in terms of two wider generalizations:

(i) The nearer is a social situation (as interpreted by members of a group) to the intergroup extreme of the interpersonal–intergroup continuum, the more uniformity will the individual members of the groups concerned show in their behaviour towards members of outgroups. Conversely, the nearer is the situation to the interpersonal end, the more variability will be shown in behaviour towards members of outgroups.

(ii) The nearer is a social situation to the intergroup extreme, the stronger tendency will there be for members of the ingroup to treat members of the outgroup as undifferentiated items in a unified social category, i.e. independently of the individual differences between them. This will be reflected simultaneously in a clear awareness of the ingroup–outgroup dichotomy, in the attribution to members of the outgroup of certain traits assumed to be common to the group as a whole, in value judgements pertaining to these traits, in the emotional significance associated with these evaluations, and in other forms of behaviour associated with the ingroup–outgroup categorization.

These two variability–uniformity continua can therefore be seen as providing a transition between the group's interpretation of a social situation as being primarily of an intergroup nature and the effects of this on various forms of social behaviour. The next section of this chapter will be concerned with some of the major social psychological conditions which are assumed to be responsible for consensual interpretations by members of a group of their relations with members of another group as being primarily of an intergroup rather than of an interpersonal character.

2. From social mobility to social movements

According to Heberle (1968), 'the term "social movement" or its equivalent in other Western languages is being used to denote a wide variety of collective attempts to bring about a change in certain social institutions or to create an entirely new order' (pp. 438–9). Toch (1965) agreed with this definition approximately (although he widened it) when he wrote that 'the key element in most definitions of social movements is the requirement that they must be *aimed at promoting or resisting change* in society at large' (p. 5, italics in the original). To distinguish social movements from other forms of collective behaviour, Toch also characterized them as consisting of 'large groups' and as being 'relatively long-lasting'. The psychological counterpart of these definitions is formulated by Toch as follows: 'A social movement represents an effort by a large number of people to solve collectively a problem that they feel they have in common' (p. 5). In turn, in a widely accepted definition, 'social mobility is the movement of individuals, families and groups from one social position to another' (Goldhamer, 1968, p. 429).

We shall narrow these definitions a little to suit as clearly as possible the purposes of the present discussion, without however departing from their general sense. Social change which, according to Toch, social movements aim at promoting or resisting, will be understood here as a change in the nature of the relations between large-scale social groups, such as socio-economic, national, religious, racial or ethnic categories; and therefore social movements will be understood on the social psychological level as, to paraphrase Toch again, efforts by large numbers of people, who define themselves and are also often defined by others as a group, to solve collectively a problem they feel they have in common, and which is perceived to arise from their relations with other groups. As to social mobility, we shall restrict the term to *individual* social mobility, i.e. to the movement of individuals and families (leaving out therefore the groups of Goldhamer's definition) from one social position to another. In turn, this individual mobility from one social position to another will refer to movement (whether it is upwards, downwards or horizontally) from one social group to another.

The basis of the distinctions previously made between interpersonal and intergroup behaviour was that in the former case individuals interact as individuals and in the latter they interact in terms of their respective group memberships. From the point of this distinction, it is not crucially important whether the 'groups' involved are face-to-face groups, large social categories, reference groups or even imaginary groups created by social consensus – as is the case in some witch hunts.

The basic *condition* for the appearance of extreme forms of intergroup behaviour (i.e. as was stated in the preceding section, behaviour in which individual differences in the outgroup matter very little or not at all) is the belief that the relevant social boundaries between the groups are sharply drawn and immutable, in the sense that, for whatever reasons, it is impossible or at least very difficult for individuals to move from one group to the other. In the same way, the basic condition for the appearance of predominantly interpersonal behaviour between individuals who assign themselves to distinct groups is the belief that the same socially relevant intergroup boundaries are flexible and that there are no special difficulties inhibiting individual social mobility from one group to another.

The grounds on which these two structures of beliefs are assumed here to determine respectively the intergroup and the interpersonal forms of social behaviour will become clearer if we consider two major examples, both taken from 'real' social situations. One of these is the existence, and/or the belief in the existence, of fairly rigid social stratifications within a society. The other is the existence of an intense conflict of interest between the groups which may or may not be related to some enduring forms of stratification. The social stratifications may be of various kinds: socio-economic, ethnic, racial, religious, national, based on criteria of birth, etc. The common feature of their rigidity is that it is impossible, or at least very difficult, for individuals to move from one group to another, and that this difficulty is created by laws, rules, sanctions and social norms designed to prevent the members of a lower-status group from penetrating into the higher-status group. At the same time, it would hardly be attractive for members of the 'higher' groups to try and join the 'lower' ones, even if there were no serious social sanctions for doing this – and such sanctions are a fairly common occurrence.

We can distinguish *a priori* between several major sets of social psychological attributes of these stratifications which are likely to determine different forms of social behaviour relating to them. The first consists of the consensus in *all* the groups involved that the criteria for the stratification are both legitimate and stable (i.e. incapable of being changed). The second consists of the consensus existing (or developing) in one or more groups that the criteria are neither legitimate nor incapable of change. The third arises when one or more groups believe that the criteria are illegitimate but unchangeable (because of, for example, drastic differences in power between the groups). And the fourth – conversely – when they are believed to be legitimate but unstable (i.e. capable of change). The third and fourth sets of attributes most probably interact in many cases – in the sense that perceived illegitimacy is likely to determine, sooner or later, attempts to change the situation; and the perceived instability (which can be translated as the development in a group of the awareness of cognitive alternatives to the existing situation) is likely to be associated, sooner or later, with the decrease in that group of the perceived legitimacy of the situation. It will be obvious that a combination of illegitimacy and instability would become a powerful incitement for attempts to change the intergroup *status quo* or to resist such changes on the part of the groups which see themselves as threatened by them. In other words, this combination will transform a potential and sometimes smouldering social conflict into one which is explicitly acknowledged as such by the groups involved. In the sense of the definitions offered at the beginning of this section, it will therefore determine a development of social movements aiming to create or to prevent social change which is conceived here as a change in the nature of the relations between the groups.

These considerations can be summarized more systematically by translating them into a description of yet another continuum relevant to the nature of intergroup behaviour. It differs from the previously described continua (interpersonal v. intergroup behaviour, and variability v. uniformity of behaviour in the ingroup and of its treatment of members of the outgroup) in that it has a *causal* function in relation to these other distinctions. It is a continuum of *structures of beliefs* concerning the nature of intergroup relations. We shall describe it as moving from the extreme of 'social mobility' to the extreme of 'social change'. The former is defined here as an individual's perception (most often shared with many others) that he can improve in important ways his position in a social situation, or more generally move from one social position to another, *as an individual*. The first direct implication of this is that the individual's system of beliefs about the society in which he lives contains the expectation that, in principle, he is able to leave his present social group or groups and move to other groups which suit him better. 'Social mobility' in this sense consists therefore of a subjective structuring of a social system (however small or large the system may be) in which the basic assumption is that the system is flexible and permeable, that it permits a fairly free movement from one group to another of the individual particles of which it consists. It does not matter very much, from the point of view of the present discussion, whether the causation of free individual movement is perceived as being due to luck, merit, hard work, talent, ability or other attributes of individuals.

'Social change', as the term is used here, refers to the other extreme of the subjective modes of structuring the social system in which an individual lives. It refers basically to his belief that he is enclosed within the walls of the social group of which he is a member; that he cannot move out of his own into another group in order to improve or change his position or his conditions of life; and that therefore the only way for him to change these conditions (or, for that matter, to resist the change of these conditions if he happens to be satisfied with them) is together with his group as a whole, as a member of it rather than as someone who leaves it, and who can act in a variety of relevant social situations as an individual independently of his group membership.

The position of an individual (or, as is more often the case, simultaneously of large numbers of individuals) on the social mobility–social change continuum of structures of belief is assumed here to be a powerful determinant of acting towards members of outgroups either on an interpersonal basis or an intergroup basis. But unless this statement is seen in the perspective of diverse forms of social reality, it is likely to lead to unwarranted over-simplifications. In one sense, the simplest case is when a rigid social stratification, on whatever criteria it may be based, is reflected in the image that the members of various groups in a social system have of the system's structure and its organization. When this reflection begins to be accompanied by the belief in some of the groups that the system lacks legitimacy and that it is capable of change, the new psychological 'problems' confronting these groups have a *finite* number of psychological solutions. These problems and solutions will be discussed in chapter 13, together with the problems and solutions pertaining to groups which wish and need to resist the threatening change in the *status quo*. But there exist at least three more variants of social conditions which determine the 'social change' structure of beliefs. They are all placed here under one and the same theoretical umbrella because they lead to similar predictions concerning the nature of social behaviour towards outgroups which is their consequence.

These three variants can be briefly described as follows: the first concerns social conditions in which the existing divisions into groups do not form a stratification preventing an individual from moving, if he so wishes, from one group to another. Correspondingly, the structure of beliefs in 'social change', if it exists, is not directly based upon this perceived impossibility of individual mobility. This is the case of *some* of the nationalist movements which are gathering strength at present. The second variant concerns certain individuals within a society who – for whatever reasons – *need* to structure their social environment in the form of beliefs about clear-cut and impenetrable distinctions between *certain* social groups. In some social conditions, these individuals may be in a position to create social movements. Much of the traditional social psychology of prejudice has been concerned with this second variant, neglecting the fact that it is no more than one instance amongst several – an instance which is by no means the most important, either socially or theoretically. The third variant concerns a direct conflict of interests between groups which is not related to any enduring status differences between the groups, or to the belief in the existence of such differences.

The first two of these three variants share two important features. One of these features is a discrepancy between the existing 'social change' beliefs and the ascertainable realities of the social situation which *does* allow for easy individual social mobility in certain important directions. The second common feature of these two variants is that, *because* of this discrepancy between beliefs and social reality, the development of the 'social change' structure of beliefs must be accompanied by a great deal of social creativity, i.e. it must be related to the development of new ideologies and attitudes and also of their emotional concomitants. These two theoretical similarities are, in a way, paradoxical because – as will be seen – there are drastic ethical, social and political differences in the implications of these first two variants.

A clear example of the first can be found in the recent development and intensification of some national movements. The relationships between the social background of some of these movements and the social psychological processes which develop in them must be distinguished from situations where there is a close correspondence between the realities of a social stratification and the corresponding 'social change' system of beliefs. For example, the socio-economic and other crucial objective differences of status and mode of life between blacks and whites in South Africa are beyond dispute, and they can easily fit in with the 'social change' structure of beliefs as soon as these differences begin to lose their perceived legitimacy and stability. To a lesser extent, but also quite clearly, the same is true of any society in which birth, religion, social background, race, language or other cultural and social characteristics of a group of people are a crippling load they continue to carry with them in a large variety of social situations and social positions. But all this is not necessarily true of many situations in which the social assimilation of an individual from one group to another presents no special difficulties. A Welshman in Britain need hardly suffer *individually* as a *Welshman*, wherever he lives in the United Kingdom, and chooses to remember and demonstrate his Welshness in a variety of ways. Despite this, there is today a rapid development of national group awareness in Wales which is shown in a number of new linguistic, cultural, educational, economic and political initiatives. There is now an important and active group of people in Wales whose aim it is to foster the 'social

change' structure of beliefs for which they use all the initiatives just
mentioned. It is not within the competence of a social psychologist to
describe or analyse in any detail the social, economic and historical
background for the development of this kind of social movement; but it
is not difficult for him to ascertain its existence and to assume that its
diffusion may have a lot to do with the operation of the processes of
'minority social influence' such as described, for example, by Moscovici
(1976).

To return to our social mobility–social change continuum of structures
of belief, we are dealing here with a group of people who are attempting
to *create* or intensify what we called earlier in this chapter a 'social
psychological group membership' and thus to shift the psychological
situation from 'social mobility' to 'social change'. The general predictions about the effects of the latter structure of beliefs still holds, in the
sense that all the initiatives which are taken attempt to increase the range
and variety of the social situations in which Welshmen would interact
with the relevant outgroup of Englishmen in terms of their respective
group membership rather than on an interpersonal basis. A recent study
by Branthwaite and Jones (1975), to which we shall return later, has
shown that these attempts have been successful even in those situations
which, on the face of it, seem to have nothing much to do with any of the
political and social dimensions of Welsh nationalism.

Our second variant of conditions inducing the social change system of
beliefs, despite their objective discrepancies from it, emerges from an
altogether different kettle of fish, or perhaps, more appropriately, a
boiling cauldron. Some people may be prejudiced and discriminating
against certain outgroups because they feel that these outgroups threaten
their interests or their way of life; others, for reasons related to certain
forms of social comparison which will be discussed in the next chapter;
others still, because they 'need' prejudice in order to deal with their
individual emotional problems or aggressions. This last group tends to
engage in a certain way of structuring their social world: they 'need' a
clear, separate and distinct 'outgroup' which can be sharply dichoto-
mized from the 'group' that they themselves, in their view, represent.
This ingroup is a cognitive *sine qua non* for the cognitive existence of the
outgroup, and one or both can be, in various conditions, either real or
mythical or somewhere in between. One *needs* the notion of 'this island's
race' with its special characteristics in order to be able to conceptualize
the deleterious effects upon it of the 'invasion' of the immutably different
'coloured' immigrants. There is nothing in this statement that is not
generally and commonsensically known, as is witnessed by the old
saying that if Jews did not exist, Hitler would have had to invent them *as*

a social entity – and, in many ways, he did just that. But there are the two interesting similarities with the case of some of the developing national movements just discussed – the discussion of these similarities *not* implying here in any way that they can be considered as similar in any other respects, e.g. moral, social or political.

The two aspects of the situation which are theoretically relevant – in the sense that they lead to similar predictions about some forms of intergroup behaviour – are, as in the previous case, that the situation need not necessarily be related *ab initio* to a clear-cut belief in the impossibility of 'passing' from one group to the other. And therefore, 'social creativity' will be needed to push in that direction the subjective structuring of the situation in those who initiate the movement, with the hope that they can also influence others. The results are clear-cut and described in many books on prejudice. In addition to the development of stereotypes which sharply dichotomize those characteristics of the two groups which are directly *relevant* to intergroup categorizations (see part II of this book), there will be a tendency, as in the case of the developing nationalisms, to increase the number and variety of social encounters in which behaviour ceases to be interpersonal and takes on the characteristics, previously described, of behaviour in terms of the participants' respective group memberships. One further point should be mentioned: in many inter-racial or inter-ethnic situations this hard work of shifting the structures of belief from the 'social mobility' to the 'social change' extremes will hardly be necessary, since the job is already done by the existing rigid social stratifications – in which case we are back to our initial general description of the social background to this social change end of the psychological continuum. In other cases, when the initial situation is more ambiguous, the prejudiced and discriminatory 'creativity', which consists of newly developing ideologies and of endowing the ingroup and the outgroup with 'relevant' characteristics, is likely – in many social conditions – to help endow the initial fiction with grim reality. We are then once again led back to our initial general case in which the 'social change' structure of belief can be shown to be related to the emerging concrete reality of rigid and objective social stratifications.

The third variant of social conditions leading to the 'social change' structure of beliefs need not be related at all to a stratification of the social system, if stratification is meant to imply consensually accepted status differentials between the groups. A sharp *division* into two or more groups may be sufficient for the purpose. A clear example is provided by two groups which are in direct conflict and which present no general status, power, domination or any other social differences – at least in the initial stages of their interaction, but very often also in the later stages.

Two football teams competing from season to season with varying fortunes are one case in point. Other cases are to be found in the competing teams of Sherif's field studies, in many other social psychological studies employing groups in competition, and in equivalent 'natural' situations. The point is that in most of these situations it is very difficult – if not impossible – for anyone to conceive that he could move individually from one group to the other. In an intense intergroup conflict of this kind the belief in the feasibility of individual social mobility is practically non-existent and the belief system of 'social change' – in the form of one's fate depending entirely upon the fortunes of one's group as they relate to the fortunes of the other group – is at a maximum. It is horrendous to imagine what could happen if, during a football match watched by tens of thousands of fans, one of the players suddenly decided to change teams; nor, one imagines, would life be very comfortable for a subject in Sherif's field studies who decided to leave his losing team in order to join the winning one. The social sanctions – both external and internal – for this kind of behaviour are extremely powerful in our cultures, although instances of 'betrayal' and decisions to become a 'renegade' do happen occasionally. The social psychological consequences of the interaction between groups which are in this kind of 'objective' competition or of sharp conflict of interests can once again be simply described in terms of the concepts previously used: a sharp social dichotomy is reflected in the predominance of the 'social change' system of beliefs which, in turn, leads to behaviour in terms of respective group membership of the participants (with a corresponding minimum of interpersonal behaviour) in a variety of situations whose nature will be determined by the nature of the conflict between the groups. But it must immediately be added that this statement is too modest and too conservative: as is well known, both from common experience and from many studies in social psychology, this 'intergroup' form of behaviour will often exceed by far the range of situations and actions which are *instrumentally* relevant to the objective outcome of the intergroup conflict or competition. The reasons for this psychological 'spilling over' will be discussed in the next chapter in the context of intergroup social comparisons.

To sum up, we distinguished between four variants of the conditions which help to determine the development of the 'social change' structure of beliefs. The first relates to the reflection in these beliefs of an existing rigid system of social stratification – at the point when, for reasons mentioned above, the perceived stability of the system begins to break down. The second concerns the *creation* of a 'social change' system of beliefs in social conditions which do not necessarily prevent individual movement from one group to another. The third finds its origins in certain individual needs for establishing clear-cut and impenetrable social dichotomies. This is the traditional area of most social psychological studies on intergroup prejudice. The fourth is a consequence of an intense and explicit conflict of interest between groups which is not related to a stable social stratification.

To conclude this chapter, it will be useful to attempt one further clarification of the differences between the approach to the social psychology of intergroup behaviour represented here and in the chapters to follow on the one hand, and many of the other approaches on the other hand. The emphasis on the psychological processes responsible for prejudice and discrimination which is found predominant even in fairly recent books on the subject such as, for example, those by Ehrlich (1973) and by Kidder and Stewart (1975), and also in most of the empirical work which these books describe and synthesize, leads to a concentration on *only one* aspect of the multiple facets and determinants of intergroup behaviour which were discussed in the present chapter. More specifically, this is confined to no more than one of the four variants just discussed: the prejudiced individual. But even this is truncated in some ways, since little attention is usually paid to the interaction between the various forms and conditions of *ingroup* affiliations of the prejudiced individuals and their consequent intergroup behaviour. In the framework presented here, prejudice and discrimination are in the nature of socially-shared *symptoms* of certain social psychological structures of intergroup relations rather than being considered as *causes* of intergroup behaviour, which are often seen in turn as deriving from certain cognitive and affective processes largely independent of their social context (see chapters 2, 3 and 7).

This individualistic emphasis may have something to do with the distinction made by the political economist Hirschman (1970) between what he called 'exit' and 'voice'. 'Exit' is for Hirschman the situation when 'some customers stop buying the firm's products or some members leave the organization' (p. 4) – in other words, it is very close to a behavioural translation to other settings of our belief system of 'social mobility'. 'Voice' is heard when 'the firm's customers or the organization's members express their dissatisfaction directly to the management or to some other authority to which management is subordinate or through general protest addressed to anyone who cares to listen' (p. 4). This seems further removed from our concept of social change than is 'exit' from social mobility, but a closer analysis does reveal certain interesting similarities and differences (see chapter 14 for a more detailed discussion). In his discussion of 'exit', Hirschman applies the concept directly to issues of social mobility:

The traditional American idea of success confirms the hold which exit has had on the national imagination. Success – or, what amounts to the same thing, upward social mobility – has long been conceived in terms of evolutionary individualism. The successful individual who starts out at a low rung of the social ladder, necessarily leaves his own group as he rises; he 'passes' into, or is 'accepted' by, the next higher group. He takes his immediate family along, but hardly anyone else. (pp. 108–9).

By contrast, Hirschman adds, 'the black power doctrine represents a totally new approach to upward mobility because of its open advocacy of the group process. It had immense shock value because it spurned and castigated a supreme value of the American society – success via exit from one's group' (p. 112). Hirschman's views about the role of 'exit' in the American social and cultural tradition have a long and distinguished history. They have been expressed earlier in Hofstadter's *Social Darwinism in American thought* (1945). It seems likely that this cultural tradition is – at least in part – responsible for the emphasis in social psychology on the explanatory necessity *and* sufficiency of intergroup theories about individuals interacting with other individuals. The understanding of the behaviour of individuals interacting with others *primarily* as members of their respective social groups had correspondingly been at variance with the powerful impact of certain social, historical and political traditions on the intellectual culture from which this 'individual' emphasis originated.

12
Social categorization, social identity and social comparison

1. Social categorization and social identity

The problems of an individual's self-definition in a social context can be restated in terms of the notion of social identity. We need to postulate that, at least in our kinds of societies, an individual strives to achieve a satisfactory concept or image of himself. This was one of the bases of Leon Festinger's early theory of social comparison (1954). Festinger, however, was almost exclusively concerned with social comparisons made between individuals and with evaluations of oneself and others made by means of these inter-individual comparisons. This inter-individual emphasis neglects an important contributing aspect of an individual's self-definition: the fact that he is a member of numerous social groups and that this membership contributes, positively or negatively, to the image that he has of himself.

Four linked concepts will be employed in order to proceed with this discussion. They are: social categorization, social identity, social comparison and psychological group distinctiveness.

The process of categorization was discussed at length in previous chapters of this book. Following these discussions and the definition of 'group' in the preceding chapter, the term 'group' denotes a cognitive entity that is meaningful to the individual at a particular point of time and must be distinguished from the way in which the term 'group' is used when it denotes a face-to-face relationship between a number of people. In other words, social categorization is a process of bringing together social objects or events in groups which are equivalent with regard to an individual's actions, intentions and system of beliefs.

The interaction between socially-derived value differentials on the one hand and the cognitive 'mechanics' of categorization on the other is particularly important in all social divisions between 'us' and 'them' – i.e. in all social categorizations in which distinctions are made between the individual's own group and the outgroups which are compared or contrasted with it. It then becomes one of the cognitive and behavioural supports of ethnocentrism (see LeVine and Campbell, 1972). The acquisition of value differentials between one's own group (or groups)

254

and other groups is part and parcel of the general processes of socialization. One important aspect of this introduction of values into the general system of differentiations between one's own and other groups is directly relevant to the present argument. This has to do with certain *consequences* of group membership to which we shall refer as 'social identity'.

For the purpose of this discussion, social identity will be understood as that *part* of an individual's self-concept which derives from his knowledge of his membership of a social group (or groups) together with the value and emotional significance attached to that membership. It will be clear that this is a limited definition of 'identity' or 'social identity'. This limitation is deliberate, and it has two aims. The first is not to enter into endless and often sterile discussions as to what 'is' identity. The second is to enable us to use this limited concept in the discussions which follow. There is no doubt that the image or concept that an individual has of himself or herself is infinitely more complex, both in its contents and its derivations, than 'social identity' as defined and circumscribed here. We are not, however, concerned in this chapter with the origins and development of individual identity or self-awareness. The aims are much more modest: the assumption is made that, however rich and complex may be the individuals' view of themselves in relation to the surrounding world, social and physical, *some* aspects of that view are contributed by the membership of certain social groups or categories. Some of these memberships are more salient than others; and some may vary in salience in time and as a function of a variety of social situations (see chapter 11). Our explicit preoccupation is with the effects of the nature and subjective importance of these memberships on those aspects of an individual's behaviour which are pertinent to intergroup relations – without in the least denying that this does not enable us to make any statements about the 'self' in general, or about social behaviour in *other* contexts. 'Social identity' as defined here is thus best considered as a shorthand term used to describe (i) limited aspects of the concept of self which are (ii) relevant to certain limited aspects of social behaviour.

Seen from this intergroup perspective of social identity, social categorization can therefore be considered as a system of orientation which helps to create and define the individual's place in society (see Berger and Luckmann, 1967; Schutz, 1932). As Berger (1966) wrote: 'Every society contains a repertoire of identities that is part of the "objective knowledge" of its members . . . Society not only defines but creates psychological reality. The individual realizes himself in society – that is, he recognizes his identity in socially defined terms and these definitions become reality as he lives in society' (pp. 106, 107).

Several consequences regarding group membership follow upon this 'recognition of identity in socially defined terms'. They can be described as follows:

(a) It can be assumed that an individual will tend to remain a member of a group and seek membership of new groups if these groups have some contribution to make to the positive aspects of his social identity; i.e. to those aspects of it from which he derives some satisfaction.

(b) If a group does not satisfy this requirement, the individual will tend to leave it *unless*: (i) leaving the group is impossible for some 'objective' reasons, or (ii) it conflicts with important values which are themselves a part of his acceptable self-image.

(c) If leaving the group presents the difficulties just mentioned, then at least two solutions are possible: (i) to change one's interpretation of the attributes of the group so that its unwelcome features (e.g. low status) are either justified or made acceptable through a reinterpretation; or (ii) to accept the situation for what it is and engage in social action which would lead to desirable changes in the situation. (Of course, there may be various combinations of (i) and (ii) such as, for example, when the negative attributes are 'justified' and social action to change them is undertaken at the same time.)

(d) No group lives alone – all groups in society live in the midst of other groups. In other words, the 'positive aspects of social identity' and the reinterpretation of attributes and engagement in social action only acquire meaning in relation to, or in comparisons with, other groups.

2. Social identity and social comparison

It is this comparative perspective which links social categorizing with social identity. In his theory of social comparison processes, Festinger (1954) hypothesized that 'there exists, in the human organism, a drive to evaluate his opinions and his abilities'. His second major hypothesis in the same paper was that 'to the extent objective, non-social means are not available, people evaluate their opinions and abilities by comparison respectively with the opinions and abilities of others'. But there are some difficulties with the conception that social comparisons only take place 'to the extent that objective non-social means are not available'. Festinger's example is that 'one could, of course, test the opinion that an object was fragile by hitting it with a hammer'. I can confirm the opinion that a bed is for lying-down-on by lying down on it until I discover that this particular bed in this particular room of the castle belonged to the Duke of Urbino and is most definitely *not* for lying-down-on. Very often, the 'objective non-social means' that may *appear* to an observer to be available for the testing of opinions do not have much validity unless they are used in conjunction with the significance that they acquire in their social setting. The cases which lie outside this range are usually trivial in the analysis of social behaviour. In addition, social reality can be as 'objective' as is non-social reality, and conversely 'objectivity' can be as 'social' as it is 'physical'. In some cultures, thunder and lightning are as indisputably signs of anger of supernatural powers as they are bursts of sound and light.

The criterion of 'objectivity' cannot be based on classifying phenomena as being of a 'social' or a 'non-social' nature, with the presumed attendant consequence that opinions about them can be tested respectively by 'social' or by 'non-social' means. It can instead be defined in terms of the awareness (or the degree of subjective probability) that there exist alternatives to the judgement one is making. A low (or nil) probability that alternatives to one's opinions exist *may* be due to the consistency over time in the checking of these opinions through non-social means, as in Festinger's example of fragility and hammer; but it may also be due to the very high social consensus about the nature of a phenomenon, independently of whether the phenomenon is thought of as being 'physical', 'natural' or 'social'. It is undoubtedly true that certainty can very often be more easily reached about the physical than about the social means of testing; but this is not a *theoretical* distinction between what appears and does not appear as 'objective reality'. It cannot be said that a human organism turns towards social means of validating opinions only when non-social means for doing so are not available. There are many examples, both in the history of science in our own culture and in the systems of knowledge of other cultures, of procedures which follow the opposite course; i.e. they do not use the means of 'physical' testing which are, in principle, available because of the very high (or complete) social consensus about the nature of a phenomenon.

Therefore, 'social comparison processes' have a fundamental and very wide range of application. This range of application includes both the social context (or significance) of 'non-social' testing, and the cases where the high social consensus about the nature of a phenomenon is sufficient to confer the mark of 'objectivity' on opinions about it. In his theory, Festinger was mainly concerned with the social testing of opinions about characteristics of *individuals*, and with the resulting 'relative similarity in opinions and abilities which are relevant to this association'. The theory was primarily addressed at the *within-group* effects of the process of social comparison (such as pressures towards uniformity in a group) while 'comparisons with members of a different status group, either higher or lower may sometimes be made on a phantasy level, but very rarely in reality'. Though Festinger qualifies this statement by adding that comparisons between groups that differ are not completely eliminated, the focus of his discussion remains on individuals comparing themselves with other individuals.

On the basis of this discussion so far, a general statement can now be made about social categorization into groups in relation to its function 'as a system of orientation which creates and defines the individual's own place in a society'. This concerns the 'objective reality' of comparisons focusing on an individual *as* an individual and comparisons based on an individual's membership of a particular social group. 'No social group is an island' is no less true than the statement that 'no man is an island'. The only 'reality' tests that matter with regard to group characteristics are tests of social reality. The characteristics of one's group as a whole (such as its status, its richness or poverty, its skin colour or its ability to reach its aims) achieve most of their significance in relation to perceived differences from other groups and the value connotation of these differences. For example, economic deprivation acquires its importance in social attitudes, intentions and actions mainly when it becomes 'relative deprivation'; easy or difficult access to means of production and consumption of goods, to benefits and opportunities become psychologically salient mainly in relation to comparisons with other groups; the definition of a group (national, racial or any other) makes no sense unless there are other groups around. A group becomes a group in the sense of being perceived as having common characteristics or a common fate mainly because other groups are present in the environment.

Thus, the psychological aspects and consequences of the membership of a group are capable, apart from some exceptional cases, of any kind of a definition *only* because of their insertion into a multi-group structure. Consequently, the social identity of an individual conceived as his knowledge that he belongs to certain social groups together with some emotional and value significance to him of his membership can only be defined through the effects of social categorizations segmenting an individual's social environment into his own group and others.

In view of this, what are the conditions which will enable a social group to preserve its contribution to those aspects of an individual's social identity which are positively valued by him? In situations which were described in the previous chapter as those of 'social mobility' as distinct from 'social change', there is not much of a problem. If adequate conditions for the preservation of positive social identity are not offered by a group, the individual will leave it – psychologically, objectively or both. In situations which are characterized by the structure of belief of 'social change', the issues become more complicated. In some conditions, to which we shall return later, a social group can fulfil its function of protecting the social identity of its members only if it manages to keep its positively-valued distinctiveness from other groups. In other conditions, this distinctiveness must be created, acquired and perhaps also fought for through various forms of relevant social action. In other conditions, yet, some or most individuals from an underprivileged group will place their bets, implicitly or explicitly, on certain processes of 'objective' social change which, they hope, will lead finally to a structure of genuine social mobility; this might imply the distant goal of the dissolution of a group which at present is mainly defined through its negative attributes when it is compared with other groups.

3. Social comparison and relative deprivation

The concept of relative deprivation, as it has been widely used in various social sciences is, of course, closely related to many aspects of the present argument. It might be said in one sense that much of it can be seen as attempting to articulate some of the social psychological processes which are responsible for the genesis and functioning of relative deprivation. But serious difficulties remain. They have to do with the theoretical links that need to be established between social comparison and relative deprivation. And here we find dichotomies which are similar to those discussed in chapter 11: between the inter-individual and the social psychology of intergroup behaviour; and between 'social mobility' and 'social change'. In the case of relative deprivation, we must reconsider the concept of social comparison from the point of view of individual versus group social comparisons; and – closely related to it – the concepts of inter-individual versus intergroup relative deprivation.

Although the concept of relative deprivation originated in social psychology (Stouffer *et al.*, 1949), it has been used rather more extensively in sociology and in political science than in social psychology. Gurr (1970), for example, made it one of the key concepts of his important book on *Why Men Rebel*. He defined relative deprivation as the

actors' perception of discrepancy between their value expectations and their value capabilities. Value expectations are the goods and conditions of life to which people believe they are rightfully entitled. Value capabilities are the goods and conditions they think they are capable of getting and keeping . . . The emphasis . . . is on the perception of deprivation; people may be subjectively deprived with reference to their expectations even though an objective observer may not judge them to be in want. Similarly, the existence of what the observer judges to be abject poverty or 'absolute deprivation' is not necessarily thought to be unjust or irremediable by those who experience it. (p. 24).

There is an interesting relationship between the concept of relative deprivation as seen from the social psychological point of view, and the same concept as it is used in other social sciences. For a political scientist, an economist, a social anthropologist or a sociologist, relative deprivation serves as an independent variable enabling them to generate hypotheses about social processes and social movements of various kinds. But, as it is clear in the cognitive emphasis of the above definition by Gurr, they have to look to social psychology for an understanding of the genesis and functioning of relative deprivation. In the history of our discipline, the social psychological texture of the concept has been supplied by two intellectual traditions: the theory of social comparison and the theory of reference groups.

We have not, however, pushed our contribution to the degree of full impact that it might have had on other social sciences. This is probably due to the fact that the inter-individual emphasis of the social comparison theory, or – in the terms used here – its 'social mobility' emphasis, fitted in more closely with the general theoretical drift of the subject than did some implications of the reference group theory. And yet, there have been clear leads, a long time ago, which could have been pursued. Consider, for example, this quotation from the classic paper on aspiration level by Chapman and Volkmann written in 1939: 'Whatever change in aspiration level is induced by a change in the frame of reference may have enormous *social consequences*: the new judgement may serve as a catalyst for major social changes in which *whole* groups abruptly revise their ambitions and perhaps their status.' (My italics.)

According to Gurr:

The scope of relative deprivation is its prevalence with respect to each class of values among the members of a collectivity. Some deprivations are characteristic of some members of all groups. Deprivation is relevant to the disposition to collective violence to the extent that many people feel discontented about the same things. Unexpected personal deprivations such as failure to obtain an expected promotion or the infidelity of a spouse ordinarily affect few people at any given time and are therefore narrow in scope. Events and patterns of conditions like the suppression of a political party, a drastic inflation or the decline of a group's status relative to its reference group are likely to precipitate feelings of relative deprivation among whole groups or categories of people and are wide in scope. Aberle dichotomizes what is here called scope into two general classes of deprivations, those that are personal and those that are group experiences. Scope is better regarded as a continuum: it should be possible to identify, for example, by survey techniques, the proportion of people in any collectivity that feels deprived with respect to any specified class of values. (p. 29).

In his book, Gurr was mainly concerned with the phenomena of collective violence and rebellion. But conceptually, some of the problems involved are very similar to those one encounters in considering the wider problems of intergroup behaviour. I have argued earlier at some length that we must provide a social psychological theory of the wide social uniformities of intergroup behaviour, and that such a theory should use linked concepts of social identity and intergroup social comparison, in addition to the inter-individual one. This fits in closely with what Gurr has to say about the continuum of the scope of relative deprivation. Three points of this continuum define its range as it relates to a social psychological theory of intergroup behaviour.

Relative deprivation in the sense used by Gurr is, psychologically speaking, a failure of expectancies, and as such it becomes an independent variable in social behaviour. This failure of expectancies can be conceived as operating along two possible dimensions: a personal one and an interpersonal one. The personal one relates to unfavourable comparisons between one's own past status or expectancies and the present status or expectancies. The interpersonal one relates to comparisons with others; and it can, of course, also itself encompass a temporal dimension; as a matter of fact, it probably does almost without exception.

It is the second, interpersonal dimension which is more directly relevant to the processes of intergroup behaviour. The three points of the continuum just mentioned can provide a useful taxonomy of the relationships between relative deprivation and intergroup behaviour. This taxonomy derives directly from the inter-individual–intergroup continuum of social behaviour discussed in chapter 11. At the individual extreme of the continuum is what can be referred to as *inter*personal *intra*group relative deprivation. This is where the inter-individual theory of social comparison is directly relevant. In the middle of the continuum there is an interesting transition. This could be described as the *inter*personal *intra*group relative deprivation which is assumed to serve as an independent variable for *inter*group behaviour; and it is at this point that theoretical difficulties arise.

The theoretical sequence assumed to be operating at this point of transition (from intragroup relative deprivation to intergroup behaviour) can be described as follows: individuals compare themselves with other individuals; the individuals chosen for purposes of comparison must not be too different from those who are doing the comparing; therefore, it is more likely that, in situations marked by strong psychological cleavages between groups, the targets of comparison will be from the individual's own group rather than from an outgroup. At this point the question arises: how are these intragroup social comparisons translated into, for

261

example, intergroup hostile behaviour? The answers to this question have been provided in various forms through theories of displaced aggression, or arousal and anger serving as a drive, of the links between this drive and aggression-eliciting cues, etc.

Before this argument proceeds, two general statements concerning hostile intergroup behaviour must again be reformulated. The first one is as follows: *some* people will display hostile intergroup behaviour under a great variety of conditions. The second statement is: in *some* conditions most people (or at least great numbers of people) will display similar hostile intergroup behaviour (see chapter 11). The distinction between these two forms of hostile intergroup behaviour concerns the transitional theoretical sequence just described: *inter*-individual *intra*group social comparison leading through the existence of an assumed motivational state in an individual to certain forms of *inter*group behaviour. This sequence can be used, and has been used with some success, to provide a theory of the phenomena of intergroup behaviour which conform to the first of the two general statements formulated above about *some* people displaying intergroup hostility in a great variety of conditions. But it has also been used to provide an explanation for the phenomena of the second kind concerning uniformities, sometimes displayed over long periods of time, in intergroup behaviour of very large numbers of people. In this form of application, it has been responsible for a dangerous narrowing of focus and scope in the relevance of social psychological theory to the psychological aspects of large-scale social problems of intergroup behaviour and social change.

Independently of this narrowing of focus, the theory is empirically inadequate, as it is based on assumptions some of which are untested and some untestable. The first untested assumption is that in conditions of psychological cleavage between groups, or of impossibility or difficulty of 'passing' from one group to another, the relevant social comparisons are confined to the intragroup horizon of an individual. The second assumption is both untested and untestable; it concerns the transposition to large-scale intergroup behaviour. This is the assumption that, in certain conditions which are sometimes long-lasting, large groups of people are in a similar internal motivational state, be it arousal, anger serving as a drive, or pent-up aggression.

A good example of a specific application of this kind of theory to a mass intergroup phenomenon can be found in a paper by Leonard Berkowitz which appeared in a special 1972 issue of the *Journal of Social Issues* devoted to collective violence and civil conflict. Berkowitz's paper, entitled 'Frustration, comparisons and other sources of emotion arousal as contributors to social unrest', deals with certain aspects of the black riots which took place in the late sixties in several American cities. His interpretation of some of the causes of the urban riots is roughly as follows: these riots are more likely in periods of 'rising expectations' when there is higher relative affluence; in such conditions, the poorer blacks have many more opportunities to compare themselves with the better off blacks than in periods of general misery; and the frustrations arising from these comparisons contribute to the riots. Why these particular social comparisons? As Berkowitz wrote:

Do poor blacks generally compare themselves with poor whites? Their economic status might be similar, but they are very different in other respects. I would like to raise the possibility that while working-class blacks might be somewhat inclined to evaluate themselves relative to working-class whites, because of their common occupational conditions, Negroes are also prone to employ other blacks as a reference group. Associations are more frequent and more intimate with other blacks, they usually are more attractive to them, and they are similar in important ways. While this seems obvious, it implies that unfavourable comparisons with other blacks contribute to social unrest *even if only in a small degree*. (p. 86)

It may be worth pointing out that precisely the opposite argument, still based on the same inter-individual social comparison theory, is made two pages earlier in the same paper. Here we are told that members of the lowest socio-economic strata, the black 'lumpenproletariat', were the least militant. The active participants in the riots 'were typically somewhat better educated than the non-rioters or less militant blacks in these cities'. As Berkowitz wrote,

The people experiencing the greatest objective deprivations, those at the bottom of the economic ladder, were presumably less hopeful than their better-off counterparts and were less aggressive at not getting the good things of life. They were deprived but not frustrated. Education has evidently awakened appetites for the pleasures of our society and intensified hopes that these pleasures might be obtained. The failure to satisfy these hopes was frustrating. (p. 83)

This example was discussed in some detail because it shows how social psychological conclusions about a social movement can be reached even by the most distinguished representatives of the 'social mobility' tradition at work. In addition to the difficulties and contradictions already discussed, there is also the small-voiced statement of theoretical failure. Leonard Berkowitz is too good a scientist to make too much of a thesis which *may* be true in some degree, but whose explanatory reach is obviously highly limited. This is why he wrote and italicized the phrase that 'unfavourable comparisons with other blacks contribute to social unrest *even if only in a small degree*'.

There is no a priori reason why, as social psychologists, we should be so modest. A consideration of the third point on the continuum of social comparison, of which the first two points were already discussed, provides promising leads for future work. The second 'transitional' point, just discussed, had to do with the assumed *inter*-individual intragroup social comparison as it was supposed to affect intergroup behaviour at large. The third point of the continuum consists of the relations between *inter*group social comparisons and *inter*group behaviour. It can be illustrated by two examples, taken from the opposite ends of the social and political spectrum. The first comes from a study, conducted in South Africa by Kurt Danziger (1963), the general conclusions of which were confirmed by Beryl Geber (1972). Both studies used as their source of data the 'future autobiographies' written by African secondary school pupils. In the case of the Geber study, there were unavoidable weaknesses in the presentation of data due to the overriding need to remove all possible clues to the identity of the respondents. But one of the general conclusions was clearly similar to that reached by Danziger: the awareness of the common group fate determined by race focused the schoolboys' aspirations away from individual goals of comparative success and towards the development of political ideologies expressed in terms of their group's aspirations. South Africa represents an extreme example of groups whose members are not able to move individually. In Festinger's terms, intergroup comparisons could only be made there on a 'phantasy level', and inter-individual comparisons outside of one's own group make very little sense. And yet, the moment the frozen system of social relationships ceases to be perceived as the only possible or feasible one, salient and relevant outgroup comparisons will be made, and in the long run their widespread diffusion becomes at one and the same time the social psychological process of 'social change' and a powerful determinant of 'objective' social changes still to come.

The second example is conceptually similar, although socially and politically it is very different. The Protestant–Catholic relationship in Northern Ireland is another instance of the impossibility or extreme difficulty of moving from one group to another. The *status quo* favourable to the Protestant majority has been increasingly threatened in the sixties by the social and economic advances of the Catholic minority. Birrell (1972) ascribed to this threat the rapid development of the extremist and militant Protestant movements. But the interesting aspect of this from our point of view is that the para-military formation of young Protestants and young Catholics roaming the streets of cities in Northern Ireland are made up on both sides, to a large extent, of people who, on any criteria other than that of their salient and dichotomous social categorization, are very similar in all respects. The militant young I.R.A. workers on the Catholic side have found, lined up in the streets against them, the militant young U.D.A. workers on the Protestant side. It would be very difficult to explain this salience of ingroup affiliation on the basis of any form of inter-individual social comparisons or individual relative deprivations. The real threat is to a particular comparative identity of a group which happens to be powerfully salient in its social and traditional context. The 'reverse' relative deprivation of the group, until recently safely esconced in its distinctive superiority, is translated for an individual into 'us' in relation to 'them' and not into 'me' in relation to 'him' or 'her'.

But the discussion of this third point of the continuum – intergroup comparisons leading to intergroup behaviour – cannot be complete unless a process is postulated which will link intergroup comparison with intergroup dissimilarity. In the case of inter-individual comparisons and the ensuing inter-individual relative deprivations, it is assumed that the scope of comparisons – and therefore also of relative deprivations – is confined within the limits of subjective similarity (not very clearly defined) between those who do the comparing and the objects of comparison. This rings intuitively true, and there is some evidence supporting this view. The present argument is that, in contrast to the similarity view, in the case of intergroup comparisons the requirements of social identity push towards comparisons between groups which may be highly dissimilar and dichotomously separate. Why then do these comparisons exist far and beyond the 'phantasy levels' and often become powerful determinants of intergroup behaviour and social action?

The answer is not far to seek. Some of it is implicit in what Durkheim had to say about the maintenance of social order. 'What is needed [he wrote] if social order is to reign is that the mass of men be content with their lot. But what is needed for them to be content, is not that they have more or less but that they be convinced that they have no right to more' (published in translation, 1959). Social comparisons between groups which may be highly dissimilar are based on the perceived legitimacy of the perceived relationships between them. The concept of social identity, as used in this chapter, is linked to the need for a positive and distinctive image of the ingroup; this is why the perceived illegitimacy of an intergroup relationship transcends the limits of intergroup similarity in the relevant social comparisons and reaches out wherever the causes of illegitimacy are thought to reside. This is by no means a new concept in social psychology. A careful review of the experimental studies on interpersonal aggression shows that the independent variable of the perceived legitimacy of aggression in an experimental situation is a more reliable predictor of overt aggressive behaviour, or of its inhibitions, than variables such as arousal, displacement, eliciting cues, or previous frustrations (see Billig, 1976).

In relation to the issue of similarity in social comparison theory, it is possible to maintain that the perceived illegitimacy of the perceived intergroup relations provides a bridge from non-comparability to comparability. This will be the case even if the groups involved are, on the face of it, highly dissimilar and have clearly marked 'impassable' boundaries. The perceived legitimacy of an intergroup relationship presents no problem for a social comparison theory, based on the assumption of similarity, when the groups are (at least potentially) of similar status on any status dimensions which are salient or relevant to the comparison – as in the case of varying fortunes of two competing athletic teams, one of which happens to be on top at the moment. Again, the assumption of similarity seems valid in the case of stable and clear-cut status differences which are perceived as legitimate, in the sense that dissimilarity implies here the *absence* of comparisons. The difficulties arise when this kind of a stable and legitimate intergroup system begins to break down. In other words, the similarity version of the social comparison theory can account for *changes* in relations in non-hierarchical intergroup systems or for the *stability* of relations in strongly hierarchical systems. It cannot account for attempts to change hierarchical systems when what has been viewed as legitimate begins to be seen as illegitimate for a great variety of historical and social reasons which need not concern us here. The important issue from the point of view of a social psychological theory is that the perceived *illegitimacy* of an existing relationship in status, power, domination or any other differential implies the development of *some* dimensions of comparability (i.e. underlying *similarity*) where none existed before. This need be no more than the idea that 'all human beings are equal' or 'all human beings have equal rights', although very often the new dimensions of comparability will tend to be defined in much greater detail in group ideologies. Paradoxically, this means that the perceived illegitimacy of the relationship between groups which are highly dissimilar leads to the acknowledgement or discovery of *new* similarities, actual or potential. For this reason, there is no inherent contradiction between the present argument and the 'similarity' theory of social comparison. The difference between the two is perhaps the difference between, respectively, a 'dynamic' and a 'static' view of similarity. In the former case, similarity – and therefore comparability – is not just conceived as something which 'is' or 'is not' there, but as something depending upon a shifting pattern of social conditions, contexts, influences, ideologies, beliefs and attitudes in a constantly changing social environment.

The perceived illegitimacy of an intergroup relationship is thus socially and psychologically the accepted and acceptable lever for social action and social change in intergroup behaviour. It is most often a *shared* perspective on the social world, actual or potential. Therefore, it provides a basis for the shared and durable ideologizing of arousal, discontent or frustration; it also provides the basis for their translation into widely diffused forms of intergroup behaviour related either to the achievement or to the preservation of an adequate form of psychological group distinctiveness. In the case of groups which are 'inferior', this leverage function is fulfilled by the perceived illegitimacy of the outcomes of intergroup comparisons; in the case of 'inferior' groups which are already on their way towards change, it is the legitimization of their new comparative image; in the case of the groups which are 'superior', it is the legitimization of the attempts to preserve a *status quo* of valued distinctiveness whenever this is perceived as being under threat.

13

The achievement of group differentiation

1. The 'minimal' intergroup experiments and 'real' social contexts

Our first studies of 'minimal groups' to which reference has already been made in chapter 11 provided, at best, suggestive evidence that some processes were at work in an intergroup situation, which, despite their leading to strong intergroup differentiation through the behaviour of the subjects, could not be attributed either to previous hostility, or to an 'objective' current conflict of interests between the groups, or to a simple version of the subjects' self-interest. These studies were in no sense crucial experiments; but rather, they served as crutches for further thinking about the issues involved.

Their aim was to establish minimal conditions in which an individual will, in his behaviour, distinguish between an ingroup and an outgroup. In order to create such minimal conditions, we attempted to eliminate from the experimental situations all the variables that normally lead to ingroup favouritism or discrimination against the outgroup. These variables were: face-to-face interaction; conflict of interests; any possibility of previous hostility between the groups; any 'utilitarian' or instrumental links between the subjects' responses and their self-interest. In addition, we enabled the subjects to choose amongst a variety of strategies in their responses, some of which were more 'rational' or 'useful' than creating a differentiation between the groups. As was mentioned in chapter 11, the subjects first performed a fairly trivial task (such as guessing numbers of dots in rapidly projected clusters, or expressing preference for the paintings of one or two fairly abstract painters, Klee and Kandinsky). They then worked separately in individual cubicles. Their task was to decide (on a number of payment matrices) about division of points worth money between two *other* subjects. They knew what was their own group membership (under- or over-estimation of dots; or preference for one or the other painter), and the group membership of those between whom they were dividing the money; but those others were designated by code numbers and their individual identity was unknown. The results were highly significant in the direction of awarding more money to members of the 'in-group'. In the second set of experiments, the matrices were so constructed that we could assess the separate 'pull' of several decision strategies. These strategies were: maximum joint profit (i.e. the strategy of awarding the maximum *joint* amount on each matrix, so that all the subjects together – who knew each other well before the experiments – could get the greatest possible amount of money out of the experimenters); maximum profit for members of the ingroup; maximum *difference* in favour of the ingroup at the price of sacrificing both the above advantages; and fairness of choices (see Tables 1 and 2). Of these strategies, the first – maximum

Table 1
Matrices used in the experiment

A

| Matrix 1 | $\frac{19}{1}$ | $\frac{18}{3}$ | $\frac{17}{5}$ | $\frac{16}{7}$ | $\frac{15}{9}$ | $\frac{14}{11}$ | $\frac{13}{13}$ | $\frac{12}{15}$ | $\frac{11}{17}$ | $\frac{10}{19}$ | $\frac{9}{21}$ | $\frac{8}{23}$ | $\frac{7}{25}$ |

| Matrix 2 | $\frac{23}{5}$ | $\frac{22}{7}$ | $\frac{21}{9}$ | $\frac{20}{11}$ | $\frac{19}{13}$ | $\frac{18}{15}$ | $\frac{17}{17}$ | $\frac{16}{19}$ | $\frac{15}{21}$ | $\frac{14}{23}$ | $\frac{13}{25}$ | $\frac{12}{27}$ | $\frac{11}{29}$ |

B

| Matrix 3 | $\frac{7}{1}$ | $\frac{8}{3}$ | $\frac{9}{5}$ | $\frac{10}{7}$ | $\frac{11}{9}$ | $\frac{12}{11}$ | $\frac{13}{13}$ | $\frac{14}{15}$ | $\frac{15}{17}$ | $\frac{16}{19}$ | $\frac{17}{21}$ | $\frac{18}{23}$ | $\frac{19}{25}$ |

| Matrix 4 | $\frac{11}{5}$ | $\frac{12}{7}$ | $\frac{13}{9}$ | $\frac{14}{11}$ | $\frac{15}{13}$ | $\frac{16}{15}$ | $\frac{17}{17}$ | $\frac{18}{19}$ | $\frac{19}{21}$ | $\frac{20}{23}$ | $\frac{21}{25}$ | $\frac{22}{27}$ | $\frac{23}{29}$ |

In each of the above matrices *one* term had to be chosen by the subject (e.g. $\frac{15}{9}$ in Matrix 1). In matrices 1 and 2 when figures in the top row represent points awarded to a member of the outgroup, maximum joint profit, maximum ingroup profit and maximum difference in favour of the ingroup all coincide at the right extreme of the matrix. When figures in the top row represent points awarded to a member of the ingroup, maximum ingroup profit and maximum difference in favour of the ingroup are at the left extreme of the matrix; maximum joint profit is still at the right extreme. All subjects completed several times both versions of the matrix.

In matrices 3 and 4, outgroup on top again represents all maxima coinciding at the right extreme of the matrix. Ingroup on top corresponds to maximum joint and maximum ingroup profits at the right, and maximum difference in favour of the ingroup at the left extreme.

The 'pull' of each of the choice strategies (M.J.P. – maximum joint profit; M.I.P. – maximum ingroup profit; M.D. – maximum difference in favour of the ingroup; F – fairness) was measured as the difference between choices made on two versions of the same matrix: the one in which outgroup was represented in the top row and the one in which it was represented in the bottom row. For details of analysis, see Tajfel *et al.*, 1971.

Table 2

Booklet for group preferring Klee

These numbers are rewards for:
Member no. 74 of Klee

group	25	23	21	19	17	15	13	11	9	7	5	3	1
Member no. 44 of	19	18	17	16	15	14	13	12	11	10	9	8	7

Kandinsky group

Please fill in below details
of the box you have just chosen:

	Amount
Reward for member no. 74 of Klee group	21
Reward for member no. 44 of Kandinsky group	17

Page of booklet, presenting a single matrix, is reproduced as a subject might have marked it. In addition to checking a box, the subject filled in the blanks below it to confirm his choice. The page heading reminded him which group he was in. The awards were made to persons identified only by number and group; the subject did not know who they were but only their group identification.

joint profit – exerted hardly any pull on the decisions; maximum ingroup profit was important, but sometimes not nearly as important as achieving a maximum difference in favour of the ingroup. Fairness was also a significant variable and served to moderate the excesses of ingroup favouritism.

Two simple and overlapping explanations were available at the time to account for these results: a 'normative' one and 'learning' one. The first was that our schoolboy subjects, aged 15 to 16 years, saw the situation as one of 'team competition' in which one should make one's own team win at whatever cost. The second was, that – in a new situation – they engaged in ingroup behaviour which had been reinforced on countless occasions in the past. Both these explanations are sensible; they are also quite 'uninteresting' – uninteresting because they are not genuinely heuristic. If our subjects had chosen strategies of choices leading to maximum joint profit, the same explanations could still serve, in one form or another. If they had chosen only the strategy of fairness without that of ingroup favouritism, one could still 'explain' their responses starting from norms and previous reinforcements. The argument put forward here is not that these explanations are invalid. It is rather that, in addition to their capacity to explain all kinds of results, they are at a level of generality which prevents them from serving as a point of departure for new and more searching insights about intergroup processes.

It is the choice by the subjects of these *particular* norms based perhaps on these *particular* reinforcements which defined the problem and provided a departure for some new questions about the psychology of intergroup relations. This is particularly so in view of the fact that the results have since been replicated in many experiments both in Britain and elsewhere. (See the previous chapter for a list of some of the recent reviews.)

Two of these results were of particular interest to us, both replicated several times at high levels of statistical significance. The first was the strong pull of the M.D. strategy against M.I.P. and M.J.P. combined (see matrices 3 and 4 in Table 1). This meant that when *relative* differentiation in favour of the ingroup conflicted with the absolute amounts of awards that could be distributed either to members of the ingroup (the M.I.P. strategy) or to all the subjects (the M.J.P. strategy), it was the achievement of this relative differentiation which tended to guide the choices. The second result concerned the choices made in the distribution of awards between two *other* members of the ingroup as compared with distribution between two members of the outgroup. These two types of choice were made on separate matrices, several times each. The findings were that the amounts awarded to two members of the ingroup were consistently and significantly nearer to the M.J.P. point of the matrices than the amounts awarded to two members of the outgroup. Here again, even more than in the case of the 'pull' of M.D., we are dealing with 'gratuitous' discrimination in favour of the ingroup: as these ingroup and outgroup choices were made on separate matrices, giving more to the outgroup did not mean that one had to give less to the ingroup. Once again, it looked as if the simplest explanation was to assume that the subjects attempted to achieve positive differentiation in favour of the ingroup, even at the cost of giving less money to members of the outgroup who, although anonymous, were from the same class at school, and presumably well acquainted with the subjects.

However, an important methodological problem had to be dealt with before the subjects' behaviour could be seen as a consequence of social categorization into groups rather than of inter-individual similarity which was, in these experiments, associated with this categorization; i.e. the criterion for group membership was a similarity between the subjects in their performance in the first part of the experiments. There is a good deal of evidence (summarized in, e.g. Byrne, 1971) that inter-individual similarities, even when they are fairly trivial, do lead the subjects in constricted experimental situations to 'prefer' those who are more 'like' them.

For this reason, further experiments were conducted in order to attempt a separation between the variables of inter-individual similarity and of 'pure' categorization into dichotomous groups. In a two-by-two design, the subjects' behaviour towards others when they were explicitly divided into groups was compared with their behaviour when division into groups was not made explicit (Billig, 1972; Billig and Tajfel, 1973). The procedure used in the earlier experiments was adapted for this purpose. In the first part of the experiment, the subjects were asked to express their preference for one or other of two painters (Klee and Kandinsky) on the basis of a number of reproductions of paintings which were shown to them on a screen. In the second part, in conditions which insured anonymity of previously-expressed preferences, each subject was asked to award points (which had monetary value) between two anonymous other subjects who were designated by code numbers. There were four experimental conditions. In one condition (categorization and similarity – CS) each subject awarded points to two others, one of whom was in his own group, the group membership being based on the previously-expressed preference (the 'Klee group' or the 'Kandinsky group'), and one in the other group. In the second condition (categorization *without* similarity – $C\tilde{S}$), the subjects awarded points to two others who were also assigned to two groups (one of which was the subject's own group) but this assignment was explicitly made random, and had nothing to do with previously-expressed picture preferences. In the third condition (similarity *without* categorization – $\tilde{C}S$), the subjects awarded points to two others whose code numbers indicated that they preferred one or the other painter, but the notion of 'groups' was not introduced or mentioned at any point during the experiment. In the fourth condition (*no* categorization and *no* similarity – $\tilde{C}\tilde{S}$) points were awarded to two other subjects without any reference either to group membership or to picture preferences. The results were as follows: in conditions of CS and $C\tilde{S}$ a significant amount of favouritism was shown towards others who were in the same group as the subject making the awards; in condition $\tilde{C}S$, there was some tendency by the subjects to favour those whose preferences were similar to their own, but this tendency did not reach the level of statistical significance; in condition $\tilde{C}\tilde{S}$ there was no bias in favour of one or the other of the recipients of the awards. The highly significant results in condition CS replicated those we obtained in the initial experiments (Tajfel *et al.*, 1971). But our main interest here was in the comparison between conditions $C\tilde{S}$ and $\tilde{C}S$. The favouritism shown towards those who were assigned to the subjects' own group without any reference to similarity in preferences (the CŠ condition) was considerably and significantly stronger than the non-significant tendency shown in the C̃S condition to favour those who, without any reference to their categorization into group, were similar to the subject in their preferences.

It cannot be said, of course, that the subjects in condition C̃S did *not* categorize as 'groups' on the basis of similarities of preferences. But the point of the experiment was that this was not an *explicit* categorization. Thus, the introduction of an explicit social categorization in condition CŠ – which was not based on any previous similarities between the individuals involved – was much more effective in producing favouritism than the introduction in condition C̃S of similarity between individuals which was not related to an explicit social categorization. These conclusions are confirmed in a study by Chase (1971; also see Hornstein, 1972) who employed a modification of the procedures used in the initial experiments (Tajfel, 1970b) with groups of subjects in New York. As in our experiments, no explicit categorization into groups was introduced; consequently, little or no discrimination was found.

Before going further, it may be worthwhile to consider the differences between the sets of results we obtained and those obtained in previous work which is relatively the nearest in its conceptions and methods to the studies described here: Sherif's work on intergroup conflict (e.g. Sherif, 1966). His aim was to investigate the effects of an explicitly- and clearly-introduced zero-sum conflict between groups on outgroup attitudes and the subsequent behaviour of his subjects. In addition, group affiliation and outgroup hostility were both intensified through prolonged intragroup interaction between the subjects. In our experiments, there was no externally defined conflict; if there was competition (i.e. actions aiming to differentiate between the groups in favour of one's own), *it was fully and actively brought into the situation by the subjects themselves* as soon as the notion of group was introduced by the experimenters. The subjects were never together as a 'group'; they neither interacted nor did they know who was in their own group and who in the other; there were no *explicit* social pressures on them to act in favour of their own group; and in no way was their own individual interest engaged in awarding more money to a member of their own group. On the contrary, a consistent use of the maximum joint profit strategy would have led to *all* of them receiving more money from the experimenters.

It is the assumed need for differentiation (or the establishment of psychological distinctiveness between the groups) which seems to provide, under some conditions, the major outcome of the sequence social categorization–social identity–social comparison. Related phenomena can be shown to exist in a large variety of social situations. One major example is provided by the wider social contexts in which the notion of 'race' is used as a criterion for social categorization. For a number of reasons 'race' has become a value-loaded term, a notion which has 'surplus' value connotations. It may therefore be instructive to identify the social situations in which this notion tends to be used or, as John Rex wrote, 'the kinds of social differentiations in which subjective social distinctions have been made' (Rex, 1969). According to Rex, these are as follows:

1. The situation of culture contact between peoples with an advanced industrial and military technology, and hunters, pastoralists and agriculturists at lower levels of development.
2. The situation on a slave plantation.
3. Class situations in the classic Marxist or Weberian sense in which men within the same society have different degrees of market power.
4. Status situations in which there is a concept of higher and lower.
5. Situations of ethnic pluralism in which groups with differing cultures and/or physical characteristics work together in the same economy but retain their social and cultural identity.
6. Situations in which a minority group occupies a pariah or scapegoat role. (Rex, 1969, p. 147)

In three of these six situations, value differentiations between groups or individuals are explicitly stated ('lower levels of development', 'criterion of esteem', 'pariah'). In the remaining three, they are not far below the surface. Whatever its other uses may be, the notion of 'race' has become in its general social usage a shorthand expression which helps to create, reflect, enhance and perpetuate the perceived differences in 'worth' between human groups or individuals. It contributes to making these differences as clear-cut and inflexible as possible. Therefore, its application in the wide range of social contexts enumerated by Rex witnesses to the introduction, whenever possible, of differentiations in terms of value which increase the dichotomous distinctiveness of social categories and thus contribute to their function as a guide for social action.

This establishment of distinctiveness is by no means, however, confined to situations connected with the notion of race. It finds its way, for example, into the complex effects that cultural and social relations have on the mutual comprehension and acceptance by interacting groups of their languages and dialects. Fishman (1968) wrote, basing his statement on linguistic evidence from West Africa, the Swahili region of

Central and East Africa, New Guinea, Scandinavia and South East Asia:

Divisiveness is an ideologized position and it can magnify minor differences; indeed, it can manufacture differences in language as in other matters almost as easily as it can capitalize on more obvious differences. Similarly, unification is also an ideologized position and it can minimize seemingly major differences or ignore them entirely, whether these be in the realm of languages, religion, culture, race, or any other basis of differentiation. (p. 45)

Fishman's 'ideologized positions' are positions in which similarities or differences, which could *in principle* be entirely 'neutral' (e.g. between languages, landscapes, flags, anthems, postage stamps, football teams and almost anything else) become endowed with emotional significance because they relate to a superordinate value, such as is the case with nationalism in Fishman's own discussion.

Nationalism, which often used to be one of the forces working towards the conservation of social systems, has become today, in many situations, one of the forces towards change. This is due to the drive of smaller ethnic groups all over the world towards a clearer establishment of a separate social identity. There is no end of examples: the French-Canadians, the American Indians, the Welsh and Scots in Britain, the Bretons in France, the Basques in France and Spain, a French-speaking minority in the Jura canton in Switzerland, etc., etc. One more detailed descriptive example is interesting because it comes from a fairly closed-in society which has had until recently very few contacts with the outside world; and yet the structure of the cognitive and behavioural push towards psychological group distinctiveness seems very similar to what one can find elsewhere.

The society in question is in Ruanda, where one of the two very nearly impermeable ethnic groups, the Tutsi, has consistently dominated the other, the Hutu, since the Tutsi conquest of four centuries ago. The description, which comes from a book by Philip Mason (1970) on race relations, is based on the extensive work in Ruanda by the social anthropologist Maquet (1961).

Separation between the two groups was not absolutely rigid; a poor Tutsi might marry the daughter of a rich Hutu but the Tutsi did not like mention of the possibility and both Tutsi and Hutu indignantly repudiated the possibility of marriage with one of the Twa, a pygmoid people, only one per cent of the population, who had been there even before the Hutu. The three groups – Tutsi, Hutu, Twa – were physically different, the Tutsis being by repute tall, fair and slender by comparison with the darker and sturdier Hutu. And in fact a difference in average height did exist in modern times, although rather less than it was reputed to be, being approximately four inches between Tutsi and Hutu and the

275

same between Hutu and Twa. But the Tutsi did all that they could to emphasize this and other differences between themselves and the Hutu.

In the first place, they emphasized the difference by training; a Tutsi youth would spend some time at Mwami's court, where he would be trained in the use of weapons, in sports and hunting and in bodily fitness, but also in poetry and legend and in the art of conversation. They were taught the qualities needed for leadership, firmness and justice, generosity and courage. It was a disgrace to show fear or betray emotion; to lose the temper was a vulgar act suitable only for Hutu. Maquet (the anthropologist who has recorded this system most complete-ly) asked both Tutsi and Hutu about the qualities each attributed to the other; he found that the Hutu regarded the Tutsi as 'intelligent, capable of command, refined, courageous and cruel'; the Hutu, according to both groups, were 'hardworking, not very clever, extrovert, quick-tempered, obedient, physically strong' – in fact, very like the stereotype of the peasant all the world over. Asked whether the characteristics could be changed by training and upbringing, both groups answered that only very limited changes could be made; the qualities were inherent.

One other point, trifling in itself, is highly significant for the general argument. The Tutsi professed to eat little if any solid food – when on a journey, they would eat none at all, living on curdled milk, banana beer and mead made from honey – never maize beer, the Hutu drink. When at home, they would eat solid food only once a day, in the evening, all Hutu servants being rigidly excluded; even then, they would not eat the standard food of the Hutu, porridge made from maize or millet, sweet potatoes or yams. In short, they were careful to adhere to a diet as different as possible from the Hutu's, and they tried to make it appear more different than in fact it was. They were superior beings and it was essential that nothing should emphasize common humanity.

(Mason, 1970, pp. 75–6).

The argument presented here postulates that the reason for this cognitive, behavioural and evaluative intergroup differentiation is in the need that the individuals have to provide social meaning through social identity to the intergroup situation, experimental or any other; and that this need is fulfilled through the creation of intergroup differences when such differences do not in fact exist, or the attribution of value to, and the enhancement of, whatever differences that do exist.

2. Strategies of intergroup differentiation

As already mentioned, the concept of social identity, as used in the previous chapter, is not an attempt to describe it for 'what it is' in a static sense – a daunting task which has baffled many social scientists of various persuasions and for which one needs a great deal of optimism and temerity. Social identity is understood here as an intervening causal mechanism in situations of 'objective' social change (see Tajfel, 1972b) –

observed, anticipated, feared, desired, or prepared by the individuals involved. From this point of view, three categories of situations appear crucial:

(i) The badly defined or marginal social situation of a group, which presents the individuals involved with difficulties of defining their place in a social system

(ii) The groups socially defined and consensually accepted as 'superior' in some important respects at a time when their position is threatened either by occurring or impending change, or by a conflict of values inherent in the 'superiority'

(iii) the groups socially defined and consensually accepted as 'inferior' in some important respects at a time when – for whatever reasons – either (a) members of a group have engaged in a shared *prise de conscience* of the illegitimacy of their inferior status; or (b) they have become aware of the *feasibility* of working towards alternatives to the existing situation; or, most often, a combination of (a) and (b), which may also imply (a) leading to (b), or (b) leading to (a).

A parenthesis is needed here concerning the meaning in this discussion of the terms 'inferior' and 'superior'. They are rough (and by no means optimal) shorthand terms referring to the psychological correlates of a number of interacting dimensions of social differentiations, such as discrepancies between groups in social status, in power, in domination, etc. These terms must be understood, of course, in the context of their social derivation. Black skin is not, outside of specific social contexts, either an inferior or a superior attribute; but it may become one, given certain social psychological conditions. In principle, *any* group characteristic could become (and most do) value-laden in this sense. One can note, for example, the persistence even today of blond hair, fair skin and blue eyes in many dauntless heroes of war comics; or the significance that long hair acquired a few years ago in a variety of social contexts, both for those who used it for its distinctiveness and for those who used it as an identifying sign of moral turpitude.

The 'dynamic' approach to problems of social identity adopted in this discussion is based on several considerations. First, and most important, it is unlikely that there exist many examples of intergroup situations which are static in the sense that they consist of an unchanging set of social relationships between the groups. The psychological counterparts of these intergroup social relations are bound to be even less static. This becomes quite clear when one reconsiders briefly the focal problem of this discussion: that of social identity understood as deriving in a comparative and 'relational' manner from an individual's group memberships.

277

For the purpose of the argument, one can distinguish between 'secure' and 'insecure' social identity. A completely secure social identity would imply a relationship between two (or more) groups in which a change in the texture of psychological distinctiveness between them is not *conceivable*. For an 'inferior' group this would imply the existence of a total consensus about the nature and the future of their inferiority. In other words, to return to our discussion in chapter 12 of 'social reality' as related to Festinger's theory of social comparison (1954), there would have to exist a complete psychological 'objectification' of a social *status quo* with no cognitive alternatives of any kind available to challenge the existing social reality. It is possible that historians and social anthropologists could provide some relevant examples in completely stable and isolated societies; these examples could hardly, however, find many counterparts in the contemporary world.

A completely secure social identity for a group consensually 'superior' is nearly an empirical impossibility. The kind of psychological distinctiveness that would insure their unchallenged superiority must not only be gained; it must also be preserved. And it can only be preserved if social conditions of distinctiveness are carefully perpetuated, together with the signs and symbols of distinctive status without which the attitudes of complete consensus about 'superior' distinctiveness are in danger of disintegrating. In this sense, therefore, even in the most rigid caste system (be it racial or any other), the social distinctions which may appear very stable are related to a continuously dynamic psychological situation in which a superior group can never stop working at the preservation of its distinctiveness. It is very difficult to think of cases of intergroup relations which would present exceptions to this statement.

For all these reasons, we shall be concerned here with cases of insecure social identity. These will be discussed in terms of a two–by–two table, in which the two criteria for categorization are: consensually 'superior' v. 'inferior' groups; and the individuals' perception of their ability to 'pass' from one group to another.

The first of these criteria, superior v. inferior, is justified because, as it will be shown, different hypotheses pertain to the two kinds of groups. The second criterion, passing or not passing, derives from our earlier discussion about the structure of belief in 'social change' and 'social mobility'. To summarize from chapter 11: in each individual's life there will be situations in which he acts mainly as an individual rather than as a member of a group; there will be others in which he acts mainly in terms of his group membership. It was assumed that one of the important determinants of an individual's choice to act in terms of self rather than in terms of his group was the 'social mobility' structure of beliefs as

Table 3
Insecure intergroup social comparisons

	Conditions conducive to leaving one's group	Conditions conducive to staying in one's group
Consensually superior groups	A	B
Consensually inferior groups	C	D

contrasted with the 'social change' structure. The former referred to situations characterized by the belief that it is relatively easy to move individually from one social group to another; so that, if a group does not contribute adequately to an individual's social identity, one of the more obvious solutions is to move, or attempt to move, to another group. In the latter class were those situations in which, for whatever reasons, 'passing' from one group to another is perceived as very difficult or impossible. It may be expected that, in these situations, there will be many occasions (and constraints) leading an individual to act as a member of his group, or at least in the knowledge that he is categorized as such. 'Social change' (as distinct from 'social mobility') will therefore refer in this discussion to the perception of changes as being based on the relationships between the groups as a whole; i.e. to expectations, fears or desires of such changes, to actions aiming at inducing or preventing them, or to intentions and plans to engage in these actions. It is therefore in the individual's awareness that many important aspects of his life, including the acquisition or preservation of an acceptable social identity, can only be based on a change (or resistance to change) in the image, position or circumstances of his group as a whole.

The resulting two-by-two classification of cases and predictions arising from them can, therefore, be presented as in Table 3.

Superior groups (Boxes A and B)

Insecure social comparisons arising within a group which is consensually defined as being of higher status can be due to two sets of conditions:

(a) The group's superior status is threatened (or perceived as threatened) by another group

(b) The superior status is related to a conflict of values, i.e. it is conceived by some members of the group as based on unfair advantages, various forms of injustice, exploitation, illegitimate use of force, etc.

In the first case, Box A (conditions conducive to leaving one's group) is not likely to contain many instances as long as the threat does not become overwhelming. It will contain hardly any instances in situations in which 'passing' is very difficult (e.g. an apartheid society). In Box B (conditions conducive to staying in one's group) one can predict an intensification of actions and precautions aiming to keep the superior group in its position. On the level of intergroup social comparison, one can predict the intensification of the existing distinctions together with the creation and use of new conditions which will enable the superior group to preserve and enhance its psychological distinctiveness. This may take many forms, such as the preservation and increase of social and psychological separation of many kinds, creation of a variety of distinctive symbols, etc. A good example of these various forms of enhancement of distinctiveness was the relationship between the Tutsi and the Hutu described earlier. Other examples abound.

In the case (b) above, that of conflict of values, three sub-cases can be distinguished:

(i) The conflict of values is of such intensity that it destroys the positive contribution to social identity that the group provides. This is Box A. Examples are provided by upper-class or middle-class revolutionaries, 'renegades' of all kinds, etc. There will be here no discrimination against the outgroup and no hostility against it. But this is hardly an interesting intergroup prediction since group membership is often cancelled for all practical purposes, or sometimes even positively reversed.

(ii) The conflict of values exists, but ingroup affiliation is sufficiently powerful to remain the determinant of attitudes and behaviour. This is Box B. The conflict of values can only be resolved through finding new justifications for the maintenance of the *status quo*. This is the condition for the creation and adoption at large by the members of a group of new 'ideologies' (e.g. the 'white man's burden', the 'inherent superiority' due to unbridgeable innate differences, the 'saving of souls', etc.). These ideologies represent the creation of new forms of psychological distinctiveness and the enhancement of those amongst the old ones which are still serviceable. The clearer are the 'objective' conditions preventing the leaving of one's group (such as self-interest, racial differences, powerfully sanctioned religious differences, etc.), the more likely it is that the conflict of values will result in the creation and wide and easy diffusion of these new and enhanced forms of psychological distinctiveness.

(iii) The third sub-case concerns situations in which the conflict of values inherent in the superiority exists but the drive towards new social identity by the 'inferior' group is not particularly relevant to the comparative social identity of the 'superior' group. This can be so for several reasons: the threat to the superior group is still relatively unimportant; or the dimensions of distinctiveness that the inferior group is seeking to achieve may be much more important to that group than to the superior group whose important social comparisons are with groups other than this particular one in a multi-group structure of comparisons. This is therefore a situation of asymmetry in which the conflict of values in the superior group and/or the relative lack of importance for it of a particular comparison of identities lead to the prediction that intergroup discrimination will be stronger in the inferior than in the superior group.

Some evidence consonant with this prediction comes from a recent experiment by Branthwaite and Jones (1975). Welsh nationalism is now rapidly gaining ground and it is becoming an increasingly salient social and political issue in Wales. This shows itself in a variety of forms of social action; for example, a great deal is being done for the revival and more widespread use of the Welsh language, there is an increasing number of symbols of Welshness, increasing demands for more auto-nomy for the region, etc. At the same time, all this is still not very much of an issue for the English. The English attitudes towards Welsh nationalism seem to be a mixture of guilty sympathy, and the hope – justified until now – that things will not reach the acute form that they have reached once again in recent years in Northern Ireland which presents a very different set of problems.

Branthwaite and Jones used as their subjects undergraduate students at University College in Cardiff in Wales who were 'asked if they preferred to be known as English or Welsh. Only those people who gave an immediate answer of "English" or "Welsh" were included as subjects. If there was any slight doubt or hesitancy they were not included in the experiment.' Fifty subjects took part, twenty-five from each of the two categories. They never met in the course of the experiment. Each subject was tested individually in a cubicle, asked to fill in a number of payment matrices chosen from those in the experiments described earlier (Tajfel *et al.*, 1971), and awarded through his choices on these matrices points worth money to two other subjects. As in the previous experiments, there were three conditions of payment: to two other subjects, one from the ingroup and one from the outgroup; to two other subjects, both from the ingroup; and to two other subjects, both from the outgroup; all these recipients of awards were identified individually and anonymously by code numbers and also as 'English' or 'Welsh'. Each subject filled forty matrices.

Table 4 (derived from the data of Branthwaite and Jones) presents the frequency distribution (in terms of mean percentages of responses on matrices) using, for each type of matrix, the four extreme responses, two favouring the ingroup and two the outgroup. Three interesting patterns are shown by these distributions. In (a), (b) and (c) in the table which

Table 4

Distribution of extreme responses in the Branthwaite and Jones (1975) study

(a) Matrices with MJP constant				(b) Matrices with MD at one end and MJP+MIP at the opposite end		
	English Ss	Welsh Ss			English Ss	Welsh Ss
Favouring ingroup	17	28		MD (in favour of ingroup)	12	32
Favouring outgroup	9	0		MJP+MIP	16	2
(c) Matrices with MIP+MD at one end and MJP at the opposite end				(d) Matrices in which MD, MIP and MJP coincide at the same end		
	English Ss	Welsh Ss			English Ss	Welsh Ss
MIP+MD	13	35		MD+MIP+ MJP	23.5	33
MJP	18	1		−(MD+MIP +MJP)	3	2

(e)
Matrices distributing between two members of the same group (ingroup or outgroup)

	English Ss	Welsh Ss
At (or near) MJP for ingroup	17	18.5
At (or near) MJP for outgroup	9	1.5

derive from matrices allowing the subjects to make choices favouring the ingroup directly over the outgroup, the Welsh subjects display these choices with markedly higher frequencies than do the English subjects. In (d), where all the advantages coincide at one end of the matrix, this end is chosen overwhelmingly more often by both groups of subjects than the opposite end. The difference in strategies between (b) and (c) on the one hand, and (d) on the other shows clearly that in (d), when a 'rational' strategy does not conflict with ingroup favouritism, it is extensively used by both groups. When, however, (as is the case for (b) and (c)) differentiation in favour of the ingroup clearly conflicts with 'rational' gains (even for one's own group, as in (b)), the Welsh group chooses the former option. The third interesting aspect of these distribu-tions is shown in (e): *both* groups display marked ingroup favouritism in awarding more often the maximum joint amount (M.J.P.) to two members of the ingroup than to two members of the outgroup. On these I/I[1] and O/O matrices, a display of ingroup favouritism is not as obvious (but just as effective) as on the I/O matrices on which the interests of the

[1] I/I   ingroup–ingroup choices.
 O/O   outgroup–outgroup choices.
 I/O   ingroup–outgroup choices.

two groups are starkly and directly confronted. When given the opportunity to indulge in this slightly more roundabout form of discrimination, the English group go some way towards joining the Welsh group in the degree of their ingroup bias.

Inferior groups (Boxes C and D)

Insecure social comparisons arising within a group which is consensually defined as being of lower status can be described as follows:

(a) Box C: Conditions conducive to leaving one's group.

These are the situations of social mobility as defined earlier: there is enough social flexibility to enable an individual to move, or hope to move, from one group to another; there are no serious social sanctions from either of the groups for moving; and no serious conflict of values involved in moving.

(b) Box D: Conditions conducive to staying in one's group.

This box presents a much greater interest from the point of view of intergroup attitudes and behaviour than the previous one. The major social conditions are: any form of caste system (whether determined by birth, race or other criteria); or any other social differentiation system which for whatever reasons, makes it difficult to move. The two major psychological conditions are: a strong conflict of values[2] inherent in leaving one's group; or the fear of powerful social sanctions for so doing; or both in combination. In most situations the social and psychological conditions will, of course, interact and reinforce each other.

The assumption is made here that, in many of these conditions, the problems of social identity of the inferior group would not necessarily express themselves in social behaviour until and unless there is some awareness that the existing social reality is not the only possible one and that alternatives to it are conceivable and perhaps attainable. If this awareness exists, the problems of social identity confronting the members of inferior groups can be solved in one of several ways, or a combination of more than one:

(i) To become, through action and reinterpretation of group characteristics, more like the superior group.

(ii) To reinterpret the existing inferior characteristics of the group, so

---

[2] It is interesting to see that conflicts of values may be expected to work in opposite directions for members of 'superior' and 'inferior' groups. In the former case, the perceived illegitimacy of the superior position of one's group may lead some of its members to leave it, even in the face of serious barriers or difficulties to 'passing'. In the latter case, a conflict of values may consist of loyalty to the group preventing the leaving of it even if 'staying' presents personal disadvantages. And therefore, in 'superior' groups, this conflict may lead to leaving despite the difficulties and disadvantages of moving 'downwards'; in the 'inferior' groups, it may lead to staying in, even if moving 'upwards' happens not to be too difficult and presents personal advantages.

that they do not appear as inferior but acquire a positively-valued distinctiveness from the superior group.

(iii) To create, through social action and/or diffusion of new 'ideologies', new group characteristics which have a positively-valued distinctiveness from the superior group.

The first solution, which is that of cultural, social and psychological assimilation of a group as a whole, is sometimes possible. One might even predict – and also infer from historical hindsight – that, given favourable conditions, it could become the solution to be tried first. In order, however, for a group as a whole to succeed in eliminating both its social and psychological inferiority, one process must first take place: the breaking down of the barriers preventing the group from obtaining improved access to conditions which it could not previously obtain. As soon as this happens, one or two psychological processes will tend to appear: if the group remains separate, a general reinterpretation of its distinctive characteristics in new and positively-valued terms; or, alternatively, the breakdown on both sides of the *psychological* barriers to 'passing'. The first of these merges with the solution (ii) which will be discussed below; the second may finally lead to the disappearance of a group as it merges with another.

It may be expected that the solutions (ii) and (iii) mentioned above will appear in conjunction with one another, and that social action will be an important ingredient of both; but for the sake of empirical distinctions they will be discussed separately. It will be remembered that both originate in situations where, for whatever reasons, the inferior group is not able to merge with the superior one, nor can the individual members of it leave their own group and join another.

Solution (ii) implies that, with the *prise de conscience* of the illegitimacy of an inferiority, a new kind of distinctiveness must be created on the basis of some *existing* group characteristics. One of the clearest recent examples of the whole process can be found in the psychological changes that are taking place amongst the American blacks. The very use of the term 'blacks' in this text, which would have had very different connotations only a few years ago, already testifies to these changes. The old *interpretations* of distinctiveness are often rejected; the old characteristics are being given a new meaning of different but equal or superior. Examples abound: the search for roots, the beauty of blackness, the African hair-do, the African cultural past and traditions, the reinterpretation of Negro music from 'entertainment' to a form of art which has deep roots in a separate cultural tradition, the taking over or re-creating, at one time, of certain ideas about *négritude*, etc. At the same time, the old attempts to be 'a little more' like the other group are often rejected: no more straightening of hair for beautiful black girls or using various procedures for lightening the skin. The accents, dialects, sway of the body, rhythms of dancing, texture of the details of interpersonal communication – all this is preserved, enhanced and re-evaluated. The *prise de conscience* starts, as it is often the case, with an active minority (see Moscovici, 1976). As and when the new-found distinctiveness does manage to do its job of creating a positive and healing new version of social identity, the prediction can be made that all its forms will find an easy and widespread diffusion at large.

Solution (iii), the creation or invention of new characteristics which establish a positively-valued group distinctiveness, is structurally similar to solution (ii). Examples of it can be found in the development of new nationalisms (see Tajfel, 1969b, 1970a). As I wrote some years ago: 'In many new nations the need is felt to stress or create common bonds in order to force the pace of the development of nationhood. The forging of bonds need not be of a "racial" kind, though it has often been of this nature, particularly in the young European nationalisms of the nineteenth century. The phenomenon is even clearer in racism old or new; the racist ideologies have always been characterized by a frantic search for common bonds of an "innate" or "instinctive" nature in the distant past so as to provide a justification for the claim of the special sort of unity that the racial group is supposed to have and of its inherent and immutable differences from other such groups.' (Tajfel, 1969b, p. 139; see, e.g. Shafer, 1955 and Mossé, 1975, for a general discussion of the creation of various categories of national myths).

The creation of new distinctive characteristics implies, however, a new problem. This problem also exists in some measure in the process of the re-evaluation of the existing characteristics (solution (ii)), but it becomes particularly clear when new forms of distinctiveness need to be either invented or created through action. It has been postulated throughout this discussion that the aim of positively-valued psychological distinctiveness is to achieve an adequate form of social identity; and that the only means by which this aim can be attained is in the establishment of appropriate kinds of intergroup comparison. There are two stages in this process which, ideally, both need to be successfully realized. The first (which is a condition *sine qua non* for the success of the enterprise) is the positive evaluation by the ingroup of its newly-created characteristics. The second stage consists of the acceptance by the outgroup of this evaluation. The issue is, however, slightly more complicated. The new characteristics of the inferior group can be of two kinds:

(a) They may consist of attributes which are already consensually highly valued by both (or more) groups, and which the inferior group

285

was previously deemed not to possess. In this case (which has been termed 'social competition' by Turner, 1975) there is no problem of re-evaluation of attributes; the issue is to shift the evaluation of a *group* on certain existing dimensions. The social comparison problem for the inferior group is: will the others acknowledge the new image, *separate* but equal or superior, on consensually-valued dimensions? An example can perhaps be found in some new and widely diffused aspects of Jewish identity (see Herman, 1970). Amongst aspects of group identity un-acceptable to the young post-war generations of Jews was their elders' passive acceptance of a wholesale slaughter of a people. The exceptions, such as the uprising of the ghetto of Warsaw or the revolts in Treblinka and other concentration camps, became therefore crucial symbols; so has the Masada story, long back from the past, and in the present, the military prowess of the new state of Israel.

(b) The second case concerns situations in which the new characteristics of an inferior group are not consensually valued to begin with. The social comparison problem of the second case for the inferior group then becomes: will the others acknowledge the new image, *different* but equal or superior? This is, therefore, the problem of acknowledgement by others through a re-evaluation of the *attributes* of a group and not the re-evaluation of a group on attributes which are already commonly valued; it also applies to the previously discussed solution (ii) in which the inferior group invests its already existing separate characteristics with a new significance. A good example can be found in some field experiments reported by Lemaine (Lemaine, 1966; Lemaine and Kasters-ztein, 1972–3; Lemaine *et al.*, 1978). In one of the studies, a competition to build huts was arranged between two groups of boys at a summer camp – but one group was given less adequate building materials than the other. Both groups were aware of the discrepancy which was based on an explicitly random distribution of resources between them. The 'inferior' group consequently engaged in two sequences of behaviour: first, they built an inferior hut but surrounded it with a small garden; and then they 'engaged in sharp discussions with the children from the other group and the adult judges to obtain acknowledgement of the legitimacy of their work. Their arguments were approximately as follows: we are willing to admit that the others have built a hut and that their hut is better than ours; but it must equally be admitted that our small garden with its fence surrounding the hut is also a part of the hut and that we are clearly superior on this criterion of comparison.' (Lemaine and Kastersztein, 1972–3, p. 675, translated from the French).

The importance of this second stage, as just discussed, from the point of view of the present argument is that its consideration leads to some crucial predictions about intergroup behaviour. The battle for legitimacy, in which Lemaine's subjects engaged, is a battle for the acceptance by others of new forms of intergroup comparison. As long as these are not consensually accepted, the new characteristics (or the re-evaluation of the old ones) cannot be fully adequate in their function of building a new social identity. At the same time, there will be many instances in which the superior group, for the sake of its own distinctive identity, cannot accept one of the three forms of change discussed above: admission (i) that, despite the previously existing stereotypes, the inferior group possesses some of the attributes which are highly valued in common; (ii) that its old attributes are at the positive end of a valued dimension; and (iii) that its newly emerging attributes are of a kind that should be positively evaluated. It is at this point of the conflict between comparative social identities that the causal processes discussed here lead to the prediction of intense hostility in intergroup attitudes and of marked discrimination in intergroup behaviour.

The results of the experimental studies so far described, together with the consideration of some 'real' social situations, lead to the conclusion that two interdependent conditions are basic in determining behaviour in terms of group rather than in terms of self (see chapter 11). They are: the dichotomization of the social world into closely distinct categories (see e.g. Hornstein, 1972, for supplementary evidence); and the impossibility or serious difficulty in 'passing' from one group to another (see the discussion of 'social mobility' v. 'social change' in chapter 11). There are, undoubtedly, many other conditions which are also important in increasing or decreasing the salience of group membership. But acting in terms of group rather than in terms of self cannot be expected to play a predominant part in an individual's behaviour unless there is present a clear cognitive structure of 'us' and 'them' and unless this structure is not perceived as capable of being easily shifted in a variety of social and psychological conditions.

14

Exit and voice in intergroup relations[1]

1. Exit and voice, mobility and change

If you customarily buy a certain brand of toothpaste, and its price goes up or its quality deteriorates, you will change – without much difficulty or conflict – to another brand. If you discover that the car you have just bought has certain features you dislike, you may decide to sell it and buy one of another manufacture; but if you cannot very well afford the new transaction you may decide to write to the manufacturer pointing out the defects and demanding improvements. If your child goes to a state school that dissatisfies you for various reasons, you may decide to change to a private school. But changing schools may be a traumatic experience for the child; or you may not be able to afford a private school; or there may be no private schools easily available; or they may not be available at all. Whenever any combination of these circumstances arises, the more strongly you feel about the quality of your child's education, the more you are likely to try to do something about the quality of his or her present school, and to find allies among other parents who feel the way you do. If you have been active for many years in a political party, and you are increasingly dissatisfied with some of its policies, you will not just leave and join another party; before you decide to do so, you will try again and again to change the present policies in a direction which suits you better, and the stronger has been your past affiliation, the more difficult you will find it to leave, and the more you will try all possible means to modify the situation from the inside. If you are miserable in your own country, you might try to emigrate. But emigration is a harsh decision to take, and sometimes it may not be possible at all. The harsher or the more nearly impossible it is, the more likely you are to join the ranks of those who try to change things from inside, even by revolutionary means.

There is nothing very startling about this list of examples. In the language used by the economist Hirschman (1970)[2] they can be arranged,

---

[1] From a chapter of the same title in L. H. Strickland, F. E. Aboud and K. J. Gergen (eds.): *Social psychology in transition*, New York: Plenum Press, 1976.

[2] All quotations from *Exit, Voice and Loyalty* used in the present text are taken from the second edition (1972); so are the page numbers of the quotations.

from those mentioned earlier above to those mentioned later, on a dimension that moves from the likelihood of the use of 'exit' to the likelihood of the use of 'voice' as an individual's way of dealing with the problems he confronts. Or, in Hirschman's terms: 'Some customers stop buying the firm's products or some members leave the organization: this is the *exit option*' (p. 4). And: 'The firm's customers or the organization's members express their dissatisfaction directly to the management or to some other authority to which management is subordinate or through general protest addressed to anyone who cares to listen; this is the *voice option*' (p. 4). Very soon we learn that 'voice is political action by excellence' (p. 16).

Hirschman's influential book *Exit, Voice and Loyalty* (1970) was concerned, as its subtitle (*Responses to Decline in Firms, Organizations and States*) indicates, with the relative efficiency of the options of exit and voice, and of their various combinations ('the elusive optimal mix of exit and voice'), in preventing a decline in the functioning of various kinds of social institutions, public or private. His analysis, grounded in economics, reached further to consider conditions for various modes of effective political action. It is not my purpose here to comment in any detail upon this analysis or to redescribe it. But the complex relationships described by Hirschman between the availability of exit to an individual and his use of voice, as they apply to his 'responses to decline' of a social institution, have a number of far-reaching implications for the social psychology of intergroup relations. These implications concern (i) a transposition of the exit–voice relationship from individual behaviour to the behaviour of a social group and (ii) the theoretical possibility that the use of voice in an intergroup context may become a powerful force towards the maintenance of the *status quo* rather than helping to prevent the decline in the functioning of an organization.

The language of exit and voice converges closely with the language of 'social mobility' and of 'social change' which I recently adopted (see the three previous chapters). But the aims of the two discussions diverge. As just stated, Hirschman's analysis of the 'responses to decline' is largely concerned with the relative efficiency of the exercise of the two options, or their various combinations, in preventing the decline in the functioning of various kinds of social institutions, public or private. The distinction between 'social mobility' and 'social change' attempts to define two (theoretical) extremes in a continuum of individuals' beliefs about the relationship between the social group or groups to which they belong and other groups. The 'behavioural' translation of this continuum of beliefs relates it to three other pairs of extremes that are associated with it, and which were discussed in chapter 11.

289

The main purpose of this continuum-splitting exercise was to contribute to a social psychological theory of intergroup relations from which predictions could be made about certain uniformities in the behaviour and attitudes of members of some social groups (or categories) towards members of other social groups (or categories). The convergences with Hirschman's exit–voice pair (I shall discuss loyalty later) are of two kinds: (i) the nature of the concepts used and of some consequences following from them and (ii) the relationship of the general approach to certain strands of an intellectual tradition.

One of the phases of Hirschman's discussion used a continuum in which the transition from a fully free (or costless) exit to its virtual impossibility interacts with the appearance of voice and with conditions for its effectiveness. We move here from the free and easy change of a brand of toothpaste to an enormous variety of social situations in which the cost of exit is, subjectively or objectively, so high as to make it impossible or unbearable, such as may be the case with family, national or political affiliations. Between these extremes, the various degrees of access to exit *may* determine the strength of voice, or of attempts to change from within a deteriorating situation. This is well summed up in the quotation by Hirschman of Erikson's (1964) dictum: 'You can actively flee, then, and you can actively stay put'.

Sometimes, of course, you cannot actively flee and you must stay put, actively or not; or, having unsuccessfully tried to flee, or seen other people try, you may come to believe that escape is impossible and that you must take the consequences of staying put. These consequences include those to which Hirschman referred in describing voice as 'political action by excellence'. For a social psychologist, they would imply the numerous behavioural and attitudinal effects on intergroup relations of the belief system previously described as 'social change'; particularly so when the effective diffusion of the idea that 'passing' individually from one's own group to another is impossible or extremely difficult causes more and more people from that group to feel and act in unison.

This form of voice in intergroup attitudes and behaviour need not only apply to those groups who wish (or need) to modify the nature of their relationships to other groups. It may also appear in groups who aim at preserving or strengthening the *status quo*. I shall return to this issue later.

The differences between the 'social mobility' and the 'social change' approaches to the social psychology of intergroup relations must be clarified in more detail before we can go further. National, racial, ethnic or social class relations may be considered as amounting together to what is the substance of social conflict. In social psychology much of the work relevant to various aspects of social conflict proceeded to extend to it the implications of the theory and research about individual and inter-individual functioning. Thus, we have been much concerned with the development of prejudiced attitudes and discriminatory behaviour in individuals – and we drew upon general theories of individual motivation and cognition or upon the etiology and the symptomatology of personality development in order to account for various forms of hostility against outgroups. The study of inter-individual behaviour provided us with theories of competition and cooperation and, more generally, of the inter-individual adjustment of goals and strategies that, as it was hoped implicitly or sometimes stated explicitly, could contribute to our understanding of the psychology of the wider forms of conflict. No doubt a great deal has been achieved, and still more can probably be done. There is also no doubt that an understanding of these individual and inter-individual processes may be *necessary* for the analysis of some aspects of the psychology of social conflict. The difficulties arise with regard to the question whether it is also *sufficient*.

These difficulties concerning sufficiency become clearer when we consider the psychological aspects of social conflict in the perspective of a phenomenon which is inseparable from it, namely, social movements. In the context of intergroup relations, social movements can be roughly described as presenting three inherent and defining characteristics: a certain duration; the participation of a significant number of people from one or more social groups; and a shared system of beliefs. The first two characteristics are explicitly quantifiable, but – to put it bluntly – it would be no less than foolish to attempt specifying the limits of minimal and maximal duration, or the minimum and maximum numbers of people that would clearly distinguish between what is and what is not a social movement. It seems more useful to attempt a list of negative examples of social phenomena that are not social movements. Such a list of examples would include an isolated and haphazard riot; a series of individual crimes of various kinds, however much on the increase; a palace conspiracy; a Watergate; vegetarian restaurants; a chamber music society, etc. These negative examples make sense when one remembers that a shared system of beliefs defining a social movement *in the context of intergroup relations* must include a set of aims relating to outgroups. In the most general way, these aims must include either changing the nature of the intergroup situation in conflict with groups wishing to maintain the *status quo*, or maintaining the intergroup *status quo* in conflict with groups wishing to change it. All the previous negative examples do not qualify either because they lack the intergroup conflictual system of beliefs; or because these beliefs are not significantly shared within a social group; or because of the ephemeral character of the social actions involved; i.e. they do not meet one or more of the relevant criteria.

The assumed 'sufficiency' of the individual or inter-individual theoretical approaches to the explanation of social movements in an intergroup context is based, to a large extent, on two conceptual transpositions, which both seem, on the face of it, highly plausible. Let us consider as an example the experiments on inter-individual games (of whatever kind) in comparison with some of the experiments introducing explicitly in their designs the notions of ingroup and outgroup, such as the studies by Sherif (e.g. 1966) and the initial Bristol experiments (Tajfel, 1970b; Tajfel *et al.*, 1971) together with studies following from them (e.g. Billig and Tajfel, 1973; Branthwaite and Jones, 1975; Caddick, 1974, 1978; Dann and Doise, 1974; Doise *et al.*, 1972; Doise and Sinclair, 1973; Tajfel and Billig, 1974; Turner, 1975, 1978a and b).

The crucial difference between Sherif's field experiments and the experimental inter-individual games of all kinds is in the nature of the extrapolations from individual to group behaviour. In the case of competitive, cooperative, 'trusting' or 'threatening' behaviour found in the various conditions in which these games are played by individual subjects, the extrapolations are based on the finding that the social behaviour of the subjects reached an acceptable level of uniformity as a function of the independent variables. The extrapolation then bridges the gap between the inter-individual and the intergroup social behaviour; the fact that a number of individuals behaved in a similar manner under similar conditions leads to the conclusion that the same individuals would behave in a similar manner if they were in a group for which would pertain conditions of competition, conflict or cooperation with another group, similar to these conditions in the games played with, or against, other individuals. The inescapable conclusions are (i) the fact that a *collection* of individuals has become a *group* composed of the same individuals makes no difference to their behaviour, since the same 'kind' of individuals are still involved and therefore (ii) the fact of those same individuals being constituted as a group in relation to another group (or groups) does not constitute a set of new independent variables, since conditions of competition, conflict or cooperation are outwardly similar to those involved in the inter-individual situations.

In sharp distinction, Sherif's conclusions were not *only* based on a number of individuals behaving in the same way; they were based on those individuals behaving in the same way together and as a group, i.e. being aware that they were a group. It does not require much methodological sophistication to conclude that, since new independent variables *may* well be involved, they need to be considered theoretically before conclusions from studies of inter-individual conflict are applied to situations of intergroup conflict. It should be made clear at this point that I am not concerned here with the behaviour of 'leaders' or others meeting face to face to represent their groups in situations of diplomatic, international, industrial or any other intergroup negotiations. Although there is some evidence that being a group representative, as distinct from representing nobody but oneself, does make a difference in the social behaviour involved (e.g. Hermann and Kogan, 1968; Lamm and Kogan, 1970; Sawyer and Guetzkow, 1965), the concern of this argument is, as mentioned earlier, with the 'social movement' aspects of intergroup behaviour in which inter-individual face to face relationships are not necessarily of crucial importance.

In the experiments of Tajfel *et al.* (1971) and others using a similar design, the inference from inter-individual to intergroup group behaviour is methodologically nearer to the inter-individual game studies than to those of Sherif. Each subject worked separately, in complete ignorance of what the others, both from the ingroup and the outgroup, were doing; and therefore it cannot be said that, as in Sherif's case, the subjects acted together as a group. The inferences to intergroup behaviour were therefore made, like in the game experiments, from the relative uniformity of a collection of individual responses. There is, however, a crucial difference between the two types of study; in the social categorization experiments the subjects, dividing rewards between two anonymous *others*, one from the ingroup and one from the outgroup, acted in terms of their group (or rather, social category) membership. There was no way to engage in this situation in any form of an inter-individual game, although responses other than those showing intergroup discrimination were fully possible and extensively used by the subjects. The crucial importance of this explicit importation of the intergroup context into the subjects' perspective on the situation was clearly shown in a recent study by Turner (1975), who introduced within the same kind of experimental design the possibility of acting in terms of self. After the preliminary induction of social categorization through aesthetic preferences, as in some of the previous experiments, in one of the experimental conditions the subjects *first* decided on a division of money between self and an alter who was either in their own group or in the outgroup; then they went on to deciding on awards between two others, one from the ingroup and one from the outgroup, as in the original experiments. Subjects in another condition had this sequence reversed: first, they worked on decisions between two others, and then went on to decisions between self and an alter who was either in the ingroup or in the outgroup. In other conditions subjects underwent identical procedures with the only difference that their decisions did not relate to amounts of money but to unspecified 'points' that had no explicit value of any kind. Out of a complex set of results, the following are the most relevant here:

(i) In all the 'other–other' conditions, outgroup discrimination was shown.

(ii) There was no outgroup discrimination (but only discrimination in favour of self) when the choice between self and an ingroup or outgroup alter came *first* in the sequence of decisions; when the choice between self and an ingroup or outgroup alter came *second* in the sequence of decisions (i.e. after a set of alter–alter decisions) the subjects, in addition to discriminating in favour of self, also allotted less to members of the outgroup than to those of the ingroup. There is little doubt that the relative salience of the intergroup perspectives, manipulated in Turner's experiment through their relative priority in the order of tasks, was responsible for the important differences in social behaviour shown in the differing experimental situations.

The inter-individual games were compared above with studies using the intergroup context directly and/or subjects acting *as* members of their group in order to argue the case that the emergence of one or both of these additional variables throws doubt on the validity of direct extrapolations from one kind of setting to the other. But the inter-individual games and strategies are no more than one example among many. I referred above to direct inferences to intergroup behaviour from studies of the 'development of prejudiced attitudes and discriminatory behaviour in individuals [which] drew upon general theories of individual motivation and cognition, or upon the etiology and symptomatology of personality development'. These inferences present exactly the same logical and methodological gaps as is the case for inter-individual games if conclusions are applied *directly* to intergroup behaviour. But it is not enough to assert that there is a gap. The need for a new social psychological analysis of social conflict must be shown to exist; such an analysis must, in order to remain valid, take for granted the achievements of the 'individual' theories, but it must also attempt to specify the nature of the new and emergent intergroup variables.

It is here that a combination of the exit–voice perspective of Hirschman, with its background in economics, with the social mobility–social change perspective, with its anchorage in social psychology, seems to prove fruitful. Social mobility corresponds to the *belief* in an easy and costless 'exit' from one's social group; social change is the corresponding no-exit situation, which may determine the use of 'voice' in the attempts to change the existing unsatisfactory situation. In other words, the 'objective' absence of access to exit, and/or the belief that this access does not exist, may lead to a certain kind of social behaviour ('political action by excellence') for which Hirschman uses the shorthand expression 'voice'. His preoccupation is essentially pragmatic: he asks questions about the utility of the two options, and of their combinations, as a recuperation mechanism for ailing social organizations. But other questions concerning intergroup behaviour can also be asked in the context of the two theoretical pairs of exit–voice and social mobility–social change. Some of these questions will be considered in the next two sections of this chapter. For the present, our concern is with the emergent intergroup variables, as seen from this particular theoretical vantage.

We noted earlier that the social mobility–social change continuum was directly and logically related to three other continua: the self–group continuum of social behaviour, the variability–uniformity continuum of behaviour of members of the ingroup towards the outgroup, and the variability–uniformity continuum in the extent of differentiation between individual members of the outgroup (e.g. from minimum to maximum stereotype). If exit in Hirschman's sense means not 'exit' from buying a product but exit from a group in order to enter another group, i.e. exit in its narrower sense of social mobility, then any number of 'individual' theories of social behaviour can be successfully used to describe the motivational and cognitive aspects of the situation. The limitations here, to be discussed later, will appear when we move from an individual's exit from his group to a group's exit from a multi-group structure. However, as long as we deal with individual exit from a group, or even a collection of individual exits, we are still within the confines of, for example, the inter-individual games and strategies, with the only difference that the individual adjusts his or her strategies to the requirements of a complex social environment rather than just to the strategies of another individual. The individual calculations predicted by, for example, the various versions of the exchange theory will yield their outcomes (usually *post hoc*) and no other *kind* of theoretical framework seems to be required.

The situation changes dramatically, however, when the other pair of equivalent terms, i.e. 'voice' and 'social change' is considered in its intergroup framework. Here, the individual has come to the conclusion that he can change his unsatisfactory situation or prevent the change in his satisfactory situation only as a member of his group, only acting as part and parcel of it, together with other members. His social environment is even more complex than is the case in the social mobility situation. There is the 'inside' of his own group, with all the usual individual, inter-individual and structural conflicts, difficulties and problems. There is the 'outside' environment consisting of other groups, which either oppose a change that he wants or want a change that he opposes. The processes of social comparison will apply, in all the relevant social situations, *directly* to these groups, however similar or dissimilar they may be to his own (see chapter 12). These same processes of social comparison compounded with the growth of a group (or social) identity will brew a powerful combination of motives, cognitions and social actions in which the more obvious individually considered reinforcements and the simple calculations of individual utility will go by the board as often as not.

The point of discussing social movements earlier was that the individual frustrations, individual reinforcements and individual personality patterns cannot account for uniformities of social action and social attitudes towards other groups shared – as they often are – for long periods of time by large masses of people. It is always possible to balance respectably the total theoretical account by throwing in notions such as conformity, common features of socialization or reward structures of social learning. But these are blunt and *post hoc* tools; blunt, because they are not capable of distinguishing theoretically between the diverse structures of various intergroup situations; *post hoc* because no one has ever been able to predict (and even less to understand) the social psychology of a social movement, be it a surge of conservative reaction or a revolution, by invoking conformity or schedules of individual reinforcements. What is more, social movements are often started by counterconforming minorities and joining them often involves the sort of individual calculation of self-interest that would drive to despair any sensible bank manager approached about a loan or an overdraft. It is the contention of the present argument that the consideration of a 'social change' structure of beliefs provides an adequate theoretical basis from which to understand these phenomena, and that its integration with other *socially shared* processes of group identity, of social comparison and of social diffusion of ideas and beliefs (such as shared evaluations and shared social expectations) provides the possibility of making differential predictions about intergroup behaviour *en masse*.

Two general additional comments need to be made to conclude this introductory discussion. The first relates to the fact that, as it will be clear from the preceding paragraphs, it would be grossly simplistic to attribute the inter-individual tradition of 'social mobility' in the social psychology of intergroup relations to nothing but the overwhelming predominance, mentioned in chapter 11, of the 'exit option' in American social history. Much of it goes back to the background of the social psychologists' theoretical concern with individual or inter-individual problems. The second point is that if Hirschman, Hofstadter (1945), and others are correct about 'the hold which exit has had on the national imagination' and about success having 'long been conceived in terms of evolutionary individualism', then it follows that 'most of our social psychology of intergroup behaviour' *should* apply 'to the behaviour of individuals who are assumed to have the belief structure of social mobility'. Undoubtedly, this is why good progress has been made in our understanding of the individual patterns of prejudice, discrimination and hostility. However, the intention of the present argument is not to question the validity of much of this work; the concern is not with its achievements but with its limitations.

The American tradition of exit developed against a background of belief in individual mobility which, although by no means exclusively American, has probably been more salient in the social history of the United States than almost anywhere else. This tradition has been weaker elsewhere and almost non-existent in some cultures (including many ex-'primitive' ones). This being the case, the question arises whether findings derived from a social context overwhelmingly dominated by the exit (or social mobility) option can be said to have a wider general validity. Moreover, an explicit social psychology of voice or 'social change' in intergroup relations is as necessary in the United States as it is anywhere else. The example of black power is one case in point, and many other similar social and national movements are not far behind – in America and elsewhere.

There is, however, one further point which is equally important. It is banal to say that in the social past (or present) of the United States, as in so many other countries, the belief in, or the myth of, individual mobility was (and is) conceived by many not to apply with indiscriminately equal generosity, liberality and force to everybody. This denial of equal opportunity (or sometimes 'ability') to scramble up the social ladder to members of some social groups is one of the psychological effects of the 'objective' intergroup conflicts of interest; but it also finds its roots in some fundamental aspects of the social comparison processes. To put it crudely, very often we are what we are because 'they' are not what we are. The psychological and 'superior' distinctiveness of a social group, sometimes achieved at the cost of strenuous efforts, must be maintained and preserved if the group is to conserve some kind of a common and valued identity. It is at this point that voice will be used, sometimes in remarkable unison, by members of the 'superior' groups, particularly since exit is very often unthinkable for them. At this point of the argument, this function of voice is stressed because it points to an additional and important limitation of the 'social mobility' approach to the psychology of intergroup relations, even against the background of the American tradition of exit. I shall return to it in more detail later in the discussion of the contribution of voice to the preservation of the *status quo* in intergroup relations and behaviour.

2. Individual exit, group exit and group chorus

We must now return to the economics of expendable products as it relates to the social psychology of intergroup relations. The change of a brand of toothpaste is the simplest paradigm of a costless exit. It is basically and inherently an individual reaction. If we can imagine a brand of toothpaste that suddenly becomes twice as expensive as all the others without any corresponding soft-sell about its unique and outstanding qualities, or that – from one day to the next without warning – begins leaving in one's mouth a powerful taste of rotten fish for three hours after use, we can easily predict a massive escape of the customers to other brands. (For theoretical purposes, we can ignore the small minority who would enjoy the lingering taste.) But even this massive escape could not be treated as a social movement inserted in a context of intergroup relations. It would be a collection of individual exits. The criteria distinguishing the collection of exits from a social movement in an intergroup social change situation are simple: even if the manufacturers of the expensive or the smelling toothpaste were considered to be an 'outgroup', the simplest solution for the members of the customers 'ingroup' is still to go away and forget all about it. Presumably, in doing so, they would form some unflattering 'stereotypes' about the manufacturers, but it is unlikely that these would be related to any form of durable, commonly shared and large-scale social action, outside of leaving in very large numbers. For the same reasons, it is just as unlikely that the abused customers would amount together to an effective social group or social category. This is so despite the fact that they would share the two most important *a priori* defining characteristics of a social group: a certain similarity between the members (they all dislike the toothpaste); and a certain equivalence of 'fate' (they all wish to change, or have to change, to another brand). The point is that they do not have to change, or wish to change, as a group; everyone can do it individually, whatever the others do or do not do.

This extreme social mobility paradigm (changing from the group of brand X users to the group of brand Y users) is unlikely to find its equivalent in most social structures in which the move from one group to another involves effort, hard work, luck, heartbreak, etc. As exit becomes more costly or more painful, Hirschman's analysis of its interaction with voice becomes increasingly pertinent in relation to the effectiveness of this interaction as a recuperation mechanism for declining organizations. It is interesting to see, however, that with the increase in the difficulty of exit and the corresponding increase in the attempts to change the situation from the inside, one important aspect of the initial simple paradigm of toothpaste exit does tend to remain a constant in Hirschman's exit–voice analysis. Exit, or the threat of it, or the use of voice, remain theoretically an individual action or a collection of individual actions. At best, this collection of individual actions becomes an organized activity (this is why voice is 'political action by excellence') aiming to change the mode of functioning of the group to which the activists belong; in other words, the implicit theoretical presupposition is that of an intragroup activity. That this is so becomes quite clear in Coleman's (1974) contribution to a recently published collection of articles on the exit and voice theme:

Intrinsic to the paradigm of exit and voice which Hirschman (1970) has set forth is the recognition that social structure is composed of two kinds of actors: *persons* and corporate actors. For it is these *persons* for whom the problem of implementing their will reduces to the dilemma of exit, that is, withdrawal of resources from the corporate actor, or voice, which attempts to control the direction of action of the corporate actor (p. 7, my italics).

A little further in the same paper, Coleman adds: 'Hirschman was largely concerned with the maintenance of the efficiency of corporate actors and with the processes through which *persons* contribute to that maintenance' (p. 7, my italics).

Before we proceed, one further conceptual distinction must be made. There is hardly anything new in asserting that members of a group will act together as a group when their individual goals converge and can only be achieved through common action as a group. It is trivially true that this is often the prime condition for the formation of a group which is likely to remain 'cohesive' for as long as the goals remain common. In this sense, it may well be that the moderating effects on intergroup hostility of Sherif's (1966) superordinate goals cannot be generalized too far, since the stringent requirements of common action in the hour of common need must have gone quite a long way towards replacing the previously separate identities of the two groups by a larger and common identity of one group confronting a hostile environment. In this final phase of one of Sherif's studies, there were no remaining divergent 'objective' interests that would have helped the groups to maintain their separate identities. Therefore, it may well be that the effectiveness of the superordinate goals was due, in part at least, to the beginning of a process of dissolution of the two separate groups towards the formation of a single group confronting 'nature'. It is difficult to know whether a similar reduction of hostility would have occurred had the initial groups been in the position of preserving clear-cut, separate goals, interests and other features of their previous distinctiveness in addition to the new and powerful requirements of their common welfare. This is undoubtedly an intergroup problem which stands in urgent need of further research.

The point of this brief diversion about Sherif's superordinate goals is that it helps to illustrate the conceptual distinction that needs to be made between the notion of group cohesion, which is generally due to common goals, and the situation in which the achievement of these goals is only possible through a change in the structure of the existing intergroup relations, or conversely through opposing such change when it is attempted or initiated by an outgroup. The difference between the two situations is quite fundamental: it is in the nature of the hostile environment confronting the ingroup. Sherif's final superordinate goals did not involve a confrontation of the total boys' camp with any other group (apart from the hidden group of the manipulating experimenters of whose dark designs the subjects were presumably unaware; see Billig, 1976, for a discussion of the relevance of this situation to the issue of 'false consciousness'). Although the details of the attitudinal and behavioural structures resulting from an intergroup social change situation cannot be discussed here, a brief list of the emergent variables, distinguishing this situation from one in which only nonsocial 'nature' is confronted (or perceived as confronted), will be sufficient to characterize its specificity. These interacting variables would include causal attributions of responsibility, processes of intergroup social comparison together with the consequent formation of a *relational* group (or social) identity, assessment of the legitimacy of the perceived intergroup situation, the relationship of this assessment to the 'objective' intergroup differences and to the consensual status differentials between the groups and the attempts to create or maintain a positively-valued distinctiveness of the ingroup from the outgroup as a major dependent variable.

So far, an attempt has been made in this chapter to argue for a theoretical specificity of a certain category of intergroup relations which would distinguish it both from problems inherent in inter-individual relations and from those encountered by a group confronting a problem common to all of its members and presented to it by a non-social or non-human 'nature'. It is to the former of these distinctions, in its variant of intragroup v. intergroup considerations, to which we must now return in pursuing the implications of the paradigm of exit and voice for the social mobility–social change paradigm. The asymmetry of the respective intragroup and intergroup points of departure has already been noted.

Social mobility is the exit of an individual from his group. Social change is the situation in which the extreme difficulty or impossibility of individual exit leads at least some of the people concerned to develop, or try to develop, an effective common voice for their group. The various modes of this voice or the conditions under which these modes may develop are not of direct concern at this point of the argument. The asymmetry between voice and 'social change' resides in the comparison of the relation, described by Coleman (1974), of persons to corporate actors with the relations of members of one group to other groups. In both cases voice will be used in its various forms. But in the case of a group, the persons composing it may be concerned with the prevention of decline in the 'efficiency' (i.e. conditions of life, status, opportunities, etc.) of the corporate actor, which in this instance is their own group. Therefore, in an organization consisting of many groups, their voice may have to be directed towards a change in the nature of the relations between their own and other groups, i.e. other corporate actors. In this process voice may become a chorus.

An example of similar asymmetry is provided by the notion of relative deprivation, as it has sometimes been used (explicitly or implicitly) in social psychology. The focus of the theories has been on individuals comparing themselves with other individuals (e.g. Festinger, 1954, on social comparison). This is entirely adequate as long as conclusions are drawn about the effects of these comparisons on inter-individual attitudes and behaviour – which is what Festinger (1954) has been aiming to do. Festinger's inter-individual emphasis is closely related to the economic version of relative deprivation, the 'relative income hypothesis', which Hirschman (1973) – after Duesenberry – described as follows: 'The welfare of an individual varies inversely with the income or the consumption of those persons with whom he associates'. (p. 546).

Difficulties begin when these inter-individual comparisons are transposed to intergroup situations. One of them concerns a basic canon of the social comparison theory in social psychology and of the relative income hypothesis in economics: people who provide the basis for comparisons must not be too different from those who are doing the comparing. I have argued elsewhere that this limitation does not hold in the case of intergroup comparisons in which the requirement of a certain degree of similarity between the comparer and the compared is replaced by the perceived legitimacy of the perceived relationship between the groups. The difference between the two kinds of comparisons is simply described: in the case of inter-individual comparisons, a person relates his position to that of other persons; in the case of intergroup comparisons, an individual compares himself *as a member of his own group* with other individuals as members of their groups, or with outgroups conceptualized as an entity. The questions are: under what conditions do these intergroup comparisons become widely diffused within a group, and what then are their social, political and psychological consequences? But these are large issues outside the scope of this chapter (see chapters 11, 12, 13 and 15).

Let us return to the asymmetry of voice and chorus. In the case of social comparison theory a collection of inter-individual comparisons is sometimes endowed with the capacity to contribute to long-term uniformities of behaviour in large masses of people (e.g. Berkowitz, 1972), although how this is supposed to happen remains a little obscure. In Hirschman's exit–voice analysis, transpositions of this kind are not made. Also in his discussion of 'changing tolerance for income inequality in the course of economic development' (Hirschman, 1973) there is a clear awareness of the psychological differences between groups that can afford to wait for a time to catch up with others and those which feel they cannot: 'the group that does not advance must be able to empathize, at least for a time, with the group that does. In other words, the two groups must not be divided by barriers that are or are felt as impassable' (p. 553). He returns to the theme in suggesting that the temporary patient waiting by some while others advance 'need not happen if each class is composed of ethnic or religious groups that are differentially involved in the growth process. Hence, the contrast between fairly unitary and highly segmented society is particularly relevant for our topic' (pp. 553–4).

In Hirschman's analysis voice comes from a collection of individuals (sometimes organized into a group) who wish to change the institution or the organization of which they feel themselves to be an inherent part. In one fundamental sense, this may also be true of a social group which attempts to change its relationship to other groups within a larger social structure common to all of them. But the question immediately arises of how, if at all, is this chorus form of voice related to the potentiality or the actuality of *group* exit.

There are two kinds of group exit discussed by Hirschman from his perspective that are of interest here. The first of these is opting out, or the ' "cop-out" movement of groups like the hippies', which is 'flight rather than fight' (1970, p. 108), i.e. exit without voice. This exit is no more than temporary for some of the people involved; but their choice to come back (or not to come back, in the case of permanent or long-term opters-out) is not dependent on the past instrumentalities of their use of voice. If they come back, it is because they have changed, or society has changed, or they think society has changed. In addition, they often become a group with well-defined common interests and a common identity only after they have opted out (e.g. in communes) rather than before; so that just as in the case of voice we are dealing, in Coleman's (1974) words, with 'the processes through which persons contribute to [the] maintenance' of a corporate actor, here we are dealing with persons who wish to get as far away as they can from a vast collection of corporate actors. In this sense, therefore, their exit cannot be considered as relevant in the context of the group exit–group voice relationship.

The other kind of group exit is boycott (Hirschman, 1970, p. 86). It is a 'phenomenon on the borderline between voice and exit', since this action 'is undertaken for the specific and explicit purpose of achieving a change of policy on the part of the boycotted organization' (p. 86) and is accompanied by 'a promise of re-entry' should the desired changes take place. To be effective, boycott (like a strike) cannot, of course, be an action by isolated individuals.

This 'true hybrid of the two mechanisms' (p. 86) raises a number of interesting psychological questions about the relationship between a dissatisfied group and the organizational or institutional structure defining the position of that group *vis-à-vis* other groups within the same structure. For example, an underprivileged group in a strongly stratified social system (i.e. a system preventing social mobility and/or a belief in this option) cannot really exit; there is nowhere to go, unless all of its members chose to emigrate, or – as in the case of ethnic or national groups – the exit option is fought for in the form of a separatist movement. The possibility of an exit that is neither emigration nor separation must be sought elsewhere, and like Hirschman's boycott, it is bound to be a 'hybrid of the two mechanisms' of exit and voice. But in the case of social groups which are strongly disaffected and see their only hope in a fundamental change of the system, it is also a hybrid from another point of view. The individuals involved are strongly identified with one of the corporate actors (their own group); but the efficiency of functioning of that corporate actor is part and parcel of the functioning of a wider system consisting of their own and other groups. Therefore, the prevention of a continuing decline in the functioning of the corporate actor (the ingroup) may be perceived as possible only through a change (more or less fundamental) in the functioning of the wider multi-group system.

In such cases, one of the solutions which may be adopted is as much of a hybrid of exit and voice as is boycott. It is obviously voice since it is a form of political or social action from within; it is also exit or threatened exit to the extent that it consists of a refusal to accept the rules by which the present relationships between the groups are regulated, and contains a 'promise of re-entry' when these rules are changed. Once again, we have a continuum here which moves from total acceptance of the rules to partial acceptance to total rejection (see chapter 15).

This continuum closely reflects a progressive transition from group voice to group exit. The relationship in this transition between the psychological and the 'objective' determinants of group exit can be considered, once again, in terms of legitimacy. But here an interaction between three forms of it would have to be taken into account: the legitimacy of the intergroup relationship as it is perceived by the disaffected group; the legitimacy of this relationship as it is perceived by the other groups involved; and an 'objective' definition (i.e. a set of rules and regulations) of legitimacy, whenever such a thing is possible.

In considering these three kinds of legitimacy, it can be assumed that group exit (or the threat of it) will be, on many occasions, the more likely the greater is the discrepancy between the first two kinds of legitimacy, and the narrower are the confines of action from within (voice) encompassed by the third. On the face of it, the second part of this statement seems to contradict Hirschman's (1970) view that 'if exit is followed by severe sanctions the very idea of exit is going to be repressed and the threat [of it] will not be uttered for fear that the sanctions will apply to the threat as well as to the act itself' (pp. 96–97). There is no doubt that this proposition holds in a vast number of cases for individual exit or a collection of individual exits. But it would be useful to consider the many important exceptions to it that may occur in the relations between separate groups within a system rather than in the relations between persons and corporate actors. It seems not unreasonable to assume that in many multi-group systems these important exceptions are likely to occur when the contribution from the disaffected group is essential to the continuing efficient functioning of the system as a whole.

Some of the social psychological consequences of this kind of actual or threatened group exit can be discussed in terms of its relationship to the impossibility or difficulty of individual exit from the ingroup. The tendency to try for this kind of individual exit, or even to conceive it as a possibility, may be in this case inversely related to the reality or the perceived potentiality of group exit. This relationship can become a powerful ingredient of ingroup loyalty. The second social psychological consequence is the increasing uniformity within the group of the relevant ingroup and outgroup attitudes and behaviour – a phenomenon mentioned earlier in this chapter in relation to the three theoretical continua associated with the transition from social mobility to social change. In this case a social psychological analysis of the situation must take explicitly into account the increased sharing by many individuals of their 'expectations about, and evaluations of, other people's behaviour'.

In turn, the positive feedback triggered into action by this sharing of social expectations and evaluations provides a parallel to the 'joys of participation' which find their place amongst Hirschman's (1974) 'new economic arguments in favour of voice' (p. 7). 'The activities connected with voice can on occasion become a highly desired end in itself' (p. 8) and thus they decrease the cost of voice and may even turn it into a benefit. But in the case of group exit it is the cost of this exit rather than of voice that is psychologically decreased in this way. This cost can sometimes be enormous for the individual concerned. Its acceptance by many would be incomprehensible without the existence of a compensating mechanism of increasing loyalty to the ingroup as the dangers of group exit loom larger and the deviant status of its members in the outside world becomes sharper and clearer.

3. Voice, status quo and social comparison in intergroup relations

In the previous section of this chapter group exit and some forms of its interaction with group voice were discussed as a recuperation mechanism for groups which perceive their position in a multi-group system as being less than satisfactory. One of the conditions in which, as Hirschman (1970) wrote, 'a no-exit situation will be superior to a situation with some limited exit [is] if exit is ineffective as a recuperation mechanism, but does succeed in draining from the firm or organization its more quality conscious, alert and potentially activist customers or members' (p. 55). It is likely, of course, that customers or members who display the qualities just mentioned are often nearer to the top of the social heap than are the more passive ones.

In the case of individual members of an organization, the greater involvement in it of those who are nearer to the top makes exit for them more costly or difficult than for others, and at the same time their voice is likely to be louder, more enthusiastic and more effective. As individuals, they may be simultaneously concerned with preventing the decline of the organization and preventing the decline of their relative position in it. The same will be true of the higher status groups when the organization consists of groups that are clearly separate from one another.

We have here a situation which is parallel to that discussed in relation to the exit of disaffected groups in the previous section of this chapter. The position of an individual belonging to a higher status group needs to be considered in relation to his group at the same time as the position of this group in relation to other groups in the organization. This can be done with regard to the possibilities of an individual's exit from his group, his group's exit from the organization, and the corresponding functions and directions of voice.

The membership of a high-status group is often satisfying in a variety of ways. Exit from it is therefore, on the whole, unlikely. But the point is that whether *some* individuals do or do not leave the group (and they may leave for a number of reasons, including a conflict of values that the 'superior' position of their groups sometimes entails) the intergroup situation within the organization remains the same. The high-status group as a whole cannot exit unless it is intent upon collective self-destruction, actual or symbolic. As distinct from the disaffected group, its members have a great deal to lose and very often nothing to gain from any form of exit – be it emigration, separation or refusal to play by the rules. From their point of view, the decline in the efficiency of the organization can take one of two forms: a decline in the over-all functioning of the system, or a decline in the relative position of their group within the system. The former without the latter would lead to the use of voice, individually or collectively, in the ways described by Hirschman. The decline in the relative position of the group, or the threat of such a decline, has certain psychological consequences relevant to the use of group voice. The relativities of the higher-status groups are, of course, concerned with the preservation of differentials.

In situations characterized by the structure of belief in social change 'a social group can fulfil its function of protecting the social identity of its members only if it manages to keep its positively valued distinctiveness from other groups'. The emergence of this structure of beliefs must be understood, in the case of high-status groups, as being dependent on the two conditions just discussed: the high cost of an individual's exit from his group and the very high cost (or impossibility) of the group's exit from the organization. These are also the conditions determining an intense use of the group's voice in the attempts to prevent its comparative decline.

We must now return to the use of voice not as a response to the comparative decline of the ingroup but as a response to the decline in the efficiency of functioning of the total organization. Assuming that differentials are perceived by members of high-status group as being eroded, three possibilities need to be considered:

(1) The comparative decline of the group is not perceived by its members as being associated in one way or another with the decline or the prevention of decline in the functioning of the organization as a whole.

(2) This comparative decline is perceived as being directly associated with the decline in the functioning of the total organization.

(3) This comparative decline is perceived as being directly associated with the *prevention* of decline in the functioning of the total organization.

These are the *psychological* alternatives. The *actual* changes in the functioning of the organization may or may not correspond to the group's perception of what happens. The point is, however, that it is these shared perceptions, tending to become more common and widespread as the group sees itself increasingly beleaguered, which will determine the intensity and the direction of the use of voice. In the first two of the three cases, there is no *perceived* conflict between responding to the threat of comparative decline of the ingroup and the wider interests at stake. It can therefore be assumed that the group's 'ethnocentric' (or more generally, sociocentric) voice will be given free rein. In turn, it can be assumed that there will be a solid wall of rationalizations (or defensive ideologies) to ward off the uncomfortable thoughts inseparable from the third case.

The emergence and diffusion of these defensive ideologies may at times determine, and at times be determined by, the use of voice. The second alternative would, of course, be predicted from dissonance theory (Festinger, 1957). Independently, however, of the nature of the psychological processes generating these ideologies, we must consider the following relationships between the use of voice by the threatened group and the realities of the decline of the total organization:

(1) As determined by some external criteria (e.g. measures of economic performance) the group is wrong in assuming that its comparative decline is *not* associated either with a decline or with a prevention of decline in the functioning of the total organization.

(2) As determined in the same manner, the group is wrong in assuming that its comparative decline is directly associated with a decline in the total functioning.

(3) The group is right in assuming that its comparative decline is directly associated with a *prevention* of decline in the total organization. But in the ensuing conflict of perceived interests, the former decline turns out to be more important than the latter.

Whenever any of these three relationships comes to materialize, the use of voice by the threatened group may prove catastrophic for the organization as a whole; and the higher is the status of the group threatened by the loss of its superior distinctiveness, the more catastrophic is its use of voice likely to become.

Two notes need to be appended to conclude this discussion of group voice. The first concerns its almost exclusive preoccupation with the 'subjective' aspects of the relationships between groups, with the psychological processes of social comparison rather than with the 'objective' conflicts of interest. This emphasis was not chosen because of a belief on my part that these social psychological processes are more important than, or primary to, the social, economic and political intergroup processes that form their context. These psychological correlates of the other relationships do, however, exist; and, as I wrote earlier in this book, the concern is

with certain points of insertion of social psychological variables into the causal spiral; and [the] argument is that, just as the effects of these variables are determined by the previous social, economic and political processes, so they also acquire in their turn an autonomous function which enables them to deflect in one direction or another the subsequent functioning of these processes.

Finally, I wish to return to the 'individual' v. 'group' dichotomy discussed earlier in this chapter. There is little doubt that many of the points discussed and conclusions presented here apply to inter-individual behaviour and attitudes as well as to the intergroup scenario. The point of departure (and of arrival) was, however, firmly kept in the area of intergroup relations because of my conviction that it is only when this is explicitly done (at some risk of neglect of other issues) that we have, as social psychologists, a good chance of making a contribution to the understanding of social processes at large.

15

The social psychology of minorities[1]

1. What is a minority group?

In asking this question, we are not concerned with definitions of social groups (or categories) in terms of the economic, social, cultural or other criteria by which they can be distinguished. Instead, we wish to know what are the psychological effects of these 'objective' factors on the people involved: do they or do they not feel themselves to be members of a particular social group which is clearly distinguished *by them* from other such groups? And what are the effects of these 'feelings' (of belonging or not belonging) on their social behaviour?

But before these questions can be discussed, we need to relate them to the solid realities of social differentiations. The 'feelings' of being a member of a group do not float in some sort of a social vacuum; and the corresponding belief systems cannot be properly understood if one considers them without taking into account their direct and intimate ties with the social realities of people's lives.

There are many definitions of social minorities which have been proposed by sociologists, political scientists and others. We shall retain here the set of criteria suggested by Wagley and Harris (1958), as quoted by Simpson and Yinger (1965) in their book on *Racial and Cultural Minorities*. According to these authors:

(1) Minorities are subordinate segments of complex state societies; (2) minorities have special physical or cultural traits which are held in low esteem by the dominant segments of the society; (3) minorities are self-conscious units bound together by the special traits which their members share and by the special disabilities which these bring; (4) membership in a minority is transmitted by a rule of descent which is capable of affiliating succeeding generations even in the absence of readily apparent special cultural or physical traits; (5) minority peoples, by choice or necessity, tend to marry within the group (Simpson and Yinger, p. 17).

It is interesting and important to see that *numbers* do not play much of a

[1] From H. Tajfel: *The social psychology of minorities*. London: Minority Rights Group, 1978. I would like to acknowledge the support of The Minority Rights Group, Benjamin Franklin House, 36 Crewes Street, London WC2N 5NG.

part in this definition. Some numerical majorities – as, for example, in South Africa – conform to all the five criteria, while some numerical minorities – such as Afrikaaners in the same country – probably only conform to the fifth: they tend to marry within the group. Again, members of women's liberation movements in this country and else-where would argue that women are a 'minority' in the sense outlined above, although they would obviously not fit some of the criteria, and often are not a numerical minority. The principle guiding the definition selected by Wagley and Harris (and many other social scientists) is not to be found in numbers but in the social *position* of the groups to which they refer as minorities.

This is a sensible approach to the problem. Quite apart from the fact that certain kinds of social disabilities, shared by certain kinds of people, are more important in understanding what happens to them and what they do then are numerical considerations, it would also be very difficult to adopt a meaningful frame of reference based on numbers. The 'social' definition is more important and much more flexible. For example, the separatist movement in Quebec is a minority movement within Canada. At the same time, as the political and social changes which recently occurred in Canada gather momentum, the problems of the English-speaking minorities in Quebec (particularly of those recent immigrants whose native language was neither French nor English, and who adopted English on their arrival) are becoming more acute (see Berry, Kalin and Taylor, 1977). In some ways, the French-speaking Quebecois still conform to the Wagley and Harris description as a 'subordinate segment' in a 'complex state society'; in other ways, they constitute a majority which is beginning to create some of the usual problems for its own minorities.

The psychological criterion for referring to certain social groups as minorities is clearly stated by Wagley and Harris. They are 'self-conscious units' of people who have in common certain similarities and certain social disadvantages. But this psychological criterion is not as simple as it may appear. Some sociologists make a sharp distinction between what they call a 'social group' and a 'social category'. For example, Morris (1968) defined ethnic groups as 'a distinct category of the population in larger society whose culture is usually different from its own'. He added that members of ethnic groups 'are, or feel themselves, or are thought to be, bound together by common ties of race or nationality or culture' (p. 167). This he distinguished from 'a mere category of the population, such as red-haired people, selected by a criterion that in the context is socially neutral and that does not prescribe uniform behaviour' (p. 168). By contrast, a genuine group must consist

310

of people 'recruited on clear principles, who are bound to one another by formal, institutionalized rules and characteristic informal behaviour'. In addition, these groups must 'be organized for cohesion and persistence; that is to say, the rights and duties of membership must regulate internal order and relations with other groups'. Having already once recognized the psychological criteria that people must 'feel themselves' or must be 'thought to be' similar to each other and distinct from others in certain ways in order to be considered as an ethnic group, Morris comes back to the 'internal' characteristics of an ethnic group membership by stating that 'members usually identify themselves with a group and give it a name' (p. 168).

These clear-cut distinctions can be useful for thinking about *some* minorities; but they may present problems if one considers many fluid and changing social situations in which men and women slowly acquire *in common* their beliefs, reactions, feelings and attitudes about their special status in a wider society. As distinct from a 'category', a social group must be, according to Morris, cohesive and long-lasting; it must also have an accepted system of internal regulations. But 'categories' and 'social groups' understood in this sense sometimes represent, respectively, the beginning and the end of a long social psychological process. There are many cases in between: a collection of people, consensually designated by a majority as somehow 'different', may begin by not accepting this difference, or by denying its interpretation. It may be a long time before this 'outside' consensus results in creating clear-cut group boundaries, formal institutionalized rules and the specific features of informal social behaviour to which Morris referred. And yet, all this time the 'feeling' of membership, of belongingness, of a common difference from others will continue to develop. A clear example of this growth of a new identity in the case of students from the West Indies coming to Britain was provided in chapter 8 of this book. The internal cohesion and structure of a minority group may sometimes come *as a result* of this development of an awareness of being considered as different. As a matter of fact, it is precisely this *development* of a special kind of awareness that some people within minorities are sometimes trying hard to achieve through social action, through initiating social and political movements (see chapter 11).

The resulting feeling of common membership of a minority comes, in many cases, long before the individuals involved have been able to construct for themselves a cohesive and organized 'group' or even to develop special modes of 'characteristic informal behaviour' for their internal usage. Very often, of course, the process is reversed, or it progresses simultaneously in two parallel directions: a group is perceived

311

as separate and different both from the inside and from the outside. But even here, there is no easy psychological dichotomy between a 'mere category' and a genuine 'social group'. It is usually a matter of complex interactions between the 'internal' and the 'external' criteria of group membership, of the conditions in which the 'felt' membership of a group or category leads to various forms of social action, social conscience, systems of attitudes and beliefs, individual or collective strategies. In order to consider this variety of issues, we must turn our attention to these internal and external criteria of minority membership and the relationship between them.

2. The internal and external criteria of minority membership

As we have seen, many of the definitions of minorities include a reference to the 'subjective' characteristics of their membership, such as stereotypes, belief systems, self-consciousness, identifications, etc. In other words, for a minority to become a distinguishable social entity, there must be amongst some, many, most or all of its members an awareness that they possess in common some socially relevant character-istics, and that these characteristics distinguish them from other social entities in the midst of which they live. But, as it is clear from the sociological definitions we discussed earlier, these 'socially relevant characteristics' must be of a certain kind in order to produce the self-awareness of being a 'minority' in the sense of the term we discussed earlier. After all, in some ways all complex societies consist of nothing but minorities: professional, regional or age groups, political affiliations and any number of others. It is only when being assigned and/or assigning oneself to a particular social entity leads at the same time to certain perceived social consequences which include discriminatory treatment from others and their negative attitudes based on some *common* criteria (however vague) of membership that the awareness of being in a minority can develop.

The crucial term in all this is 'in common'. In order to understand the psychological realities of 'feeling' a member of a minority, it is important to make a clear distinction between *individual* differences and *group* differences. Although a lot of people may be red-haired, or obese or of small stature, they are unlikely to acquire an awareness of being 'members' of corresponding 'minorities'. These characteristics, although shared by large numbers of people, retain their *individual* significance in a person's life. It would be very difficult to think of detrimental 'group' social consequences following upon obesity, left-handedness or stam-mering. Obviously, any of these individual features can acquire an enormous importance in a person's life; and, just as obviously, they may create for such people a number of social handicaps. And yet, we are much less likely to find in a newspaper an item which would start: 'A fat man (or a stammerer), Mr. X., is helping police with their enquiries' than 'A Pakistani, Mr. X.,' etc.[2]

The difference between an 'individual' attribute, such as fatness, and one which designates the membership of a minority, such as 'a Pakistani', is that the former is not a characteristic of a person from which *other* social inferences can easily be made. One type of inference which is usually *not* made from 'fat' is quite crucial for the understanding of the different social consequences of various kinds of categorization. It has to do with *other* characteristics of *other* people who are in the same category. Fatness or stammering or small stature are not used as criteria in a social typology. Socially relevant characteristics of other people who share the same attribute are randomly related to that attribute; in other words, they have very limited implications for the social attributes of others who share the same characteristic.

The result is that fat people, or short people, or people using a certain kind of toothpaste, are collections of individuals, while Pakistanis or (at one point of time) long-haired teenagers, or ex-inmates of prisons are, or may easily become minorities. The three examples just mentioned are similar in some important ways and different in others. The similarities are that all these designations are associated with widespread negative stereotypes about the people involved; 'stereotypes' consisting of a number of *other* characteristics assigned to all, or most, of those who share the attribute. The differences are in the degree of acceptance by the people involved that they are indeed bound together in some important ways which distinguish them from people in other social categories.

This acceptance of being *together* in a low-status minority depends upon a large number of social and psychological conditions which can only be briefly discussed here. In many cases, there is a long history of

---

[2] The following item (by no means exceptional) appeared in *The Times* of 6 Sept. 1978: 'A young British hitch-hiker was charged with murder by the police at Katerini, south of Salonika, today . . . Mr. X., aged 20, a British passport-holder of Sinhalese extraction, whose home is in Birmingham, was remanded in custody pending trial. He is accused of killing one of two gypsies who attacked his girl companion . . . he and Miss Y., aged 20, of Solihull, Birmingham, had been hiking to Salonika. They were picked-up by two gypsies driving a small pick-up van . . . The two Britons were forced out of the car by one gypsy holding a double-barrelled shot-gun, while the other attacked the girl.' The Sinhalese and the two gypsies are identified as such. For Miss Y., who, judging from her name, is a member of the 'majority', no other identification, apart from her provenance from Birmingham, seems necessary. In the case of Mr. X., also from Birmingham, we are additionally informed of his 'extraction'. We do not know whether the two gypsies are Greek (or any other) 'passport-holders'. It is apparently enough to know that they are gypsies. (See Husband, 1977, 1979, for reviews of evidence and a discussion about newspaper reports of this kind).

social or cultural differences between the minority and other groups in the society. It is easy to find examples of categories which are definitely 'groups', in the sense that they conform to all the sociological criteria which we discussed earlier. The South Moluccans in Holland, the Arabs in Israel, the German-speaking inhabitants of Alto Adige in Italy, the racial groups in South Africa, the Kurds in Iraq, the Maronites in the Lebanon, are obvious examples. But, once again, it is important to remember that, psychologically speaking, we are dealing here with a continuum and not a simple and clear-cut distinction. The awareness of being a member of a separate minority group and the identification with it following upon this awareness depend upon the *perceived* clarity of the boundaries separating in common the members of that group from others.

In turn, the perceived clarity of these boundaries depends upon the existence and wide diffusion in the group of certain beliefs about themselves and the wider society. Three systems of belief are particularly important in this respect. The first is that the criteria for their pervasive categorization as 'separate' from and by others are such that it is impossible, or at least difficult, for a member of the minority to move out *individually* from the group and become a member of the 'majority' indistinguishable from others. In other words, it is the belief that individual social mobility (e.g. becoming a teacher, a lawyer, a doctor, a factory manager, a foreman) will not affect, in many important social situations, the identification of the individual by others as a member of the minority. The second and related belief is that this assignment by others to a certain group, largely independent as it is of the individual differences between the people so assigned as long as they share the defining criterion of the minority (e.g. colour of skin, descent, language, etc.) has certain social consequences which are common to all, or most, members of the group. The third system of beliefs concerns the minority members' *own* views about their common differences from others.

We have already discussed one way in which these views about separateness may develop. This is when they are mainly imposed from the outside, when they result from social categorizations created and consistently used by 'others'. This was the case of the West Indian students mentioned earlier. Once this happens, a minority enters a spiral of psychological separateness in which the 'outside' social categorizations are associated with their 'inside' acceptance by the group in a mutually reinforcing convergence.

The second case concerns a minority which already has a tradition of separateness created by its cultural, social and historical differences from others. The belief that 'passing' or leaving the group is impossible or difficult may then be determined not only by the constraints imposed by others but also by powerful social pressures internal to the minority. This has often been the case with religious minorities of various kinds, with some national or ethnic minorities, with political or ideological movements.

Finally, there are some minorities which, although they are aware of their cultural, social, political or historical differences, claim at the same time the right to shed some or most of these differences as and if they wish to do so. If no continuing obstacles are laid in their path, these minorities may merge sooner or later into the surrounding society even while maintaining some of their special characteristics. The Scots living in England or the catholics in Britain and in the United States can probably serve as examples here. In such cases, the psychological constraints, both internal and external, on leaving the group weaken with time, and the dilution of the sociological criteria of social disadvantages and discrimination is associated with the weakening of the major psychological condition for the existence of a minority: the perception of the existence of clear boundaries confining the group.

The story is very different when, for whatever reasons, the claims of the minority to merge if, when and how they wish are met by strong social and psychological resistance from the outside. We shall come back to this issue when discussing the psychological strategies employed by minorities to deal with these problems. For the present, it will be sufficient to say that this conflict between the push outwards from the minority and the creation of barriers by others may create, in time, a new consciousness of belonging, give a new strength to old affiliations, and it may finally lead to powerful internal constraints against leaving the group.

To sum up: we distinguished between three general sets of conditions which all lead to the appearance or strengthening of ingroup affiliations in members of minorities. In the first of these, a common identity is thrust upon a category of people because they are at the receiving end of certain attitudes and treatment from the 'outside'. In the second case, a group already exists in the sense of wishing to preserve its separate identity, and this is further reinforced by an interaction between the 'inside' and the 'outside' attitudes and patterns of social behaviour. In the third case, an existing group might wish to dilute in a number of ways its differences and separateness from others; when this is resisted, new and intense forms of a common group identity may be expected to appear.

3. From social stability to social change: the psychological effects of minority membership

The relations – social and psychological – between minorities and other groups in society vary continuously, as a function of social conditions changing with time and of the diversity of the groups by which the minorities are surrounded. Also, each social group has its own internal structure which places different individuals in different social positions; and each group has a considerable range of individual differences in personality, abilities, social roles, family backgrounds, achievements, opportunities and luck. How, then, is it possible to talk blandly about *the* psychological effects of minority membership?

The simple answer is that this is not possible. It cannot be assumed in any discussion of these effects that facile generalizations would emerge which could be applied to all, most or even many members of one or another minority group. All the 'effects' we shall be describing apply to *some* members of *some* minorities, and a variety of patterns can be found within any one minority. All that can be achieved is to identify some patterns which appear more important than others because they are adopted by a variety of people in a variety of groups in a variety of circumstances. The generalizations of social psychology are (thankfully) limited by the creative and boundless diversity and flexibility of human social behaviour.

These reservations must be kept clearly in mind when we think about the social behaviour, attitudes, feelings and affiliations of people who belong to minorities. In a sense, a 'social psychology of minorities' has no more of a claim to a separate existence than would have a 'social psychology of majorities'. Or rather, its claims must be modest from the outset, and they need to be based on clearly stated preliminary assumptions. This is why we embarked earlier upon a lengthy discussion of what, psychologically speaking, 'is' a minority. The preliminary assumptions on which the remainder of this paper is based are quite simple, and they are closely related to our previous discussion: members of minorities, as defined earlier, have some problems in common; there is only a limited number of possible psychological solutions (or attempts at solutions) to these problems; the kind of solution adopted is closely related to the social conditions in which minorities live.

The awareness of interdependence presently growing all over the world has evolved together with a world-wide push towards differentiation originating from minorities which are often at great distance from each other geographically as well as in their cultural and historical diversity. There is one crucially important element which is common to many of these movements towards differentiation: the new claims of the minorities are based on their right to decide to be different (preserve their separateness) as defined *in their own terms* and not in terms implicitly adopted or explicitly dictated by the majorities. The increasing inter-dependence has led to ever wider multi-national economic and political structures; it has also resulted in a backlash of demands for decentralization coming from smaller social entities which wish to preserve their right to take their own decisions and keep their own 'identity'.

This trend towards differentiation often represents, socially and politi-cally, a rejection of the *status quo* by groups which perceive themselves as separate and socially disadvantaged. The rejection also represents an important psychological development. As the French sociologist, Col-ette Guillaumin (1972), argued in her excellent book about racist ideologies, an important cleavage between social majorities and minor-ities is in the fact that, as she put it,

a majority is a form of response to minority groups: its existence can only be conceived through the absence of clear-cut, limiting criteria as distinct from groups which are explicitly categorized and narrowly defined. Or, in other words, the membership of a majority is based on the latitude to deny that one belongs to a minority. It is conceived as a freedom in the definition of oneself, a freedom which is never granted to members of minorities and which they are not in a position to give to themselves (p. 196, translated from the French).

Although it is doubtful that this characterization can be indiscrimi-nately applied to *all* social minorities, Guillaumin makes an important point about the social psychological aspects of many majority–minority situations. As we have seen earlier, minorities are often defined on the basis of criteria originating from, and developed by, the majorities. They are different in certain ways which are socially important, but they are different from something which, itself, need not be clearly defined. The contemporary trend towards differentiation represents an explicit rejec-tion of these one-sided definitions. It represents an attempt to create or preserve criteria of group definition which are not imposed from the outside. Rather than consisting of departures from the 'norm', these newly developing criteria reflect attempts to develop a positively-valued identity for the group in which its 'separateness' is not compounded of various stigmas of assumed inferiorities. Social action is often closely related to these redefinitions of who and what one is. We shall return later to the psychological 'strategies' adopted by minority groups in order to achieve these new definitions of themselves.

This powerful and world-wide push to achieve a positive differentia-tion represents one extreme of a social psychological continuum of the minorities' attitudes towards their position in the wider society – a continuum which moves from the total acceptance to the total rejection of that position. No doubt, most minorities are somewhere in the middle of that continuum, nearer one or the other of its extremes. The important questions are as follows: what are the psychological determinants and effects of acceptance and rejection? What are the psychological processes contributing to, and resulting from, a transition from acceptance to rejection?

(a) The transition from acceptance to rejection

We start with the second of these two questions because, in considering it, we can already begin to discuss in a preliminary way some aspects of acceptance and rejection. An acceptance by the minority of its social and psychological inferiority must first be looked at in the framework of 'objective' social conditions – but an analysis of such conditions is a job of sociologists, economists, historians and political scientists. It is therefore beyond the scope of our discussion here. There is little doubt, however, that the prime condition for the maintenance of a *status quo* of inequality, formal or informal, is in the unequal distribution of power – political, economic or military. Two major psychological correlates of this unequal distribution of resources help to ensure the maintenance of its stability: the perception of the system of inequalities as being *stable* or *legitimate* or both simultaneously.

It is important to stress at this point that we are concerned here with the *perceived* stability or legitimacy of the prevailing relations between groups rather than with their formal and institutional characteristics or the realities of physical or economic power. Thus, from a social psychological perspective, the perceived stability of a system of inter-group relations consists of an absence of cognitive alternatives to the existing situation. As far as the minority groups are concerned, this implies that, at the 'acceptance' extreme of our continuum, there is no *conceivable* prospect of any change in the nature and the future of the existing inferiorities. Although some exceptional individuals may be able to improve their position and mode of life within the existing situation, and they may even be accepted and highly respected by some members of the majority, this does not affect the position of their group as a whole; as a matter of fact, such individuals are explicitly seen on both sides of the boundary as more or less surprising exceptions to the general rule. Their breaking through some of the barriers separating the groups has two important characteristics: they are often still regarded by the majority as remaining in some important ways specimens of the social category to which they originally belonged; and, whatever they may be

318

or might have become is not seen as generalizing to other, more 'typical', members of the minority. Examples of these attitudes of the majority which remain unchanged, despite the outstanding achievements of some minority individuals, go far back in history. They can be found in the descriptions provided by Sherwin-White (1967) of reactions in imperial Rome to revolts by Greek and other slaves. Longinus who, as Sherwin-White wrote, was 'a severe and inhuman legalist' felt that 'you can only control the foreign scum by fear'; but

> The kindly Pliny, famous for his humanitarian attitude towards his servants, betrays exactly the same reaction as Longinus when he relates the murder of Lucius Maredo. This man had been a master of exceptional brutality. It was no great surprise when his slaves attacked him in his bath and flung him on to the furnace to finish him off. The household was duly punished, and Pliny, like Cassius, approved. He ends the account with an interestingly irrational outburst: 'See what dangers and insults we are exposed to. You cannot hope to secure your safety by kindliness and indulgence. They murder us indiscriminately, out of sheer criminality.' (p. 84)

Another interesting example, even if in part fictitious, is provided in William Styron's novel *The Confessions of Nat Turner*. Turner was the leader of what was 'in August 1831, in a remote region of southeastern Virginia . . . the only effective, sustained revolt in the annals of American Negro slavery'. He had outstanding personal qualities which led to relations closer than usual and, in some ways, at a more equal level than usual, with some members of his master's family. But this had no effects upon the general attitudes in the family towards the master–slave relationship.

Thus, it is highly unlikely that the perceived stability of the existing relations between a majority and a minority can be seriously affected by the opportunity afforded to a few exceptional or exceptionally lucky members of the minority to escape the inflexibility of the system. Something else is needed to shake the acceptance of what appears as inevitable. The building up of 'cognitive alternatives' to what appears as unshakeable social reality must depend upon the conviction, growing at least amongst some members of the minority, that some cracks are visible in the edifice of impenetrable social layers, and that therefore the time has come to push *as a group*. This pushing as a group can take a number of forms, including *unexceptional* individual social mobility encouraged by visible changes in the system. We shall return to these issues later. In today's conditions, there is very little doubt that, whatever may have been the reasons for the first appearance of visible cracks in one or another system of rigid stratifications still existing in the contemporary world, the growth of the mass media of communication has helped enormously to transplant from one social location to another the *perceived possibility* of causing new cracks. This is one of the ways in which the increasing interdependence, which we discussed earlier, has also led to increasing trends towards differentiation.

The perceived stability of the system (i.e. the absence of realistic alternative conceptions of the social order) is one important foundation of the various patterns of acceptance by the minority. The perceived legitimacy of the existing order is at least as important. Daniel Bell (1977), writing in *The Fontana Dictionary of Modern Thought*, defined legitimacy as 'the rightful rule or exercise of power, based on some principle (e.g. consent) jointly accepted by the ruler and the ruled' (p. 491). The *Concise O.E.D.* describes 'legitimate' as, amongst other things, lawful, proper, regular, logically admissible. In the case which interests us here, that of a social order based on clear-cut differences between the majority and a 'lower' minority, the perceived legitimacy would therefore imply an acceptance (or consent, in Bell's terms) of the differentiation as based on some principles acceptable to both sides and accepted by them. This was presumably the case for some of the social divisions in the feudal societies or in the Indian caste system at the time when they were still very stable. When, for whatever reasons, this consent begins to break down, an interaction between three forms of legitimacy must be taken into account: 'the legitimacy of the intergroup relationship as it is perceived by the disaffected group; the legitimacy of this relationship as it is perceived by the other groups involved; and an "objective" definition (i.e. a set of rules and regulations) of legitimacy, whenever such a thing is possible' (see chapter 14).

There is little doubt that an unstable system of social divisions between a majority and a minority is more likely to be perceived as illegitimate than a stable one; and that, conversely, a system perceived as illegitimate will contain the seeds of instability. It is this interaction between the perceived instability and illegitimacy of the system of differentials which is likely to become a powerful ingredient of the transition from the minority's acceptance of the *status quo* to the rejection of it. It is, however, possible – at least in theory, but also probably in some concrete contexts – that perceived instability and illegitimacy need not always be inseparable to begin with (see Turner and Brown, 1978), even if it is true that, sooner or later, one is likely to lead to the other. It is, for example, conceivable that a certain kind of social or political order is so powerfully maintained by those in charge that it appears very stable, however deeply held are the convictions about its illegitimacy. In a recent television programme broadcast for the tenth anniversary of the invasion of

Czechoslovakia in 1968, one of the exiled Czechs was asked in an interview whether he believed that a return of any form of the 'Prague spring' was possible, at least in the foreseeable future. His answer was negative. In this case, as in the case of the minorities which see the system as illegitimate but extremely stable, a conception of the illegitimacy of the situation will continue to exert its powerful influence on actions, attitudes, beliefs and affiliations in the teeth of what appears as unshakeable. The converse can also occur: a system of differentials affecting a minority may retain, at least for a time, its perceived legitimacy even when it is seen as unstable. But although we have a good deal of evidence, both from 'real life' and from some experimental studies in social psychology (e.g. Turner and Brown, 1978; Caddick, 1978; Commins and Lockwood, 1979), that a system of relations between social groups seen as illegitimate will lead to the rejection of the *status quo* by the disadvantaged group, there is less convincing evidence that the same would happen in a system perceived as legitimate but unstable. The psychological importance in the determination of social actions of their perception as legitimate or illegitimate is further confirmed (at least in our culture) by a very large number of social psychological studies on inter-individual aggression. Although it would be preposterous to equate a minority's rejection of its status with 'aggression', the weight of evidence from these studies is sufficiently impressive to appear relevant to a variety of large-scale social situations (see Billig, 1976, for a detailed review). It must, however, be stressed again that a theoretical separation of perceived instability and illegitimacy cannot be taken very far without losing touch with social reality. Very often they merge, either from their very inception, or because each of them can contribute to changes in the social situation in a way which causes the other to make its appearance. It is then that, as we said earlier, a rapid transition from acceptance to rejection by the minorities of their status and of their beliefs about the 'inferiority' of their group can be safely predicted to occur.

(b) Patterns of acceptance

Social position carries with it certain experiences, attitudes, and activities not shared by people at other levels, which do modify self-evaluation and general outlook on life . . . It therefore seems valid and useful to talk of a person's social personality; meaning that part of his make-up which is contributed by the society in which he lives and moves and which he shares in large measure with all other persons living under the same conditions. This social personality is obviously different from his personal temperament or psychological individuality, which is developed by another set of factors entirely. (Warner et al., 1941, pp. 25–7)

This description of a 'social personality', written nearly forty years ago, is still largely valid today, although many of us would find it difficult to agree with the sharp distinction made by the authors between what 'is contributed by the society' and what is 'developed by another set of factors entirely'. We are more likely today to conceive these different sets of factors, the 'individual' and the 'social', to be almost inseparable and interacting very closely from the beginning of an individual's life, one setting the stage for the development of the other, one creating or inhibiting the potentialities or the restrictions determined by the other (see, e.g. Bruner and Garton, 1978). Be this as it may Lloyd Warner and his colleagues were right in stressing the importance in a person's life and 'make-up' of 'what he *shares* in large measure with all other persons living under the same conditions'.

People who are members of the kind of minorities with which we are concerned here share one difficult psychological problem which can be described, in its most general terms, as a conflict between a satisfactory self-realization and the restrictions imposed upon it by the realities of membership of a minority group. 'Satisfactory self-realization' is a hopelessly vague, synthetic term which can mean so much that it is in danger of meaning very little at all. We shall therefore confine ourselves here to one of its important aspects. We shall assume, both on the basis of common experience and of an endless stream of psychological studies, that it is a fairly general human characteristic to try to achieve or preserve one's self-respect and the respect of others; that it is important for most of us to have and keep as much of a positive self-image as we can manage to scrape together; and that having to live with a contemptuous view of oneself, coming from inside or from other people, constitutes a serious psychological problem (see chapters 12 and 13).

The value-loaded comparisons with other groups or their individual members may become an important aspect of a person's self-image, particularly so when he or she belongs to a minority which is considered to be clearly separate from others and (explicitly or implicitly) 'inferior' to them in some important ways. We discussed earlier certain relationships between the external and the internal criteria of minority membership. As long as the external criteria and the value connotations associated with them continue to predominate, as long as the membership of a minority is defined by general consensus as a departure from some ill-defined 'norm' inherent, as Guillaumin wrote (see previous section), in the majority, the self-image and self-respect problems of minority individuals will continue to be acute.

A large number of clear examples of this has been found in many studies about the phenomenon known as 'ethnocentrism'. The term was first introduced by William Graham Sumner in his book on *Folkways* written in 1906, and has since then gained wide currency in the social sciences and elsewhere. As he wrote:

Ethnocentrism is the technical name for this view of things in which one's own group is the centre of everything, and all others are scaled and rated with reference to it . . . Each group nourishes its own pride and vanity, boasts itself superior, exalts its own divinities, and looks with contempt on outsiders. Each group thinks its own folkways the only right ones, and if it observes that other groups have other folkways, these excite its scorn. Opprobrious epithets are derived from these differences . . . For our present purpose the most important fact is that ethnocentrism leads a people to exaggerate and intensify everything in their own folkways which is peculiar and which differentiates them from others. (pp. 12–13)

This 'universal syndrome of ethnocentrism' turned out to be considerably less universal than Sumner assumed it to be three quarters of a century ago (see LeVine and Campbell, 1972, for a recent review of some of the evidence). An enormous amount of work has been done, since Sumner wrote, on the forms, conditions and development of ethnocentrism. The 'differentiation from others' to which he referred can be understood as fulfilling two main functions, one for the group as a whole and one for its individual members. For the group as a whole, it 'strengthens the folkways', i.e. it contributes to the continuation of the group as an articulate social entity. For individual members of the group, positively-valued differentiations from others contribute favourably to their self-image and boost their self-respect. As I wrote elsewhere, this amounts to saying to oneself: 'We are what we are because *they* are not what we are.'

One of the important exceptions to the world-wide generality of ethnocentrism has been found in the attitudes towards themselves, their own group and other groups displayed, under certain conditions, by members of minorities. The conditions are usually those previously discussed: a general consensus in society about the nature of the characteristics attributed to the minority; some measures of acceptance, within the minority, of these defining criteria derived from the outside; the absence of well-established alternatives which would be based on the idea that the present situation is not legitimate and not necessarily permanent; the difficulty of 'passing' from the stigmatized group to another one; the fact that some instances of successful individual social mobility out of the minority group have not affected the nature of the generally established relations and differences between the minority and the others. But these are the 'maximum' conditions. A reversal of ethnocentrism (i.e. the devaluation of themselves and of their groups by

323

members of minorities) can also occur in social conditions which present much less of a drastic social division between the minorities and others. Social differentiations between groups, even when they take on fairly subtle forms, are reflected, as we have seen in chapter 9, with an amazing sensitivity in the attitudes of the people who are adversely affected.

One of the extreme forms of this internalization by members of minorities of the 'outside' views about them has been well described by the eminent black American psychologist, Kenneth Clark (1965), when he wrote:

Human beings who are forced to live under ghetto conditions and whose daily experience tells them that almost nowhere in society are they respected and granted the ordinary dignity and courtesy accorded to others will, as a matter of course, begin to doubt their own worth. Since every human being depends upon his cumulative experiences with others for clues as to how he should view and value himself, children who are consistently rejected understandably begin to question and doubt whether they, their family and their group really deserve no more respect from the larger society than they receive. These doubts become the seeds of a pernicious self- and group-hatred, the Negro's complex and debilitating prejudice against himself . . . Negroes have come to believe in their own inferiority. (As quoted in Milner, 1975, p. 100)

This belief in one's own inferiority is, as Clark wrote, a complex and important issue; but it is no less crucial to understand the many and important exceptions to it and the conditions in which it is likely to disappear. We shall return to this issue in the next section of this paper, concerned with the minorities' 'patterns of rejection'. For the present, we must look in a little more detail at this acceptance of inferiority and the effects it has on the lives of those suffering from it. This is by no means confined to the social contexts in which the recognition of a minority member as such is immediate and certain (as is the case for skin colour) or in which a very large proportion of the minority are confined to *de jure* or *de facto* ghettoes. For example, the phenomenon of the 'Jewish self-hatred' has been known for a long time (Karl Marx was one of its more famous victims), and contributed in important ways to Jean-Paul Sartre's *Reflections on the Jewish question*, first drafted in 1944, when the shock of the Nazi mass murders was still stunning the conscience of the world. Sartre's reflections about self-hatred are not very different from those of Clark.

It is not the man but the *Jew* that Jews try to know in themselves through introspection; and they want to know him so that they can deny him . . . This is how can be explained the special quality of Jewish irony which is most often used against the Jew himself and which is a perpetual attempt at looking at oneself from the outside. The Jew, knowing that he is being watched, gets there first and tries to look at himself with the eyes of others. This objectivity applied to himself is yet another ruse of inauthenticity: while he contemplates himself with the detachment of someone else, he feels in effect *detached* from himself, he becomes someone else, a pure witness. (Translated from the 1948 French edition, pp. 117–18)

The process starts from early childhood, and evidence of its existence comes from many countries and many cultures (see Milner, 1975, for an excellent recent review). In the late thirties, the Clarks (see Clark and Clark, 1947) published the first of a long series of studies demonstrating that black children in the United States could be directly and objectively shown to have serious identity, identification and group preference problems already at the age of six or seven, or even earlier. The methods used by Clark and Clark, and in many subsequent studies, consisted of presenting each child 'with a variety of dolls or pictures representing the various racial groups in the child's environment', and then asking the children a number of questions about which of the dolls they looked like, which ones they would prefer to have for a friend, to play with, to be at school together, etc. It was found that the minority children (e.g. the blacks in America, the Maoris in New Zealand, children of the various 'coloured' minorities in Britain) sometimes mis-identified themselves in the tests (i.e. they said that they were 'more like' the white than the black doll) and that most of them 'preferred' in various tests the white to the other dolls. Doubts have been raised, on methodological grounds, about the validity of the first of these findings – concerning mis-identification of the child's own group membership. But there is a considerable weight of evidence, from several countries including Britain, supporting the findings about marked 'outgroup preference' of the minority children at ages from six or so until eleven, and sometimes well beyond. Even in a study on children of Asian origin conducted in Glasgow by Jahoda and his colleagues (1972), in which all possible care was taken to counteract such 'artifactual' effects, as, for example, the experimenter being a member of the majority, (it was, in this case, 'a charming and attractive' young Indian woman), by the age of ten the children shifted their preferences towards the majority. This study is mentioned here because it probably presents a *minimum* of the effects as compared with many of the others. In a large-scale study conducted in England, Milner was able to confirm and extend many of the previous findings, from America and elsewhere, about the development of these 'outgroup preferences' in children from racial minorities (see chapter 9 of his book). In a series of studies on Maori and Pakeha (European-descended) children conducted by Graham Vaughan in New Zealand over a period of more than ten years, a similar pattern of outgroup preferences emerged for the Maori

325

children (see, e.g. Vaughan, 1978a). As Milner summarized it, the research by Vaughan has shown that the Maori children favoured other-race children when assigning desirable or undesirable attributes to members of their own and other groups; preferred other-race figures as playmates; and preferred other-race dolls to 'take home'. At the same time, recent favourable changes in the social environment of the Maori children had a drastic effect in the direction of *reducing* the disparagement of their own ethnic group in their responses to the tests (see Vaughan, 1978b). A similar effect, which can again be ascribed to variations in the social conditions, has been found by Morland (1969) who compared Chinese children in Hong Kong with the American black and white children. Hong Kong is, in Morland's words, a 'multi-racial setting in which no race is clearly dominant'. He found that preferences for their own group were displayed by 82% of the white American children, 65% of the Hong Kong Chinese and only 28% of the black Americans.

It is, of course, difficult to establish solid links of evidence between this early rejection by children of their own group and its effects on their later developmen. and behaviour. 'Longitudinal' studies on this subject, which could trace such a development in the same individuals over a number of years, are very difficult to organize and conduct. We can only guess, and our guesses can be helped by what we know of the deleterious effects of the 'self-hatred', about which Clark and Sartre wrote, in some adult members of minorities. Alienation from the society at large is often the result of social conditions, such as poverty, unemployment, family disintegration, overcrowding, etc.; but the search for some possibilities of regaining self-respect can also be a contributing factor to 'deviant' social behaviour. Withdrawal from the wider community's system of norms, values, prescriptions and achievements, and the creation of groups which have their own values, divergent from those which are generally approved, is one *possible* effect (not by any means confined to minorities) of what is now fashionably called a 'search for identity'. This withdrawal is rooted in the *acceptance* by the minorities of the image of themselves imposed by the society at large; and it may result in turn in the *rejection* of this image through means which are, at best, ineffective in changing the social situation, and, at worst, reinforce the existing stereotypes and divisions. Some examples of this kind of 'acceptance', which seems to exist even in conditions less tense than those of inter-racial tensions, were provided in chapters 5 and 9.

It would be a mistake, however, to exaggerate the importance of all these findings, whether concerned with children or with adults, as indicators of serious problems of *personal* identity amongst members of minorities. Their common element is that the judgements made in these

326

studies by members of minorities about their own groups are requested in contexts which are directly and explicitly comparative with the majority. There is, as we have seen, substantial evidence that in such conditions an unfavourable self-image has come to be internalized. But not all 'natural' social contexts include the need or the requirement for intergroup comparisons, and a person's idea about himself or herself is at least as much (and probably much more) dependent upon continuous and daily interactions with individuals from the same social group. When this group happens to have its own strongly integrated norms, traditions, values and functions, a 'negative' self-image elicited in comparisons with other groups need not by any means become the central focus of an individual's identity. This is why one can remain happy and contented inside a ghetto, as long as this ghetto has not become socially disintegrated. An excellent example of this can be found in the Jewish *shtetls* which led, at the turn of the century, their isolated lives in Russia and elsewhere in eastern Europe. The internal norms and cultural prescriptions of these small communities together with their tremendous power in guiding the lives of their members have been reflected and beautifully transmitted in the short stories of Sholem Aleichem and other writers of the period. The 'deviant' groups, to which we referred earlier, can serve as another contemporary example, providing that they can manage to create a mini-culture which is powerful enough to protect the self-respect of their members from the cold winds of disapproval blowing from the outside.

But it remains true that, fundamentally, this internal minority protection of individual self-respect is yet another facet of the minority's *acceptance* of the *status quo*. It is, as we have said earlier, a form of withdrawal from the society at large, a delicately poised and hard-won equilibrium which can be easily destroyed. In this kind of a situation, a community (or a deviant group) must manage to be virtually sealed off from the outside world in those aspects of their lives which really matter to them; and, in turn, those aspects of their lives which really matter are bound to be selected, in the long run, on the criterion of their safe insulation from comparability with other people who become inherently different, and thus partly irrelevant. The question is: for how long can they remain irrelevant unless the difficult achievement of social and psychological isolation is maintained? When it cannot be, the practical implications of a comparative (and negative) self-image come again to the fore. Irwin Katz, an American social psychologist, has done a good deal of work on the academic achievement of black pupils in segregated and mixed schools. Some of his earlier conclusions, based on the work done in the sixties, may well have to be revised today; but this does not

327

detract from their importance in suggesting what happens in situations of intergroup contact and comparison, when comparisons have to be made in terms of criteria generally accepted by the society. Here are some examples: 'where feelings of inferiority are acquired by Negro children outside the school, minority-group newcomers in integrated classrooms are likely to have a low expectancy of academic success; consequently, their achievement motivation should be low'. Or: 'Experiments on Negro male college students by the author and his associates have shown that in work teams composed of Negro and white students of similar intellectual ability, Negroes are passively compliant, rate their own performance as inferior when it is not, and express less satisfaction with the team experience than do their white companions.' Or again: 'Among Florida Negro college students, anticipated intellectual comparison with Negro peers was found to produce a higher level of verbal performance than anticipated comparison with white peers, in accordance with the assumption that the subjective probability of success was lower when the expected comparison was with whites.' (Katz, 1968, pp. 283–4)

There exists, however, a half-way house between the two extremes, one of which is the psychological isolation from the surrounding society, such as was the case of a Jewish *shtetl* in Tsarist Russia or for some deviant groups in today's large cities, and the other the damaging acceptance by the minority of the majority's prevailing images. As we have seen, the first of these extremes is a psychological withdrawal from comparisons with others which is made possible by the development of separate and socially powerful criteria of personal worth; the second is the result of a social (and consequently, psychological) disintegration of a group and of its inability to create an articulate social entity with its own forms of interaction, its own values, norms and prescriptions. Needless to say, most of the minorities fall somewhere between these two extremes. Their identity is then simultaneously determined by the socially prevailing views of the majority and by the psychological effects of their own cultural and social organization. Cases of that nature are still near to the 'acceptance' end of our acceptance–rejection continuum. The continuous and daily interactions with the outside world, and the consequent *psychological* participation of a group in the system of values and the network of stereotypes of the society at large create a degree of acceptance by the minority of its deleterious image; at the same time, *some* measure of protection is offered by the social and cultural links surviving within the group. A good example of this is provided in David Milner's research in England (Milner, 1975), in which he compared the negative self-images of the West Indians and the Asian children. His description of the differences in the cultural background and the corresponding initial attitudes toward the host society is as follows:

It seemed likely that the British component of the West Indians' culture, and the 'white bias' in their racial ordering of West Indian society, would enhance their children's orientation and positive feeling towards whites in this country. In addition, the West Indians' original aspirations to integrate ensured more contact with the white community – and its hostility – than was experienced by the Asian community. Not only did the Asians' detached stance *vis-à-vis* the host community insulate them to some extent, they also had entirely separate cultural traditions which provided a strong sense of identity. In the American studies many black children internalized the racial values that were imposed on them by the dominant white group, such that they had difficulty in identifying with their own group, and were very positively disposed towards whites. For the reasons discussed, it seemed likely that this response to racism would be more prevalent among West Indian children than among the Asian children. (pp. 117–18)

The comparisons, in Milner's work, between the two categories of children showed that 'while the Asian and the West Indian children equally reproduce white values about their groups, they do not equally accept the implications for themselves . . . the derogatory personal identity is less easily imposed on Asian children. It is as though the same pressure simply meets with more resistance' (p. 138).

And herein lies the problem. For how long can this partial resistance be maintained in succeeding generations? The cultural pressures from the surrounding society are bound to become more effective, the cultural separateness to decrease. The Asian minorities in this country, or any other minorities anywhere which live in the kind of half-way house to which we previously referred, have at their disposal a limited number of *psychological* solutions to their problems of self-respect and human dignity. Some of these solutions are, at least for the present and the foreseeable future, simply not realistic. The first is that of a *complete* assimilation, of merging in the surrounding society. This is not possible as long as the attitudes of prejudice and the realities of discrimination remain what they are. The second is that of a cultural and psychological insulation from others. This, again, is not possible, for two reasons at least. One is that the new generations cannot be expected to remain immune to the increasing pressures of the surrounding cultural values and social influences. As the same time, the economic and social requirements of everyday life make it both impossible and undesirable to withdraw from the network of entanglements with the outside society together with its pecking order of stereotyped images. Thus, in the last analysis, 'psychological' solutions must give precedence to social and economic changes. Minority groups cannot respond to the outside images by the creation of their own counter-images floating in a social vacuum. They must rely on the creation of social changes from which new psychological solutions can derive. Some of the 'patterns of rejection', which we shall discuss next, are relevant to this issue.

(c) Patterns of rejection

The focus of much of the previous discussion was on the effects that the psychological status of minorities has on the ideas of personal worth and dignity, on the self-image and the self-respect of their individual members. As we have seen, these effects exist with particular clarity in situations which elicit direct comparisons between members of the minority and the majority. But there is little doubt that they do not entirely disappear even in the psychologically 'safer' social interactions confined to the minority itself and its separate cultural prescriptions.

Underlying this centrality of a positive self-image and of its erosion was the conception that *social comparisons* are crucial in the development of our image of ourselves (see chapter 12). In the relations between minorities and majorities (or between any other distinct social groups), the comparisons between the groups, or between individuals clearly identified as belonging to one group or another, make an important contribution to this image of oneself. In situations of considerable intergroup tension or conflict this can become, for a time, one of the most important facets of this image. This is one of the reasons why comparisons which are made in such situations are often associated with powerful emotions. Even differences between groups which might be emotionally neutral to begin with may then acquire strong value connotations and a powerful emotional charge. This is often the case with nationalism. The importance of these intergroup comparisons is also well-exemplified in the large number of industrial conflicts which have to do with differentials. As Elliot Jaques exclaimed in desperation in a letter to *The Times* (29 Oct. 1974): 'Is it not apparent to all that the present wave of disputes had to do with relativities, relativities and nothing but relativities?' We found in some laboratory experiments (see chapters 11 to 13) that the establishment of a *difference* between two groups in favour of their own was often more important to the schoolboys with whom we worked than the absolute amounts of monetary rewards that they could get. Starting from the results of these studies, Brown (1978) found a similar pattern when doing research in a large factory with shop stewards belonging to different unions. As we know from common experience and from many sociological and psychological studies, 'relative deprivation' can be, within limits, a more important determinant of attitudes and social behaviour than are the 'absolute' levels of deprivation (see Runciman, 1966; and chapter 12 for more extensive discussions of this issue).

As we have seen in the previous section, the 'comparative' self-image of members of minorities is often derogatory. The question is: what can they do about it? This is by no means a 'theoretical' or an 'academic' issue. In the preface to his book on *Ethos and Identity*, Epstein (1978) wrote recently:

I found myself asking how such groups manage to survive as groups at all, and why they should strive so consciously to retain their sense of group identity. At the same time, I am keenly aware that if I achieved any insight into these situations it was because they touched some chord of response that echoed my own ethnic experience as a Jew of the Diaspora. Reflecting on all this, the major conviction that emerged was the powerful emotional charge that appears to surround or underlie so much of ethnic behaviour. (p. xi)

There is little doubt that personal problems of worth, dignity and self-respect involved in being a member of a minority and shared with others who are in the same situation are an important ingredient of this high 'emotional charge'. I have defined elsewhere in this book 'social identity' of individuals as consisting of those aspects of their self-image and its evaluation which derive from membership of social groups that are salient to them; and, in turn, much of that self-image and of the values attached to it derive from comparisons with other groups which are present in the social environment. These comparisons are rarely 'neutral'. They touch a 'chord of response' which echoes the past, the present and a possible future of 'inferiority'. It is therefore not surprising that emotions and passions will rise in the defence of one's right to have and keep as much self-respect as has the next man or woman.

As we asked earlier: what can the minorities do about it? One obvious answer for some of their members is assimilation to the majority, whenever this is possible. Assimilation, as Simpson (1968) wrote,

is a process in which persons of diverse ethnic and racial backgrounds come to interact, free of these constraints, in the life of the larger community. Wherever representatives of different racial and cultural groups live together, some individuals of subordinate status (whether or not they constitute a numerical minority) become assimilated. Complete assimilation would mean that no separate social structures based on racial or ethnic concepts remained. (p. 438)

There are many variants of this process, psychologically as well as socially. From the psychological point of view, a distinction can be made between at least four kinds of assimilation. The first, which would present no particular problems to the assimilating individuals, is when there are no constraints to social mobility imposed by either of the two

331

groups involved. But whenever this happens (as has been the case, for example, for *some* immigrant ethnic groups in the United States), the minority ceases to exist as such, sooner or later. There is a psychological merging in which, even when the defining label is maintained and invoked from time to time, it has lost most of the characerics which define a 'minority', both psychologically and socially. Individual assimilation has then become the assimilation of a social group as a whole, the case to which Simpson referred as the disappearance of 'separate social structures based on racial or ethnic concepts'.

The second kind of assimilation presents more difficulties to the assimilating individual. This is when, although the people who moved from one group to another may well interact in their new setting in many ways which are 'free of constraints', they have not been fully accepted by the majority. Paradoxically, they are regarded as still typifying in some important ways the unpleasant characteristics attributed to their group and at the same time as 'exceptions' to the general rule. A classic example of this kind of situation was provided between the late eighteenth century and very recent times in some European countries with a strong tradition of anti-Semitism. Despite this, a number of Jews managed to break through the barriers of prejudice and discrimination, and some even achieved very high positions in the 'outside' society. But the breaking of the barriers by some did not succeed in breaking them for the group as a whole nor did it eliminate the widespread prejudice. At the turn of the century, the Dreyfus affair in France provided a dramatic case history of this inherent ambiguity. This was one of the turning points for the Viennese journalist Herzl, one of the founders of Zionism, in his search for alternative solutions for the Jewish minorities in Europe.

Dreyfus himself was probably a good example of the psychological problems encountered in this kind of assimilation. His identification with the majority, as a Frenchman and an officer in the army, not different from any other Frenchman, was total. A little later, the German-Jewish industralist and statesman Rathenau, who was assassinated by right-wing nationalists in 1922 when he was minister for foreign affairs, was able to write, no more than twenty years before Hitler's accession to power: 'what made the conquerors the masters, what made the few capable of subduing the many was fearlessness, toughness and a purer spirit; and there is no way of preserving these advantages during periods of tedious inaction or of protecting the nobler blood against interbreeding . . . Thus has the earth squandered its noblest racial stocks' (as quoted by James Joll in the *T.L.S.*, 25 Aug. 1978).

We cannot speculate here about Dreyfus's or Rathenau's possible emotional problems caused by their total adherence to their identity as members of the majority. It is, however, a fair assumption that, as long as the subordinate minority is conceived by others (and sometimes also from the inside) as inherently different and separate, assimilation, even when free of many constraints, is likely to create personal conflicts and difficulties. One of its well-known effects is the leaning-over-backwards in the acceptance of the majority's derogatory views about the minority; and this is probably another determinant of some of the Jewish 'self-hatred' to which we referred in the preceding section of this paper. A more drastic example can be found in the acceptance by some inmates of concentration camps during World War Two, who belonged to many ethnic or national groups, of the attitudes, values and behaviour of their jailers.

What is more important from the point of view of wider generalizations about the social psychology of minorities is that, in conditions of marked prejudice and discrimination, the assimilation of the few does not solve the problems of the many. It is an uneasy compromise, in those who have succeeded in assimilating, between the acceptance and the rejection of their inferior status as members of the minority. Rejection, because they have attempted to leave behind them some at least of the distinguishing marks of their 'inferiority'; acceptance, because they must often do this by achieving and emphasizing a psychological distance between themselves and other members of their previous group. It needs to be stressed once again that this kind of compromise remains uneasy and full of potential personal conflicts only when no more than a small back door is open for a passage from one group to another, when most of the members of the subordinate groups are firmly kept in their place, and when the existing prejudice and discrimination are not markedly affected by the presence of a few 'exceptions' who are often considered to 'prove the rule' in one way or another. It is because of these personal conflicts that the French colonial policies of selective cultural assimilation, based on stringent criteria for deciding which members of the native populations could be considered as more or less French, proved to be a breeding ground for discontent and revolt amongst some of those who passed the tests. Frantz Fanon was one of the more famous examples; so were Aimé Césaire, a poet from Martinique, and Léopold Senghor, also a poet and later the President of Senegal, who both developed the idea of *négritude*, a positive conception of Negro identity.

The third kind of assimilation presents problems similar to the previous one but made more acute by the fact that it is 'illegitimate'. In the case of Dreyfus, Rathenau, Fanon, Césaire or Senghor, everyone knew that they were Jews or Negroes. Hiding one's origins in order to 'pass' is a different matter altogether. The innocuous forms of it are quite frequent in countries such as Britain or the United States where changing one's name does not present much of a legal difficulty and can often get one off the hook of being foreign born or of foreign descent. There was a time in England when a physician called Goldsmith could get more easily his first job in a hospital than one called Goldschmidt. The same was true in, for example, some banks and some of the more 'exclusive' large commercial emporia. It is, however, a very different matter when 'passing' is illegal, as it is in South Africa or was in Nazi Germany, or when it must imply a total and very careful hiding of one's origins, as in the case of light-skinned Negroes in the United States.

The 'illegitimate' forms of assimilation lead to an identification with the new group and a rejection of the old one which are sometimes even stronger than in many cases of 'legitimate' assimilation. Paradoxically, this might occur even when assimilation is in the opposite direction – from the majority to the minority. Arthur Miller, in his novel *Focus* written in the early forties, provided a beautifully analysed fictitious account, and the American journalist J. H. Griffin supplemented it with a counterpart of real experiences in his book *Black Like Me* (1962). The hero of Miller's story is a fairly anti-Semitic 'average' American who must start wearing spectacles because of his declining sight. This makes him look like a Jew. He finds it impossible to persuade anyone around him that he has not been until now a wolf in sheep's clothing, a Jew who successfully 'passed'. His whole life is changed as a result, he encounters discrimination in many of his basic daily activities, and for a time struggles vainly proclaiming his innocence. He finally gives up and makes a conscious choice of a strong Jewish identification. Poetic licence allowed Miller to use a few initial improbabilities to set his stage. But this subsequent analysis rings true and it is confirmed by the account of Griffin who chemically darkened his skin in order to see, from the other side of the fence, what it was like, in the late fifties, to *feel* a black in a Southern state. His subsequent attitudes were not very different from those described by Miller.

To sum up in returning to the more usual forms of 'illegitimate' assimilation: the threats and insecurities of their lives undoubtedly contribute to the attitudes of those who managed to 'pass' and constantly face the danger of being unmasked. One of the precautions they can take is to proclaim their dislike of the 'inferior' minority. It does not take much to set this pattern into motion. In a recent experimental study conducted in a classroom with schoolgirls, Glynis Breakwell (1979) managed to create two groups of different status, the assignment to higher or lower status being based on the level of performance in a fairly trivial task. At the same time, it was possible to cheat in order to find oneself in the higher group. The 'illegitimate' members of the higher group showed, in some of the subsequent tests, a more marked differentiation in favour of that group than did its legitimate members. It must be hoped that the study also served as a useful educational experience for its participants: complete anonymity was preserved, but in a subsequent 'debriefing' session the purpose and implications of the study were carefully explained to them.

The fourth kind of assimilation is so different from those previously discussed that it is probably inappropriate to use the same term in referring to it. Some sociologists call it 'accommodation', and John Turner (1975) discussed its social psychological aspects in terms of what he called 'social competition' (see chapter 13). The ambiguities and conflicts of the simultaneous acceptance and rejection of minority status, present in the second and third forms of assimilation which we have just discussed, do not usually make their appearance here. 'Accommodation' or 'social competition' consist of the minority's attempts to retain their own identity and separateness while at the same time becoming more like the majority in their opportunities of achieving goals and marks of respect which are generally valued by the society at large. There are usually two important preliminary conditions, one or both of which are necessary for this 'social competition' to occur. The first is that the previous successful assimilation by *some* individual members of the minority has not affected, or has not appeared to affect, the *general* inferior status of the minority and the prevailing negative attitudes towards it. The second consists of the existence of strong separate cultural norms and traditions in the minority which many or most of its members are not willing to give up. The first of these conditions cannot remain for long unrelated to the attempts, within the minority, of creating the second; we shall return later to a discussion of some forms of this relationship. From the psychological point of view, their common elements are, once again, in the attempts to create or preserve a self-respect associated with being a member of a social group which does not get its due share of respect from others; and in trying to achieve this, *in part*, through establishing comparisons with others which will not remain unfavourable on the criteria which are commonly valued by all groups in the society.

The development of black social movements in the United States since World War Two provides an example of several of these processes simultaneously at work. Some of the earlier leaders of the National Association for the Advancement of Coloured People (N.A.A.C.P.) believed that the way ahead was in the assimilation in the wider society of as many blacks as possible and that this would finally lead to the label 'black' becoming more or less irrelevant to a person's status or social image. Although there is no doubt that this kind of integration has made great strides in the last thirty years or so, both socially and psychologically, it is also true that prejudice, discrimination and the differences in status and opportunities have by no means disappeared. An important aspect of the militant black movements of the sixties has been a new affirmation of black identity best reflected in the famous slogan: 'Black is beautiful'. There is the affirmation here that the black minority does not have to become like the others in order to 'merit' the granting to it of equal economic and social chances and opportunities. On the contrary, there is a stress on a separate cultural identity, traditions and roots which found its most popular expression in the novel of Alex Haley and the television film based on it. There is also the rejection of certain value judgements which have hitherto been implicitly accepted inside the minority. This is the case with the negative cultural connotations of blackness. It is not only that having black skin does not matter and should be 'forgotten' in a genuinely free human interaction. The declared aim is not to neutralize these traditional and deeply implanted value judgements but to reverse them.

In other words, this is a movement towards 'equal but different'; but it would be highly misleading, for a number of obvious reasons, to equate it with the similar slogan of the South African apartheid. Underlying this kind of social movement (of which there are by now many examples amongst minorities all over the world) are certain psychological issues which need further discussion.

We have previously characterized 'social competition' as based on the minority's aims to achieve parity with the majority; but in other ways, the minority aims to remain different. As we have seen, in some cases, such as for the American blacks, this kind of movement develops after the attempts to obtain a straightforward integration into the wider society have been perceived by some as a failure. This means that, in the eyes of some people, the expectation or the hope that there is a chance to integrate *as individuals* and on the basis of individual actions alone has more or less vanished. The remaining alternative, both for changing the present 'objective social situation of the group and for preserving or regaining its self-respect, is in acting in certain directions not as individuals but as members of a separate and distinct group. In conditions of rigid social stratification this can reach very deeply. Some years ago Beryl Geber (1972) conducted research on the attitudes of African school children in Soweto, the African township near Johannesburg, in which very serious riots occurred in recent times. One of the tasks the children were asked to complete was to write their 'future autobiography'. As Geber reported, in many of these autobiographies, the *personal* future was tightly bound up with the future of the Africans as a whole, with future personal decisions and actions which aimed not so much at the achievement of individual success as at doing something, as a member of the group, for the group as a whole. (A description of some of this research will be published as a book in 1980.)

These attitudes towards the present and the future, based on group membership rather than on individual motives and aspirations, are diametrically different from those which underlie the attempts at individual assimilation. They imply that, in addition to obtaining some forms of parity, efforts must also be made to delete, modify or reverse the traditional negative value connotations of the minority's special characteristics. In social competition for parity, the attempt is to shift the position of the *group* on certain value dimensions which are generally accepted by the society at large. In the simultaneous attempts to achieve an honourable and acceptable form of separateness or differentiation, the problem is not to shift the group's position within a system of values which is already accepted, but to change the *values* themselves. We must now turn to a discussion of this second aspect of 'equal but different'.

There is now a good deal of evidence (see e.g. Lemaine and Kastersztein, 1974, Lemaine *et al.*, 1978) that the achievement of some forms of clear differentiation from others is an important ingredient of people's ideas about their personal worth and self-respect. This is true in many walks of life, and – predictably – it becomes particularly marked when individuals or small groups of people are engaged in creating new forms of human endeavour – for example, in art or in science. The race amongst scientists to be the 'first' with a discovery (see e.g. the account by Watson in *The Double Helix*, 1968) is not only explicable in terms of a hope to reap the rewards and honours which may be awaiting the winner. To be creative is to be different, and there have been many painters and composers who endured long years of hardship, derision, hostility or public indifference in defence of their right or compulsion to break out of the accepted moulds. At the same time, differentiation from others is, *by definition*, a comparison with others. The creation of something *new* is not possible unless there is something *old* which serves as a criterion for the establishment of a difference from it. No doubt, this powerful tendency to differentiate has sometimes led, in art, in science and also in the 'mass' culture, to the creation of worthless fads whose only notable characteristic is their 'shock value', their capacity to appear as clearly different from what went on before. It is this same tendency which also sometimes results in the attempts by the aspiring innovators to magnify and exaggerate small or trivial differences between what they are doing and what has been done by others.

337

Whether genuinely creative or not, these are some of the examples of the process of social comparison upon which, as we have said earlier, must be based most of the attempts to create, achieve, preserve or defend a positive conception of oneself, a satisfactory self-image. This is true of social groups as well as of individuals. In the case of minorities, this 'social creativity' may take a number of forms. For groups who wish to remain (or become) separate, and yet obtain equality, this creation of *new* forms of comparison with the majority will be closely associated with social competition which we have previously discussed. Sometimes, when direct social competition is impossible or very difficult, social creativity of this kind may become, for a time, a compensatory activity, an attempt to maintain some kind of integrity through the only channels which remain available.

In principle, there are two major forms of the minorities' social creativity, and although they often appear together in 'real life', it is still useful, for the purposes of our discussion, to distinguish between them (see chapter 13). The first is to attempt a re-evaluation of the *existing* group characteristics which carry an unfavourable connotation, often both inside and outside the group. We have already seen an example of this with 'Black is beautiful'. The second is to search in the past of the group for some of its old traditions or separate attributes, to revitalize them and to give them a new and positive significance. A version of this can also be the *creation* of some new group characteristics which will be endowed with positive values through social action and/or through an attempt to construct new attitudes.

There are many examples of each of these forms of attempting to achieve a new group distinctiveness. A strong emotional charge often accompanies movements towards a re-establishment of equal or high status for the separate language of an ethnic minority. The national language easily becomes one of the major symbols of separateness with dignity, of a positive self-definition (see Giles, 1977 and 1978 for extensive discussion). This has been the case in Belgium, in Québec, in the Basque country, in a predominantly Swiss–German *canton* containing a French-speaking minority which fought for secession; it was also an important ingredient of several nationalist movements which were faced, in the central and eastern Europe of nineteenth century, with attempts at cultural Russification or Germanization by the governing authorities from Petersburg, Vienna or Berlin. In cases when this leads to a general acceptance of bilingualism, both official and public, the results can be sometimes a little paradoxical. In the Friesian region of The Netherlands one can see, on entering some villages, *two* identical signposts offering information about the name of the village; this is so because it happens that the name is the same in Dutch and in Friesian. Some years ago, at the time of the intense battle in Belgium for establishing the social and cultural parity of Flemish with French, it was sometimes easier in Antwerp to obtain information when asking for it in English than in French, although it was quite obvious that the respondent's French was much better than his or her English. These anecdotal examples reflect a deeper and more serious psychological reality: if one considered no more than the possible 'objective' advantages, social, political or economic, which may flow from the re-establishment of a high or equal status for an ethnic minority's language, one would miss the crucial part that it plays as one of the most evident and powerful symbols of distinctive identity. The increasing predominance of French in Québec (which, in some cases, even blots out the official policy of bilingualism) may well create some new 'objective' difficulties in a continent so overwhelmingly dominated by another language; and yet, the separatist linguistic pressure remains steady in the Province.

It may be useful to return briefly from these linguistic considerations to 'Black is beautiful'. As I wrote some time ago (see chapter 13):

The very use of the term 'blacks' in this text, which would have had very different connotations only a few years ago already testifies to these changes. The old *interpretations* of distinctiveness are rejected; the old characteristics are given a new meaning of different but equal or superior. Examples abound: the beauty of blackness, the African hair-do, the African cultural past and traditions, the reinterpretation of Negro music from 'entertainment' to a form of art which has deep roots in a *separate* cultural tradition . . . At the same time, the old attempts to be a little more like the other people are often rejected: no more straightening of hair for beautiful black girls or using of various procedures for lightening the skin. The accents, dialects, sway of the body, rhythms of dancing, texture of the details of interpersonal communication – all this is preserved, enhanced and re-evaluated.

The interesting aspect of this list of newly evaluated attributes is that some of them have not been, by any means, negatively evaluated in the past. Negro music and dance, or Negro prowess in athletics have long been a part of the general stereotype, used both inside and outside the group. But they were perceived as largely irrelevant to the *rest* of the Negro image; in some subtle ways they probably contributed to the general stigma of inferiority. A similar phenomenon appears in anti-Semitism. As Billig (1978) recently pointed out, there are many examples in the publications of the National Front of Jews being referred to as impressive in their achievements, 'intelligent', capable of great solidarity and self-sacrifice, etc. This only serves to enhance the dire warnings about their plot to take over the world. The evaluations attached to any presumed attributes of a minority cannot be properly understood when they are considered in isolation. Their social and psychological signifi-cance only appears when they are placed in the context of the general conceptual and social category of which they are a part. Their meaning changes with the context. This is why some of the well-intentioned efforts to present minority groups as having various 'nice' attributes have often failed to produce a decrease in prejudice.

The second major form of the search for a positive distinctiveness finds again some of its striking examples in the domain of language. The attempts to revitalize the use of Welsh are a crucial part of Welsh nationalism. But perhaps the most dramatic example known in history is Hebrew becoming, in a period of no more than about thirty years, the undisputed first (and often the only) language of well over two million people. Once again, it is easy to point to the concrete need for having a common language in a country to which people came, in the span of one or two generations, from all over the world and from many cultures. And yet, there have been some controversies in the early years as to whether modern Hebrew should continue to be written in its own alphabet or whether the Latin alphabet should be adopted. The latter solution would have been an easier one for a number of reasons. The first alternative, backed by cultural tradition and, at the same time, streng-thening the distinctive new identity, was finally chosen.

Ethnic minorities in which national movements develop usually have at their disposal the possibility of backing their claims by returning to the past. Language is only one of these distinctive traditions emerging from recent or remote history. The claim for a new separate unity *now* can be made much more effective in the minds of people if it is supported by ideas about about the existence of a separate unity in the distant past. And thus, each of these movements must rely on a combination of myths, symbols and historical realities which all help to stress the *distinctive* nature of the group and its right to continue its distinctiveness. In his book on *The Nationalization of the Masses*, the historian George Mossé (1975) discussed what he called the 'aesthetics of politics'. Taking the example of the development of mass nationalism in Germany in the nineteenth and twentieth centuries, to which he referred as 'the growth of a secular religion', he also wrote: 'As in any religion, the theology expressed itself through liturgy: festivals, rites and symbols which remained constant in an ever-changing world' (p. 16). In all this, the internal unit of a national 'group' can become indissolubly linked to its *inherent* and *immutable* differences from others. At this point, nationalism is capable of shading into racism. But, in the case of many national movements growing inside ethnic minorities, this need not be the case, and very often it is not. With the creation and revival of distinct symbols, of cultural traditions, of modes of social behaviour sanctified by a real or a mythical past, and of new stereotypes stressing the differences between the 'ingroup' and the 'outgroups', the enhanced separate identity of the group can become powerfully reflected in the feelings and attitudes of its members. As we have already seen, this is closely linked to the image they have of their *personal* integrity, dignity and worth.

There are, however, minority groups which cannot find very much in the past in the way of symbols and traditions of a separate identity. The differences from others must then be created or enhanced, and re-evaluated in the present, as soon as possible. Women's liberation movements went through some developments, whose nature can be attributed to the overriding need for creating a conception of *different* but equal. In the early times, when the suffragettes made the headlines, the main idea in relation to men seems to have been that 'whatever you can do, I can do better' (or at least as well). This was therefore a fairly pure form of John Turner's 'social competition' in which two groups aim to achieve the same goals by the same means. The increasing sophistication of the movement, particularly as it developed in the last ten years or so, shifted the stress to a synthesis of social competition with the conception of a differentiation *in* equality (see e.g. Williams and Giles, 1978). In these more recent developments, there is still a continuing insistence that there are many jobs which women can do as well as men, although they are often debarred from them by the past and present sex discrimination and the corresponding dominant public attitudes partly determined by the way we socialize our children.[2]

The feminist movement also insists, however, that many of the things women traditionally do, or are uniquely capable of doing, have been debased and devalued in society. This is, therefore, another example of an attempt to re-evaluate positively certain distinctive characteristics of the group rather than trying to become more like the 'superior' group. This strategy is justified as there is evidence (see Williams and Giles, 1978) that in some cases the straightforward 'social competition' does not achieve its objectives: some jobs and professions in which the number of

[2] That this direct social competition is still fully justified is clearly shown in a recent research report from the United States (summarized in the *Newsletter of the Institute for Social Research*, University of Michigan, Spring 1978): 'In 1975 the average hourly earnings of white men were 36 per cent higher than for black men, 60 per cent higher than for white women, and 78 per cent higher than for black women . . . But findings from the Survey Research Center's Panel Study of Income Dynamics clearly shows that . . . average differences in . . . qualifications account for less than one-third of the wage gap between white men and black women, less than half of the gap between white men and white women, and less than two-thirds of the gap between white men and black men'. In addition, 'differences in what economists call "attachment to the labour force" explain virtually none of the differences in earning between men and women' (p. 7).

women has increased suffered a corresponding decrease in their social status or prestige.

All these various examples contain at least three important implications for our discussion. The first is that certain social conditions resulting in the 'inferiority' of a group lead to genuine social creativity, to a search for new constructive dimensions of social comparison. The second is that one of the major problems likely to be encountered by minority groups engaging in this kind of creativity is in gaining a *legitimization* of their efforts. This legitimization has two sides to it. First, the newly created or newly evaluated attributes of the minority must gain a wide and positive acceptance inside the group itself. This may often prove difficult, as it can only be done if and when the patterns of acceptance by the minority of their 'inferiority', which we discussed earlier, can be broken down. What is likely to prove even more difficult is obtaining from other groups the legitimization of the new forms of parity. In addition to the conflicts of objective interests, which are often bound to be involved, the positively-valued 'social identity' of the majority and of its individual members depends no less on the outcomes of certain social comparisons than do the corresponding conceptions in the minority. One is back to 'we are what we are *because* they are not what we are', or as good as we are. Some of the cyclical changes in fashions used to reflect this need of 'superior' groups for marking their continuing differentiation from others. If a certain style or detail of dress, clearly pointing to the 'superior' status of the wearer, began to be imitated by those 'from below', appropriate changes were made (see Laver, 1964). Unfortunately, social changes of more profound impact are not as easy to invent as changes in fashion; and therefore, some of the new 'creations' by minorities must be stopped or denied their validity rather than walked away from.

Finally, our discussion implies a possible *inevitability* of certain forms of competitive or conflicting intergroup social comparisons and actions if and when minorities are ready to reject their inferior status and the ideas about their 'inferior' attributes. As long as complex societies exist, distinct social groups will continue to exist. As we have seen, intergroup differences easily acquire value connotations which may be of profound personal importance to those who are adversely affected; but the preservation and defence of certain outcomes of these comparisons are also important to those who benefit from them in the 'social image' they can create for themselves. This is not quite like an irresistible force encountering an immovable object, because neither is the force irresistible nor is the object immovable; social situations rarely, if ever, end up in this kind of suspended animation. But the seeds of conflict and tension are always there, although it is scientifically superficial as well as dubious to attribute them to some vaguely conceived, inherent human tendencies of social 'aggression'. We are not dealing in this field with haphazard and unorganized collections of individual aggressions.

There are no easy solutions in sight. It is true that different social groups may be able to derive their self-respect and integrity from excelling in different directions which are not directly competitive. But, in the first place, these different directions are also very often socially ranked according to their prestige; and, secondly, the self-respect of any group *must* be based, in many important ways, on comparisons with other groups from which a favourable distance must therefore be achieved or maintained.

These fairly pessimistic conclusions have not taken into account the unavoidable persistence of conflicts of objective interests between social groups. But perhaps it is here that, paradoxically, we can place some of our hopes for the future. The present conditions of interdependence also imply that few social conflicts between groups can be of a 'zero-sum' variety, all gain to one of the parties, all loss to the other. In the present conditions, there is always bound to be some distribution of gains and losses across the line. This being the case, it may be useful to see in each intergroup situation whether and how it might be possible for each group to achieve, preserve or defend its vital interests, or the interests which are perceived as vital, in such a way that the self-respect of other groups is not adversely affected at the same time. We must hope that the increasing complexity and interweaving of conflicts between groups will lead to a progressive rejection of simple 'all-or-none' solutions, of the crude divisions of mankind into 'us' and 'them'. To achieve this we need less hindsight and more planning. There is no doubt that the planning must involve two crucial areas of human endeavour: education and social change which must be achieved through genuinely effective legislative, political, social and economic programmes. This will not be easy and starry-eyed optimism will not help; nor will good intentions alone, however sincere they may be. But there is no doubt that the solution of the social and psychological problems which concerned us here is one of the most urgent and fundamental issues which will have to be directly confronted in a very large number of countries (of whatever 'colour' or political system) before the century is over.

References

1. The following previous publications are used in this book in a revised or shortened form by permission of the publishers:

Chapter 2
H. Tajfel: Introduction; Experiments in a vacuum. From J. Israel and H. Tajfel (eds.): *The context of social psychology: A critical assessment.* (European Monographs in Social Psychology, No. 2), London: Academic Press, 1972.

Chapter 3
H. Tajfel: Individuals and groups in social psychology. *British Journal of Social and Clinical Psychology*, 1979, **18,** 183–90.

Chapter 4
H. Tajfel: Value and the perceptual judgement of magnitude. *Psychological Review*, 1957, **64,** 192–204. © 1957, the American Psychological Society.
H. Tajfel and S. D. Cawasjee: Value and the accentuation of judged differences: A confirmation. *Journal of Abnormal and Social Psychology*, 1959, **59,** 436–9. © 1959, the American Psychological Society.
H. Tajfel: Quantitative judgement in social perception. *British Journal of Psychology*, 1959, **50,** 16–29.

Chapter 5
H. Tajfel and A. L. Wilkes: Classification and quantitative judgement. *British Journal of Psychology*, 1963, **54,** 101–14.
H. Tajfel and A. L. Wilkes: Salience of attributes and commitment to extreme judgements in the perception of people. *British Journal of Social and Clinical Psychology*, 1964, **2,** 40–9.
H. Tajfel, A. A. Sheikh and R. C. Gardner: Content of stereotypes and the inference of similarity between members of stereotyped groups. *Acta Psychologica*, 1964, **22,** 191–201. North Holland Publishing Company.
H. Tajfel: A note on Lambert's 'Evaluation reactions to spoken languages'. *Canadian Journal of Psychology*, 1959, **13,** 86–92. © 1959 Canadian Psychological Association.

Chapter 6
H. Tajfel: Cognitive aspects of prejudice. *Journal of Biosocial Science*, 1969, Supplement No. 1, 173–91.

344

References

Chapter 7

H. Tajfel: Social stereotypes and social groups. From J. C. Turner and H. Giles (eds.): *Intergroup behaviour*. Oxford: Blackwell, 1981 (in press).

Chapter 8

H. Tajfel and J. L. Dawson: Epilogue. From H. Tajfel and J. L. Dawson (eds.): *Disappointed guests*. Oxford University Press, 1965.

Chapter 9

H. Tajfel, C. Nemeth, G. Jahoda, J. D. Campbell and N. B. Johnson: The development of children's preference for their own country: A cross-national study. *International Journal of Psychology*, 1970, **5**, 245–53.

H. Tajfel, G. Jahoda, C. Nemeth, Y. Rim and N. B. Johnson: Devaluation by children of their own national or ethnic group: Two case studies. *British Journal of Social and Clinical Psychology*, 1972, **11**, 235–43.

Chapter 10

H. Tajfel and G. Jahoda: Development in children of concepts and attitudes about their own and other nations: A cross-national study. *Proceedings of the XVIIIth International Congress of Psychology*, Symposium 36, 17–33, Moscow, 1966.

N. B. Johnson, M. R. Middleton and H. Tajfel: The relationship between children's preferences for and knowledge about other nations. *British Journal of Social and Clinical Psychology*, 1970, **9**, 232–40.

Chapters 11, 12 and 13

H. Tajfel: The psychological structure of intergroup relations. Part I in H. Tajfel (ed.): *Differentiation between social groups: Studies in the social psychology of intergroup relations*. (European Monographs in Social Psychology, No. 14), London: Academic Press, 1978.

Chapter 14

H. Tajfel: Exit, voice and intergroup relations. From L. H. Strickland, F. E. Aboud and K. J. Gergen (eds.): *Social psychology in transition*. New York: Plenum Press, 1976.

Chapter 15

H. Tajfel: *The social psychology of minorities*. London: Minority Rights Group, 1978.

2. Other references:

Abelson, R. P., Aronson, E., McGuire, W. J., Newcomb, T. M., Rosenberg, M. J. and Tannenbaum, P. H. (eds.) 1968. *Theories of cognitive consistency*. Chicago: Rand McNally.

Adorno, T. W., Frenkel-Brunswik, E., Levinson, D. J. and Sanford, R. N. 1950. *The authoritarian personality*. New York: Harper.

Allport, G. W. 1954. *The nature of prejudice*. Cambridge, Mass.: Addison-Wesley.

Allport, G. W. and Kramer, B. M. 1946. Some roots of prejudice. *Journal of Psychology*, **22**, 9–39.

References

Allport, G. W. and Postman, L. 1947. *The psychology of rumour*. New York: Holt.
Apfelbaum, E. and Herzlich, C. 1971. La théorie de l'attribution en psychologie sociale. *Bulletin de Psychologie*, **24**, 961–76.
Armistead, N. (ed.) 1974. *Reconstructing social psychology*. Harmondsworth: Penguin Books.
Asch, S. E. 1956. Studies on independence and conformity: A minority of one against a unanimous majority. *Psychological Monographs*, **10**, 516.
Banton, M. 1967. *Race relations*. London: Tavistock Publications.
Barbiero, N. C. 1974. *Noi e gli altri: Attegiamenti e pregiudizi nel bambino*. Naples: Guida Editori.
Bartlett, F. C. 1932. *Remembering: A study in experimental and social psychology*. Cambridge University Press.
Bell, D. 1977. Power. In A. Bullock and O. Stallybrass (eds.): *The Fontana Dictionary of Modern Thought*. London: Fontana/Collins.
Berger, P. L. 1966. Identity as a problem in the sociology of knowledge. *European Journal of Sociology*, **7**, 105–15.
Berger, P. L. and Luckmann, T. 1967. *The social construction of reality*. London: Allen Lane.
Berkowitz, L. 1962. *Aggression: A social psychological analysis*. New York: McGraw-Hill.
    1972. Frustration, comparisons and other sources of emotion arousal as contributors to social unrest. *Journal of Social Issues*, **28**, 1, 77–91.
Berkowitz, L. and Walster, E. (eds.) 1976. *Equity theory: towards a general theory of social interaction*. (Advances in experimental social psychology, Vol. 9). New York: Academic Press.
Berry, J. W., Kalin, R. and Taylor, D. M. 1977. *Multiculturalism and ethnic attitudes in Canada*. Ottawa: Minister of Supply and Services.
Bevan, W. and Bevan, D. C. 1956. Judged size and personal relevance: An exercise in quasi-representative design. *Journal of General Psychology*, **54**, 203–7.
Billig, M. 1972. Social categorization and intergroup relations. Unpublished Ph.D. thesis, University of Bristol.
    1976. *Social psychology and intergroup relations*. (European Monographs in Social Psychology, No. 9). London: Academic Press.
    1977. The new social psychology and 'fascism'. *European Journal of Social Psychology*, **7**, 393–432.
    1978. *Fascists: A social psychological view of the National Front*. (European Monographs in Social Psychology, No. 15). London: Academic Press.
Billig, M. and Tajfel, H. 1973. Social categorization and similarity in intergroup behaviour. *European Journal of Social Psychology*, **3**, 27–52.
Birrell, D. 1972. Relative deprivation as a factor in conflict in Northern Ireland. *Sociological Review*, **20**, 317–43.
Bittner, E. 1973. Objectivity and realism in sociology. In G. Psathas (ed.): *Phenomenological sociology: Issues and applications*. New York: Wiley.
Blalock, H. M. 1967. *Toward a theory of minority-group relations*. New York: Wiley.

References

Bodmer, W. and Cavalli-Sforza, L. 1970. Intelligence and race. *Scientific American*, **223** (4), 19–29.

Bourhis, R. Y. and Giles, H. 1977. The language of intergroup distinctiveness. In H. Giles (ed.), *op. cit.*

Bourhis, R. Y., Giles, H. and Tajfel, H. 1973. Language as a determinant of Welsh identity. *European Journal of Social Psychology*, **3**, 447–60.

Bourhis, R. Y. and Hill, P. 1981. Intergroup perceptions in British higher education. In H. Tajfel (ed.), *op. cit.*

Branthwaite, A. and Jones, J. E. 1975. Fairness and discrimination: English vs. Welsh. *European Journal of Social Psychology*, **5**, 323–38.

Breakwell, G. 1979. Illegitimate membership and intergroup differentiation. *British Journal of Social and Clinical Psychology*, **18**, 141–9.

Brehm, J. W. and Cohen, A. R. 1962. *Explorations in cognitive dissonance*. New York: Wiley.

Brewer, M. B. 1979. Ingroup bias in the minimal intergroup situation: A cognitive–motivational analysis. *Psychological Bulletin*, **86** (2), 307–24.

Brewer, M. B. and Campbell, D. T. 1976. *Ethnocentrism and intergroup attitudes*. New York: Wiley.

Brown, D. R. 1953. Stimulus-similarity and the anchoring of subjective scales. *American Journal of Psychology*, **66**, 199–214.

Brown, R. J. 1976. Similarity and intergroup behaviour. Mimeo, University of Bristol.

1977. Similarity in cooperative and competitive contexts. Mimeo, University of Bristol.

1978. Divided we fall: An analysis of relations between sections of a factory workforce. In H. Tajfel (ed.), *op. cit.*

Brown, R. J. and Turner, J. C. 1979. The criss-cross categorization effect in intergroup discrimination. *British Journal of Social and Clinical Psychology*, **18**, 371–83.

1981. Interpersonal and intergroup behaviour. In J. C. Turner and H. Giles (eds.), *op. cit.*

Bruner, J. S. 1957. On perceptual readiness. *Psychological Review*, **64**, 123–51.

1962. Myth and identity. In: *On knowing: Essays for the left hand*. Cambridge, Mass.: Harvard University Press.

Bruner, J. S. and Garton, A. (eds.) 1978. *Human growth and development*. Oxford: Clarendon Press.

Bruner, J. S. and Goodman, C. C. 1947. Value and need as organizing factors in perception. *Journal of Abnormal and Social Psychology*, **42**, 33–44.

Bruner, J. S., Goodnow, J. J. and Austin, G. A. 1956. *A study of thinking*. New York: Wiley.

Bruner, J. S. and Klein, G. S. 1960. The functions of perceiving: New look retrospect. In B. Kaplan and S. Wapner (eds.): *Perspectives in psychological theory: Essays in honour of Heinz Werner*. New York: International Universities Press.

Bruner, J. S. and Postman, L. 1948. Symbolic value as an organizing factor in perception. *Journal of Social Psychology*, **27**, 203–8.

References

Bruner, J. S. and Potter, M. C. 1964. Interference in visual recognition. *Science*, **144,** 424–5.

Bruner, J. S. and Rodrigues, J. S. 1953. Some determinants of apparent size. *Journal of Abnormal and Social Psychology*, **48,** 17–24.

Brunswik, E. 1947. *Systematic and representative design of psychological experiments with results in physical and social perception.* Berkeley, Calif.: University of California Press.

Buss, A. R. 1978. Causes and reasons in attribution theory: A conceptual critique. *Journal of Personality and Social Psychology*, **36,** 1311–21.

Byrne, D. 1971. *The attraction paradigm.* New York: Academic Press.

Caddick, B. 1974. Experimental Report. Unpublished ms., University of Bristol.

  1977. The sources of perceived illegitimacy in intergroup behaviour. Mimeo, University of Bristol.

  1978. Status, legitimacy and the social identity concept in intergroup relations. Unpublished Ph.D. thesis, University of Bristol.

Cairns, E. 1981, Intergroup conflict in Northern Ireland, In H. Tajfel (ed.) *op. cit.*

Capozza, D., Bonaldo, E. and Di Maggio, A. 1979. *Problemi di identità e di conflitto sociale: Ricerche condotte su gruppi etnici in Italia.* Padua: Antoniana Spa.

Carey, A. T. 1956. *Colonial students.* London: Secker and Warburg.

Carlson, E. R. 1956. Attitude change through modification of attitude structure. *Journal of Abnormal and Social Psychology*, **52,** 256–61.

Carswell, E. A. and Rommetveit, R. (eds.) 1971. *Social contexts of messages.* (European Monographs in Social Psychology, No. 1). London: Academic Press.

Carter, L. F. and Schooler, K. 1949. Value, need and other factors in perception. *Psychological Review*, **56,** 200–7.

Chapman, D. W. and Volkmann, J. 1939. A social determinant of the level of aspiration. *Journal of Abnormal and Social Psychology*, **34,** 225–38.

Chapman, L. J. 1967. Illusory correlations in observational report. *Journal of Verbal Learning and Verbal Behaviour*, **6,** 151–5.

Chase, M. 1971. Categorization and affective arousal: Some behavioural and judgemental consequences. Unpublished Ph.D. thesis, Columbia University.

Cheyne, W. M. 1970. Stereotyped reactions to speakers with Scottish and English regional accents. *British Journal of Social and Clinical Psychology*, **9,** 77–9.

Child, I. L. and Doob, L. F. 1943. Factors determining national stereotypes. *Journal of Social Psychology*, **17,** 203–19.

Clark, K. B. 1965. *Dark ghetto.* New York.

Clark, K. B. and Clark, M. P. 1947. Racial identification and preference in Negro children. In T. M. Newcomb and E. L. Hartley (eds.): *Readings in social psychology.* New York: Holt.

Cohen, D. 1977. *Psychologists on psychology.* London: Routledge and Kegan Paul.

Cohn, N. 1967. *Warrant for genocide.* New York: Harper.

References

Coleman, J. 1974. Processes of concentration and dispersal of power in social systems. *Social Science Information*, **13** (2), 7–18.

Commins, B. and Lockwood, J. 1979. The effects of status differences, favoured treatment and equity on intergroup comparisons. *European Journal of Social Psychology*, **9**, 281–9.

Crook, J. H. 1978. Evolution and social behaviour. In H. Tajfel and C. Fraser (eds.): *Introducing social psychology*. Harmondsworth: Penguin Books.

Crosby, F. 1976. A model of egoistical relative deprivation. *Psychological Review*, **83**, 85–113.

Dann, H. D. and Doise, W. 1974. Ein neuer methodologischer Ansatz zur experimentellen Erforschung von Intergruppen-Beziehungen. *Zeitschrift für Sozialpsychologie*, **5**, 2–15.

Danziger, K. 1963. The psychological future of an oppressed group. *Social Forces*, **62**, 31–40.

Davies, A. F. 1968. The child's discovery of nationality. *Australian and New Zealand Journal of Sociology*, **4**, 107–25.

Dawson, J. L. M. 1961. An analysis of the degree of adaptation achieved by Oxford University African and Asian students. Paper read to J.A.C.A.R.I.

Deschamps, J. C. 1977. *L'attribution et la catégorisation sociale*. Bern: Peter Lang.
  1978. La perception des causes du comportement. In W. Doise, J. C. Deschamps and G. Mugny, *op. cit.*

Deschamps, J. C. and Doise, W. 1978. Crossed category memberships in intergroup relations. In H. Tajfel (ed.), *op. cit.*

Deutsch, M. 1973. *The resolution of conflict*. New Haven, Conn.: Yale University Press.
  1974. The social psychological study of conflict: Rejoinder to a critique. *European Journal of Social Psychology*, **4**, 441–56.

Deutsch, M. and Krauss, R. M. 1965. *Theories in social psychology*. New York: Basic Books.

Doise, W. 1978a. Les préjugés et la différenciation catégorielle. In W. Doise, J. C. Deschamps and G. Mugny, *op. cit.*
  1978b. *Groups and individuals*. London: Cambridge University Press.

Doise, W., Csepeli, G., Dann, H. D., Gouge, C. and Larsen, W. 1972. An experimental investigation into the formation of intergroup representations. *European Journal of Social Psychology*, **2**, 202–4.

Doise, W., Deschamps, J. C. and Mugny, G. 1978. *Psychologie sociale expérimentale*. Paris: Armand Colin.

Doise, W. and Sinclair, A. 1973. The categorization process in intergroup relations. *European Journal of Social Psychology*, **3**, 145–57.

Doise, W. and Weinberger, M. 1972–3. Représentations masculines dans différentes situations de rencontres mixtes. *Bulletin de Psychologie*, **26**, 649–57.

Dukes, W. F. and Bevan, W. 1952. Size estimation and monetary value: A correlation. *Journal of Psychology*, **34**, 43–53.

Duncan, B. L. 1976. Differential social perception and attribution of inter-group violence: Testing the lower limits of stereotyping of Blacks. *Journal of Personality and Social Psychology*, **34**, 590–8.

349

References

Durkheim, E. 1959. In A. W. Gouldner (ed.): Translated by C. Sattler: *Socialism and Saint Simon*. London: Routledge and Kegan Paul.

Eaves, L. J. and Eysenck, H. L. 1974. Genetics and the development of social attitudes. *Nature,* **249,** 288–9.

Edwards, A. L. 1968. *Experimental design in psychological research,* 3rd edn. New York: Holt, Rinehart and Winston.

Ehrlich, H. J. 1973. *The social psychology of prejudice.* New York: Wiley.

Eiser, J. R. 1980. *Cognitive social psychology.* London: McGraw-Hill.

Eiser, J. R., Van der Pligt, J. and Gossop, M. R. 1979. Categorization, attitude and memory for the source of attitude statements. *European Journal of Social Psychology,* **9,** 243–51.

Eiser, J. R. and Stroebe, W. 1972. *Categorization and social judgement.* (European Monographs in Social Psychology, No. 3). London: Academic Press.

Emerson, R. 1960. *From empire to nation.* Cambridge, Mass.: Harvard University Press.

Epstein, A. L. 1978. *Ethos and identity.* London: Tavistock Publications.

Eriksen, C. W. and Hake, H. W. 1955. Multidimensional stimulus differences and accuracy of discrimination. *Journal of Experimental Psychology,* **50,** 153–60.

Erikson, E. 1964. *Insight and responsibility.* New York: Norton.

Eysenck, H. J. and Wilson, G. D. (eds.) 1978. *The psychological basis of ideology.* Lancaster: M.T.P. Press.

Faucheux, C. 1976. Cross-cultural research in experimental social psychology. *European Journal of Social Psychology,* **6,** 269–322.

Ferguson, C. K. and Kelley, H. H. 1964. Significant factors in over-evaluation of own group's product. *Journal of Abnormal and Social Psychology,* **69,** 223–8.

Festinger, L. 1954. A theory of social comparison processes. *Human Relations,* **7,** 117–40.

   1957. *A theory of cognitive dissonance.* Evanson, Ill.: Row, Peterson.

Fishbein, M. and Ajzen, I. 1975. *Attitudes, beliefs, intention and behaviour.* Reading, Mass.: Addison-Wesley.

Fishman, J. A. 1968. Nationality–nationalism and nation–nationism. In J. A. Fishman, C. A. Ferguson and J. D. Gupta, (eds.): *Language problems of developing countries.* New York: Wiley.

Forgas, J. P. 1979. *Social episodes: The study of interaction routines.* (European Monographs in Social Psychology, No. 17). London: Academic Press.

Frijda, N. and Jahoda, G. 1966. On the scope and methods of cross-cultural research. *International Journal of Psychology,* **1,** 110–27.

Geber, B. A. 1972. Occupational aspirations and expectations of South African high school children. Unpublished Ph.D. thesis, University of London.

Gerard, H. B. and Hoyt, M. F. 1974. Distinctiveness of social categorization and attitude towards ingroup members. *Journal of Personality and Social Psychology,* **29,** 836–42.

Gerard, H. B. and Miller, N. 1967. Group dynamics. *Annual Review of Psychology,* Vol. 18.

Gibson, J. J. 1953. Social perception and the psychology of perceptual learning.

References

in M. Sherif and M. O. Wilson (eds.): *Group relations at the crossroads*. New York: Harper.

Gilbert, G. M. 1951. Stereotype persistence and change among college students. *Journal of Abnormal and Social Psychology*, **46**, 245–54.

Giles, H. (eds.) 1977. *Language, ethnicity and intergroup relations*. (European Monographs in Social Psychology, No. 13.) London: Academic Press.

1978. Linguistic differentiation in ethnic groups. In H. Tajfel (ed.), *op. cit.*

1979. Ethnicity markers in speech. In K. R. Scherer and H. Giles (eds.): *Social markers in speech*. Cambridge University Press.

Giles, H., Bourhis, R. Y. and Taylor, D. M. 1977a. Towards a theory of language in ethnic group relations. In H. Giles (ed.), *op. cit.*

Giles, H., Taylor, D. M. and Bourhis, R. Y. 1977b. Dimensions of Welsh identity. *European Journal of Social Psychology*, **7**, 29–39.

Goldhamer, H. 1968. Social mobility. In *International Encyclopedia of the Social Sciences*, Vol. 14. New York: Macmillan and the Free Press.

Gombrich, E. H. 1960. *Art and illusion*. London: Phaidon.

Goodman, M. E. 1964. *Race awareness in young children*. Revised edn. New York: Collier.

Grace, H. A. 1954. Education and the reduction of prejudice. *Education Research Bulletin*, **33**, 169–75.

Grace H. A. and Neuhaus, J. O. 1952. Information and social distance as predictors of hostility toward nations. *Journal of Abnormal and Social Psychology*, **47**, 540–5.

Griffin, J. H. 1962. *Black like me*. London: Collins.

Guillaumin, C. 1972. *L'idéologie raciste: Genèse et langage actuel*. Paris: Mouton.

Gurr, T. R. 1970. *Why men rebel*. Princeton: Princeton University Press.

Hamilton, D. L. 1976. Cognitive biases in the perception of social groups. In J. S. Carroll and J. W. Payne (eds.): *Cognition and social behaviour*. Hillsdale, N. J.: Erlbaum.

Hamilton, D. L. and Gifford, R. K. 1976. Illusory correlations in interpersonal perception: A cognitive basis of stereotypic judgements. *Journal of Experimental Social Psychology*, **12**, 392–407.

Hamilton, V. L. 1978. Who is responsible? Towards a *social* psychology of responsibility attribution. *Social Psychology*, **41**, 316–28.

Harré, R. 1972. The analysis of episodes. In J. Israel and H. Tajfel (eds.), *op. cit.*

1974. Blueprint for a new science. In N. Armistead (ed.), *op. cit.*

1977a. On the ethogenic approach: Theory and practice. In L. Berkowitz (ed.): *Advances in experimental social psychology*, Vol. 10. New York: Academic Press.

1977b. Automatisms and autonomics: In reply to Professor Schlenker. In L. Berkowitz (ed.): *Advances in experimental social psychology*, Vol. 10. New York: Academic Press.

Harré, R. and Secord, P. F. 1972. *The explanation of social behaviour*. Oxford: Blackwell's.

Hastorf, A. H., Richardson, S. A. and Dornbusch, S. M. 1958. The problem of relevance in the study of person perception. In R. Tagiuri and L. Petrullo

351

References

(eds.): *Person perception and interpersonal behaviour*. Stanford University Press.

Hayek, F. A. 1969. The primacy of the abstract. In A. Koestler and J. R. Smythies (eds.): *Beyond reductionism: New perspectives in the life sciences.* London: Hutchinson.

Heberle, R. 1968. Social movements. In *International Encyclopedia of the Social Sciences*, Vol. 14. New York: Macmillan and the Free Press.

Heintz, R. K. 1950. The effect of remote anchoring points upon the judgement of lifted weights. *Journal of Experimental Psychology*, **40**, 584–91.

Helson, H. 1948. Adaptation-level as a basis for a quantitative theory of frames of reference. *Psychological Review*, **55**, 297–313.

Herman, S. 1970. *Israelis and Jews: The continuity of an identity*. New York: Random House.

Hermann, N. and Kogan, N. 1968. Negotiation in leader and delegate groups. *Journal of Conflict Resolution*, **12**, 332–44.

Hewstone, M. and Jaspars, J. 1981. Intergroup relations and attribution processes. In H. Tajfel (ed.), *op. cit.*

Hinde, R. A. 1979. *Towards understanding relationships*. (European Monographs in Social Psychology, No. 18). London: Academic Press.

Hirschman, A. O. 1970. *Exit, voice and loyalty: Responses to decline in firms, organizations and states*. 2nd edn., 1972. Cambridge, Mass.: Harvard University Press.

1973. The changing tolerance for income inequality in the course of economic development. *Quarterly Journal of Economics*, **87**, 544–66.

1974. 'Exit, voice and loyalty': Further reflections and a survey of recent contributions. *Social Science Information*, **13**, (1), 7–26.

Hofstadter, R. 1945. *Social Darwinism in American thought*. Philadelphia: University of Pennsylvania Press.

Holmes, R. 1965. Freud, Piaget and democratic leadership. *British Journal of Sociology*, **16**, 123.

Homans, G. C. 1961. *Social behaviour: Its elementary forms*. New York: Harcourt, Brace and World.

Hornstein, H. A. 1972. Promotive tension: The basis of prosocial behaviour from a Lewinian perspective. *Journal of Social Issues*, **28** (3), 191–218.

Horowitz, E. L. 1936. Development of attitudes towards Negroes. *Archives of Psychology*, No. 194.

1940. Some aspects of the development of patriotism in children. *Sociometry*, **3**, 329–41.

Hovland, I. and Sherif, M. 1952. Judgemental phenomena and scales of attitude measurement: Item displacement in Thurstone scales. *Journal of Abnormal and Social Psychology*, **47**, 822–32.

Husband, C. 1977. News media, language and race relations: A case study in identity maintenance. In H. Giles (ed.), *op. cit.*

1979. Social identity and the language of race relations. In H. Giles and B. Saint-Jacques (eds.): *Language and ethnic relations*. Oxford: Pergamon Press.

Irle, M. 1975. *Lehrbuch der Sozialpsychologie*. Göttingen: Hogrefe.

(ed.) 1978. *Kursus der Sozialpsychologie*. Darmstadt: Luchterhand.

References

Israel, J. 1972. Stipulations and construction in the social sciences. In J. Israel and H. Tajfel (eds.), *op. cit.*

Israel, J. and Tajfel, H. (eds.) 1972. *The context of social psychology: A critical assessment.* (European Monographs in Social Psychology, No. 2). London: Academic Press.

Jahoda, G. 1962. Development of Scottish children's ideas and attitudes about other countries. *Journal of Social Psychology,* **58,** 91–108.

1963a. The development of children's ideas about country and nationality. I. The conceptual framework. *British Journal of Educational Psychology,* **33,** 47–60.

1963b. The development of children's ideas about country and nationality. II. National symbols and themes. *British Journal of Educational Psychology,* **33,** 142–53.

1970. A cross-cultural perspective in psychology. *The Advancement of Science,* **27,** 57–70.

1979. A cross-cultural perspective on experimental social psychology. *Personality and Social Psychology Bulletin,* **5,** 142–8.

Jahoda, G. and Thomson, S. S. 1970. Ethnic identity and preference among Pakistani immigrant children in Glasgow. Unpublished ms., University of Strathclyde.

Jahoda, G., Thomson, S. S. and Bhatt, S. 1972. Ethnic identity and preferences among Asian immigrant children in Glasgow: A replicated study. *European Journal of Social Psychology,* **2,** 19–32.

James, H. E. O. and Tenen, C. 1951. Attitudes towards other peoples. *International Social Science Bulletin,* **3,** 553–61.

Jaspars, J., van de Geer, J. P., Tajfel, H. and Johnson, N. B. 1973. On the development of national attitudes. *European Journal of Social Psychology,* **3,** 347–69.

Jaspars, J. and Wernaen, S. 1981. Intergroup relations, ethnic identity and self-evaluation in Indonesia. In H. Tajfel (ed.), *op. cit.*

Jaulin, R. 1973. *Gens du soi, gens de l'autre.* Paris: Union Générale d'Edition.

Johnson, N. B. 1966. What do children learn from war comics? *New Society,* **8,** 7–12.

Jones, E. J. and Gerard, H. B. 1967. *Foundations of social psychology.* New York: Wiley.

Kamin, L. J. 1977. *The science and politics of I.Q.* Harmondsworth: Penguin Books.

Katz, D. and Braly, K. 1933. Social stereotypes of one hundred college students. *Journal of Abnormal and Social Psychology,* **28,** 280–90.

Katz, I. 1968. Factors influencing Negro performance in the desegregated school. In M. Deutsch, I. Katz and H. R. Jensen (eds.): *Social class, race and psychological development.* New York: Holt, Rinehart and Winston.

Kelley, H. H. and Thibaut, J. W. 1969. Group problem solving. In G. Lindzey and E. Aronson (eds.): *The handbook of social psychology,* Vol. 4. Reading, Mass.: Addison-Wesley.

Kidder, L. H. and Stewart, V. M. 1975. *The psychology of intergroup relations.*

References

New York: McGraw-Hill.

Kiernan, V. G. 1972. *The lords of human kind: European attitudes to the outside world in the imperial age*. Harmondsworth: Penguin Books.

Klein, G. S., Schlesinger, H. J. and Meister, D. E. 1951. The effect of values on perception: An experimental critique. *Psychological Review*, **58**, 96–112.

Klineberg, O. 1968. Prejudice. I. The Concept. In *International Encyclopedia of the Social Sciences*, Vol. 12. New York: Macmillan and the Free Press.

Kluckhohn, C. 1944. *Navaho witchcraft*. Harvard University, Peabody Museum Papers, Vol. 22, No. 2.

van Knippenberg, A. F. M. 1978. *Perception and evaluation of intergroup differences*. University of Leiden.

Lambert, W. E., Hodgson, R. C., Gardner, R. C. and Fillenbaum, S. 1960. Evaluational reactions to spoken languages. *Journal of Abnormal and Social Psychology*, **60**, 44–51.

Lambert, W. E. and Klineberg, O. 1959. A pilot study of the origin and development of national stereotypes. *International Social Science Journal*, **11**, 221–38.

  1967. *Children's views of foreign peoples: A cross-national study*. New York: Appleton Century Crofts.

Lambert, W. W., Solomon, R. L. and Watson, P. D. 1949. Reinforcement and extinction as factors in size estimation. *Journal of Experimental Psychology*, **39**, 637–41.

Lamm, H. and Kogan, N. 1970. Risk taking in the context of intergroup negotiation. *Journal of Experimental Social Psychology*, **6**, 351–63.

Laver, J. 1964. Costume as a means of social aggression. In J. D. Carthy and F. J. Ebling (eds.): *The natural history of aggression*. London: Academic Press.

Lawrence, D. H. and Festinger, L. 1962. *Deterrents and reinforcements: The psychology of insufficient reward*. Stanford University Press.

Lawson, E. D. 1963. The development of patriotism in children. A second look. *Journal of Psychology*, **55**, 279–86.

Lemaine, G. 1966. Inégalité, comparaison et incomparabilité: Esquisse d'une théorie de l'originalité social. *Bulletin de Psychologie*, **20**, 24–32.

Lemaine, G. and Kastersztein, J. 1972–3. Recherches sur l'originalité sociale, la différenciation et l'incomparabilité. *Bulletin de Psychologie*, **25**, 673–93.

Lemaine, G., Kastersztein, J. and Personnaz, B. 1978. Social differentiation. In H. Tajfel (ed.), *op. cit.*

Lent, R. H. 1970. Binocular resolution and perception of race in United States. *British Journal of Psychology*, **61**, 521–33.

Lévi-Strauss, C. 1966. *The savage mind*. University of Chicago Press.

LeVine, R. A. 1965. Socialization, social structure and intersocietal images. In H. Kelman (ed.): *International behaviour: A social psychological analysis*. New York: Holt, Rinehart and Winston.

LeVine, R. A. and Campbell, D. T. 1972. *Ethnocentrism: Theories of conflict, ethnic attitudes and group behaviour*. New York: Wiley.

Liebkind, K. 1979. *The social psychology of minority identity: A case study of intergroup identification*. Research Reports, University of Helsinki.

References

Lilli, W. 1975. *Soziale Akzentuierung.* Stuttgart: Kohlhammer.

Lilli, W. and Winkler, E. 1972. Scale usage and accentuation: Perceptual and memory estimations. *European Journal of Social Psychology,* **2,** 323–6.

1973. Accentuation under serial and non-serial conditions: Further evidence in favour of the relative concept. *European Journal of Social Psychology,* **3,** 209–12.

Lindzey, G. and Rogolsky, S. 1950. Prejudice and identification of minority group membership. *Journal of Abnormal and Social Psychology,* **45,** 279–86.

Lorenz, K. 1964. Ritualized fighting. In J. D. Carthy and F. J. Ebling (eds.): *The natural history of aggression.* London: Academic Press.

Louche, C. 1976. Les effets de la catégorisation sociale et de l'interaction collective dans la préparation et le déroulement d'une négociation inter-groupe. *Bulletin de Psychologie,* **28,** 18, 941–7.

Lubin, A. 1965. The care and feeding of correlated means. *Psychological Reports,* **17,** 457–8.

Ludmerer, K. M. 1972. *Genetics and American society.* Baltimore: Johns Hopkins University Press.

Lysak, W. and Gilchrist, J. C. 1955. Value, equivocality and goal availability. *Journal of Personality,* **23,** 500–1 (Abstract).

Manis, M. 1960. The interpretation of opinion statements as a function of recipient attitude. *Journal of Abnormal and Social Psychology,* **60,** 340–4.

Mann, J. F. and Taylor, D. M. 1974. Attribution of causality: Role of ethnicity and social class. *Journal of Social Psychology,* **94,** 3–13.

Maquet, J. J. 1961. *The premise of inequality in Ruanda.* London: Oxford University Press.

Mason, P. 1970. *Race relations.* London: Oxford University Press.

Mead, G. H. 1934. *Mind, self and society.* Chicago: University of Chicago Press.

Meenes, M. 1943. A comparison of racial stereotypes of 1930 and 1942. *Journal of Social Psychology,* **17,** 327–36.

Meltzer, H. 1939. Group differences in nationality and race preferences of children. *Sociometry,* **2,** 86–105.

1941. Hostility and tolerance in children's nationality and race attitudes. *Journal of Genetic Psychology,* **56,** 662–75.

Merton, R. K. 1957. *Social theory and social structure.* Glencoe, Illinois: Free Press.

Middleton, M., Tajfel, H. and Johnson, N. B. 1970. Cognitive and affective aspects of children's national attitudes. *British Journal of Social and Clinical Psychology,* **9,** 122–34.

Milner, D. 1970. Ethnic identity and preference in minority-group children. Unpublished Ph.D. thesis, University of Bristol.

1975. *Children and race.* Harmondsworth: Penguin Books.

Montagu, Ashley M. F. (ed.) 1968. *Man and aggression.* Oxford University Press.

Morin, E. 1969. *La rumeur d'Orléans.* Paris: Seuil.

Morland, J. K. 1966. A comparison of race awareness in Northern and Southern children. *American Journal of Orthopsychiatry,* **36,** 22.

1969. Race awareness among American and Hong Kong Chinese children. *American Journal of Sociology,* **75,** 360–74.

355

References

Morris, H. S. 1968. Ethnic groups. In *International Encyclopedia of the Social Sciences*, Vol. 5. New York: Macmillan and the Free Press.

Moscovici, S. 1972. Society and theory in social psychology. In J. Israel and H. Tajfel (eds.), *op. cit.*

1976. *Social influence and social change.* (European Monographs in Social Psychology, No. 10). London: Academic Press.

1979. A rejoinder. *British Journal of Social and Clinical Psychology*, **18**, 181.

Moscovici, S. and Faucheux, C. 1972. Social influence, conformity bias and the study of active minorities. In L. Berkowitz (ed.): *Advances in Experimental Social Psychology*, Vol. 6. New York: Academic Press.

Mossé, G. L. 1975. *The nationalization of the masses.* New York: Meridian.

Newcomb, T. 1943. *Personality and social change.* New York: Rinehart and Winston.

Orne, M. T. 1962. On the social psychology of the psychological experiment with particular reference to the demand characteristics and their implications. *American Psychologist*, **17**, 776–83.

Osgood, C. E., Suci, G. J. and Tannenbaum, P. H. 1957. *The measurement of meaning.* Urbana: University of Illinois Press.

Palmonari, A., Carugati, F., Ricci Bitti, P. and Sarchielli, G. 1979. *Identità imperfette.* Bologna: Il Mulino.

Political and Economic Planning 1955. *Colonial students in Britain.* London: Political and Economic Planning.

Perret-Clermont, A.-N. 1980. *Cognitive development and social interaction in children.* (European Monographs in Social Psychology, No. 19). London: Academic Press.

Peters, R. S. 1960. *The concept of motivation*, 2nd edn. London: Routledge and Kegan Paul.

Peters, R. S. and Tajfel, H. 1957. Hobbes and Hull – metaphysicians of behaviour. *British Journal for the Philosophy of Science*, **8**, 29, 30–44.

Pettigrew, T. F. 1958. Personality and sociocultural factors in intergroup attitudes: A cross-national comparison. *Journal of Conflict Resolution*, **2**, 29.

Pettigrew, T. F., Allport, G. W. and Barnett, E. O. 1958. Binocular resolution and perception of race in South Africa. *British Journal of Psychology*, **49**, 265–78.

Piaget, J. 1928. *Judgement and reasoning in the child.* New York: Harcourt, Brace. 1932. *The moral judgement of the child.* London: Routledge and Kegan Paul.

Piaget, J. and Inhelder, B. 1969. The gaps in empiricism. In A. Koestler and J. R. Smythies, (eds.): *Beyond reductionism: New perspectives in the life sciences.* London: Hutchinson.

Piaget, J. and Weil, A. M. 1951. The development in children of the idea of homeland, and of relations with other countries. *International Social Science Bulletin*, **3**, 561–78.

Plamenatz, J. 1970. *Ideology.* London: Macmillan.

Plon, M. 1972. Sur quelques aspects de la rencontre entre la psychologie sociale et la théorie des jeux. *La Pensée*, **161**, 2–30.

1974. On the meaning of the notion of conflict and its study in social psychology. *European Journal of Social Psychology,* **4,** 389–436.

Poitou, J. P. 1978. *La dynamique des groupes: Une idéologie au travail.* Paris: Éditions C.N.R.S.

Popper, K. 1961. *The poverty of historicism.* London: Routledge and Kegan Paul.

Proshansky, H. M. 1966. The development of intergroup attitudes. In I. W. Hoffman and M. L. Hoffman (eds.): *Review of child development,* Vol. 2. New York: Russell Sage Foundation.

Rabbie, J. M. and Wilkens, G. 1971. Intergroup competition and its effect on intragroup and intergroup relations. *European Journal of Social Psychology,* **1,** 215–34.

Razran, G. 1950. Ethnic dislikes and stereotypes: A laboratory study. *Journal of Abnormal and Social Psychology,* **45,** 7–27.

Rex, J. 1969. Race as a social category. *Journal of Biosocial Science,* Suppl. No. 1, 145–52.

Rim, Y. 1968. The development of national stereotypes in children. *Megamot,* 45–50.

Rivers, W. H. R. 1905. Observations on the senses of the Todas. *British Journal of Psychology,* **1,** 321.

Rokeach, M. 1960. *The open and closed mind.* New York: Basic Books.

Rosenberg, M. J. 1960. Cognitive reorganization in response to the hypnotic reversal of attitudinal affect. *Journal of Personality,* **28,** 39–63.

Rosenthal, R. 1966. *Experimenter effects in behavioural research.* New York: Appleton.

Ross, R. T. 1939. Optimal orders in the method of paired comparisons. *Journal of Experimental Psychology,* **25,** 414–24.

Rothbart, M., Fulero, S., Jensen, C., Howard, J. and Birrell, P. 1978. From individual to group perspectives: Availability heuristics in stereotype formation. *Journal of Experimental Social Psychology,* **14,** 237–55.

Runciman, W. G. 1966. *Relative deprivation and social justice.* London: Routledge and Kegan Paul.

Sartre, J.-P. 1948. *Réflexions sur la question juive.* Paris: Gallimard.

Sawyer, J. and Guetzkow, H. 1965. Bargaining and negotiation in international relations. In H. C. Kelman (ed.): *International behaviour.* New York: Holt, Rinehart and Winston.

Schachter, S. 1970. The assumption of identity and peripheralist–centralist controversies in motivation and emotion. In M. Arnold (ed.): *Feelings and emotions.* New York: Academic Press.

Schlenker, B. R. 1977. On the ethogenic approach: Etiquette and revolution. In L. Berkowitz (ed.): *Advances in experimental social psychology,* Vol. 10. New York: Academic Press.

Schönbach, P. 1981. *Intergroup attitudes and education.* (European Monographs in Social Psychology). London: Academic Press, in press.

Schutz, A. 1932. *Der sinnhafte Aufbau der sozialen Welt.* Vienna: Springer. In translation: *The phenomenology of the social world,* 1967. London: Heinemann.

Scodel, A. and Austrin, H. 1957. The perception of Jewish photographs by non-Jews and Jews. *Journal of Abnormal and Social Psychology,* **54,** 278–80.

References

Secord, P. F., Bevan, W. and Katz, B. 1956. The Negro stereotype and perceptual accentuation. *Journal of Abnormal and Social Psychology*, **53**, 78–83.

Segall, M. H., Campbell, D. T. and Herskovits, M. J. 1966. *The influence of culture on visual perception*. Indianapolis: Bobbs-Merrill.

Shafer, B. C. 1955. *Nationalism: Myth and reality*. New York: Harcourt Brace Jovanovich.

Sheikh, A. A. 1963. The role of stereotypes in interpersonal perception. Unpublished M.A. thesis, University of Western Ontario.

Sherif, M. 1951. A preliminary experimental study of intergroup relations. In J. H. Rohrer and M. Sherif (eds.): *Social psychology at the crossroads*. New York: Harper.

1966. *Group conflict and cooperation: Their social psychology*. London: Routledge and Kegan Paul.

Sherif, M., Harvey, O. J., White, B. J., Hood, W. R. and Sherif, C. W. 1961. *Intergroup conflict and cooperation: The robbers cave experiment*. Norman, Oklahoma: University of Oklahoma Book Exchange.

Sherif, M. and Hovland, C. I. 1961. *Social judgement. Assimilation and contrast effects in communication and attitude change*. New Haven, Conn.: Yale University Press.

Sherif, M. and Sherif, C. W. 1953. *Groups in harmony and tension*. New York: Harper.

Sherif, M., Taub, D. and Hovland, C. I. 1958. Assimilation and contrast effects of anchoring stimuli on judgement. *Journal of Experimental Psychology*, **55**, 150–5.

Sherwin-White, A. N. 1967. *Racial prejudice in imperial Rome*. Cambridge University Press.

Shuval, J. T. 1963. *Immigrants on the threshold*. New York: Atherton Press.

Siegel, S. 1956. *Nonparametric statistics for the behavioural sciences*. New York: McGraw-Hill.

Simon, M. D., Tajfel, H. and Johnson, N. B. 1967. Wie erkennt man einen Österreicher? *Kölner Zeitschrift für Soziologie und Sozialpsychologie*, **19**, 511–37.

Simpson, G. E. 1968. Assimilation. In *International Encyclopedia of the Social Sciences*, Vol. 1. New York: Macmillan and the Free Press.

Simpson, G. E. and Yinger, J. M. 1965. *Racial and cultural minorities*. New York: Harper and Row.

Singh, K. A. 1963. *Indian students in Britain*. New York: Asia Publishing House.

Skevington, S. M. 1980. Intergroup relations and nursing. *British Journal of Social and Clinical Psychology*, **19**, 3, 201–13.

Smith, K. R., Parker, G. B. and Robinson, G. A. 1951. An exploratory investigation of autistic perception. *Journal of Abnormal and Social Psychology*, **46**, 324–6.

Smith, P. M. 1978. Sex roles in speech: An intergroup perspective. Paper delivered in Section 3 of the Sociolinguistics Program in the 9th World Congress of Sociology, Uppsala, August 1978.

Stallybrass, O. 1977. Sterotype. In A. Bullock and O. Stallybrass (eds.): *The*

References

Fontana Dictionary of Modern Thought. London: Fontana/Collins.

Steiner, I. D. 1974. Whatever happened to the group in social psychology? *Journal of Experimental Social Psychology*, **10**, 94–108.

Stephan, W. 1977. Stereotyping: Role of ingroup–outgroup differences in causal attribution of behaviour. *Journal of Social Psychology*, **101**, 255–66.

Stevens, S. S. and Galanter, E. H. 1956. Ratio scales and category scales for a dozen perceptual continua. *U.S. Navy, Project No. 142–201, Report PNR-186*.

Stouffer, S. A., Lumsdaine, A. A., Lumsdaine, M. H., Williams, R. M. Jr., Smith, M. B., Janis, I. L., Star, S.A. and Cottrell, L. S. Jr. 1949. *The American soldier: Conflict and its aftermath*. Princeton: Princeton University Press.

Strickland, L., Aboud, F. and Gergen, K. (eds.) 1976. *Social psychology in transition*. New York: Plenum Press.

Stroebe, W. 1979. The level of social psychological analysis: A plea for a more social social psychology. In L. Strickland (ed.): *Soviet and Western perspectives in social psychology*. Oxford: Pergamon Press.

Styron, W. 1966. *The confessions of Nat Turner*. London: Jonathan Cape.

Sumner, G. A. 1906. *Folkways*. New York: Ginn.

Tagiuri, R. 1969. Person perception. In G. Lindzey and E. Aronson (eds.): *The handbook of social psychology*, 2nd edn, Vol. 3. Reading, Mass.: Addison-Wesley.

Tajfel, H. 1959. The anchoring effects of value in a scale of judgements. *British Journal of Psychology*, **50**, 294–304.

1969a. Social and cultural factors in perception. In G. Lindzey and E. Aronson (eds.): *The handbook of social psychology*, 2nd edn, Vol. 3. Reading, Mass.: Addison-Wesley.

1969b. The formation of national attitudes: A social psychological perspective. In M. Sherif (ed.): *Interdisciplinary relationships in the social sciences*. Chicago: Aldine.

1970a. Aspects of national and ethnic loyalty. *Social Science Information*, **9** (3), 119–44.

1970b. Experiments in intergroup discrimination. *Scientific American*, **223** (5), 96–102.

1972a. La catégorisation sociale. In S. Moscovici (ed.): *Introduction à la psychologie sociale*. Paris: Larousse.

1972b. Some developments in European social psychology. *European Journal of Social Psychology*, **2**, 307–22.

1974. Social identity and intergroup behaviour. *Social Science Information*, **13** (2), 65–93.

1976. Against biologism. *New Society*, **37**, 240–2.

1977. Social psychology and social reality. *New Society*, **39**, 653–4.

(ed.) 1978a. *Differentiation between social groups: Studies in the social psychology of intergroup relations*. (European Monographs in Social Psychology, No. 14). London: Academic Press.

1978b. The structure of our views about society. In H. Tajfel and C. Fraser (eds.): *Introducing social psychology*. Harmondsworth: Penguin Books.

1979. Human intergroup conflict: Useful and less useful forms of analysis. In M. von Cranach, K. Foppa, W. Lepenies and D. Ploog (eds.): *Human ethology: The claims and limits of a new discipline*. Cambridge University Press.

1980a. The 'New Look' and social differentiations: A semi-Brunerian perspective. In D. Olson (ed.): *The social foundations of language and thought: Essays in honor of J. S. Bruner*. New York: Norton.

1980b. Experimental studies of intergroup behaviour. In M. Jeeves (ed.): *Survey of psychology, No. 3*. London: George Allen and Unwin.

(ed.) 1981. *Social identity and intergroup relations*. Cambridge University Press and Paris: Editions de la Maison des Sciences de l'Homme, in press.

Tajfel, H. and Billig, M. 1974. Familiarity and categorization in intergroup behaviour. *Journal of Experimental Social Psychology*, **10**, 159–70.

Tajfel, H., Flament, C., Billig, M. and Bundy, R. P. 1971. Social categorization and intergroup behaviour. *European Journal of Social Psychology*, **1**, 149–78.

Tajfel, H. and Turner, J. C. 1979. An integrative theory of intergroup conflict. In W. G. Austin and S. Worchel (eds.): *The social psychology of intergroup relations*. Monterey, Calif.: Brooks/Cole.

Taylor, D. M. and Aboud, F. E. 1973. Ethnic stereotypes: Is the concept necessary? *Canadian Psychologist*, **14**, 330–8.

Taylor, D. M. and Brown, R. J. 1979. Towards a more social social psychology? *British Journal of Social and Clinical Psychology*, **18**, 173–9.

Taylor, D. M. and Giles, H. 1979. At the crossroads of research into language and ethnic relations. In H. Giles and B. Saint-Jacques (eds.): *Language and ethnic relations*. Oxford: Pergamon Press.

Taylor, D. M. and Guimond, S. 1978. The belief theory of prejudice in an intergroup context. *Journal of Social Psychology*, **105**, 11–25.

Taylor, D. M. and Jaggi, V. 1974. Ethnocentrism and causal attribution in a South Indian context. *Journal of Cross-Cultural Psychology*, **5**, 162–71.

Taylor, S. E., Fiske, S. T., Etcoff, N. L. and Ruderman, A. 1978. Categorical and contextual bases of person memory and stereotyping. *Journal of Personality and Social Psychology*, **36**, 778–93.

Thomas, K. 1971. *Religion and the decline of magic*. London: Weidenfeld and Nicholson. Reprinted in 1973, Penguin Books.

Toch, H. 1965. *The social psychology of social movements*. Indianapolis: Bobbs-Merrill.

Triandis, H. C. 1971. *Attitude and attitudes change*. New York: Wiley.

Turner, J. C. 1975. Social comparison and social identity: Some prospects for intergroup behaviour. *European Journal of Social Psychology*, **5**, 5–34.

1978a. Social categorization and social discrimination in the minimal group paradigm. In H. Tajfel (ed.), *op. cit.*

1978b. Social comparison, similarity and ingroup favouritism. In H. Tajfel (ed.), *op. cit.*

Turner, J. C. and Brown, R. J. 1978. Social status, cognitive alternatives and intergroup relations. In H. Tajfel (ed.), *op. cit.*

Turner, J. C. and Giles, H. (eds.) 1981. *Intergroup behaviour*. Oxford: Blackwell's,

References

in press.

Tversky, A. and Kahnemann, D. 1973. Availability: A heuristic for judging frequency and probability. *Cognitive Psychology*, **5**, 207–32.

Upmeyer, A. 1971. Social perception and signal detection theory: Group influence on discrimination and usage of scale. *Psychologische Forschung*, **34**, 283–94.

Upmeyer, A. and Layer, H. 1974. Accentuation and attitude in social judgement. *European Journal of Social Psychology*, **4**, 469–88.

Vaughan, G. M. 1964. The development of ethnic attitudes in New Zealand school children. *Genetic Psychology Monographs*, **70**, 135.

1978a. Social change and intergroup preferences in New Zealand. *European Journal of Social Psychology*, **8**, 297–314.

1978b. Social categorization and intergroup behaviour in children. In H. Tajfel (ed.), *op. cit.*

Vroom, V. H. 1957. Design and estimated size of coins. *Canadian Journal of Psychology*, **11**, 89–92.

Wagley, C. and Harris, M. 1958. *Minorities in the New World*. New York: Columbia University Press.

Walster, E., Berscheid, E. and Walster, G. W. 1976. New directions in equity research. In L. Berkowitz and E. Walster (eds.), *op. cit.*

Warner, W. L., Junker, B. H. and Adams, W. A. 1941. *Colour and human nature: Negro personality development in a Northern city*. A.C.E.

Watson, J. B. 1968. *The double helix*. New York: Athenaum.

Wilkes, A. L. and Tajfel, H. 1966. Types de classification et importance du contraste relatif. *Bulletin du C.E.R.P.*, **15**, 71–81.

Williams, J. and Giles, H. 1978. The changing status of women in society: An intergroup perspective. In H. Tajfel (ed.), *op. cit.*

Wittgenstein, L. 1953. *Philosophical investigations*. Oxford: Blackwell's.

Zimbardo, P. G. 1969. *The cognitive control of motivation*. Glenview, Illinois: Scott and Foresman.

Author index

365

Subject index

Subject index

Holocaust, 2, 7, 241, 286, 324, 333

ideologies, 15–16, 36, 38, 139–41, 146, 154–7, 248, 250, 264, 266, 275, 280, 284, 307
illusory correlations, 144, 149–50
ingroup devaluation, 122–6, 135–6, 166, 174, 196–206, 324–30
instinct, 130, 131
Institute of Race Relations, 168
intergroup relations, 3, 4, 8–9, 19–20, 30–40, 42–3, 45–53, 61, 83, 122–6, 128–41, 161, 223–343
inter-individual similarity, 237–8, 271–3
international preferences
   and factual information, 207–20
   in children, 207–20
interpersonal attraction, 42, 50
interpersonal–intergroup continuum, 238–43, 244–53, 261–5

judgements
   anchoring effects in, 92
   assimilation effects in, 92–3
   contrast effects in, 92–3
   of compound stimuli, 68–9
   of length, 90, 91–104, 115, 133
   of people, 104–14
   of skin colour, 77–8, 81, 82, 83, 84, 85, 132, 170, 214
   polarization of, 59–60, 70–5, 85–6, 90–114, 115–16, 133, 148, 151, 159, 226

legitimacy, 48, 245–6, 247, 248, 265–7, 277, 283, 284, 286–7, 300, 301, 304, 318, 320–1, 323, 342
L'Enfant Sauvage, 28
locus of control, 155, 160
loyalty, 290, 304–5

marginality, 277, 332–4, 335
mass media
   and interdependence, 320
   and stereotypes, 143–4, 195–6
   in children's national preferences, 219–20
   in race relations, 178, 185, 313
   see also war comics
'minimal' group experiments, 233–8, 241, 268–73, 292–4
moral judgement, 134–5

national attitudes, 38, 174–5, 184, 247, 248–9, 275, 281, 285, 340–1
   and cognitive decentration, 207
   in children, 4, 8, 137, 166–7, 187–97, 198–206, 207–19

role of language in, 274–5, 338–9, 340
National Front, 339–40
National Socialism, 16, 140
Négritude, 184, 284, 333
New Look, 8, 62–3
norms, 36–9, 270–1

perceptual overestimation, 3, 8, 57, 58, 62–75, 79–80, 86, 226
person perception, 58, 90, 151
   description categories of, 106–7, 113
   favourable ratings in, 113
   polarization of judgements in, 104–14
   salience of attributes in, 105–9, 110–14
'physiognomic ecology', 193–4, 195–6, 204–5
political attitudes, 15–16
positive group distinctiveness, 254, 259, 264, 265, 266–7, 271, 273–4, 275–87, 297–8, 300, 306, 317–18, 323, 340–1
prejudice, 2, 4, 9, 58, 76, 77, 84, 143, 147, 153, 239, 248, 249–50, 252, 291, 329, 333, 341
   belief similarity theory of, 42, 50–1, 52
   cognitive aspects of, 127–42
   experience of, 168–86
public knowledge, 127–8

Race Relations Act, 228
racism, 38, 50, 77, 140, 169, 171–2, 176–81, 274, 285, 317
relative deprivation, 25, 42, 258, 259–67, 301, 330–1
relative income hypothesis, 301–2
response bias, 153–4
rules in behaviour, 35–40
rumour, 160

self-definition, 14, 48, 135, 137, 139–40, 225, 254–6, 258, 322, 326–8, 330, 331, 338
self-hate, 324–5, 326, 332
self-interest, 36, 37, 38, 268, 296
semantic differential scales, 118
signal detection theory, 59
slavery, 319
social accentuation theory, 57, 58, 59, 61, 63–89, 226
   see also judgements, polarization of
social attitudes, 16, 39, 59–60, 105–6, 114
social categorization, 8, 14, 45–7, 48, 49, 50–1, 58, 61, 62, 90, 116, 132–4, 145, 147–50, 158–9, 160–1, 226, 228, 231, 240, 243, 254–6, 258, 264, 272–4, 293–4, 310–12, 313

368